Best Prep for SOA Exam P

Updated for 2025 Syllabi

Now Includes
Explanations for all the
627 SOA Sample Questions

Faisal Kaleem, PhD

Associate Professor of Mathematics

Reprinted with updates on December 23, 2024

Special thanks to Grace Cho, one of the first buyers, for catching many typos and mistakes in the earlier days of this book. She is an angel sent by God to help me.

Special Thanks to Sumiksha Koirala for helping me with one of the earlier updates.

Special thanks to SOA for providing sample Exam P questions on their website. This book, among other things, provides clear and detailed explanations to all of these questions.

Special thanks to my former student Yogesh Agrawal for all his input and help in the preparation of this manuscript.

Special thanks to Riley Cooper for agreeing to be on the cover of the book.

Preface

The salient features of this book are:

1) It is comprehensive. It contains everything you need to know to do well in Exam P. It breaks the official SOA sample questions into small portions, introduces the tools needed for each portion, provides detailed explanations for the problems, and (up to the first 319 SOA sample problems) follows up with a quiz (with detailed solutions) based on the portion. At the end, I provide a comprehensive tool sheet for the entire exam, 2 full-length practice exams containing fresh problems and detailed solutions to these practice exams. Altogether, the quizzes and exams contain about 300 fresh problems which are similar to SOA problems and will provide excellent preparation for the actual P exam.
2) It is concise and to the point. Despite being comprehensive, this book completely avoids all those details which may be good to know in general, but which are not really needed for the exam. My explanations are mathematically rigorous for the most part, but there are times when such rigor gets in the way of a quick, efficient, and easily understandable solution of a problem, and in that case, I always go for speed, efficiency, and easier understanding over unnecessary mathematical rigor.
3) It has a unique presentation style in that it is centered around the sequence of the official SOA sample questions. I start by concisely introducing the ideas needed to understand problems 1-16. Then I present very clear solutions to these problems. These solutions are easier to understand than any other solutions I have come across. I then follow up with a quiz (with detailed solutions) based on these problems. Every problem on the quiz is a serious practice problem for Exam level questions. The process is then repeated for the next set of few problems, and so on, up to the first 319 SOA sample questions. This way, sometimes the same formulas are mentioned multiple times. Such repetition is a great way for a deeper understanding, effortless memorization, and convenient finding of the necessary tools. This is a better and more efficient way to prepare for the P exam instead of reading a text which is divided by topics.
4) It provides clear and detailed explanations for each of the 627 SOA sample questions (ignoring the duplicates). The link for the SOA sample questions is: https://www.soa.org/4a1b24/globalassets/assets/files/edu/edu-exam-p-sample-quest.pdf So, all together, the book contains detailed solutions for almost 1000 problems.
5) The explanations provided for the official SOA problems synchronize with the videos of my YouTube channel titled: "Best Actuarial and Statistics Solutions" which contains explanation videos for most of these problems.
6) This revised edition of the book is in synchronization with the most updated SOA sample questions (2025 Syllabus). If you have any suggestions, comments, questions, or if you are interested in receiving tutoring for Exams P or FM, you can contact me at: bestactuarialsolutions@gmail.com
7) I am a tenured faculty of mathematics in USA. I am also the author of the book titled "Best Prep for SOA Exam FM". I played a major role in starting the Actuarial Science concentration in the Mathematics program of the university that I currently teach in, and then in getting the SOA UCAP recognition for it. We offer year-long prep courses for the P and FM exams, and I am the one who teaches both these sequences. The success rate in SOA Exams of students taking my courses has been extremely high. I am also the liaison between SOA and our university. I achieved a perfect score on Exam P. I have tried to capture all my successful experience and teaching techniques in this book.

Table of Contents

Tools needed for problems 1-16

Addition Rule

For 2 events: $P(A \cup B) = P(A) + P(B) - P(AB)$.

For 3 events: $P(A \cup B \cup C) = P(A) + P(B) + P(C) - P(AB) - P(AC) - P(BC) + P(ABC)$

Note that we will regularly be using the shorthand $P(AB)$ for $P(A \cap B)$

Complement Rule: $P(A') = 1 - P(A)$

Partition Rule: $P(A) = P(AB) + P(AB')$

Two events A, B are independent, if and only if $P(AB) = P(A)P(B)$

Conditional Rule:

$$P(A\ given\ B) = \frac{P(AB)}{P(B)}$$

Sum of a geometric series with 1st term a and common ration r is:

$$S = \frac{a}{1 - r}$$

(Note: I will not be writing the statements for the SOA Sample Questions in this book. These can be found on the SOA website. The link is given in the preface.)

SOA Sample Question 1 Explanation:

We will first find the probability of those who watched at least one sport and then use the complement rule to find the probability of those watching none.

Let G, B, S be the percentages who watch gymnastics, baseball, and soccer, respectively.

Probability of at least one of the 3 events is the same as the probability of their union:

$$P(G \cup B \cup S) = P(G) + P(B) + P(S) - P(GB) - P(BS) - P(GS) + P(GBS)$$

$$= 28 + 29 + 19 - 14 - 12 - 10 + 8 = 48$$

$$P(none) = 100\% - P(at\ least\ 1)$$

$$= 100\% - 48\%$$

$$= 52\%$$

The correct answer is **D**.

SOA Sample Question 2 Explanation:

Let L be the event of lab work and S be the event of referral to specialist.

Let x be the probability that a visit results in both lab work and referral to a specialist.

The problem is captured by the following Venn diagram:

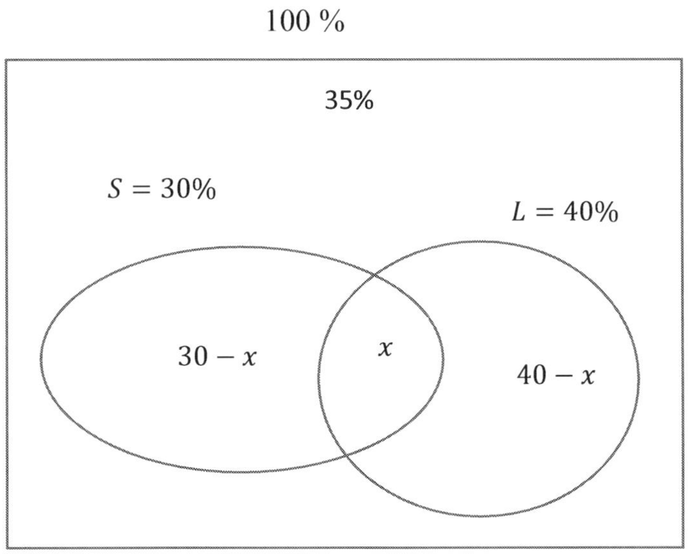

From the diagram we see that:

$$(30 - x) + x + (40 - x) + 35 = 100$$

$$x = 5\%$$

The correct answer is **A**.

SOA Sample Question 3 Explanation:

Prime means complement. Also, we shall always in this book be using the convention that:

$$AB = A \cap B$$

Now recall from elementary set theory that:

$$A = AB \ \cup \ AB'$$

And since the two sets in the union on the right side are disjoint, so:

$$P(A) = P(AB) + P(AB') \quad (1)$$

Finally, we use the addition rule for both $A \cup B$ and $A \cup B'$

$$P(A \cup B) = P(A) + P(B) - P(AB)$$

$$0.7 = P(A) + P(B) - P(AB) \qquad (2)$$

$$P(A \cup B') = P(A) + P(B') - P(AB')$$

$$0.9 = P(A) + [1 - P(B)] - P(AB')$$

$$-0.1 = P(A) - P(B) - P(AB') \quad (3)$$

Adding (2) and (3) we get:

$$.6 = 2P(A) - [P(AB) + P(AB')]$$

$$.6 = 2P(A) - P(A)$$

Where we have used (1). Thus, we have:

$$P(A) = .6$$

The correct answer is **D**.

SOA Sample Question 4 Explanation:

4 R

6 B

Total $= 10$

16 R

x B

Total $x + 16$

$$P(RR) + P(BB) = .44$$

$$\frac{4}{10} \cdot \frac{16}{x+16} + \frac{6}{10} \cdot \frac{x}{x+16} = .44$$

$$64 + 6x = .44(10)(x + 16)$$

$$x = 4$$

The correct answer is **A**.

SOA Sample Question 5 Explanation:

Young Single Girls = Young Girls – Young Married Girls

= (Total Young – Young Boys) – (Young Married – Young Married Boys)

= (3000 – 1320) – (1400 – 600)

= 880

The correct answer is **D**.

SOA Sample Question 6 Explanation:

The word "given" in the last sentence tells us that this is a conditional probability problem. Although we have a well-known formula for this, it is sometimes simpler to do these problems by thinking that whatever is "given" is the whole universe and we can simply ignore anything else. In this case, it is given that neither parent suffers from heart disease. Since 312 out of 937 had at least one suffering parent, so 937 – 312 will have no suffering parent. Thus, our grand total is 625. We need to know how many of these 625 died of heart related issues.

Total deaths $= 210$

Number of deaths with at least one suffering parent $= 102$

So, number deaths with no suffering parent $= 210 - 102 = 108$

P (Died of heart issues given no parent suffered) $= 108/625$

$= .173$

The correct answer is **B**.

***SOA Sample Question 7 Explanation*:**

The situation is summarized in the diagram below:

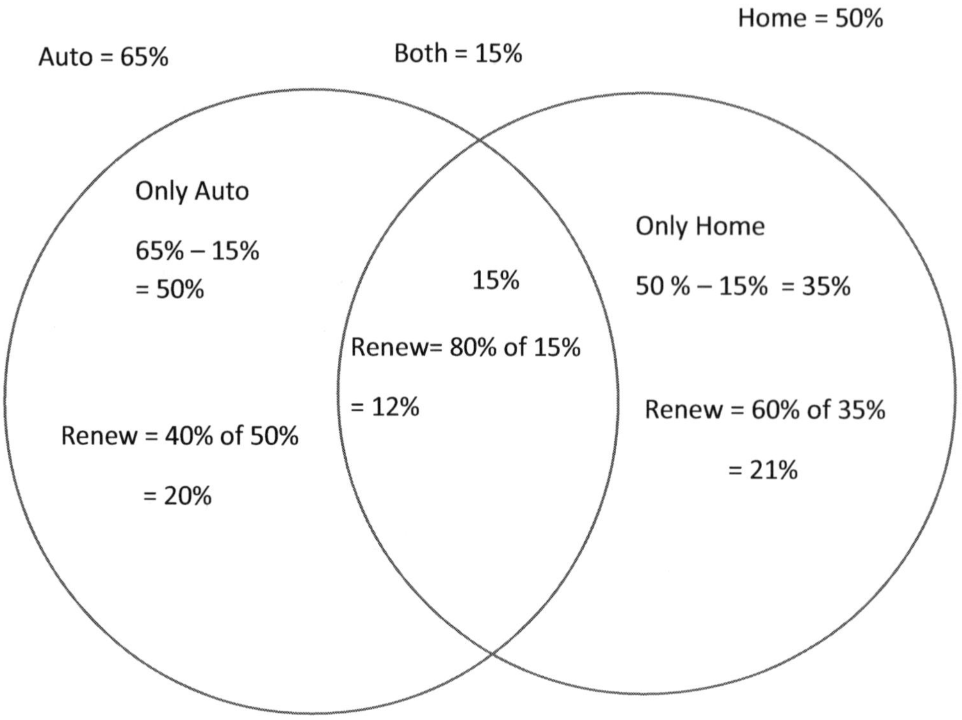

Total Renewed = 20 + 12 + 21 = 53%

The correct answer is **D**.

SOA Sample Question 8 Explanation:

Let the probability of visiting a physical therapist $= x$

Then the probability of visiting a chiropractor $= .14 + x$

Once again, Venn diagrams are useful.

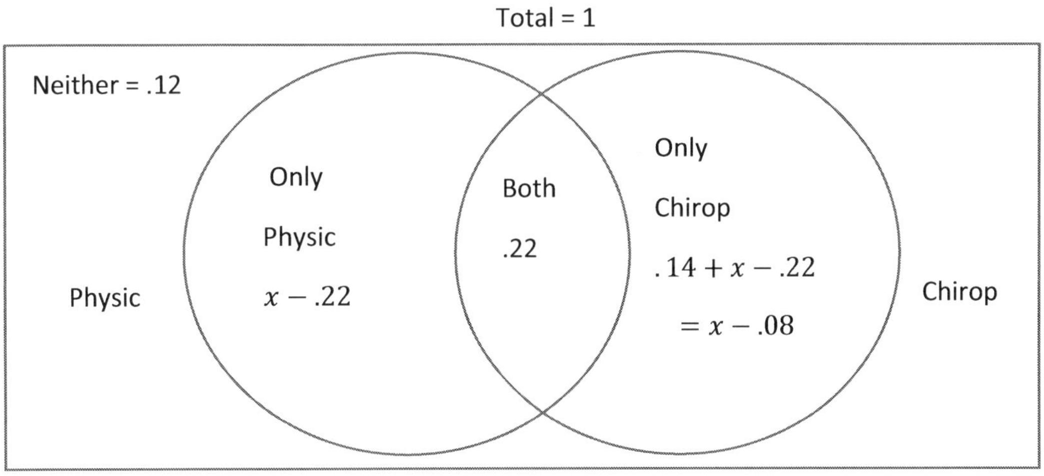

All the possible probabilities should add up to 1. That is:

$$(x - .22) + .22 + (x - .08) + .12 = 1$$

$$x = .48$$

The correct answer is **D**.

SOA Sample Question 9 Explanation:

Suppose there are 100 customers who insure at least 1 car. Consider the table below:

Total = 100

Exactly one = 30	More than one = 70
Let non-sports = x	Sports = 15% of 70 = .15(70) = 10.5
Then sports = 30 – x	Non-Sports = 70 – 10.5 = 59.5

The sum of the sports cars of the two groups should equal 20. Thus:

$$30 - x + 10.5 = 20$$

$$x = 20.5$$

So, 20.5 out of the 100 customers insure exactly one car and that car is not a sports car.

That gives a probability of $20.5/100$, which equals $.205$.

This rounds to choice **B**.

SOA Sample Question 10 Explanation:

Let Probability of purchasing disability coverage $= d$

Then, probability of purchasing collision coverage $= 2d$

Recall that for independent events, $P(AB) = P(A)P(B)$

So, conditions (ii) and (iii) give:

$$0.15 = d \cdot 2d$$

$$d = .274$$

$$2d = .548$$

$$P\ (C\ or\ D) = P(C) + P(D) - P(CD)$$

$$= .548 + .274 - .15$$

$$= .672$$

$$P\ (neither\ C\ nor\ D) = 1 - P\ (C\ or\ D)$$

$$= 1 - .672$$

$$= .328$$

This rounds to choice **B**.

SOA Sample Question 11 Explanation:

With so many variables, a table is easier than a Venn Diagram.

	High BP	Low BP	Normal BP	Total
Regular Heartbeat	$.14 - .05$ $= .09$ (Step 3)	$.22 - .02 = \boldsymbol{.2}$ (Step 6)	*.56*	$1 - .15$ $= .85$ (Step 4)
Irregular Heartbeat	1/3 of .15 =*.05* (Step 1)	$.15 - .05 - .08 = .02$ (Step 5)	1/8 of .64 = .08 (Step 2)	.15
Total	.14	.22	*.64*	1

Given values are written in normal font, while the calculated entries are italicized.

Calculation order can be followed by the step numbers.

Bold italicized entry is what was asked.

So, the answer is 20%

The correct answer is **E**.

SOA Sample Question 12 Explanation:

Letting $P(ABC) = x,\ P(none\ of\ A, B, C) = y$, we have the following:

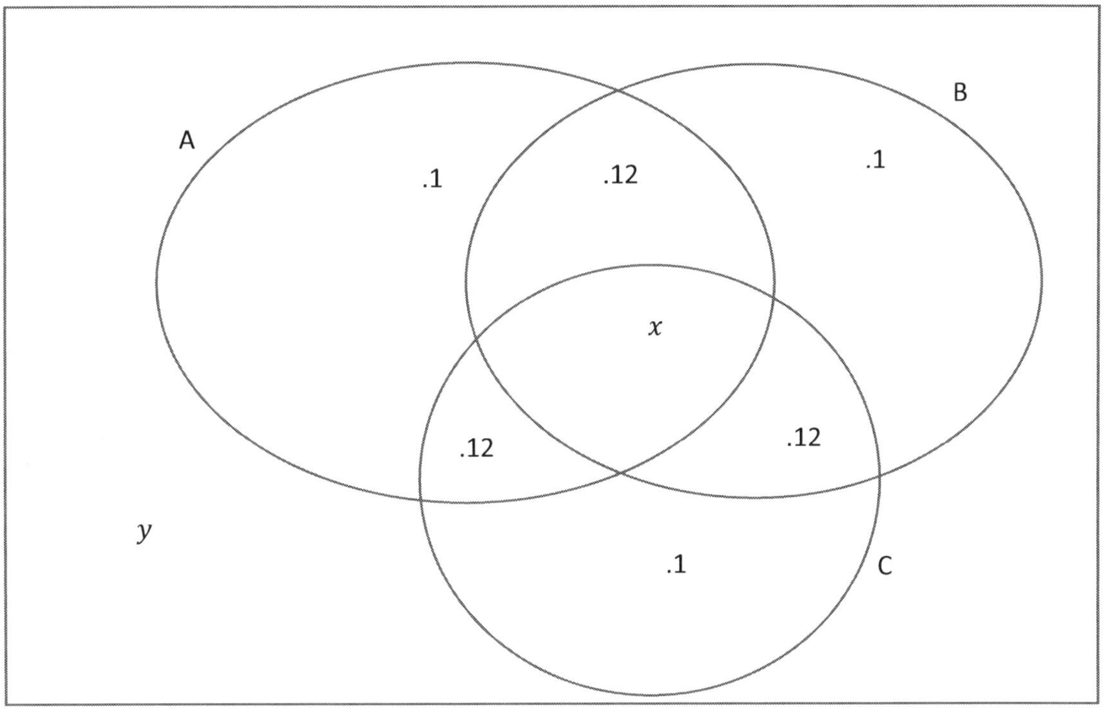

We know that $P(ABC\ given\ AB) = 1/3$. That is,

$$\frac{P(ABC)}{P(AB)} = \frac{1}{3}$$

$$\frac{x}{x + .12} = \frac{1}{3}$$

$$3x = x + .12$$

$$x = .06$$

$$y = 1 - 3(.1) - 3(.12) - .06$$

$$= .28$$

$$P(None\ of\ A, B, C\ given\ A') = \frac{P(none\ of\ A, B, C)}{P(A')}$$

$$= \frac{y}{.1 + .1 + .12 + y}$$

$$= \frac{.28}{.32 + .28}$$

$$= .467$$

The correct answer is **C**.

SOA Sample Question 13 Explanation:

$$p(1) = .2p(0)$$

$$p(2) = .2p(1) = .2[.2p(0)] = .04p(0)$$

$$p(3) = .2p(2) = .2[.04p(0)] = .008p(0)$$

etc. The sum of all possible probabilities is 1. That is:

$$p(0) + p(1) + p(2) + p(3) + \cdots = 1$$

$$p(0) + .2p(0) + .04p(0) + .008p(0) + \cdots = 1$$

$$p(0)[1 + .2 + .04 + .008 + \cdots] = 1 \quad (1)$$

Recall that the sum of a geometric series equals:

$$\frac{a}{1-r}$$

where a is the 1st term, and r is the common ratio. Thus, (1) becomes:

$$p(0)\left[\frac{1}{1-.2}\right] = 1$$

$$p(0) = .8$$

$$p(1) = .2p(0)$$

$$= .2(.8)$$

$$= .16$$

We need $p(n > 1)$, which is easily done through the complement. So,

$$p(n > 1) = 1 - p(0) - p(1)$$

$$= 1 - .8 - .16$$

$$= .04$$

The correct answer is **A**.

SOA Sample Question 14 Explanation:

See the figure. Since only exactly 2 coverages are possible, so the only non-zero portions are the intersections of two of A, B, C, and the part outside of all 3 which indicates no coverage.

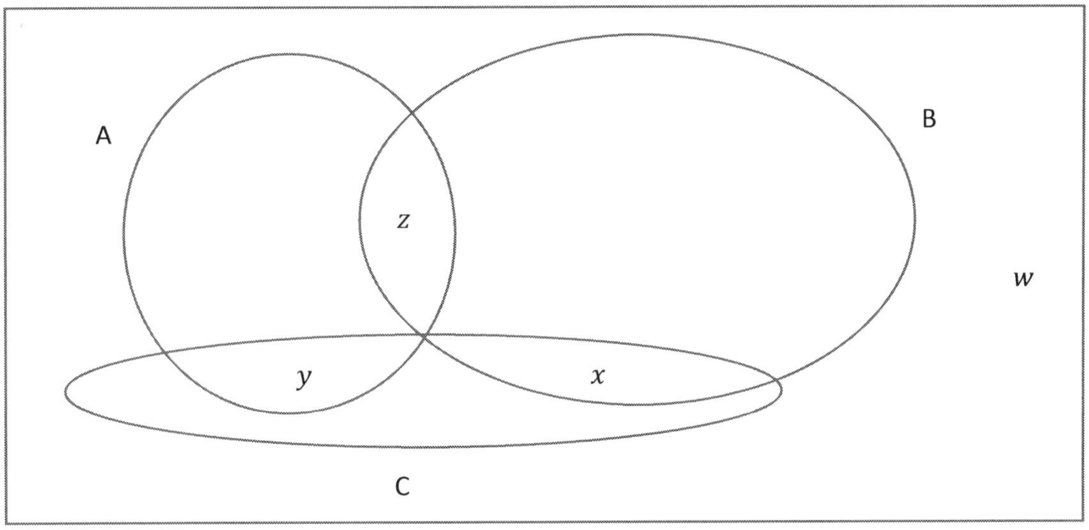

By the given conditions:

$$y + z = \frac{1}{4}$$

$$x + z = \frac{1}{3}$$

$$x + y = \frac{5}{12}$$

We need to find w which equals $1 - x - y - z = 1 - (x + y + z)$.

We can solve the above equations to get the values of the 3 variables but we don't have to because if we just add the 3 equations, we get what we need. So, adding the equations gives:

$$2x + 2y + 2z = \frac{1}{4} + \frac{1}{3} + \frac{5}{12}$$

$$2x + 2y + 2z = 1$$

$$x + y + z = \frac{1}{2}$$

$$w = 1 - (x + y + z)$$

$$= 1 - \frac{1}{2}$$

$$= \frac{1}{2}$$

The correct answer is **C**.

SOA Sample Question 15 Explanation:

Note that we can have a total of 7 claims in the 2 weeks in 8 possible ways indicated by the pairs:

$$(0,7), (1,6), (2,5), (3,4), (4,3), (5,2), (6,1), (7,0)$$

where the 1st entry of each pair represents the claims in the 1st week, and the 2nd entry represents the claims in the 2nd week.

We see from the above pairs that if there are n claims in the 1st week, then there are $7 - n$ claims in the 2nd week. The probability of this happening is:

$$P(n)P(7-n) = \frac{1}{2^{n+1}} \cdot \frac{1}{2^{7-n+1}}$$

$$= \frac{1}{2^9}$$

$$= \frac{1}{512}$$

And this can happen in 8 ways because there are 8 pairs. So the total probability is:

$$8\left(\frac{1}{512}\right) = \frac{1}{64}$$

The correct answer is **D**.

SOA Sample Question 16 Explanation:

Let E be the event that a claim includes emergency room charges.

Let O be the event that a claim includes operating room charges. We are given that:

$$P(E \cup O) = .85$$

$$P(E') = .25$$

Using complement rule, we get:

$$P(E) = 1 - .25 = .75.$$

Since we are told that the two types of claims are independent of each other, so

$$P(EO) = P(E)P(O)$$

We now use the addition rule.

$$P(E \cup O) = P(E) + P(O) - P(EO)$$

$$.85 = P(E) + P(O) - P(EO)$$

$$.85 = P(E) + P(O) - P(E)P(O)$$

$$.85 = .75 + P(O) - .75P(O)$$

$$.1 = .25P(O)$$

$$P(O) = .4$$

The correct answer is **D**.

Quiz 1

1. All the people in a town were interviewed and it was found that:

- 44% liked apples
- 48% liked oranges
- 29% liked apples and oranges
- 25% liked apples and bananas
- 32% liked oranges and bananas
- 18% liked all the 3 fruits
- 31% liked none of the 3 fruits

What percentage of the town people liked bananas?

A) 41%
B) 45%
C) 49%
D) 53%
E) 57%

Solution:

Let A, O, B be the events of liking apples, oranges, bananas, respectively.

$$P(A \cup O \cup B) = P(A) + P(O) + P(B) - P(AO) - P(AB) - P(OB) + P(AOB) \quad (1)$$

We also note that whole union is the probability of at least one, which is the complement of none. Thus:

$$P(A \cup O \cup B) = 1 - .31$$

$$= .69$$

Equation (1) becomes:

$$.69 = .44 + .48 + P(B) - .29 - .25 - .32 + .18$$

$$P(B) = .45$$

The correct answer is **B**.

2. Given $P(A \cup B) = .7,\ \ P(A' \cup B) = .8,\ \ $ Find $P(B)$

A) .25
B) .3
C) .4
D) .5
E) .6

Solution:

Using addition rule for both the unions we get:

$$.7 = P(A \cup B) = P(A) + P(B) - P(AB) \qquad (1)$$

$$.8 = P(A') + P(B) - P(A'B) = 1 - P(A) + P(B) - P(A'B) \qquad (2)$$

Adding (1) and (2) we have:

$$1.5 = 1 + 2P(B) - P(AB) - P(A'B)$$

$$.5 = 2P(B) - [P(AB) + P(A'B)] \quad (3)$$

Now recall that $P(BA) + P(BA') = P(B)$

So, (3) becomes:

$$.5 = 2P(B) - P(B) = P(B)$$

The correct answer is **D**.

3. A class in University A has 7 girls and 5 boys, while a class in university B has 6 boys and y girls. If one student is picked from each class, the probability of the two picks being of opposite gender is .4755. Find y.

A) 9
B) 10
C) 11
D) 12
E) 13

Solution:

$$.4755 = P(GB) + P(BG)$$

$$.4755 = \frac{7}{12} \cdot \frac{6}{y+6} + \frac{5}{12} \cdot \frac{y}{6+y}$$

$$.4755(12)(y+6) = 42 + 5y$$

$$5.706y + 34.236 = 42 + 5y$$

$$y = 11$$

The correct answer is **C**.

4. 130 of the 500 children in a school have blue eyes. Also, 204 children have at least one blue-eyed parent, and a third of these 204 children have blue eyes. Find the probability that a child in this school will have blue eyes given that neither parent has blue eyes.

A) .124
B) .136
C) .168
D) .209
E) .230

Solution:

A third of 204 is 68. So, 68 blue-eyed children have at least one blue-eyed parent.

It means the remaining 130 – 68 = 62 blue eyed children have no blue-eyed parent.

The total number of non-blue-eyed parents is 500 – 204 = 296.

Remember that in a conditional probability problem, whatever is given becomes the universe and everything else can be ignored. Thus, the non-blue-eyed parents is the whole universe here, and so, for the probability of a child with blue eyes given neither parent has blue eyes, we will only consider the blue-eyed children with neither parent blue eyed, and it will be 62/296 = .209

Correct answer is **D**.

5. 12% of the students in a university like both Math and Stats while 30% like neither. The probability that a student likes Stats is twice the probability that s/he likes Math. Find the probability that a randomly chosen student at this university likes Math.

A) .15
B) .19
C) .23
D) .27
E) .31

Solution:

Let the probability of a student liking Math $= x$

Then the probability of a student liking Stats $= 2x$

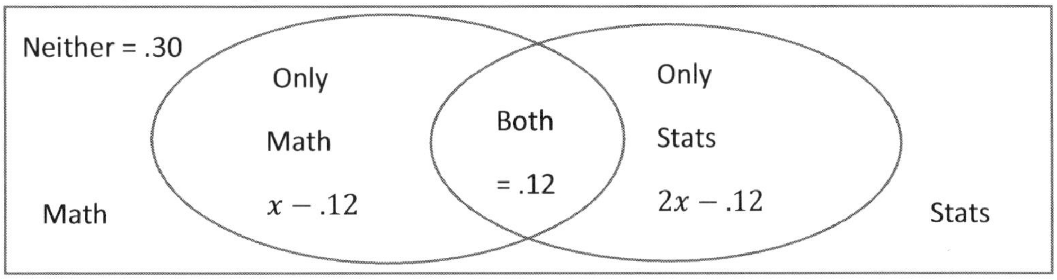

All the possible probabilities should add up to 1. That is:

$$(x - .12) + .12 + (2x - .12) + .3 = 1$$

$$x = .2733$$

This rounds to choice **D**.

6. You are 3 times as likely to buy a computer as a car next month. The event that you buy a computer is independent of the event that you buy a car. The probability that you buy both is .21. Calculate the probability that you buy neither?

A) .15
B) .17
C) .19
D) .21
E) .23

Solution:

Let the probability of buying a car be x.

Then the probability of buying a computer will be $3x$.

$$\text{P (car or computer)} = \text{P (car)} + \text{P (computer)} - \text{P (car and computer)}$$

Also, since the events are independent, we have:

$$\text{P (car and computer)} = \text{P (car)} \cdot \text{P (computer)}.$$

This gives:

$$.21 = 3x \cdot x$$

$$x = .2646$$

$$\text{P (car or computer)} = .2646 + 3(.2646) - .21$$

$$= .85$$

$$\text{P (neither car nor computer)} = 1 - \text{P (car or computer)}$$

$$= 1 - .85$$

$$= .15$$

The correct answer is **A**.

7. In a certain country

- 8% have green eyes
- 24% have blue eyes
- 40% are males
- 10% of the males have green eyes
- A quarter of those whose eyes are neither green nor blue are males

What percentage of the county is composed of blue-eyed females?

A) 5%
B) 6%
C) 7%
D) 8%
E) 9%

With so many variables, a table is easier than a Venn Diagram.

	Green Eyes	Blue Eyes	Other Eyes	Total
Females	*.04* (Step 2)	***.05*** (Step 7)	*.51* (Step 6)	*.60* (Step 3)
Males	*.04* (10% of .40) (Step 1)		*.17* (1/4 of .68) (Step 5)	.40
Total	.08	.24	*.68* (Step 4)	1

The given entries are in normal font, the calculated entries are italicized.

Required entry is italicized and bold.

The correct answer is **A**.

8. The probability of a married couple having n children satisfies: $p(n+1) = .6p(n)$, where $p(n)$ is the probability of the couple having n children. What is the probability of a married couple having 4 or more children?

A) .11
B) .12
C) .13
D) .14
E) .15

Solution:

$$p(1) = .6p(0)$$

$$p(2) = .6p(1) = .6[.6p(0)] = .36p(0)$$

$$p(3) = .6p(2) = .6[.36p(0)] = .216p(0)$$

$$p(0) + p(1) + p(2) + p(3) + \cdots = 1$$

$$p(0) + .6p(0) + .36p(0) + .216p(0) + \cdots = 1$$

$$p(0)[1 + .6 + .36 + .216 + \cdots] = 1 \quad (1)$$

Recall that the sum of a geometric series equals:

$$\frac{a}{1-r}$$

where a is the 1st term, and r is the common ratio. Thus, (1) becomes:

$$p(0)\left[\frac{1}{1-.6}\right] = 1$$

$$p(0) = .4$$

Using the equations developed at the start of the solution we get:

$$p(1) = .6(.4) = .24$$

$$p(2) = .36(.4) = .144$$

$$p(3) = .216(.4) = .0864$$

$$p(n \geq 4) = 1 - p(0) - p(1) - p(2) - p(3)$$

$$= 1 - .4 - .24 - .144 - .0864$$

$$= .13$$

The correct answer is **C**.

9. A certain high school gives its students the opportunity to take calculus, physics, and statistics during their senior year. However, if a student selects one of these 3 subjects, they must select another one of these 3 as well, otherwise they cannot take any of the 3. Also, no student can take all the 3. The proportions of seniors who end up taking calculus, physics, and statistics are .1, .15, and .2 respectively. Find the probability that a randomly selected senior chose none of the 3.

A) .375
B) .475
C) .575
D) .675
E) .775

Let C, P, S represent students who take calculus, physics, and statistics, respectively.

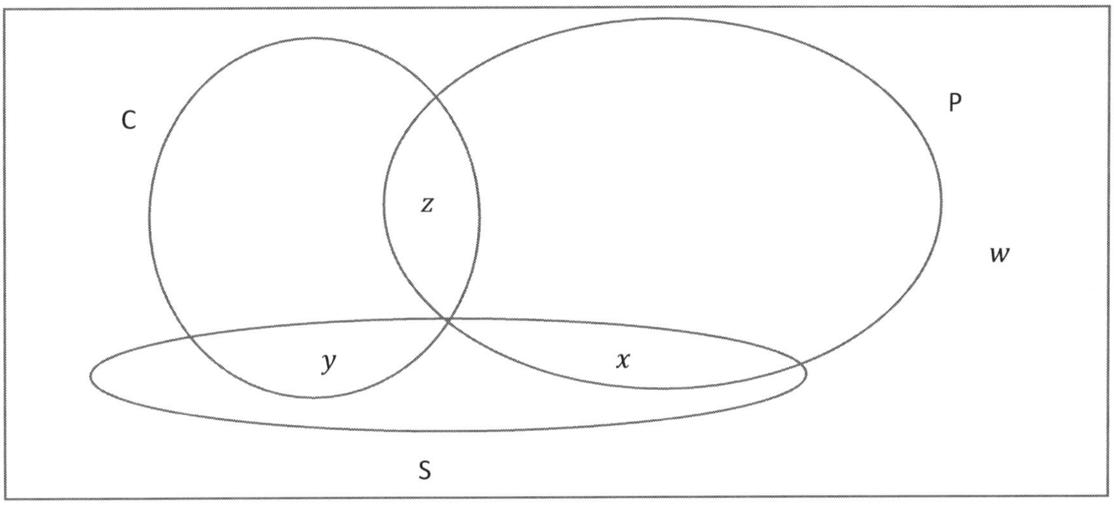

Since exactly 2 subjects are possible, so the only non-zero portions are the intersections of two of C,P, and S, and the part outside of all 3 which indicates none of the 3. By give conditions:

$$y + z = .1$$

$$x + z = .15$$

$$x + y = .2$$

Adding these 3 equations we get:

$$2x + 2y + 2z = .1 + .15 + .2 = .45$$

$$x + y + z = .225$$

We need to find w.

$$w = 1 - x - y - z$$

$$= 1 - (x + y + z).$$

$$= 1 - .225$$

$$= .775$$

The correct answer is **E**.

10. 90% of 1st semester college freshmen take Math or English. If 42% of them do not take Math, what proportion takes English? Assume that taking Math and English are independent events.

A) .76
B) .80
C) .84
D) .88
E) .92

Solution:

Let E be the event of a 1st semester freshman taking English.

Let M be the event of a 1st semester freshman taking Math.

We are given that:

$$P(E \cup M) = .9$$

$$P(M') = .42$$

Using complement rule, and independence rule we get:

$$P(M) = 1 - .42 = .58.$$

$$P(EM) = P(E)P(M)$$

We next use the addition rule:

$$P(E \cup M) = P(E) + P(M) - P(EM)$$

$$.9 = P(E) + P(M) - P(EM)$$

$$.9 = P(E) + P(M) - P(E)P(M)$$

$$.9 = P(E) + .58 - .58P(E)$$

$$.32 = .42P(E)$$

$$P(E) = .76$$

The correct answer is **A**.

Tools needed for problems 17-27

If X is normally distributed with mean μ and standard deviation σ, the standard score is given by:

$$z = \frac{x - \mu}{\sigma}$$

If X, Y are independent normal variables, and $N = aX + bY$, then:

$$\mu_N = a\mu_X + b\mu_Y$$

$$\sigma_N = \sqrt{a^2 {\sigma_X}^2 + b^2 {\sigma_Y}^2}$$

The probability of x successes in n binomial trials is given as:

$$f(x) = \binom{n}{x} p^x (1-p)^{n-x}, \qquad x = 0,1,2, \ldots$$

where p is the probability of success in each trial.

Bayes Theorem says that if events $A_1, \ldots, A_n$ form a partition of the sample space S, and B is any event, then for $i = 1, \ldots, n$:

$$P(A_i \; given \; B) = \frac{P(A_i B)}{P(A_1 B) + \cdots + P(A_n B)}$$

Standard Deviation = $\sqrt{Variance}$

SOA Sample Question 17 Explanation:

Let X_1, X_2 be the two measurement errors. The average of these two is:

$$Y = \frac{X_1 + X_2}{2} = \frac{1}{2}X_1 + \frac{1}{2}X_2$$

The sum and constant multiple of two normal variables is normal with mean and variance given by:

$$\mu_Y = \frac{1}{2}\mu_{X_1} + \frac{1}{2}\mu_{X_2} = \frac{1}{2}(0) + \frac{1}{2}(0) = 0$$

$$Var\ Y = \left(\frac{1}{2}\right)^2 VarX_1 + \left(\frac{1}{2}\right)^2 VarX_2 = \frac{(.0056h)^2 + (.0044h)^2}{4} = .00001268h^2$$

Standard deviation of $Y = \sigma_Y = \sqrt{Var\ Y} = \sqrt{.00001268h^2} = .00356h$

We are asked to calculate $P(-.005h \le Y \le .005h)$.

Since we need to use standard normal table to calculate the required probability, so we need to change $Y = -.005h,\ Y = .005h$ into standard normal values through the formula:

$$z = \frac{Y - \mu_Y}{\sigma_Y} = \frac{Y}{.00356h}$$

$$z_1 = \frac{-.005h}{.00356h} = -1.4, \quad z_2 = \frac{.005h}{.00356h} = 1.4$$

$$P(-.005h \le Y \le .005h) = P(-1.4 \le z \le 1.4)$$

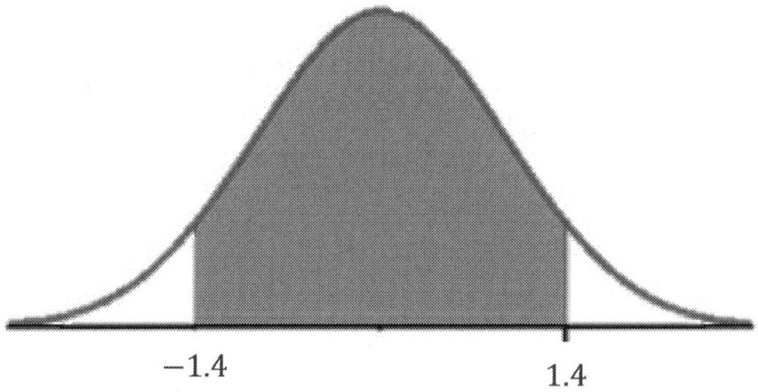

Exam tables give area to the left of the positive standard values. From the figure, we see that:

$$P(-1.4 \le z \le 1.4) = P(z \le 1.4) - P(z \le -1.4) = P(z \le 1.4) - [1 - P(z \le 1.4)]$$
$$= 2P(z \le 1.4) - 1 = 2(.9192) - 1$$

$$= .84$$

The correct answer is **D**.

SOA Sample Question 18 Explanation:

Age of Driver	Probability of Accident	Portion of Insured Drivers	Probability of insured and accident
16-20	.06	.08	$.06(.08) = .0048$
21-30	.03	.15	$.03(.15) = .0045$
31-65	.02	.49	$.02(.49) = .0098$
66-99	.04	.28	$.04(.28) = .0112$

Note that since having an accident and being insured are independent, so the entries in the last column are obtained by multiplying the entries of columns 2 and 3 because we know that if two events A, B are independent, then $P(AB) = P(A)P(B)$

We next use the formula:

$$P(A \text{ } given \text{ } B) = \frac{P(A \text{ } and \text{ } B)}{P(B)}$$

$$P\,(16-\ 20 \text{ } given \text{ } Insured \text{ } \& \text{ } Accident) = \frac{P\,(16-20 \text{ } and \text{ } Insured \text{ } \& \text{ } Accident)}{P\,(Insured \text{ } \& \text{ } Accident)}$$

$$= \frac{.0048}{.0048+.0045+.0098+.0112}$$

$$= .16$$

The correct answer is **B**.

SOA Sample Question 19 Explanation:

Type	Proportion	Death Probability	P (Given Policy and Death)
Standard	.5	.01	$.5(.01) = .005$
Preferred	.4	.005	$.4(.005) = .002$
Ultra-Preferred	.1	.001	$.1(.001) = .0001$

Just like the previous question, this is also a conditional probability problem, with the given condition being the death of a policy holder. So,

$$P(Ultra \text{ } Preferred \text{ } given \text{ } Death) = \frac{P(Ultra \text{ } Preferred \text{ } \& \text{ } Death)}{P(Death)}$$

$$= \frac{.0001}{.005+.002+.0001}$$

$$= .0141$$

The correct answer is **D**.

SOA Sample Question 20 Explanation:

Here, we are asked to find P(Serious given Survived).

The main difference between this problem and the two previous ones is that although death probabilities are given, but the question is asking for survival probabilities.

Therefore, in our table, we will also write a column for survival probabilities.

Condition	Proportion	Death Probability	Survival Probability = 1−Death Probability.	P(Condition & Survived)
Critical	.1	.4	.6	$.1(.6) = .06$
Serious	.3	.1	.9	$.3(.9) = .27$
Stable	$1 - .1 - .3 = .6$	.01	.99	$.6(.99) = .594$

$$P(Serious\ given\ Survived) = \frac{P(Serious\ and\ Survived)}{P(Survived)}$$

$$= \frac{.27}{.06 + .27 + .594}$$

$$= .29$$

The correct answer is **B**.

SOA Sample Question 21 Explanation:

Here, the death probabilities are not given directly.

We need to calculate them before making the table.

Let x be the probability of death of non-smokers.

Then probability of death of light smokers will be $2x$,

And the probability of death of heavy smokers will be $4x$.

Since sum of all these probabilities has to be 1, so:

$$x + 2x + 4x = 1$$

This gives:

$$x = \frac{1}{7}, \qquad 2x = \frac{2}{7}, \qquad 4x = \frac{4}{7}$$

We thus get the following table:

Person Type	Proportion	Death Probability (D)	P (Person Type & Death)
Heavy Smoker (H)	.2	4/7	$.2\left(\frac{4}{7}\right)$
Light Smoker (L)	.3	2/7	$.3\left(\frac{2}{7}\right)$
Non-Smoker (N)	.5	1/7	$.5\left(\frac{1}{7}\right)$

Here, we are given that the patient dies. So, we need to find:

$$P(H\ given\ D) = \frac{P(H\ and\ D)}{P(D)}$$

$$= \frac{.2\left(\frac{4}{7}\right)}{.2\left(\frac{4}{7}\right) + .3\left(\frac{2}{7}\right) + .5\left(\frac{1}{7}\right)}$$

$$= .42$$

The correct answer is **D**.

SOA Sample Question 22 Explanation:

Type of Driver	% of all Drivers	Collision Probability (C)	Driver Type and Collision Probability
Teen (T)	8%	.15	$.08(.15) = .012$
Young Adult (Y)	16%	.08	$.16(.08) = .0128$
Midlife (M)	45%	.04	$.45(.04) = .018$
Senior (S)	31%	.05	$.31(.05) = .0155$
Total	100%		

$$\text{P (Young Adult given Collision)} = \frac{P(Young\ Adult\ and\ Collision)}{P(Collision)}$$

$$= \frac{.0128}{.012 + .0128 + .018 + .0155}$$

$$= .22$$

The correct answer is **D**.

SOA Sample Question 23 Explanation:

$$P(N \geq 1\ given\ N \leq 4) = \frac{P(N \geq 1\ and\ N \leq 4)}{P(N \leq 4)}$$

$$= \frac{P(N = 1,2,3,4)}{P(N = 0,1,2,3,4)} \quad (1)$$

Let us tabulate all the required values.

n	$P(n) = \dfrac{1}{(n+1)(n+2)}$
0	1/2
1	1/6
2	1/12
3	1/20
4	1/30

Equation (1) becomes:

$$P(N \geq 1\ given\ N \leq 4) = \frac{P(1) + P(2) + P(3) + P(4)}{P(0) + P(1) + P(2) + P(3) + P(4)}$$

$$= \frac{\frac{1}{6} + \frac{1}{12} + \frac{1}{20} + \frac{1}{30}}{\frac{1}{2} + \frac{1}{6} + \frac{1}{12} + \frac{1}{20} + \frac{1}{30}}$$

$$= \frac{2}{5}$$

The correct answer is **B**.

SOA Sample Question 24 Explanation:

Person Type	Proportion	Tests Positive	Person Type and Tests Positive
Has Disease	1%	95%	$.01(.95) = .0095$
Doesn't have Disease	99%	.5%	$.99(.005) = .00495$

$$P(a\ person\ actually\ has\ disease, given\ test\ is\ positive)$$

$$= \frac{P(a\ person\ actually\ has\ disease\ and\ tests\ positive)}{P(tests\ positive)}$$

$$= \frac{.0095}{.0095 + .00495}$$

$$= .657$$

The correct answer is **B**.

SOA Sample Question 25 Explanation:

Here the smoking probabilities are not given but we can find them.

Let x be the probability of smoking without circulation problem.

Then $2x$ is the probability of smoking with circulation problem.

$$x + 2x = 1$$

This gives:

$$x = \frac{1}{3},\ \ 2x = \frac{2}{3}$$

Person Type	Probability	Smoker	Person Type and Smoker
Circulation Problem	.25	2/3	$.25\left(\frac{2}{3}\right)$
No Circulation Problem	.75	1/3	$.75\left(\frac{1}{3}\right)$

P(Circulation Problem given Smoker) = $P(C\ given\ S)\ =\ P(CS)\ /\ P(S)$

$$= \frac{.25\left(\frac{2}{3}\right)}{.25\left(\frac{2}{3}\right) + .75\left(\frac{1}{3}\right)}$$

$$= .4$$

$$= \frac{2}{5}$$

The correct answer is **C**.

SOA Sample Question 26 Explanation:

We will need only the data for 2012, 2013, and 2014.

Year	Proportion of all Cars	Accident Probability	Year and Accident Probability
2014	.16	.05	$.16(.05) = .008$
2013	.18	.02	$.18(.02) = .0036$
2012	.2	.03	$.2(.03) = .006$

$$P(2014\ Accident, given\ 2014, 2013, or\ 2012\ Accident)$$

$$= \frac{P(2014\ Accident)}{P(2014\ Accident\ and\ \ 2014, 2013, or\ 2012\ Accident)}$$

$$= \frac{.008}{.008 + .0036 + .006}$$

$$= .45$$

The correct answer is **D**.

SOA Sample Question 27 Explanation:

The main idea here is to find the probability of 1 defective vial out of 30 for each company. This will be done by using the binomial distribution.

$$f(x) = \binom{30}{x} p^x (1-p)^{30-x}$$

$$f(1) = \binom{30}{1} p^1 (1-p)^{30-1}$$

$$= 30p(1-p)^{29}$$

Company	Vials Proportion	Ineffective probability p	Probability that 1 out of 30 vials ineffective $f(1) = 30p(1-p)^{29}$	Vials Proportion and $f(1)$
X	1/5 = .2	.1	$30(.1)(.9)^{29} = .141$	$.2(.141) = .0282$
Rest (R)	4/5 = .8	.02	$30(.02)(.98)^{29} = .334$	$.8(.334) = .2672$

$$P(X\ given\ f(1)\ ) = \frac{P(X\ and\ f(1))}{P(f(1))}$$

$$= \frac{.0282}{.0282 + .2672}$$

$$= .1$$

The correct answer is **A**.

Quiz 2.

1. A man commutes for work from Monroe to Shreveport. The amount of gas he uses for going to Shreveport every morning is a normal random variable X with mean 3 gallons and standard deviation 0.3 gallon. The amount of gas he uses for returning to Monroe every evening is a normal random variable with mean 3.4 gallons and standard deviation .4 gallon. X and Y are independent. Find the probability that on a certain day, he uses more than 6 gallons for his complete round trip.
   A) .71
   B) .73
   C) .75
   D) .77
   E) .79

   Solution:
   We need to first find the mean μ and standard deviation σ for the complete round trip which will be captured by the sum of X and Y.
   Since X and Y are independent normal variables, so their sum will also be a normal variable with mean and variance given by:

$$\begin{aligned}\mu &= \mu_X + \mu_Y \\ &= 3 + 3.4 \\ &= 6.4\end{aligned}$$

$$\begin{aligned}\sigma &= \sqrt{\sigma_X{}^2 + \sigma_Y{}^2} \\ &= \sqrt{.3^2 + .4^2} \\ &= .5\end{aligned}$$

   Next, we need to convert 6 into the standard score so that we can use the standard normal tables given in the P exam.

$$\begin{aligned}z &= \frac{6 - 6.4}{.5} \\ &= -.8\end{aligned}$$

   We need $P(z > -.8)$
   This is the same as $P(z < .8)$. From the tables:

$$P(z < .8) = .7881$$

   The correct answer is **E**.

2. A company hires 10%, 12%, and 15% of its employees who graduate from the universities X, Y, and Z respectively while the remaining hires are from other universities. The probability of an employee of this company becoming a millionaire during the next year is .02, .03, .04, and .06 for those coming from X, Y, Z, and other universities respectively. If an employee becomes a millionaire during the next year, what is the probability that he graduated from University X?
   A) .01
   B) .02
   C) .03
   D) .04
   E) .05

   Solution:

$$P\ (X\ given\ millionaire) = \frac{P(X\ and\ millionaire)}{P\ (millionaire)}$$

$$= \frac{.1(.02)}{.1(.02) + .12(.03) + .15(.04) + .63(.06)}$$

$$= .04$$

   The correct answer is **D**.

3. Students taking the P exam in a certain month were surveyed. 25% said that they loved Math, 35% said they were ok with Math, while the remaining said that they hated Math. It turned out that those who were ok with Math were thrice as likely to pass the exam than those who hated Math, but only half as likely to pass as those who loved Math. Given that a student passed the exam, what is the probability that s/he loved Math?
   A) .51
   B) .53
   C) .55
   D) .57
   E) .59

   Solution:
   Let x be the pass probability of a student who hated Math.
   Then $3x$ is the pass probability of a student who was ok with Math,
   And $6x$ is the pass probability of a student who loved Math.

$$x + 3x + 6x = 1$$

$$x = .1, \qquad 3x = .3, \qquad 6x = .6$$

$$P\ (loved\ Math\ given\ Pass) = \frac{P(loved\ Math\ and\ Passed)}{P(passed)}$$

$$= \frac{.25(.6)}{.25(.6) + .35(.3) + .4(.1)} = .51$$

   The correct answer is **A**.

4. The probability of x car accidents per day in a town is 2^{-x-1}.

Calculate the probability of at least three accidents during a day, given that there has been at least one accident during that day.

(A) 1/2

(B) 1/3

(C) 1/4

(D) 1/5

(E) 1/6

Solution:

$$P(X \geq 3\ given\ X \geq 1) = \frac{P(N \geq 3\ and\ X \geq 1)}{P(X \geq 1)}$$

$$= \frac{P(X \geq 3)}{P(X \geq 1)}$$

$$= \frac{1 - P(X = 0,1, or\ 2)}{1 - P(X = 0)} \qquad (1)$$

Let us tabulate all the required values.

x	$P(x) = \frac{1}{2^{x+1}}$
0	1/2
1	1/4
2	1/8

Equation (1) then becomes:

$$P(X \geq 3\ given\ X \geq 1) = \frac{1 - [P(0) + P(1) + P(2)]}{1 - P(0)}$$

$$= \frac{1 - \left(\frac{1}{2} + \frac{1}{4} + \frac{1}{8}\right)}{1 - \frac{1}{2}}$$

$$= \frac{1}{4}$$

The correct answer is **C.**

5. A test indicates the presence of an infection 80% of the time when a person actually has the infection. It also falsely indicates infection 1% of the time when the person does not have the infection. In a certain country 5% of the population actually has the infection. Find the probability that a person does not have the infection given that the test indicates infection.
A) .17
B) .19
C) .23
D) .21
E) .25

Solution:

$$P(person\ doesn't\ have\ infection, given\ test\ is\ positive) = \frac{P(person\ doesn't\ have\ infection\ and\ tests\ positive)}{P(tests\ positive)}$$

Person Type	Proportion	Tests Positive	Person Type and Test Positive
Has Infection	5%	80%	$.05(.8) = .04$
Does not have Infection	95%	1%	$.95(.01) = .0095$

Thus, the required probability is:

$$P(person\ doesn't\ have\ infection, given\ test\ is\ positive) = \frac{.0095}{.0095 + .04} = .19$$

The correct answer is **B**.

6. A food bank receives 40% of its donations from Mike and 60% from Anna. Both send their donations in large truck loads. Mike's donation items always contain 10% fruit while Anna's donation items contain 15% fruit. It was found that 12 randomly chosen items in a truck load contained 2 pieces of fruit. What is the probability that the truck load was sent by Anna.
   A) 66%
   B) 70%
   C) 74%
   D) 78%
   E) 82%

Solution:

The main idea here is to find the probability of 2 fruits out of 12 for each donor. This will be done by using the binomial distribution.

$$f(2) = \binom{12}{2} p^2(1-p)^{12-2}$$

$$= 66p^2(1-p)^{10}$$

Person	Donation Proportion	Fruit Probability p	Probability that 2 out of 12 items were fruit $f(2) = 66p^2(1-p)^{10}$	P(person and $f(2)$)
Anna (A)	$.60$	.15	$66(.15)^2(.85)^{10} = .292$	$.6(.292) = .18$
Mike (M)	$.40$	.10	$66(.1)^2(.9)^{10} = .230$	$.4(.23) = .09$

$$\text{P(A given } f(2)) = \frac{\text{P(A and } f(2))}{\text{P}(f(2))}$$

$$= \frac{.18}{.18 + .09}$$

$$= .66$$

The correct answer is **A**.

Tools needed for problems 28-40

- The multinomial probability mass function is given as:

$$\boldsymbol{f(x_1, \ldots., x_k; n; p_1, \ldots.., p_k) = \frac{n!}{x_1! * \ldots * x_k!} p_1^{x_1} * \ldots . p_k^{x_k}}$$

Where $n =$ number of trials,
$x_1, \ldots, x_k$, are the number of instances of events $1, \ldots, k$ respectively,
$p_1, \ldots, p_k$, are the probabilities of events $1, \ldots, k$ respectively. Note that the binomial formula is a special case of this with only 2 events.

Density function, or probability density function (pdf) of a continuous random variable X is denoted by a lowercase function, for example, $f(x)$.

Cumulative Density function (cdf) of a continuous random variable X is denoted by the uppercase function corresponding to the lowercase pdf.

For example, $F(x)$ is the cdf corresponding to the pdf $f(x)$. Cdf is generally the integral of pdf:

$$F(x) = P(X \leq x) = \int_{-\infty}^{t} f(t)\, dt$$

In continuous variables $P(X \leq x) = P(X < x)$. Thus, it does not matter whether we include the equality sign with the inequality or not.

- The cumulative distribution function of an exponential distribution with mean k is:

$$F(x) = 1 - e^{-\frac{x}{k}}$$

- If X, Y are independent normal variables, and $N = aX + bY$, then:

$$\mu_N = a\mu_X + b\mu_Y$$
$$\sigma_N = \sqrt{a^2{\sigma_X}^2 + b^2{\sigma_Y}^2}$$

- For a normal distribution:

$$z = \frac{x - mean}{SD}$$
$$P(z > k) = 1 - P(z \leq k)$$
$$P(z > -k) = P(z < k)$$

SOA Sample Question 28 Explanation:

The cdf of an exponential distribution with mean k is given as:

$$F(x) = 1 - e^{-\frac{x}{k}}$$

Here, x is the number of days elapsed.

We are given that $F(50) = .3$. So, we get:

$$.3 = 1 - e^{-\frac{50}{k}}$$

$$e^{-\frac{50}{k}} = .7$$

$$-\frac{50}{k} = \ln(.7)$$

$$k = -\frac{50}{\ln(.7)}$$

$$= 140.2$$

We need to find $F(80)$.

$$F(80) = 1 - e^{-\frac{80}{140.2}}$$
$$= .43$$

The correct answer is **C**.

SOA Sample Question 29 Explanation:

The pdf for a Poisson distribution with x successes and mean k is:

$$f(x) = \frac{k^x e^{-k}}{x!}$$

The variance of Poisson distribution is also k.

We are given that $f(2) = 3f(4)$. So, we get:

$$\frac{k^2 e^{-k}}{2!} = 3\frac{k^4 e^{-k}}{4!}$$

$$\frac{k^2}{2} = \frac{3k^4}{24}$$

$$4 = k^2$$

$$k = 2$$

The correct answer is **D**.

SOA Sample Question 30 Explanation:

Let X denote the number of employees who achieve the high-performance level.

Then X follows a binomial distribution with parameters $n = 20, p = .02$.

We want the probability of inadequacy of funds to be less than 1%.

This means that we want the probability of adequacy of funds to be more than 99%.

The binomial formula is:

$$f(x) = \binom{n}{x} p^x (1-p)^{20-x}$$

$$f(x) = \binom{20}{x} .02^x (.98)^{20-x}$$

Since each employee gets C, so if x employees get the reward, then total reward will be xC.

Now because the total reward limit is 120 and since we want to maximize C, so we need to find the minimum x such that $P(X \leq x) > .99$.

Using the formula, we keep finding the values of the probability function until the cumulative value exceeds .99.

We have the following table:

x	$P(x) = \binom{20}{x} .02^x (.98)^{20-x}$	$P(X \leq x)$
0	.6676	.6676
1	.2725	.9401
2	.0528	.9929

Thus, there is more than 99% probability (99.29%) that 2 or less persons receive the award.

Note that we cannot stop at 1 since cumulative probability at that point is only 94.01% which is less than the required 99%.

Setting $xC = 120$, we get:

$$2C = 120,$$

$$C = 60$$

The correct answer is **D**.

SOA Sample Question 31 Explanation:

This is a trinomial distribution which is a special case of the multinomial distribution. The multinomial probability mass function is given as:

$$f(x_1, ..., x_k; n; p_1, ..., p_k) = \frac{n!}{x_1! * ... * x_k!} p_1^{x_1} * .... * p_k^{x_k}$$

Where n = number of trials,
$x_1, ..., x_k$, are the number of instances of events $1, ..., k$ respectively,
$p_1, ..., p_k$, are the probabilities of events $1, ..., k$ respectively,
This is a trinomial distribution. Let:
X_1 represent then number of low risk drivers,
X_2 represent then number of medium risk drivers,
X_3 represent then number of high risk drivers.

Here, $n = 4$ because we are selecting 4 drivers in our study. Also,

$$p_1 = .5, \qquad p_2 = .3, \qquad p_3 = .2$$

$$f(x_1, x_2, x_3) = \frac{4!}{x_1!\, x_2!\, x_3!}(.5)^{x_1}(.3)^{x_2}(.2)^{x_3}$$

We are to find $P(X_3 \geq X_1 + 2)$ subject to the condition $X_1 + X_2 + X_3 = 4$

All possible cases in which this happens are listed in the table below:

x_1	x_2	x_3	$f(x_1, x_2, x_3)$
0	0	4	.0016
0	1	3	.0096
0	2	2	.0216
1	0	3	.016

Adding all the values in the last column we get:

$$P(X_3 \geq X_1 + 2) = .0016 + .0096 + .0216 + .016$$

$$= .0488$$

This rounds to choice **D**.

SOA Sample Question 32 Explanation:

$$P(X > 16\ given\ X > 8) = \frac{P(X > 16\ and\ X > 8)}{P(X > 8)}$$

$$= \frac{P(X > 16)}{P(X > 8)}$$

$$P(X > 16) = \int_{16}^{\infty} f(x)dx$$

$$= \int_{16}^{20} .005(20 - x)\,dx$$

$$= .005\frac{(20 - x)^2}{-2}\Big|_{16}^{20}$$

$$= -.0025[(20 - 20)^2 - (20 - 16)^2]$$

$$= .04$$

$$P(X > 8) = \int_{8}^{\infty} f(x)dx$$

$$= \int_{8}^{20} .005(20 - x)\,dx$$

$$= .005\frac{(20 - x)^2}{-2}\Big|_{8}^{20}$$

$$= -.0025[(20 - 20)^2 - (20 - 8)^2]$$

$$= .36$$

$$P(X > 16\ given\ X > 8) = \frac{.04}{.36}$$

$$= \frac{1}{9}$$

The correct answer is **B**.

SOA Sample Question 33 Explanation:

We are given that:

$$f(x) = k(10 + x)^{-2}, \qquad 0 < x < 40$$

where k is a constant which can be found by using the fact that the integral of any pdf is 1.

$$\int_{-\infty}^{\infty} f(x)\,dx = 1$$

$$\int_{0}^{40} k\,(10 + x)^{-2} dx = 1$$

$$k\,\frac{(10 + x)^{-1}}{-1}\Big|_{0}^{40} = 1$$

$$\frac{-k}{10 + x}\Big|_{0}^{40} = 1$$

$$-\frac{k}{50} + \frac{k}{10} = 1$$

$$k = 12.5$$

Thus, the pdf is:

$$f(x) = 12.5(10 + x)^{-2}$$

We need to find $P(X < 6)$. Using the pdf with the appropriate limits we get:

$$P(X < 6) = \int_{-\infty}^{6} f(x)\,dx$$

$$= \int_{0}^{6} 12.5\,(10 + x)^{-2} dx$$

$$= \frac{-12.5}{10 + x}\Big|_{0}^{6}$$

$$= -\frac{12.5}{16} + \frac{12.5}{10}$$

$$= .47$$

The correct answer is **C**.

SOA Sample Question 34 Explanation:

$$f(y) = \begin{cases} k(1-y)^4, & 0 < y < 1 \\ 0, & otherwise \end{cases}$$

We begin by finding k. This is done by setting the integral of the pdf equal to 1.

$$\int_{-\infty}^{\infty} f(y)\,dy = 1$$

$$\int_0^1 k(1-y)^4 dy = 1$$

$$\frac{-k}{5}(1-y)^5\Big|_0^1 = 1$$

$$\frac{k}{5} = 1$$

$$k = 5$$

We need to find $P(V > 40000, given\ V > 10000)$.

$$P(V > 40000, given\ V > 10000) = \frac{P(V > 40000\ and\ V > 10000)}{P(V > 10000)}$$

$$= \frac{P(V > 40000)}{P(V > 10000)}$$

$$= \frac{P(100000Y > 40000)}{P(100000Y > 10000)}$$

$$= \frac{P(Y > .4)}{P(Y > .1)}$$

Note that we needed to change V in terms of Y because the pdf we have is for Y. We now integrate the pdf with the appropriate limits.

$$P(Y > .4) = \int_{.4}^{1} 5(1-y)^4 dy = -(1-y)^5\Big|_{.4}^{1} = .07776$$

$$P(Y > .1) = \int_{.1}^{1} 5(1-y)^4 dy = -(1-y)^5\Big|_{.1}^{1} = .59049$$

$$P(V > 40000, given\ V > 10000) = \frac{.07776}{.59049} = .13$$

The correct answer is **B**.

SOA Sample Question 35 Explanation:

Let T be the random variable representing the lifetime of the printer. The cdf of an exponential distribution with mean 2 is:

$$F(t) = P(T \leq t) = 1 - e^{-\frac{t}{2}}$$

$$\text{P(Failure during 1}^{\text{st}}\text{ year)} = P(T \leq 1)$$

$$= F(1)$$

$$= 1 - e^{-\frac{1}{2}}$$

$$= .3935$$

$$\text{P(Failure during 2}^{\text{nd}}\text{ year)} = P(1 \leq T \leq 2)$$

$$= F(2) - F(1)$$

$$= .2386$$

$$\text{Expected Refund per Printer} = .3935(200) + .2386(100)$$

$$= 102.56$$

$$\text{Expected Refund for 100 Printers} = 100(102.56)$$

$$= 10256$$

The correct answer is **D**.

SOA Sample Question 36 Explanation:

$$f(x) = \begin{cases} 3x^{-4}, & x > 1 \\ 0, & otherwise \end{cases}$$

$$P(X < 2 \; given \; X \geq 1.5) = \frac{P(X < 2 \; and \; X \geq 1.5)}{P(X \geq 1.5)}$$

$$= \frac{P(1.5 \leq X < 2)}{P(X \geq 1.5)}$$

$$P(1.5 \leq X < 2) = \int_{1.5}^{2} f(x)dx$$

$$= \int_{1.5}^{2} 3x^{-4}dx$$

$$= 3\frac{x^{-3}}{-3}\Big|_{1.5}^{2}$$

$$= -(2^{-3} - 1.5^{-3})$$

$$= .1713$$

$$P(X \geq 1.5) = \int_{1.5}^{\infty} 3x^{-4}dx$$

$$= 3\frac{x^{-3}}{-3}\Big|_{1.5}^{\infty}$$

$$= -(\infty^{-3} - 1.5^{-3})$$

$$= .2963$$

We have used the fact that:

$$\infty^{-3} = \frac{1}{\infty^3} = 0$$

$$P(X < 2 \; given \; X \geq 1.5) = \frac{.1713}{.2963}$$

$$= .578$$

The correct answer is **A**.

SOA Sample Question 37 Explanation:

Let X be a random variable denoting the number of hurricanes in 20 years.

Then X follows a binomial distribution with $n = 20,\ p = .05$.

$$f(x) = \binom{20}{x}(.05)^x(1-.05)^{20-x}$$

We need:

$$P(X < 3) = P(X = 0, 1, or\ 2)$$

$$= f(0) + f(1) + f(2)$$

x	$f(x) = \binom{20}{x}(.05)^x(.95)^{20-x}$
0	$\binom{20}{0}(.05)^0(.95)^{20-0} = .358$
1	$\binom{20}{1}(.05)^1(.95)^{20-1} = .377$
2	$\binom{20}{2}(.05)^2(.95)^{20-2} = .189$

$$P(X < 3) = .358 + .377 + .189$$

$$= .92$$

The correct answer is **E**.

SOA Sample Question 38 Explanation:

Let Y be insurance payment.

For a loss less than C, no payment is made because C is the deductible.

For a loss bigger than C, the payment is $X - C$. So,

$$Y = X - C, \qquad X > C$$

We are given that:

$$P(Y < .5) = .64$$

Substituting the value of Y we get:

$$P(X - C < .5) = .64$$

$$P(X < C + .5) = .64$$

$$\int_{-\infty}^{C+.5} f(x)\, dx = .64$$

$$\int_{0}^{C+.5} 2x\, dx = .64$$

$$x^2\Big|_0^{C+.5} = .64$$

$$(C + .5)^2 = .64$$

$$C + .5 = \pm .8$$

$$C = .3, -1.3$$

The negative value is rejected because $0 < C < 1$.

Thus $C = .3$

The correct answer is **B**.

SOA Sample Question 39 Explanation:

Each group has 10 participants.

The number of participants who complete the study in each group follows a binomial distribution with $n = 10, p = .8$ because if probability of dropping out is .2, then the probability of successfully completing is $1 - .2 = .8$.

$$f(x) = \binom{10}{x}(.8)^x(.2)^{10-x}$$

P (at least 9 complete in a group) $= f(9) + f(10)$

$$= \binom{10}{9}(.8)^9(.2)^{10-9} + \binom{10}{10}(.8)^{10}(.2)^{10-10}$$

$$= .2684 + .1074$$

$$= .3758$$

Since less than 9 is the complement of at least 9, so:

P (less than 9 complete in a group) $= 1 - .3758$

$$= .6242$$

P (at least 9 complete in one group but not the other)

= P (at least 9 complete in 1st group and less than 9 complete in 2nd group, or at least 9 complete in 2nd group and less than 9 complete in 1st group)

$$= .3758(.6242) + .3758(.6242)$$

$$= .469$$

The correct answer is **E**.

SOA Sample Question 40 Explanation:

Let A be a random variable denoting the claim amount for company A.

Let B be a random variable denoting the claim amount for company B.

We are to find $P(B > A)$. There are 2 cases where this can happen:

Case 1: No claim is made by company A. In this case, as long as a claim is made by company B, its amount exceeds that of company A. So,

$P_1(B > A) = P$(no claim is made by A)*P(a claim is made by B).

$$= .6(.3)$$

$$= .18$$

Case 2: A claim is made by company A. In this case, not only company B will also need to have a claim, but this would need to exceed the claim of company A. Since in this case both our random variables are normally distributed, so if:

$$X = B - A,$$

then X is normally distributed with parameters:

$$\mu_X = \mu_B - \mu_A = 9000 - 10000 = -1000$$

$$\sigma_X = \sqrt{{\sigma_B}^2 + (-1)^2{\sigma_A}^2} = \sqrt{2000^2 + 2000^2} = 2828.4$$

$$P(B > A) = P((B - A) > 0) = P(X > 0)$$

So, we need to find the z-score for 0 in order to proceed.

$$z = \frac{X - \mu_X}{\sigma_X}$$

$$z = \frac{0 - (-1000)}{2828.4}$$

$$= .35$$

$$P(X > 0) = P(z > .35) = 1 - P(z \leq .35) = 1 - .6368 = .3632$$

Hence, $P_2(B > A) = P$(a claim is made by both A and B)*$P(z > .35)$

$$= .4(.3)(.3632) = .0436$$

$$P(B > A) = P_1(B > A) + P_2(B > A) = .18 + .0436 = .2236$$

This is closest to choice D. The difference is because of roundings.

The correct answer is **D**.

Quiz 3

1. The lifetime of a bulb is exponentially distributed. The probability that the bulb will work for no more than 100 hours is .25. Find the probability that it will work for more than 200 hours.
   A) .125
   B) .438
   C) .500
   D) .562
   E) .657

Solution:

The cdf of an exponential distribution with mean k is given as:

$$F(x) = 1 - e^{-\frac{x}{k}}$$

Here, x is the number of hours elapsed before the bulb is out.

We are given that $F(100) = .25$. So, the cdf equation becomes:

$$.25 = 1 - e^{-\frac{100}{k}}$$

$$e^{-\frac{100}{k}} = .75$$

$$-\frac{100}{k} = \ln(.75)$$

$$k = -\frac{100}{\ln(.75)}$$

$$= 347.6$$

$$F(200) = 1 - e^{-\frac{200}{347.6}}$$

$$= .438$$

We need to find $1 - F(200)$.

Note that $F(200)$ gives the probability that lifetime is less than 200 hrs. Thus:

$$P(X > 200) = 1 - F(200)$$

$$= 1 - .438$$

$$= .562$$

The correct answer is **D**.

2. The number of children that a couple can have has a Poisson distribution. The probability that the couple has 3 children is half of the probability that they will have 2 children. Find the probability of them having only 1 child.
   A) .11
   B) .16
   C) .22
   D) .28
   E) .33

Solution:

The pdf for a Poisson distribution with x successes and mean k is:

$$f(x) = \frac{k^x e^{-k}}{x!}$$

We are given that $f(3) = .5f(2)$. So, we get:

$$\frac{k^3 e^{-k}}{3!} = .5\frac{k^2 e^{-k}}{2!}$$

$$\frac{k^3}{6} = \frac{k^2}{4}$$

$$k = 1.5$$

$$f(1) = \frac{1.5^1 e^{-1.5}}{1!}$$

$$= .33$$

The correct answer is **E**.

3. A high school has a total reward of $60,000 from which equal prizes will be given to any of the 15 grade 12 teachers whose class averages 29 or more in MATH ACT at the end of school year. However, the individual prize amount must be announced at the beginning of the school year. Past data shows that the probability of 29+ MATH ACT in a class is .05. What individual prize amount should be announced so that the probability of there being sufficient funds for every qualifying teacher is at least 98%.
A) 4000
B) 5000
C) 15000
D) 20000
E) 30000

Solution:

Let X denote the number of teachers who achieve the high-performance level.

Let M denote the maximum individual award.

Then X follows a binomial distribution with parameters n = 15 and p = 0.05.

We want the probability of adequacy of funds to be more than 98%.

The binomial formula is:

$$f(x) = \binom{15}{x}.05^x(.95)^{15-x}$$

Since each employee gets M, so if x employees get the reward, then total reward will be xM. Now because the total reward limit is 60000 and since we want to maximize M, so we need to find the minimum x such that $P(X \leq x) > .98$.

Using the formula, we keep finding the values of the probability function until the cumulative value exceeds .98. We have the following table:

x	$f(x) = \binom{15}{x}.05^x(.95)^{15-x}$	$P(X \leq x)$
0	$\binom{15}{0}.05^0(.95)^{15-0} = .4633$	.4633
1	$\binom{15}{1}.05^1(.95)^{15-1} = .3658$	.8291
2	$\binom{15}{2}.05^2(.95)^{15-2} = .1348$	.9639
3	$\binom{15}{3}.05^3(.95)^{15-3} = .0307$	.9946

Thus, there is more than 98% probability that 3 or less persons receive the award.

Setting $3M = 60000$, we get $M = 20000$

The correct answer is **D.**

4. At a certain university, half of the students are from Louisiana, and a third of the students are from Texas. What is the probability that among 3 randomly selected students, there is exactly one more student from Louisiana than from Texas?
   A) .292
   B) .346
   C) .397
   D) .445
   E) .483

Solution:

This is a trinomial distribution which is a special case of the multinomial distribution. The multinomial probability mass function is given as:

$$f(x_1, \dots, x_k; n; p_1, \dots, p_k) = \frac{n!}{x_1! * \dots * x_k!} {p_1}^{x_1} * \dots * {p_k}^{x_k}$$

Where n = number of trials,
$x_1, \dots, x_k$, are the number of instances of events $1, \dots, k$ respectively,
$p_1, \dots, p_k$, are the probabilities of events $1, \dots, k$ respectively,
This is a trinomial distribution. Let:
X_1 represent then number of students from Louisiana,
X_2 represent then number of students from Texas,
X_3 represent then number of students from other places

Here, $n = 3$ because we are selecting 3 students in our study. Also,

$$p_1 = \frac{1}{2}, \qquad p_2 = \frac{1}{3}, \qquad p_3 = 1 - \frac{1}{2} - \frac{1}{3} = \frac{1}{6}$$

$$f(x_1, x_2, x_3) = \frac{3!}{x_1!\, x_2!\, x_3!} \left(\frac{1}{2}\right)^{x_1} \left(\frac{1}{3}\right)^{x_2} \left(\frac{1}{6}\right)^{x_3}$$

We are to find $P(X_1 = X_2 + 1)$ subject to the condition $X_1 + X_2 + X_3 = 3$

All possible cases in which this happens are listed in the table below:

x_1	x_2	x_3	$f(x_1, x_2, x_3)$
1	0	2	.0417
2	1	0	.25

$$\text{Required probability} = .0417 + .25$$
$$= .2917$$

This rounds to .292.

The correct answer is **A.**

5. In a certain country, divorce is not possible during the 1st year of marriage. Other than that, the random variable T, denoting the number of years after marriage which a divorce occurs has the pdf:

$$f(t) = \frac{1}{t^2}, \qquad t > 1$$

Find the probability that a divorce happened within the 1st ten years of marriage, given that it happened during the 1st twenty years of marriage.

A) .91
B) .93
C) .95
D) .97
E) .99

Solution:

$$P(T < 10 \; given \; T < 20) = \frac{P(T < 10 \; and \; T < 20)}{P(T < 20)}$$

$$= \frac{P(T < 10)}{P(T < 20)}$$

$$P(T < 10) = \int_1^{10} t^{-2} \, dt = -\frac{1}{t}\Big|_1^{10}$$

$$= .9$$

$$P(T < 20) = \int_1^{20} t^{-2} \, dt = -\frac{1}{t}\Big|_1^{20}$$

$$= .95$$

$$P(T < 10 \; given \; T < 20) = \frac{.9}{.95}$$

$$= .95$$

The correct answer is **C**.

6. If you pass a quiz in less than 10 minutes, your probability of passing a corresponding exam is given by the probability density function $f(t)$, where $f(t)$ is proportional to $(2+t)^{-1}$. If you take more than 10 minutes, you have no chance of passing the exam. Calculate the probability of passing the exam if you take more than 8 minutes to pass the quiz.
   A) 6%
   B) 8%
   C) 10%
   D) 12%
   E) 14%

Solution:

We need to find $P(T > 8)$.

We are given that:

$$f(t) = k(2+t)^{-1}$$

where k is a constant.

We can find k by using the fact that the integral of any pdf is 1.

$$\int_0^{10} k\,(2+t)^{-1} dt = 1$$

$$k \ln(2+t)\,\Big|_0^{10} = 1$$

$$k(\ln 12 - \ln 2) = 1$$

$$k \ln \frac{12}{2} = 1$$

$$k = \frac{1}{\ln 6}$$

Thus, the pdf that we have is:

$$f(t) = \frac{(2+t)^{-1}}{\ln 6}$$

$$P(T > 8) = \int_8^{10} \frac{(2+t)^{-1}}{\ln 6} dt$$

$$= \frac{\ln(2+t)}{\ln 6}\Big|_8^{10}$$

$$= \frac{\ln 12}{\ln 6} - \frac{\ln 10}{\ln 6}$$

$$.10 = 10\%$$

The correct answer is **C**.

7. The lifetime of a computer costing 500 is exponentially distributed with mean 10 years. The manufacturer agrees to pay a full refund to a buyer if the computer fails during the first month following its purchase, and 75% refund if it fails during the remaining of the 1st year, and no refund for failure after that. The sale of how many computers will result in an expected total refund of approximately 2570?
A) 60
B) 70
C) 80
D) 90
E) 100

Solution:
Let T be the random variable representing the lifetime of the computer in months.

The cdf of an exponential distribution with mean 120 months is:

$$F(t) = P(T \leq t)$$

$$= 1 - e^{-\frac{t}{120}}$$

$$\text{P(Failure during 1}^{\text{st}}\text{ month)} = P(T \leq 1)$$

$$= F(1)$$

$$= 1 - e^{-\frac{1}{120}}$$

$$= .0083$$

$$\text{P(Failure during next 11 months)} = P(1 \leq T \leq 12)$$

$$= F(12) - F(1)$$

$$= .0869$$

$$\text{Expected Refund per Computer} = .0083(500) + .0869(.75)(500)$$

$$= 36.74$$

If x computers give a total refund of 2570, then:

$$36.74x = 2570$$

$$x = 70$$

The correct answer is **B**.

8. An insurance policy pays for a random loss X subject to a deductible of 100. The loss amount is modeled as a continuous random variable with density:

$$f(x) = \frac{x}{80000}, 0 < x < 400$$

The loss amount can never exceed 400.

For a given loss, find the probability that the company pays less than 90

(A) 0.226

(B) 0.332

(C) 0.447

(D) 0.512

(E) 0.604

Solution:

Let Y be a random variable representing the insurance payment.

Note that for a loss less than 100, no payment is made because 100 is the deductible.

For a loss bigger than 100, the payment is X – 100. So,

$$Y = \{X - 100, \quad X > 100$$

$$P(Y < 90) = P(X - 100 < 90)$$

$$= P(X < 190)$$

$$= \int_0^{190} \frac{x}{80000} dx$$

$$= \frac{x^2}{160000} \Big|_0^{190}$$

$$= .226$$

The correct answer is **A**.

9. A college has a 90% graduation rate. Find the probability that among 7 boys and 7 girls, all randomly chosen from this college, all the girls but not all the boys will graduate.
A) .05
B) .15
C) .20
D) .25
E) .50

Solution:

Each group has 7 students and the number of students who graduate in each group follows a binomial distribution with $n = 7, p = .9$

P (all girls graduate) = $f(7)$, where

$$f(x) = \binom{7}{x}(.9)^x(.1)^{7-x}$$

Therefore, P (all girls graduate) = $\binom{7}{7}(.9)^7(.1)^{7-7}$

$$= .4783$$

Note that probability of any event is the same whether we deal with boys or girls.

Thus, probability of all boys graduating is the same as that of all girls graduating. So,

P (not all boys graduate) = 1 − P (all boys graduate)

$$= 1 - .4783$$

$$= .5217$$

P (all girls graduate but not all boys) = $.4783(.5217)$

$$= .25$$

The correct answer is **D**.

10. Because of the pandemic, a job seeker in country X is only 55% likely to find a job in 2021, but if a job is found, then the annual salary will be normally distributed with mean 30000 and standard deviation 5000. Also, a job seeker in country Y is only 65% likely to find a job, but if a job is found, then the annual salary will be normally distributed with mean 20000 and standard deviation 3000. The salaries in the two countries are independent. Find the probability that the salary of a job seeker in 2021 in country X will be more than that of a person in country Y.

A) .53
B) .62
C) .71
D) .84
E) .96

Solution:

Let X be a random variable denoting the salary amount in Country X.

Let Y be a random variable denoting the salary amount in Country Y.

We are to find $P(X > Y)$. There are 2 cases where this can happen:

Case 1: The Person in Country Y is Jobless. In this case, as long as, the person in country X gets a job, their amount exceeds that of the one in Country Y. In this case, $P_1(X > Y) =$ P(person in Country Y is jobless)*P(person in Country X has a job). So, we have:

$$P_1(X > Y) = .35(.55) = .1925$$

Case 2: The Person in Country Y has a Job. In this case, not only will the person in Country X need to have a job, but their salary would need to exceed the salary of Country Y person. Since in this case both our random variables are normally distributed, so if N is the random variable equaling $X - Y$, then N is normally distributed with:

$$\mu_N = \mu_X - \mu_Y = 30000 - 20000 = 10000$$

$$\sigma_N = \sqrt{\sigma_X{}^2 + \sigma_Y{}^2} = \sqrt{5000^2 + 3000^2} = 5831$$

We are looking for $P(X > Y) = P((X - Y) > 0) = P(N > 0)$

So, we need to find the z-score for 0 in order to proceed.

$$z = \frac{0 - 10000}{5831} = -1.71$$

Thus, we need $P(z >. -1.71) = P(z < 1.71) = .9564$

Hence, $P_2(X > Y) = P$(Both person have a job)*$P(z > -1.71)$

$$= .55(.65)(.9564) = .3419$$

$$P(X > Y) = P_1(X > Y) + P_2(X > Y) = .1925 + .3419 = .5344$$

The correct answer is **A**.

Tools Needed for Problems 41-52

Binomial Distribution pmf: $f(x) = \binom{n}{x}(.p)^x(1-p)^{n-x}$

Poisson Distribution pmf:

$$f(x) = \frac{m^x e^{-m}}{x!}, \qquad x = 0,1,2,3,\ldots$$

where m = mean

For a continuous random variable, with pdf $f(x)$, the expected value is:

$$E[X] = \int_{-\infty}^{\infty} x\, f(x)\, dx$$

For a discrete random variable, with pmf $f(x)$, the expected value is:

$$E[X] = \sum x\, f(x)$$

$$|x| = \begin{cases} -x, & x < 0 \\ x, & x \geq 0 \end{cases}$$

The pdf, and cdf, respectively, of an exponential distribution with mean k are:

$$f(x) = \frac{1}{k} e^{-\frac{x}{k}}, \qquad 0 < x < \infty$$

$$F(x) = 1 - e^{-x/k}$$

Integration by parts shortcut:

$$\int (x+k)e^{ax} dx = \frac{(x+k)e^{ax}}{a} - \frac{e^{ax}}{a^2}$$

$$Var\ aX = a^2\ Var\ X$$

SOA Sample Question 41 Explanation:

We are being asked the probability of there being at least 4 non-accident months before the 4th accident month.

This will happen if in the first 7 months, there are at least 4 non-accident months, because if there are less than 4 non-accident months in the first 7, then it means we have already had 4 accident months before 4 non-accident months.

Number of non-accident months, X, in first 7 months is binomial with $n = 7,\ p = .4$. Thus:

$$f(x) = \binom{7}{x}(.4)^x(.6)^{7-x}$$

P (at least 4 non-accident months in the first 7) = $P(X \geq 4)$

$$= f(4) + f(5) + f(6) + f(7)$$

$$= \binom{7}{4}(.4)^4(.6)^{7-4} + \binom{7}{5}(.4)^5(.6)^{7-5} + \binom{7}{6}(.4)^6(.6)^{7-6} + \binom{7}{7}(.4)^7(.6)^{7-7}$$

$$= .29$$

The correct answer is **D**.

SOA Sample Question 42 Explanation:

The appropriate values are tabulated below:

Number of Hospital Days (k)	$P(k) = \frac{6-k}{15}$	Payment (y)	$yP(k)$
1	1/3	100	100/3
2	4/15	200	160/3
3	1/5	300	60
4	2/15	350	140/3
5	1/15	400	80/3

$$\text{Expected payment} = \sum yP(k)$$

$$= 220$$

which is obtained by adding the entries of the last column.

The correct answer is **C**.

***SOA Sample Question 43 Explanation**:*

For a continuous random variable, the expected value is:

$$E[X] = \int_{-\infty}^{\infty} x\, f(x)\, dx$$

Now there is no direct formula for integrating the absolute value function.

So, we have to break it up by recalling that:

$$|x| = \begin{cases} -x, & x < 0 \\ x, & x \geq 0 \end{cases}$$

The pdf given here is:

$$f(x) = \begin{cases} \dfrac{|x|}{10}, & -2 \leq x \leq 4 \\ 0, & otherwise \end{cases}$$

Splitting up the integral appropriately, and omitting the parts where pdf is 0 we get:

$$E[X] = \int_{-2}^{0} x\left(-\frac{x}{10}\right) dx + \int_{0}^{4} x\left(\frac{x}{10}\right) dx$$

$$= \int_{-2}^{0} -\frac{x^2}{10}\, dx + \int_{0}^{4} \frac{x^2}{10}\, dx$$

$$= -\frac{x^3}{30}\bigg|_{-2}^{0} + \frac{x^3}{30}\bigg|_{0}^{4}$$

$$= -\left(\frac{0^3}{30} - \frac{(-2)^3}{30}\right) + \left(\frac{4^3}{30} - \frac{0^3}{30}\right)$$

$$= \frac{28}{15}$$

The correct answer is **D**.

SOA Sample Question 44 Explanation:

The formula for the pdf of an exponential distribution with mean 3 is:

$$f(t) = \frac{1}{3}e^{-\frac{t}{3}}, \ t \geq 0$$

Next, we note that:

$$X = \max(T, 2) = \begin{cases} 2, & 0 \leq T \leq 2 \\ T, & T > 2 \end{cases}$$

$$E[X] = E[\max(T, 2)]$$

$$= \int_0^\infty \max(t, 2)\, f(t)\, dt$$

$$= \int_0^2 \max(t, 2)\, f(t)\, dt + \int_2^\infty \max(t, 2)\, f(t)\, dt$$

$$\int_0^2 2\left(\frac{1}{3}e^{-\frac{t}{3}}\right) dt + \int_2^\infty t\left(\frac{1}{3}e^{-\frac{t}{3}}\right) dt$$

Recall from calculus that:

$$\int e^{ax} dx = \frac{e^{ax}}{a}$$

The 2nd integral requires integration by parts which can be done by the shortcut:

$$\int x\, e^{ax} dx = \frac{x\, e^{ax}}{a} - \frac{e^{ax}}{a^2}$$

Here, $a = -\frac{1}{3}$ for both the integrals. So, pulling the constants out:

$$E[X] = -2e^{-\frac{t}{3}}\Big|_0^2 + \left(-t\, e^{-\frac{t}{3}} - 3e^{-\frac{t}{3}}\right)\Big|_2^\infty$$

Also, recall that:

$$e^{-\infty} = 0, \quad \infty e^{-\infty} = 0$$

Note that the correct mathematical way to write these is in terms of limits, but I am using loose notation as it is more convenient and time saving, and serves our purpose adequately. We get:

$$E[X] = -2e^{-\frac{2}{3}} + 2 + \left(2e^{-\frac{2}{3}} + 3e^{-\frac{2}{3}}\right)$$

$$= 2 + 3e^{-\frac{2}{3}}$$

The correct answer is **D**.

***SOA Sample Question 45 Explanation**:*

Here, we can use the cdf of exponential distribution.

Note that using cdf instead of pdf saves you from integration and makes your work shorter.

Since the mean is 10, the cdf becomes:

$$F(t) = 1 - e^{-t/10}$$

Expected Payment equals:

(pmt in 1st year) P(failure in1st year) + (pmt in 2nd or 3rd year) P(failure in 2nd or 3rd year).

This gives:

$$1000 = x\,P(X \leq 1) + \;.5x\,P(1 \leq X \leq 3)$$
$$1000 = x\,F(1) + \;.5x\,[F(3) - F(1)]$$
$$1000 = x\left(1 - e^{-1/10}\right) + .5x\left[\left(1 - e^{-3/10}\right) - \left(1 - e^{-1/10}\right)\right]$$
$$1000 = .0952x + .5x(.164)$$
$$1000 = .1772x$$
$$x = 5643$$

The slight discrepancy of this from choice D is because of rounding.

The correct answer is **D**.

***SOA Sample Question 46 Explanation**:*

Probability of not failing in a given year when it is still alive at the beginning of the year is:

$$1 - .4 = .6$$

Failure in Year	Probability (p)	Payment (X)	pX
1	$.4$	4000	1600
2	$.6(.4) = .24$	3000	720
3	$.6(.6)(.4) = .144$	2000	288
4	$.6(.6)(.6)(.4) = .0864$	1000	86.4

$$\text{Expected value } = \sum pX$$

$$= 1600 + 720 + 288 + 86.4$$

$$= 2694$$

The correct answer is **E**.

SOA Sample Question 47 Explanation:

The pmf of the Poisson distribution with mean 1.5 is:

$$f(x) = \frac{1.5^x e^{-1.5}}{x!}, \qquad x = 0,1,2,3,...$$

Also, the mean of any discrete distribution equals $\sum x\, f(x)$. So, we get:

$$1.5 = \sum_{x=1}^{\infty} x\, \frac{1.5^x e^{-1.5}}{x!} = \sum_{x=1}^{\infty} \frac{1.5^x e^{-1.5}}{(x-1)!} \qquad (1)$$

Note that we started the summation from 1 instead of 0 because the 1st sum above shows that there is no contribution to the sum when $x = 0$. This equation will be needed later.

We are given that there is no payment for 0 or 1 snowstorms, and a payment of 10000 per snowstorm thereafter. So, for 2 snowstorms, the payment is 10000; for 3 snowstorms, it is 20000, for 4 snowstorms, it is 30000, and so on. Hence:

The payment for x snowstorms is $10000(x-1)$.

So, the total expect payment is given as:

$$E = \sum_{x=1}^{\infty} 10000(x-1)\, f(x)$$

$$= \sum_{x=1}^{\infty} 10000(x-1)\, \frac{1.5^x e^{-1.5}}{x!}$$

$$= \sum_{x=1}^{\infty} 10000\, x \frac{1.5^x e^{-1.5}}{x!} - \sum_{x=1}^{\infty} 10000\, \frac{1.5^x e^{-1.5}}{x!}$$

$$= 10000 \sum_{x=1}^{\infty} \frac{1.5^x e^{-1.5}}{(x-1)!} - 10000 \sum_{x=1}^{\infty} \frac{1.5^x e^{-1.5}}{x!}$$

The 1st sum equals 1.5 by equation (1). The 2nd sum, if it had started from 0 instead of 1, would have equaled 1 because the sum of all the possible probabilities in a probability space is 1. So, we add and subtract the term corresponding to $x = 0$ in the 2nd sum. Thus:

$$E = 10000(1.5) - 10000 \sum_{x=0}^{\infty} \frac{1.5^{x-1} e^{-1.5}}{x!} + 10000 \frac{(1.5)^0 e^{-1.5}}{0!}$$

$$= 15000 - 10000(1) + 10000e^{-1.5}$$

$$= 7231$$

The correct answer is **C**.

SOA Sample Question 48 Explanation:

Let Y represent unpaid losses. If loss amount is less than 2, then all that amount is unpaid. If loss amount is greater than or equal to 2, then the unpaid amount is 2. So, we have:

$$Y = \begin{cases} X, & X < 2 \\ 2, & X \geq 2 \end{cases}$$

We need mean of unpaid losses, which is the expected value of Y.

$$E[Y] = \int_{-\infty}^{\infty} y\, f(x)\, dx$$

$$= \int_{-\infty}^{2} x\, f(x)\, dx + \int_{2}^{\infty} 2\, f(x)\, dx$$

$$= \int_{.6}^{2} x\, \frac{2.5(.6)^{2.5}}{x^{3.5}}\, dx + \int_{2}^{\infty} 2\, \frac{2.5(.6)^{2.5}}{x^{3.5}}\, dx$$

$$= 2.5(.6)^{2.5} \int_{.6}^{2} x^{-2.5} dx + 5\,(.6)^{2.5} \int_{2}^{\infty} x^{-3.5} dx$$

$$= .697\left(\frac{x^{-1.5}}{-1.5}\right)\Big|_{.6}^{2} + 1.394\left(\frac{x^{-2.5}}{-2.5}\right)\Big|_{2}^{\infty}$$

$$= -.465(2^{-1.5} - .6^{-1.5}) - .558(\infty^{-2.5} - 2^{-2.5})$$

Note that $\infty^{-2.5} = \frac{1}{\infty^{2.5}} = \frac{1}{\infty} = 0$. Thus:

$$E[Y] = .93$$

The correct answer is **C**.

***SOA Sample Question 49 Explanation*:**

$$P(N) = \frac{K}{N}$$

By adding all the possible probabilities to 1, we have:

$$P(1) + P(2) + P(3) + P(4) + P(5) = 1$$

$$\frac{K}{1} + \frac{K}{2} + \frac{K}{3} + \frac{K}{4} + \frac{K}{5} = 1$$

$$K\left(1 + \frac{1}{2} + \frac{1}{3} + \frac{1}{4} + \frac{1}{5}\right) = 1$$

$$K\left(\frac{60 + 30 + 20 + 15 + 12}{60}\right) = 1$$

$$K = \frac{60}{137} = .438$$

Remember that there is deductible of 2.

We need to find the expected value of the paid amount. The necessary values are tabulated below:

Loss (N)	Payment (X) (subject to a deductible of 2)	Probability= $p = \frac{K}{N} = \frac{.438}{N}$	Xp
1	0	.438	0
2	0	.219	0
3	1	.146	.146
4	2	.1095	.219
5	3	.0876	.263

Since the probability of a loss occurring is .05, so:

$$E(X) = .05 \sum Xp$$

$$= .05(0 + 0 + .146 + .219 + .263)$$

$$= .031$$

The correct answer is **A**.

SOA Sample Question 50 Explanation:

Let X be a random variable that represents the benefit amount. Then:

$$X = \begin{cases} Y, & Y \le 10 \\ 10, & Y > 10 \end{cases}$$

$$E[X] = \int_{-\infty}^{\infty} x\, f(y)$$

$$= \int_{-\infty}^{10} y\, f(y)\, dy + \int_{10}^{\infty} 10\, f(y)\, dy$$

$$= \int_{1}^{10} y\, 2y^{-3} dy + \int_{10}^{\infty} 10\, (2y^{-3})\, dy$$

$$\int_{1}^{10} 2y^{-2} dy + \int_{10}^{\infty} 20\, y^{-3}\, dy$$

$$= \frac{2y^{-1}}{-1}\bigg|_{1}^{10} + \frac{20y^{-2}}{-2}\bigg|_{10}^{\infty}$$

$$= -2(10^{-1} - 1^{-1}) - 10(\infty^{-2} - 10^{-2})$$

Note that:

$$\infty^{-2} = \frac{1}{\infty^2} = \frac{1}{\infty} = 0$$

So, the expected value is:

$$E[X] = 1.9$$

The correct answer is **D**.

SOA Sample Question 51 Explanation:

Let Y be a random variable representing the claim payment. Then:

$$Y = \begin{cases} X - 1, & 1 < X < 15 \\ 15 - 1, & X = 15 \end{cases}$$

Now since there is .04 probability of partial loss, and .02 probability of total loss, the expected claim payment (in thousands) will equal:

.04(Expected value of Y in case of partial loss) + .02(Expected value of Y in case of total loss)

$$= .04 \int_1^{15} yf(x)\,dx + .02(15 - 1)$$

$$= .04 \int_1^{15} (x - 1)(.5003)e^{-\frac{x}{2}}\,dx + .02(15 - 1)$$

The short cut for this integration by parts is:

$$\int (x + k)e^{ax}dx = \frac{(x + k)e^{ax}}{a} - \frac{e^{ax}}{a^2}$$

Here, $k = -1, a = -\frac{1}{2}$. Thus, the expected claim payment is:

$$.020012\left[(x - 1)\left(-2e^{-\frac{x}{2}}\right) - 4e^{-\frac{x}{2}}\right]_1^{15} + .02(14)$$

$$= .020012\left[-28e^{-\frac{15}{2}} - 4e^{-\frac{15}{2}} + 4e^{-\frac{1}{2}}\right] + .28$$

$$= .329$$

This answer is in thousands.

So the value is 329 which calls for choice B.

The difference is because of the rounding that they have done in their calculations.

The correct answer is **B**.

SOA Sample Question 52 Explanation:

$$f(x) = k(1+x)^{-4}$$

The first step is to find the constant by integrating the pdf to 1.

$$\int_0^\infty k(1+x)^{-4}dx = 1$$

$$\frac{k(1+x)^{-3}}{-3}\Big|_0^\infty = 1$$

$$= -\frac{k}{3}[(1+\infty)^{-3} - (1+0)^{-3}] = 1$$

Note that $(1+\infty)^{-3} = \infty^{-3} = \frac{1}{\infty^3} = \frac{1}{\infty} = 0$. So, we get:

$$\frac{k}{3} = 1$$

$$k = 3$$

To get the expected value, we use the formula:

$$E[X] = \int_{-\infty}^{\infty} x\, f(x)\, dx$$

$$= \int_0^\infty x\, 3(1+x)^{-4}\, dx$$

Let $u = 1 + x \Rightarrow du = dx$. When $x = 0, u = 1$. When $x = \infty, u = \infty$

$$E[X] = 3\int_1^\infty (u-1)(u)^{-4}\, du$$

$$E[X] = 3\int_1^\infty u^{-3} - u^{-4}\, du$$

$$= 3\left(\frac{u^{-2}}{-2} - \frac{u^{-3}}{-3}\right)\Big|_1^\infty$$

$$= 3\left(-\frac{1}{2u^2} + \frac{1}{3u^3}\right)\Big|_1^\infty$$

$$= 3\left(-\frac{1}{2\infty^2} + \frac{1}{3\infty^3} + \frac{1}{2} - \frac{1}{3}\right)$$

$$= \frac{1}{2}$$

The correct answer is **C**.

Quiz 4

1. I move at the beginning of a year to an area where the probability of a flood in any given year is .45. Flood(s) occurring or not in different years are independent. What is the probability that I see at least 3 flood-free years before the 2nd flood year?
   A) .35
   B) .39
   C) .43
   D) .47
   E) .51

Solution:

We are being asked the probability of there being at least 3 flood-free years before the 2nd flood year.

This will happen if in the first 4 years, there are at least 3 non-flood years, because if there are less than 3 non-flood years in the first 4, then it means we have already had 2 flood years before 3 non-flood years.

P (at least 3 non-flood years in the first 4) = $f(3) + f(4)$

$$\text{where } f(x) = \binom{4}{x}(.55)^x(.45)^{4-x},$$

as this is a binomial distribution with $n = 4,\ p = .55,\ X =$ number of non-flood years.

Thus:

$$P(X \geq 3) = \binom{4}{3}(.55)^3(.45)^{4-3} + \binom{4}{4}(.55)^4(.45)^{4-4}$$

$$= .39$$

The correct answer is **B**.

2. A university reimburses 200 for each of the first two actuarial exams that a student passes, and 100 each for the 3rd and 4th exam. No one passes more than 4 exams during their undergraduate career. All reimbursements to a student are done together at the time of their graduation. The number of exams X that a requesting student passes has the pmf:

$$f(X = x) = \frac{7 - kx}{12}, \qquad x = 1,2,3,4$$

Find the expected reimbursement to a requesting student.

A) 258
B) 298
C) 338
D) 378
E) 418

Solution:

We start by finding k, by adding all possible pmf values to 1.

$$f(1) + f(2) + f(3) + f(4) = 1$$

$$\frac{7 - k}{12} + \frac{7 - 2k}{12} + \frac{7 - 3k}{12} + \frac{7 - 4k}{12} = 1$$

$$\frac{28 - 10k}{12} = 1$$

$$28 - 10k = 12$$

$$k = 1.6$$

$$f(X = x) = \frac{7 - 1.6x}{12}, \qquad x = 1,2,3,4$$

The appropriate values are tabulated below:

No. of Exams Passed (x)	$f(x) = \frac{7 - 1.6x}{12}$	Payment (y)	$yf(x)$
1	$.45$	200	90
2	$.32$	400	128
3	$.18$	500	90
4	$.05$	600	30

$$E = \sum y\,f(x) = 90 + 128 + 90 + 30$$

$$= 338$$

The correct answer is **C**.

3. Let X be a continuous random variable with pdf:

$$f(x) = \frac{4|x|^3}{17}, -1 < x < 2$$

Find the expected value of X.

A) 124/85
B) 128/85
C) 132/85
D) 137/85
E) 141/85

Solution:
For a continuous random variable, the expected value is:

$$E[X] = \int_{-\infty}^{\infty} x\, f(x)\, dx$$

Now there is no direct formula for integrating the absolute value function.

So, we have to break it up by recalling that:

$$|x| = \begin{cases} -x, & x < 0 \\ x, & x \geq 0 \end{cases}$$

Splitting up the integral appropriately, and omitting the 0 region gives:

$$E[X] = \int_{-1}^{0} x\left(-\frac{4x^3}{17}\right) dx + \int_{0}^{2} x\left(\frac{4x^3}{17}\right) dx$$

$$= \int_{-1}^{0} -\frac{4x^4}{17}\, dx + \int_{0}^{2} \frac{4x^4}{17}\, dx$$

$$= -\frac{4x^5}{85}\bigg|_{-1}^{0} + \frac{4x^5}{85}\bigg|_{0}^{2}$$

$$= \frac{124}{85}$$

The correct answer is **A**.

4. If X is a non-negative exponentially distributed random variable with mean 2, and $Y = \min\{X, 5\}$, find the expected value of Y.
A) 1.44
B) 1.54
C) 1.64
D) 1.74
E) 1.84

Solution:

The formula for the pdf of an exponential distribution with mean 2 is:

$$f(x) = \frac{1}{2}e^{-\frac{x}{2}},\ x > 0$$

Next, note that:

$$\min(X,5) = \begin{cases} X, & 0 \le X \le 5 \\ 5, & X > 5 \end{cases}$$

$$E[Y] = E[\min(X,5)]$$

$$= \int_0^\infty \min(x,5)\, f(x)\, dx$$

$$= \int_0^5 \min(x,5)\, f(x)\, dx + \int_5^\infty \min(x,5)\, f(x)\, dx$$

$$\int_0^5 x\left(\frac{1}{2}e^{-\frac{x}{2}}\right) dx + \int_5^\infty 5\left(\frac{1}{2}e^{-\frac{x}{2}}\right) dx$$

The 1st integral requires integration by parts. In case you forgot, you can remember the following special case because this is the form that will mostly be needed for Exam P:

$$\int x\, e^{ax} dx = \frac{x\, e^{ax}}{a} - \frac{e^{ax}}{a^2}$$

Here, $a = -\frac{1}{2}$. So, pulling the constants out we get:

$$E[X] = -xe^{-\frac{x}{2}} - 2e^{-\frac{x}{2}}\Big|_0^5 - 5e^{-\frac{x}{2}}\Big|_5^\infty$$

Also, recalling that $e^{-\infty} = 0$, we get:

$$E[X] = -5e^{-\frac{5}{2}} - 2e^{-\frac{5}{2}} + 0 + 2e^0 - 5e^{-\infty} + 5e^{-\frac{5}{2}}$$

$$= 1.84$$

The correct answer is **E**.

5. You will be refunded the full purchase price of a computer if it breaks within a year of purchase, but if it breaks during 2nd, 3rd, or 4th year, you will be refunded only 25% of the price. No refund is made after that. The lifetime of the computer is exponentially distributed with mean 8 years. If your expected refund amount is 150, what is the purchase price?
A) 500
B) 600
C) 700
D) 800
E) 900
Solution:
Here, we can use the cdf of exponential distribution. Note that using cdf instead of pdf saves you from integration and makes your work shorter. Since the mean is 8,
$$F(t) = 1 - e^{-t/8}$$
Let the price be X. Expected Payment equals:

(pmt in 1st year) P(failure in1st year) + (pmt in 2nd/3rd/4th year)P(failure in 2nd/3rd /4thyear).

$$150 = X\,F(1) + .25X\,[F(4) - F(1)]$$
$$150 = .1175X + .25X(.3935 - .1175)$$
$$150 = .1865X$$
$$X = 804 \approx 800$$
The correct answer is **D**

.

6. You buy an insurance policy on your new computer. The policy will pay 600 if your computer gets stolen during the 1st year, and the payment keeps decreasing by 200 each year until it reaches 0. The probability that your computer will not be stolen in any particular year given that it has not been stolen by the start of that year is 0.9. What is the expected insurance payment under this policy?
A) 110
B) 112
C) 114
D) 116
E) 118

Solution:

Stolen in Year	Probability (p)	Payment (X)	pX
1	$.1$	600	60
2	$.9(.1) = .09$	400	36
3	$.9(.9)(.1) = .081$	200	16.2

$$\text{Expected value} = \sum pX = 60 + 36 + 16.2$$
$$= 112.2 \approx 112$$

The correct answer is **B.**

7. Your home annual repair expenses X (in thousands) have the pdf:

$$f(x) = \begin{cases} x^{-2}, & x > 1 \\ 0, & otherwise \end{cases}$$

You insure these with an annual deductible of 1200. What is the expected value of the expense that you will have to pay yourself?

A) 1082
B) 1182
C) 1282
D) 1382
E) 1482

Solution:
Let Y be the random variable that represents your out of pocket expenses.
If loss amount it less than 1.2 (in thousands), then all that amount is unpaid.
If loss amount is greater than or equal to 1.2, then the unpaid amount is 1.2.
So, we have:

$$Y = \begin{cases} X, & X < 1.2 \\ 1.2, & X > 1.2 \end{cases}$$

We need mean of unpaid expenses, which is the expected value of Y.

$$E[Y] = \int_{-\infty}^{\infty} y\, f(x)$$

$$= \int_{-\infty}^{1.2} x\, f(x)\, dx + \int_{1.2}^{\infty} 1.2\, f(x)\, dx$$

$$= \int_{1}^{1.2} x \frac{1}{x^2}\, dx + \int_{1.2}^{\infty} 1.2 \frac{1}{x^2}\, dx$$

$$= \int_{1}^{1.2} \frac{1}{x} dx + 1.2 \int_{1.2}^{\infty} x^{-2} dx$$

$$= \ln x \,|_{1}^{1.2} + 1.2 \frac{x^{-1}}{-1} |_{1.2}^{\infty}$$

$$= \ln(1.2) - \ln(1) - 1.2(\infty^{-1} - 1.2^{-1})$$

$$= 1.182\ thousands.$$

$$= 1182$$

The correct answer is **B**.

8. In a country, if something happens to your bank account, the government will pay you the lost balance, up to a maximum of 200000. The sum X (in hundreds of thousands) taken out from an account in case of a bank robbery has pdf:

$$f(x) = \begin{cases} 3x^{-4}, & x > 1 \\ 0, & x \le 1 \end{cases}$$

Find the expected amount paid by the government in case of a bank robbery.

(A) 107500

(B) 117500

(C) 127500

(D) 137500

(E) 147500

Solution:

Let Y be a random variable that represents the government payment. Then:

$$Y = \begin{cases} X, & X \le 2 \\ 2, & X > 2 \end{cases}$$

$$E[Y] = \int_{-\infty}^{\infty} y\, f(x)$$

$$= \int_{-\infty}^{2} x\, f(x)\, dx + \int_{2}^{\infty} 2\, f(x)\, dx$$

$$= \int_{1}^{2} x\, 3x^{-4} dx + \int_{2}^{\infty} 2\,(3x^{-4})\, dx$$

$$\int_{1}^{2} 3x^{-3} dx + \int_{2}^{\infty} 6\, x^{-4}\, dx$$

$$= \frac{3x^{-2}}{-2}\Bigg|_{1}^{2} + \frac{6x^{-3}}{-3}\Bigg|_{2}^{\infty}$$

$$= -\frac{3}{2}(2^{-2} - 1^{-2}) - 2(\infty^{-3} - 2^{-3})$$

Note that: $\infty^{-3} = \frac{1}{\infty^3} = \frac{1}{\infty} = 0$. So, the expected value is:

$$E[X] = 1.375 \text{ hundred thousand}$$

$$= 137500$$

The correct answer is **D**.

9. You insure your car worth 20,000 for one year under a policy with a 3,000 deductible, and a maximum payment equal to the price of the car minus the deductible. During the policy year there is a 10% chance of partial damage to the car less than the price of the car, and a 1% chance of damage more than the price of the car. If there is partial damage to the car, the amount *X* of damage follows an exponential distribution with mean 5000. Calculate the expected claim payment.

(A) 234

(B) 328

(C) 404

(D) 500

(E) 630

Solution:

The pdf of damage amount in case of partial loss is:

$$f(x) = \frac{1}{5000} e^{-x/5000}, \qquad x > 0$$

Let *Y* be a random variable representing the claim payment. Then:

$$Y = \begin{cases} X - 3000, & 3000 < X < 20000 \\ 17000, & X > 20000 \end{cases}$$

Now since there is .1 probability of partial loss, and .01 probability of total loss, the expected claim amount will equal:

.1(Expected value of Y in case of partial loss) + .01(Expected value of Y in case of total loss)

$$= .1 \int_{3000}^{20000} (x - 3000)(\frac{1}{5000})\, e^{-\frac{x}{5000}}\, dx \; + .01(17000)$$

The short cut for this integration by parts is:

$$\int (x + k)e^{ax} dx = \frac{(x + k)e^{ax}}{a} - \frac{e^{ax}}{a^2}$$

Here, $k = -3000, a = -\frac{1}{5000}$. Thus, the expected claim amount is:

$$\frac{.1}{5000}\left[(x - 3000)\left(-5000e^{-\frac{x}{5000}}\right) - 25000000e^{-\frac{x}{5000}}\right]_{3000}^{20000} + 170$$

$$= \frac{.1}{5000}\left[-85000000e^{-4} - 25000000e^{-4} + 25000000e^{-\frac{3}{5}}\right] + 170$$

$$= 404$$

The correct answer is **C**.

Tools Needed for Problems 53-64

For a uniform $[a, b]$ distribution, the pdf and expected value are given as:

$$f(x) = \frac{1}{b-a}, \qquad a \leq x \leq b,$$

$$E[X] = \frac{a+b}{2}$$

The pdf and cdf of an exponential distribution with mean k are:

$$f(x) = \frac{1}{k}e^{-x/k}, \qquad x > 0, \qquad F(x) = 1 - e^{-x/k}$$

If X is a discrete random variable, then $E[X^n] = \sum x^n f(x)$

If X is a continuous random variable, then $E[X^n] = \int_{-\infty}^{\infty} x^n\, f(x)dx$

$$Var\,[X] = E[X^2] - (E[X])^2$$

$$SD = \sqrt{Var}$$

If $Y = aX$, then:

$$Var\,Y = a^2\,Var\,X$$

Pmf of Poisson Distribution of mean m:

$$f(x) = \frac{m^x e^{-m}}{x!}, \qquad x = 0,1,2,3,\ldots$$

$$\int (x+k)e^{ax}dx = \frac{(x+k)e^{ax}}{a} - \frac{e^{ax}}{a^2}$$

The pth percentile of a random variable is the value x_p such that:

$$F(x_p) = \frac{p}{100}$$

Median is the 50th percentile.

Interquartile range is the difference between 75th and 25th percentile.

SOA Sample Question 53 Explanation:

Expected payment without deductible = Expected payment of full loss = $E[X]$.

For a uniform $[a, b]$ distribution, the pdf and expected value are given as:

$$f(x) = \frac{1}{b-a}, \qquad a \le x \le b$$

$$E[X] = \frac{a+b}{2}$$

So, for the loss distribution of this problem, since $a = 0,\ b = 1000$, we have:

$$f(x) = \frac{1}{1000}, \qquad 0 \le x \le 1000$$

$$E[X] = \frac{0+1000}{2} = 500$$

Let Y be a random variable representing the payment under the deductible d. Then:

$$Y = \begin{cases} 0, & X < d \\ X - d, & X > d \end{cases}$$

Also remember that $0 \le X \le 1000$. Thus:

$$E[Y] = \int_{-\infty}^{\infty} y\, f(x)\, dx$$

$$= \int_{d}^{1000} (x-d) \left(\frac{1}{1000}\right) dx$$

$$= \frac{(x-d)^2}{2000} \Big|_{d}^{1000}$$

$$= \frac{(1000-d)^2}{2000}$$

We are given that $E[Y] = .25\, E[X]$. Thus:

$$\frac{(1000-d)^2}{2000} = .25(500)$$

$$(1000-d)^2 = 250000$$

$$1000 - d = \pm 500$$

$$d = 500, 1500$$

A deductible of 1500 makes no sense since the maximum loss is 1000. Thus, $d = 500$.

The correct answer is **C**.

SOA Sample Question 54 Explanation:

When 2 or more percentiles are to be calculated, it saves work if we calculate the cdf.

$$F(x) = \int_{200}^{x} f(t)\,dt, \quad x > 200$$

$$= \int_{200}^{x} \frac{2.5(200)^{2.5}}{t^{3.5}}\,dt, \quad x > 200$$

$$= 2.5(200)^{2.5} \frac{t^{-2.5}}{-2.5} \Big|_{200}^{x}$$

$$= -(200)^{2.5} x^{-2.5} + 1$$

The pth percentile is the random variable value x_p such that:

$$F(x_p) = \frac{p}{100}$$

$$-(200)^{2.5} x_p^{-2.5} + 1 = \frac{p}{100}$$

$$1 - \frac{p}{100} = (200)^{2.5} x_p^{-2.5}$$

$$\left(1 - \frac{p}{100}\right)(200)^{-2.5} = x_p^{-2.5}$$

$$x_p = 200\left(1 - \frac{p}{100}\right)^{-1/2.5}$$

$$x_{30} = 200\left(1 - \frac{30}{100}\right)^{-\frac{1}{2.5}} = 230.67$$

$$x_{70} = 200\left(1 - \frac{70}{100}\right)^{-\frac{1}{2.5}} = 323.73$$

Subtracting the two percentiles we get:

$$x_{70} - x_{30} = 93$$

The correct answer is **B**.

SOA Sample Question 55 Explanation:

Let X denote the annual cost before taxes were introduced.

Let Y denote the annual cost after taxes came. Then:

$$Y = 1.2X$$

We know that if $Y = aX$, then:

$$\begin{aligned} Var\,Y &= a^2\,Var\,X \\ &= 1.2^2\,Var\,X \\ &= 1.2^2(260) \\ &= 374 \end{aligned}$$

The correct answer is **E**.

SOA Sample Question 56 Explanation:

$$F(x) = \begin{cases} 0, & x < 1 \\ \dfrac{x^2 - 2x + 2}{2}, & 1 \leq x < 2 \\ 1, & x \geq 2 \end{cases}$$

$$Var\,X = E[X^2] - (E[X])^2$$

In order to find these expected values, we need the pdf.

If the cdf is differentiable everywhere, which is generally the case, then we simply take its derivative to get the pdf.

However, the cdf of this problem is a tricky one.

Since $F(1) = 1/2$, F is not even continuous at 1, because the value just before 1 is 0 as can be seen from the first piece of the cdf. In other words, the pdf has a jump at 1.

There is no jump at 2 because the values at 2 from the 2nd and 3rd piece of cdf are the same.

Thus, other than the jump at 1, it is the usual business of taking the derivative of each piece of the cdf to get the pdf. We get:

$$f(x) = \begin{cases} 0, & x < 1 \\ \dfrac{1}{2}, & x = 1 \\ \dfrac{2x - 2}{2}, & 1 < x < 2 \\ 0, & x \geq 2 \end{cases}$$

To get the required expected values we will need to use expected value formulas for both discrete and continuous variables.

$$E[X] = 1\left(\frac{1}{2}\right) + \int_1^2 x\frac{(2x-2)}{2}dx$$

$$= \frac{1}{2} + \int_1^2 x^2 - x\, dx$$

$$= \frac{1}{2} + \left(\frac{x^3}{3} - \frac{x^2}{2}\right)|_1^2$$

$$= \frac{1}{2} + \frac{8}{3} - 2 - \left(\frac{1}{3} - \frac{1}{2}\right)$$

$$= \frac{4}{3}$$

$$E[X^2] = 1^2\left(\frac{1}{2}\right) + \int_1^2 x^2\frac{(2x-2)}{2}dx$$

$$= \frac{1}{2} + \int_1^2 x^3 - x^2\, dx$$

$$= \frac{1}{2} + \left(\frac{x^4}{4} - \frac{x^3}{3}\right)|_1^2$$

$$= \frac{1}{2} + 4 - \frac{8}{3} - \left(\frac{1}{4} - \frac{1}{3}\right)$$

$$= \frac{23}{12}$$

We are now ready to apply the variance formula:

$$Var\,X = E[X^2] - (E[X])^2$$

$$= \frac{23}{12} - \left(\frac{4}{3}\right)^2$$

$$= \frac{5}{36}$$

The correct answer is **C**.

SOA Sample Question 57 Explanation:

$$Y = \min\{X, 4\}$$

$$= \begin{cases} X, & X \leq 4 \\ 4, & X > 4 \end{cases}$$

$$E[Y] = \int_{-\infty}^{\infty} y\, f(x)\; dx$$

$$= \int_{-\infty}^{4} x\, f(x)\; dx + \int_{4}^{\infty} 4\, f(x)\; dx$$

$$= \int_{0}^{4} x \left(\frac{1}{5}\right) dx + \int_{4}^{5} 4 \left(\frac{1}{5}\right) dx$$

$$= \frac{x^2}{10}\Big|_0^4 + \frac{4x}{5}\Big|_4^5$$

$$= \frac{16}{10} + \frac{20}{5} - \frac{16}{5}$$

$$= 2.4$$

$$E[Y^2] = \int_{-\infty}^{\infty} y^2\, f(x)$$

$$\int_{-\infty}^{4} x^2 f(x)\; dx + \int_{4}^{\infty} 4^2\, f(x)\; dx$$

$$\int_{0}^{4} x^2 \left(\frac{1}{5}\right) dx + \int_{4}^{5} 16 \left(\frac{1}{5}\right) dx$$

$$= \frac{x^3}{15}\Big|_0^4 + \frac{16x}{5}\Big|_4^5$$

$$\frac{64}{15} + \frac{80}{5} - \frac{64}{5}$$

$$= \frac{112}{15}$$

$$Var\, Y = E[Y^2] - (E[Y])^2$$

$$= \frac{112}{15} - (2.4)^2$$

$$= 1.7$$

The correct answer is **C**.

SOA Sample Question 58 Explanation:

Claim Size	Probability
20	.15
30	.1
40	.05
50	.2
60	.1
70	.1
80	.3

The mean and standard deviation can be found most quickly on calculator as I explain in my youtube video whose link is:

https://www.youtube.com/watch?v=QNlw_TX-vEI&t=69

We get:

$$\mu = 55, \quad \sigma = 21.79$$

We are interested in the portion within 1 standard deviation of mean.

$$(\mu - \sigma, \mu + \sigma) = (55 - 21.79, 55 + 21.79)$$

$$= (33.2, 76.8)$$

The claims of 40, 50, 60, and 70 fall in this interval.

Adding up their corresponding probabilities we get:

$$.05 + .2 + .1 + .1 = .45$$

The correct answer is **A**.

SOA Sample Question 59 Explanation:

Let X, Y be random variables representing repair cost, and insurance payment respectively. We know pdf for a uniform $[a, b]$ variable X:

$$f(x) = \frac{1}{b-a}, a \le x \le b$$

For the variable X in this problem, $a = 0,\ b = 1500$. So:

$$f(x) = \frac{1}{1500}, 0 \le x \le 1500$$

$$Y = \begin{cases} 0, & 0 \le X \le 250 \\ X - 250, & X > 250 \end{cases}$$

$$Var\ Y = E[Y^2] - (E[Y])^2$$

$$E[Y] = \int_{-\infty}^{\infty} yf(x)\, dx$$

$$E[Y] = \int_{250}^{1500} (x-250)\left(\frac{1}{1500}\right) dx$$

$$= \frac{(x-250)^2}{3000}\Big|_{250}^{1500}$$

$$= \frac{1250^2}{3000} = 521$$

$$E[Y^2] = \int_{250}^{1500} (x-250)^2\left(\frac{1}{1500}\right) dx$$

$$= \frac{(x-250)^3}{4500}\Big|_{250}^{1500}$$

$$= \frac{1250^3}{4500} = 434028$$

$$Var\ Y = 434028 - (521)^2$$

$$= 162587$$

$$SD = \sqrt{Var}$$

$$= \sqrt{162587}$$

$$= 403$$

The correct answer is **B**.

SOA Sample Question 60 Explanation:

Let X represent the number of consecutive rainy days starting April 1.

We know that the pmf of a Poisson variable with mean $.6$ is:

$$f(x) = \frac{.6^x e^{-.6}}{x!}, x = 0,1,2, \ldots$$

The insurance company will pay if it rains for 1 or 2,3,4… days.

x	$f(x)$	Payment (y)
0	$.5488$	0
1	$.3293$	1000
$2,3,4,\ldots$	$1 - f(0) - f(1) =$ $1 - .5488 - .3293 = .1219$	2000

The mean and standard deviation can be found most quickly on calculator as I explain in my youtube video whose link is:

https://www.youtube.com/watch?v=QNlw_TX-vEI&t=69

From calculator, SD = 699

The correct answer is **B**.

SOA Sample Question 61 Explanation:

$$f(x) = ce^{-.004x}, \qquad x \geq 0$$

is an exponential distribution pdf:

$$f(x) = ce^{-cx}, \qquad x \geq 0$$

Thus, $c = .004$. So, the cdf will be:

$$F(x) = 1 - e^{-.004x}$$

Let x_m be the median of this function by ignoring the maximum benefit.

Median is the variable value such that $F(x_m) = .5$

$$1 - e^{-.004x_m} = .5$$

$$e^{-.004x_m} = .5$$

$$-.004x_m = \ln .5$$

$$x_m = 173$$

Since this is below the maximum benefit, so it is the median benefit for the policy.

Note that if the median of the exponential distribution had come out to be more than 250 the answer would have been 250.

The correct answer is **C**.

SOA Sample Question 62 Explanation:

The cdf of an exponential distribution is:

$$F(x) = 1 - e^{-c\,x}$$

Since the median is 4.

This means that at $x = 4,\ F(x) = .5$. So,

$$.5 = 1 - e^{-4c}$$

$$e^{-4c} = .5$$

$$-4c = \ln .5$$

$$c = .1733$$

$$F(x) = 1 - e^{-.1733\,x}$$

$$P(X \geq 5) = 1 - P(X < 5)$$

$$= 1 - F(5)$$

$$= 1 - .58$$

$$= .42$$

The correct answer is **D**.

SOA Sample Question 63 Explanation:

We can use the memoryless property of the exponential function to find the 95th percentile of the loss and then shift it by 100. Let q be the 95th percentile of the loss. Then

$$.95 = 1 - e^{-q/300}$$

$$e^{-\frac{q}{300}} = .05$$

$$-\frac{q}{300} = \ln .05$$

$$q = 899$$

So, 95th percentile of losses exceeding the deductible of a 100 is $899 + 100 = 999$

This rounds to choice **E**.

SOA Sample Question 64 Explanation

Let the 3 claim amounts be represented by X_1, X_2, X_3. Let $Y = \max\{X_1, X_2, X_3\}$.

We are to find expected value of Y. For this we will need its pdf. We first find the cdf of Y.

$$G(y) = P(Y \le y)$$
$$= P(\max\{X_1, X_2, X_3\} \le y)$$
$$= P(X_1 \le y, and\ X_2 \le y, and\ X_3 \le y)$$
$$= P(X_1 \le y) \bullet P(X_2 \le y) \bullet P(X_3 \le y)$$
$$= F(y) \bullet F(y) \bullet F(y) = [F(y)]^3$$

We use the same F for cdf of all three variables because each has same pdf.

$$F(y) = \int_{-\infty}^{y} f(x)\,dx$$
$$= \int_{1}^{y} \frac{3}{x^4}\,dx$$
$$= 3\frac{x^{-3}}{-3}\Big|_1^y$$
$$= 1 - y^{-3}$$
$$G(y) = (1 - y^{-3})^3$$
$$g(y) = G'(y)$$
$$= 3(1 - y^{-3})^2(3y^{-4})$$
$$= 9y^{-4}(1 - 2y^{-3} + y^{-6})$$
$$E[Y] = \int_{-\infty}^{\infty} y\,g(y)\,dy$$
$$= \int_{1}^{\infty} y\,(9y^{-4})(1 - 2y^{-3} + y^{-6})dy$$
$$= \int_{1}^{\infty} 9y^{-3} - 18y^{-6} + 9y^{-9}\,dy$$
$$= 9\frac{y^{-2}}{-2} - 18\frac{y^{-5}}{-5} + 9\frac{y^{-8}}{-8}\Big|_1^\infty$$
$$= \frac{9}{2} - \frac{18}{5} + \frac{9}{8} = 2.025\ thousand$$

The correct answer is **A**.

Quiz 5

1. An insurance policy is written to cover a computer that you buy for P. The loss on the computer has a uniform distribution on [0, P]. The policy has a deductible of 100, and the expected payment under the policy is half of what it would be with no deductible. Calculate P.

(A) 294

(B) 341

(C) 402

(D) 525

(E) 616

Solution:

Let X be a random variable representing the loss.

Expected payment without deductible = Expected loss = $E[X]$.

For a uniform $[a, b]$ distribution, the pdf and expected value are given as:

$$f(x) = \frac{1}{b-a}, \qquad a \le x \le b$$

$$E[X] = \frac{a+b}{2}$$

So, for the loss distribution of this problem, since $a = 0,\ b = P$, we have:

$$f(x) = \frac{1}{P}, \qquad 0 \le x \le P$$

$$E[X] = \frac{0+P}{2} = \frac{P}{2}$$

Let Y be a random variable representing the payment under the deductible.

$$Y = \begin{cases} 0, & X < 100 \\ X - 100, & X > 100 \end{cases}$$

$$E[Y] = \int_{-\infty}^{\infty} y\, f(x)$$

$$= \int_{100}^{P} (x - 100)\left(\frac{1}{P}\right) dx$$

$$= \frac{(x-100)^2}{2P}\Big|_{100}^{P}$$

$$\frac{(P-100)^2}{2P}$$

We are given that $E[Y] = .5\ E[X]$.

Thus:

$$\frac{(P-100)^2}{2P} = \frac{.5P}{2}$$

$$(P-100)^2 = .5P^2$$

$$P - 100 = \pm .707P$$

$$.293P = 100, or\ 1.707P = 100$$

$$P = 341, 59$$

A price of 59 makes no sense since it is less than the deductible. Thus, $P = 341$.

The correct answer is **B**.

2. The time to failure of a device has an exponential distribution with 25th percentile of 3 hours. Calculate the probability that device will fail within 4 hours.

(A) 0.17

(B) 0.24

(C) 0.32

(D) 0.50

(E) 0.68

Solution:

The cdf of an exponential distribution is $F(x) = 1 - e^{-cx}$

Since the 25th percentile is 3, so $x = 3 \Rightarrow F(x) = .25$. We get:

$$.25 = 1 - e^{-3c}$$

$$e^{-3c} = .75$$

$$-3c = \ln .75$$

$$c = .0959$$

$$F(x) = 1 - e^{-.0959\,x}$$

$$P(X \leq 4) = F(4)$$

$$= .32$$

The correct answer is **C**.

3. An insurance company sells a policy that covers losses incurred by a policyholder, subject to a deductible of 300. Losses incurred follow an exponential distribution with mean 500. Calculate the median of losses that are more than twice the deductible.

(A) 867

(B) 887

(C) 907

(D) 927

(E) 947

Solution:

Let X represent the loss amount. Exponential cdf with mean 500 is:

$$F(x) = 1 - e^{-x/500}$$

Let p be the median of losses exceeding twice the deductible. Then:

$$P(X < p \; given \; X > 600) = .5$$

$$\frac{P(X < p \; and \; X > 600)}{P(X > 600)} = .5$$

$$\frac{P(600 < X < p)}{1 - P(X \leq 600)} = .5$$

$$\frac{F(p) - F(600)}{1 - F(600)} = .5$$

$$\frac{1 - e^{-\frac{p}{500}} - \left(1 - e^{-\frac{600}{500}}\right)}{1 - \left(1 - e^{-\frac{600}{500}}\right)} = .5$$

$$\frac{e^{-\frac{6}{5}} - e^{-\frac{p}{500}}}{e^{-\frac{6}{5}}} = .5$$

$$e^{-\frac{6}{5}} - e^{-\frac{p}{500}} = .5e^{-\frac{6}{5}}$$

$$.5e^{-\frac{6}{5}} = e^{-\frac{p}{500}}$$

$$.1506 = e^{-\frac{p}{500}}$$

$$\ln .1506 = -\frac{p}{500}$$

$$p = 947$$

The correct answer is **E**.

4. Find the interquartile range (that is, the difference between the 75th and 25th percentiles) of the random variable X with pdf:

$$f(x) = \frac{1}{x^2}, x > 1$$

A) 4/3
B) 2
C) 7/3
D) 8/3
E) 4

Solution:

Interquartile range is the difference between 75th and 25th percentiles. When 2 or more percentiles are to be calculated, it is convenient to calculate the cdf. Here,

$$F(x) = \int_1^x f(t)\, dt, \ \ x > 1$$

$$= \int_1^x \frac{1}{t^2}\, dt, \ \ t > 1$$

$$= \frac{t^{-1}}{-1}\Big|_1^x$$

$$= -x^{-1} + 1$$

The pth percentile is the random variable value x_p such that:

$$F(x_p) = \frac{p}{100}$$

$$-x_p{}^{-1} + 1 = \frac{p}{100}$$

$$1 - \frac{p}{100} = \frac{1}{x_p}$$

$$\frac{100 - p}{100} = \frac{1}{x_p}$$

$$x_p = \frac{100}{100 - p}$$

$$x_{25} = \frac{100}{100 - 25} = \frac{4}{3}$$

$$x_{75} = \frac{100}{100 - 75} = 4$$

$$x_{75} - x_{25} = 4 - \frac{4}{3}$$

$$= \frac{8}{3}$$

The correct answer is **D**.

5. A random variable X has the probability distribution function:

$$f(x) = \begin{cases} 0, & x < 1 \\ 1, & 1 \le x < 1.5 \\ .5, & x = 1.5 \end{cases}$$

Calculate the variance of X.

(A) .022

(B) .024

(C) .026

(D) .028

(E) .030

Solution:

$$Var\ X = E[X^2] - (E[X])^2$$

Note that the pdf is partly continuous and partly discrete.

$$E[X] = 1.5(.5) + \int_1^{1.5} x(1)dx$$

$$= .75 + \left(\frac{x^2}{2}\right)\Big|_1^{1.5}$$

$$= .75 + 1.125 - .5 = 1.375$$

$$E[X^2] = 1.5^2(.5) + \int_1^{1.5} x^2(1)dx$$

$$1.125 + \left(\frac{x^3}{3}\right)\Big|_1^{1.5}$$

$$1.125 + 1.125 - 1/3 = 1.9167$$

$$Var\ X = 1.9167 - (1.375)^2 = .026$$

The correct answer is **C**.

6. Probability distribution of the claim sizes for a policy is given in the table below:

Claim Size	Probability
100	.15
200	.15
300	.25
400	.25
500	.2

Calculate the percentage of claims that are within two standard deviations of the mean claim size.

(A) 45%

(B) 55%

C) 68%

(D) 85%

(E) 100%

Solution:

The mean and standard deviation can be found most quickly on calculator as I explain in my youtube video whose link is:

https://www.youtube.com/watch?v=QNlw_TX-vEI&t=69

We get:

$$\mu = 320, \quad \sigma = 132.7$$

We are interested in the portion within 2 standard deviations of mean.

$$(\mu - 2\sigma, \mu + 2\sigma) = (320 - 265.4, 320 + 265.4)$$
$$= (54.6, 585.4)$$

All claims fall in this interval.

Thus the answer is 100%

The correct answer is **E**.

7. The number of annual snowstorms in a state follows Poisson distribution with mean 2. Your insurance will pay you 1500 for the 1st, 1000 for the 2nd, 500 for the 3rd snowstorm, and no more in a year. What is your expected annual benefit?

A) 1645

B) 2053

C) 2499

D) 3116

E) 3568

Solution:

Let X represent the number of annual snowstorms.

$$f(x) = \frac{2^x e^{-2}}{x!}, x = 0,1,2,...$$

The insurance company will pay if it rains for 1 or 2,3,4... days.

x	$f(x)$	Payment (y)
0	$.1353$	0
1	$.2707$	1500
2	$.2707$	2500
3,4,5, ...	$1 - f(0) - f(1) - f(2) = .3233$	3000

$$\text{Expected Payment} = \sum yf(x)$$

$$= 1500(.2707) + 2500(.2707) + 3000(.3233)$$

$$= 2053$$

The correct answer is **B**.

8. Annual dental expenses of a man follow an exponential distribution with mean 400. A dental insurance will cover these expenses up to a maximum of 1000. Find the 90th percentile of the covered expenses.

A) 816

B) 877

C) 921

D) 952

E) 1000

Solution:

The cdf of expenses will be:

$$F(x) = 1 - e^{-\frac{x}{400}}$$

For the time being, let us find the 90th percentile, x_p, of expenses by ignoring the maximum benefit.

Setting $F(x_p) = .9$

$$1 - e^{-\frac{x_p}{400}} = .9$$

$$e^{-\frac{x_p}{400}} = .1$$

$$-\frac{x_p}{400} = \ln .1$$

$$x_p = 921$$

Since this is below the maximum benefit, so it is the 90th percentile of covered expenses.

Note that if x_p had come out to be more than 1000 the answer would have been 1000.

The correct answer is **C**.

9. Annual cost of tax-free home repairs in a city averages 2000 with standard deviation of 25. The city introduces a tax for these repairs that will result in raising their standard deviation to 29. What is the tax rate?

(A) 16%

(B) 18%

(C) 20%

(D) 22%

(E) 24%

Solution:

Let X denote the annual cost before taxes were introduced.

Let Y denote the annual cost after taxes came.

Let the tax rate be r. Then:

$$Y = (1 + r)X$$

$$Var\ Y = (1 + r)^2\ Var\ X$$

$$29^2 = (1 + r)^2 25^2$$

$$29 = 25(1 + r)$$

$$1.16 = 1 + r$$

$$r = .16$$

The correct answer is **A**.

10. Two batteries are used in a device. The lifetime of each battery has pdf:

$$f(x) = \begin{cases} \dfrac{2}{x^3}, & x > 1 \\ 0, & otherwise \end{cases}$$

Lifetimes of the 2 batteries are independent. In order to keep running, the device needs at least one battery to be alive. In other words, we care for the larger of the two battery lifetimes. Find the expected lifetime of the device.

A) 2/3
B) 4/3
C) 2
D) 8/3
E) 10/3

Solution:

Let the 2 lifetimes be represented by X_1, X_2.

Let $Y = \max\{X_1, X_2\}$. We are to find the expected value of Y. For this, we will need the pdf of Y. For this, we first find the cdf of Y.

$$G(y) = P(Y \leq y)$$

$$= P(\max\{X_1, X_2\} \leq y)$$

$$= P(X_1 \leq y, and\ X_2 \leq y)$$

$$= P(X_1 \leq y) \bullet P(X_2 \leq y)$$

$$= F(y) \bullet F(y) = [F(y)]^2$$

Note that we have used the same F for the cdf of the two variables because each of the 2 variables have the same density function $f(x)$.

The next step is to find $F(y)$.

$$F(y) = P(X \leq y)$$

$$= \int_{-\infty}^{y} f(x)\, dx$$

$$= \int_{1}^{y} \frac{2}{x^3}\, dx$$

$$= 2\frac{x^{-2}}{-2} \Big|_1^y$$

$$= 1 - y^{-2}$$

$$G(y) = (1 - y^{-2})^2$$

$$g(y) = G'(y)$$

$$= 2(1 - y^{-2})(2y^{-3})$$

$$= 4(y^{-3} - y^{-5})$$

$$E[Y] = \int_{-\infty}^{\infty} y\, g(y)\, dy$$

$$= \int_{1}^{\infty} y\, [4(y^{-3} - y^{-5})] dy$$

$$= 4\int_{1}^{\infty} y^{-2} - y^{-4}\, dy$$

$$= 4\frac{y^{-2}}{-1} - 4\frac{y^{-3}}{-3} \Big|_1^{\infty}$$

$$= 4 - \frac{4}{3}$$

$$= \frac{8}{3}$$

The correct answer is **D**.

Central Limit Theorem

If population is normal, or if sample size, $n > 30$, then the sampling distribution of means and sums is approximately normal with mean and standard deviation:

$$\mu_{\bar{X}} = \mu$$

$$\sigma_{\bar{X}} = \frac{\sigma}{\sqrt{n}}$$

$$\mu_{sum} = n\mu$$

$$\sigma_{sum} = \sqrt{n}\,\sigma$$

where μ and σ are the mean and standard deviation of each of the n identical variables.

For independent variables X, Y, the joint pdf is:

$$h(x, y) = f(x)g(y)$$

The mean and standard deviation for a uniform (a, b) distribution are:

$$\mu = \frac{a+b}{2}$$

$$\sigma = \sqrt{\frac{(b-a)^2}{12}}$$

$$E[X+Y] = E[X] + E[Y]$$

$$Var[X+Y] = Var[X] + Var[Y] + 2Cov[X, Y]$$

For independent variables $X, Y,\ Cov[X, Y] = 0$

Continuity Correction:

Continuity correction is used when a discrete variable is approximated by a continuous variable. It says that:

$$P(X > n) = P(X \geq n + .5)$$

$$P(X < n) = P(X \leq n - .5)$$

Variance of a Poisson distribution equals its mean.

SOA Sample Question 65 Explanation:

Central Limit Theorem tells us that the distribution of the sum of more than 30 identically distributed variables is approximately normal.

Here we have way more 30 variables (2025 to be exact).

It also tells us that if there are n such variables, then the mean μ and standard deviation σ of the sum are given as:

$$\mu = n(mean\ of\ each)$$

$$= 2025(3125)$$

$$= 6328125$$

$$\sigma = \sqrt{n}\ (SD\ of\ each)$$

$$= \sqrt{2025}\ (250)$$

$$= 11250$$

To find the 90th percentile, we first find the standard score z from the table that corresponds to a cumulative probability of .90. From the bottom row of the exam table, we get $z = 1.2816$

$$z = \frac{x - \mu}{\sigma}$$

$$1.2816 = \frac{x - 6328125}{11250}$$

$$x = 6342543$$

$$= 6343000$$

If we round to the nearest thousand, as all the answer choices are, this is 6343000.

The correct answer is **C**.

SOA Sample Question 66 Explanation:

By central limit theorem, if μ and σ are the mean and standard deviation of each of the n identical variables, then the mean and standard deviation of their average are:

$$\mu_{\bar{X}} = \mu = 19400$$

$$\sigma_{\bar{X}} = \frac{\sigma}{\sqrt{n}} = \frac{5000}{\sqrt{25}} = 1000$$

$$z = \frac{\bar{X} - \mu_{\bar{X}}}{\sigma_{\bar{X}}} = \frac{20000 - 19400}{1000} = .6$$

$$P(\bar{X} > 20000) = P(z > .6) = 1 - P(z \leq .6) = 1 - .7257 = .27$$

The correct answer is **C**.

SOA Sample Question 67 Explanation:

Central limit theorem applies because we have a sample size of 1250 which is way more than 30. The distribution of the sum of claims is thus approximately normal.

Also, the variance of a Poisson distribution equals its mean, that is, 2. Thus, standard deviation of each claim is $\sqrt{2}$. Hence, the mean and standard deviation of the sum are given as:

$$\mu = n(mean\ of\ each) = 1250(2) = 2500$$

$$\sigma = \sqrt{n}\,(SD\ of\ each) = \sqrt{1250}\,(\sqrt{2}) = 50$$

We need to convert both 2450 and 2600 into standard scores.

$$z_1 = \frac{2450 - 2500}{50} = -1$$

$$z_2 = \frac{2600 - 2500}{50} = 2$$

If X is the total annual claim, then:

$$P(2450 < X < 2600) = P(-1 < z < 2)$$

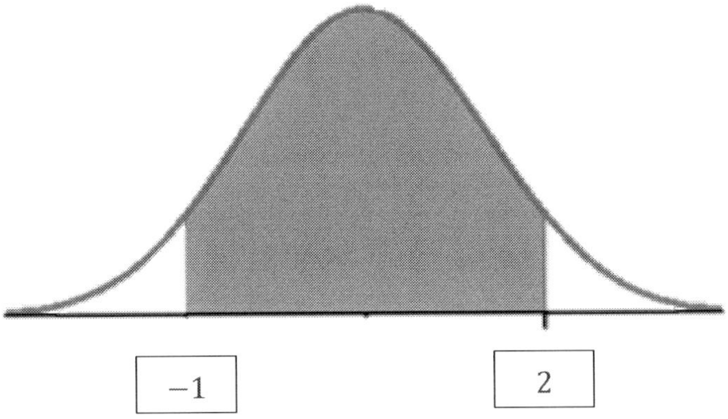

From the figure, we see that:

$$P(-1 \le z \le 2) = P(z \le 2) - P(z \le -1)$$

$$= P(z \le 2) - [1 - P(z \le 1)]$$

$$= P(z \le 2) + P(z \le 1) - 1$$

Using the appropriate table value, we have:

$$P(-1 \le z \le 2) = .9772 + .8413 - 1$$

$$= .82$$

Note that even though Poisson is a discrete distribution, our calculations are done through normal approximation which is continuous, and hence we can switch between $<$ and $\le$.

The correct answer is **B**.

SOA Sample Question 68 Explanation:

Let n be the number of bulbs purchased, and X represent the total lifetime of these bulbs. Then:

$$\mu_X = 3n$$

$$\sigma_X = \sqrt{n}\sqrt{1} = \sqrt{n}$$

We want $P(X \geq 40)$ to be at least .9772. We first solve the equality:

$$P(X \geq 40) = .9772 \quad (1)$$

The z value from the table corresponding to probability of .9772 is 2. So

$$P(z \leq 2) = .9772$$

We need to make this last equation appear like equation (1) so that we can set up our standard score equation. Since $P(z \leq a) = P(z \geq -a)$ we write:

$$P(z \geq -2) = .9772 \quad (2)$$

From (1) and (2) we see that the $z = -2$ corresponds to $X = 40$.

$$z = \frac{X - \mu_X}{\sigma_X}$$

$$\Rightarrow -2 = \frac{40 - 3n}{\sqrt{n}}$$

$$-2\sqrt{n} = 40 - 3n$$

$$3n - 2\sqrt{n} - 40 = 0$$

Let $\sqrt{n} = y$. So, the above equation becomes:

$$3y^2 - 2y - 40 = 0$$

$$(3y + 10)(y - 4) = 0$$

$$y = 4$$

The other value is rejected because square root is positive by default.

$$\sqrt{n} = 4$$

$$n = 16$$

So, 16 is the least number of bulbs that will ensure a total lifetime of at least 40 months with probability at least .9772 because this is the answer we got by setting the probability equal to the smallest value allowed, which was .9772.

For a higher probability of the same total lifetime, more bulbs might be needed, so the least number needed will still be 16.

The correct answer is **B**.

SOA Sample Question 69 Explanation:

Let W be the number of watching hours spent by one person. Then:

$$W = X + Y$$

$$E[W] = E[X + Y]$$

$$= E[X] + E[Y]$$

$$= 50 + 20$$

$$= 70$$

$$Var[W] = Var[X] + Var[Y] + 2Cov[X, Y]$$

$$= 50 + 30 + 2(10)$$

$$= 100$$

Note that if X and Y were independent, then their covariance would be 0. So, they are obviously not independent in this problem. Thus:

$$\mu_W = 70$$

$$\sigma_W = \sqrt{100} = 10$$

Since T is the total watch time of 100 people, central limit theorem applies because the sample size is bigger than 30. We have:

$$\mu_T = 100\mu_W$$

$$= 100(70)$$

$$= 7000$$

$$\sigma_T = \sqrt{100}\sigma_W$$

$$= 10(10)$$

$$= 100$$

We need to change 7100 to standard score.

$$z = \frac{7100 - 7000}{100} = 1$$

$$P[T < 7100] = P[z < 1]$$

$$= .8413$$

Thus, the correct answer is **B**.

SOA Sample Question 70 Explanation:

The given pdf for the total claim amount is

$$f(x) = \frac{1}{1000}e^{-\frac{x}{1000}}, \qquad x > 0$$

We recognize this as the pdf of an exponential distribution with mean (expected value) 1000.

Also, remember that standard deviation of an exponential distribution equals its mean. Hence:

$$\mu_X = 1000, \qquad \sigma_X = 1000.$$

Since the premium is the expected total claim plus 100, so premium for each policy is 1100.

Premium for 100 policies will be $100(1100) = 110000$

Since the sample size is 100 (which is greater than 30), central limit theorem applies and the distribution of 100 claim amounts is approximately normal.

Mean and standard deviation for 100 policies are given as:

$$\mu = 100\mu_X$$

$$= 100(1000)$$

$$= 100000$$

$$\sigma = \sqrt{100}\,\sigma_X$$

$$= 10(1000)$$

$$= 10000$$

If T is the total claim amount for 100 policies, we need $P(T > 110000)$.

We therefore need to find the z-score for 110000.

$$z = \frac{110000 - \mu}{\sigma}$$

$$= \frac{110000 - 100000}{10000} = 1$$

$$P(T > 110000) = P(z > 1)$$

$$= 1 - P(z \leq 1)$$

$$= 1 - .8413$$

$$= .159$$

The correct answer is **B**.

SOA Sample Question 71 Explanation:

Let X be the number of pensions a recruit gets at retirement, where we are also counting the husband's pension in the recruit's pension.

The probability of a recruit getting 1 pension $= .4(.25) = .1$

The probability of a recruit getting 2 pensions $= .4(.75) = .3$

Central Limit Theorem applies because number of recruits is greater than 30.

Let T be the total pensions among 100 recruits.

# of Pensions x	Probability $f(x)$	$xf(x)$	$x^2f(x)$
1	$.1$	$.1$	$.1$
2	$.3$	$.6$	1.2

Mean for 1 recruit $= \mu = \sum xf(x) = .7$

Mean for 100 recruits $= \mu_T = 100\mu = 100(.7) = 70$

SD for 1 recruit $= \sigma = \sqrt{\sum x^2 f(x) - \mu^2} = \sqrt{1.3 - .7^2} = .9$

SD for 100 recruits $= \sigma_T = \sqrt{100}\sigma = 10(.9) = 9$

$$P(T \leq 90) = P(T < 90.5)$$

where, for the first time in this course, we are applying the continuity correction when using Normal approximation for a discrete situation. We did not use this correction until now because either the original distributions were continuous, or the numbers involved were so big that it made very little difference whether we applied it or not. In this case, the distribution is discrete, and the numbers involved are not that large. So, we should apply the correction.

Changing 90.5 into z:

$$z = \frac{90.5 - \mu_T}{\sigma_T} = 2.28$$

$$(T < 90.5) = P(z < 2.28)$$

$$= .9887$$

This rounds to choice **E**.

__SOA Sample Question 72 Explanation__:

The mean and standard deviation for a uniform (a,b) distribution are:

$$\mu = \frac{a+b}{2} = \frac{-2.5+2.5}{2} = 0$$

$$\sigma = \sqrt{\frac{(b-a)^2}{12}} = \sqrt{\frac{(2.5-(-2.5))^2}{12}} = \sqrt{\frac{25}{12}}$$

This is the mean and standard deviation of one age difference. Our sample size is 48 which is greater than 30. So, central limit theorem applies and the distribution of mean of 48 age differences, $\bar{X}$, is approximately normal with mean and standard deviation given as:

$$\mu_{\bar{X}} = \mu = 0$$

$$\sigma_{\bar{X}} = \frac{\sigma}{\sqrt{48}} = \sqrt{\frac{25}{12(48)}} = \frac{5}{24}$$

We are asked to find $P(-.25 < \bar{X} < .25)$

$$z - \text{score for } .25 = \frac{.25 - \mu_{\bar{X}}}{\sigma_{\bar{X}}} = \frac{.25 - 0}{5/24} = 1.2$$

By symmetry of normal distribution, z-score for $-.25$ is -1.2. So,

$$P(-.25 < \bar{X} < .25) = P(-1.2 < z < 1.2)$$

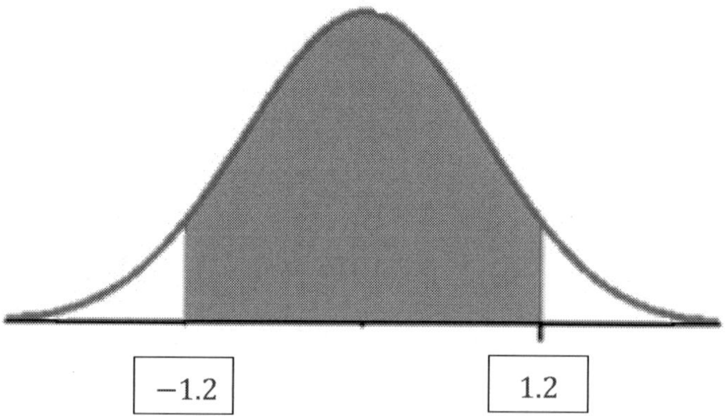

However, table values that are provided to us on the exam give us the area to the left of the positive standard values and not the in between area. From the figure, we see that:

$$P(-1.2 \le z \le 1.2) = P(z \le 1.2) - P(z \le -1.2)$$

$$= P(z \le 1.2) - [1 - P(z \le 1.2)]$$

$$= 2P(z \le 1.2) - 1 = 2(.8849) - 1$$

$$= .77$$

The correct answer is **D**.

SOA Sample Question 73 Explanation:

Let X be waiting time for 1st claim from a good driver.

Let Y be waiting time for 1st claim from a bad driver. Then,

$$F(x) = 1 - e^{-x/6}$$

$$G(y) = 1 - e^{-y/3}$$

Because of independence, we have:

$$P(X \leq 3 \; and \; Y \leq 2) = P(X \leq 3)P(Y \leq 2)$$

$$= F(3)G(2)$$

$$= (1 - e^{-\frac{3}{6}})(1 - e^{-\frac{2}{3}})$$

$$= 1 - e^{-\frac{2}{3}} - e^{-\frac{1}{2}} + e^{-\frac{7}{6}}$$

The correct answer is **C**.

SOA Sample Question 74 Explanation

Let X be the number of people who show up.

<u>Case I: 20 or fewer people show up</u>

If 20 or fewer people show up, revenue is $21(50) = 1050$

This is a binomial situation with $n = 21, \; p = .98$

$$f(x) = \binom{n}{x} p^x (1-p)^{n-x}$$

$$f(x) = \binom{21}{x} .98^x (.02)^{21-x}$$

$$P(X \leq 20) = 1 - f(21)$$

$$= 1 - .654$$

$$= .346$$

<u>Case II: 21 people show up</u>

If 21 people show up, revenue is $1050 - 100 = 950$

$$P(X = 21) = f(21)$$

$$= .654$$

$$\text{Expected Revenue} = \text{Expected Revenue from Case I} + \text{Expected Revenue from Case II}$$

$$= 1050(.346) + 950(.654)$$

$$= 985$$

The correct answer is **E**.

Quiz 6

1. In a country, the age at which males start having vision problems is exponentially distributed with mean 16, while the age at which females start having vision problems is exponentially distributed with mean 16.8. The problems of the 2 genders are independent of each other. What is the probability that a male will start having vision problems before age 10, while a female will start having vision problems after the age of 11.24?
   A) .203
   B) .216
   C) .227
   D) .238
   E) .274

Solution:

Let X be the starting age for male vision problems.

Let Y be the starting age for female vision problems. Then,

$$F(x) = 1 - e^{-x/16}$$

$$G(y) = 1 - e^{-y/16.8}$$

$$P(X < 10 \text{ and } Y > 11.24) = F(10)[1 - G(11.24)]$$

$$= (1 - e^{-\frac{10}{16}})(e^{-\frac{11.24}{16.8}})$$

$$= .238$$

The correct answer is **D**.

2. It is a common practice to round your age down to the nearest integer. For example, if you are 18.75 years old, you will usually say that your age is 18. The difference (in years) between the true age and the rounded down integer age is uniform in the interval (0,1). Find the probability that the mean of true ages of a random sample of 64 people is different from the mean of their rounded down ages by more than 5 months.
A) .0104
B) .1023
C) .5833
D) .8977
E) .9896
Solution:

The mean and standard deviation for a uniform (a, b) distribution are:

$$\mu = \frac{a+b}{2} = \frac{0+1}{2} = 0.5$$

$$\sigma = \sqrt{\frac{(b-a)^2}{12}} = \sqrt{\frac{(1-0)^2}{12}} = \sqrt{\frac{1}{12}}$$

This is the mean and standard deviation of one age difference. Our sample size is 64 which is greater than 30. So, central limit theorem applies and the distribution of mean of 64 age differences, $\bar{X}$, is approximately normal with parameters:

$$\mu_{\bar{X}} = \mu = 0.5$$

$$\sigma_{\bar{X}} = \frac{\sigma}{\sqrt{64}}$$

$$= \sqrt{\frac{1}{12(64)}}$$

$$= .036$$

We are asked to find $P(\bar{X} > 5/12)$

z-score for 5/12 is:

$$\frac{5/12 - \mu_{\bar{X}}}{\sigma_{\bar{X}}} = \frac{5/12 - .5}{.036} = -2.31$$

$$P(\bar{X} > 5/12) = P(z > -2.31)$$

$$= P(z < 2.31)$$

$$= .9896$$

The correct answer is **E**.

3. Last year, 100 auto insurance claims are filed in a city. Claim amounts were independent and identically distributed with mean 1200 and variance 400. Approximate the 75th percentile for the sum of all the amounts.
   A) 120135
   B) 121350
   C) 122700
   D) 135300
   E) 147000

Solution:

Central Limit Theorem tells us that the distribution of the sum of more than 30 identically distributed variables (100 here) is approximately normal.

Also if there are n such variables, then the mean and standard deviation of the sum are:

$$\mu = n(mean\ of\ each)$$

$$= 100(1200)$$

$$= 120000$$

$$\sigma = \sqrt{n}\,(SD\ of\ each)$$

$$= \sqrt{100}\,\sqrt{400}$$

$$= 200$$

To find the 75th percentile, we first find the standard score z from the table that corresponds to a cumulative probability of .75.

We see that a probability of .7486 corresponds to $z = .67$, while a probability of .7517 corresponds to $z = .68$.

We use linear interpolation:

$$\frac{.75 - .7486}{.7517 - .7486} = .5$$

So, we go .5 of the way between .67 and .68. Thus, we have:

$$z = .675$$

$$z = \frac{x - \mu}{\sigma}$$

$$.675 = \frac{x - 120000}{200}$$

$$x = 120135$$

The correct answer is **A**.

4. The ages of all the people who go to gym in a town are normally distributed with mean 24 and standard deviation 10. Find the probability that the average age of 19 randomly selected gym goers between 20 and 23.
   A) .1891
   B) .2891
   C) .3891
   D) .4891
   E) .5891

   Solution:

   By central limit theorem, if μ and σ are the mean and standard deviation of each of the n identical variables, then the mean and standard deviation of their average are:

$$\mu_{\bar{X}} = \mu = 24$$

$$\sigma_{\bar{X}} = \frac{\sigma}{\sqrt{n}} = \frac{10}{\sqrt{19}}$$

$$= 2.294$$

   We find the z-score corresponding to the average ages of 20 and 23:

$$z_1 = \frac{\bar{X} - \mu_{\bar{X}}}{\sigma_{\bar{X}}}$$

$$= \frac{20 - 24}{2.294}$$

$$= -1.74$$

$$z_2 = \frac{23 - 24}{2.294}$$

$$= -.44$$

$$P(20 < \bar{X} < 23) = P(-1.74 < z < -.44)$$

$$= P(.44 < z < 1.74)$$

$$= P(z < 1.74) - P(z < .44)$$

$$= .9591 - .67$$

$$= .2891$$

   The correct answer is **B**.

5. A research group decides to study earthquakes in the 36 most vulnerable countries of the world. Historical data shows that the number of annual earthquakes in each of these countries is a Poisson random variable with mean 100. Assume the number of earthquakes in different countries are mutually independent. Find the approximate probability of there being a total of between 3500 and 3700 earthquakes in these countries next year.
   A) .1
   B) .2
   C) .5
   D) .8
   E) .9

Solution:

Central limit theorem applies because the sample size of 36 is more than 30.

The distribution of the sum of earthquakes is thus approximately normal.

Also, the variance of a Poisson distribution equals its mean.

Thus, standard deviation of each claim is $\sqrt{100}$

So, the mean and standard deviation of the sum are:

$$\mu = n(mean\ of\ each) = 36(100) = 3600$$

$$\sigma = \sqrt{n}\ (SD\ of\ each) = \sqrt{36}\left(\sqrt{100}\right) = 60$$

We need to convert both 3500 and 3700 into standard scores.

$$z_1 = \frac{3500 - 3600}{60} = -1.67$$

$$z_2 = \frac{3700 - 3600}{60} = 1.67$$

If X is the annual total of the earthquakes, then:

$$P(3500 < X < 3700) = P(-1.67 < z < 1.67)$$

$$= P(z \leq 1.67) - P(z \leq -1.67)$$

$$= P(z \leq 1.67) - [1 - P(z \leq 1.67)]$$

$$= 2P(z \leq 1.67) - 1$$

$$= 2(.9525) - 1$$

$$= .9$$

The correct answer is **E**.

6. A shelter will keep getting aid from a rich family as long as they shelter a dog. The shelter takes in each dog as a new-born puppy and keeps it until its death upon which they immediately take in another new-born puppy, so that they have only one dog at any given time. The life of each dog is normally distributed with mean 11 years and standard deviation 2.5 years. Find the minimum number of total dogs the shelter will take in so that the aid from the rich family continues for at least 100 years with probability at least .95.
A) 9
B) 10
C) 11
D) 12
E) 13
Solution:

Let n be the number of dogs, and X represent their total lifetimes. Then:

$$\mu_X = 11n$$

$$\sigma_X = 2.5\sqrt{n}$$

We want $P(X \geq 100)$ to be at least .95. We first solve the equality:

$$P(X \geq 100) = .95 \quad (1)$$

The z value from the table corresponding to probability of .95 is 1.645 because it lies in the middle of 1.64 and 1.65, which are the z values corresponding to probabilities of .9495 and .9505, and .95 is exactly in the middle of these 2.

$$P(z \leq 1.645) = .95$$

We need to make this last equation appear like equation (1) so that we can set up our standard score equation. We therefore write:

$$P(z \geq -1.645) = .95 \quad (2)$$

From (1) and (2) we see that the $z = -1.645$ corresponds to $X = 100$.

$$z = \frac{X - \mu_X}{\sigma_X}$$

$$\Rightarrow -1.645 = \frac{100 - 11n}{2.5\sqrt{n}}$$

$$-4.1125\sqrt{n} = 100 - 11n$$

$$11n - 4.1125\sqrt{n} - 100 = 0$$

Let $\sqrt{n} = y$.

So, the above equation becomes:

$$11y^2 - 4.1125y - 100 = 0$$

$$y = \frac{4.1125 \pm \sqrt{4.1125^2 + 4(11)(100)}}{22}$$

$$y = 3.2078$$

The negative value is rejected because square root is positive by default.

$$\sqrt{n} = 3.2078$$

$$n = 10.29$$

So, 11 is the least number of dogs that will ensure a total lifetime of at least 100 years with probability at least .95 because 10.29 is the lowest value of n that guarantees the required probability. 10 dogs will give less than the required probability.

Thus, the minimum number is 11.

The correct answer is **C**.

7. In order to encourage recruitment and retention of extremely talented students, university X announces special scholarships for those entering freshmen in the year 2025 who have a perfect math ACT or SAT score. Each scholarship will pay a million dollars, but only after the student has completed graduation from university X by 2029. If, in addition, the student ends up with a 4.0 college GPA, then another million is added to the scholarship. 40 students enter University X with the perfect test scores in 2025. It is estimated that 70% of them will complete their graduation from University X by 2029, and 20% of these graduating students will also end up with a college GPA of 4.0. Find the probability that University X will end up paying more than 40 million to these 40 students.
A) .045
B) .093
C) .28
D) .907
E) .955
Solution:

Let Y be the number of millions a student gets upon graduation.

The probability of a student getting 1 M $= .7(.8) = .56$

The probability of a student getting 2 M $= .7(.2) = .14$

Central Limit Theorem applies because number of students is greater than 30.

Let T be the total millions among 40 students.

Millions y	Probability $f(y)$	$yf(y)$	$y^2f(y)$
1	$.56$	$.56$	$.56$
2	$.14$	$.28$	$.56$

Mean for 1 student $= \mu = \sum yf(y) = .84$

Mean for 40 students $= \mu_T = 40\mu = 40(.84) = 33.6$

SD for 1 student is:

$$\sigma = \sqrt{\sum y^2 f(y) - \mu^2}$$

$$= \sqrt{1.12 - .84^2}$$

$$= .6437$$

SD for 40 students is:

$$\sigma_T = \sqrt{40}\sigma$$

$$= 4.07$$

Using continuity correction:

$$P(T > 40) = P(T \geq 40.5)$$

Changing 40.5 into z:

$$z = \frac{40.5 - \mu_T}{\sigma_T}$$

$$= \frac{40.5 - 33.6}{4.07}$$

$$= 1.70$$

$$(T > 40.5) = P(z > 1.70)$$

$$= P(1 - z \leq 1.70)$$

$$= 1 - .9554$$

$$= .0446$$

The correct answer is **A**.

8. Let X, Y be the number of hours per school week that a randomly selected English major spends in reading course books and extracurricular books, respectively. We know that:

$$E(X) = 20, E(Y) = 5, Var(X) = 3, Var(Y) = 2, Cov(X, Y) = 1.$$

The totals of hours that different students spend in reading are independent. Approximate the probability that the total number of weekly hours that 70 randomly selected English majors spend in reading books is more than 1800.

A) .003
B) .006
C) .009
D) .012
E) .015

Solution:

Let W be the number of reading hours spent by one person. Then:

$$W = X + Y$$

$$E[W] = E[X + Y]$$

$$= E[X] + E[Y]$$

$$= 20 + 5 = 25$$

$$Var[W] = Var[X] + Var[Y] + 2Cov[X, Y]$$

$$= 3 + 2 + 2(1) = 7$$

$$\mu_W = E[W] = 25$$

$$\sigma_W = \sqrt{Var[W]} = \sqrt{7}$$

Since T is the total reading time of 70 students, central limit theorem applies because the sample size is bigger than 30. We have:

$$\mu_T = 70\mu_W = 70(25) = 1750$$

$$\sigma_T = \sqrt{70}\sigma_W = \sqrt{70}\,\sqrt{7} = 22.136$$

We need to change 1800 to standard score.

$$z = \frac{1800 - 1750}{22.136} = 2.26$$

$$P[T > 1800] = P[z > 2.26]$$

$$= 1 - P[z \leq 2.26]$$

$$= 1 - .9881$$

$$= .012$$

The correct answer is **D**.

9. A hotel has 30 rooms. It does only non-refundable bookings, each for \$65. It estimates that the probability of a person not showing up is .1, and so it does 32 bookings for each day. If more than 30 bookings show up on a day, the extra show(s) above the 30 each get back their booking price plus and extra \$100. Find the expected daily revenue of the hotel.

A) 1755

B) 1864

C) 1989

D) 2049

E) 2108

Solution:

Let X be the number of people who show up.

If 30 or fewer people show up, revenue is $32(65) = 2080$

This is a binomial situation with $n = 32,\ p = .9$

$$f(x) = \binom{n}{x} p^x (1-p)^{n-x}$$

$$f(x) = \binom{32}{x} .9^x (.1)^{32-x}$$

$$P(X \leq 30) = 1 - f(31) - f(32)$$

$$= 1 - .1221 - .0343$$

$$= .8436$$

If 31 people show up, revenue is $2080 - 165 = 1915$

$$P(X = 31) = f(31)$$

$$= .1221$$

If 32 people show up, revenue is $2080 - 2(165)$

$$= 1750$$

$$P(X = 32) = f(32)$$

$$= .0343$$

Expected Revenue $= 2080(.8436) + 1915(.1221) + 1750(.0343)$

$$= 2049$$

The correct answer is **D**.

Tools Needed for Problems 75-83

For any random variables, $E[X+Y+\cdots]=E[X]+E[Y]+\cdots$

If the joint pdf of 2 variables is constant/uniform over a domain, then it equals the reciprocal of the area of the domain.

If X and Y are independent, then so are any other functions involving them.

If X and Y are independent, then $E[XY]=E[X]\,E[Y]$

Expected value of a discrete random variable R is:

$$E(R)=\sum r\,f(r)$$

$$Var\,(aW+bZ+c)=a^2\,Var\,W+b^2\,Var\,Z+2ab\,Cov\,(W,Z)$$

If X and Y are independent, then $Cov\,(X,Y)=0$

SD $=\sqrt{Var}$

Variance of an exponential variable with mean k is k^2

Cdf of an exponential distribution with mean k is:

$$F(x)=1-e^{-x/k}$$

If X and Y have the joint probability $f(x,y)$ then:

$$f(y|x)=\frac{f(x,y)}{f_X(x)}$$

The joint pdf of independent variables is the product of their individual pdf's.

Then X,Y are independent random variables. Here, $g(x),h(y)$ are the pdf's of X,Y, respectively.

$$Cov(X,Y)=E[XY]-E[X]E[Y]$$

Covariance of independent random variables is 0.

The joint density function of X and Y can always be given by both:

$$f(x,y)=g(x)\,h(y\ given\ x)=f_X(x)f_Y(y|x)$$

$$f(x,y)=h(y)\,g(x\ given\ y)=f_Y(y)f_X(x|y)$$

$$Cov(aX+bY,cX+dY)=acVarX+(ad+bc)Cov(X,Y)+bdVarY$$

$$Var[X+Y]=Var\,X+Var\,Y+2Cov\,(X,Y)$$

$$Var\,X=\ E[X^2]-(E[X])^2$$

SOA Sample Question 75 Explanation

Total benefit after the revision is:

$$T = X + 100 + 1.10Y$$

We have:

$$17000 = Var(X + Y)$$

$$17000 = Var\ X + Var\ Y + 2\ Cov\ (X, Y)$$

$$17000 = 5000 + 10000 + 2Cov\ (X, Y)$$

$$Cov\ (X, Y) = 1000$$

This covariance will be needed in our calculations. We know that:

$$Var\ (aW + bZ + c) = a^2\ Var\ W + b^2\ Var\ Z + 2ab\ Cov\ (W, Z)$$

$$Var\ T = Var\ X + 1.1^2\ Var\ Y + 2(1)(1.1)\ Cov\ (X, Y)$$

$$= 5000 + 1.21(10000) + 2.2(1000)$$

$$= 19300$$

The correct answer is **C**.

SOA Sample Question 76 Explanation

x	$f(x)$
0	$1/6$
1	$\frac{1}{12} + \frac{1}{6} = 1/4$
2	$\frac{1}{12} + \frac{1}{3} + \frac{1}{6} = 7/12$

This can be done most quickly on calculator as explained earlier. The video link is:

https://www.youtube.com/watch?v=QNlw_TX-vEI&t=69

From calculator:

$$\text{SD} = .7592$$

$$Var\ X = .7592^2$$

$$= .58$$

The correct answer is **B**.

SOA Sample Question 77 Explanation

We know that:

$$Var\ (aX + bY + c) = a^2\ Var\ X + b^2\ Var\ Y + 2ab\ Cov\ (X, Y)$$

We also know that if X, Y are independent, then:

$$Cov\ (X, Y) = 0$$

So:

$$Var\ Z = Var\ (3X - Y - 5)$$

$$= 3^2\ Var\ X + (-1)^2\ Var\ Y$$

$$= 9(1) + 1(2)$$

$$= 11$$

The correct answer is **D**.

SOA Sample Question 78 Explanation

Let X, Y be the lifetimes of the 2 generators.

We need $Var(X + Y)$.

The lifetimes of the 2 generators are obviously independent and so:

$$Var(X + Y) = Var\ X + Var\ Y$$

We know that variance of an exponential variable with mean k is k^2.

Thus,

$$Var\ X = Var\ Y$$

$$= 10^2$$

$$= 100$$

Hence,

$$Var(X + Y) = 100 + 100$$

$$= 200$$

The correct answer is **E**.

SOA Sample Question 79 Explanation

Let X, Y, Z be the losses due to storm, fire, and theft, respectively.

The cdf's are:

$$F(x) = 1 - e^{-\frac{x}{1}}$$

$$G(y) = 1 - e^{-\frac{y}{1.5}}$$

$$H(z) = 1 - e^{-\frac{z}{2.4}}$$

Let $M = Max\ \{X, Y, Z\}$.

We need to find $P(M > 3)$.

$$P(M > 3) = 1 - P(M \leq 3)$$

$$= 1 - P(X \leq 3)P(Y \leq 3)P(Z \leq 3)$$

$$= 1 - F(3)G(3)H(3)$$

$$= .414$$

The correct answer is **E**.

SOA Problem 80 Explanation

First note that:

$$C_2 = X + 1.2Y$$

So, we get:

$$Cov(C_1, C_2) = Cov(X + Y, X + 1.2Y)$$

In general, we have the formula:

$$Cov(aX + bY, cX + dY) = acVarX + (ad + bc)Cov(X, Y) + bdVarY$$

Here, $a = 1, b = 1, c = 1, d = 1.2$.

So, the formula becomes:

$$Cov(X + Y, X + 1.2Y) = Var\,X + 2.2\,Cov\,(X, Y) + 1.2\,Var\,Y \qquad (1)$$

We need to find the quantities on the right side of (1).

$$Var\,X = E[X^2] - (E[X])^2$$

$$= 27.4 - 5^2$$

$$= 2.4$$

$$Var\,Y = E[Y^2] - (E[Y])^2$$

$$= 51.4 - 7^2$$

$$= 2.4$$

We know that:

$$Cov\,(X, Y) = E[XY] - E[X]E[Y]$$

But since we are not given $E[XY]$, we use another way to find the covariance. We know that:

$$Var[X + Y] = Var\,X + Var\,Y + 2Cov\,(X, Y)$$

$$8 = 2.4 + 2.4 + 2Cov\,(X, Y)$$

$$Cov\,(X, Y) = 1.6$$

Now we have all the values needed on the right side of equation (1).

$$Cov(X + Y, X + 1.2Y) = Var\,X + 2.2\,Cov\,(X, Y) + 1.2\,Var\,Y$$

$$= 2.4 + 2.2\,(1.6) + 1.2\,\,(2.4)$$

$$= 8.8$$

The correct answer is **A**.

SOA Problem 81 Explanation

Since husband survives, the only way a claim could occur is if the wife died within the 10 years.

$$\text{P(wife dies | husband lives)} = \frac{P(wife\ dies\ and\ husband\ lives)}{P(husband\ lives)}$$

$$\text{P(husband lives)} = P(only\ the\ husband\ lives) + P(both\ live)$$

$$= .01 + .96$$

$$= .97$$

Thus:

$$P\ (wife\ dies\ |\ husband\ lives) = \frac{.01}{.97} = \frac{1}{97}$$

$$\text{Expected Claim} = \text{(Claim Amount) (Probability of Claim)}$$

$$= 10000\left(\frac{1}{97}\right) = 103$$

$$\text{Total premium} = 2(500) = 1000$$

$$\text{Expected excess of Premiums over Claims} = \text{Expected Premium} - \text{Expected Claim}$$

$$= 1000 - 103 = 897.$$

The correct answer is **E**.

SOA Problem 82 Explanation

$$P[Y = 0|X = 1] = \frac{P[Y = 0\ and\ X = 1]}{P[X = 1]}$$

$$= \frac{.05}{P[X = 1, Y = 0] + P[X = 1, Y = 1]}$$

$$= \frac{.05}{.05 + .125} = .286$$

$$P[Y = 1|X = 1] = 1 - P[Y = 0|X = 1]$$

$$= 1 - .286 = .714$$

The relevant values are tabulated below:

$Y\|X = 1$	$P[Y\|X = 1]$
0	$.286$
1	$.714$

From calculator (as explained for problem 58):

$$\text{SD} = .452$$

$$Var = (.452)^2 = .20$$

The correct answer is **C**.

SOA Sample Question 83 Explanation

Let the joint pmf be $f(q,p)$.

We need conditional pmf:

$$f(q|p=0)=\frac{f(q,0)}{f_P(0)}$$

Here,

$$f_P(0)=.12+.06+.05+.02$$
$$=.25$$

$q\|p=0$	$f(q,0)$	$f[q\|p=0]=\frac{f(q,0)}{.25}$
0	.12	12/25
1	.06	6/25
2	.05	5/25
3	.02	2/25

The standard deviation can be found most quickly on calculator as I explain in my youtube video whose link is:

https://www.youtube.com/watch?v=QNlw_TX-vEI&t=69s

From calculator:

$$\text{SD}=.9928$$
$$Var=.9928^2$$
$$=.99$$

The correct answer is **D**.

Quiz 7

1. The daily amounts of auto and home insurance claims that an insurance company receives are exponentially distributed with means 500 and 1000 respectively. Find the probability that on any given day, the higher of these two claims is less than 2000.
   A) .15
   B) .19
   C) .81
   D) .85
   E) .89
   Solution:

   Let X, Y be the daily amounts of auto and home insurance claims, respectively.

   The cdf's are:

$$F(x) = 1 - e^{-\frac{x}{500}}$$

$$G(y) = 1 - e^{-\frac{y}{1000}}$$

   Let $M = Max\,\{X, Y\}$.

   We need to find $P(M < 2000)$.

$$P(M < 2000) = P(X < 2000\ and\ Y < 2000)$$

$$= F(2000)G(2000)$$

$$= \left(1 - e^{-\frac{2000}{500}}\right)\left(1 - e^{-\frac{2000}{1000}}\right)$$

$$= .85$$

   The correct answer is **D**.

2. The lifetime of a bulb is exponentially distributed with mean 72 hours. You use it in a lamp that is always on, and when the bulb goes out, you replace it with a similar bulb. Find the standard deviation (in hours) of the total working life of the two bulbs in the lamp.
   Solution:
   A) 102
   B) 104
   C) 10368
   D) 10816
   E) 12000

   Let X, Y be the lifetimes of the 2 bulbs.

   We need $SD\ (X + Y)$.

   The lifetimes of the 2 bulbs are obviously independent and so:

$$Var(X + Y) = Var\ X + Var\ Y$$

   We know that variance of an exponential variable with mean k is k^2. Thus:

$$Var\ X = Var\ Y$$
$$= 72^2$$
$$= 5184$$

Hence,

$$Var(X + Y) = 5184 + 5184 = 10368$$
$$SD(X + Y) = \sqrt{Var(X + Y)}$$
$$= \sqrt{10368} = 102$$

The correct answer is **A**.

3. Let X represent the monthly rent and Y represent the monthly grocery expense for a person in a certain city. We know that:

$$Var\ X = 200, \qquad Var\ Y = 150, \qquad Var(X + Y) = 400$$

Next year, the rent is expected to increase by 5% and the grocery bill for each person is expected to increase by 10. Find the variance of the sum of the monthly rent and the grocery bill after these changes.

Solution:

A) 410
B) 417
C) 423
D) 431
E) 436

Total expense after the increase is: $T = 1.05X + Y + 10$. We have:

$$400 = Var(X + Y) = Var\ X + Var\ Y + 2\ Cov\ (X, Y)$$
$$400 = 200 + 150 + 2Cov\ (X, Y)$$
$$Cov\ (X, Y) = 25$$

This covariance will be needed in our calculations because we know:

$$Var\ (aW + bZ + c) = a^2\ Var\ W + b^2\ Var\ Z + 2ab\ Cov\ (W, Z)$$
$$Var\ T = 1.05^2 Var\ X + \ Var\ Y + 2(1.05)(1)\ Cov\ (X, Y)$$
$$= 1.05^2(200) + 150 + 2.1(25)$$
$$= 423$$

The correct answer is **C**.

4. A car dealer sells 0, 1, or 2 luxury cars on any day. When selling a car, the dealer also tries to persuade the customer to buy an extended warranty for the car. Let X denote the number of luxury cars sold in a given day, and let Y denote the number of extended warranties sold.

$$P[X = 0, Y = 0] = 1/6$$

$$P[X = 1, Y = 0] = 1/12$$

$$P[X = 1, Y = 1] = 1/6$$

$$P[X = 2, Y = 0] = 1/12$$

$$P[X = 2, Y = 1] = 1/3$$

$$P[X = 2, Y = 2] = 1/6$$

Calculate the variance of Y.

(A) 0.47

(B) 0.58

(C) 0.83

(D) 1.42

(E) 2.58

Solution:

y	$f(y)$
0	$\frac{1}{6}+\frac{1}{12}+\frac{1}{12}=\frac{1}{3}$
1	$\frac{1}{3}+\frac{1}{6}=\frac{1}{2}$
2	$\frac{1}{6}$

This can be done most quickly on calculator as explained earlier. Once again, the video link is:

https://www.youtube.com/watch?v=QNlw_TX-vEI&t=69

From calculator:

$$\text{SD} = .6872$$

$$Var\ Y = .6872^2$$

$$= .47$$

The correct answer is **A**.

5. A high school summer camp needs a counsellor and gets applications from candidates whose ages are uniformly distributed between 19 and 23 years. A team of selectors comes up with the top 2 qualified applicants. If the ages of these two applicants differ by more than 6 months, then the younger one is automatically selected, otherwise both are invited for an in-person interview. What is the probability of an in-person interview?

(A) 0.21

(B) 0.23

(C) 0.50

(D) 0.77

(E) 0.79

Solution:

Let X, Y be the ages of the top 2 applicants. We are asked to find:

$$P(|Y - X| < .5)$$

$$= P(X - .5 < Y < X + .5)$$

Since both the age distributions are uniform (19, 23) we have:

$$f(x) = \frac{1}{4}, \qquad 19 < x < 23$$

$$g(y) = \frac{1}{4}, \qquad 19 < y < 23$$

The ages of the 2 candidates can reasonably be assumed to be independent, the joint pdf is the product of individual ones.

$$h(x, y) = f(x)\, g(y)$$

$$= \frac{1}{16}, \quad 19 < x < 23, \quad 19 < y < 23$$

Total region is the square with area 16. Required region is the white region between the 2 triangles.

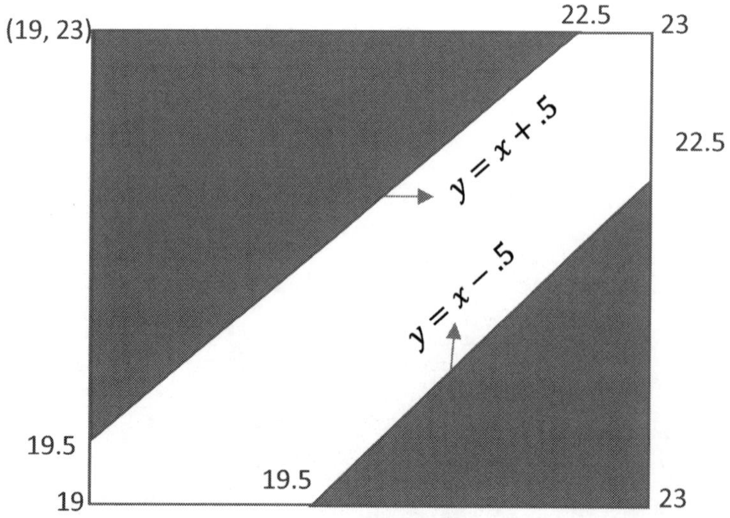

Instead of finding the white area directly, we can see from the figure that it is easier to calculate the total area of the 2 triangles and then subtract it from the area of the outer square to get the required area.

$$\text{The area of each blue triangle} = (.5)\ (\text{base})\ (\text{height})$$

$$= (.5)(3.5)(3.5)$$

$$= 6.125$$

$$\text{Area of both triangles} = 2(6.125)$$

$$= 12.25$$

$$\text{White area} = 16 - 12.25$$

$$= 3.75.$$

Required probability is:

$$\frac{3.75}{16}$$

$$= .23$$

The correct answer is **B**.

6. In case of a car accident, the loss is uniformly distributed from 0 to 15000, and in case of a hurricane, the home damage is uniformly distributed from 0 to 15000. Auto insurance has a deductible of 1000 and home insurance has a deductible of 3000. If a man experiences exactly one car accident and exactly one hurricane, find the probability that the amount paid by insurance company is less than 9000?

A) .35

B) .42

C) .50

D) .58

E) .65

Solution:

Let X be the loss in car accident, and Y be the home damage by hurricane. For uniform distributions, we can just calculate the appropriate areas and divide by the total area of the rectangle. Here, $0 \leq X \leq 15000$, $0 \leq Y \leq 15000$, so the total area is $(15000 - 0)(15000 - 0) = 225M$. We need to consider the following cases in which the total benefit is less than or equal to 9000:

Case 1: $\boldsymbol{0 \leq X \leq 1000}$

In this case, there is no benefit from the car policy. Thus, the benefit from home policy needs to be maximum 9000. Hence $0 \leq Y \leq 12000$. The conditions on X, Y give a total area of $(1000 - 0)(12000 - 0) = 12M$

Case 2: $\boldsymbol{1000 < X \leq 10000}$

In this case, the benefit from car policy is $X - 1000$. Hence, the benefit from the home policy needs to be less than $9000 - (X - 1000) = 10000 - X$. Thus, the home loss needs to be less than $13000 - X$, that is, $Y < 13000 - X$. The graph of this case is shown below, where for brevity, we have used the standard notation K to represent a thousand:

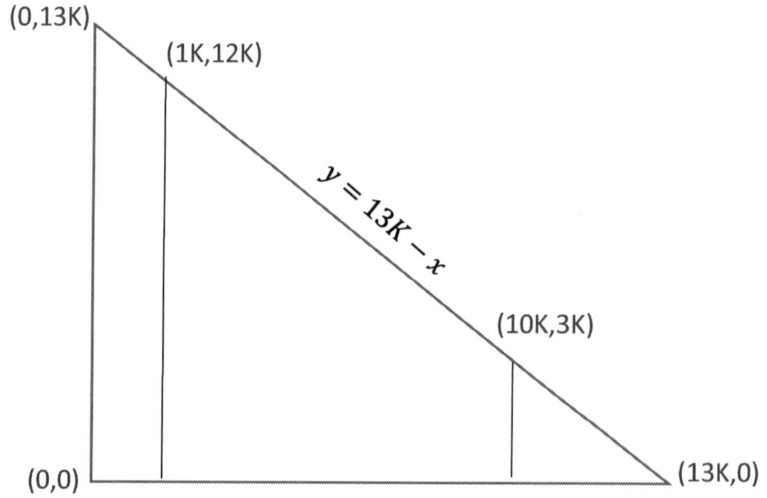

The required area is the area of the trapezoid $= \frac{1}{2}(b)(h_1 + h_2)$

$$= \frac{1}{2}(10000 - 1000)(12000 + 3000) = 67.5M$$

Thus, the required area $= 12M + 67.5 = 79.5M$

$$Required\ probability = \frac{Required\ Area}{Total\ Area} = \frac{79.5M}{225M} = .35$$

The correct answer is **A**.

7. Let X denote the physician's fee and Y denote the lab fee paid by an insurance company to a hospital. Let $C_1 = X + Y$.

$$E[X] = 70, E[X^2] = 5000, E[Y] = 150, E[Y^2] = 23000, Var[X + Y] = 1000$$

However, the hospital does not get this full amount but there is a 10% tax cut. Let C_2 denote the amount the hospital gets after taxes. Calculate Cov (C_1, C_2) .

A) 700
B) 900
C) 1100
D) 1300
E) 1500

Solution:

First note that $C_2 = .9C_1 = .9(X + Y) = .9X + .9Y$. So we have:

$$Cov(C_1, C_2) = Cov(X + Y, .9X + .9Y)$$

In general, we have the formula:

$$Cov(aX + bY, cX + dY) = acVarX + (ad + bc)Cov(X, Y) + bdVarY$$

Here, $a = 1, b = 1, c = .9, d = .9$. So, the formula becomes:

$$Cov(X + Y, .9X + .9Y) = .9Var\ X + 1.8\ Cov\ (X, Y) + .9\ Var\ Y \qquad (1)$$

Thus, we need to find the quantities on the right side of (1).

$$Var\ X = E[X^2] - (E[X])^2 = 5000 - 70^2 = 100$$

$$Var\ Y = E[Y^2] - (E[Y])^2 = 23000 - 150^2 = 500$$

To find $Cov\ (X, Y)$, we use the fact that:

$$Var[X + Y] = Var\ X + Var\ Y + 2Cov\ (X, Y)$$

$$1000 = 100 + 500 + 2Cov\ (X, Y)$$

$$Cov\ (X, Y) = 200$$

Now we have all the values needed on the right side of equation (1).

$$Cov(X + Y, .9X + .9Y) = .9(100) + 1.8(200) + .9(500)$$

$$= 900$$

The correct answer is **B**.

8. Life insurance policies, each with a death benefit of 10,000 and a one-time premium of 500, are sold to 3 married couples, one for each person. The policies will expire at the end of 30 years from now. For each couple, the probability that only the wife will survive at least 30 years is 0.025, the probability that only the husband will survive at least 30 years is 0.01, and the probability that both partners will survive at least 30 years is 0.9. Calculate the expected excess of premiums over claims, given that the wives survive at least 30 years.
   A) 730
   B) 1088
   C) 1526
   D) 2189
   E) 2441

Solution:

We are given that the wife survives for each couple, so the only way a claim could occur is if the husband died within the 30 years.

$$\text{P (husband dies | wife lives)} = \frac{P(husband\ dies\ and\ wife\ lives)}{P(wife\ lives)}$$

$$P(wife\ lives) = P(only\ the\ wife\ lives) + P(both\ live)$$

$$= .025 + .9$$

$$= .925$$

Thus:

$$P\ (husband\ dies \mid wife\ lives) = \frac{.025}{.925}$$

$$= \frac{1}{37}$$

Expected Claim for dead 3 husbands = (Claim Amount for) (Probability of Claim)

$$= 30000\left(\frac{1}{37}\right)$$

$$= 811$$

$$\text{Total premium for 3 couples } = 6(500)$$

$$= 3000$$

$$\text{Expected excess of Premiums over Claims} = \text{Expected Premium} - \text{Expected Claim}$$

$$= 3000 - 811$$

$$= 2189.$$

The correct answer is **D**.

9. A diagnostic test for the presence of a disease has two possible outcomes: 1 for disease present and 0 for disease not present. Let X denote the disease state (0 or 1) of a patient and let Y denote the outcome of the diagnostic test. The joint probability function of X and Y is given by:

$$P[X = 0, Y = 0] = .800$$

$$P[X = 1, Y = 0] = .050$$

$$P[X = 0, Y = 1] = .025$$

$$P[X = 1, Y = 1] = .125$$

Calculate $Var[Y|X = 0]$

(A) 0.0194

(B) 0.0294

(C) 0.0394

(D) 0.0494

(E) 0.0594

Solution:

$$P[Y = 0|X = 0] = \frac{P[Y = 0 \text{ and } X = 0]}{P[X = 0]}$$

$$= \frac{.8}{P[X = 0, Y = 0] + P[X = 0, Y = 1]}$$

$$= \frac{.8}{.8 + .025} = .9697$$

$$P[Y = 1|X = 0] = 1 - P[Y = 0|X = 0]$$

$$= 1 - .9697 = .0303$$

The relevant values are tabulated below:

$Y\|X = 0$	$P[Y\|X = 0]$
0	.9697
1	.0303

The standard deviation can be found most quickly on calculator as I explain in my youtube video whose link is:

https://www.youtube.com/watch?v=QNlw_TX-vEI&t=69s

$$\text{SD} = .1714$$

$$Var = .1714^2 = .0294$$

The correct answer is **B.**

10. The annual number of tornadoes in counties P and Q are jointly distributed as follows:

Annual Number of Tornadoes in County Q

		0	1	2	3
Annual Number of Tornadoes In County P	0	.12	.06	.05	.02
	1	.13	.15	.12	.03
	2	.05	.15	.10	.02

Calculate the conditional variance of the annual number of tornadoes in county P, given that there is one tornado in county Q.

(A) 0.52
(B) 0.72
(C) 1.02
(D) 1.62
(E) 2.72

Solution:

If the joint pmf is $f(p,q)$, we need conditional pmf:

$$f(p|1) = \frac{f(p,1)}{f_Q(1)}$$

$$f_Q(1) = .06 + .15 + .15 = .36$$

$p|1$	$f(p,1)$	$f[p|1] = \frac{f(p,1)}{.36}$
0	.06	$6/36$
1	.15	$15/36$
2	.15	$15/36$

The standard deviation can be found most quickly on calculator as I explain in my youtube video whose link is:

https://www.youtube.com/watch?v=QNlw_TX-vEI&t=69s

SD = .7217

$$Var = .7217^2 = .52$$

The correct answer is **A**.

Tools Needed for Problems 84-95

Pdf, expected value, and variance of uniform (a, b) distribution are:

$$f(x) = \frac{1}{b-a}, \quad a < x < b, \quad E[X] = \frac{(a+b)}{2}, \qquad Var\ X = \frac{(b-a)^2}{12}$$

If X and Y are independent, then:

$$(i)\ Var[X|Y < y] = Var[X|Y > y] = Var[X|Y = y] = Var\ X$$

$$(ii)\ f(x, y) = f_X(x) f_Y(y)$$

For exponential variable X with mean k, variance is k^2. For this distribution we also have:

$$f(x) = \frac{1}{k} e^{-\frac{x}{k}}, x > 0 \qquad F(x) = 1 - e^{-\frac{x}{k}} \qquad Var[X|X > a] = Var\ X$$

If joint pdf is constant, then any required probability can be found be finding the area of the appropriate region. For any continuous variable:

$$P(a < X < b) = \int_a^b f(x)\, dx$$

If population is normal, or if sample size, $n > 30$, then the sampling distribution of means and sums is approximately normal with mean and standard deviation:

$$\mu_{\bar{X}} = \mu \qquad \sigma_{\bar{X}} = \frac{\sigma}{\sqrt{n}} \qquad \mu_{sum} = n\mu \qquad \sigma_{sum} = \sqrt{n}\,\sigma$$

where μ and σ are the mean and standard deviation of each of the n identical variables.

$$Var\ X = E[X^2] - (E[X])^2$$

Geometric distribution gives the probability of the 1st success requiring k independent trials, each with success probability p. The pmf is:

$$f(k) = p(1-p)^{k-1}$$

The mean, or expected value of geometric distribution is $1/p$

For Poisson distribution of mean k, variance is k

Conditional Variance Formula, or Law of Total Variance:

$$Var(X) = E[Var(X|\lambda)] + \text{Var}[\text{E}(\text{X}|\lambda)], \text{where } \lambda \text{ is a parameter of } X$$

By hypergeometric, if we have N items, of which a items are of type A, b items are of type B, then the probability of selecting n items, of which x items are of type A is:

$$\frac{\binom{a}{x}\binom{b}{n-x}}{\binom{N}{n}}$$

Law of Total Expectation:

$$E(X|Y = a) = \sum_x P(X = x|Y = a) E[X|X = x, Y = a]$$

SOA Sample Question 84 Explanation

The cdfs of exponential distributions with means 5 and 8 are:

$$F(s) = 1 - e^{-s/5}$$

$$G(s) = 1 - e^{-s/8}$$

For claim amount to be between 4 and 8, *N* has to be 1 or greater.

So, by law of total probability:

$$P(4 < S < 8) = P(N = 1)P(4 < S < 8|N = 1) + P(N > 1)P(4 < S < 8|N > 1)$$

$$= \frac{1}{3}[F(8) - F(4)] + \frac{1}{6}[G(8) - G(4)]$$

$$= .12$$

The correct answer is **C**.

SOA Sample Question 85 Explanation

By condition (ii) we have:

$$p(n+1) - p(n) = c, \qquad n = 0,1,2,3,4$$

This gives:

$$p(1) = p(0) + c$$

$$p(2) = p(1) + c = p(0) + c + c = p(0) + 2c$$

$$p(3) = p(2) + c = p(0) + 2c + c = p(0) + 3c$$

$$p(4) = p(3) + c = p(0) + 3c + c = p(0) + 4c$$

$$p(5) = p(4) + c = p(0) + 4c + c = p(0) + 5c$$

We also know that the sum of all probabilities is 1.

$$p(0) + p(1) + p(2) + p(3) + p(4) + p(5) = 1$$

$$p(0) + p(0) + c + p(0) + 2c + p(0) + 3c + p(0) + 4c + p(0) + 5c = 1$$

$$6p(0) + 15c = 1 \qquad (1)$$

By condition (iii),

$$p(0) + p(1) = .4$$

$$p(0) + p(0) + c = .4$$

$$2p(0) + c = .4$$

$$c = .4 - 2p(0)$$

Substituting this value of c in (1) we get:

$$6p(0) + 15[.4 - 2p(0)] = 1$$

$$6p(0) + 6 - 30p(0) = 1$$

$$p(0) = 5/24$$

$$c = .4 - 2p(0) = .4 - 2\left(\frac{5}{24}\right) = -\frac{.4}{24}$$

$$p(4) = p(0) + 4c = \frac{5}{24} - 4\left(\frac{.4}{24}\right) = \frac{3.4}{24}$$

$$p(5) = p(0) + 5c = \frac{5}{24} - 5\left(\frac{.4}{24}\right) = \frac{3}{24}$$

$$P(more\ than\ 3\ claims) = p(4) + p(5) = \frac{6.4}{24} = .27$$

The correct answer is **C**.

SOA Sample Question 86 Explanation

Let X represent each loss, and Y represent each payout. Then:

$$f(x) = \frac{1}{20000}, \qquad 0 < x < 20000$$

$$Y = \begin{cases} 0, & X \leq 5000 \\ X - 5000, & X > 5000 \end{cases}$$

We start by finding the mean and standard deviation of each payout.

$$\mu_Y = E[Y] = \int_{-\infty}^{\infty} y\, f(x)dx = \int_{5000}^{20000} (x - 5000)\left(\frac{1}{20000}\right) dx$$

$$= \frac{(x-5000)^2}{40000}\Big|_{5000}^{20000} = 5625$$

$$E[Y^2] = \int_{-\infty}^{\infty} y^2\, f(x)dx = \int_{5000}^{20000} (x - 5000)^2\left(\frac{1}{20000}\right) dx$$

$$= \frac{(x-5000)^3}{60000}\Big|_{5000}^{20000} = 56250000$$

$$\sigma_Y = \sqrt{E[Y^2] - (E[Y])^2} = \sqrt{56250000 - 5625^2} = 4961$$

Since we have more than 30 payouts, central limit theorem applies. Let T denote the total payout on 200 losses. Then:

$$\mu_T = 200\mu_Y = 200(5625) = 1125000$$

$$\sigma_T = \sqrt{200}\sigma_Y = \sqrt{200}(4961) = 70159$$

Next, we need to change 1,000,000 and 1,200,000 into standard scores.

$$z_1 = \frac{1000000 - \mu_T}{\sigma_T} = -1.78$$

$$z_2 = \frac{1200000 - \mu_T}{\sigma_T} = 1.07$$

$$P(1000000 < T < 1200000) = P(-1.78 < z < 1.07)$$

$$= P(z < 1.07) - P(z < -1.78) = P(z < 1.07) - P(z > 1.78)$$

$$= P(z < 1.07) - [1 - P(z < 1.78)]$$

$$= .8577 - (1 - .9625) = .8202$$

The small discrepancy from choice D is because of rounding.

The correct answer is **D**.

SOA Sample Question 87 Explanation

Let A, H, R be the % that have auto, homeowners, and renter's insurance, respectively.

Homeowners and renters insurance are mutually exclusive, meaning someone who has one of them does not have the other. So, in the diagram, there is no overlap between H and R.

Condition (iii) tells us that $H = 2R$.

The Venn diagram is shown below:

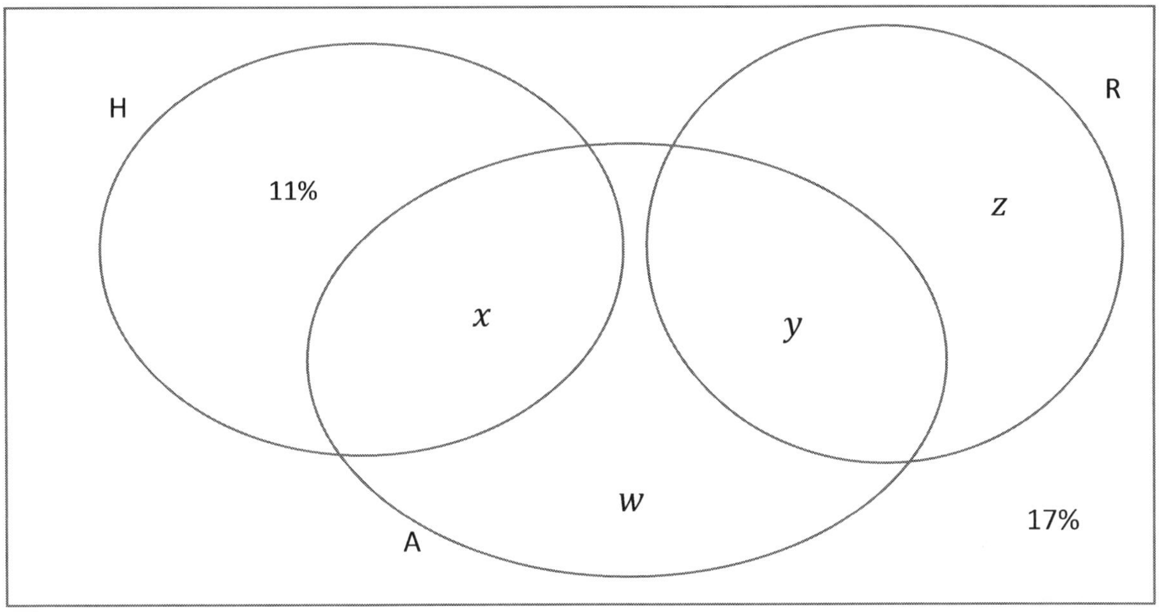

We are to find y. Since $H = 2R$, we have:

$$11 + x = 2(y + z) \quad (1)$$

Conditions (ii) and (iv) give:

$$x + y + w = 64 \quad (2)$$

$$x + y = 35 \quad (3)$$

From equations (2) and (3), $w = 29$. Also, the total sum is 100%. So,

$$11 + x + y + z + 29 + 17 = 100$$

$$\Rightarrow y + z = 43 - x \quad (4)$$

Substituting this value of $y + z$ from (4) in (1) we get:

$$11 + x = 2(43 - x)$$

$$\Rightarrow x = 25$$

Substituting this in (3) we get $y = 10$.

The correct answer is **B**.

SOA Sample Question 88 Explanation

Let Y be the reimbursement.

The reimbursement is positive if the cost is greater than 20. Thus:

$$G(115) = P(Y < 115|Y > 0)$$

$$= P(Y < 115|X > 20)$$

$$= \frac{P(Y < 115 \text{ and } X > 20)}{P(X > 20)} \quad (1)$$

Now if the loss is 120, the reimbursement is 100.

So, for the reimbursement to be 115, which is 15 more than 100, we need an extra loss of 30 above the 120, because the losses above 120 are reimbursed at 50%.

Thus, if the cost is 150, the reimbursement is:

100 (for the cost up to 120) + 50% (the extra cost of 150 − 120 = 30)

$$= 100 + .5(30)$$

$$= 115$$

Hence, for reimbursement to be less than 115, loss needs to be less than 150.

Equation (1) thus becomes:

$$G(115) = \frac{P(X < 150 \text{ and } X > 20)}{P(X > 20)}$$

$$= \frac{P(20 < X < 150\,)}{1 - P(X \leq 20)}$$

$$= \frac{F(150) - F(20)}{1 - F(20)}$$

$$= \frac{1 - e^{-\frac{150}{100}} - \left(1 - e^{-\frac{20}{100}}\right)}{1 - \left(1 - e^{-\frac{20}{100}}\right)}$$

$$= .727$$

The correct answer is **B**.

SOA Sample Question 89 Explanation

Let us first talk about geometric distribution. Geometric distribution gives the probability of the 1st success requiring k independent trials, each with success probability p. The pmf is:

$$f(k) = p(1-p)^{k-1}$$

The mean, or expected value of geometric distribution is $1/p$

Now we start solving this problem. We are to find $E[N_2|N_1 = 2]$. For this we need $P(n_2|N_1 = 2)$. We use our basic formula:

$$P(n_2|N_1 = 2) = \frac{P(2, n_2)}{P(N_1 = 2)}$$

$$= \frac{\left(\frac{3}{4}\right)\left(\frac{1}{4}\right)e^{-2}(1-e^{-2})^{n_2-1}}{P(N_1 = 2)} \qquad (1)$$

Now the denominator is found by summing over all values of N_2.

$$P(N_1 = 2) = \sum_{n_2=1}^{\infty}\left(\frac{3}{4}\right)\left(\frac{1}{4}\right)e^{-2}(1-e^{-2})^{n_2-1}$$

$$= \frac{3}{16}e^{-2}\sum_{n_2=1}^{\infty}(1-e^{-2})^{n_2-1}$$

The sum is a geometric series with 1st term 1, and ratio $1 - e^{-2}$. So,

$$P(N_1 = 2) = \frac{3}{16}e^{-2}\frac{1}{1-(1-e^{-2})}$$

$$= \frac{3}{16}$$

So, equation (1) becomes:

$$P(n_2|N_1 = 2) = \frac{\left(\frac{3}{4}\right)\left(\frac{1}{4}\right)e^{-2}(1-e^{-2})^{n_2-1}}{\frac{3}{16}}$$

$$= e^{-2}(1-e^{-2})^{n_2-1}$$

We recognize this as the pmf of a geometric series with $p = e^{-2}$

Thus, its expected value is:

$$\frac{1}{e^{-2}}$$

$$= e^2$$

The correct answer is **E**.

SOA Sample Question 90 Explanation

Source	#	% Defective	# Defective	# Fine
A	30	20%	$30(.2) = 6$	$30 - 6 = 24$
B	50	8%	$50(.08) = 4$	$50 - 4 = 46$
Total	80		10	70

Out of a sample of 5, we want 2 defective, and hence 3 fine.

# of ways to choose 2 defective modems out of 10 = $\binom{10}{2} = 45$

# of ways to choose 3 fine modems out of 70 = $\binom{70}{3} = 54740$

# of ways to choose 5 total modems out of 80 = $\binom{80}{5} = 24040016$

Using the hypergeometric Formula:

$$P(2\ out\ of\ 5\ defective) = \frac{(\text{\# of ways to choose 2 defective })(\text{\# of ways to choose 3 fine})}{\text{\# of ways to choose 5 total}}$$

$$= \frac{45(54740)}{24040016}$$

$$= .102$$

The correct answer is **C**.

SOA Sample Question 91 Explanation

The probability of the man dying before his 50th birthday is $P(t < 50|t > 40)$ because it is given to us that he already has lived 40 years.

$$P(t < 50|t > 40) = \frac{P(t < 50\ and\ t > 40)}{P(t > 40)}$$

$$= \frac{P(40 < t < 50)}{1 - P(t \leq 40)}$$

$$= \frac{F(50) - F(40)}{1 - F(40)}$$

$$= \frac{1 - .8901 - (1 - .9567)}{1 - (1 - .9567)}$$

$$= .0696$$

$$Expec\ pmt = (Payment\ in\ Case\ of\ Death\ before\ 50)(Probability\ of\ death\ before\ 50)$$

$$= 5000\ P(t < 50|t > 40)$$

$$= 5000(.0696)$$

$$= 348$$

The correct answer is **B**.

SOA Sample Question 92 Explanation

Let K, Q, T be the number of king, queen, and twin mattresses sold, respectively. So:

$$\text{Total mattress sold} = K + Q + T$$

We need to find $P(K\ or\ Q)$.

$$P(K\ or\ Q) = \frac{K + Q}{K + Q + T}$$

We are given that:

$$Q = \frac{1}{4}(K + T) \quad (1)$$

$$K = 3T \quad (2)$$

Substituting (2) in (1) we get:

$$Q = \frac{1}{4}(3T + T) = T$$

$$P(K\ or\ Q) = \frac{K + Q}{K + Q + T}$$

$$= \frac{3T + T}{3T + T + T}$$

$$= \frac{4T}{5T}$$

$$= .8$$

The correct answer is **C**.

SOA Sample Question 93 Explanation

For this problem, we need the following very rarely seen conditional variance formula:

$$Var(N) = E[Var(N|\lambda)] + \mathrm{Var}[\mathrm{E}(\mathrm{N}|\lambda)] \quad (1)$$

Now $\mathrm{E}(\mathrm{N}|\lambda)$ is just the expected value or mean of a Poisson distribution given that its mean is λ. So it simply equals λ. That is:

$$\mathrm{E}(\mathrm{N}|\lambda) = \lambda$$

Also, $\mathrm{Var}(\mathrm{N}|\lambda)$ is just the variance of a Poisson distribution given that its mean is λ.

So it equals λ because mean and variance of a Poisson distribution are equal. That is:

$$\mathrm{Var}(\mathrm{N}|\lambda) = \lambda$$

Thus, (1) becomes:

$$Var(N) = E[\lambda] + \mathrm{Var}[\lambda]$$

But λ is uniform [0, 3], and the mean and variance of uniform $[a, b]$ are:

$$E[\lambda] = \frac{a+b}{2}$$

$$= \frac{0+3}{2}$$

$$= 1.5$$

$$Var[\lambda] = \frac{(b-a)^2}{12}$$

$$= \frac{(3-0)^2}{12}$$

$$= .75$$

This gives:

$$Var(N) = E[\lambda] + \mathrm{Var}[\lambda]$$

$$= 1.5 + .75$$

$$= 2.25$$

The correct answer is **E**.

SOA Sample Question 94 Explanation

To get $E(X|Y=2)$, we will need to find $f(x|Y=2)$.

We note that X has a geometric distribution.

Since the probability of getting a 5 on each roll is 1/6, we have $p = 1/6$.

Since expected value of geometric distribution is $1/p$, so:

$$E[X] = \frac{1}{p}$$

$$= \frac{1}{\left(\frac{1}{6}\right)}$$

$$= 6$$

Y also has a geometric distribution, and $Y = 2$ tells us that the first 6 happens on the 2nd roll.

We therefore know that the first roll was not a 6.

Thus, the first roll has to be 1,2,3,4, or 5.

So, because of 5 choices on 1st roll:

$$P(\,5\ on\ 1st\ roll|Y=2) = \frac{1}{5} = .2$$

We also know the 2nd roll was not a 5 (because it was a 6).

So, if the first 5 does not occur on the 1st roll, then it occurs on roll# 3 or later.

$x|Y=2$	$P(X=x|Y=2)$
1	$.2$
$3\ or\ 4\ or\ 5\ or\ \ldots$	$1-.2=.8$

Now $E[X|X \geq 3, Y=2]$ equals the number of rolls expected to get the first 5 given that there is no 5 on the first 2 rolls. So it is just the expected value of X with 2 added on, that is:

$$E[X|X \geq 3, Y=2] = 6+2 = 8$$

Using Law of Total Expectation:

$$E(X|Y=2) = \sum_x P(X=x|Y=2)E[X|X=x,Y=2]$$

$$E(X|Y=2) = .2\ E[X|X=1,Y=2] + .8\ E[X|X \geq 3, Y=2]$$

$$= .2(1) + .8(8)$$

$$= 6.6$$

The correct answer is **D**.

SOA Sample Question 95 Explanation

Let T be the number of people hospitalized. Then $T = 0,1, or\ 2$.

When $T = 0\ or\ 1$, the total loss, L, is less than 1 since each loss is distributed over (0,1).

However, when $T = 2$, the total loss, L, could be between 0 and 2, and the probability of the total loss being less than 1 will be 0.5.

t	$f(t)$	$P(L < 1)$	$P(T = t\ and\ L < 1)$
0	$.7(.7) = .49$	1	$.49(1) = .49$
1	$.7(.3) + .3(.7) = .42$	1	$.42(1) = .42$
2	$.3(.3) = .09$	$.5$	$.09(.5) = .045$

$$P(L < 1) = \sum_{t=0,1,2} P(T = t\ and\ L < 1)$$

$$= .49 + .42 + .045$$

$$= .955$$

To find $E[T|L < 1]$, we need $f(t|L < 1)$.

$$f(t|L < 1) = \frac{P(T = t\ and\ L < 1)}{P(L < 1)}$$

$$= \frac{P(T = t\ and\ L < 1)}{.955}$$

Using the above table we get:

$t\|L < 1$	$P(T = t\ and\ L < 1)$	$f(t\|L < 1) = \frac{P(T = t\ and\ L < 1)}{.955}$
0	$.49(1) = .49$	$.5131$
1	$.42(1) = .42$	$.4398$
2	$.09(.5) = .045$	$.0471$

$$E[T|L < 1] = 0(.5131) + 1(.4398) + 2(.0471)$$

$$= .534$$

The correct answer is **B**.

Quiz 8

1. You are given the following information about N, the annual number of claims for a randomly selected insured:

$$P(N=0)=\frac{1}{3}, \qquad P(N=1)=\frac{1}{2}, \qquad P(N>1)=\frac{1}{6}$$

Let X denote the total annual claim amount for an insured. When $N=1, X$ is uniformly distributed on [100,1000]. When $N>1, X$ is exponentially distributed with mean 500. Calculate $P(50<X<400)$.

A) .04
B) .14
C) .24
D) .34
E) .44

Solution:

The pdf of the uniform distribution is:

$$g(x)=\frac{1}{1000-100}=\frac{1}{900}, \qquad 100<x<1000$$

The cdf of the exponential distribution is:

$$F(x)=1-e^{-x/500}$$

For claim amount to be between 50 and 400, *N* has to be 1 or greater. So:

$$\begin{aligned} &P(50<X<400) \\ &\quad = P(N=1)P(50<X<400|N=1) \\ &\quad + P(N>1)P(50<S<400|N>1) \end{aligned}$$

$$=\frac{1}{2}\int_{100}^{400}\frac{1}{900}\,dx+\frac{1}{6}[F(400)-F(50)]$$

$$=\frac{1}{1800}(400-100)+\frac{1}{6}\left[\left(1-e^{-\frac{400}{500}}\right)-\left(1-e^{-\frac{50}{500}}\right)\right]$$

$$=.24$$

The correct answer is **C**.

2. Several job openings are announced for which only married couples can apply. It is possible that none, one, or both of the partners get selected. The probability of an applicant being selected is .6. In case of selection, the salary of a person will be uniformly distributed on [50000, 100000]. If a couple applies for the jobs, find the expected number of persons among them who get the job, given that the total couple salary is less than 150000.

A) .96
B) .98
C) 1.00
D) 1.02
E) 1.04

Solution: Let T be the persons getting the job. Then $T = 0{,}1, or\ 2$.
When $T = 0\ or\ 1$, the total salary, S, is less than 150K since each salary is between 50K and100K.
When $T = 2$, the total salary is between 100K and 200K.
So the probability of the total being less than 150000 will be 0.5.

t	$f(t)$	$P(S < 150K)$	$P(T = t\ and\ S < 150K)$
0	$.4(.4) = .16$	1	$.16(1) = .16$
1	$.4(.6) + .6(.4) = .48$	1	$.48(1) = .48$
2	$.6(.6) = .36$	$.5$	$.36(.5) = .18$

$$P(S < 150K) = \sum_{t=0,1,2} P(T = t\ and\ S < 150K)$$

$$= .16 + .48 + .18$$

$$= .82$$

$$f(t|S < 150K) = \frac{P(T = t\ and\ S < 150K)}{P(S < 150K)}$$

$$= \frac{P(T = t\ and\ S < 150K)}{.82}$$

$t\|L < 1$	$P(T = t\ and\ S < 150K)$	$f(t\|L < 1) = \frac{P(T = t\ and\ S < 150K)}{.82}$
0	$.16(1) = .16$	$.1951$
1	$.48(1) = .48$	$.5854$
2	$.36(.5) = .18$	$.2195$

$$E[T|S < 150K] = 0(.1951) + 1(.5854) + 2(.2195)$$

$$= 1.02$$

The correct answer is **D.**

3. A fair die is rolled repeatedly. Let X be the number of rolls needed to get a 5 and Y the number of rolls needed for a 6. Find $E(X|Y = 3)$.

A) 5.6
B) 5.8
C) 6.0
D) 6.3
E) 6.6

Solution:

To get $E(X|Y = 3)$, we will need to find $f(x|Y = 3)$.

We note that X has a geometric distribution.

Since the probability of getting a 5 on each roll is 1/6, we have $p = 1/6$.

So, its expected value is $1/p$, that is, 6.

Y also has a geometric distribution, and $Y = 3$ tells us that the first 6 happens on the 3rd roll. We therefore know that neither the 1st nor the 2nd roll was a 6. The 1st and 2nd rolls were 1,2,3,4, or 5. So, because of 5 choices on 1st and 2nd rolls:

$$P(\,5\ on\ 1st\ roll|Y = 3) = \frac{1}{5} = .2$$

$$P(\,5\ on\ 2nd\ roll|Y = 3) = P(not\ 5\ on\ 1st\ roll\ and\ 5\ on\ 2nd\ roll|Y = 3)$$
$$= (1 - .2)(.2) = .16$$

We also know the 3rd roll was not a 5 (because it was a 6).

So, if the first 5 does not occur on the 1st or 2nd rolls, then it occurs on roll# 4 or later.

$x|Y = 3$	$f(x|Y = 3)$
1	.2
2	.16
$4\ or\ 5\ or\ 6\ or\ \ldots$	$1 - .2 - .16 = .64$

Now $E[X|X \geq 4, Y = 3]$ equals the number of rolls expected to get the first 5 given that there is no 5 on the first 3 rolls.

So it is just the expected value of X with 3 added on, that is, $6 + 3 = 9$

$$E(X|Y = 3) = .2\,E[X|X = 1, Y = 3] + .16\,E[X|X = 2, Y = 3] + .64\,E[X|X \geq 4, Y = 3]$$
$$= .2(1) + .16(2) + .64(9)$$
$$= 6.3$$

The correct answer is **D**.

4. The loss X due to fire in a house in US follows an exponential distribution with mean λ. The parameter λ is a random variable that is determined by the location, and is uniformly distributed on [1000, 10000]. Find Var(X).

A) 43.75 million
B) 48.75 million
C) 53.75 million
D) 58.75 million
E) 90 million

Solution:

For this problem, we need the law of total variance:

$$Var(X) = E[Var(X|\lambda)] + \mathrm{Var}[\mathrm{E}(\mathrm{X}|\lambda)] \quad (1)$$

E(X|λ) is the expected value of an exponential distribution given that its mean is λ. So:

$$\mathrm{E}(\mathrm{X}|\lambda) = \lambda \quad (2)$$

Also, Var(X|λ) is the variance of an exponential distribution given that its mean is λ. So:

$$\mathrm{Var}(\mathrm{X}|\lambda) = \lambda^2 \quad (3)$$

because variance of an exponential distribution equals square of its mean.

Substituting (2) and (3) in (1).

$$Var(X) = E[\lambda^2] + \mathrm{Var}[\lambda]$$

But λ is uniform [1000, 10000], and the mean and variance of uniform $[a, b]$ are:

$$E[\lambda] = \frac{a+b}{2} = \frac{1000 + 10000}{2} = 5500$$

$$Var[\lambda] = \frac{(b-a)^2}{12} = \frac{(10000 - 1000)^2}{12} = 6750000$$

$$Var[\lambda] = E[\lambda^2] - (E[\lambda])^2$$

$$6750000 = E[\lambda^2] - 5500^2$$

$$E[\lambda^2] = 37M$$

$$Var(X) = E[\lambda^2] + \mathrm{Var}[\lambda]$$

$$= 37\mathrm{M} + 6.75\mathrm{M}$$

$$= 43.75\mathrm{M}$$

The correct answer is **A**.

5. Members a gym are classified as children, adults, and seniors. There are twice as many adults as the children and seniors combined. The number of children is a third of the number of seniors. Find the probability that a randomly chosen member will be a child or an adult.

A) .55
B) .6
C) .65
D) .7
E) .75

Solution:

Let C, A, S be the number of children, adults, and seniors, respectively.

So, total members $= C + A + S$. We need to find:

$$P(C \text{ or } A) = \frac{C + A}{C + A + S}$$

We are given that:

$$A = 2(C + S) \quad (1)$$

$$C = \frac{S}{3} \quad (2)$$

Substituting (2) in (1) we get:

$$A = 2\left(\frac{S}{3} + S\right)$$

$$= \frac{8S}{3}$$

$$P(C \text{ or } A) = \frac{C + A}{C + A + S}$$

$$= \frac{\frac{S}{3} + \frac{8S}{3}}{\frac{S}{3} + \frac{8S}{3} + S}$$

$$= \frac{3S}{4S}$$

$$= .75$$

The correct answer is **E.**

6. A high school has 32 students of which 10 are seniors. 60% of the seniors are girls, while half of the non-seniors are girls. Find the probability that there will be exactly 7 girls among 12 randomly chosen students.

A) .20
B) .22
C) .24
D) .26
E) .28

Solution:

Classification	#	% girls	# girls	# boys
Seniors	10	60%	$10(.6) = 6$	$10 - 6 = 4$
Non-Seniors	22	50%	$22(.5) = 11$	$22 - 11 = 11$
Total	32		17	15

Out of a sample of 12, we want 7 girls, and hence 5 boys.

# of ways to choose 7 girls out of 17 = $\binom{17}{7} = 19448$

# of ways to choose 5 boys out of 15 = $\binom{15}{5} = 3003$

# of ways to choose 12 total students out of 32 = $\binom{32}{12} = 225792840$

$$P(7\ out\ of\ 12\ girls) = \frac{19448(3003)}{225792840}$$

$$= .26$$

The correct answer is **D**.

7. In case of a hurricane, the expense to repair the roof of a home is uniformly distributed on [0,6000]. An insurance company will cover these expenses subject to a deductible of 1000. Find the probability that after a hurricane, the insurance company has to pay a total of more than 100,000 on 50 insured homes.

A) .24
B) .36
C) .48
D) .64
E) .80

Solution:

Let X represent each expense, and Y represent each payout. Then:

$$f(x) = \frac{1}{6000}, \qquad 0 < x < 6000$$

$$Y = \begin{cases} 0, & X \leq 1000 \\ X - 1000, & X > 1000 \end{cases}$$

We start by finding the mean and standard deviation of each payout.

$$\mu_Y = E[Y] = \int_{-\infty}^{\infty} y\, f(x)dx$$

$$= \int_{1000}^{6000} (x - 1000) \left(\frac{1}{6000}\right) dx$$

$$= \frac{(x-1000)^2}{12000} \Big|_{1000}^{6000}$$

$$= 2083$$

$$E[Y^2] = \int_{-\infty}^{\infty} y^2\, f(x)dx$$

$$= \int_{1000}^{6000} (x - 1000)^2 \left(\frac{1}{6000}\right) dx$$

$$= \frac{(x-1000)^3}{18000} \Big|_{1000}^{6000}$$

$$= 6944444$$

$$\sigma_Y = \sqrt{E[Y^2] - (E[Y])^2}$$

$$= \sqrt{6944444 - 2083^2} = 1614$$

Since we have more than 30 payouts, central limit theorem applies. Let T denote the total payout on 50 homes. Then:

$$\mu_T = 50\mu_Y = 50(2083) = 104150$$

$$\sigma_T = \sqrt{50}\sigma_Y = \sqrt{50}(1614) = 11413$$

Next, we need to change 100,000 into standard score.

$$z = \frac{100000 - \mu_T}{\sigma_T} = -.36$$

$$P(T > 100000) = P(z > -.36)$$

$$= P(z < .36)$$

$$= .64$$

The correct answer is **D**.

8. In a country, i) 55% of adults wear glasses. ii) Number of adults with blue eyes is thrice the number of adults with hazel eyes. iii) 30% of adults wear glasses and have either blue or hazel eyes. iv) 16% of the adults have blue eyes and don't wear glasses. v) 20% adults neither wear glass, nor have blue or hazel eyes. What percentage of adults wear glasses and have hazel eyes?

A) 4.75
B) 5.75
C) 6.75
D) 7.75
E) 8.75

Solution:

Let G be the % that wear glasses.
Let B be the % that has blue eyes.
Let H be the % that has hazel eyes.
Note that there can be no overlap between B and H.
The Venn diagram is shown below:

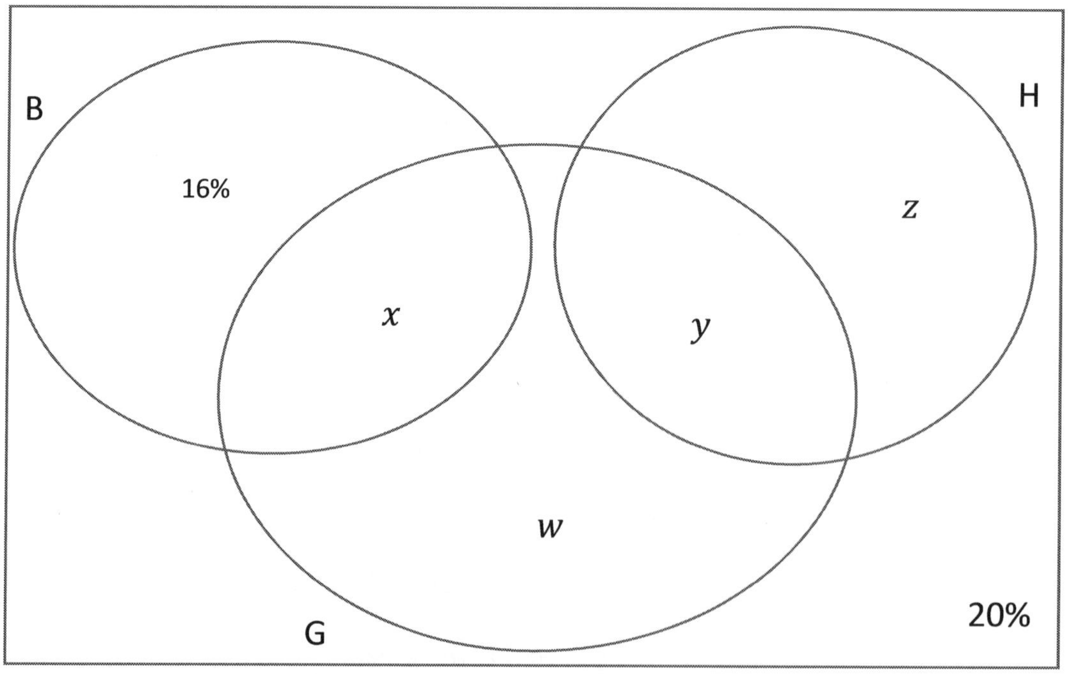

We are to find y. Since $B = 3H$, we have:

$$16 + x = 3(y + z) \quad (1)$$

Conditions (i) and (iii) give:

$$x + y + w = 55 \quad (2)$$

$$x + y = 30 \quad (3)$$

From equations (2) and (3):

$$w = 25$$

Also, the total sum is 100%. So,

$$16 + x + y + z + 25 + 20 = 100$$

$$\Rightarrow y + z = 39 - x \quad (4)$$

Substituting this value of $y + z$ from (4) in (1) we get:

$$16 + x = 3(39 - x)$$

$$\Rightarrow x = 25.25$$

Substituting this in (3) we get $y = 4.75$.

The correct answer is **A**.

9. Under an insurance policy, a maximum of four claims may be filed per year by a policyholder. Let $p(n)$ be the probability that a policyholder files n claims during a given year, where $n = 0,1,2,3,4$. An actuary makes the following observations:

i) $p(n) \geq p(n+1)$ for $n = 0, 1, 2, 3, 4$

ii) The difference between $p(n)$ and $p(n+1)$ is the same for $n = 0,1,2,3$

iii) 75% of policyholders file fewer than three claims during a given year.

Find the probability that a random policyholder will file 4 claims in a year.

A) .1
B) .2
C) .3
D) .4
E) .5

Solution:

By condition (ii) we have:

$$p(n+1) - p(n) = c, \qquad n = 0,1,2,3,4$$

This gives:

$$p(1) = p(0) + c$$
$$p(2) = p(1) + c = p(0) + c + c = p(0) + 2c$$
$$p(3) = p(2) + c = p(0) + 2c + c = p(0) + 3c$$
$$p(4) = p(3) + c = p(0) + 3c + c = p(0) + 4c$$

We also know that the sum of all probabilities is 1.

$$p(0) + p(1) + p(2) + p(3) + p(4) = 1$$

$$p(0) + p(0) + c + p(0) + 2c + p(0) + 3c + p(0) + 4c = 1$$

$$5p(0) + 10c = 1 \quad (1)$$

By condition (iii),

$$p(0) + p(1) + p(2) = .75$$

$$p(0) + p(0) + c + p(0) + 2c = .75$$

$$3p(0) + 3c = .75$$

$$c = .25 - p(0)$$

Substituting this value of c in (1) we get:

$$5p(0) + 10[.25 - p(0)] = 1$$

$$5p(0) + 2.5 - 10p(0) = 1$$

$$p(0) = .3$$

$$c = .25 - p(0) = .25 - .3 = -.05$$

$$p(4) = p(0) + 4c = .3 - 4(.05) = .1$$

The correct answer is **A**.

Tools Needed for Problems 96-106

N has **negative binomial distribution** if the probability of needing n trials to get r successes is:

$$P(N = n) = \binom{n-1}{r-1} p^r (1-p)^{n-r}$$

where p is the probability of success in each trial.

Mode: The mode of a variable X is the value x for which $f(x)$ is maximum.

Combinations and Permutations are related by the formula:

$$n\,C\,r = \frac{n\,P\,r}{r!}$$

To find $P(X+Y > c)$ it may be easier to find $P(X+Y \le c)$ and then take comp.

$$Var[Y|X = a] = E[Y^2|X = a] - (E[Y|X = a])^2$$

$$P(A \cup B \cup C) = P(A) + P(B) + P(C) - P(AB) - P(AC) - P(BC) + P(ABC)$$

$$\binom{n}{x} = \frac{n!}{x!\,(n-x)!}$$

By hypergeometric, if we have N items, of which a items are of type A, b items are of type B, then the probability of selecting n items, of which x items are of type A is:

$$\frac{\binom{a}{x}\binom{b}{n-x}}{\binom{N}{n}}$$

For Poisson distribution of mean k, variance is k

For exponential distribution of mean k, variance is k^2

Conditional Variance Formula or Law of Total Variance

$$Var(X) = E[Var(X|\lambda)] + \mathrm{Var}[\mathrm{E}(\mathrm{X}|\lambda)], \text{where } \lambda \text{ is a parameter of X}$$

The mean and variance of ***binomial distribution*** are:

$$E[X] = np \qquad Var[X] = np(1-p)$$

For any distribution X,

$$E[aX] = aE[X] \qquad Var[aX] = a^2 Var[X]$$

If a loss distribution is exponential, and the payout has a deductible so that the expected value of the payout is reduced by $a\%$ compared to the expected value of the loss, then the variance of the payout reduces by $(a\%)^2$ compared to the variance of the loss.

Set addition rule

If the number of elements in 3 sets are X, Y, Z, then the number of elements in their union is:

$$X \text{ or } Y \text{ or } Z = X + Y + Z - X\&Y - X\&Z - Y\&Z + X\&Y\&Z$$

If T is the sum of N independent identical variables X, then:

$$E[T|N] = NE[X] \quad Var[T|N] = NVar[X]$$

SOA Sample Question 96 Explanation

Let N be the number of hurricanes it takes for 2 losses to occur.

Then N has negative binomial distribution, which says that the probability of needing n trials to get r successes is:

$$P(N = n) = \binom{n-1}{r-1} p^r (1-p)^{n-r}$$

where p is the probability of success in each trial.

Here, $r = 2, p = .4$.

So, the pmf is:

$$f(n) = \binom{n-1}{2-1} (.4)^2 (1-.4)^{n-2}$$

$$= .16(n-1)(.6)^{n-2} \quad (1)$$

We need the mode of N, that is, the value of n which maximizes $f(n)$.

The easiest way is to find the first few values from eq (1)

$$f(2) = .16,$$

$$f(3) = .192,$$

$$f(4) = .1728,$$

$$f(5) = .1382$$

We see that after the initial increase, the values keep decreasing.

So, mode is 3.

The correct answer is **B**.

__SOA Sample Question 97 Explanation__

There are 30 ways to select the 1st item. Once that has been selected, we cannot select anything from the row or column of that item. So, for the 2nd item, we have $30 - 10 = 20$ choices. For example, if A_1 was the 1st item picked, we get the picture below:

~~A_1~~	~~A_2~~	~~A_3~~	~~A_4~~	~~A_5~~
~~A_6~~	A_7	A_8	A_9	A_{10}
~~A_{11}~~	A_{12}	A_{13}	A_{14}	A_{15}
~~A_{16}~~	A_{17}	A_{18}	A_{19}	A_{20}
~~A_{21}~~	A_{22}	A_{23}	A_{24}	A_{25}
~~A_{26}~~	A_{27}	A_{28}	A_{29}	A_{30}

Once the 2nd item is picked, we cannot pick anything more from that row and column, which leaves 12 choices for the 3rd pick. See figure:

~~A_1~~	~~A_2~~	~~A_3~~	~~A_4~~	~~A_5~~
~~A_6~~	~~A_7~~	~~A_8~~	~~A_9~~	~~A_{10}~~
~~A_{11}~~	~~A_{12}~~	A_{13}	A_{14}	A_{15}
~~A_{16}~~	~~A_{17}~~	A_{18}	A_{19}	A_{20}
~~A_{21}~~	~~A_{22}~~	A_{23}	A_{24}	A_{25}
~~A_{26}~~	~~A_{27}~~	A_{28}	A_{29}	A_{30}

So, the number of ways in picking the 1st, 2nd and 3rd entries this way is:

$$30(20)(12) = 7200$$

However, the strategy we have used is giving the number of permutations of the 3 entries because a change in order of counting entries can result in counting the same 3 entries multiple times. To get the number of combinations, we use the fact that:

$$n\,C\,r = \frac{n\,P\,r}{r!}$$

$$= \frac{7200}{3!}$$

$$= 1200$$

The correct answer is **C**.

SOA Sample Question 98 Explanation

Among the 400 low-risk drivers, each driver will either have 0 accident or non-zero accidents per month.

Hence, the number of zero accidents for low risk drivers is binomial with:

$$n = 400, \qquad p = .9$$

The mean of a binomial distribution is np. So,

Mean of Low-risk Drivers with 0 monthly accident = $400(.9) = 360$

Similarly, the zero accidents for high-risk drivers also form a binomial experiment with:

$$n = 600, \qquad p = .8$$

Mean of High-risk Drivers with 0 monthly accident = $600(.8) = 480$

Mean of total drivers having 0 monthly accident = $360 + 480 = 840$

Thus:

Expected Monthly payment = (Payment for each driver) (Expected # of drivers with 0 accidents)

$$= 5(840)$$

$$= 4200$$

Expected Yearly payment = 12 (expected monthly payment)

$$= 12(4200)$$

$$= 50400$$

The correct answer is **B**.

SOA Sample Question 99 Explanation

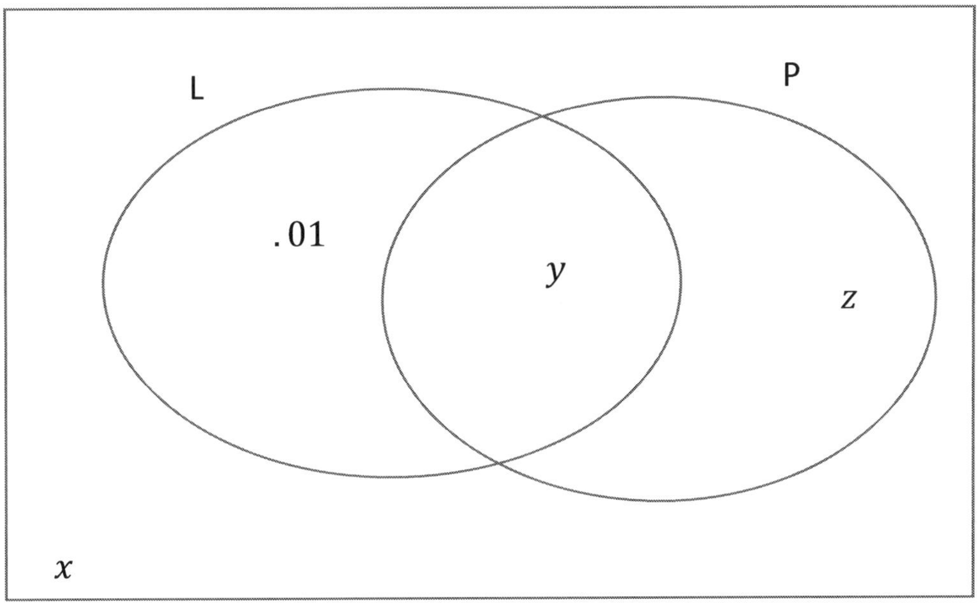

We have to find x.

We are given that:

$$.01 + y = .04 \quad (1)$$

$$y + z = .1 \quad (2)$$

From (1),

$$y = .03$$

Substituting this value in (2) we get:

$$z = .07$$

Since the rectangle is the whole universe, we also have:

$$.01 + y + z + x = 1$$

$$.01 + .03 + .07 + x = 1$$

$$x = .89$$

The correct answer is **E**.

SOA Sample Question 100 Explanation

Let the number who watched CBS, NBC, ABC, HGTV be X, Y, Z, H, respectively.

Using the set addition rule:

$$X\ or\ Y\ or\ Z = X + Y + Z - X\&Y - X\&Z - Y\&Z + X\&Y\&Z$$

$$= 34 + 15 + 10 - 7 - 6 - 5 + 4$$

$$= 45$$

Since $(X\ or\ Y\ or\ Z)\ and\ H$ are disjoint, we have:

$$(X\ or\ Y\ or\ Z)\ or\ H = (X\ or\ Y\ or\ Z) + H$$

$$= 45 + 18$$

$$= 63$$

Those who watched none of the channels is the complement of this.

Those who viewed neither = Total – Those who viewed at least one.

$$= 100 - 63$$

$$= 37$$

The correct answer is **B**.

SOA Sample Question 101 Explanation

The quickest way to do this problem is to remember that if a loss distribution is exponential, and the payout has a deductible so that the expected value of the payout is reduced by $a\%$ compared to the expected value of the loss, then the variance of the payout reduces by $(a\%)^2$ compared to the variance of the loss.

So here, the variance of the payout will reduce by:

$$(10\%)^2 = \left(\frac{10}{100}\right)^2$$

$$= \frac{1}{100}$$

$$= 1\%$$

The correct answer is **A**.

SOA Sample Question 102 Explanation

Let N be the number of hurricanes during the ten years, and X be the loss due to each hurricane. Since N is Poisson, and X is exponential:

$$Var\ N = E[N]$$

$$= 4$$

$$Var\ X = (E[X])^2$$

$$= 1000^2$$

$$= 1000000$$

Let T be the total loss due to N hurricanes. We are to find $Var[T]$.

Now T is the sum of N independent losses X. So by the last 2 formulas in the tool sheet:

$$E[T|N] = NE[X]$$

$$= 1000N$$

$$Var[T|N] = NVar[X]$$

$$= 1000000N$$

By law of total variance:

$$Var(T) = E[Var(T|\mathrm{N})] + \mathrm{Var}[\mathrm{E}(\mathrm{T}|\mathrm{N})]$$

$$= E[1000000N] + Var[1000N]$$

$$= 1000000E[N] + 1000^2 Var[N]$$

$$= 1000000(4) + 1000000(4)$$

$$= 8000000$$

The correct answer is **C**.

SOA Sample Question 103 Explanation

If X is the number of accidents, then X is binomial with $n = 3,\ p = .25$

$$E[X] = np$$

$$= 3(.25)$$

$$= .75$$

$$Var[X] = np(1 - p)$$

$$= .75(1 - .25)$$

$$= .5625$$

Let L be the loss due to each accident. L is exponential with mean .8.

$$E[L] = .8$$

$$Var[L] = .8^2$$

$$= .64$$

If Y the un-reimbursed loss due to each accident, then:

$$Y = .3L$$

$$E[Y] = .3E[L]$$

$$= .3(.8)$$

$$= .24$$

$$Var[Y] = .3^2 Var[L]$$

$$= .09(.64)$$

$$= .0576$$

Let T be the total un-reimbursed loss due to X accidents. Then:

$$E[T|X] = XE[Y] = .24X$$

$$Var[T|X] = XVar[Y] = .0576X$$

Using conditional variance formula:

$$Var(T) = E[Var(T|\mathrm{X})] + \mathrm{Var}[\mathrm{E}(\mathrm{T}|\mathrm{X})]$$

$$= E[.0576X] + Var[.24X]$$

$$= .0576E[X] + .24^2 Var[X]$$

$$= .0576(.75) + .24^2(.5625)$$

$$= .0756$$

The correct answer is **B**.

SOA Sample Question 104 Explanation

$$P(0\ accident) = .8$$

$$P(more\ than\ 1\ accident) = 0$$

$$\Rightarrow P(\ 1\ accident) = 1 - .8 - 0 = .2$$

The payout occurs when there is an accident. See figure below:

We see that the 95th percentile is three quarters of the way into the accident region. The formal calculation is:

$$\frac{95 - 80}{100 - 80} = \frac{3}{4} = 75\%$$

So, 95th percentile of payout = 75th percentile of payout given accident.

In other words, we need the 75th percentile of loss minus deductible.

The cdf of loss is:

$$F(x) = 1 - e^{-x/3000}$$

If p is the 75th percentile of loss, then:

$$.75 = 1 - e^{-p/3000}$$

$$e^{-\frac{p}{3000}} = .25$$

$$-\frac{p}{3000} = \ln .25$$

$$p = 4159$$

75th percentile of payout = 75th percentile of loss – deductible

$$= p - 500$$

$$= 4159 - 500$$

$$= 3659$$

The correct answer is **B**.

SOA Sample Question 105 Explanation

Let r be the number of pieces that are insured in the total 27 pieces.

Then $27 - r$ is the number of uninsured pieces.

# of ways to get 4 damaged pieces in 27 is $\binom{27}{4}$

# of ways in which 1 damaged piece is insured (and so 3 damaged pieces are uninsured) is:

$$\binom{r}{1}\binom{27-r}{3}$$

Using hypergeometric formula:

$$P(\,1\ damaged\ piece\ insured) = p_1 = \frac{\binom{r}{1}\binom{27-r}{3}}{\binom{27}{4}} \qquad (1)$$

$$P(\,no\ damaged\ piece\ insured) = p_0 = \frac{\binom{r}{0}\binom{27-r}{4}}{\binom{27}{4}} \qquad (2)$$

We are given that $p_1 = 2p_0$. So, from (1) and (2):

$$\frac{\binom{r}{1}\binom{27-r}{3}}{\binom{27}{4}} = 2\frac{\binom{r}{0}\binom{27-r}{4}}{\binom{27}{4}} \qquad (3)$$

Recall that:

$$\binom{n}{x} = \frac{n!}{x!\,(n-x)!}$$

So, (3) becomes:

$$r\frac{(27-r)!}{3!\,(24-r)!} = 2\frac{(27-r)!}{4!\,(23-r)!}$$

$$r\frac{4!}{3!} = 2\frac{(24-r)!}{(23-r)!}$$

$$4r = 2(24-r)$$

$$r = 8$$

$$P(\,2\ damaged\ pieces\ insured) = \frac{\binom{8}{2}\binom{27-8}{4-2}}{\binom{27}{4}}$$

$$= .27$$

The correct answer is **C**.

SOA Sample Question 106 Explanation

If both of them simultaneously examine one policy at a time until at least one of them finds a claim, then at each examination, there are 4 mutually exclusive possibilities:

(i) Both find a claim. Probability $= .1(.2) = .02$

(ii) Rahul finds a claim, Toby doesn't. Probability $= .1(.8) = .08$

(iii) Toby finds a claim, Rahul doesn't. Probability $= .2(.9) = .18$

(iv) None of them find a claim. Probability $= .9(.8) = .72$

For Rahul to examine fewer policies than Toby before a claim is found we must end with Case (ii). So:

P(Rahul needs fewer policies) =

P(Rahul finds a claim, Toby doesn't, given that a claim is found)

$$= \frac{\text{P(Rahul finds a claim, Toby doesn't)}}{\text{P(a claim is found)}}$$

$$= \frac{.08}{.02 + .08 + .18}$$

$$= .2857$$

The correct answer is **A**.

Quiz 9

1. Meg and Liz play a game in which Meg rolls a fair die and Liz tosses a fair coin at the same time. The game stops if Meg gets a 6 and/or Liz gets a head. If only one of them gets the game-stopping result, she wins. Find the probability that Meg will win.
   A) .14
   B) .18
   C) .23
   D) .27
   E) .33

Solution:
Meg's probability of getting a 6 on a roll = 1/6
Liz's probability of getting a head on a toss = 1/2

At each turn, there are 4 mutually exclusive possibilities:

a. Meg gets a 6, Liz gets a head. Probability $= \frac{1}{6}\left(\frac{1}{2}\right) = \frac{1}{12}$
b. Meg gets a 6, Liz does not get a head. Probability $= \frac{1}{6}\left(\frac{1}{2}\right) = \frac{1}{12}$
c. Meg does not get a 6, Liz gets a head. Probability $= \frac{5}{6}\left(\frac{1}{2}\right) = \frac{5}{12}$
d. Meg does not get a 6, Liz does not get a head. Probability $= \frac{5}{6}\left(\frac{1}{2}\right) = \frac{5}{12}$

Meg wins only in Case (ii) above. So:

P(Meg wins) = P(Meg gets a 6, Liz doesn't get a head given a 6 or a head appears)

$$= \frac{\text{P(Meg gets a 6, Liz doesn't get a head)}}{\text{P(a 6 or a head appears)}}$$

$$= \frac{1/12}{1/12 + 1/12 + 5/12}$$

$$= .14$$

The correct answer is **A**.

2. A bus carrying 16 passengers has an accident in which 5 of the passengers get injured. The probability that only one of the injured passengers is male is 5 times the probability that none of the injured passengers is male. Find the probability that exactly 2 of the 5 injured ones is male.
   A) .33
   B) .37
   C) .41
   D) .45
   E) .49

   Solution:

   Let r be the number of males among the 16.
   Then $16 - r$ is the number of females.

   Number of ways to get 5 injured persons in 16 is: $\binom{16}{5}$

   Number of ways in which 1 injured person is male (and so 4 injured persons are female) is: $\binom{r}{1}\binom{16-r}{4}$. So,

$$P(\,1\ injured\ person\ is\ male) = p_1 = \frac{\binom{r}{1}\binom{16-r}{4}}{\binom{16}{5}} \qquad (1)$$

   Similarly,

$$P(\,no\ no\ injured\ person\ is\ male) = p_0 = \frac{\binom{r}{0}\binom{16-r}{5}}{\binom{16}{5}} \qquad (2)$$

   We are given that $p_1 = 5p_0$. So, from (1) and (2):

$$\frac{\binom{r}{1}\binom{16-r}{4}}{\binom{16}{5}} = 5\frac{\binom{r}{0}\binom{16-r}{5}}{\binom{16}{5}} \qquad (3)$$

   Recall that:

$$\binom{n}{x} = \frac{n!}{x!\,(n-x)!}$$

   So, (3) becomes:

$$r\frac{(16-r)!}{4!\,(12-r)!} = 5\frac{(16-r)!}{5!\,(11-r)!}$$

$$r\frac{5!}{4!} = 5\frac{(12-r)!}{(11-r)!}$$

$$5r = 5(12-r)$$

$$r = 6$$

$$P(\,2\ injured\ persons\ are\ male) = \frac{\binom{6}{2}\binom{10}{3}}{\binom{16}{5}} = .41$$

   The correct answer is **C.**

3. An insurance company issues a policy with annual deductible of 400. In any year, the probability is 0.9 that there will be no accident. If there is one or more accident, the total annual loss is exponentially distributed with mean 2000. Find the 95th percentile of the insurance company payout.
   A) 886
   B) 986
   C) 1186
   D) 1286
   E) 1386

   Solution:

$$P(0\ accident) = .9$$

$$P(1\ or\ more\ accident) = 1 - .9 = .1$$

The payout occurs when there is an accident. See figure below:

We see that the 95th percentile is mid-way into the accident region. The formal calculation is:

$$\frac{95-90}{100-90} = \frac{1}{2} = 50\%$$

So, 95th percentile of payout = 50th percentile of payout given accident(s).
In other words, we need the 50th percentile of loss minus deductible.
The cdf of loss is:

$$F(x) = 1 - e^{-x/2000}$$

If p is the 50th percentile of loss, then:

$$.5 = 1 - e^{-p/2000}$$

$$e^{-\frac{p}{2000}} = .5$$

$$-\frac{p}{2000} = \ln .5$$

$$p = 1386$$

50th percentile of payout = 50th percentile of loss – deductible

$$= p - 400$$

$$= 1386 - 400$$

$$= 986$$

The correct answer is **B.**

4. There is a 10% probability that a truck crash will result in the death of driver. Annual income loss for a death is exponentially distributed with mean 50000. Losses are mutually independent and independent of the number of deaths. State gives 80% of each lost income to the family. Find the variance (in millions) of the total State benefit for 9 truck crashes.
A) 2136
B) 2336
C) 2536
D) 2736
E) 2936
Solution:

If X is the number of deaths, then X is binomial with $n = 9,\ p = .1$

$$E[X] = np = 9(.1) = .9$$

$$Var[X] = np(1 - p) = .9(1 - .1) = .81$$

Let L be the income loss due to each death. L is exponential with mean 50000.

$$E[L] = 50000$$

$$Var[L] = 50000^2 = 2500M$$

If Y the reimbursed income due to each death, then:

$$Y = .8L$$

$$E[Y] = .8E[L] = .8(50000) = 40000$$

$$Var[Y] = .8^2 Var[L] = .64(2500M) = 1600M$$

Let T be the total reimbursed income due to X deaths. Then:

$$E[T|X] = XE[Y] = 40000X$$

$$Var[T|X] = XVar[Y] = 1600000000X$$

$$Var(T) = E[Var(T|\mathrm{X})] + \mathrm{Var}[\mathrm{E}(\mathrm{T}|\mathrm{X})]$$

$$= E[1600000000X] + Var[40000X]$$

$$= 1600000000E[X] + 40000^2 Var[X]$$

$$= 1600M(.9) + 40000^2(.81)$$

$$= 2736\ M$$

The correct answer is **D.**

5. Every time a loaded coin is tossed, there is a 60% probability of getting a head. Find the mode of the number of tosses needed to get 2 heads.
   A) 1
   B) 2
   C) 3
   D) 4
   E) There is no single mode

Solution:

Let N be the number of tosses it takes for 2 heads.

Then N has negative binomial distribution, and so the probability of needing n trials to get r successes is:

$$P(N = n) = \binom{n-1}{r-1} p^r (1-p)^{n-r}$$

where p is the probability of success in each trial.

Here, $r = 2, p = .6$. So, the pmf is:

$$f(n) = \binom{n-1}{2-1} (.6)^2 (1-.6)^{n-2}$$

$$= .36(n-1)(.4)^{n-2} \quad (1)$$

We need the mode of N, that is, the value of n which maximizes $f(n)$.

The easiest way is to find the first few values from eq (1)

$$f(2) = .36$$

$$f(3) = .288$$

$$f(4) = .1728$$

The values keep decreasing.

So, mode is 2.

The correct answer is **B.**

6. Twenty distinct items are arranged in a 4 by 5 array (4 rows and 5 columns). Find the number of ways to form a set of four distinct items such that no two of the selected items are in the same row or same column.
   A) 80
   B) 90
   C) 100
   D) 110
   E) 120

   Solution:

   There are 20 ways to select the 1st item. Once that has been selected, So, for the 2nd item, we have $20 - 8 = 12$ choices. See picture below:

A_1	A_2	A_3	A_4	A_5
A_6	A_7	A_8	A_9	A_{10}
A_{11}	A_{12}	A_{13}	A_{14}	A_{15}
A_{16}	A_{17}	A_{18}	A_{19}	A_{20}

For illustration, we assumed that A_1 was the 1st item picked.

Once the 2nd item is picked, say A_7, we have 6 choices for the 3rd. See figure

A_1	A_2	A_3	A_4	A_5
A_6	A_7	A_8	A_9	A_{10}
A_{11}	A_{12}	A_{13}	A_{14}	A_{15}
A_{16}	A_{17}	A_{18}	A_{19}	A_{20}

Once the 3rd item is picked, say A_{13}, there are only 2 choices left for the 4th pick.

So, the number of ways in picking the 1st, 2nd, 3rd, and 4th entries this way is:

$$20(12)(6)(2) = 2880$$

However, the strategy we have used is giving the number of permutations of the 4 entries. To get the number of combinations, we use the fact that:

$$n\,C\,r = \frac{n\,P\,r}{r!}$$

$$= \frac{2880}{4!}$$

$$= 120$$

The correct answer is **E.**

7. A senior high school class consisting of 40 girls and 30 boys is about to take an ACT exam. Records show that a senior girl taking ACT has a 25% probability of scoring 30+ in Math ACT, while a senior boy has a 20% probability of doing so. Everyone who scores 30+ in Math ACT will be awarded 500. Find the expected award amount for this senior class.
   A) 5000
   B) 6000
   C) 7000
   D) 8000
   E) 9000

   Solution:

   Among the 40 girls, each will either score 30+ or not.

   Hence, it is a binomial situation with $n = 40,\ p = .25$.

   The mean of a binomial distribution is np.

   So,

   Mean number of girls with 30+ ACT $= 40(.25) = 10$

   Similarly, the 30 boys also form a binomial experiment.

   Mean number of boys with 30+ ACT $= 30(.2) = 6$

   Mean total students having 30+ACT $= 10 + 6 = 16$

   Thus:

$$\text{Expected Award} = 500(16)$$
$$= 8000$$

   The correct answer is **D**.

8. A survey of 250 university students showed that:

i) 40 liked Math

ii) 60 liked English.

iii) 70 liked Art.

iv) 20 liked Math and English.

v) 30 liked Math and Art.

vi) 50 liked English and Art.

vii) 10 liked Math, English, and Art.

viii) 80 liked History, but liked neither Math, nor English, nor Art.

How many of the 250 students did not like any of the 4 subjects?

A) 50
B) 60
C) 70
D) 80
E) 90

Solution:

$$M \text{ or } E \text{ or } A = M + E + A - M\&E - M\&A - E\&A + M\&E\&A$$

$$= 40 + 60 + 70 - 20 - 30 - 50 + 10$$

$$= 80$$

Since $(M \text{ or } E \text{ or } A) \text{ and } H$ are disjoint, we have:

$$(M \text{ or } E \text{ or } A) \text{ or } H = (M \text{ or } E \text{ or } A) + H$$

$$= 80 + 80$$

$$= 160$$

Those who liked neither = Total – Those who liked at least one.

$$= 250 - 160$$

$$= 90$$

The correct answer is **E.**

Tools Needed for Problems 107-117

$$Var[aX] = a^2 VarX$$

$$Var\,X = E[X^2] - (E[X])^2$$

$$Var[X+Y] = Var\,X + Var\,Y + 2\,Cov\,(X,Y)$$

$$\int (x+k)e^{ax}dx = \frac{(x+k)e^{ax}}{a} - \frac{e^{ax}}{a^2}$$

The mean k and variance of Poisson distribution are equal and the pmf is:

$$f(x) = \frac{k^x e^{-k}}{x!}$$

For an exponential distribution with mean k, the variance is k^2, and pdf is:

$$f(x) = \frac{1}{k}e^{-\frac{x}{k}}, x > 0$$

The correlation coefficient between two random variables is:

$$r = \frac{Cov(X,Y)}{\sqrt{(Var\,X)(Var\,Y)}}$$

In intervals where the cdf is differentiable, pdf is the derivative of cdf, except at end points. At endpoints, we need to find out separately what might be going on.

If a distribution is a mixture of continuous parts and point masses, then the expected value is calculated by calculating the expected values of each portion, multiplying by their respective probabilities, and adding up the products.

If a pair of n −side dice is rolled, there are n^2 possible outcomes.

The nth moment of X is $E[X^n]$.

If U is uniform $[a,b]$, and $X = cU$, where c is constant, then X is uniform $[ac, bc]$

For a binomial distribution:

$$\mu = np, \qquad \sigma = \sqrt{np(1-p)}$$

Continuity Correction for a discrete distribution implies that:

$$P(X > n) = P(X \geq n + .5) \quad and \quad P(X < n) = P(X \leq n - .5)$$

The sum of N independent Poisson variables with means $k_1, k_2, \ldots, k_N$, is also Poisson with mean $k_1 + k_2 + \cdots + k_N$

The geometric sum of n terms equals:

$$\frac{a(1-r^n)}{1-r}$$

where a is the 1st term and r is the common ratio.

$$P(y = a|x = b) = \frac{P(x = a, y = b)}{P(x = b)}$$

SOA Sample Question 107 Explanation

The nth moment of X is $E[X^n]$.

Since X and Y are Poisson, their means equal their variances.

Let a be the mean and variance of X

Let b be the mean and variance of Y.

Condition (ii) gives:

$$E[X] = E[Y] - 8$$

$$a = b - 8 \quad (1)$$

Condition (iii) gives:

$$E[X^2] = .6E[Y^2]$$

However, we know that:

$$Var\ X = E[X^2] - (E[X])^2,$$

$$Var\ Y = E[Y^2] - (E[Y])^2$$

This gives:

$$E[X^2] = (E[X])^2 + Var\ X = a^2 + a,$$

$$E[Y^2] = (E[Y])^2 + Var\ Y = b^2 + b$$

So, condition (iii) becomes:

$$a^2 + a = .6(b^2 + b) \quad (2)$$

Substituting a from (1) in (2) we get:

$$(b-8)^2 + b - 8 = .6(b^2 + b)$$

$$b^2 - 16b + 64 + b - 8 = .6b^2 + .6b$$

$$.4b^2 - 15.6b + 56 = 0$$

$$b = \frac{15.6 \pm \sqrt{15.6^2 - 4(.4)(56)}}{2(.4)}$$

$$= 35 \text{ or } 4$$

However, if $b = 4, a = 4 - 8 = -4$ from (1). This is not possible because variance cannot be negative. Hence,

$$Var\ Y = b = 35$$

The correct answer is **E**.

SOA Sample Question 108 Explanation

Suppose there are n red sectors. The game is won if we miss all the red sectors. The total area of all the red sectors is:

$$\sum_{i=1}^{n}\left(\frac{9}{20}\right)^{i}$$

This is a geometric sum with 1st term $9/20$ and common ratio 9/20.

We know that a geometric sum of n terms equals:

$$\frac{a(1-r^n)}{1-r}$$

where a is the 1st term and r is the common ratio. Here, $a = r = 9/20$

Thus, the total area of the red sectors is:

$$\frac{9\left[1-\left(\frac{9}{20}\right)^n\right]}{20\left(1-\frac{9}{20}\right)} = \frac{9}{11}\left[1-\left(\frac{9}{20}\right)^n\right] = \frac{9}{11}-\frac{9}{11}\left(\frac{9}{20}\right)^n$$

The winning probability is the complement of the red area

$$= 1-\left[\frac{9}{11}-\frac{9}{11}\left(\frac{9}{20}\right)^n\right]$$

$$= \frac{2}{11}+\frac{9}{11}\left(\frac{9}{20}\right)^n$$

We want the winning probability to be less than .2, that is:

$$\frac{2}{11}+\frac{9}{11}\left(\frac{9}{20}\right)^n < .2$$

$$\frac{9}{11}\left(\frac{9}{20}\right)^n < \frac{.2}{11}$$

$$\left(\frac{9}{20}\right)^n < \frac{.2}{9}$$

$$n\ln\left(\frac{9}{20}\right) < \ln\left(\frac{.2}{9}\right)$$

When we divide both sides by $\ln\left(\frac{9}{20}\right)$ (a negative number), the inequality gets reversed. So:

$$n > 4.767$$

The minimum integer n that meets this requirement is 5.

The correct answer is **C**.

SOA Sample Question 109 Explanation

Let U be the uniform [0, 10,000] variable denoting claim amount. Then:

$$X = \frac{U}{1000}$$

We know that if U is uniform $[a, b]$, and $X = cU$, where c is constant,then X is uniform $[ac, bc]$. Here, $a = 0, b = 10000, c = 1/1000$. So, X is uniform $[0, 10]$. Thus,

$$f(x) = \frac{1}{10}, 0 \leq x \leq 10$$

$$4^{\text{th}} \text{ moment of } X = E[X^4] = \int_{-\infty}^{\infty} x^4 f(x)\, dx$$

$$= \int_0^{10} (x)^4 \frac{1}{10}\, dx$$

$$= \frac{x^5}{50}\Big|_0^{10} = 2000$$

The possible x −values, corresponding y −values, and the pdf are tabulated below:

$x-interval$	$y = x \; rounded \; to \; nearest \; integer$	$f(y) = \frac{Interval\ length}{10}$
[0,.5)	0	.05
[.5,1.5)	1	.1
[1.5,2.5)	2	.1
[2.5,3.5)	3	.1
[3.5,4.5)	4	.1
[4.5,5.5)	5	.1
[5.5,6.5)	6	.1
[6.5,7.5)	7	.1
[7.5,8.5)	8	.1
[8.5,9.5)	9	.1
[9.5,10]	10	.05

Since Y is a discrete variable, its 4th moment is given by:

$$Y = E[Y^4] = \sum_{y=0}^{10} y^4 f(y)$$

$$= (1^4 + 2^4 + 3^4 + \cdots + 9^4)(.1) + 10^4(.05)$$

$$= 2033$$

Absolute value of the difference between the 4th moment of X and the 4th moment of Y is:

$$2033 - 2000 = 33$$

The correct answer is **B**.

SOA Sample Question 110 Explanation

We need to examine the cases where $x + y = 2$

$$P(y = a|x = b) = \frac{P(x = a, y = b)}{P(x = b)}$$

$$\Rightarrow \quad P(x = a, y = b) = P(y = a|x = b)P(x = b)$$

x	y	$P(x) = .5^{x+1}$	$P(y\|x)$	$P(x,y) = P(y\|x)P(x)$
0	2	.5	.05	.025
1	1	.25	.3	.075
2	0	.125	.25	.03125

$$P(exactly\ 2\ losses) = .025 + .075 + .03125 = .131$$

The correct answer is **E**.

SOA Sample Question 111 Explanation

$$E[X] = \int_{-\infty}^{\infty} xf(x)\,dx = \int_{1}^{\infty} x\,\frac{p-1}{x^p}\,dx = (p-1)\int_{1}^{\infty} x^{1-p}\,dx = (p-1)\frac{x^{2-p}}{2-p}\Big|_{x=1}^{x=\infty}$$

$$= \frac{p-1}{2-p}(\infty^{2-p} - 1^{2-p}) \quad (1)$$

We know that

$$\infty^k = \begin{cases} 0, & k < 0 \\ \infty, & k > 0 \end{cases}$$

Thus, for expected value to be finite, we must have:

$$2 - p < 0$$

$$p > 2$$

In this case, (1) becomes:

$$E[X] = \frac{p-1}{2-p}(0-1) = \frac{1-p}{2-p}$$

Setting that equal to 2, because we want the expected value to be 2, we get:

$$\frac{1-p}{2-p} = 2$$

$$1 - p = 4 - 2p$$

$$p = 3$$

The correct answer is **C**.

SOA Sample Question 112 Explanation

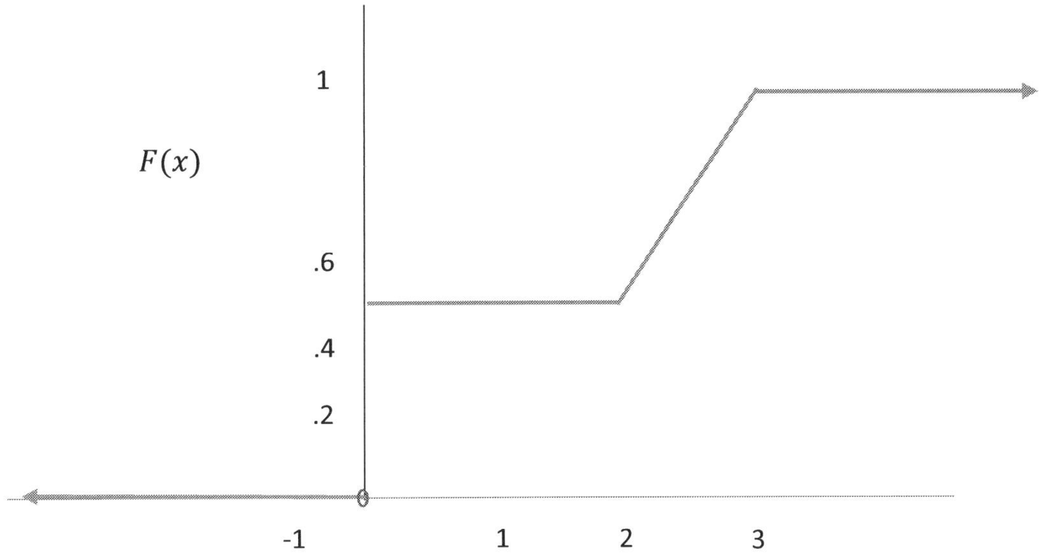

From the graph, we see tha

$$F(x) = \begin{cases} 0, & x < 0 \\ .5, & 0 \le x \le 2 \\ .5x - .5, & 2 < x < 3 \\ 1, & x \ge 3 \end{cases}$$

Note that the 3rd piece is the equation of a line through (2,.5) and (3,1).

We first find the pdf. Recall that in intervals where the cdf is differentiable, pdf is the derivative of cdf. At endpoints, we can look at the graph to figure out what might be going on. We see that the cdf takes a jump from 0 to 0.5 at $x = 0$. Thus:

$$f(x) = \begin{cases} 0, & x < 0 \\ .5, & x = 0 \\ 0, & 0 < x < 2 \\ .5, & 2 < x < 3 \\ 0, & x > 3 \end{cases}$$

We see that the only 2 non-zero parts of the pdf are the point mass of .5 at $x = 0$, and a uniform spread of .5 for $2 < x < 3$. In other words, x takes the value 0 half of the time, and is uniform on (2,3) half of the time (since both probabilities are .5). The average of uniform (a, b) is:

$$\frac{a+b}{2}$$

This gives the expected value to be:

$$E[X] = 0(.5) + \left(\frac{2+3}{2}\right)(.5)$$

$$= 1.25$$

The correct answer is **D**.

SOA Sample Question 113 Explanation

We know that when a pair of dice is rolled, there are 36 equally likely outcomes.

The pairs where the absolute value of the difference between the 2 numbers are less than 3 are:

(1,1), (1,2), (1,3), (2,1), (2,2), (2,3), (2,4), (3,1), (3,2), (3,3), (3,4), (3,5), (4,2), (4,3), (4,4), (4,5), (4,6), (5,3), (5,4), (5,5), (5,6), (6,4), (6,5), and (6,6).

The above are 24 of the 36 usual pairs. So

$$P(X < 3) = \frac{24}{36}$$

$$= \frac{2}{3}$$

The correct answer is **E**.

SOA Sample Question 114 Explanation

The correlation coefficient between two random variables is:

$$r = \frac{Cov(M,N)}{\sqrt{(Var\ M)(Var\ N)}}$$

This gives:

$$Cov(M,N) = r\sqrt{(Var\ M)(Var\ N)}$$

$$= .64\sqrt{1600(900)}$$

$$= 768$$

$$Var(M+N) = Var\ M + Var\ N + 2Cov(M,N)$$

$$= 1600 + 900 + 2(768)$$

$$= 4036$$

The correct answer is **D**.

SOA Sample Question 115 Explanation

Let X represent the loss, and Y represent the claim payment.

$$f(x) = \frac{1}{2}e^{-\frac{x}{2}}, x > 0$$

$$Y = \begin{cases} 0\,, & X < 1 \\ X - 1\,, & 1 \le X \le 6 \\ 5\,, & X > 6 \end{cases}$$

$$E[Y] = \int_{-\infty}^{\infty} y\, f(x)\, dx$$

$$= \int_{1}^{6} (x-1)\frac{1}{2}e^{-\frac{x}{2}}\, dx + \int_{6}^{\infty} 5\left(\frac{1}{2}e^{-\frac{x}{2}}\right) dx$$

Recall the shortcut we learnt earlier:

$$\int (x+k)e^{ax}dx = \frac{(x+k)e^{ax}}{a} - \frac{e^{ax}}{a^2}$$

$$E[Z] = \frac{1}{2}\left[(x-1)(-2)e^{-\frac{x}{2}} - 4e^{-\frac{x}{2}}\right]_1^6 + 5\left(\frac{1}{2}\right)(-2)e^{-\frac{x}{2}}\Big|_6^{\infty}$$

$$= \frac{1}{2}\left(-10e^{-3} - 4e^{-3} + 4e^{-1/2}\right) + 5e^{-3}$$

$$= -2e^{-3} + 2e^{-1/2}$$

The correct answer is **C**.

SOA Sample Question 116 Explanation

For a binomial distribution with $n = 40, p = .5$, mean and SD are:

$$\mu = np = 40(.5) = 20$$

$$\sigma = \sqrt{np(1-p)} = \sqrt{20(1-.5)} = \sqrt{10}$$

Let X be the number of correctly answered questions. We are given:

$$P(X > N) > .1$$

$$P(X > N + 1) < .1$$

The standard score for N with continuity correction is:

$$z = \frac{N + .5 - \mu}{\sigma}$$

$$= \frac{N + .5 - 20}{\sqrt{10}}$$

$$z = \frac{N - 19.5}{\sqrt{10}}$$

$$P(X > N) = .1$$

$$\Rightarrow P(X \leq N) = .9$$

$$\Rightarrow P\left(z \leq \frac{N - 19.5}{\sqrt{10}}\right) = .9$$

The probability of $.9$ corresponds to $z = 1.28$ from the table.

$$\Rightarrow \frac{N - 19.5}{\sqrt{10}} = 1.28$$

$$N = 23.55$$

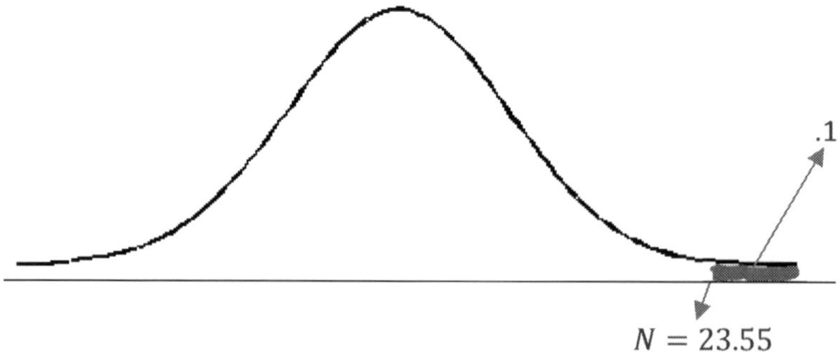

This is saying that probability of answering more than 23.55 questions equals 0.1. Thus, probability of answering more than 23 questions will be higher than 0.1, while the probability of answering more than 24 questions will be lower than 0.1. This gives $N = 23$

The correct answer is **A**.

SOA Sample Question 117 Explanation

The sum of N independent Poisson variables with means $k_1, k_2, \ldots, k_N,$ is also Poisson with mean $k_1 + k_2 + \cdots + k_N$

The means of July, Aug, Sep, Oct, Nov are 1,1,.5,.5,.5 respectively.

So, the mean accidents in these months equal:

$$1 + 1 + .5 + .5 + .5$$

$$= 3.5$$

The probability of getting x Poisson successes with mean k is:

$$f(x) = \frac{k^x e^{-k}}{x!}$$

Here, $x = 2, k = 3.5$. So,

$$f(2) = \frac{3.5^2 e^{-3.5}}{2!}$$

$$= .185$$

The correct answer is **B**.

Quiz 10

1. The number of snowstorms during each month in a country is Poisson random variable. The mean number of snowstorms during each of Jan, Feb, and Dec is 2. The mean for each of March, April, and November is 1.5. The mean for each of remaining months is 1. Assume that these 12 random variables are mutually independent. Find probability that exactly four snowstorm occurs in February through May.
   A) .117
   B) .134
   C) .152
   D) .170
   E) .196

   Solution:

   The sum of N independent Poisson variables with means $k_1, k_2, \ldots, k_N$, is also Poisson with mean $k_1 + k_2 + \cdots + k_N$

   The means of Feb, Mar, Apr, May are 2,1.5,1.5,1, respectively.

   So, the mean snowstorms in these months = $2 + 1.5 + 1.5 + 1 = 6$

   The probability of getting x Poisson successes with mean k is

$$f(x) = \frac{k^x e^{-k}}{x!}$$

   Here, $x = 4, k = 6$. So,

$$f(4) = \frac{6^4 e^{-6}}{4!}$$

$$= .134$$

   The correct answer is **B**.

2. In a town of 120 adults, there is a 60% probability that an adult will vote for candidate X. The probability that more than N adults will vote for candidate X is greater than .2. The probability that more than $N+1$ adults will vote for candidate X is less than .2. Find N using normal approximation.
   A) 72
   B) 76
   C) 80
   D) 84
   E) 88

Solution:

For a binomial distribution with $n = 120, p = .6$, mean and SD are

$$\mu = np = 120(.6) = 72$$

$$\sigma = \sqrt{np(1-p)} = \sqrt{72(1-.6)} = 5.3666$$

Let X be the number of adults voting for candidate X. We have:

$$P(X > N) > .2$$

The standard score for N with continuity correction is:

$$z = \frac{N + .5 - \mu}{\sigma}$$

$$= \frac{N + .5 - 72}{5.3666}$$

$$z = \frac{N - 71.5}{5.3666}$$

$$P(X > N) = .2$$

$$\Rightarrow P(X \le N) = .8$$

$$\Rightarrow P\left(z \le \frac{N - 71.5}{5.3666}\right) = .8$$

The probability of $.8$ corresponds to $z = .84$ from the table.

$$\Rightarrow \frac{N - 71.5}{5.3666} = .84$$

$$N = 76.01$$

The situation is illustrated in the figure below:

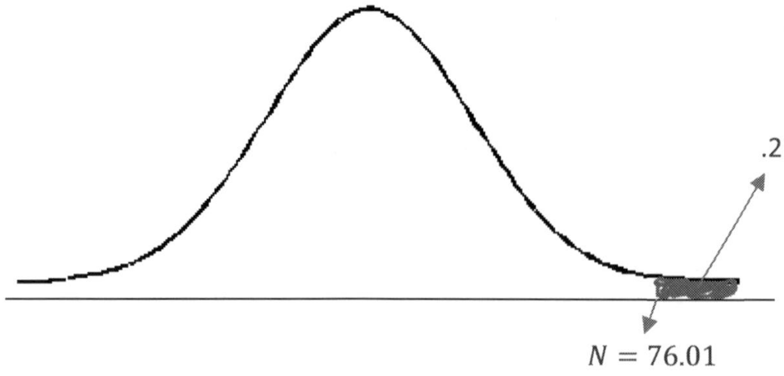

That is to say probability of more than 76.01 adults voting for candidate X equals 0.2.

Thus, probability of more than 76 adults voting for candidate X will be higher than 0.2, while the probability of more than 77 candidates voting for candidate X will be lower than 0.2.

This gives $N = 76$

The correct answer is **B**.

3. Ages of people in a town are uniform on the interval [0, 100]. If X is the actual age divided by 10, and Y is X rounded to the nearest integer, find the sum of the 5th moment of X and the 5th moment of Y.
   A) 33150
   B) 33350
   C) 33550
   D) 33750
   E) 33950
   Solution:

   Let U be the uniform [0, 100] variable denoting age of a person. Then

$$X = \frac{U}{10}$$

   If U is uniform $[a, b]$, and $X = cU$, where c is constant, then X is uniform $[ac, bc]$. Here:

$$a = 0, b = 100, c = 1/10$$

   So, X is uniform $[0, 10]$. Thus,

$$f(x) = \frac{1}{10}, 0 \le x \le 10$$

   5th moment of X is given by:

$$E[X^5] = \int_{-\infty}^{\infty} x^5 f(x)\, dx$$

$$= \int_0^{10} (x)^5 \frac{1}{10}\, dx$$

$$= \frac{x^6}{60}\Big|_0^{10}$$

$$5^{th}\ moment\ of\ X = 16667$$

The possible x −values, corresponding y −values, and the pdf is tabulated below:

$x - interval$	$y =\ x\ rounded\ to\ nearest\ integer$	$f(y) = \frac{Interval\ length}{10}$
[0,.5)	0	.05
[.5,1.5)	1	.1
[1.5,2.5)	2	.1
[2.5,3.5)	3	.1
[3.5,4.5)	4	.1
[4.5,5.5)	5	.1
[5.5,6.5)	6	.1
[6.5,7.5)	7	.1
[7.5,8.5)	8	.1
[8.5,9.5)	9	.1
[9.5,10]	10	.05

Since Y is a discrete variable, its 5th moment is given by:

$$E[Y^5] = \sum_{y=0}^{10} y^5 f(y)$$

$$= (1^5 + 2^5 + 3^5 + \cdots + 9^5)(.1) + 10^5(.05)$$

$$= 17083$$

Sum of the two 5th moments is $16667 + 17083 = 33750$

The correct answer is **D**.

4. i) X and Y are exponentially distributed.

ii) The first moment of X is twice the first moment of Y.

iii) The second moment of X is 1 more than the second moment of Y.

Calculate the variance of Y.

A) 1/2
B) 2/3
C) 2/5
D) 1/5
E) 1/6

Solution:

The nth moment of $X = E[X^n]$.

Let a be the mean of X, and b be the mean of Y.

Since X and Y are exponential:

$$Var\ X = a^2$$

$$Var\ Y = b^2$$

By condition (i):

$$E[X] = 2E[Y]$$

$$a = 2b \qquad (1)$$

$$Var\ X = E[X^2] - (E[X])^2,$$

$$Var\ Y = E[Y^2] - (E[Y])^2$$

$$E[X^2] = (E[X])^2 + Var\ X = a^2 + a^2 = 2a^2,$$

$$E[Y^2] = (E[Y])^2 + Var\ Y = b^2 + b^2 = 2b^2$$

So, by condition (ii):

$$E[X^2] = 1 + E[Y^2]$$

$$2a^2 = 1 + 2b^2 \qquad (2)$$

Substituting a from (1) in (2) we get:

$$2(2b)^2 = 1 + 2b^2$$

$$6b^2 = 1$$

$$Var\ Y = b^2 = \frac{1}{6}$$

The correct answer is **E**.

5. Let X be a continuous random variable with density function

$$f(x) = \frac{p-1}{x^p}, \qquad x > 1$$

Find p such that $E[X^2] = 5$

(A) 3.5

(B) 4.5

(C) 6

(D) 7

(E) There is no such p.

Solution:

$$E[X^2] = \int_{-\infty}^{\infty} x^2 f(x)\, dx$$

$$= \int_{1}^{\infty} x^2 \frac{p-1}{x^p} dx$$

$$= (p-1)\int_{1}^{\infty} x^{2-p}\, dx$$

$$= (p-1)\frac{x^{3-p}}{3-p}\Big|_{x=1}^{x=\infty}$$

$$= \frac{p-1}{3-p}(\infty^{3-p} - 1^{3-p}) \qquad (1)$$

We know that:

$$\infty^k = \begin{cases} 0, & k < 0 \\ \infty, & k > 0 \end{cases}$$

Thus, for $E[X^2]$ to be finite, we must have:

$$3 - p < 0$$

$$p > 3$$

In this case, (1) becomes:

$$E[X^2] = \frac{p-1}{3-p}(0-1)$$

$$= \frac{1-p}{3-p}$$

Setting that equal to 5 we get:

$$\frac{1-p}{3-p} = 5$$

$$1 - p = 15 - 5p$$

$$p = 3.5$$

The correct answer is **A**.

6. The cumulative distribution function of X is:

$$F(x) = \begin{cases} 0, & x < 1 \\ .5, & 1 \le x \le 3 \\ .5x - 1, & 3 < x < 4 \\ 1, & x \ge 4 \end{cases}$$

Find $E[X]$

A) 1.5
B) 1.75
C) 2
D) 2.25
E) 2.5

Solution:

We first find the pdf. Recall that in intervals where the cdf is differentiable, pdf is the derivative of cdf. At endpoints, we need to find out what might be going on. We see that the cdf takes a jump from 0 to 0.5 at $x = 1$. So

$$f(x) = \begin{cases} 0, & x < 1 \\ .5, & x = 1 \\ 0, & 1 < x < 3 \\ .5, & 3 < x < 4 \\ 0, & x > 4 \end{cases}$$

We see that the only 2 non-zero parts are the point mass of .5 at $x = 1$, and a uniform spread of .5 for $3 < x < 4$.

In other words, x takes the value 1 half of the time, and is uniform on (3,4) half of the time (since both probabilities are .5).

Recall that the average of uniform (a, b) is $(a + b)/2$. Thus:

$$E[X] = 1(.5) + \left(\frac{3+4}{2}\right)(.5)$$

$$= 2.25$$

The correct answer is **D**.

7. Two square boxes, each open at both ends and each having 4 faces numbered 1,2,3,4 fall from a height and each is equally likely to settle on any of the 4 numbers. Find the probability that the sum of the 2 settled numbers is divisible by 3.

A) 1/16

B) 3/16

C) 5/16

D) 7/16

E) 9/16

Solution:

There are $4(4) = 16$ equally likely outcomes.

The following 5 pairs have sums that are divisible by 3:

$$(1,2), (2,1), (2,4), (3,3), (4,2)$$

Hence the required probability is:

$$\frac{\#\ of\ pairs\ divisible\ by\ 3}{\#\ of\ Total\ pairs} = \frac{5}{16}$$

The correct answer is **C**.

8. Given $Var\ X = 10, Var\ Y = 6$, correlation coefficient between $X\ and\ Y = -.9$, Find $Var[X + Y]$.

A) 2.1

B) 2.3

C) 2.5

D) 2.7

E) 2.9

Solution:

The correlation coefficient between two random variables is:

$$r = \frac{Cov(X,Y)}{\sqrt{(Var\ X)(Var\ Y)}}$$

$$Cov(X,Y) = -.9\sqrt{10(6)}$$

$$= -6.97$$

$$Var(X + Y) = Var\ X + Var\ Y + 2Cov(X,Y)$$

$$= 10 + 6 - 2(6.97)$$

$$= 2.1$$

The correct answer is **A**.

9. An insurance policy has a deductible of 50 and a maximum benefit of 500 for every dental claim filed. Dental expenses follow an exponential distribution with mean 300. Find the expected benefit for a dental claim.

A) 176

B) 186

C) 196

D) 206

E) 216

Solution:

Let X represent the expense, and Y represent the benefit.

$$f(x) = \frac{1}{300}e^{-\frac{x}{300}}, x > 0$$

$$Y = \begin{cases} 0, & X < 50 \\ X - 50, & 50 \leq X \leq 550 \\ 500, & X > 550 \end{cases}$$

$$E[Y] = \int_{-\infty}^{\infty} y\, f(x)\, dx$$

$$= \int_{50}^{550} (x - 50)\frac{1}{300}e^{-\frac{x}{300}}\, dx + \int_{550}^{\infty} 500\left(\frac{1}{300}e^{-\frac{x}{300}}\right) dx$$

Using our shortcut:

$$\int (x + k)e^{ax}dx = \frac{(x + k)e^{ax}}{a} - \frac{e^{ax}}{a^2}$$

$$E[Y] = \frac{1}{300}\left[(x - 50)(-300)e^{-\frac{x}{300}} - 90000e^{-\frac{x}{300}}\right]_{50}^{550} + 500\left(\frac{1}{300}\right)(-300)e^{-\frac{x}{300}}\Big|_{550}^{\infty}$$

$$= \frac{1}{300}\left(-150000e^{-\frac{550}{300}} - 90000e^{-\frac{550}{300}} + 90000e^{-\frac{50}{300}}\right) + 500e^{-\frac{550}{300}}$$

$$= 206$$

The correct answer is **D**.

Tools Needed for Problems 118-130

$$Var\ X = E[X^2] - (E[X])^2$$

$$Var[aX + bY] = a^2 Var\ X + b^2 Var\ Y + 2ab\ Cov(X, Y)$$

If X, Y are independent, their covariance is 0.

The cdf of an exponential distribution with mean k is:

$$F(x) = 1 - e^{-\frac{x}{k}}$$

The sample space of two tosses of a coin is $\{HH, HT, TH, TT\}$

X and Y are independent if and only if $P(XY) = P(X)P(Y)$

A, B, C are mutually independent if an only if $P(ABC) = P(A)P(B)P(C)$

If a collection has N items, where K items are of type A, and we pick n of those without replacement, then the probability that x of those n are of type A is:

$$\frac{\binom{K}{x}\binom{N-K}{n-x}}{\binom{N}{n}}$$

Every odd moment of a variable with symmetric pdf is 0.

Pmf of a binomial distribution is:

$$f(x) = \binom{n}{x} p^x (1-p)^{n-x}$$

Law of Total Probability:

If $B_1, B_2, B_3, \ldots$ are disjoint events whose union is the whole sample space, and if A is any event in the sample space, then:

$$P(A) = \sum_i P(AB_i)$$

Where, by our usual convention the product AB_i means the intersection of A and B_i

SOA Sample Question 118 Explanation

Since the 300 payment kicks in only after full 10 inches exceeding 40 inches, there is no payment for a rainfall in the [0,50) range, which is made up of the first 4 intervals.

Total probability of 0 payment is thus:

$$.06 + .18 + .26 + .22 = .72$$

So, we have the following table of non-zero probabilities:

Inches	[0,50)	[50,60)	[60,70)	[70,80)	[80,90)
Probability	.72	.14	.06	.04	.04
Payment	0	300	600	700	700

Note that we have omitted the [90,inf) entry because its probability was 0.

Note that if we were finding SD by hand, we can omit the 0-payment entry but we must include it if we are doing it on calculator, which I am. From calculator:

$$SD = 235$$

The correct answer is **B**.

SOA Sample Question 119 Explanation

$$P(X > 10 \text{ } given \text{ } X > 2) = \frac{P(X > 10 \text{ } and \text{ } X > 2)}{P(X > 2)} = \frac{P(X > 10)}{P(X > 2)} \quad (1)$$

$$P(X > 10) = \int_{10}^{\infty} f(x)\,dx = \int_{10}^{20} c(x^2 - 60x + 800)\,dx = c\left(\frac{x^3}{3} - 30x^2 + 800x\right)\Big|_{10}^{20}$$

$$= c\left(\frac{20^3}{3} - 30(20)^2 + 800(20)\right) - c\left(\frac{10^3}{3} - 30(10)^2 + 800(10)\right) = \frac{4000c}{3}$$

$$P(X > 2) = \int_{2}^{\infty} f(x)\,dx = \int_{2}^{20} c(x^2 - 60x + 800)\,dx = c\left(\frac{x^3}{3} - 30x^2 + 800x\right)\Big|_{2}^{20}$$

$$= c\left(\frac{20^3}{3} - 30(20)^2 + 800(20)\right) - c\left(\frac{2^3}{3} - 30(2)^2 + 800(2)\right) = 5184c$$

Equation (1) thus becomes:

$$P(X > 10 \text{ } given \text{ } X > 2) = \frac{4000c}{3(5184c)} = .26$$

The correct answer is **D**.

SOA Sample Question 120 Explanation

It is clear each die and the sum is equally likely to be odd or even. So

$$P(A) = P(B) = P(C) = .5$$

It is also clear that A and B are independent since what appears on one die has nothing to do with what appears on the other.

Second Roll

First Roll	1	2	3	4	5	6
1	11	12	13	14	15	16
2	21	22	23	24	25	26
3	31	32	33	34	35	36
4	41	42	43	44	45	46
5	51	52	53	54	55	56
6	61	62	63	64	65	66

We know that X and Y are independent if $P(XY) = P(X)P(Y)$. Now from the picture above we see that there are 9 pairs where the 1st number is odd, and the sum is also odd, namely:

(1,2), (1,4), (1,6), (3,2), (3,4), (3,6), (5,2), (5,4), (5,6). So,

$$P(AC) = P(1st\ die\ odd, sum\ odd) = \frac{9}{36} = .25 \quad (1)$$

$$P(A)P(C) = .5(.5) = .25 \quad (2)$$

From (1) and (2) we see that:

$$P(AC) = P(A)P(C)$$

Thus, A and C are independent

Similarly, B and C are independent.

Hence, each pair is independent.

But the 3 events cannot occur all together because if each die is odd, then the sum is even. Thus:

$$P(ABC) = 0 \quad (3)$$

$$P(A)P(B)P(C) = .5(.5)(.5) = .125 \quad (4)$$

From (3) and (4) we see that

$$P(ABC) \neq P(A)P(B)P(C)$$

Thus A, B, C are not mutually independent. Since each pair is independent, so:

The correct answer is **A**.

SOA Sample Question 121 Explanation

$$P(\,6\,from\ \ 1st\ or\ 2nd\ die) = \frac{1}{6}$$

$$P(\,6\,from\ \ 3rd\ die) = \frac{2}{6}$$

$$P(\,6\,from\ \ 4th\ die) = 1$$

$$P(Two\ 6's\,from\ \ 1st\ die) = \frac{1}{6}\left(\frac{1}{6}\right) = \frac{1}{36}$$

$$P(Two\ 6's\,from\ \ 2nd\ die) = \frac{1}{6}\left(\frac{1}{6}\right) = \frac{1}{36}$$

$$P(Two\ 6's\,from\ \ 3rd\ die) = \frac{2}{6}\left(\frac{2}{6}\right) = \frac{4}{36}$$

$$P(Two\ 6's\,from\ \ 4th\ die) = 1(1) = 1$$

Each die has probability $1/4$ of being picked. So:

$$P(two\ 6's) = P(1st\ die\ and\ two\ 6's) + P(2nd\ die\ and\ two\ 6's) + P(3rd\ die\ and\ two\ 6's) + P(4th\ die\ and\ two\ 6's)$$

$$= \frac{1}{4}\left(\frac{1}{36}\right) + \frac{1}{4}\left(\frac{1}{36}\right) + \frac{1}{4}\left(\frac{4}{36}\right) + \frac{1}{4}(1) = .292$$

The correct answer is **C**.

SOA Sample Question 122 Explanation

Number of ways to pick 2 auto out of 6 = $\binom{6}{2} = 15$

Number of ways to pick 2 home out of 4 = $\binom{4}{2} = 6$

Number of ways to pick 2 life out of 2 = $\binom{2}{2} = 1$

Number of ways to pick 2 auto, 2 home, and 2 life = $15(6)(1) = 90$

Number of ways to pick 6 total out of 12 = $\binom{12}{6} = 924$

$$P(2\ auto, 2\ home, 2\ life) = \frac{\#\ of\ ways\ to\ pick\ 2\ auto,\ 2\ home,\ 2\ life}{\#\ of\ ways\ to\ pick\ 6\ total}$$

$$= \frac{90}{924}$$

$$= .097$$

The correct answer is **D**.

SOA Sample Question 123 Explanation

Let N be the number of claims

<u>With no claim ($N = 0$)</u>:

$$P(Total\ Benefit \leq 48) = .7$$

<u>With one claim ($N = 1$)</u>:

$$P(Total\ Benefit \leq 48) = \frac{48 - 0}{60 - 0} = .8$$

<u>With 2 claims ($N = 2$)</u>:

If X, Y are the benefits of 1st and 2nd claims respectively, then:

$$P(Total\ Benefit \leq 48) = P(X + Y \leq 48)$$

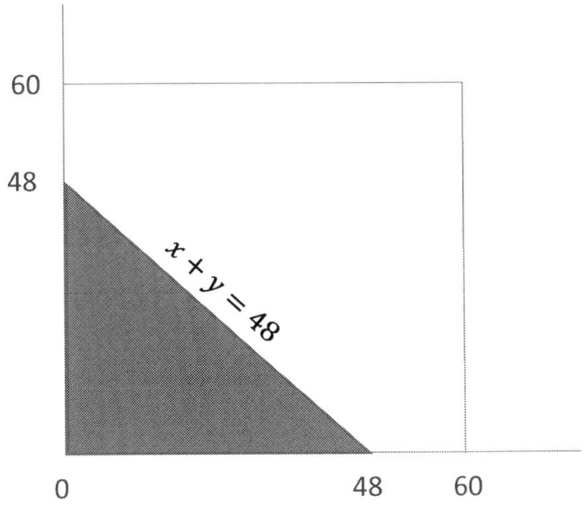

Total region is the outer square. The shaded region is $x + y \leq 48$. Thus, in case of two claims,

$$P(X + Y \leq 48) = \frac{area\ of\ triangle}{area\ of\ square}$$

$$= \frac{\frac{1}{2}(48)(48)}{60(60)}$$

$$= .32$$

So, by law of total probability, if T is the total benefit, we have:

$$P(T \leq 48) = P(N = 0\ and\ T \leq 48) + P(N = 1\ and\ T \leq 48) + P(N = 2\ and\ T \leq 48)$$

$$= .7(1) + .2(.8) + .1(.32)$$

$$= .892$$

The correct answer is **D**.

SOA Sample Question 124 Explanation

We know that the sum of 3 independent Poisson variables with means k_1, k_2, k_3 is Poisson with mean $k_1 + k_2 + k_3$.

So, the number of tornadoes in a 3-week period is Poisson with mean:

$$k = 2 + 2 + 2$$

$$= 6.$$

The probability of x Poisson successes is:

$$f(x) = \frac{k^x e^{-k}}{x!}$$

$$= \frac{6^x e^{-6}}{x!}$$

$$P(X < 4) = f(0) + f(1) + f(2) + f(3)$$

$$= .15$$

The correct answer is **B**.

SOA Sample Question 125 Explanation

The number of failed components X is binomial with $n = 3, p = .05$.

The system fails if there are 2 or 3 failed components.

The pmf is:

$$f(x) = \binom{n}{x} p^x (1-p)^{n-x}$$

$$= \binom{3}{x} .05^x (.95)^{3-x}$$

$$P(X \geq 2) = f(2) + f(3)$$

$$= \binom{3}{2} .05^2 (.95)^{3-2} + \binom{3}{3} .05^3 (.95)^{3-3}$$

$$= .007$$

The correct answer is **A**.

SOA Sample Question 126 Explanation

Let X be the annual profit. We are to find $P(X \leq 60|X > 0)$.

$$P(X \leq 60|X > 0) = \frac{P(X \leq 60 \ and \ X > 0)}{P(X > 0)} = \frac{P(0 < X \leq 60\ )}{P(X > 0)} \qquad (1)$$

So, we need to change 0 and 60 into standard scores.

$$Z = \frac{X - \mu}{\sigma} = \frac{X - 100}{\sqrt{400}} = \frac{X - 100}{20}$$

$$Z_0 = \frac{0 - 100}{20} = -5$$

$$Z_{60} = \frac{60 - 100}{20} = -2$$

Equation (1) becomes:

$$P(X \leq 60|X > 0) = \frac{P(-5 < Z \leq -2\ )}{P(Z > -5)} = \frac{P(2 < Z \leq 5\ )}{P(Z < 5)} = \frac{F(5) - F(2)}{F(5)}$$

The correct answer is **E**.

SOA Sample Question 127 Explanation

Let B be the event that someone has high blood pressure.

Let C be the event that someone has high cholesterol. Then:

$$P(B) = .2$$

$$P(C) = .3$$

$$P(BC) = .25(.2) = .05$$

$$P(B|C) = \frac{P(BC)}{P(C)} = \frac{.05}{.3} = \frac{1}{6}$$

The correct answer is **A**.

SOA Sample Question 128 Explanation

P(exactly 1 low risk) = P(1st low, 2nd high) + P(1st high, 2nd low)

$$= \frac{20}{25}\left(\frac{5}{24}\right) + \frac{5}{25}\left(\frac{20}{24}\right)$$

$$= .333$$

The correct answer is **D**.

SOA Sample Question 129 Explanation

$$E\left[\frac{X}{1-X}\right] = \int_{-\infty}^{\infty} \frac{x}{1-x} f(x)\, dx$$

$$= \int_{0}^{1} \frac{x}{1-x} 60x^3(1-x)^2\, dx$$

$$= \int_{0}^{1} 60x^4(1-x)\, dx$$

$$= 60\int_{0}^{1} x^4 - x^5\, dx$$

$$= 60\left(\frac{x^5}{5} - \frac{x^6}{6}\right)\Big|_0^1$$

$$= 2$$

$$E\left[\left(\frac{X}{1-X}\right)^2\right] = \int_{-\infty}^{\infty} \left(\frac{x}{1-x}\right)^2 f(x)\, dx$$

$$= \int_{0}^{1} \left(\frac{x}{1-x}\right)^2 60x^3(1-x)^2\, dx$$

$$= \int_{0}^{1} 60x^5\, dx$$

$$= 60\left(\frac{x^6}{6}\right)\Big|_0^1$$

$$= 10$$

$$Var\left[\frac{X}{1-X}\right] = E\left[\left(\frac{X}{1-X}\right)^2\right] - \left(E\left[\frac{X}{1-X}\right]\right)^2$$

$$= 10 - 2^2$$

$$= 6$$

The correct answer is **C**.

SOA Sample Question 130 Explanation

Let E be the event of at least one emergency room visit.

Let H be the event of at least one hospital stay.

We are to find $P(EH)$.

$$P(E) = 1 - .7$$

$$= .3$$

$$P(H) = 1 - .85$$

$$= .15$$

$$P(E \text{ or } H) = 1 - P(\text{neither } E \text{ nor } H)$$

$$= 1 - .61$$

$$= .39$$

$$P(E \text{ or } H) = P(E) + P(H) - P(EH)$$

$$.39 = .3 + .15 - P(EH)$$

$$P(EH) = .06$$

The correct answer is **B**.

Quiz 11.

1. 90% of college students don't like Math, 70% don't like English, and 65% like neither Math nor English. What is the probability that a randomly chosen college student likes both Math and English?
   A) .05
   B) .1
   C) .15
   D) .2
   E) .25

Solution:

Let M be the event that the student likes Math.

Let E be the event that the student likes English. We are to find $P(EM)$.

$$P(E) = 1 - .7 = .3$$

$$P(M) = 1 - .9 = .1$$

$$P(E \text{ } or \text{ } M) = 1 - P(neither \text{ } E \text{ } nor \text{ } M) = 1 - .65 = .35$$

$$P(E \text{ } or \text{ } M) = P(E) + P(M) - P(EM)$$

$$.35 = .3 + .1 - P(EM)$$

$$P(EM) = .05$$

The correct answer is **A**.

2. Fire damage to a home is exponentially distributed with mean 5000. A fire insurance has a deductible of 1000 per fire. After a fire a home suffered more damage than the deductible. Find the probability that the damage was more than 7000.
   A) .18
   B) .21
   C) .24
   D) .27
   E) .30

Solution:
Let X be the damage amount. The cdf is:

$$F(x) = 1 - e^{-\frac{x}{5000}}, \qquad x > 0$$

We are given that the damage was more than deductible. So we need:

$$P(X > 7000|X > 1000) = \frac{P(X > 7000 \text{ } and \text{ } X > 1000)}{P(X > 1000)} = \frac{P(X > 7000)}{P(X > 1000)}$$

$$P(X > 7000) = 1 - P(X \leq 7000) = 1 - F(7000) = .2466$$

$$P(X > 1000) = 1 - P(X \leq 1000) = 1 - F(1000) = .8187$$

$$P(X > 7000|X > 1000) = \frac{.2466}{.8187} = .30$$

The correct answer is **E**.

3. Two fair coins are tossed. Let A be the event that the first coin shows head. Let B be the event that the 2nd coin shows tail. Let C be the event that the same thing shows up on both coins. Which of the following is true?
(A) A, B, and C are not mutually independent, but each pair is.
(B) A, B, and C are mutually independent.
(C) Exactly one pair of the three events is independent.
(D) Exactly two of the three pairs are independent.
(E) No pair of the three events is independent.

Solution:

Since each coin is equally likely to show head or tail, so

$$P(A) = P(B) = .5$$

The sample space of two tosses is $\{HH, HT, TH, TT\}$.

From this we see that the probability of both coins showing the same thing is also .5. That is: $P(C) = .5$

Since X and Y are independent if $P(XY) = P(X)P(Y)$, so, from sample space:

$$P(AC) = P(1st\ coin\ head, and\ both\ same)$$

$$= \frac{1}{4} = .25 \quad (1)$$

$$P(A)P(C) = .5(.5) = .25 \quad (2)$$

From (1) and (2) we see that:

$$P(AC) = P(A)P(C)$$

Thus, A and C are independent.

Similarly, B and C are independent.

It is obvious that A and B are independent since two coins have nothing to do with each other.

Hence, each pair is independent.

However, the 3 events cannot occur all together because if 1st is head and 2nd is tail, they both cannot show the same thing. Thus:

$$P(ABC) = 0 \quad (3)$$

$$P(A)P(B)P(C) = .5(.5)(.5) = .125 \quad (4)$$

From (3) and (4) we see that

$$P(ABC) \neq P(A)P(B)P(C)$$

Thus, A, B, C are not mutually independent. Therefore:

The correct answer is **A**.

4. Box A contains all odd single digits while boxes B and C each contain all digits 0 through 9. You randomly select a box, draw a number and put it back in that box. You then pick a number from the same box. Find the probability that you first picked a 7 and then a 9.
   A) .01
   B) .02
   C) .04
   D) .09
   E) .10

   Solution:

   Box A has a total of 5 numbers, while B and C each have 10 numbers.

$$P(7\ and\ 9\ from\ A) = \frac{1}{5}\left(\frac{1}{5}\right) = \frac{1}{25}$$

$$P(7\ and\ 9\ from\ B) = \frac{1}{10}\left(\frac{1}{10}\right) = \frac{1}{100}$$

$$P(7\ and\ 9\ from\ C) = \frac{1}{10}\left(\frac{1}{10}\right) = \frac{1}{100}$$

   Each Box has a probability 1/3 of being selected. By law of total probability:

$$P(79) = P(A)P(79\ from\ A) + P(B)P(79\ fom\ B) + P(C)P(79\ fom\ C)$$

$$= \frac{1}{3}\left(\frac{1}{25}\right) + \frac{1}{3}\left(\frac{1}{100}\right) + \frac{1}{3}\left(\frac{1}{100}\right) = .02$$

   The correct answer is **B**.

5. From 8 freshmen, 7 sophomores, 5 juniors, and 6 seniors from a college, we randomly pick 10 members for SGA. Find the probability that there are 3 freshmen, 2 sophomores, 1 junior and 4 seniors in the SGA.
   A) .0166
   B) .0266
   C) .0366
   D) .0466
   E) .0566

   Solution:

   Number of ways to pick 3 freshmen out of 8 = $\binom{8}{3} = 56$

   Number of ways to pick 2 sophomores out of 7 = $\binom{7}{2} = 21$

   Number of ways to pick 1 junior out of 5 = $\binom{5}{1} = 5$

   Number of ways to pick 4 seniors out of 6 = $\binom{6}{4} = 15$

   Number of ways to pick 3 freshmen, 2 sophomores, 1 junior, and 4 seniors is:

$$56(21)(5)(15) = 88200$$

   Total initial students = $8 + 7 + 5 + 6 = 26$

   Number of ways to pick 10 total out of 26 = $\binom{26}{10} = 5311735$

$$P(\text{3 freshmen, 2 sophomores, 1 junior, 4 seniors}) = \frac{88200}{5311735} = .0166$$

   The correct answer is **A**.

6. There are two homes around a park. A fire in the park has 15% probability of causing damage to only one home, and 25% probability of causing damage to both homes. The loss amounts of each home damage are uniformly distributed on [0, 100000] and are independent. Calculate the probability that after a fire, the total loss amount on both homes is more than 80000.

A) .2

B) .4

C) .5

D) .6

E) .8

Solution:

The probability of no damage $= 1 - .15 - .25 = .6$

It is easier to calculate the probability of total loss being less than 80000.

With no damage, $P(Total\ Loss \leq 80000) = .6$

With one damage, $P(Total\ Loss \leq 80000) = \frac{80000-0}{100000-0} = .8$

With 2 damages, if X, Y are the losses of 1st and 2nd homes respectively,

$$P(Total\ Loss \leq 80000) = P(X + Y \leq 80000)$$

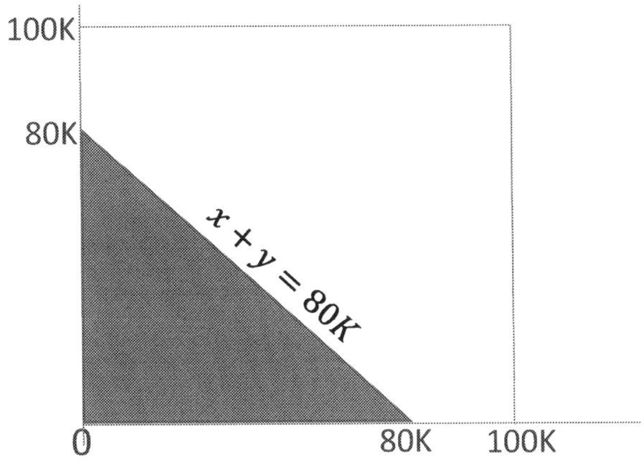

Total region is the outer square.

Shaded region is $x + y \leq 80000$. So, in case of two losses:

$$P(X + Y \leq 80000) = \frac{area\ of\ triangle}{area\ of\ square}$$

$$= \frac{\frac{1}{2}(80000)(80000)}{100000(100000)}$$

$$= .32$$

So, by law of total probability, if T is the total loss, and N is the number of claims, we have:

$$P(T \leq 80000)$$

$$= P(N = 0 \text{ and } T \leq 80000) + P(N = 1 \text{ and } T \leq 80000) + P(N = 2 \text{ and } T \leq 80000)$$

$$= .6(1) + .15(.8) + .25(.32)$$

$$= .8$$

$$P(T > 80000) = 1 - P(T \leq 80000)$$

$$= 1 - .8$$

$$= .2$$

The correct answer is **A**.

7. Monthly salaries of recent graduates in a certain country are normally distributed with mean 2600 and variance 8100. Let Z be normally distributed with mean 0 and variance 1 and let F be the cumulative distribution function of Z. Find the probability that a monthly salary is at most 2500, given that it is more than 2400.

A) .06

B) .09

C) .12

D) .15

E) .18

Solution:

Let X be the monthly salary. We are to find $P(X \leq 2500|X > 2400)$.

$$P(X \leq 2500|X > 2400) = \frac{P(X \leq 2500 \text{ and } X > 2400)}{P(X > 2400)}$$

$$= \frac{P(2400 < X \leq 2500)}{P(X > 2400)} \quad (1)$$

So we need to change 2400 and 2500 into standard scores.

$$Z = \frac{X - \mu}{\sigma} = \frac{X - 2600}{\sqrt{8100}} = \frac{X - 2600}{90}$$

$$Z_{2400} = \frac{2400 - 2600}{90} = -2.22$$

$$Z_{2500} = \frac{2500 - 2600}{90} = -1.11$$

Equation (1) becomes:

$$P(X \leq 2500|X > 2400) = \frac{P(-2.22 < Z \leq -1.11)}{P(Z > -2.22)}$$

$$= \frac{P(1.11 < Z \le 2.22)}{P(Z < 2.22)}$$

$$= \frac{F(2.22) - F(1.11)}{F(2.22)}$$

$$= \frac{.9868 - .8665}{.9868}$$

$$= .12$$

The correct answer is **C**.

8. A student is taking a 5-question multiple choice test. Each question has 5 possible answers. To pass the exam, a minimum score of 60% is needed. What is the probability that a student who randomly guesses all answers will pass?

A) .0512

B) .0525

C) .0546

D) .0563

E) .0579

Solution:

$$60\% \ of \ 5 = 3$$

So, to pass, the student needs to answer 3 or 4 or 5 questions correctly.

The number of correct answers X is binomial with $n = 5, p = .2$.

$$f(x) = \binom{n}{x} p^x (1-p)^{n-x}$$

$$= \binom{5}{x} (.2)^x (.8)^{5-x}$$

$$P(X \ge 3) = f(3) + f(4) + f(5)$$

$$= \binom{5}{3} (.2)^3 (.8)^{5-3} + \binom{5}{4} (.2)^4 (.8)^{5-4} + \binom{5}{5} (.2)^5 (.8)^{5-5}$$

$$= .0579$$

The correct answer is **E**.

Tools Needed for Problems 131-140

For uniform (a, b) distribution:

$$f(x) = \frac{1}{b-a}, \qquad a < x < b$$

$$P(A|B) = \frac{P(AB)}{P(B)}$$

$$F(x) = P(X \leq x) = \int_{-\infty}^{x} f(t)dt$$

For a binomial random variable, the pmf, mean, and variance are:

$$f(x) = \binom{n}{x} p^x (1-p)^{n-x}$$

$$mean = np$$

$$Var = np(1-p)$$

Continuity Correction is used when normal approximation is applied to a discrete variable. It says:

$$P(X \geq n) = P(X > n - .5)$$

$$P(X \leq n) = P(X < n + .5)$$

$$z = \frac{X - \mu}{\sigma}$$

The pmf of a Poisson distribution with mean λ is:

$$f(x) = \frac{e^{-\lambda} \lambda^x}{x!}$$

For independent variables $X, Y, Z,$ the mean and variance of $aX + bY + cZ$ are:

$$\mu = a\mu_X + b\mu_Y + c\mu_Z$$

$$Var = a^2 VarX + b^2 VarY + c^2 VarZ$$

SOA Sample Question 131 Explanation

Let Y be the loss, and X be the benefit.

The probability of the benefit being less than 0 is 0, and so is the cumulative probability. Hence:

$$P(X \leq x) = 0, \qquad x < 0 \quad (1)$$

The maximum benefit is 4.

So, the probability of the benefit being less than or equal to any number greater than or equal to 4 is 1. That is:

$$P(X \leq x) = 1, \qquad x \geq 4 \quad (2)$$

The pdf of the loss is:

$$g(y) = \frac{1}{5}, 0 < y < 5$$

When $0 \leq X < 4$, loss and benefit are the same, that is, $Y = X$. Here,

$$P(X \leq x) = P(Y \leq x)$$

$$= \int_0^x f(y)\,dy$$

$$= \int_0^x \frac{1}{5}\,dy$$

$$= \frac{y}{5}\Big|_0^x$$

$$= \frac{x}{5}$$

$$= .2x, \qquad 0 \leq x < 4 \quad (3)$$

Piecing together (1), (2) and (3) we get:

$$F(x) = \begin{cases} 0, & x < 0 \\ .2x, & 0 \leq x < 4 \\ 1, & x \geq 4 \end{cases}$$

The correct answer is **A**.

SOA Sample Question 132 Explanation

Let M be the total number of males.

Let F be the total number of females.

$$M = .54(900) = 486$$

$$F = 900 - 486 = 414$$

$$F \text{ over } 25 = .43(414) = 178$$

$$F \text{ under } 25 = F - F\ over\ 25 = 414 - 178 = 236$$

$$\text{Total under } 25 = Total - Total\ over\ 25 = 900 - 395 = 505$$

$$M\ under\ 25 = Total\ under\ 25 - F\ under\ 25 = 505 - 236 = 269$$

We are given that a person under 25 is selected. So,

$$P(Male|under\ 25) = \frac{P(Male\ and\ under\ 25)}{P(under\ 25)} = \frac{269}{505} = .53$$

The correct answer is **B**.

SOA Sample Question 133 Explanation

Total Cars $= 300 + 700 = 1000$

Probability of selecting a red car is:

$$\frac{300}{1000} = .3$$

Probability of selecting a green car is:

$$\frac{700}{1000} = .7$$

$$P(Red\ and\ Accident) = .3(.1) = .03$$

$$P(Green\ and\ Accident) = .7(.05) = .035$$

$$P(Red\ Accident|Exceeds) = \frac{P(Red\ Accident\ and\ Exceeds)}{P(Exceeds)}$$

$$= \frac{.03(.9)}{.03(.9) + .035(.8)}$$

$$= .491$$

The correct answer is **C**.

SOA Sample Question 134 Explanation

Let X, Y be the selected numbers.

Paul wins if $|X - Y| \leq 3$.

There are total of $20(20) = 400$ possible outcomes.

Paul wins when:

$$X = 1, Y = 1,2,3,4 \ (4 \ points)$$

$$X = 2, Y = 1,2,3,4,5 \ (5 \ points)$$

$$X = 3, Y = 1,2,3,4,5,6 \ (6 \ points)$$

For each of $X = 4,5,6,7, \dots, 17$, Y can be either 3 numbers below, 3 numbers above, or equal to X for the difference to be 3 or less.

Thus each of $X = 4,5,6,7, \dots, 17$ will give 7 points. Between 4 and 17, there are 14 values.

So we have another $14(7) = 98$ points. Finally,

$$X = 18, Y = 15,16,17,18,19,20 \ (6 \ points)$$

$$X = 19, Y = 16,17,18,19,20 \ (5 \ points)$$

$$X = 20, Y = 17,18,19,20 \ (4 \ points)$$

$$P(Paul \ wins) = \frac{4+5+6+98+6+5+4}{400} = \frac{128}{400} = .32$$

The correct answer is **B.**

SOA Sample Question 135 Explanation

Question Type	Proportion	Probability correct
Knows	$\frac{N}{20}$	1
Guesses	$\frac{20-N}{20}$	$\frac{1}{2}$

$$P(knows|correct) = \frac{P(knows \ and \ correct)}{P(correct)}$$

$$.824 = \frac{\frac{N}{20}(1)}{\frac{N}{20}(1) + \left(\frac{20-N}{20}\right)\left(\frac{1}{2}\right)}$$

$$.824 = \frac{2N}{2N + 20 - N}$$

$$.824(N + 20) = 2N$$

$$N = 14$$

The correct answer is **C**.

SOA Sample Question 136 Explanation

Number of cables that do not break under a force of 12400 is a binomial variable with $n = 400$. We need to find p, the probability that a cable will not break under the force of 12400.

Let Y be the minimum force needed to break a cable.

If a cable does not break under a force of 12,400, it means that the minimum force needed to break it is greater than 12,400. So,

P(a cable does not break under force of 12,400) $= P(Y > 12400)$

So, we need to change 12400 into standard score.

$$z = \frac{12400 - 12432}{25}$$

$$= -1.28$$

$$P(Y > 12400) = P(z > -1.28)$$

$$= P(z < 1.28)$$

$$= .8997$$

Thus, the number of cables X that will not break under a force of 12400 is a binomial variable with $n = 400,\ p = .8997$. So:

$$\mu = np = 400(.8997) = 359.88$$

$$\sigma = \sqrt{np(1-p)} = \sqrt{359.88(1 - .8997)} = 6.01$$

Using normal approximation with continuity correction:

$$P(X \geq 349) = P(X \geq 348.5)$$

So we need to change 348.5 to standard score.

$$Z = \frac{X - \mu}{\sigma}$$

$$= \frac{348.5 - 359.88}{6.01}$$

$$= -1.89$$

$$P(X \geq 348.5) = P(Z \geq -1.89)$$

$$= P(Z \leq 1.89)$$

$$= .97$$

The correct answer is **D**.

SOA Sample Question 137 Explanation

Let X be the number of policies sold.

The pmf of a Poisson distribution with mean m is:

$$f(x) = \frac{e^{-m}\, m^x}{x!}$$

Since both 2 and 3 are modes, so pmf is maximum at 2 and 3, and:

$$f(2) = f(3)$$

$$\frac{e^{-m}\, m^2}{2!} = \frac{e^{-m}\, m^3}{3!}$$

$$\frac{3!}{2!} = \frac{m^3}{m^2}$$

$$m = 3$$

To find K we tabulate the cumulative probabilities and their complements until the complement gets less than 25%.

x	$f(x) = \frac{e^{-3}\, 3^x}{x!}$	$P(X \le x)$ $= f(0) + \cdots + f(x)$	Probability of selling more than x policies $P(X > x) = 1 - P(X \le x)$
0	.0498	.0498	.9502
1	.1494	.1992	.8008
2	.2240	.4232	.5768
3	.2240	.6472	.3528
4	.1680	.8152	.1848

We see from the table that the smallest integer K such that the probability of selling more than K policies is less than 25% is 4.

The correct answer is **D**.

SOA Sample Question 138 Explanation

Let the 1st die be red, and the 2nd green.

Sample space is shown below:

	Second Roll					
First Roll	**1**	**2**	**3**	**4**	**5**	**6**
1	11	12	13	14	15	16
2	21	22	23	24	25	26
3	31	32	33	34	35	36
4	41	42	43	44	45	46
5	51	52	53	54	55	56
6	61	62	63	64	65	66

There are 15 pairs (highlighted in the table) in which first number is larger.

Of these 15 pairs, the following have odd sum:

(2,1), (3,2), (4,1), (4,3), (5,2), (5,4), (6,1), (6,3), (6,5)

These are 9 pairs.

Recall that if something is given, then that becomes our entire sample space, or entire total. So:

$$P(Odd\ Sum | 1st\ number\ is\ larger) = \frac{9}{15}$$

$$= \frac{3}{5}$$

The correct answer is **E**.

SOA Sample Question 139 Explanation

We first need to find z −score of mother.

This is the z value corresponding to a probability of .93.

In the table, .9292 corresponds to $z = 1.47$, and .9306 corresponds to $z = 1.48$.

By interpolation:

$$\frac{.93 - .9292}{.9306 - .9202} = .6$$

This means that the score is .6 of the way between 1.47 and 1.48. That is, $z = 1.476$.

Next we find the mother's numerical score.

$$z_{mom} = \frac{X_{mom} - mean}{SD}$$

$$1.476 = \frac{X_{mom} - 503}{\sqrt{9604}}$$

$$X_{mom} = 647.65$$

But we are told that the scores are multiples of 10.

So the mom's score is the nearest multiple of 10, that is, 650.

That is also Abby's score.

$$z_{Abby} = \frac{650 - 521}{\sqrt{10201}}$$

$$= 1.28$$

This corresponds to a cumulative probability of .8997.

Thus, Abby's percentile was 89.97 which rounds to 90.

The correct answer is **B**.

SOA Sample Question 140 Explanation

Let X, Y, Z be the 3 lifetimes.

We are to find $P(X+Y>1.9Z)$, that is:

$$P(X+Y-1.9Z>0)$$

Let $W = X+Y-1.9Z$.

This means we are to find $P(W>0)$.

We know that any linear combination of independent normal variables is normal.

So, W is normal.

Also, for independent variables X, Y, Z, the mean and variance of $aX+bY+cZ$ are:

$$\mu = a\mu_X + b\mu_Y + c\mu_Z$$

$$Var = a^2 VarX + b^2 VarY + c^2 VarZ$$

$$\mu_W = \mu_X + \mu_Y - 1.9\mu_Z$$

$$= 10 + 10 - 1.9(10)$$

$$= 1$$

$$Var\ W = Var\ X + Var\ Y + 1.9^2 Var\ Z$$

$$= 3^2 + 3^2 + 1.9^2(3^2)$$

$$= 50.49$$

$$\sigma_W = \sqrt{50.49}$$

$$= 7.106$$

Since we are to find $P(W>0)$, so we need to change 0 into z-score

$$z = \frac{0-\mu_W}{\sigma_W}$$

$$= \frac{0-1}{7.106}$$

$$= -.14$$

$$P(W>0) = P(z>-.14)$$

$$= P(z<.14)$$

$$= .5557$$

This rounds to .556.

The correct answer is **C**.

Quiz 12

1. A university has 8000 students of whom 61% are females. The total number of freshmen is 2500. If a male student is randomly chosen, the probability he is a freshman is 0.28. Find the probability that a randomly selected student is female if it is known that the student is not a freshman.
   A) .50
   B) .53
   C) .56
   D) .59
   E) .62

Solution:

We need to work our way towards all info about non-freshmen.

Total Females $= .61(8000) = 4880$

Total Males $= 8000 - 4880 = 3120$

Male Freshmen $= .28(3120) = 874$

$$\text{Male Non-Freshmen} = Males - Male\ Freshmen$$

$$= 3120 - 874$$

$$= 2246$$

$$\text{Total Non-Freshmen} = Total - Total\ Freshmen$$

$$= 8000 - 2500$$

$$= 5500$$

$$\text{Female NonFreshmen} = Total\ NonFreshmen - Male\ NonFreshmen$$

$$= 5500 - 2246$$

$$= 3254$$

We are given that a non-freshman is selected. So,

$$P(Female|NonFreshman) = \frac{P(Female\ and\ NonFreshman)}{P(NonFreshman)}$$

$$= \frac{3254}{5500}$$

$$= .59$$

The correct answer is **D**.

2. A company insures 80 homes and 40 cars in a town against earthquake damage. The deductible is the same for both home and auto insurance. There is a .3 probability that an earthquake will damage a home, and .9 probability that this damage will exceed the deductible. There is .06 probability that an earthquake will damage a car and .75 probability that this damage will exceed the deductible. The actuary randomly picks a claim from all claims that exceed the deductible. Calculate the probability that the claim is on a home.
   A) .903
   B) .923
   C) .943
   D) .963
   E) .983

Solution.

Total Insured items equal:

$$80 + 40$$

$$= 120$$

Probability of selecting a home equals:

$$\frac{80}{120}$$

$$= \frac{2}{3}$$

Probability of selecting a car equals:

$$\frac{40}{120} = \frac{1}{3}$$

$$P(Home\ and\ Damage) = \frac{2}{3}(.3) = .2$$

$$P(Car\ and\ Damage) = \frac{1}{3}(.06) = .02$$

$$P(Home\ Damage|Exceeds) = \frac{P(Home\ Damage\ and\ Exceeds)}{P(Exceeds)}$$

$$= \frac{.2(.9)}{.2(.9) + .02(.75)}$$

$$= .923$$

The correct answer is **B**.

3. A box has numbers 1 to 9. You randomly draw a number, replace it, and then again randomly draw a number. Find the probability that the two numbers drawn differ from each other by less than 3 in absolute value.

Solution:

A) 22/81
B) 44/81
C) 13/27
D) 53/100
E) 65/121

Solution:

Let X, Y be the selected numbers in 1st and 2nd picks.

We need $P(|X - Y| < 3)$.

There are total of $9(9) = 81$ possible outcomes.

The required outcomes are:

$$X = 1, Y = 1,2,3\ (3\ points)$$

$$X = 2, Y = 1,2,3,4\ (4\ points)$$

$$X = 3, Y = 1,2,3,4,5\ (5\ points)$$

$$X = 4, Y = 2,3,4,5,6\ (5\ points)$$

$$X = 5,6,7\ also\ give\ 5\ points\ each\ \ (15\ points)$$

$$X = 8, Y = 6,7,8,9\ (4\ points)$$

$$X = 9, Y = 7,8,9\ (3\ points)$$

So, there are a total of $3 + 4 + 5 + 5 + 15 + 4 + 3 = 39$ required points.

$$P(|X - Y| < 3) = \frac{39}{81}$$

$$= \frac{13}{27}$$

The correct answer is **C**.

4. A student takes the P exam consisting of 30 multiple choice questions, each with 5 answer choices. The student knows answers to N of the questions, which are answered correctly, and guesses the rest. The conditional probability that the student knows the answer to a question, given that the student answered it correctly, is 0.77. Find N.
A) 10
B) 12
C) 14
D) 16
E) 18

Solution:

Question Type	Proportion	Probability correct
Knows	$\frac{N}{30}$	1
Guesses	$\frac{30-N}{30}$	$\frac{1}{5}$

$$P(knows|correct) = \frac{P(knows\ and\ correct)}{P(correct)}$$

$$.77 = \frac{\frac{N}{30}(1)}{\frac{N}{30}(1) + \left(\frac{30-N}{30}\right)\left(\frac{1}{5}\right)}$$

Multiply the numerator and denominator on right side by 150.

$$.77 = \frac{5N}{5N + 30 - N}$$

$$.77(4N + 30) = 5N$$

$$N = 12$$

The correct answer is **B**.

5. The minimum wind speed that will damage the roof of a home is normally distributed with mean 60 mph and variance 36. Find the probability that out of 100 randomly chosen homes in a town, the roofs of at most 10 will be damaged by a wind speed of under 50 mph.
A) .9177
B) .9332
C) .9591
D) .9788
E) .9965

Solution:

At most 10 damaged means at least 90 are not damaged out of the 100.

The number of undamaged roofs with wind-speed under 50 mph is a binomial variable with $n = 100$. We need to do some work to find p, the probability that a roof will be undamaged if the wind-speed is under 50 mph.

Let Y be the minimum wind-speed that will damage a roof.

If a roof is undamaged when the wind-speed is under 50 mph, it means that the minimum wind-speed needed to damage it is greater than 50 mph. So,

P(a roof is undamaged with wind-speed under 50 mph) = $P(Y > 50)$

So, we need to change 50 into standard score.

$$z = \frac{50 - 60}{\sqrt{36}} = -1.67$$

$$P(Y > 50) = P(z > -1.67) = P(z < 1.67) = .9525$$

Thus, the number of roofs X that will not damage with wind-speed under 50 mph is a binomial variable with $n = 100,\ p = .9525$. So:

$$\mu = np = 100(.9525) = 95.25$$

$$\sigma = \sqrt{np(1-p)} = \sqrt{95.25(1 - .9525)} = 2.127$$

Using normal approximation with continuity correction:

$$P(X \geq 90) = P(X \geq 89.5)$$

So we need to change 69.5 to standard score.

$$Z = \frac{X - \mu}{\sigma} = \frac{89.5 - 95.25}{2.127} = -2.70$$

$$P(X \geq 89.5) = P(Z \geq -2.70)$$

$$= P(Z \leq 2.70)$$

$$= .9965$$

The correct answer is **E**.

6. The annual number of storms in a city follows Poisson distribution. The probability of there being 3 storms in a year is equal to the probability of there being 4 storms in a year. M is the smallest integer such that the probability of there being more than M storms is less than 0.8. Find M.

A) 1
B) 2
C) 3
D) 4
E) 5

Solution:

Let X be the number of annual storms.

The pmf of a Poisson distribution with mean λ is:

$$f(x) = \frac{e^{-\lambda}\,\lambda^x}{x!}$$

$$f(3) = f(4)$$

$$\frac{e^{-\lambda}\,\lambda^3}{3!} = \frac{e^{-\lambda}\,\lambda^4}{4!}$$

$$\frac{4!}{3!} = \frac{m^4}{m^3}$$

$$m = 4$$

To find M we tabulate the cumulative probabilities and their complements until the complement gets less than 0.8.

x	$f(x) = \dfrac{e^{-4}\,4^x}{x!}$	$P(X \le x) = f(0) + \cdots + f(x)$	Probability of more than x storms $P(X > x) = 1 - P(X \le x)$
0	.0183	.0183	.9817
1	.0733	.0916	.9084
2	.1465	.2381	.7619

We see from the table that the smallest integer M such that the probability of more than K storms is less than 0.8 is 2.

The correct answer is **B**.

7. Two fair dice are tossed. One is red and one is green. Find the probability that the sum of the numbers on the two dice is even given that the number that shows on the red die is at least double the number that shows on the green die.

(A) .44

(B) .48

(C) .52

(D) .56

(E) .60

Solution:

Let the 1st die be red, and the 2nd green. Sample space is shown below:

Second Roll

First Roll

	1	2	3	4	5	6
1	11	12	13	14	15	16
2	21	22	23	24	25	26
3	31	32	33	34	35	36
4	41	42	43	44	45	46
5	51	52	53	54	55	56
6	61	62	63	64	65	66

Pairs in which 1st number is at least double the 2nd number are:

(2,1), (3,1), (4,1), (4,2), (5,1), (5,2), (6,1), (6,2), (6,3)

These are 9 pairs.

Of these 9 pairs, the following have even sum:

(3,1), (4,2), (5,1), (6,2)

These are 4 pairs.

Recall that if something is given, it becomes the entire sample space, or the entire total.

$$P(Even\ Sum|1st\ number\ is\ atleast\ double\ of\ 2nd) = \frac{4}{9}$$

$$= .44$$

The correct answer is **A**.

8. The year in which Mary's mom turned 18, the average height of 18-year-old American girls was 63 inches and the standard deviation was 4 inches, and the height of Mary's mom was at the 85th percentile in this group. Many years later, when Mary turned 18, the average height of 18-year-old American girls was 64 inches at that time and the standard deviation was 5 inches. Mary was exactly as tall at 18 as her mom was at 18. The heights of 18-year old American girls are normally distributed and are reported to the nearest whole number in inches. Find Mary's percentile in her respective group and year when she turned 18.

A) 64

B) 67

C) 70

D) 73

E) 76

Solution:

The z-score of mom is the value corresponding to a cumulative probability of .85.

In the table, .8485 corresponds to $z = 1.03$, and .8508 corresponds to $z = 1.04$.

$$\frac{.85 - .8485}{.8508 - .8485} = .7$$

Thus, by interpolation, $z = 1.037$.

Next, we find the mom's height.

$$z_{mom} = \frac{X_{mom} - mean}{SD}$$

$$1.037 = \frac{X_{mom} - 63}{4}$$

$$X_{mom} = 67$$

to the nearest inch. That is also Mary's height.

$$z_{Mary} = \frac{67 - 64}{5}$$

$$= .6$$

This corresponds to a cumulative probability of .7257.

Thus, Mary's percentile was 72.57 which rounds to 73.

The correct answer is **D**.

9. In a city, the average age of men is 60 years with variance 121. Find the probability that the sum of ages of 2 randomly chosen men will be less than 1.5 times the age of a 3rd randomly chosen man. All ages are mutually independent.

A) .0534

B) .0734

C) .0934

D) .9066

E) .9466

Solution:

Let X, Y, Z be the 3 ages. We are to find $P(X + Y < 1.5Z)$, that is:

$$P(X + Y - 1.5Z < 0)$$

Let $W = X + Y - 1.5Z.$

Then we are to find $P(W < 0).$

$W,$ being linear combination of independent normal variables is normal.

Also, for independent variables $X, Y, Z,$ the mean and variance of $aX + bY + cZ$ are:

$$\mu = a\mu_X + b\mu_Y + c\mu_Z$$

$$Var = a^2VarX + b^2VarY + c^2VarZ$$

$$\mu_W = \mu_X + \mu_Y - 1.5\mu_Z = 60 + 60 - 1.5(60) = 30$$

$$Var\ W = Var\ X + Var\ Y + 1.5^2Var\ Z$$

$$= 121 + 121 + 1.5^2(121) = 514.25$$

$$\sigma_W = \sqrt{514.25} = 22.677$$

Since we are to find $P(W < 0),$ so we need to change 0 into z-score

$$z = \frac{0 - \mu_W}{\sigma_W} = \frac{0 - 30}{22.677} = -1.32$$

$$P(W < 0) = P(z < -1.32)$$

$$= P(z > 1.32)$$

$$= 1 - P(z \leq 1.32)$$

$$= 1 - .9066$$

$$= .0934$$

The correct answer is **C**.

Tools Needed for Problems 141-151

In case of a deductible d, if X is the payout, and $a > d$ it is simpler to calculate $P(X < a)$ by finding $P(X \geq a)$ and taking the complement.

where $\rho = correlation\ coefficient\ between\ X\ and\ Y$

$$\sigma_X{}^2 = Variance\ of\ X,\ \ \sigma_Y{}^2 = Variance\ of\ Y$$

The pdf and cdf of an exponential distribution with mean m are:

$$f(x) = \frac{1}{m}e^{-\frac{x}{m}}, \qquad x > 0$$

$$F(x) = 1 - e^{-\frac{x}{m}}$$

Mode of a distribution is the x value for which $f(x)$ is maximum.

For a geometric distribution, the pdf is:

$$g(x) = (1 - P)^{x-1}P,$$

and the mean is $1/P$.

If N has negative binomial distribution, the probability of needing n trials to get r successes is:

$$P(N = n) = \binom{n-1}{r-1}p^r(1-p)^{n-r}$$

where p is the probability of success in each trial.

An integral of the form:

$$\int_a^b \left[\frac{k - nx}{m - x}\right] dx$$

can be done by making the substitution $u = m - x$ and then splitting fraction.

The variance of a horizontally shifted pdf is same as that of the original.

SOA Sample Question 141 Explanation

Let X be the loss and Y be the payout.

$$f(x) = \frac{1}{2}, \qquad 0 < x < 2$$

$$Y = \begin{cases} 0, & X \le d \\ X - d, & X > d \end{cases}$$

We first use the given probability to find the deductible.

$$P(Y \ge 1.2) = .3$$

$$P(X - d \ge 1.2) = .3$$

$$P(X \ge 1.2 + d) = .3$$

$$\int_{1.2+d}^{\infty} f(x)\,dx = .3$$

$$\int_{1.2+d}^{2} \frac{1}{2}\,dx = .3$$

$$\frac{x}{2}\Big|_{1.2+d}^{2} = .3$$

$$\frac{1}{2}(2 - 1.2 - d) = .3$$

$$.8 - d = .6$$

$$d = .2$$

$$P(Y \ge 1.44) = P(X - d \ge 1.44)$$

$$= P(X \ge 1.44 + d)$$

$$= \int_{1.44+d}^{\infty} f(x)\,dx$$

$$= \int_{1.44+.2}^{2} \frac{1}{2}\,dx$$

$$= \frac{x}{2}\Big|_{1.64}^{2}$$

$$= \frac{1}{2}(2 - 1.64)$$

$$= .18$$

The correct answer is **C**.

SOA Sample Question 142 Explanation

Let X be the lifespan.

$$F(x) = 1 - e^{-kx}$$

$$.3 = P(X > 4)$$

$$.3 = 1 - P(X \leq 4)$$

$$.3 = 1 - F(4)$$

$$.3 = 1 - (1 - e^{-4k})$$

$$.3 = e^{-4k}$$

$$\ln(.3) = -4k$$

$$k = -\frac{1}{4}\ln(.3)$$

$$F(x) = 1 - e^{\frac{x}{4}\ln(.3)}$$

$$f(x) = F'(x)$$

$$= -\frac{\ln(.3)}{4}e^{\frac{x}{4}\ln(.3)}$$

$$= -\frac{\ln(.3)}{4}e^{\ln(.3)\frac{x}{4}}$$

$$= \frac{-\ln(0.3)}{4}(0.3)^{x/4}$$

The correct answer is **E**.

SOA Sample Question 143 Explanation

$$f(x) = \frac{c\,x^2}{1+x^3}, \qquad 0 < x < 5$$

where c is a constant. Mode is the x value for which $f(x)$ is maximum.

Recall from calculus that the absolute maximum and minimum are found by evaluating the function value at the end points and critical points. Here, the endpoints are not included.

So we only need the critical points which are those where the derivative is 0 or undefined.

$$f'(x) = \frac{2cx(1+x^3) - c\,x^2(3\,x^2)}{(1+x^3)^2} = \frac{2cx - cx^4}{(1+x^3)^2} = \frac{cx(2-x^3)}{(1+x^3)^2}$$

This is undefined at $x = -1$ but that point is out of the interval (0,5).

So, we only need to see where it is 0.

A fraction is 0 if numerator is 0. So:

$$cx(2-x^3) = 0$$

$c \neq 0$ because pdf cannot be always 0, while $x = 0$ is not in (0,5). So

$$2 - x^3 = 0$$

$$x = \sqrt[3]{2} = 1.26$$

The correct answer is **C**.

SOA Sample Question 144 Explanation

$$f(x) = c\,xe^{-x^2}, \qquad 0 < x < 1$$

where c is a constant. Mode is the x value for which $f(x)$ is maximum.

Recall from calculus that the absolute maximum and minimum are found by evaluating the function value at the end points and critical points. Here, the endpoints are not included.

So we only need the critical points which are those where the derivative is 0 or undefined.

$$f'(x) = c\left[1\left(e^{-x^2}\right) + xe^{-x^2}(-2x)\right] = ce^{-x^2}(1-2x^2)$$

This is always defined. So, we set it to 0 to find critical points.

Note that $c \neq 0$, and an exponential function is also never 0. Thus, we get:

$$(1-2x^2) = 0$$

$$x^2 = 1/2$$

$$x = .71$$

The correct answer is **C**.

SOA Sample Question 145 Explanation

Since each admission costs 20000, the total hospital cost will be less than 50000 if there are 2 or fewer admissions.

The number of admitted employees, X is binomial with $n = 5,\ p = .20$

$$f(x) = \binom{n}{x} p^x (1-p)^{n-x} = \binom{5}{x} (.2)^x (.8)^{5-x} \quad (1)$$

Also, the number of visits V in case an employee is admitted is geometric with mean 1.50. So:

$$g(v) = (1-P)^{v-1}P,$$

The mean of geometric distribution is $1/P$. So,

$$P = \frac{1}{1.5} = \frac{2}{3}$$

$$g(v) = \left(1 - \frac{2}{3}\right)^{v-1} \left(\frac{2}{3}\right)$$

$$= \left(\frac{1}{3}\right)^{v-1} \left(\frac{2}{3}\right)$$

$$\Rightarrow g(1) = \frac{2}{3},\ \ g(2) = \frac{2}{9}$$

Two or fewer total admissions can happen in the following scenarios:

<u>Case 1</u>: No employees are admitted. Probability of this is found by substituting $x = 0$ in (1)

$$f(0) = \binom{5}{0} (.2)^0 (.8)^{5-0} = .32768$$

<u>Case 2</u>: One employee goes, and has 1 admission; others have none.

P (Only 1 employee goes, and has only 1 visit) = $f(1)g(1)$

$$= \binom{5}{1} (.2)^1 (.8)^{5-1} \left(\frac{2}{3}\right) = .27307$$

<u>Case 3</u>: One employee goes, and has 2 admissions; others have none.

P (Only 1 employee goes, and has only 2 visits) = $f(1)g(2)$

$$= \binom{5}{1} (.2)^1 (.8)^{5-1} \left(\frac{2}{9}\right) = .09102$$

<u>Case 4</u>: Two employees go, each has 1 admission; others have none.

P (2 employees go, first has 1 visit, and 2nd has 1 visit) = $f(2)g(1)g(1)$

$$= \binom{5}{2} (.2)^2 (.8)^{5-2} \left(\frac{2}{3}\right)\left(\frac{2}{3}\right) = .09102$$

$$P(less\ than\ 2\ adm) = .32768 + .27307 + .09102 + .09102 = \mathbf{.78}$$

The correct answer is **E**.

SOA Sample Question 146 Explanation

Let N be the number of days it takes for 3rd malfunction to occur.

Then N has negative binomial distribution, which says that the probability of needing n trials to get r successes is:

$$P(N = n) = \binom{n-1}{r-1} p^r (1-p)^{n-r}$$

where p is the probability of success in each trial.

Here, $n = 5, r = 3,\ p = .4$. So:

$$f(5) = \binom{5-1}{3-1} (.4)^3 (1-.4)^{5-3} = .13824$$

$$P(3\ malfunctions\ in\ 1st\ 3\ days) = .4(.4)(.4) = .064$$

$$P(Not\ 3\ malfunctions\ in\ 1st\ 3\ days) = 1 - .064 = .936$$

$$P(3rd\ MF\ on\ 5th\ day | not\ 3\ MF\ on\ 1st\ 3\ days) = \frac{P(3rd\ MF\ on\ 5th\ day, and\ not\ 3\ MF\ on\ 1st\ 3\ days)}{P(Not\ 3\ malfunctions\ in\ 1st\ 3\ days)} \quad (1)$$

Note that when we say that there were not 3 malfunctions in the 1st three days, we are not saying that each of the 1st three days was a fine day; we are only saying that there could be 0, or 1, or 2 total malfunctions in the 1st three days, but not 3.

Also, in order to even have the possibility of the 3rd MF being on 5th day, we must have only 0,1, or 2 total MF in the 1st 3 days, and not 3, because if we had 3 MF in the 1st 3days, then we have already had the 3rd MF on the 3rd day and there is no way can have the 3rd MF on the 5th day.

So, the given condition has no overlap with the 3rd MF being on 5th day. Thus,

$$P(3rd\ MF\ on\ 5th\ day, and\ not\ 3\ MF\ on\ 1st\ 3\ days) = P(3rd\ MF\ on\ 5th\ day)$$

$$= f(5)$$

$$= .13824$$

So, equation (1) becomes:

$$P(3rd\ MF\ on\ 5th\ day | not\ 3\ MF\ on\ 1st\ 3\ days) = \frac{.13824}{.936}$$

$$= .148$$

The correct answer is **C**.

SOA Sample Question 147 Explanation

Let p_i , $i = 0,1,2,3,4$ be the probability of stage i cancer in the group.

We are asked to find p_1.

According to conditions (i), (ii), and (iii), and by basic probability laws:

$$p_0 + p_1 + p_2 = .75 \quad (1)$$

$$p_1 + p_2 + p_3 + p_4 = .8 \quad (2)$$

$$p_0 + p_1 + p_3 + p_4 = .8 \quad (3)$$

$$p_0 + p_1 + p_2 + p_3 + p_4 = 1 \quad (4)$$

From (2) and (4),

$$p_0 + .8 = 1$$

$$p_0 = .2$$

Substituting this value of p_0 in (1) and (3) we get:

$$.2 + p_1 + p_2 = .75$$

$$p_1 + p_2 = .55 \quad (5)$$

$$.2 + p_1 + p_3 + p_4 = .8$$

$$p_1 + p_3 + p_4 = .6 \quad (6)$$

Substituting (5) in (2)

$$.55 + p_3 + p_4 = .8$$

$$p_3 + p_4 = .25 \quad (7)$$

Substituting (7) in (6)

$$p_1 + .25 = .6$$

$$p_1 = .35$$

The correct answer is **C**.

SOA Sample Question 148 Explanation

Let the first failure occur after t years. The cdf is:

$$F(t) = 1 - e^{-\frac{t}{2}}, \qquad t > 0$$

Let p_i be the probability that 1st failure occurs in last quarter of year i.

$$p_i = F(i) - F(i - .25)$$

$$= 1 - e^{-\frac{i}{2}} - \left(1 - e^{-\frac{(i-.25)}{2}}\right)$$

$$= e^{-\frac{i}{2}+\frac{.25}{2}} - e^{-\frac{i}{2}}$$

$$= e^{-\frac{i}{2}}(e^{.125} - 1)$$

The last quarter failure can occur in year 1, or 2, or 3, or…. So,

$$P(1st\ failure\ in\ last\ quarter\ of\ a\ year) = p_1 + p_2 + p_3 + \cdots$$

$$= \sum_{i=1}^{\infty} p_i$$

$$= (e^{.125} - 1)\sum_{i=1}^{\infty} e^{-\frac{i}{2}}$$

The sum of a geometric series with 1st term a, and common ratio r is

$$\frac{a}{1-r}$$

The geometric series here has 1st term $e^{-\frac{1}{2}}$ and common ratio $e^{-\frac{1}{2}}$. So,

$$P(1st\ failure\ in\ last\ quarter\ of\ a\ year) = (e^{.125} - 1)\frac{e^{-\frac{1}{2}}}{1 - e^{-\frac{1}{2}}}$$

$$= .205$$

The correct answer is **D.**

SOA Sample Question 149 Explanation

Total undamaged packages $= 20 - 7 = 13$

If the 4th damaged package appears on the 12th inspection, it means that:

there were 3 damaged packages after 11 inspections, and;

therefore $11 - 3 = 8$ undamaged packages after 11 inspections.

Number of ways to choose 3 out of 7 damaged $= \binom{7}{3} = 35$

Number of ways to choose 8 out of 13 undamaged $= \binom{13}{8} = 1287$

Number of ways to choose 11 out of 20 total $= \binom{20}{11} = 167960$

$$P(3\ of\ 1st\ 11\ damaged) = \frac{(\#\text{of ways 3 damaged})(\#\text{of ways 8 undamaged})}{\#\ of\ ways\ to\ choose\ 11}$$

$$= \frac{35(1287)}{167960}$$

$$= .2682$$

If 3 are damaged out of 11 inspections, then before the 12th inspection, there are:

$20 - 11 = 9$ total packages left to be inspected, out of which $7 - 3 = 4$ are damaged. So,

$$P(12th\ damaged | 3\ of\ first\ 11\ damaged) = \frac{4}{9}$$

$$P(4th\ damage\ on\ 12th\ inspection)$$
$$= [P(3\ of\ 1st\ 11\ damaged)]\ [P(12th\ damaged | 3\ of\ first\ 11\ damaged)]$$

$$= .2682\left(\frac{4}{9}\right)$$

$$= .119$$

The correct answer is **B**.

SOA Sample Question 150 Explanation

Let M be the size of family visiting the park, and N be the number of family members riding the roller coaster.

We need $P(M = 6|N = 5)$.

Since N has a discrete uniform distribution on $\{1, \dots , m\}$, so:

$$P(N = 1) = P(N = 2) = P(N = 3) = \cdots P(N = m) = 1/m$$

Note that a discrete uniform distribution is different from the usual (continuous) uniform distribution that we mostly work with.

Also note that in order to have 5 rollercoaster rides, the family size should be 5,6, or 7.

$$P(M = 6|N = 5) = \frac{P(M = 6 \; and \; N = 5)}{P(N = 5)}$$

The values of interest are tabulated below:

m	$P(M = m) = \frac{8 - m}{28}$	$P(N = 5) = \frac{1}{m}$
5	$\frac{8-5}{28} = \frac{3}{28}$	$\frac{1}{5}$
6	$\frac{8-6}{28} = \frac{2}{28}$	$\frac{1}{6}$
7	$\frac{8-7}{28} = \frac{1}{28}$	$\frac{1}{7}$

$$P(M = 6 \; and \; N = 5) = \frac{2}{28}\left(\frac{1}{6}\right)$$

$$P(N = 5) = \frac{3}{28}\left(\frac{1}{5}\right) + \frac{2}{28}\left(\frac{1}{6}\right) + \frac{1}{28}\left(\frac{1}{7}\right)$$

$$P(M = 6|N = 5) = \frac{\frac{2}{28}\left(\frac{1}{6}\right)}{\frac{3}{28}\left(\frac{1}{5}\right) + \frac{2}{28}\left(\frac{1}{6}\right) + \frac{1}{28}\left(\frac{1}{7}\right)}$$

$$= .31$$

The correct answer is **E**.

SOA Sample Question 151 Explanation

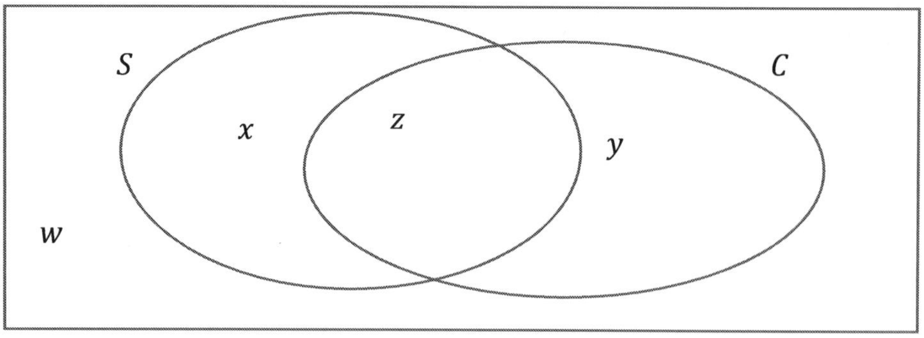

Let S be the probability of defaulting on at least one student loan.

Let C be the probability of defaulting on at least one car loan.

Condition (i) gives:

$$x + z = .3 \quad (1)$$

Condition (ii) gives:

$$z = .4(y + z)$$

$$\Rightarrow z = \frac{2y}{3} \quad (2)$$

Condition (iii) gives:

$$y = .28(w + y)$$

$$y + w = \frac{y}{.28} \quad (3)$$

$$x + y + z + w = 1 \quad (4)$$

Substituting (3) in (4) we get:

$$x + z + \frac{y}{.28} = 1 \quad (5)$$

Substituting the value of $x + z$ from (1) in (5)

$$.3 + \frac{y}{.28} = 1$$

$$y = .196$$

$$z = \frac{2(.196)}{3} = .131$$

$$x = .3 - .131 = .169$$

$$P(C|S) = \frac{P(CS)}{P(S)} = \frac{z}{x + z} = \frac{.131}{.169 + .131} = .44$$

The correct answer is **C**.

Quiz 13

1. A dental insurance pays for each visit to a dentist subject to a deductible d. Dental costs for each visit are uniform on [0, 1500]. There is a 25% probability that the payout is at least 500 on a random dental visit. Find the probability that the payout on a random visit is less than 600.

A) .18
B) .36
C) .50
D) .64
E) .82

Solution:

Let X be the loss and Y be the payout.

$$f(x) = \frac{1}{1500}, \qquad 0 < x < 1500$$

$$Y = \begin{cases} 0, & X \leq d \\ X - d, & X > d \end{cases}$$

We first use the given probability to find the deductible.

$$P(Y \geq 500) = .25$$

$$P(X - d \geq 500) = .25$$

$$P(X \geq 500 + d) = .25$$

$$\int_{500+d}^{\infty} f(x)\,dx = .25$$

$$\int_{500+d}^{1500} \frac{1}{1500}\,dx = .25$$

$$\frac{x}{1500}\Big|_{500+d}^{1500} = .25$$

$$\frac{1}{1500}(1500 - 500 - d) = .25$$

$$1000 - d = 375$$

$$d = 625$$

$$P(Y \geq 600) = P(X - d \geq 600)$$

$$= P(X \geq 600 + d)$$

$$= \int_{600+d}^{\infty} f(x)\,dx$$

$$= \int_{600+625}^{1500} \frac{1}{1500}\,dx$$

$$= \frac{x}{1500}\Big|_{1225}^{1500}$$

$$= \frac{1}{1500}(1500 - 1225)$$

$$= .18$$

$$P(Y < 600) = 1 - P(Y \geq 600)$$

$$= 1 - .18$$

$$= .82$$

The correct answer is **E**.

2. The lifetime of a bulb is exponentially distributed. The probability that the lifetime is more than 100 hours is .8. Find the probability that the lifetime is more than 150 hours.
   A) .7155
   B) .7355
   C) .7555
   D) .7755
   E) .7955

Solution:

$$F(x) = 1 - e^{-kx}$$

$$.8 = P(X > 100) = 1 - P(X \leq 100) = 1 - F(100)$$

$$.8 = 1 - (1 - e^{-100k})$$

$$.8 = e^{-100k}$$

$$\ln(.8) = -100k$$

$$k = -.01\ln(.8)$$

$$F(x) = 1 - e^{.01x\ln(.8)}$$

$$P(X > 150) = 1 - P(X \leq 150)$$

$$= 1 - F(150)$$

$$= 1 - \left(1 - e^{.01(150)\ln(.8)}\right)$$

$$= .7155$$

The correct answer is **A**.

3. The lifetime of a computer has a pdf proportional to

$$\frac{x^3}{2 + x^4}, \qquad 0 < x < 10$$

Calculate the mode of this distribution.

A) 1.3
B) 1.6
C) 1.9
D) 2.2
E) 2.5

Solution:

$$f(x) = \frac{c\,x^3}{2 + x^4}, \qquad 0 < x < 10$$

where c is a constant.

Mode is the x value for which $f(x)$ is maximum.

Recall from calculus that the absolute maximum and minimum are found by evaluating the function value at the end points and critical points.

Here, the endpoints are not included.

So we only need the critical points which are those where the derivative is 0 or undefined.

$$f'(x) = \frac{3cx^2(2 + x^4) - c\,x^3(4\,x^3)}{(2 + x^4)^2} = \frac{6cx^2 - cx^6}{(2 + x^4)^2} = \frac{cx^2(6 - x^4)}{(2 + x^4)^2}$$

This is always defined. So we only need to see where it is 0.

$$cx^2(6 - x^4) = 0$$

$c \neq 0$ because pdf cannot be always 0, while $x = 0$ is not in (0,10). So

$$6 - x^4 = 0$$

$$x^4 = 6$$

$$x = 6^{\frac{1}{4}}$$

$$= 1.6$$

The correct answer is **B**.

4. A family has 4 members. Each year, each member independently has a 6% probability of catching flue. If a member gets flue, the number of doctor visits is modeled by a geometric distribution with a mean of 2. Numbers of doctor visits of different members are mutually independent. Each visit costs 500. Calculate the probability that the family's total doctor costs in a year are more than 900.
A) .10
B) .12
C) .14
D) .16
E) .18

Solution:

Since 1 visit costs 500, 2 visits will cost 1000 which is more than 900. So, we are really being asked the probability of 2 or more total visits.

It is simpler to go through the complement and find the probability of less than 2 visits.

The number of members catching flue, X, is binomial with $n = 4,\ p = .06$

$$f(x) = \binom{n}{x} p^x (1-p)^{n-x} = \binom{4}{x} (.06)^x (.94)^{4-x} \quad (1)$$

Also, the number of visits V if a member is admitted is geometric with mean 2. So:

$$g(v) = (1-P)^{v-1}P,$$

The mean for geometric distribution is $1/P$. So,

$$P = \frac{1}{2}$$

$$g(v) = \left(1 - \frac{1}{2}\right)^{v-1} \left(\frac{1}{2}\right)$$

$$= \left(\frac{1}{2}\right)^{v-1} \left(\frac{1}{2}\right)$$

$$\Rightarrow g(1) = \frac{1}{2}$$

Less than 2 visits can happen in exactly the following scenarios:

Case 1: No one gets flue.

The probability of this is found by substituting $x = 0$ in (1)

$$f(0) = \binom{4}{0} (.06)^0 (.94)^{4-0} = .78075$$

Case 2: One member gets flue, and has 1 visit; others have none.

P (Only 1 member gets flue, and has only 1 visit) = $f(1)g(1)$

$$= \binom{4}{1} (.06)^1 (.94)^{4-1} \left(\frac{1}{2}\right)$$

$$= .099675$$

$$P(Less\ than\ 2\ visits) = .78075 + .099675 = .88$$

$$P(2\ or\ mor\ visits) = 1 - .88 = .12$$

The correct answer is **B**.

5. Students in a Math class got A, B, C, D, or F in an exam.

i) 40% of the students got C or lower.

ii) 95% of the students did not get an F.

iii) 75% of the students got a grade other than C.

One student is randomly selected. Calculate the probability that the student had a D.

A) .1
B) .15
C) .2
D) .25
E) .3

Solution:

Let p_X be the probability of getting grade X. We are asked to find p_D.

According to conditions (i), (ii), and (iii), and by basic probability laws:

$$p_C + p_D + p_F = .4 \quad (1)$$

$$p_A + p_B + p_C + p_D = .95 \quad (2)$$

$$p_A + p_B + p_D + p_F = .75 \quad (3)$$

$$p_A + p_B + p_C + p_D + p_F = 1 \quad (4)$$

From (2) and (4),

$$p_F + .95 = 1$$

$$p_F = .05$$

Substituting this value of p_F in (1) and (3) we get:

$$p_C + p_D + .05 = .4$$

$$p_C + p_D = .35 \quad (5)$$

$$p_A + p_B + p_D + .05 = .75$$

$$p_A + p_B + p_D = .7 \quad (6)$$

Substituting (5) in (2)

$$p_A + p_B + .35 = .95$$

$$p_A + p_B = .6 \quad (7)$$

Substituting (7) in (6)

$$.6 + p_D = .7$$

$$p_D = .1$$

The correct answer is **A**.

6. The time in years after high school graduation that the first person of a certain graduating class will die is exponentially distributed with mean 60. Find the probability that this first death of this class will occur in some October, November, or December.

A) .15
B) .2
C) .25
D) .3
E) .35

Solution:
We are asked to find the death probability in the last quarter of a year.

Let the first death occur after t years. The cdf is:

$$F(t) = 1 - e^{-\frac{t}{60}}, \qquad t > 0$$

Let p_i be the probability that 1st death occurs in last quarter of year i.

$$p_i = F(i) - F(i - .25)$$

$$= 1 - e^{-\frac{i}{60}} - \left(1 - e^{-\frac{(i-.25)}{60}}\right)$$

$$= e^{-\frac{i}{60}+\frac{.25}{60}} - e^{-\frac{i}{60}}$$

$$= e^{-\frac{i}{60}}\left(e^{.25/60} - 1\right)$$

The last quarter death can occur in year 1, or 2, or 3, or…. So,

$$P(1st\ death\ in\ last\ quarter\ of\ a\ year) = p_1 + p_2 + p_3 + \cdots$$

$$= \sum_{i=1}^{\infty} p_i = \left(e^{.25/60} - 1\right)\sum_{i=1}^{\infty} e^{-\frac{i}{60}}$$

The sum of a geometric series with 1st term a, and common ratio r is

$$\frac{a}{1-r}$$

The geometric series here has 1st term $e^{-\frac{1}{60}}$ and common ratio $e^{-\frac{1}{60}}$. So,

$$P(1st\ death\ in\ last\ quarter\ of\ a\ year) = \left(e^{.25/60} - 1\right)\frac{e^{-\frac{1}{60}}}{1 - e^{-\frac{1}{60}}} = .25$$

The correct answer is **C**.

7. Considering all the adults in a certain city:

i) 40% own at least one vehicle.

ii) Of those who own at least one home, 90% own at least one vehicle.

iii) Of those who do not own a vehicle, 5% own at least one home.

You randomly select an adult in this city and observe that s/he owns at least one vehicle. Find the probability that the selected person owns at least one home.

A) .175
B) .350
C) .525
D) .675
E) .750

Solution:

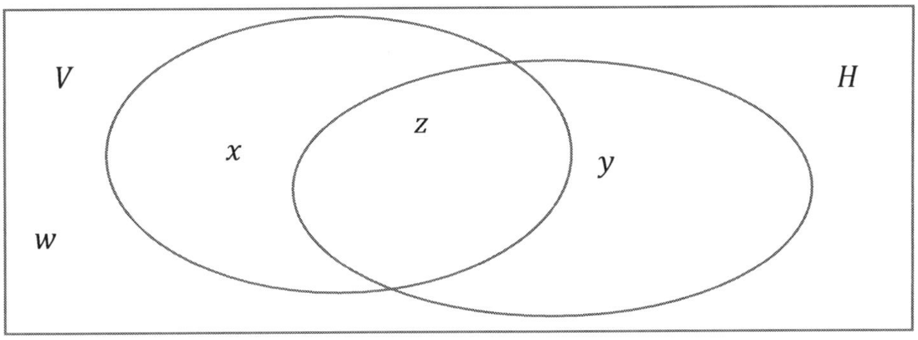

Let V be the probability of owning at least one vehicle.

Let H be the probability of owning at least one home.

Condition (i) gives:

$$x + z = .4 \quad (1)$$

The proportion who own at least one home is $y + z$. So, condition (ii) gives:

$$z = .9(y + z)$$

$$z = .9y + .9z$$

$$z = 9y \quad (2)$$

The proportion who do not own a vehicle is $w + y$. So, condition (iii) gives:

$$y = .05(w + y)$$

$$y + w = \frac{y}{.05} = 20y \quad (3)$$

$$x + y + z + w = 1 \quad (4)$$

Since we are given that the selected person owns a vehicle, we need $P(H|V)$.

$$P(H|V) = \frac{P(HV)}{P(V)} = \frac{z}{x + z}$$

Substituting (3) in (4) we get:

$$x + z + 20y = 1 \quad (5)$$

Substituting the value of $x + z$ from (1) in (5)

$$.4 + 20y = 1$$

$$y = .03$$

$$z = 9y = 9(.03) = .27$$

$$x = .4 - z = .4 - .27 = .13$$

$$P(C|S) = \frac{z}{x + z} = \frac{.27}{.13 + .27} = .675$$

The correct answer is **D**.

8. A bag contains 11 quarters and 4 dimes. Coins are randomly removed from the bag, one at a time, without replacement, until the 3rd quarter is removed. Calculate the probability that exactly 6 coins were removed.

A) .066

B) .184

C) .243

D) .375

E) .500

Solution:

If the 3rd quarter is the 6th removal, then there were 2 quarters removed after 5 removals, and therefore $5-2=3$ dimes removed after 5 removals.

Number of ways to choose 2 out of 11 quarters $=\binom{11}{2}=55$

Number of ways to choose 3 out of 4 dimes $=\binom{4}{3}=4$

Number of ways to choose 5 out of 15 total coins $=\binom{15}{5}=3003$

$$P(2\ of\ 1st\ five\ removals\ are\ quarters)=\frac{55(4)}{3003}=.07326$$

Now if 2 are quarters out of 5 removals, then before the 6th removal, there are:

$15-5=10$ total coins still in the bag, out of which $11-2=9$ are quarters. So,

$$P(6th\ removal\ is\ quarter|2\ of\ first\ five\ are\ quarters)=\frac{9}{10}=.9$$

$$\begin{aligned}&P(3rd\ quarter\ on\ 6th\ removal)\\&=[P(2\ of\ 1st\ five\ are\ quarters)]\,[P(6th\ quarter|2\ of\ 1st\ five\ quarters)]\\&=.07326(.9)\\&=.066\end{aligned}$$

The correct answer is **A**.

The pdf, mean and variance of a uniform $[a, b]$ distribution are:

$$f(x) = \frac{1}{b-a}, \qquad a < x < b$$

$$E[X] = \frac{a+b}{2}$$

$$Var\ X = \frac{(b-a)^2}{12}$$

If a collection has N items, where K items are of type A, and we pick n of those without replacement, then the probability that x of those n are of type A is:

$$\frac{\binom{K}{x}\binom{N-K}{n-x}}{\binom{N}{n}}$$

The sum of independent Poisson variables is also Poisson with mean equal to the sum of individual means.

The pmf of a Poisson distribution with mean m is:

$$f(x) = \frac{m^x e^{-m}}{x!}$$

The cdf of an exponential function is:

$$F(x) = 1 - e^{-kx}$$

The integral of a pdf over its entire range is 1

SOA Sample Question 152 Explanation

Let X be the damage and Y be the payout.

$$f(x) = \frac{1}{b}, \qquad 0 < x < b$$

$$Var\,X = \frac{(b-0)^2}{12}$$

$$SD\,(X) = \frac{b}{\sqrt{12}}$$

$$Y = \begin{cases} 0\,, & X < 0.1b \\ X - 0.1b\,, & 0.1b < X < b \end{cases}$$

$$E(Y) = \int_{-\infty}^{\infty} y\, f(x)\, dx = \int_{0.1b}^{b} (x - 0.1b)\left(\frac{1}{b}\right) dx = \int_{0.1b}^{b} \frac{x}{b} - 0.1\, dx$$

$$= \left(\frac{x^2}{2b} - 0.1x\right)\Big|_{x=.1b}^{x=b}$$

$$= \left(\frac{b^2}{2b} - 0.1b\right) - \left(\frac{(.1b)^2}{2b} - 0.1(.1b)\right) = \frac{b}{2} - .1b - \frac{.01b}{2} + .01b = .405b$$

$$E(Y^2) = \int_{-\infty}^{\infty} y^2\, f(x)\, dx = \int_{0.1b}^{b} (x - 0.1b)^2\left(\frac{1}{b}\right) dx$$

$$= \frac{1}{b}\left(\frac{(x-.1b)^3}{3}\right)\Big|_{x=.1b}^{x=b} = \frac{1}{b}\left(\frac{(b-.1b)^3}{3}\right) = \frac{(.9b)^3}{3b} = .243b^2$$

$$SD(Y) = \sqrt{E(Y^2) - (E[Y])^2} = \sqrt{.243b^2 - (.405b)^2} = .281b$$

Dividing the two standard deviations we get:

$$\frac{SD(Y)}{SD(X)} = \frac{.281b}{\frac{b}{\sqrt{12}}} = .9735$$

The correct answer is **E**.

SOA Sample Question 153 Explanation

Solution:

$F \cap G$ = One accident in year 1, and one or more accidents in year 2.

Only (iii) and (iv) say exactly the same information.

So, exactly 2.

The correct answer is **C**.

SOA Sample Question 154 Explanation

Let x be the death probability of a low-risk policy holder.

So, $3x$ is the death probability of a medium-risk, and $6x$ is the death probability of a high-risk.

Type	Proportion	Death Probability
Low Risk (L)	$.45$	x
Medium Risk (M)	$.35$	$3x$
High Risk (H)	$1 - .45 - .35 = .2$	$6x$

Let D be the event of death of a policy holder.

$$P(D) = P(L\ and\ D) + P(M\ and\ D) + P(H\ and\ D)$$

$$.009 = .45x + .35(3x) + .2(6x)$$

$$x = \frac{1}{300}$$

$$P(D|H) = \frac{P(D\ and\ H)}{P(H)} = \frac{.2(6x)}{.2} = 6x = 6\left(\frac{1}{300}\right) = .02$$

The correct answer is **B**.

SOA Sample Question 155 Explanation

Let d be the deductible. If $d \le 60$, the expected claim payment will be:

$$.1(60 - d) + .05(200 - d) + .01(3000 - d) = 30$$

$$6 - .1d + 10 - .05d + 30 - .01d = 30$$

$$16 = .16d$$

$$d = 100$$

This contradicts our assumption that $d \le 60$.

So d must be greater than 60.

If $60 < d < 200$, the expected claim payment will be:

$$.05(200 - d) + .01(3000 - d) = 30$$

$$10 - .05d + 30 - .01d = 30$$

$$10 = .06d$$

$$d = 167$$

This does not contradict the assumption that $60 < d < 200$.

Hence this is the correct deductible.

The correct answer is **C**.

SOA Sample Question 156 Explanation

$$P(all\ 3\ are\ non-insured) = \frac{k}{10}\left(\frac{k-1}{9}\right)\left(\frac{k-2}{8}\right)$$

So

$$\frac{k}{10}\left(\frac{k-1}{9}\right)\left(\frac{k-2}{8}\right) = \frac{1}{120}$$

Multiplying both sides by 720 we get:

$$k(k-1)(k-2) = 6$$

Since k has to be integer between 0 and 10, we note that $k = 3$ is a solution of this equation.

We thus know that out of the 10, there are 3 non-insured and hence 7 insured.

$$P(at\ most\ 1\ of\ 3\ insured) = P(0\ insured) + P(1\ insured)$$

$$P(\ 0\ insured) = P(all\ 3\ are\ non-insured)$$

$$= \frac{1}{120}$$

$$P(1\ insured) = P(1\ insured\ and\ 2\ non-insured)$$

$$= \frac{\binom{7}{1}\binom{3}{2}}{\binom{10}{3}}$$

$$= .175$$

$$P(at\ most\ 1\ of\ 3\ insured) = \frac{1}{120} + .175$$

$$= \frac{11}{60}$$

The correct answer is **C**.

SOA Sample Question 157 Explanation

Total Integers = 12

Integers picked by gambler = 4

So, integers not picked by gambler = 8

We need the probability that the casino picks a total of 9 numbers including 4 numbers of the gambler, and thus 5 numbers not picked by the gambler.

Using hypergeometric formula, the required probability is:

$$\frac{(\#\ of\ ways\ to\ pick\ 4\ numbers\ of\ gambler)(\#of\ ways\ to\ pick\ 5\ other\ numbers)}{\#\ of\ ways\ to\ pick\ 9\ numbers\ from\ 12}$$

$$= \frac{\binom{4}{4}\binom{8}{5}}{\binom{12}{9}}$$

$$= .255$$

The correct answer is **B**.

SOA Sample Question 158 Explanation

We know that the sum of independent Poisson variables is also Poisson with mean equal to the sum of individual means.

We are interested in a 3-month period.

Since the mean for each month is 1, the mean for 3 months is 3.

Let X be the number of sick days in 3 months.

The pmf is:

$$f(x) = \frac{3^x e^{-3}}{x!}$$

$$P(X > 2) = 1 - P(X \leq 2)$$

$$= 1 - [f(0) + f(1) + f(2)]$$

$$= 1 - \frac{3^0 e^{-3}}{0!} - \frac{3^1 e^{-3}}{1!} - \frac{3^2 e^{-3}}{2!}$$

$$= .577$$

The correct answer is **D**.

SOA Sample Question 159 Explanation

Let $q(x)$ be the pmf of the number of weekly accidents at Q.

$$q(x) = \frac{3^x e^{-3}}{x!}$$

$$A = P(X > 3) = 1 - P(X \leq 3) = 1 - [q(0) + q(1) + q(2) + q(3)] = .353$$

Let $r(y)$ be the pmf of the number of weekly accidents at R.

$$r(y) = \frac{1.5^y e^{-1.5}}{y!}$$

$$B = P(Y > 1.5) = P(Y \geq 2) = 1 - P(Y < 2) = 1 - [r(0) + r(1)] = .442$$

$$B - A = .442 - .353 = .09$$

The correct answer is **B**.

SOA Sample Question 160 Explanation

Let X be the loss. The cdf of loss is:

$$F(x) = 1 - e^{-kx}$$

The payment happens in policy A if loss is greater than 1.44. So,

$$P(X > 1.44) = .64$$

$$P(X \leq 1.44) = 1 - P(X > 1.44)$$

$$F(1.44) = 1 - .64$$

$$F(1.44) = .36$$

$$1 - e^{-1.44k} = .36$$

$$.64 = e^{-1.44k}$$

$$k = .3099$$

The payment happens in policy B if loss is greater than d. So,

$$P(X > d) = .512$$

$$P(X \leq d) = 1 - P(X > d)$$

$$F(d) = 1 - .512$$

$$F(d) = .488$$

$$1 - e^{-kd} = .488$$

$$.512 = e^{-.3099d}$$

$$d = 2.160$$

The correct answer is **E**.

SOA Sample Question 161 Explanation

$$.4871 = P(X < 3.75) = \int_{-\infty}^{3.75} f(x)\,dx = \int_{0}^{3.75} cx^{a}\,dx$$

$$.4871 = \frac{c\,x^{a+1}}{a+1}\Big|_{x=0}^{x=3.75}$$

$$.4871(a+1) = c(3.75)^{a+1} \qquad (1)$$

We also know that the integral of a pdf over its entire range is 1.

$$1 = \int_{0}^{5} cx^{a}\,dx$$

$$1 = \frac{c\,x^{a+1}}{a+1}\Big|_{x=0}^{x=5}$$

$$(a+1) = c(5)^{a+1} \qquad (2)$$

Dividing (1) by (2) we get:

$$.4871 = \left(\frac{3.75}{5}\right)^{a+1}$$

$$.4871 = (.75)^{a+1}$$

$$\ln .4871 = (a+1)\ln .75$$

$$a+1 = \frac{\ln .4871}{\ln .75} = 2.5$$

$$a = 1.5$$

Substituting the value of $a + 1$ in (2) we get:

$$2.5 = c(5)^{2.5}$$

$$c = 2.5(5)^{-2.5} = .0447$$

$$f(x) = .0447x^{1.5}, \qquad 0 < x < 5$$

$$P(X > 4) = \int_{4}^{5} .0447x^{1.5}dx$$

$$= .0447\left(\frac{x^{2.5}}{2.5}\right)\Big|_{4}^{5}$$

$$= .0179(5^{2.5} - 4^{2.5}) = .428$$

The correct answer is **B**.

SOA Sample Question 162 Explanation

The number of claims X has the pmf:

$$f(x) = \frac{c^x e^{-c}}{x!}$$

We are given that $f(0) = .6$. So:

$$.6 = \frac{c^0 e^{-c}}{0!}$$

$$\ln .6 = -c$$

$$c = .5108$$

The pmf thus becomes:

$$f(x) = \frac{(.5108)^x (.6)}{x!}$$

Expected payment is given as:

$$E = 0f(0) + 0f(1) + 5000f(2) + 10000f(3) + 15000f(4) + \cdots$$

$$= 5000[f(2) + 2f(3) + 3f(4) + \cdots]$$

$$= 5000[f(1) - f(1) + 2f(2) - f(2) + 3f(3) - f(3) + \cdots]$$

$$= 5000[f(1) + 2f(2) + 3f(3) + \cdots]$$

$$-5000[f(1) + f(2) + f(3) + \cdots]$$

$$= 5000[0f(0) + 1f(1) + 2f(2) + 3f(3) + \cdots]$$

$$-5000[f(0) + f(1) + f(2) + f(3) + \cdots] + 5000f(0)$$

$$= 5000\sum_{x=0}^{\infty} xf(x) - 5000\sum_{x=0}^{\infty} f(x) + 5000f(0)$$

$$= 5000E[X] - 5000(1) + 5000(.6)$$

$$= 5000(.5108) - 5000 + 3000$$

$$= 554$$

The correct answer is **A**.

SOA Sample Question 163 Explanation

Let X be the loss and Y be the unreimbursed portion of loss.

$$f(x) = \frac{1}{b}, \qquad 0 < x < b$$

When loss is less than or equal to 180, all of it is unreimbursed.

When loss is greater than 180, then 180 is unreimbursed.

That is:

$$Y = \begin{cases} X, & X \le 180 \\ 180, & X > 180 \end{cases}$$

$$E[Y] = \int_{-\infty}^{\infty} y\, f(x) dx$$

$$= \int_{0}^{180} x\left(\frac{1}{b}\right) dx + \int_{180}^{b} 180\left(\frac{1}{b}\right) dx$$

$$= \frac{x^2}{2b}\Big|_{x=0}^{x=180} + \frac{180x}{b}\Big|_{x=180}^{x=b}$$

$$= \frac{180^2}{2b} + \frac{180}{b}(b - 180)$$

$$= \frac{16200}{b} + 180 - \frac{32400}{b}$$

$$= 180 - \frac{16200}{b}$$

Setting it equal to the given value of 144 we get:

$$180 - \frac{16200}{b} = 144$$

$$36 = \frac{16200}{b}$$

$$b = \frac{16200}{36}$$

$$b = 450$$

The correct answer is **D**.

Quiz 14

1. The lifetime, T, in years, of a machine is uniform on [0, 12]. A warranty pays a benefit of 3000 if failure occurs between times $t = 1$ and $t = 9$ years. The present value, W, of this benefit is

$$W = \begin{cases} 0, & 0 \le T < 1 \\ 3000e^{-.06t}, & 1 \le T < 9 \\ 0, & 9 \le T \le 12 \end{cases}$$

Find the probability that that present value of the benefit is less than 2000.

A) .43
B) .46
C) .49
D) .52
E) .55

Solution:

$$f(t) = \frac{1}{12}, \qquad 0 \le T \le 12$$

The main calculation is when $1 \le T < 9$. In this case:

$$\begin{aligned} P(W < 2000) &= P(3000e^{-.06T} < 2000) \\ &= P(e^{-.06T} < .6667) \\ &= P(-.06T < \ln .6667) \\ &= P(T > 6.76 \text{ and } 1 \le T < 9) \\ &= P(T \text{ is between } 6.76 \text{ and } 9) \\ &= \frac{9 - 6.76}{12 - 0} \\ &= .1867 \end{aligned}$$

Note that in this case, we also have $W > 0$. So we can say that:

$$P(0 < W < 2000) = .1867$$

Also, $W = 0$ when $0 \le T < 1$ or when $9 \le T \le 12$. So $P(W = 0)$ is found by dividing the combined lengths of these intervals by total length of the given interval.

$$P(W = 0) = \frac{1 + 3}{12} = .3333$$

We thus have:

$$\begin{aligned} P(W < 2000) &= P(W = 0) + P(0 < W < 2000) \\ &= .3333 + .1867 = .52 \end{aligned}$$

The correct answer is **D**.

2. The amount of damage a car undergoes in an accident is uniform on $[0, b]$. An insurance policy payout is subject to a deductible of $b/5$. A policyholder experiences automobile damage. Find the ratio of the expected payout to the expected amount of the damage.
   A) .18
   B) .36
   C) .5
   D) .64
   E) .82

   Solution:

   Let X be the damage and Y be the payout.

$$f(x) = \frac{1}{b}, \qquad 0 < x < b$$

$$E[X] = \frac{b+0}{2} = \frac{b}{2}$$

$$Y = \begin{cases} 0\,, & X < 0.2b \\ X - 0.2b\,, & 0.2b < X < b \end{cases}$$

$$E(Y) = \int_{-\infty}^{\infty} y\, f(x)\, dx$$

$$= \int_{0.2b}^{b} (x - 0.2b)\left(\frac{1}{b}\right) dx$$

$$= \int_{0.2b}^{b} \frac{x}{b} - 0.2\, dx$$

$$= \left(\frac{x^2}{2b} - 0.2x\right)\Big|_{x=.2b}^{x=b}$$

$$= \left(\frac{b^2}{2b} - 0.2b\right) - \left(\frac{(.2b)^2}{2b} - 0.2(.2b)\right)$$

$$= \frac{b}{2} - .2b - \frac{.04b}{2} + .04b$$

$$= .32b$$

Dividing the two we get:

$$\frac{E[Y]}{E[X]} = \frac{.32b}{.5b}$$

$$= .64$$

The correct answer is **D**.

3. Members of a gym are classified as children, adults, and seniors. 60% of the members are adults, and 25% are seniors. On a Friday, a child is half as likely to come as a senior, and a senior is twice as likely to come as an adult. The probability of a member coming to a gym on Friday is 0.1. Find the probability of a child coming to gym on a Friday?
A) .04
B) .08
C) .12
D) .16
E) .2

Solution:

Let x be probability of a child coming to the gym.

So $2x$ will be the probability of a senior coming to the gym,

and x will be probability of an adult coming to the gym.

Type	Proportion	Coming Probability
Child (C)	$1 - .6 - .25 = .15$	x
Adult (A)	$.6$	x
Senior (S)	$.25$	$2x$

Let Y be the event of a member coming to the gym.

$$P(Y) = P(C \text{ and } Y) + P(A \text{ and } Y) + P(S \text{ and } Y)$$

$$= .15x + .6x + .25(2x) = 1.25x = .1$$

$$x = \frac{.1}{1.25}$$

$$= .08$$

The correct answer is **B**.

4. A 1-year warranty covers the entire home subject to a deductible. During the year, only one of the following problems can occur:
   (i) The roof may need to be replaced at a cost of 5000. The probability of this happening is 10%.
   (ii) The heater may need to be replaced at a cost of 2000. The probability of this happening is 15%.
   (iii) The stove may need to be replaced at a cost of 1000. The probability of this happening is 20%.

   What deductible would produce an expected claim payment of 400?

   A) 1333
   B) At least 1400 but less than 1450
   C) At least 1450 but less than 1500
   D) At least 1500 but less than 1550
   E) Greater than 1550.

Solution:

Let d be the deductible.

If $d \leq 1000$, the expected claim payment will be:

$$.1(5000 - d) + .15(2000 - d) + .2(1000 - d) = 400$$

$$500 - .1d + 300 - .15d + 200 - .2d = 400$$

$$600 = .45d$$

$$d = 1333$$

This contradicts out supposition that $d \leq 1000$.

So d must be greater than 1000.

If $1000 < d < 2000$, the expected claim payment will be:

$$.1(5000 - d) + .15(2000 - d) = 400$$

$$500 - .1d + 300 - .15d = 400$$

$$400 = .25d$$

$$d = 1600$$

This is consistent with our assumption that $1000 < d < 2000$.

Hence this is the correct deductible.

The correct answer is **E**.

5. In a class of 12 students, there are x boys. Three of the students catch flue. The probability that all these three are boys is 1/55. Find that probability that at most one girl catches flue.
   A) .16
   B) .18
   C) .2
   D) .22
   E) .24

Solution:

$$P(all\ 3\ are\ boys) = \frac{x}{12}\left(\frac{x-1}{11}\right)\left(\frac{x-2}{10}\right)$$

$$\frac{x}{12}\left(\frac{x-1}{11}\right)\left(\frac{x-2}{10}\right) = \frac{1}{55}$$

$$x(x-1)(x-2) = 24$$

Since x has to be integer between 0 and 12, we note that $x = 4$ is a solution of this equation.

So, out of the 12, there are 4 boys and hence 8 girls.

$$P(at\ most\ 1\ of\ 3\ flues\ is\ a\ girl) = P(0\ girl\ flue) + P(1\ girl\ flue)$$

$$P(\ 0\ girl\ flue) = P(all\ 3\ flues\ are\ boys)$$

$$= \frac{1}{55}$$

$$P(1\ girl\ flue) = P(1\ girl\ and\ 2\ boys\ flue)$$

$$= \frac{\binom{8}{1}\binom{4}{2}}{\binom{12}{3}}$$

$$= .2182$$

$$P(at\ most\ 1\ of\ 3\ flues\ is\ for\ a\ girl) = \frac{1}{55} + .2182$$

$$= .2364$$

The correct answer is **E**.

6. In a city, the number of days it rains every week follows a Poisson distribution with mean 1.5. The numbers of rainy days in different weeks are mutually independent. Calculate the probability that it there are more than 3 rainy days in a 4-week period.
   A) .85
   B) .87
   C) .89
   D) .91
   E) .93
   Solution:

   Sum of independent Poisson variables is Poisson with mean equal to sum of individual means.

   Since the mean for each week is 1.5, the mean for 4 weeks is $1.5(4) = 6$.

   Let X be the number of rainy days in 4 weeks. The pmf is:

$$f(x) = \frac{6^x e^{-6}}{x!}$$

$$P(X > 3) = 1 - P(X \leq 3)$$

$$= 1 - [f(0) + f(1) + f(2) + f(3)]$$

$$= 1 - \frac{6^0 e^{-6}}{0!} - \frac{6^1 e^{-6}}{1!} - \frac{6^2 e^{-6}}{2!} - \frac{6^3 e^{-6}}{3!}$$

$$= .85$$

   The correct answer is **A**.

7. Hospital costs for a driver after a car accident are exponentially distributed. A driver has to choose between two different insurance policies. Policy A has a deductible of 1000. For a random loss, the probability is 0.9 that under this policy, the insurer will pay some

money to the driver. Policy B has a deductible of d. For a random loss, the probability is 0.8 that under this policy, the insurer will pay some money to the driver. Calculate d.
A) 2118
B) 2318
C) 2518
D) 2718
E) 2918
Solution:

Let X be the loss.

The cdf of loss is:

$$F(x) = 1 - e^{-kx}$$

The payment happens in policy A if loss is greater than 1000. So,

$$P(X > 1000) = .9$$

$$P(X \leq 1000) = 1 - P(X > 1000)$$

$$F(1000) = 1 - .9$$

$$F(1000) = .1$$

$$1 - e^{-1000k} = .1$$

$$.9 = e^{-1000k}$$

$$\ln .9 = -1000k$$

$$k = .00010536$$

The payment happens in policy B if loss is greater than d. So,

$$P(X > d) = .8$$

$$P(X \leq d) = 1 - P(X > d)$$

$$F(d) = 1 - .8$$

$$F(d) = .2$$

$$1 - e^{-kd} = .2$$

$$.8 = e^{-.00010536d}$$

$$d = 2118$$

The correct answer is **A**.

8. The distribution of the size of claims paid under an insurance policy has probability density function

$$f(x) = cx^a, \qquad 0 < x < 9$$

where $a > 0,\ c > 0$.

For a random claim, the probability that the size of the claim is less than 5 is 0.3. Find the probability that the size of a randomly selected claim is greater than 6.

A) .327
B) .436
C) .564
D) .667
E) .673

Solution:

$$.3 = P(X < 5) = \int_{-\infty}^{5} f(x)\, dx$$

$$.3 = \int_{0}^{5} cx^a\, dx$$

$$.3 = \frac{c\, x^{a+1}}{a+1}\Big|_{x=0}^{x=5}$$

$$.3(a+1) = c(5)^{a+1} \qquad (1)$$

We also know that the integral of a pdf over its entire range is 1.

$$1 = \int_{0}^{9} cx^a\, dx$$

$$1 = \frac{c\, x^{a+1}}{a+1}\Big|_{x=0}^{x=9}$$

$$(a+1) = c(9)^{a+1} \qquad (2)$$

Dividing (1) by (2) we get:

$$.3 = \left(\frac{5}{9}\right)^{a+1}$$

$$\ln .3 = (a+1)\ln\left(\frac{5}{9}\right)$$

$$a + 1 = \frac{\ln .3}{\ln\left(\frac{5}{9}\right)} = 2.0483$$

$$a = 1.0483$$

Substituting the value of $a + 1$ in (2) we get:

$$2.0483 = c(9)^{2.0483}$$

$$c = .02274$$

$$f(x) = .02274x^{1.0483}, \qquad 0 < x < 9$$

$$P(X > 6) = \int_6^9 .02274x^{1.0483}dx$$

$$= .02274\left(\frac{x^{2.0483}}{2.0483}\right)\Big|_6^9$$

$$= .564$$

The correct answer is **C**.

9. A company provides a warranty on computers. Each year, the number of warranty claims follows a Poisson distribution with mean m. The probability that at least one claim is received in a year is 0.3. The company purchases an insurance policy hoping to reduce warranty claim payment costs. The insurance policy will pay nothing for the first warranty claim received and 200 for each claim thereafter until the end of the year. Find the expected amount of annual insurance policy payments to the company.

(A) 11

(B) 13

(C) 15

(D) 17

(E) 19

Solution:

The number of claims X has the pmf:

$$f(x) = \frac{m^x e^{-m}}{x!}$$

$$f(0) = P(X = 0)$$

$$f(0) = 1 - P(X \geq 1)$$

$$f(0) = 1 - .3$$

$$f(0) = .7$$

$$\frac{m^0 e^{-m}}{0!} = .7$$

$$\ln .7 = -m$$

$$m = .3567$$

The pdf becomes:

$$f(x) = \frac{(.3567)^x(.7)}{x!}$$

Expected payment is given as:

$$0f(0) + 0f(1) + 200f(2) + 400f(3) + 600f(4) + \cdots$$

$$= 200[f(2) + 2f(3) + 3f(4) + \cdots]$$

$$= 200[f(1) - f(1) + 2f(2) - f(2) + 3f(3) - f(3) + \cdots]$$

$$= 200[f(1) + 2f(2) + 3f(3) + \cdots] - 200[f(1) + f(2) + f(3) + \cdots]$$

$$= 200[0f(0) + 1f(1) + 2f(2) + 3f(3) + \cdots]$$

$$-200[f(0) + f(1) + f(2) + f(3) + \cdots] + 200f(0)$$

$$= 200\sum_{x=0}^{\infty} xf(x) - 200\sum_{x=0}^{\infty} f(x) + 200f(0)$$

$$= 200E[X] - 200(1) + 200(.7)$$

$$= 200(.3567) - 200 + 140$$

$$= 11$$

The correct answer is **A**.

10. Auto repair costs are uniformly distributed on $[0, b]$. An insurance policy has a deductible of 100 and the expected value of the unreimbursed portion of the costs is 60. Calculate b.
A) 100
B) 125
C) 150
D) 175
E) 200
Solution:

Let X be the loss and Y be the unreimbursed portion of loss.

$$f(x) = \frac{1}{b}, \qquad 0 < x < b$$

When loss is less than or equal to 100, all of it is unreimbursed.

When loss is greater than 100, then 100 is unreimbursed. That is:

$$Y = \begin{cases} X, & X \leq 100 \\ 100, & X > 100 \end{cases}$$

$$E[Y] = \int_{-\infty}^{\infty} y f(x) dx$$

$$= \int_{0}^{100} x\left(\frac{1}{b}\right) dx + \int_{100}^{b} 100\left(\frac{1}{b}\right) dx$$

$$= \frac{x^2}{2b}\Big|_{x=0}^{x=100} + \frac{100x}{b}\Big|_{x=100}^{x=b}$$

$$= \frac{100^2}{2b} + \frac{100}{b}(b - 100)$$

$$= \frac{5000}{b} + 100 - \frac{10000}{b}$$

$$= 100 - \frac{5000}{b}$$

Setting it equal to the given value of 60 we get:

$$100 - \frac{5000}{b} = 60$$

$$40 = \frac{5000}{b}$$

$$b = 125$$

The correct answer is **B**.

Tools Needed for Problems 164-172

The standard pth percentile is the z corresponding to a cumulative probability p. The absolute values of the z-scores corresponding to cumulative probabilities p and $1-p$ are equal.

Linear interpolation should be used to find a z value corresponding to a cumulative probability that is not listed in the table.

The variance is unchanged by a horizontal shift of any pdf.

The exponential pdf:

$$g(x) = \frac{1}{m} e^{\frac{-x}{m}}, \qquad x > 0$$

has mean m and variance m^2

By the memoryless property of the exponentially distributed variable X,

$$Var[X|X > k] = Var\ X$$

If population is normal, or if sample size, $n > 30$, then the sampling distribution of means and sums is approximately normal with mean and standard deviation:

$$\mu_{\bar{X}} = \mu$$

$$\sigma_{\bar{X}} = \frac{\sigma}{\sqrt{n}}$$

$$\mu_{sum} = n\mu$$

$$\sigma_{sum} = \sqrt{n}\,\sigma$$

where μ and σ are the mean and standard deviation of each of the n identical variables.

$$\mu_{aX+b} = a\mu_X + b$$

$$\sigma_{aX+b} = |a|\,\sigma_X$$

If joint distribution of 2 continuous random variables is uniform, pdf is reciprocal of the area of region.

For a discrete random variable:

$$E[X] = \sum xf(x), \qquad E[X^2] = \sum x^2 f(x)$$

$$Var\ X = E[X^2] - (E[X])^2$$

SOA Sample Question 164 Explanation

12th percentile is the standard score corresponding to a cumulative probability of 0.12.

However, the Exam table only gives the cumulative probabilities greater than or equal to .5.

By symmetry, absolute standard value of 12th percentile equals that of $100 - 12 = 88^{th}$ percentile.

From tables, the standard score corresponding to a probability of .88 is exactly midway between 1.17 (corresponding to .8790) and 1.18 (corresponding to .8810).

Thus, the 88th percentile has standard score 1.175. Hence 12th percentile has $z = -1.175$.

$$z = \frac{X - \mu}{\sigma}$$

$$-1.175 = \frac{X - 10}{\sqrt{4}}$$

$$X = 7.65$$

The correct answer is **B**.

SOA Sample Question 165 Explanation

Let X be the 14th percentile of A's profit.

Then X is also the pth percentile of company B's profit.

The means μ are same for both profits. Let standard deviation of A's profit $= \sigma$

Then standard deviation of B's profit $= \sqrt{2.25}\sigma = 1.5\sigma$

14th percentile is the standard score corresponding to a cumulative probability of .14.

However, the Exam table only gives the cumulative probabilities greater than or equal to .5.

By symmetry, absolute standard value of 14th percentile equals that of $100 - 14 = 86^{th}$ percentile.

We find a probability of .8599 in the table corresponding to z −score of 1.08.

So the 14th percentile is $z = -1.08$

$$-1.08 = \frac{X - \mu}{\sigma}$$

Dividing both sides by 1.5 gives the standard p^{th} percentile of B's profit :

$$-.72 = \frac{X - \mu}{1.5\ \sigma}$$

Thus the pth percentile of company B's profit has $z = -.72$

From table, $z = .72$ corresponds to a probability of .7642.

Thus $z = -.72$ corresponds to a cumulative probability of $1 - .7642 = .2358$.

Thus $z = -.72$ corresponds to the 23.58^{th} percentile. Hence $p = 23.6$

The correct answer is **D**.

SOA Sample Question 166 Explanation

$$f(x) = \frac{1}{5}e^{\frac{-(x-5)}{5}}, \qquad x > 5$$

This is a horizontal shift of the basic exponential pdf which has mean 5 and variance $5^2 = 25$.

We know that the variance is unchanged by a horizontal shift of any pdf.

Also, by the memoryless property of the exponential distribution,

$$Var[X|X > k] = Var[X|X > 10] = Var\ X = 25$$

The correct answer is **C**.

SOA Sample Question 167 Explanation

Let the common mean of annual profit for both companies be μ. Then:

$$\sigma_A = \mu/2 \quad (1)$$

Let X, Y be profits of A and B respectively. Then:

$$P(Y < 0) = .9P(X < 0)$$

$$z_A = \frac{0-\mu}{\sigma_A} = \frac{-\mu}{\mu/2} = -2$$

$$P(X < 0) = P(z_A < -2) = P(z_A > 2) = 1 - P(z_A \leq 2) = 1 - .9772 = .0228$$

$$P(Y < 0) = .9P(X < 0) = .9(.0228) = .0205$$

To get the z −score corresponding to a cumulative probability of .0205, we find the z −score corresponding to the cumulative probability of $1 - .0205 = .9795$. From table, .9793 corresponds to 2.04, and .9798 corresponds to 2.05.

$$\frac{.9795 - .9793}{.9798 - .9793} = .4$$

By interpolation, z −score corresponding to the cumulative probability of $.9795$ is .4 of the way between 2.04 and 2.05, that is, 2.044. Hence, by symmetry, the z −score for a cumulative probability of .0205 is -2.044. Thus, this is the z −score corresponding to 0 for company B. So,

$$z_B = \frac{0-\mu}{\sigma_B}$$

$$-2.044 = \frac{-\mu}{\sigma_B}$$

$$\sigma_B = \frac{\mu}{2.044} \quad (2)$$

Dividing (2) by (1) we get:

$$\frac{\sigma_B}{\sigma_A} = \frac{2}{2.044} = .98$$

The correct answer is **C**.

SOA Sample Question 168 Explanation

By central limit theorem, if μ_Y and σ_Y are the mean and standard deviation of each of the n identical variables, then the mean and standard deviation of their average are:

$$\mu_{\bar{Y}} = \mu_Y$$

$$= 1.04\mu_X + 5$$

$$= 1.04(100) + 5$$

$$= 109$$

$$\sigma_{\bar{Y}} = \frac{\sigma_Y}{\sqrt{n}} \quad (1)$$

$$Var\ Y = 1.04^2 Var\ X$$

$$= 1.04^2(25)^2$$

$$\sigma_Y = 1.04(25) = 26$$

Equation (1) becomes:

$$\sigma_{\bar{Y}} = \frac{26}{\sqrt{25}} = 5.2$$

We are to find:

$$P(100 < \bar{Y} < 110)$$

Thus, we need to change 100 and 110 into standard scores.

$$z_{100} = \frac{100 - \mu_{\bar{Y}}}{\sigma_{\bar{Y}}} = \frac{100 - 109}{5.2} = -1.73$$

$$z_{110} = \frac{110 - \mu_{\bar{Y}}}{\sigma_{\bar{Y}}} = \frac{110 - 109}{5.2} = .19$$

$$P(100 < \bar{Y} < 110) = P(-1.73 < z < .19)$$

$$= P(z < .19) - P(z < -1.73)$$

$$= P(z < .19) - P(z > 1.73)$$

$$= P(z < .19) - [1 - P(z \leq 1.73)]$$

$$= .5753 - (1 - .9582)$$

$$= .53$$

The correct answer is **B**.

SOA Sample Question 169 Explanation

We first find c by summing the probability function to 1.

$$f(0,0)+f(0,1)+f(0,2)+f(0,3)+f(1,1)+f(1,2)+f(1,3)+f(2,2)+f(2,3)+f(3,3) = 1$$

$$c(0+2+4+6+3+5+7+6+8+9)=1$$

$$c=\frac{1}{50}$$

$$=.02$$

Number of tornadoes that result in less than 50 million in losses $= Y - X$

(x,y)	(0,0)	(0,1)	(0,2)	(0,3)	(1,1)	(1,2)	(1,3)	(2,2)	(2,3)	(3,3)
$y-x$	0	1	2	3	0	1	2	0	1	0
$x+2y$	0	2	4	6	3	5	7	6	8	9

$$E[Y-X] = .02\sum(y-x)\,(x+2y) = .02(2+8+18+5+14+8) = 1.1$$

The correct answer is **E**.

SOA Sample Question 170 Explanation

There are 6 outcomes in which the difference between republicans and democrats is not 0.

The 3 outcomes in which the difference is 0 are: RD, DR, and II, and these have been excluded from the table.

1st letter is for the 1st person interviewed; 2nd letter is for the 2nd person interviewed.

Outcome	RR	DD	RI	IR	DI	ID
Probability	$\frac{3}{10}\left(\frac{2}{9}\right)=\frac{1}{15}$	$\frac{2}{10}\left(\frac{1}{9}\right)=\frac{1}{45}$	$\frac{3}{10}\left(\frac{5}{9}\right)=\frac{1}{6}$	$\frac{5}{10}\left(\frac{3}{9}\right)=\frac{1}{6}$	$\frac{2}{10}\left(\frac{5}{9}\right)=\frac{1}{9}$	$\frac{5}{10}\left(\frac{2}{9}\right)=\frac{1}{9}$
$\lvert R-D\rvert$	2	2	1	1	1	1

$$E[|R-D|] = 2\left(\frac{1}{15}\right)+2\left(\frac{1}{45}\right)+1\left(\frac{1}{6}\right)+1\left(\frac{1}{6}\right)+1\left(\frac{1}{9}\right)+1\left(\frac{1}{9}\right)$$

$$=\frac{11}{15}$$

The correct answer is **D**.

SOA Sample Question 171 Explanation

Let $Z = XY$.

Then Z can be 0, 1, or 2.

Let f be the probability function of Z.

Let $a = f(0) = P(Z = 0) = P(X = 0 \text{ or } Y = 0)$.

So, we are asked to find a.

Let $b = f(1) = P(Z = 1) = P(X = 1 \text{ and } Y = 1) = p(1,1)$.

Let $c = f(2) = P(Z = 2) = P(X = 1 \text{ and } Y = 2) = p(1,2) = 3p(1,1) = 3b$.

$$E[Z] = \sum zf(z) = 0f(0) + 1f(1) + 2f(2)$$

$$= 0a + 1b + 2c = b + 2c$$

$$= b + 2(3b) = 7b$$

$$E[Z^2] = \sum z^2 f(z) = 0^2 f(0) + 1^2 f(1) + 2^2 f(2)$$

$$= b + 4c = b + 4(3b) = 13b$$

$$Var\ Z = E[Z^2] - (E[Z])^2$$

$$= 13b - 49b^2$$

We are told that $p(1,1) = b$ maximizes $Var\ Z$. We also know from calculus that $Var\ Z$ is maximum where its derivative is 0. Setting derivative equal to 0:

$$(Var\ Z)' = 13 - 98b = 0$$

$$b = \frac{13}{98}$$

$$c = 3b$$

$$= 3\left(\frac{13}{98}\right)$$

$$= \frac{39}{98}$$

Also, by basic probability law,

$$a + b + c = 1$$

$$a + \frac{13}{98} + \frac{39}{98} = 1$$

$$a = \frac{23}{49}$$

The correct answer is **C**.

SOA Sample Question 172 Explanation

Let J be the annual number of severe storms in city J.

Let K be the annual number of severe storms in city K.

We are to find $E[J|K=5]$.

We first find the corresponding probability function.

We are given that m storms in city J result in $m, m+1, or\ m+2$ storms in city K.

In other words, the number of storms in city J either equals, is one less, or is two less than the number of storms in city K.

So, if there are 5 storms in city K, then city J has 3, 4, or 5 storms.

$j\|k=5$	Prob (p)	$f(j) = \binom{5}{j}(.6)^j(.4)^{5-j}$	$P(J=j\ and\ K=5) = pf(j)$	$P(J=j\|K=5) = \frac{P(J=j\ and\ K=5)}{P(K=5)}$
3	1/6	.3456	.0576	.315
4	1/3	.2592	.0864	.472
5	1/2	.07776	.03888	.213
			$P(K=5)=.18288$	

$$E[J|K=5] = \sum (j|k=5)P(J=j|K=5)$$

$$= 3(.315) + 4(.472) + 5(.213)$$

$$= 3.9$$

The correct answer is **C**.

Quiz 15

1. The mean height of all the 18-year-old girls in USA is 64 inches and the standard deviation is 4 inches. Find the 25th percentile of these heights.

(A) 61.30

(B) 62.65

(C) 63.41

(D) 63.95

(E) 64.70

Solution:

25th percentile is the standard score corresponding to a cumulative probability of 0.25.

However, the table provided to us in the Exam only gives the cumulative probabilities greater than or equal to .5. By symmetry, the absolute standard value of the 25th percentile is the same as that of the 100 – 25 = 75th percentile.

In table, $z = .67$ corresponds to cumulative probability .7486, and $z = .68$ corresponds to cumulative probability .7517. Using interpolation:

$$\frac{.75 - .7486}{.7517 - .7486} = .4$$

Thus, the 75thth percentile has standard score .674. So, the 25th percentile has $z = -.674$

$$z = \frac{X - \mu}{\sigma}$$

$$-.674 = \frac{X - 64}{4}$$

$$-.674(4) = X - 64$$

$$X = 61.3$$

The correct answer is **A**.

2. The annual incomes of men and women in a country are normally distributed with the same mean. The variance of women's income is 9 times the variance of men' income. The 90th percentile of men's income is the same as the pth percentile of women's income. Calculate p.

A) 61

B) 63

C) 65

D) 67

E) 69

Solution:

Let X be the 90th percentile of men's income.

Then X is also the pth percentile of women's income.

The means μ are same for both profits.

Let standard deviation of men's income $= \sigma$

Then standard deviation of women's income $= \sqrt{9}\sigma = 3\sigma$

90th percentile is the standard score corresponding to cumulative probability of .9.

We find probability of .8997 in the table corresponds to $z = 1.28$, and probability of .9015 corresponds to $z = 1.29$. By interpolation,

$$\frac{.9 - .8997}{.9015 - .8997} = .2$$

So the 90th percentile is $z = 1.282$

$$z = \frac{X - \mu}{\sigma}$$

$$1.282 = \frac{X - \mu}{\sigma}$$

Dividing both sides by 3 gives the standard p^{th} percentile of women's income:

$$\frac{1.282}{3} = \frac{X - \mu}{3\,\sigma}$$

$$.43 = \frac{X - \mu}{3\,\sigma}$$

Thus the pth percentile of women's income has $z = .43$ which corresponds to a cumulative probability of .6664, or 66.64th percentile.

This rounds to 67.

The correct answer is **D**.

3. Amount of damage to a roof caused by a hurricane is modeled by a normal random variable X with mean 2000 and variance 8100. The reimbursement for the damage by an insurance company is modeled by the random variable

$$Y = 0.9X - 300.$$

Calculate the probability that the total reimbursement for a random sample of 10 roofs damaged by a hurricane is greater than 14500.

A) .026
B) .056
C) .500
D) .944
E) .974

Solution:

By central limit theorem, if μ_Y and σ_Y are mean and standard deviation of each of n identical variables, then the mean and standard deviation of their sum, X, are:

$$\mu = n\mu_Y$$

$$= 10(.9\mu_X - 300)$$

$$= 10[.9(2000) - 300]$$

$$= 15000$$

$$\sigma = \sqrt{n}\,\sigma_Y$$

$$= \sqrt{10}\,(.9)\,\sigma_X$$

$$= \sqrt{10}\,(.9)\sqrt{8100} = 256$$

We need to change 14500 into standard score.

$$z_{14500} = \frac{14500 - 15000}{256} = -1.95$$

$$P(X > 14500) = P(z > -1.95) = P(z \leq 1.95)$$

$$= .9744$$

The correct answer is **E**.

4. A insurance will cover fire losses for up to 2 fires in a home per year. Let X be the number of fires that result in at least 10000 in losses, and let Y be the total number of fires in a year. The joint probability function for X and Y is

$$p(x,y) = c(3x + y), \qquad x = 0,1,2, \qquad y = 0,1,2, \qquad x \leq y$$

where c is constant. Find expected number of fires causing fewer than 10000 in losses.

A) .1
B) .2
C) .3
D) .4
E) .5

Solution:

We first find c by summing the probability function to 1.

$$f(0,0) + f(0,1) + f(0,2) + f(1,1) + f(1,2) + f(2,2) = 1$$

$$c(0 + 1 + 2 + 4 + 5 + 8) = 1$$

$$c = \frac{1}{20} = .05$$

Number of fires that result in less than 10000 in losses $= Y - X$

(x,y)	(0,0)	(0,1)	(0,2)	(1,1)	(1,2)	(2,2)
$y - x$	0	1	2	0	1	0
$3x + y$	0	1	2	4	5	8
$(y - x)(3x + y)$	0	1	4	0	5	0

$$E[Y - X] = \sum (y - x)\,p(x) = .05 \sum (y - x)\,(3x + y)$$

$$= .05(1 + 4 + 5) = .5$$

The correct answer is **E**.

5. A committee has 8 members including 4 undergraduate students, 3 graduate students, and 1 faculty member. Two members quit. Find the expectation of the absolute value of the difference between the number of undergraduate students quitting and the number of graduate students quitting.

A) .7

B) .9

C) 1

D) 1.2

E) 1.5

Solution:

There are 6 possible outcomes in which the difference between the quitting undergraduate quitting and graduate students is not 0. These are tabulated below.

The ones in which the difference is 0 do not contribute to the expected value.

1st letter is for the 1st quitting member; 2nd letter is for the 2nd quitting member. U for undergraduate, G for graduate, F for faculty.

Outcome	UU	GG	UF	FU	GF	FG
Probability	$\frac{4}{8}\left(\frac{3}{7}\right) = \frac{3}{14}$	$\frac{3}{8}\left(\frac{2}{7}\right) = \frac{3}{28}$	$\frac{4}{8}\left(\frac{1}{7}\right) = \frac{1}{14}$	$\frac{1}{8}\left(\frac{4}{7}\right) = \frac{1}{14}$	$\frac{3}{8}\left(\frac{1}{7}\right) = \frac{3}{56}$	$\frac{1}{8}\left(\frac{3}{7}\right) = \frac{3}{56}$
$\lvert U-G\rvert$	2	2	1	1	1	1

$$E[|U-G|] = 2\left(\frac{3}{14}\right) + 2\left(\frac{3}{28}\right) + 1\left(\frac{1}{14}\right) + 1\left(\frac{1}{14}\right) + 1\left(\frac{3}{56}\right) + 1\left(\frac{3}{56}\right)$$

$$= .9$$

The correct answer is **B**.

6. The random variables X and Y have joint probability function

$$p(x,y), \qquad x = 0,1,2, \qquad y = 0,1.$$

Suppose $p(1,1) = 2p(2,1)$, and $p(1,1)$ maximizes the variance of XY. Calculate the probability that neither X nor Y is 0.

(A) 5/16

(B) 7/16

(C) 9/16

(D) 11/16

(E) 13/16

Solution:

Let $Z = XY$. Then Z can be 0, 1, or 2. Let f be the probability function of Z.

Let $a = f(0) = P(Z = 0) = P(X = 0\ or\ Y = 0)$.

Let $b = f(1) = P(Z = 1) = P(X = 1\ and\ Y = 1) = p(1,1)$.

Let $c = f(2) = P(Z = 2) = P(X = 2\ and\ Y = 1) = p(2,1) = .5p(1,1) = .5b$.

It is easier to work this through the compliment. That is, we will first calculate a, which is the probability that at least one of X, Y is 0.

$$E[Z] = \sum zf(z) = 0f(0) + 1f(1) + 2f(2)$$

$$= 0a + 1b + 2c$$

$$= b + 2c$$

$$= b + 2(.5b)$$

$$= b + b = 2b$$

$$E[Z^2] = \sum z^2 f(z) = 0^2 f(0) + 1^2 f(1) + 2^2 f(2)$$

$$= b + 4c$$

$$= b + 4(.5b) = 3b$$

$$Var\ Z = E[Z^2] - (E[Z])^2$$

$$= 3b - 4b^2$$

We are told that $p(1,1) = b$ maximizes $Var\ Z$.

We also know that $Var\ Z$ is maximum where its derivative is 0.

Setting derivative equal to 0:

$$(Var\ Z)' = 3 - 8b = 0$$

$$b = \frac{3}{8}$$

$$c = .5b$$

$$= .5\left(\frac{3}{8}\right)$$

$$= \frac{3}{16}$$

Also, by basic probability law,

$$a + b + c = 1$$

$$a + \frac{3}{8} + \frac{3}{16} = 1$$

$$a = \frac{7}{16}$$

a is the probability that at least one of X, Y is 0. Probability that neither X nor Y is 0 is the complement of this. Thus,

$$P(\text{ neither } X \text{ nor } Y \text{ is } 0) = 1 - \frac{7}{16} = \frac{9}{16}$$

The correct answer is **C**.

7. The lifetime X of a bulb, and the lifetime Y of a battery have joint pdf:

$$f(x,y) = x + 1.5y^2, \qquad 0 \le x \le 1, \qquad 0 \le y \le 1$$

Find the average lifetime of the battery, given that the lifetime of the bulb is .7

A) .3
B) .4
C) .5
D) .6
E) .7

Solution:

We are to find $E[Y|X = .7]$. First, we find the corresponding conditional pdf.

$$f(y|x = .7) = \frac{f(.7,y)}{f_X(.7)} = \frac{.7 + 1.5y^2}{f_X(.7)} \qquad (1)$$

$$f_X(x) = \int_{-\infty}^{\infty} f(x,y)dy$$

$$f_X(.7) = \int_{-\infty}^{\infty} f(.7,y)dy$$

$$= \int_0^1 .7 + 1.5y^2 dy$$

$$= .7y + 1.5\frac{y^3}{3}\Big|_0^1$$

$$= 1.2$$

So, (1) becomes:

$$f(y|x = .7) = \frac{.7 + 1.5y^2}{1.2}, \qquad 0 \le y \le 1$$

$$E[Y|X = .7] = \int_0^1 y\, f(y|x = .7)\ dy$$

$$= \int_0^1 y\, \frac{.7 + 1.5y^2}{1.2}\, dy$$

$$= \frac{1}{1.2} \int_0^1 .7y + 1.5y^3 \; dy$$

$$= \frac{1}{1.2} \left(.7\frac{y^2}{2} + 1.5\frac{y^4}{4} \right) |_0^1$$

$$= \frac{1}{1.2} \left[\frac{.7}{2} + \frac{1.5}{4} \right]$$

$$= .6$$

The correct answer is **D**.

8. Number of crimes in city A in a year follows a binomial distribution with $n = 8, p = .3$. Given that m crimes occur in city A in a year, number of crimes that occur in city B in the same year is $m + 1$ with probability .6, and $m + 2$ with probability .4. Find expected number of crimes that occur in city A in a year during which 2 crimes occur in city B.

(A) .44

(B) .54

(C) .64

(D) .74

(E) .84

Solution:

Let A, B be the annual number of crimes in city A, B, respectively.

We are to find $E[A|B = 2]$.

We first find the corresponding probability function.

We are given that m crimes in city A result in $m + 1$ or $m + 2$ crimes in city B.

In other words, the number of crimes in city A is either one less, or is two less than the number of crimes in city B. So, if there are 2 crimes in city B, then city A has 1 or 0 crimes.

The relevant values are tabulated below:

$a\|b = 2$	Prob (p)	$f(a) = \binom{8}{a}(.3)^a(.7)^{8-a}$	$P(A = a, B = 2) = pf(a)$	$P(A = a\|B = 2) = \frac{P(A = a, B = 2)}{P(B = 2)}$
0	.4	.05765	.0231	.163
1	.6	.19765	.1186	.837
			$P(B = 2) = .1417$	

$$E[A|B = 2] = \sum (a|b = 5)P(A = a|B = 2)$$

$$= 0(.163) + 1(.837) = .837$$

The correct answer is **E**.

Tools Needed for Problems 173-181

$$Var\,X = E[X^2] - (E[X])^2$$

The mean and standard deviation of exponential distribution are equal.

If population is normal, or if sample size, $n > 30$, then the sampling distribution of means and sums is approximately normal with mean and standard deviation:

$$\mu_{\bar{X}} = \mu$$

$$\sigma_{\bar{X}} = \frac{\sigma}{\sqrt{n}}$$

$$\mu_{sum} = n\mu$$

$$\sigma_{sum} = \sqrt{n}\,\sigma$$

where μ and σ are the mean and standard deviation of each of the n identical variables.

$$\mu_{aX+b} = a\mu_X + b$$

$$\sigma_{aX+b} = |a|\,\sigma_X$$

$$Var(aX + bY) = a^2 Var\,X + b^2 Var\,Y + 2abCov(X, Y)$$

For independent variables, $Cov(X, Y) = 0$

Expected value of a binomial distribution is np and variance is $np(1 - p)$

Mode of a discrete random variable is the value of the variable that corresponds to maximum probability.

If X, Y are discrete random variables, then:

$$E[Y] = \sum_k P(X = k)E[Y|X = k]$$

Hypergeometric Formula:

If a collection has N items, where K items are of type A, and we pick n of those without replacement, then the probability that x of those n are of type A is:

$$\frac{\binom{K}{x}\binom{N-K}{n-x}}{\binom{N}{n}}$$

$$\binom{n}{r} = \frac{n!}{r!\,(n-r)!}$$

Law of total expectation:

$$E[A] = \sum_k P(X = k)E[A|X = k]$$

SOA Sample Question 173 Explanation

We tabulate the info for the (N, S) pairs where $N + S = 2$

(n, s)	$f((n,s))$	n	$P(N = n \mid N + S = 2) = \dfrac{f((n,s))}{P(N+S=2)}$
(0,2)	.10	0	.25
(1,1)	.18	1	.45
(2,0)	.12	2	.3
	$P(N + S = 2) = .4$		

From calculator, using the last 2 columns, the standard deviation is .74

$$Var(N \mid N + S = 2) = .74^2 = .55$$

The correct answer is **B**.

SOA Sample Question 174 Explanation

It can be shown that if there are equal number of claims in each territory (which is the case here) then the probability of each claim amount can be found be averaging the probabilities of that claim amount in the 3 territories.

I will provide a demonstration of this at the end of this problem. Let us assume it for now. So:

$$P(100) = \frac{.9 + .8 + .7}{3} = .8$$

$$P(500) = \frac{.08 + .11 + .2}{3} = .13$$

$$P(1000) = \frac{.02 + .09 + .1}{3} = .07$$

If X is the claim amount, then from calculator:

$$SD(X) = 253.53$$

Now here is the demonstration promised at the beginning of the problem:

Suppose each territory has 200 claims. Then we have the following situation:

Claim Amount (X)	100	500	1000
Claims in Territory 1	$.9(200) = 180$	$200(.08) = 16$	$200(.02) = 4$
Claims in Territory 2	$.8(200) = 160$	$200(.11) = 22$	$200(.09) = 18$
Claims in Territory 3	$.7(200) = 140$	$200(.2) = 40$	$200(.1) = 20$
Total Claims	480	78	42
$P(X) = \dfrac{Total\ Claims}{600}$	.8	.13	.07

The entries in the last row are the same as the average probabilities we obtained before.

The correct answer is **A**.

SOA Sample Question 175 Explanation

Let A be the amount added, and R be the amount removed during the week.

By central limit theorem:

$$\mu_A = 20(mean\ of\ each\ load\ added) = 20(1.5) = 30$$

$$\sigma_A = \sqrt{20}\,(SD\ of\ each\ load\ added) = \sqrt{20}\,(.25)$$

$$\mu_R = 4(mean\ of\ each\ load\ removed) = 4(7.25) = 29$$

$$\sigma_R = \sqrt{4}\,(SD\ of\ each\ load\ removed) = \sqrt{4}\,(.5) = 1$$

Let $X = A - R$.

We are asked to find $P(X > 0)$.

$$\mu_X = \mu_A - \mu_R = 30 - 29 = 1$$

$$Var\ X = Var\ A + (-1)^2 Var\ R$$

$$= 20(.25)^2 + 1^2$$

$$= 2.25$$

$$\sigma_X = \sqrt{Var\ X}$$

$$= \sqrt{2.25}$$

$$= 1.5$$

Since we have to find $P(X > 0)$, we need to change 0 into z-score.

$$z = \frac{0 - \mu_X}{\sigma_X}$$

$$= -\frac{1}{1.5}$$

$$= -.67$$

$$P(X > 0) = P(z > -.67)$$

$$= P(z < .67)$$

$$= .7486$$

This rounds to .75.

The correct answer is **D**.

SOA Sample Question 176 Explanation

Since each driver can have a maximum of 3 claims, the total number of claims between the two of them could be 0,1,2,3,4,5, or 6.

So, we need to calculate that probability of each of these numbers.

The number corresponding to the highest probability will be the mode.

# of Claims	(G,B) causing them	Probability (p)	Remaining Probability
0	(0,0)	$.5(.2) = .1$	$1 - .1 = .9$
1	(0,1),(1,0)	$.5(.3) + .3(.2) = .21$	$.9 - .21 = .69$
2	(0,2),(1,1),(2,0)	$.5(.4) + .3(.3) + .2(.2) = .33$	$.69 - .33 = .36$
3	(0,3),(1,2),(2,1),(3,0)	$.5(.1) + .3(.4) + .2(.3) = .23$	$.36 - .23 = .13$

Remaining probability of .13 after 3 claims shows that the probabilities of each 4,5, or 6 claims will not exceed .13.

So, 4,5, or 6 cannot be modes because we already have a probability of .33 corresponding to 2, which is higher than .13 and also higher than any other probability.

So, the mode is 2.

The correct answer is **C**.

SOA Sample Question 177 Explanation

Let R be the number of patients who undergo radiation.

Let C be the number of patients who undergo chemotherapy.

Then the total payment, X, is:

$$X = 2R + 3C$$

Now since $R \text{ } and \text{ } C$ are independent, $Cov\ (R, C) = 0$.

We thus have:

$$Var\ X = 2^2 Var\ R + 3^2 Var\ C$$

$$= 4\ Var\ R + 9\ Var\ C \quad (1)$$

R is binomial with $n = 15, p = .9$. So:

$$Var\ R = np(1-p)$$

$$= 15(.9)(.1)$$

$$= 1.35$$

C is binomial with $n = 15, p = .4$. So:

$$Var\ C = np(1-p)$$

$$= 15(.4)(.6)$$

$$= 3.6$$

Equation (1) becomes:

$$Var\ X = 4\ Var\ R + 9\ Var\ C$$

$$= 4(1.35) + 9(3.6)$$

$$= 37.8$$

The correct answer is **B**.

SOA Sample Question 178 Explanation

Let X, A be the number of patients with early and advanced cancer, respectively.

We are to find $E[A|X \geq 1]$. By law of total expectation:

$$E[A] = \sum_k P(X = k)E[A|X = k]$$

$$E[A] = P(X = 0)E[A|X = 0] + P(X \geq 1)E[A|X \geq 1]$$

$$\Rightarrow E[A|X \geq 1] = \frac{E[A] - P(X = 0)E[A|X = 0]}{P(X \geq 1)} \qquad (1)$$

We now go about finding the quantities on the right side of (1).

The number of patients with early stage cancer, X, is binomial with $n = 6,\ p = .2$

$$P(no\ patient\ has\ early\ stage\ cancer) = P(X = 0)$$

$$= \binom{6}{0}(.2)^0(1 - .2)^{6-0} = .262144$$

$$P(at\ least\ one\ has\ early\ stage\ cancer) = P(X \geq 1)$$

$$= 1 - P(X = 0) = 1 - .262144 = .737856$$

The number of patients having advanced stage cancer, A, is binomial with $n = 6,\ p = .1$. So:

$$E[A] = np = 6(.1) = .6.$$

We now have all we need except $E[A|X = 0]$. For this, we note that $A|X = 0$ means the number of advanced stage patients, given that there are no early stage patients among the 6 chosen ones.

$$P(advanced|not\ early) = \frac{P(advanced\ and\ not\ early)}{P(not\ early)}$$

$$= \frac{.1}{1 - .2}$$

$$= \frac{1}{8}$$

So, $A|X = 0$ is binomial with $n = 6,\ p = 1/8$. Thus,

$$E[A|X = 0] = np = 6\left(\frac{1}{8}\right) = .75$$

We now have all the values on the right side of (1). So,

$$E[A|X \geq 1] = \frac{.6 - .262144(.75)}{.737856}$$

$$= .547$$

The correct answer is **C**.

SOA Sample Question 179 Explanation

Whichever of the 4 integers are chosen from the first 12, since X is the 2nd largest of the four, there must be exactly one larger than it, and two smaller than it. We can never have two smaller integers than either 1 or 2, and we can never have a larger integer than 12. So, $X \neq 1, 2, or\ 12$.

x	Larger Integers	# ways of to get one Larger Integer	Smaller Integers	# ways to get two Smaller Integers
3	4,5,6,…,12	$9 = 12 - 3$	1,2	$\binom{2}{2}$
4	5,6,7,…,12	$8 = 12 - 4$	1,2,3	$\binom{3}{2}$
5	6,7,8,…,12	$7 = 12 - 5$	1,2,3,4	$\binom{4}{2}$

The pattern is now clear. There are:

$$12 - x \text{ ways to get an integer larger than } x$$

$$\binom{x-1}{2} \text{ ways to get two integers smaller than } x.$$

Also, there are $\binom{12}{4}$ ways of selecting 4 integers out of 12. So,

$$p(x) = \frac{\text{Number of ways in which } X \text{ is the 2nd largest integer in four}}{\text{ways to select 4 integers out of 12}}$$

$$= \frac{(\text{ways to get an integer} > X)(\text{ways to get 2 integers} < X)}{\text{ways to select 4 integers out of 12}}$$

$$= \frac{(12 - x) * \binom{x-1}{2}}{\binom{12}{4}}$$

$$p(x) = \frac{(12 - x) * \frac{(x-1)!}{2!\,(x-1-2)!}}{\binom{12}{4}}$$

$$= \frac{(12 - x) * \frac{(x-1)!}{2(x-3)!}}{495}$$

$$= \frac{(12 - x) * \frac{(x-1)!}{2(x-3)!}}{495}$$

$$= \frac{(12 - x) * \frac{(x-1)(x-2)(x-3)!}{2(x-3)!}}{495}$$

$$= \frac{(12 - x)(x-1)(x-2)}{990}$$

The correct answer is **A**.

SOA Sample Question 180 Explanation

Let X be the loss. We are told that $P(X < k) = .9582$, and:

$$P(X < k|X > 10000) = .95$$

$$\frac{P(X < k, and\ X > 10000)}{P(X > 10000)} = .95$$

$$\frac{P(10000 < X < k)}{P(X > 10000)} = .95$$

$$\frac{P(X < k) - P(X < 10000)}{P(X > 10000)} = .95$$

$$\frac{.9582 - P(X < 10000)}{1 - P(X < 10000)} = .95$$

Let $P(X < 10000) = y$. Then the above equation becomes:

$$\frac{.9582 - y}{1 - y} = .95$$

$$.9582 - y = .95 - .95y$$

$$.9582 - .95 = y - .95y$$

$$.0082 = .05y$$

$$y = .164$$

$$P(X < 10000) = .164$$

We now find the z-score corresponding to a cumulative probability of .164. All the table probability values are greater than or equal to .5. So, we will find the z-score corresponding to a cumulative probability of $1 - .164 = .836$ and negate it.

From the table, $z = .97$ corresponds to .8340, and $z = .98$ corresponds to .8365.

$$\frac{.836 - .8340}{.8365 - .8340} = .8$$

Thus, by interpolation, $z = .978$ corresponds to a cumulative probability of .836. By symmetry of the normal curve, $z = -.978$ corresponds to a cumulative probability of .164. This z-score corresponds to $X = 10000$. So,

$$z = \frac{X - mean}{SD}$$

$$-.978 = \frac{10000 - 12000}{c}$$

$$c = 2045$$

The correct answer is **A**.

SOA Sample Question 181 Explanation

Let X be the loss and Y be the reimbursement.

$$Y = \begin{cases} 0\,, & X \le 250 \\ X - 250\,, & X > 250 \end{cases}$$

We have the following picture:

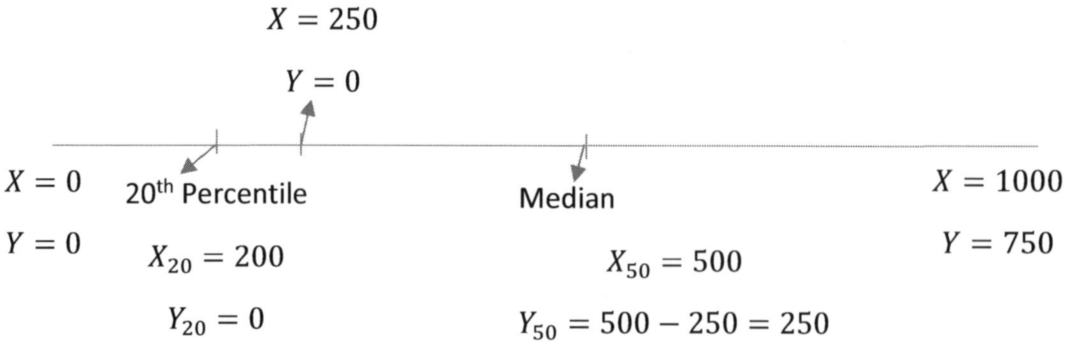

From the picture, we see that:

$$\begin{aligned} Y_{50} - Y_{20} &= 250 - 0 \\ &= 250 \end{aligned}$$

The correct answer is **B**.

Quiz 16

1. At the start of a month a deep well has some water in it. During the month it rains 5 times. Each rain adds a volume of water to the well that is normally distributed with mean 100 cubic feet and standard deviation 40 cubic feet. During the month, there are 20 days when people remove water from the well. The amount of water removed on each of these 20 days is normally distributed with mean 24 cubic feet and standard deviation 14 cubic feet. The amounts added to the well or removed from the well are all independent of each other. Find the probability that the well contains more water at the end of the month than it had at the start of the month. Assume that rains never cause it to overflow.

A) .43

B) .5

C) .57

D) .64

E) .71

Solution:

Let A be the amount added, and R be the amount removed during the month.

By central limit theorem:

$$\mu_A = 5(mean\ of\ each\ addition) = 5(100) = 500$$

$$\sigma_A = \sqrt{5}\,(SD\ of\ each\ addition) = \sqrt{5}\,(40) = 89.44$$

$$\mu_R = 20(mean\ of\ each\ removal) = 20(24) = 480$$

$$\sigma_R = \sqrt{20}\,(SD\ of\ each\ removal) = \sqrt{20}\,(14) = 62.61$$

Let $X = A - R$. We are asked to find $P(X > 0)$.

$$\mu_X = \mu_A - \mu_R = 500 - 480 = 20$$

$$Var\ X = Var\ A + (-1)^2 Var\ R$$

$$= (89.44)^2 + (62.61)^2 = 11920$$

$$\sigma_X = \sqrt{Var\ X}$$

$$= \sqrt{11920} = 109.18$$

Since we have to find $P(X > 0)$, we need to change 0 into z-score.

$$z = \frac{0 - \mu_X}{\sigma_X} = -\frac{20}{109.18} = -.18$$

$$P(X > 0) = P(z > -.18) = P(z < .18)$$

$$= .5714$$

This rounds to .57 which is choice **C**.

2. The table below gives the probability of a given number of major earthquakes occurring in countries A and B during a year.

Number of Earthquakes	Probability for Country A p_A	Probability for Country B p_B
0	.1	.5
1	.3	.2
2	.4	.2
3	.2	.1

The number of earthquakes occurring in the 2 countries are independent. Calculate the mode of the distribution of the combined total of major earthquakes occurring in the 2 countries.

(A) 1

(B) 2

(C) 3

(D) 4

(E) 5

Solution:

Since each country can have a maximum of 3 earthquakes, the total number of earthquakes between the two of them could be 0,1,2,3,4,5, or 6.

So, we need to calculate that probability of each of these numbers.

The number corresponding to the highest probability will be the mode.

# of EQ	Relevant (A,B)	Probability ($p = p_A p_B$)	Remaining Probability
0	(0,0)	$.1(.5) = .05$	$1 - .05 = .95$
1	(0,1),(1,0)	$.1(.2) + .3(.5) = .17$	$.95 - .17 = .78$
2	(0,2),(1,1),(2,0)	$.1(.2) + .3(.2) + .4(.5) = .28$	$.78 - .28 = .5$
3	(0,3),(1,2),(2,1),(3,0)	$.1(.1) + .3(.2) + .4(.2) + .2(.5) = .25$	$.5 - .25 = .25$

Remaining probability of .25 after 3 earthquakes shows that the probabilities of each 4,5, or 6 earthquakes will not exceed .25.

So 4,5,6 cannot be modes because we already have a probability of .28 corresponding to 2, which is higher than .25 and also higher than any other probability.

So, mode is 2.

The correct answer is **B**.

3. A company offers vision insurance to its employees. 40 employees opt for it. Next month each of these policy holders has a .6 probability of buying eyeglasses, and a .5 probability of buying contact lenses. Both these choices are independent. Also, any choices made by different employees are mutually independent. The insurance pays 200 for eyeglasses and 250 for contact lenses that are bought. Calculate the variance of the total amount in insurance pays for eyeglasses and contact lenses bought next month by these 40 policyholders.

A. 1001000

B. 1003000

C. 1005000

D. 1007000

E. 1009000

Solution:

Let G be the number of policyholders who buy eyeglasses.

Let C be the number of policyholders who buy contact lenses.

Then the total payment, X, is:

$$X = 200G + 250C$$

Now since G and C are independent, $Cov\ (G, C) = 0$.

We thus have:

$$Var\ X = 200^2 Var\ G + 250^2 Var\ C$$

$$= 40000 Var\ G + 62500 Var\ C$$

G is binomial with $n = 40, p = .6$. So:

$$Var\ G = np(1 - p) = 40(.6)(.4) = 9.6$$

C is binomial with $n = 40, p = .5$. So:

$$Var\ C = np(1 - p) = 40(.5)(.5) = 10$$

$$Var\ X = 40000\ Var\ G + 62500\ Var\ C$$

$$= 40000(9.6) + 62500(10)$$

$$= 1009000$$

The correct answer is **E**.

4. In a gym, 20% of the members are under 16, 45% are between ages $16 - 59$, and remaining members are 60 or older. Four members are randomly selected. Find the expected number of under 16 members given that at least one of the selected members was over 60.

A) .7

B) .8

C) .9

D) 1.0

E) 1.1

Solution:

$100\% - 20\% - 45\% = 35\%$ of the members are over 60.

Let X be the number of under 16 members selected.

Let Y be the number of over 60 members selected.

We are to find $E[X|Y \geq 1]$.

Here we will use the law of total expectation:

$$E[X] = \sum_k P(Y = k)E[X|Y = k]$$

$$= P(Y = 0)E[X|Y = 0] + P(Y \geq 1)E[X|Y \geq 1]$$

This gives:

$$E[X|Y \geq 1] = \frac{E[X] - P(Y = 0)E[X|Y = 0]}{P(Y \geq 1)} \qquad (1)$$

We now go about finding the quantities on the right side of (1).

Y is binomial with $n = 4, p = .35$

$$P(no\ over\ 60\ member\ is\ selected) = P(Y = 0)$$

$$= \binom{4}{0}(.35)^0(1 - .35)^{4-0} = .1785$$

$$P(at\ least\ one\ \ over\ 60\ member\ is\ selected) = P(Y \geq 1) = 1 - P(Y = 0)$$

$$= 1 - .1785 = .8215$$

X is also binomial with $n = 4$, $p = .2$. So

$$E[X] = np = 4(.2) = .8$$

We now have all we need except $E[X|Y = 0]$.

For this, we note that $X|Y = 0$ means the number of under 16 members selected, given that there are no over 60 members among the 4 selected.

$$P[under\ 16|not\ over\ 60] = \frac{P(under\ 16\ and\ not\ over\ 60)}{P(not\ over\ 60)} = \frac{.2}{1-.35} = \frac{4}{13}$$

So, $X|Y = 0$ is binomial with $n = 4,\ p = \frac{4}{13}$. Thus,

$$E[X|Y = 0] = np = 4\left(\frac{4}{13}\right) = 1.2308$$

We now have all the values on the right side of (1). So,

$$E[X|Y \geq 1] = \frac{.8 - .1785(1.2308)}{.8215} = .7$$

The correct answer is **A**.

5. Three distinct integers are chosen randomly and without replacement from the first nine positive integers. Let X be the random variable representing the second largest of the three selected. Let p be the probability function for X.

   Find $p(x)$ for integer values of x, where $p(x) > 0$.

   A. $\frac{(8-x)(x-1)}{84}$

   B. $\frac{(8-x)(x-1)}{168}$

   C. $\frac{(9-x)(x-1)}{84}$

   D. $\frac{(9-x)(x-1)}{168}$

   E. $\frac{(9-x)(x-2)}{84}$

Solution:

No matter which of the 3 integers are chosen from the first nine, since X is the 2nd largest of the three, so there must be exactly one larger than it, and one smaller than it.

We can never have a smaller integer than 1, and we can never have a larger integer than 9. So, $X \neq 1\ or\ 9$.

x	Larger Integers	# of ways to get a larger integer	Smaller integers	# of ways to get a smaller integer
2	3,4,5,6,7,8,9	$7 = 9 - 2$	1	$\binom{1}{1}$
3	4,5,6,7,8,9	$6 = 9 - 3$	1,2	$\binom{2}{1}$
4	5,6,7,8,9	$5 = 9 - 4$	1,2,3	$\binom{3}{1}$

The pattern is now clear. There are:

$$9 - x \text{ ways to get an integer larger than x}$$

$$\binom{x-1}{1}\ ways\ to\ get\ an\ integer\ smaller\ than\ x$$

Also, there are $\binom{9}{3}$ ways of selecting three integers out of nine. So:

$$p(x) = \frac{Number\ of\ ways\ in\ which\ X\ is\ the\ 2nd\ largest\ integer\ in\ three}{ways\ to\ select\ three\ integers\ out\ of\ nine}$$

$$= \frac{(ways\ to\ get\ an\ integer > X)(ways\ to\ get\ an\ integer < X)}{ways\ to\ select\ three\ integers\ out\ of\ nine}$$

$$= \frac{(9-x) * \binom{x-1}{1}}{\binom{9}{3}}$$

Recall that:

$$\binom{n}{r} = \frac{n!}{r!\,(n-r)!}$$

So,

$$p(x) = \frac{(9-x) * \frac{(x-1)!}{1!\,(x-1-1)!}}{\binom{9}{3}}$$

$$= \frac{(9-x) * \frac{(x-1)!}{(x-2)!}}{84}$$

$$= \frac{(9-x) * \frac{(x-1)(x-2)!}{(x-2)!}}{84}$$

$$= \frac{(9-x) * (x-1)}{84}$$

The correct answer is **C**.

6. Auto losses covered by an insurance policy are uniform on [0, 3000]. An insurance company reimburses losses in excess of a deductible of 500. Calculate the difference between the 75th and the 25th percentile of the insurance company reimbursement, over all losses.

(A) 1250

(B) 1500

(C) 1750

(D) 2000

(E) 2250

Solution:

Let X be the loss and Y be the reimbursement.

$$Y = \begin{cases} 0, & X \leq 500 \\ X - 500, & X > 500 \end{cases}$$

We have the following picture:

$X = 500$

$Y = 0$

$X = 0$ 25th Percentile 75th percentile $X = 3000$

$Y = 0$ $X_{25} = 750$ $X_{75} = .75(3000)$ $Y = 750$

$Y_{25} = 750 - 500 = 250$ $= 2250$

$Y_{75} = 2250 - 500$

$= 1750$

The required difference is:

$$Y_{75} - Y_{25} = 1750 - 250$$
$$= 1500$$

The correct answer is **B**.

Tools Needed for Problems 182-193

A and B are independent if and only if $P(AB) = P(A)P(B)$

The binomial pmf is:

$$f(x) = \binom{n}{x}(p)^x(1-p)^{n-x}$$

$$P(A|B) = \frac{P(AB)}{P(B)}$$

$$P(A \cup B \cup C) = P(A) + P(B) + P(C) - P(AB) - P(AC) - P(BC) + P(ABC)$$

If A and B are mutually exclusive events, then $P(AB) = 0$.

If $P(AB) = 0$, then for any event X, we have:

$$P(ABX) = 0$$

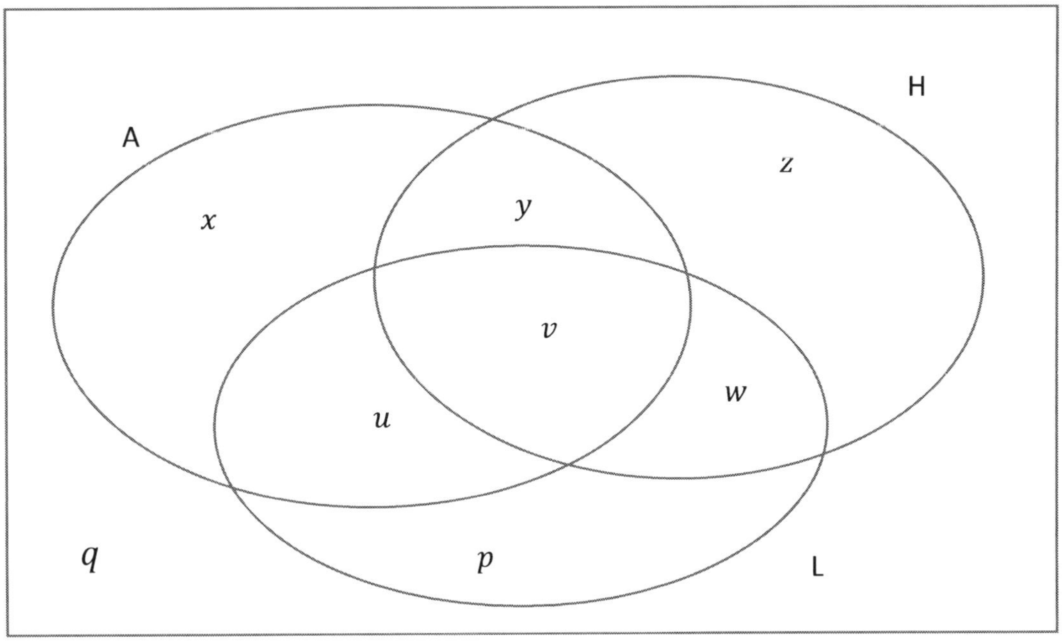

Using diagram and conditions (i) through (vii) we get the following equations:

$$x + y + u + v = 243 \quad (1)$$

$$y + z + v + w = 207 \quad (2)$$

$$v + w = 55 \quad (3)$$

$$y + v = 96 \quad (4)$$

$$\boldsymbol{v = 32} \quad (5)$$

$$x = p + 76 \quad (6)$$

$$x + z + p = 270 \quad (7)$$

We are to find $x + y + z + u + v + w + p$.

Substituting the value of v from (5) in (3) and (4) we get.

$$w = 23$$

$$y = 64$$

Substituting the value of v, w, y in (2) we get:

$$64 + z + 32 + 23 = 207$$

$$z = 88$$

From (6) we get $p = x - 76$. Substituting this, and $z = 88$ in (7), we have:

$$x + 88 + x - 76 = 270$$

$$x = 129$$

Substituting the value of v, x, y in (1) we get:

$$129 + 64 + u + 32 = 243$$

$$u = 18$$

$$p = x - 76$$

$$= 129 - 76$$

$$= 53$$

$$x + y + z + u + v + w + p = 129 + 64 + 88 + 18 + 32 + 23 + 53$$

$$= 407$$

The correct answer is **B**.

SOA Sample Question 183 Explanation

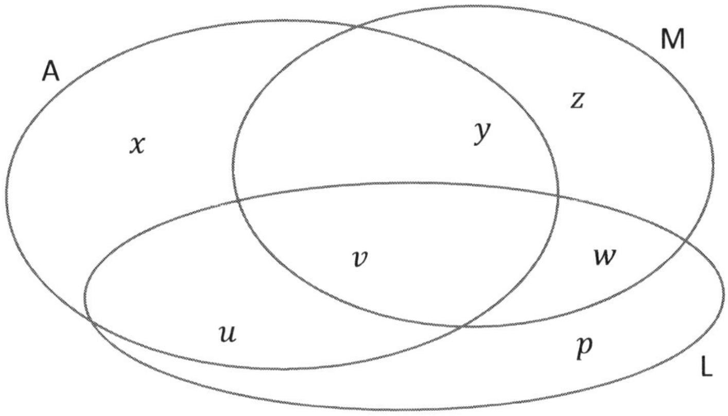

using diagram and conditions (i) through (vii) we get the following equations:

$$x + y + u + v = 228 \quad (1)$$

$$y + z + v + w = 220 \quad (2)$$

$$v + w = 98 \quad (3)$$

$$y + v = 93 \quad (4)$$

$$\boldsymbol{v} = \mathbf{16} \quad (5)$$

$$p = x + 45 \quad (6)$$

$$x + z + p = 290 \quad (7)$$

We are to find $x + y + z + u + v + w + p$.

Substituting the value of v from (5) in (3) and (4) we get.

$$w = 82 \qquad y = 77$$

Substituting the value of v, w, y in (2) we get:

$$77 + z + 16 + 82 = 220$$

$$z = 45$$

Substituting the value of p From (6) , and $z = 45$ in (7), we have:

$$x + 45 + x + 45 = 290$$

$$x = 100$$

Substituting the value of v, x, y in (1) we get:

$$100 + 77 + u + 16 = 228$$

$$u = 35$$

$$p = x + 45 = 100 + 45 = 145$$

$$x + y + z + u + v + w + p = 100 + 77 + 45 + 35 + 16 + 82 + 145 = 500$$

The correct answer is **D**.

SOA Sample Question 184 Explanation

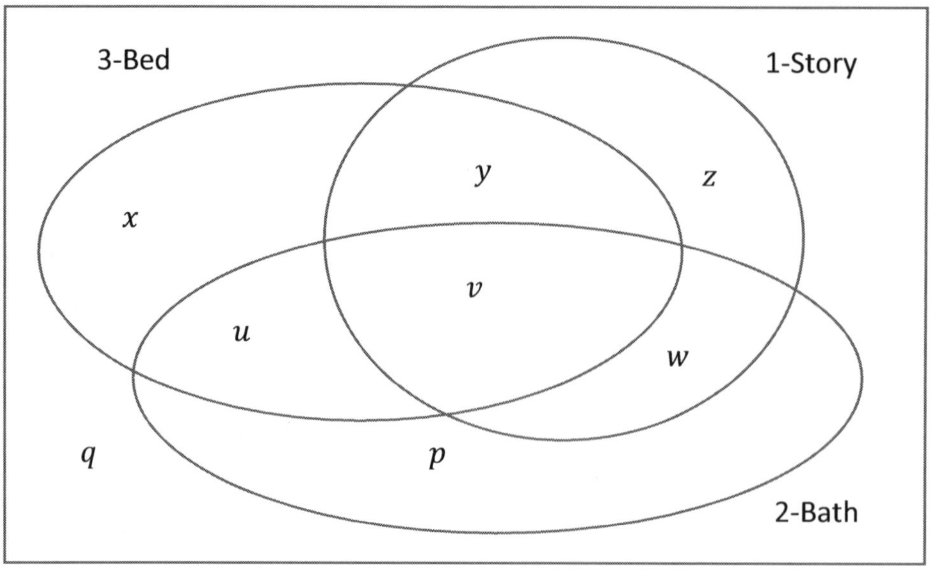

Using diagram and conditions (i) through (vii) we get the following equations:

$$x + y + u + v = 130 \quad (1)$$

$$y + z + v + w = 280 \quad (2)$$

$$u + v + w + p = 150 \quad (3)$$

$$u + v = 30 \quad (4)$$

$$v + w = 50 \quad (5)$$

$$v + y = 40 \quad (6)$$

$$v = 10 \quad (7)$$

We are to find q.

Substituting the value of v from (7) in (4),(5) and (6) we get.

$$u = 20$$

$$w = 40$$

$$y = 30$$

Substituting the value of v, u, y in (1) we get:

$$x + 30 + 20 + 10 = 130$$

$$x = 70$$

Substituting the value of v, w, y in (2) we get:

$$30 + z + 10 + 40 = 280$$

$$z = 200$$

Substituting the value of u, v, w in (3) we get:

$$20 + 10 + 40 + p = 150$$

$$p = 80$$

$$q = 1000 - (x + y + z + u + v + w + p)$$

$$= 1000 - (70 + 30 + 200 + 20 + 10 + 40 + 80) = 550$$

The correct answer is **D**.

SOA Sample Question 185 Explanation

In essence, we need to find the number of possible subcommittees with a chair.

Number of Possible 4-member subcommittees from 7 persons $= \binom{7}{4} = 35$

Number of ways to choose a chair from the 4 sub-committee members $= 4$

Number of ways to have a 4-member sub-committee, and a chair $= 35(4) = 140$

Thus, under the given conditions, we can have 140 different possibilities.

Since a possible committee change happens every week, so 140 is the maximum number of weeks that can elapse without a repetition.

The correct answer is **B**.

SOA Sample Question 186 Explanation

Bowl 1 contains $8 + 6 = 14$ balls.

Ways to pick 4 from 14 $= \binom{14}{4} = 1001.$

Given the ball selected from bowl II is blue, the 4 balls transferred must have at least one blue.

Transfer	# of Transfers	$P(Transfer)$	P(Transfer and pick Blue)
0R, 4B	$\binom{8}{0}\binom{6}{4} = 15$	$\frac{15}{1001}$	$\frac{15}{1001}\left(\frac{4}{4}\right) = .015$
1R, 3B	$\binom{8}{1}\binom{6}{3} = 160$	$\frac{160}{1001}$	$\frac{160}{1001}\left(\frac{3}{4}\right) = .12$
2R, 2B	$\binom{8}{2}\binom{6}{2} = 420$	$\frac{420}{1001}$	$\frac{420}{1001}\left(\frac{2}{4}\right) = .21$
3R, 1B	$\binom{8}{3}\binom{6}{1} = 336$	$\frac{336}{1001}$	$\frac{336}{1001}\left(\frac{1}{4}\right) = .084$

$$P(2R, 2B\ transferred | pick\ B) = \frac{P(2R, 2B\ transferred\ and\ pick\ B)}{P(pick\ B)}$$

$$= \frac{.21}{.015 + .12 + .21 + .084} = .49$$

The correct answer is **D**.

SOA Sample Question 187 Explanation

A policy will have same number of claims on both cars if there are either 0 or 1 or 2 or 3 claims on both cars.

Let $P(A), P(B)$ be the probabilities of the selected policy being A or B respectively.

$$P(A) = .4(.4) + .3(.3) + .2(.2) + .1(.1)$$

$$= .3$$

$$P(B) = .25(.25) + .25(.25) + .25(.25) + .25(.25)$$

$$= .25$$

$$P(randomly\ selected\ policy\ has\ equal\ claims\ on\ both\ cars)$$
$$= P(Policy\ A\ and\ equal\ claims, or\ Policy\ B\ and\ equal\ claims)$$

$$= .7(.3) + .3(.25)$$

$$= .285$$

The policies, X, that have equal claims for both cars is binomial $n = 4, p = .285$

$$f(x) = \binom{4}{x}(.285)^x(1 - .285)^{4-x}$$

$$P(X = 1) = f(1)$$

$$= .417$$

The correct answer is **D**.

SOA Sample Question 188 Explanation

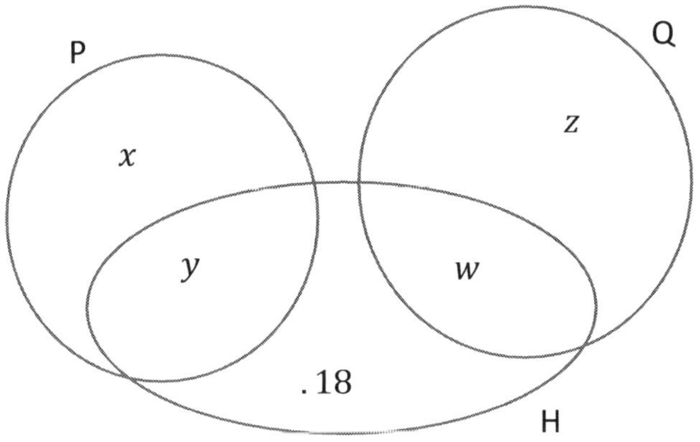

Condition (i) tells us that there is no intersection between P and Q

Condition (iv) gives the .18 in the diagram.

We are asked to find $x + z + .18$

Condition (ii) gives:

$$x + y = 2(z + w) \quad (1)$$

Condition (iii) gives:

$$y + w + .18 = .45$$

$$y + w = .27 \quad (2)$$

Condition (v) gives:

$$P(Health\ and\ Life) = P(Health)P(Life)$$

$$y + w = (y + w + .18)(x + y + z + w) \quad (3)$$

Substituting eq (2) in eq (3) we get:

$$.27 = (.27 + .18)(x + z + .27)$$

$$(x + z + .27) = .6$$

$$x + z = .33$$

$$x + z + .18 = .33 + .18$$

$$= .51$$

The correct answer is **A**.

SOA Sample Question 189 Explanation

The state gets a total revenue of 800,000 (1 per entry).

State will lose money if there are 2 or more total winners because each winner gets 500,000.

Number of ways to choose 6 integers from 30 is $\binom{30}{6}$.

Only one of these combinations wins.

So, the probability of success of a single person is:

$$p = \frac{1}{\binom{30}{6}}$$

$$= \frac{1}{593775}$$

The total number of winners, X, is binomial with $n = 800000,\ p = \frac{1}{593775}$

$$f(x) = P(X = x)$$

$$= \binom{800000}{x}\left(\frac{1}{593775}\right)^{x}\left(1 - \frac{1}{593775}\right)^{800000-x}$$

We are looking for the probability of 2 or more winners, that is, $P(X \geq 2)$.

$$P(X \geq 2) = 1 - P(X < 2)$$

$$= 1 - f(0) - f(1)$$

$$= 1 - .26 - .35$$

$$= .39$$

The correct answer is **B**.

SOA Sample Question 190 Explanation

The number of applications with errors, X, is binomial with $n = 100,\ p = .03$

$$f(x) = \binom{100}{x}(.03)^{x}(.97)^{100-x}$$

95 or less applications being error free means 5 or more have errors.

$$P(X \geq 5) = 1 - P(X < 5)$$

$$= 1 - f(0) - f(1) - f(2) - f(3) - f(4)$$

$$= 1 - .04755 - .14707 - .22515 - .22747 - .17061$$

$$= .18$$

The correct answer is **E**.

SOA Sample Question 191 Explanation

The independence conditions give:

$$P(AB) = P(A)P(B)$$

$$P(BC) = P(B)P(C)$$

The mutually exclusive condition gives:

$$P(AC) = 0$$

This also implies that $P(ABC) = 0$, because if A and C cannot occur at the same time, then A, B, and C can also not occur at the same time.

We now use the generalized addition rule:

$$P(A \cup B \cup C) = P(A) + P(B) + P(C) - P(AB) - P(AC) - P(BC) + P(ABC)$$

$$= P(A) + P(B) + P(C) - P(A)P(B) - 0 - P(B)P(C) + 0$$

$$= .2 + .1 + .3 - .2(.1) - .1(.3)$$

$$= .55$$

The correct answer is **D**.

SOA Sample Question 192 Explanation

The probability of a union of events equals the sum of individual event probabilities if the events are disjoint or mutually exclusive, that is, the occurrence of any one of the events rules out all others in the union.

(A) Is the correct choice because if any one of A, B, or E occurs, it rules out the other 2. For example, if A occurs, then there are no thefts in 3 years. This means B cannot occur because B says that there is a theft in the 2nd year. Also, E cannot occur because E says that there is a theft in the 3rd year.
(B) Is not true because C and E can occur at the same time.
(C) Is not true because A and D can occur at the same time.
(D) Is not true because B and C can occur at the same time.
(E) Is not true because B and C can occur at the same time.

The correct answer is **A**.

SOA Sample Question 193 Explanation

Let the letters and envelopes be numbered 1,2,3, and 4.

P (at least one letter in correct envelope) = P (letter 1 in correct envelope, or letter 1 in wrong envelope and at least one of the others in correct envelope) (1)

$$P(Letter\ 1\ in\ correct\ envelope) = \frac{1}{4}$$

$$P(Letter\ 1\ in\ wrong\ envelope) = \frac{3}{4}$$

So, eq (1) becomes:

$$P(at\ least\ one\ correct\ envelope)$$
$$= \frac{1}{4} + \frac{3}{4} P(one\ of\ others\ in\ correct\ given\ 1st\ wrong) \quad (2)$$

Given that 1st is in wrong envelope, suppose it was put in the envelope for 2nd letter.

So now, we are left with letters 2,3,4, and envelopes 1,3,4.

Now, the possibilities for the remaining letters are:

$$P_1 = \begin{pmatrix} L & 2\,3\,4 \\ E & 1\,3\,4 \end{pmatrix}, P_2 = \begin{pmatrix} L & 2\,3\,4 \\ E & 1\,4\,3 \end{pmatrix}, P_3 = \begin{pmatrix} L & 2\,3\,4 \\ E & 3\,1\,4 \end{pmatrix},$$

$$P_4 = \begin{pmatrix} L & 2\,3\,4 \\ E & 3\,4\,1 \end{pmatrix}, P_5 = \begin{pmatrix} L & 2\,3\,4 \\ E & 4\,1\,3 \end{pmatrix}, P_6 = \begin{pmatrix} L & 2\,3\,4 \\ E & 4\,3\,1 \end{pmatrix}$$

Of these 6 possibilities, exactly half, i.e, P_1, P_3, P_6 have one correct placement. So,

$$P(one\ of\ others\ in\ correct\ given\ 1st\ wrong) = \frac{3}{6} = \frac{1}{2}$$

Hence, equation (2) becomes:

$$P(at\ least\ one\ correct\ envelope) = \frac{1}{4} + \frac{3}{4}\left(\frac{1}{2}\right)$$

$$= \frac{5}{8}$$

The correct answer is **D**.

Quiz 17

1. A club offers only tennis, golf, and swimming as its activities.

i) 120 members like tennis.

ii) 110 members like golf.

iii) 60 members like golf and swimming.

iv) 55 members like tennis and golf.

v) 11 members like all the three activities.

vi) 24 more members like only swimming than ones who like only tennis.

vii) 130 members like only one of the 3 activities.

Calculate the total number of gym members.

A) 241
B) 243
C) 245
D) 247
E) 249

Solution:

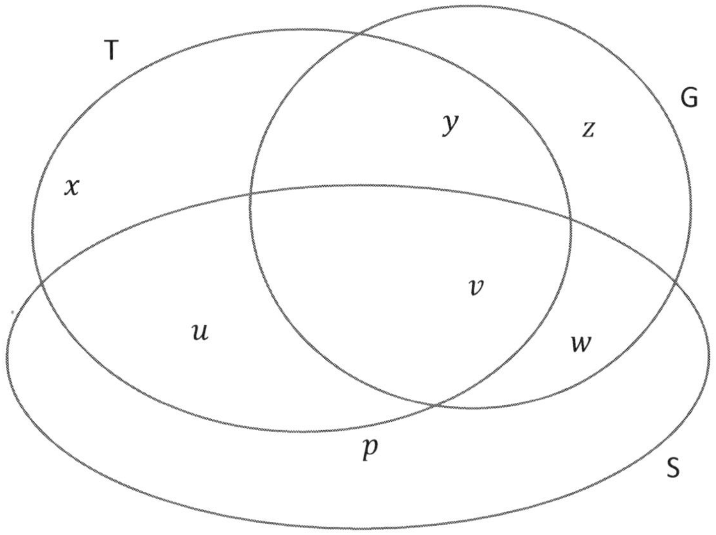

Using diagram and conditions (i) through (vii) we get the following equations:

$$x + y + u + v = 120 \quad (1)$$

$$y + z + v + w = 110 \quad (2)$$

$$v + w = 60 \quad (3)$$

$$y + v = 55 \quad (4)$$

$$\boldsymbol{v = 11} \quad (5)$$

$$p = x + 24 \quad (6)$$

$$x + z + p = 130 \quad (7)$$

We are to find $x + y + z + u + v + w + p$.

Substituting the value of v from (5) in (3) and (4) we get.

$$w = 49$$

$$y = 44$$

Substituting the value of v, w, y in (2) we get:

$$44 + z + 11 + 49 = 110$$

$$z = 6$$

Substituting the value of p From (6) , and $z = 6$ in equation (7), we have:

$$x + 6 + x + 24 = 130$$

$$x = 50$$

Substituting the value of v, x, y in (1) we get:

$$50 + 44 + u + 11 = 120$$

$$u = 15$$

$$p = x + 24 = 50 + 24 = 74$$

$$x + y + z + u + v + w + p = 50 + 44 + 6 + 15 + 11 + 49 + 74 = 249$$

The correct answer is **E**.

2. In every session of a yoga group of 8 persons, three people are randomly placed in the 1st row, and one of those three is chosen as the leader for the session. Find the number of ways in which this can be done.

A) 168

B) 204

C) 240

D) 288

E) 336

Solution:

Number of ways to choose three 1st rowers from 8 = $\binom{8}{3} = 56$

Number of ways to choose a leader from the three 1st rowers = 3

Number of ways to choose three 1st rowers, and a leader = $56(3) = 168$

The correct answer is **A**.

3. There are 12 children at an orphanage, 7 boys and 5 girls. A couple adopts 3 of these children. An interviewer speaks to one of these adopted children, who happens to be a girl. Find the probability that she was the only girl adopted.

A) .35

B) .38

C) .41

D) .44

E) .47

Solution:

She would be the only girl adopted if 2 boys and 1 girl were adopted.

Ways to pick 3 children from 12 = $\binom{12}{3} = 220$.

Given the child interviewed is a girl, the 3 adoptions must have at least one girl.

All such possible 3-child adoptions are tabulated below:

Adoption	# of ways	$P(Adoption)$	P(Adoption and girl interviewed)
0B, 3G	$\binom{7}{0}\binom{5}{3} = 10$	$\frac{10}{220}$	$\frac{10}{220}\left(\frac{3}{3}\right) = \frac{1}{22}$
1B, 2G	$\binom{7}{1}\binom{5}{2} = 70$	$\frac{70}{220}$	$\frac{70}{220}\left(\frac{2}{3}\right) = \frac{7}{33}$
2B, 1G	$\binom{7}{2}\binom{5}{1} = 105$	$\frac{105}{220}$	$\frac{105}{220}\left(\frac{1}{3}\right) = \frac{7}{44}$

$$P(2B, 1G\ adopted | G\ interviewed) = \frac{P(2B, 1G\ adopted\ and\ G\ interviewed)}{P(G\ interviewed)}$$

$$= \frac{\frac{7}{44}}{\frac{1}{22} + \frac{7}{33} + \frac{7}{44}}$$

$$= .38$$

The correct answer is **B**.

4. In city X, of all the people who have exactly one home and exactly one car insured, 40% use insurance company A for both home and car, and 60% use insurance company B for both home and car. The number of claims on different homes and cars across all policies are mutually independent. The annual distributions of the number of claims for different people are tabulated:

Number of claims	Company A	Company B
0	10%	15%
1	30%	25%
2	45%	35%
3	15%	25%

Three policy holders are selected at random. Calculate the probability that exactly one of the three has the same number of home and auto claims.

A) .40
B) .42
C) .44
D) .46
E) .48

Solution:

A policy holder will have same number of claims on both home and auto if there are either 0 or 1 or 2 or 3 claims on both.

Let $P(A), P(B)$ be probabilities of the selected person having policy being A or B respectively.

$$P(A) = .1(.1) + .3(.3) + .45(.45) + .15(.15)$$

$$= .325$$

$$P(B) = .15(.15) + .25(.25) + .35(.35) + .25(.25)$$

$$= .27$$

$$P(same\ home\ and\ auto\ claims)$$
$$= P(Policy\ A\ and\ equal\ claims, or\ Policy\ B\ has\ equal\ claims)$$

$$= .4(.325) + .6(.27)$$

$$= .292$$

The policies, X, that have equal claims for both things is binomial $n = 3, p = .292$

$$f(x) = \binom{3}{x}(.292)^x(1 - .292)^{3-x}$$

$$P(X = 1) = f(1)$$

$$= .44$$

The correct answer is **C**.

5. Students at a university were surveyed about Math, Dance and Biology:

i) No student liked both Math and Dance.

ii) Thrice as many students liked Dance as Math.

iii) 55% students liked Biology.

iv) 26% students liked only Biology.

v) The event that a student liked Biology was independent of the event that he or she liked any of the other two subjects.

Find the probability that a random student liked exactly 1 of the 3 subjects.

(A) 0.50

(B) 0.52

(C) 0.54

(D) 0.56

(E) 0.58

Solution:

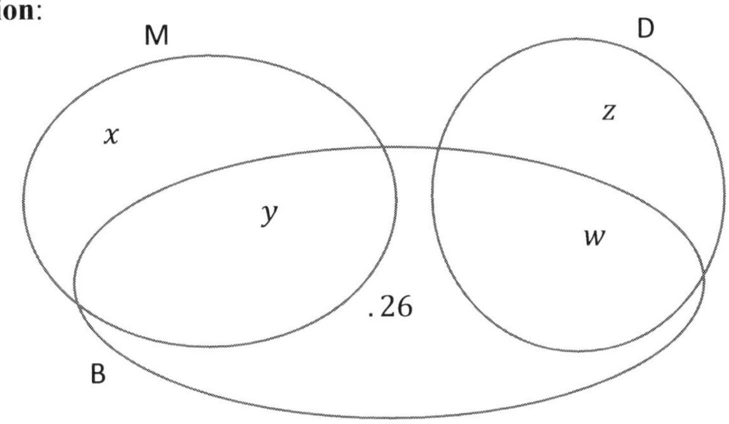

Condition (i) tells us that there is no intersection between M and D.

Condition (iv) gives the .26 in the diagram.

We are asked to find $x + z + .26$

Condition (ii) gives:

$$z + w = 3(x + y) \quad (1)$$

Condition (iii) gives:

$$y + w + .26 = .55$$

$$y + w = .29 \quad (2)$$

Condition (v) gives:

$$P(Biology\ and\ Others) = P(Bilogy)P(Others)$$

$$y + w = (y + w + .26)(x + y + z + w) \quad (3)$$

Substituting eq (2) in eq (3) we get:

$$.29 = (.29 + .26)(x + z + .29)$$

$$(x + z + .29) = .53$$

$$x + z = .24$$

$$x + z + .26 = .24 + .26$$

$$= .5$$

The correct answer is **A**.

6. A state is starting a lottery. To enter this lottery, a player selects four distinct numbers from among the first 20 positive integers. The lottery runners also randomly select four distinct numbers from the same 20 positive integers. A winning entry must match the same set of four numbers that the lottery selected. The entry fee is 3, each winning entry receives a prize amount of 40,000, and all other entries receive no prize. Find the probability that the state will win money, given that 50,000 entries are purchased.

A) .00516

B) .00616

C) .00716

D) .00816

E) .00916

Solution:

The state gets a total revenue of 150,000 (3 per entry).

State will win money if there are 3 or less total winners because each winner gets 40,000, and so 3 winners will get a total of 120,000 which is still less than the state revenue of 150,000.

But 4 winners will mean a total prize of 160,000 and state loses.

Number of ways to choose 4 integers from 20 is $\binom{20}{4}$. Only one of these combinations wins. So, the probability of success of a single person is:

$$p = \frac{1}{\binom{20}{4}} = \frac{1}{4845}$$

The total number of winners, X, is binomial with $n = 50000,\ p = \frac{1}{4845}$

$$f(x) = P(X = x)$$

$$= \binom{50000}{x}\left(\frac{1}{4845}\right)^{x}\left(1 - \frac{1}{4845}\right)^{50000-x}$$

We are looking for the probability of 3 or fewer winners, that is, $P(X \leq 3)$.

$$P(X \leq 3) = f(0) + f(1) + f(2) + f(3)$$

$$= .000033 + .000340 + .001754 + .006036$$

$$= .00816$$

The correct answer is **D**.

7. There is a 6% probability that a person in a certain town will catch flue during October. Find the probability that among 30 randomly chosen residents of the town, 80% or fewer will not catch flue.

A) .005

B) .008

C) .011

D) .014

E) .017

Solution:

If X is the number of people who catch flue, it is binomial $n = 30,\ p = .06$

$$f(x) = \binom{30}{x}(.06)^x(.94)^{30-x}$$

80% of 30 is $(.8)(30) = 24$.

So we are asked to find the probability that 24 or fewer do not catch flue.

24 or less out of 30 being flue-free means 6 or more catch flue.

$$P(X \geq 6) = 1 - P(X < 6)$$

$$= 1 - f(0) - f(1) - f(2) - f(3) - f(4) - f(5)$$

$$= 1 - .1563 - .2992 - .2769 - .165 - .0711 - .0236$$

$$= .008$$

The correct answer is **B**.

8. Let A, B, and C be events such that $P[A] = 0.3, P[B] = 0.4$, and $P[C] = 0.1$. The events A and B are independent, the events A and C are independent, and the events B and C are mutually exclusive. Calculate $P[A \; U \; B \; U \; C]$.

A) .50

B) .55

C) .60

D) .65

E) .70

Solution:

The independence conditions give:

$$P(AB) = P(A)P(B)$$

$$P(AC) = P(A)P(C)$$

The mutually exclusive condition gives:

$$P(BC) = 0$$

This also implies that $P(ABC) = 0$, because if B and C cannot occur at the same time, then A, B, and C can also not occur at the same time.

We now use the generalized addition rule:

$$P(A \cup B \cup C) = P(A) + P(B) + P(C) - P(AB) - P(AC) - P(BC) + P(ABC)$$

$$= P(A) + P(B) + P(C) - P(A)P(B) - P(A)P(C) - 0 + 0$$

$$= .3 + .4 + .1 - .3(.4) - .3(.1)$$

$$= .65$$

The correct answer is **D**.

9. Ann, Kate, Liz, and Mary are not related, and they all write letters to their moms. Each letter is then randomly sent to one of the four moms. Find the probability that none of the moms receive her daughter's letter.

A) .125

B) .250

C) .375

D) .500

E) .625

Solution:

Let the letters be called A, K, L, M.

P (at least one letter to correct mom) = P (letter A to correct mom, or letter A to wrong mom and at least one of the other letters to correct mom)   (1)

$$P(Letter\ A\ to\ correct\ mom) = \frac{1}{4}$$

$$P(Letter\ A\ to\ wrong\ mom) = \frac{3}{4}$$

So, eq (1) becomes:

$$P(at\ least\ one\ correct\ sending)$$
$$= \frac{1}{4} + \frac{3}{4} P(one\ of\ others\ in\ correct\ given\ A\ wrong) \quad (2)$$

Given that A is sent wrong, suppose it was sent to K's mom.

So now, we are left with letters K, L, M and moms of A, L, M.

Now, the possibilities for the remaining letters are (top rows for letters, bottom rows for moms):

$$P_1 = \begin{pmatrix} K\ L\ M \\ A\ L\ M \end{pmatrix}, P_2 = \begin{pmatrix} K\ L\ M \\ A\ M\ L \end{pmatrix}, P_3 = \begin{pmatrix} K\ L\ M \\ L\ A\ M \end{pmatrix},$$

$$P_4 = \begin{pmatrix} K\ L\ M \\ L\ M\ A \end{pmatrix}, P_5 = \begin{pmatrix} K\ L\ M \\ M\ L\ A \end{pmatrix}, P_6 = \begin{pmatrix} K\ L\ M \\ M\ A\ L \end{pmatrix}$$

Of these 6 possibilities, exactly half, i.e, P_1, P_3, P_5 have one correct placement. So

$$P(one\ of\ others\ in\ correct\ given\ A\ wrong) = \frac{3}{6} = \frac{1}{2}$$

Hence, equation (2) becomes:

$$P(at\ least\ one\ letter\ to\ correct\ mom) = \frac{1}{4} + \frac{3}{4}\left(\frac{1}{2}\right) = \frac{5}{8}$$

$$P(no\ letter\ to\ correct\ mom) = 1 - \frac{5}{8}$$

$$= .375$$

The correct answer is **C**.

Tools Needed for Problems 194-207

$$F(k) = P(X \leq k)$$

A and B are independent if and only if $P(AB) = P(A)P(B)$

The pmf of geometric distribution is:

$$f(n) = (1-p)^{n-1}p$$

Where n is the number of trials for 1st success, and p is the probability of success on each trial.

The binomial pmf is:

$$f(x) = \binom{n}{x}(p)^x(1-p)^{n-x}$$

$$P(A|B) = \frac{P(AB)}{P(B)}$$

$$P(A \cup B) = P(A) + P(B) - P(AB)$$

$$\binom{n}{r} = \frac{n!}{r!\,(n-r)!}$$

The pmf of a Poisson variable X with mean m is:

$$f(x) = \frac{m^x e^{-m}}{x!}, x = 0,1,2,3, \ldots$$

$$z = \frac{X-\mu}{\sigma}$$

The pdf and cdf of an exponential distribution with mean m are:

$$f(x) = \frac{1}{m}e^{-\frac{x}{m}}, \qquad x > 0$$

$$F(x) = 1 - e^{-\frac{x}{m}}$$

$$P(a \leq X \leq b) = F(b) - F(a)$$

All measurements, for example, heights, weights, times, are continuous variables.

For continuous variables it makes no difference whether the probability expressions have strict inequalities or non-strict inequalities.

SOA Sample Question 194 Explanation

Cost will exceed deductible in case of 4 or more visits because then the cost will be 400 or more.

For 3 visits, the cost is 300 which is less than deductible.

We are given that the policy cost exceeds deductible, that is, $V \geq 4$.

$$P(V = 5|V \geq 4) = \frac{P(V = 5 \text{ and } V \geq 4)}{P(V \geq 4)}$$

$$= \frac{P(V = 5)}{P(V \geq 4)}$$

$$= \frac{.02}{.04 + .02 + .01}$$

$$= .286$$

The correct answer is **C**.

SOA Sample Question 195 Explanation

$$P(A) = .8$$

$$P(B) = .6$$

$$P(A \cup B) = .9$$

We need to find $P(B|A)$.

$$P(B|A) = \frac{P(AB)}{P(A)} \quad (1)$$

To find $P(AB)$ we use the addition rule:

$$P(A \cup B) = P(A) + P(B) - P(AB)$$

$$.9 = .8 + .6 - P(AB)$$

$$P(AB) = .5$$

Equation (1) becomes:

$$P(B|A) = \frac{.5}{.8}$$

$$= \frac{5}{8}$$

The correct answer is **C**.

SOA Sample Question 196 Explanation

Number of ways to pick 1 worker compensation claim out of 2 = $\binom{2}{1}$

Number of ways to pick 2 homeowners claims out of 4 = $\binom{4}{2}$

Number of ways to pick 3 auto claims out of 7 = $\binom{7}{3}$

Total Number of ways to pick 6 claims out of 13 = $\binom{13}{6}$

Using hypergeometric formula:

$$P(1W, 2H, 3A) = \frac{(\#\ of\ ways\ 1W)(\#\ of\ ways\ 2H)(\#\ of\ ways\ 3A)}{\#\ of\ ways\ to\ pick\ 6\ claims}$$

$$= \frac{\binom{2}{1}\binom{4}{2}\binom{7}{3}}{\binom{13}{6}}$$

$$= .245$$

The correct answer is **D**.

SOA Sample Question 197 Explanation

It is possible to draw 4 different colors in the first 4 draws, but then the 5th draw will definitely produce an already drawn color because there are only 4 total colors.

So, the maximum number of draws for a matching pair is 5.

To get 4 different colors in the first four draws we must have the following:

For the 1st draw, the total available socks are 8, and we can pick any of these 8. *Probability* 8/8.

For the 2nd draw, the total available socks are 7, but to get a different color, draw must be from one from the remaining 3 pairs (6 socks). *Probability* 6/7.

For the 3rd draw, the total available socks are 6, but to get a different color, draw must be from one from the remaining 2 pairs (4 socks). *Probability* 4/6.

For the 4th draw, the total available socks are 5, but to get a different color, draw must be from one from the remaining 1 pairs (2 socks). *Probability* 2/5.

$$P(5\ draws\ until\ a\ pair) = \frac{8}{8}\left(\frac{6}{7}\right)\left(\frac{4}{6}\right)\left(\frac{2}{5}\right)$$

$$= .2286$$

The correct answer is **E**.

SOA Sample Question 198 Explanation

Let M be the event that a person applies for mortgage.

Let A be the event that a person initially spoke to an attendant.

Let S be the event that a person left number and were called back the same day.

Let N be the event that a person left number and were called back the next day.

We are to find $P(A|M)$.

$$P(M) = P(A\&M) + P(S\&M) + P(N\&M)$$

$$= .6(.8) + .4(.75)(.6) + .4(.25)(.4)$$

$$= .7$$

$$P(A|M) = \frac{P(A\&M)}{P(M)}$$

$$= \frac{.6(.8)}{.7}$$

$$= .69$$

The correct answer is **E**.

SOA Sample Question 199 Explanation

Lifting Type	Proportion	Claim Probability	P (Lifting Type and Claim)
No (N)	.4	.05	$.4(.05) = .02$
Moderate (M)	.5	.08	$.5(.08) = .04$
Heavy (H)	.1	.2	$.1(.2) = .02$

$$P(M \text{ or } H, \text{given Claim}) = \frac{P(M \text{ or } H, \text{and Claim})}{P(Claim)}$$

$$= \frac{P(M \text{ and Claim}) + P(H \text{ and Claim})}{P(Claim)}$$

$$= \frac{.04 + .02}{.02 + .04 + .02}$$

$$= .75$$

The correct answer is **A**.

SOA Sample Question 200 Explanation

Let X be the number of accidents in a day in Coralville. Then:

$$P(x\ accidents) = f(x) = \frac{5^x e^{-5}}{x!}$$

P(no accident with uninsured driver) $= P(all\ accidents\ with\ insured\ drivers)$

There can be 0,1,2,3,... total accidents. So,

$$P(all\ accidents\ with\ insured\ drivers)$$

$$= \sum_{k=0}^{\infty} P(k\ accidents\ and\ all\ of\ the\ k\ drivers\ insured)$$

$$= \sum_{k=0}^{\infty} P(k\ accidents)\ P(all\ of\ the\ k\ drivers\ insured)$$

$$P(driver\ insured) = 1 - .25$$

$$= .75$$

$$P(k\ drivers\ insured) = .75^k$$

$$P(all\ accidents\ with\ insured\ drivers) = \sum_{k=0}^{\infty} \left(\frac{5^k e^{-5}}{k!}\right)(.75)^k$$

$$= \sum_{k=0}^{\infty} \left(\frac{e^{-5}}{k!}\right)(.75 * 5)^k$$

$$= \sum_{k=0}^{\infty} \left(\frac{e^{-5}}{k!}\right)(3.75)^k$$

$$= \sum_{k=0}^{\infty} \left(\frac{e^{-3.75-1.25}}{k!}\right)(3.75)^k$$

$$= \sum_{k=0}^{\infty} \left(\frac{e^{-3.75}e^{-1.25}}{k!}\right)(3.75)^k$$

$$= e^{-1.25} \sum_{k=0}^{\infty} \left(\frac{e^{-3.75}}{k!}\right)(3.75)^k$$

$$= e^{-1.25}(sum\ of\ all\ values\ of\ a\ Poisson\ pmf\ with\ mean\ 3.75)$$

$$= e^{-1.25}(1)$$

$$= .287$$

The correct answer is **E**.

SOA Sample Question 201 Explanation

If exactly n patients are tested, this means that the nth patient was the first one who tested positive for more than one risk factors.

This reminds us of a geometric distribution where the first success occurs on the nth trial, the success here being that a patient tests positive for one or more risk factors.

Let G be the probability of a patient testing positive for more than one risk factor.

Let X be the number of risk factors for which a patient tests positive.

Then X is binomial with $n = 3, p = p$, and pmf:

$$f(x) = \binom{3}{x} (p)^x (1-p)^{3-x}$$

$$G = P(X > 1)$$

$$= f(2) + f(3)$$

$$= \binom{3}{2} (p)^2 (1-p)^{3-2} + \binom{3}{3} p^3 (1-p)^{3-3}$$

$$= 3p^2(1-p) + p^3$$

Now, using the formula for the geometric distribution:

$$P(Y = n) = (1 - G)^{n-1} G$$

$$= [1 - 3p^2(1-p) - p^3]^{n-1}[3p^2(1-p) + p^3]$$

The correct answer is **B**.

SOA Sample Question 202 Explanation

If more than 3 calls are needed to have a completed survey, it means that the first three calls produced uncompleted surveys.

$$P(uncompleted\ survey\ in\ one\ call) = 1 - .25$$

$$= .75$$

P(uncompleted survey in 1st three calls) $= .75^3$

$$= .42$$

The correct answer is **B**.

SOA Sample Question 203 Explanation

No matter which of the 4 integers are chosen from the first 12, since X is the 2nd smallest of the four, so there must be exactly one smaller than it, and two larger than it. We can never have two larger integers than either 11 or 12, and we can never have a smaller integer than 1. So, $X \neq 1, 11, or\ 12$. We have the following:

x	Larger Integers	# of ways to get 2 Larger Integers	Smaller Integers	# of ways to get a Smaller Integer
2	3,4,5,…,12 (10 total)	$\binom{10}{2}$	1	1
3	4,5,6,…,12 (9 total)	$\binom{9}{2}$	1,2	2
4	5,6,7,…,12 (8 total)	$\binom{8}{2}$	1,2,3	3
5	6,7,8,…,12 (7 total)	$\binom{7}{2}$	1,2,3,4	4

The pattern is now clear. There are:

$$\binom{12-x}{2}\ ways\ to\ get\ two\ integers\ larger\ than\ x.$$

$$x-1\ ways\ to\ get\ an\ integer\ smaller\ than\ x.$$

Also, there are $\binom{12}{4}$ ways of selecting 4 integers out of 12. So,

$$p(x)=\frac{Number\ of\ ways\ in\ which\ X\ is\ the\ 2nd\ smallest\ integer\ in\ four}{ways\ to\ select\ 4\ integers\ out\ of\ 12}$$

$$=\frac{(ways\ to\ get\ 2\ integers > X)(ways\ to\ get\ 1\ integer < X)}{ways\ to\ select\ 4\ integers\ out\ of\ 12}$$

$$=\frac{\binom{12-x}{2}(x-1)}{\binom{12}{4}}$$

$$p(x)=\frac{\frac{(12-x)!}{2!\,(12-x-2)!}(x-1)}{\binom{12}{4}}$$

$$=\frac{\frac{(12-x)!\,(x-1)}{2(10-x)!}}{495}$$

$$=\frac{\frac{(x-1)(12-x)(11-x)(10-x)!}{2(10-x)!}}{495}$$

$$=\frac{(x-1)(12-x)(11-x)}{990}$$

The correct answer is **B**.

SOA Sample Question 204 Explanation

Let X be the loss. The cdf of an exponential distribution with mean 100 is:

$$F(x) = 1 - e^{-\frac{x}{100}}$$

$$P(40 < X < 50) = F(50) - F(40)$$

$$= .0638 \quad (1)$$

$$P(60 < X < r) = F(r) - F(60)$$

$$= 1 - e^{-\frac{r}{100}} - \left(1 - e^{-\frac{60}{100}}\right)$$

$$= .5488 - e^{-\frac{r}{100}} \quad (2)$$

By the given condition, the probabilities in (1) and (2) are equal. So,

$$.0638 = .5488 - e^{-\frac{r}{100}}$$

$$e^{-\frac{r}{100}} = .485$$

$$-\frac{r}{100} = \ln .485$$

$$r = 72.36$$

The correct answer is **D**.

SOA Sample Question 205 Explanation

Let X be the number of days until next car accident.

$$F(x) = 1 - e^{-\frac{x}{200}}$$

No accident during 1st 365 days and at least one accident during next 365 days is equivalent to the statement that:

The number of days it takes for the 1st accident to occur is between 365 and 730.

So, we are to find $P(365 < X < 730)$.

$$P(365 < X < 730) = F(730) - F(365)$$

$$= .135$$

The correct answer is **B**.

SOA Sample Question 206 Explanation

Let X be the annual profit.

$$P(X \leq 2000) = .7642$$

From tables, $z = .72$ corresponds to a cumulative probability of .7642. So, in

$$z = \frac{X - \mu}{\sigma}$$

we have $z = .72$ when $X = 2000$.

$$.72 = \frac{2000 - \mu}{\sigma}$$

$$\mu = 2000 - .72\sigma \quad (1)$$

$$P(X \leq 3000) = .9066$$

From tables, $z = 1.32$ corresponds to a cumulative probability of .9066.

So, we have $z = 1.32$ when $X = 3000$.

$$1.32 = \frac{3000 - \mu}{\sigma}$$

$$\mu = 3000 - 1.32\sigma \quad (2)$$

Comparing (1) and (2) we have:

$$2000 - .72\sigma = 3000 - 1.32\sigma$$

$$.6\sigma = 1000$$

$$\sigma = \frac{5000}{3}$$

Substituting in (1)

$$\mu = 2000 - .72\left(\frac{5000}{3}\right) = 800$$

We are to find $P(X \leq 1000)$. So, we need to change 1000 into z-score.

$$z = \frac{X - \mu}{\sigma} = \frac{1000 - 800}{\frac{5000}{3}} = .12$$

$$P(X \leq 1000) = P(z \leq .12)$$

$$= .5478$$

The correct answer is **C**.

SOA Sample Question 207 Explanation

The given cdf is:

$$F(l) = \begin{cases} \frac{3}{4}\left(\frac{l}{V}\right)^3 , & 0 \le l < V \\ 1 - \frac{1}{10}e^{-\frac{l-V}{V}}, & V \le l \end{cases}$$

Therefore:

$$P(L > V) = 1 - P(L \le V)$$

$$= 1 - F(V)$$

$$= 1 - \left(1 - \frac{1}{10}e^{-\frac{V-V}{V}}\right)$$

$$= 1 - \left(1 - \frac{1}{10}e^{0}\right)$$

$$= .1$$

The correct answer is **B**.

Quiz 18

1. The probability that a husband will be alive 50 years after marriage is .35, and the probability that a wife will be alive 50 years after marriage is .55. The probability that at least one of them will be alive 50 years after marriage is .7. Find the probability that 50 years after marriage the wife is alive given that the husband is alive.
A) .57
B) .62
C) .67
D) .72
E) .77
Solution:

$$P(H) = .35$$

$$P(W) = .55$$

$$P(H \cup W) = .7$$

We need to find $P(W|H)$.

$$P(W|H) = \frac{P(WH)}{P(H)} \qquad (1)$$

To find $P(WH)$ we use the addition rule:

$$P(W \cup H) = P(W) + P(H) - P(WH)$$

$$.7 = .35 + .55 - P(WH)$$

$$P(WH) = .2$$

Equation (1) becomes:

$$P(W|H) = \frac{.2}{.35}$$

$$= \frac{4}{7}$$

$$= .57$$

The correct answer is **A**.

2. Nine students are surveyed in a class of 20 students that comprises of 2 freshmen, 4 sophomores, 6 juniors, and 8 seniors. Find the probability the 9 surveyed include 4 seniors, 3 juniors, 1 freshman, and 1 sophomore.
A) .027
B) .037
C) .047
D) .057
E) .067

Solution:

Number of ways to pick 4 seniors out of 8 = $\binom{8}{4} = 70$

Number of ways to pick 3 juniors out of 6 = $\binom{6}{3} = 20$

Number of ways to pick 1 sophomore out of 4 = $\binom{4}{1} = 4$

Number of ways to pick 1 freshman out of 2 = $\binom{2}{1} = 2$

Number of ways to pick 9 students out of 20 = $\binom{20}{9} = 167960$

$$P(4sen, 3jun, 1soph, 1fresh) = \frac{70(20)(4)(2)}{167960} = .067$$

The correct answer is **E**.

3. Three siblings and their spouses play a game in the names of all the 6 persons are written on pieces of paper and one piece is randomly drawn at a time without replacement until the names of both a husband and his wife are drawn. Find the probability of maximum number of draws.
   A) .35
   B) .4
   C) .45
   D) .5
   E) .55
   Solution:

   It is possible to draw 3 persons that do not include a couple in the first 3 draws, but then the 4th draw will definitely be a spouse of someone already drawn because there are only 3 total couples.

   So, the maximum number of draws for a couple is 4.

   To get 3 persons that do not include a couple in the first three draws we must have the following:

   For 1st draw, the total available persons are 6, and we can pick any of these 6. *Probability* 6/6.

   For 2nd draw, the total available persons are 5, but to avoid a couple, draw must be from one from the remaining 2 couples (4 persons). *Probability* 4/5.

   For 3rd draw, the total available persons are 4, but to avoid a couple, draw must be from the remaining couple (2 persons). *Probability* 2/4.

$$P(4\ draws\ until\ a\ couple) = \frac{6}{6}\left(\frac{4}{5}\right)\left(\frac{2}{4}\right)$$

$$= .4$$

   The correct answer is **B**.

4. Students considering entering university X email a professor in their fields. 75% of these students receive a courteous response within 3 days while the remainder receive a rude or no response within 3 days. Of those who receive a courteous response within 3 days, 30% receive it the same day. Those who receive a courteous response the same day have .9 probability of coming to university X. Those who receive a courteous response 1 to 3 days later have a .6 probability of coming to university X, while the remaining students have a .2 probability of coming to university X. Find the probability that a student received a courteous response the same day given that she came to university X.
A) .16
B) .26
C) .36
D) .46
E) .56
Solution:

Let C be the event that a student comes to university X.

Let R be the event that a student got a rude or no reply within 1-3 days.

Let S be the event that a student got a courteous reply the same day.

Let N be the event that a student got a courteous reply within 1-3 days.

We are to find $P(S|C)$.

$$P(R) = 100\% - 75\% = .25$$

$$P(C) = P(R\&C) + P(S\&C) + P(N\&C)$$

$$= .25(.2) + .75(.3)(.9) + .75(.7)(.6) = .5675$$

$$P(S|C) = \frac{P(S\&C)}{P(C)}$$

$$= \frac{.75(.3)(.9)}{.5675} = .36$$

The correct answer is **C**.

5. Of all the people above 30 in a city, 20% call themselves non-religious, 70% call themselves somewhat religious, while 10% call themselves very religious. Every day a self-called non-religious person has a probability .25 of visiting the city park, a self-called somewhat religious person has probability .15 of visiting the city park, and a self-called very religious person has probability .05 of visiting the city park. One day, a man was interviewed in the city park. Find the probability that the man called himself somewhat or very religious.
A) .66
B) .69
C) .72
D) .75
E) .78

Solution:

Religion Type	Proportion	Park Probability	P (Religion Type and Park)
No (N)	.2	.25	$.2(.25) = .05$
Somewhat (S)	.7	.15	$.7(.15) = .105$
Very (V)	.1	.05	$.1(.5) = .005$

$$P(S\ or\ V, given\ Park) = \frac{P(S\ or\ V, and\ Park)}{P(Park)}$$

$$= \frac{P(S\ and\ Park) + P(V\ and\ Park)}{P(Park)}$$

$$= \frac{.105 + .005}{.05 + .105 + .005}$$

$$= .69$$

The correct answer is **B**.

6. The number of daily deaths in a city is Poisson distributed with mean 3. The probability that any given person who dies in the city is a male is .6. Find the probability that on any given day in the city no male dies.

A) .105
B) .125
C) .145
D) .165
E) .185

Solution:

Let X be the number of daily deaths in the city. Then:

$$P(x\ deaths) = f(x) = \frac{3^x e^{-3}}{x!}$$

$P(\text{no male deaths}) = P(all\ dead\ are\ female)$

There can be 0,1,2,3,... total deaths. So,

$$P(all\ dead\ are\ female) = \sum_{k=0}^{\infty} P(k\ deaths\ and\ all\ of\ them\ female)$$

$$= \sum_{k=0}^{\infty} P(k\ deaths)\ P(all\ of\ the\ k\ dead\ are\ female)$$

$$P(dead\ is\ a\ female) = 1 - .6 = .4$$

$$P(k\ dead\ are\ all\ female) = .4^k$$

$$P(all\ dead\ are\ female) = \sum_{k=0}^{\infty} \left(\frac{3^k e^{-3}}{k!}\right)(.4)^k$$

$$= \sum_{k=0}^{\infty} \left(\frac{e^{-3}}{k!}\right)(.4 * 3)^k$$

$$= \sum_{k=0}^{\infty} \left(\frac{e^{-3}}{k!}\right)(1.2)^k$$

$$= \sum_{k=0}^{\infty} \left(\frac{e^{-1.2-1.8}}{k!}\right)(1.2)^k$$

$$= \sum_{k=0}^{\infty} \left(\frac{e^{-1.2}e^{-1.8}}{k!}\right)(1.2)^k$$

$$= e^{-1.8} \sum_{k=0}^{\infty} \left(\frac{e^{-1.2}}{k!}\right)(1.2)^k$$

$$= e^{-1.8}(sum\ of\ all\ values\ of\ a\ Poisson\ pmf\ with\ mean\ 1.2)$$

$$= e^{-1.8}(1)$$

$$= .165$$

The correct answer is **D**.

7. The value of an insured home is V. The cost of repair C after a flood is a random variable with cumulative distribution function

$$F(C) = \begin{cases} \frac{3}{4}\left(\frac{C}{V}\right)^3, & 0 \le C < V \\ 1 - \frac{1}{10}e^{-\frac{C-V}{V}}, & V \le C \end{cases}$$

Find the probability that the loss on a randomly selected insured home is greater than half its value.

A) .87

B) .89

C) .91

D) .93

E) .95

Solution:

$$P(C > .5V) = 1 - P(C \le .5V)$$

$$= 1 - F(.5V)$$

Since $.5V < V$, so we have to use the upper half of the definition to find $F(.5V)$.

$$P(C > .5V) = 1 - \left(\frac{3}{4}\left(\frac{.5V}{V}\right)^3\right)$$

$$= 1 - \frac{3}{4}(.5)^3$$

$$= .91$$

The correct answer is **C**.

8. Heights of 20-year old girls in US are normally distributed. Probability that the height of a randomly chosen 20-year old girl in US is less than 66 inches is .9418, and the probability that the height of a randomly chosen 20-year old girl in US is less than 67 inches is .9834. Find the probability that the height of a randomly chosen 20-year old girl in US is greater than 65 inches.

   A) .1562

   B) .2090

   C) .3085

   D) .6915

   E) .8438

   Solution:

   Let X be the height of a 20-year old US girl.

$$P(X < 66) = .9418$$

   From tables, $z = 1.57$ corresponds to a cumulative probability of .9418. So, in

$$z = \frac{X - \mu}{\sigma}$$

   we have $z = 1.57$ when $X = 66$.

$$1.57 = \frac{66 - \mu}{\sigma}$$

$$\mu = 66 - 1.57\sigma \quad (1)$$

$$P(X < 67) = .9834$$

   From tables, $z = 2.13$ corresponds to a cumulative probability of .9834.

   So, we have $z = 2.13$ when $X = 67$.

$$2.13 = \frac{67 - \mu}{\sigma}$$

$$\mu = 67 - 2.13\sigma \quad (2)$$

   Comparing (1) and (2) we have:

$$66 - 1.57\sigma = 67 - 2.13\sigma$$

$$.56\sigma = 1$$

$$\sigma = 1.786$$

Substituting in (1)

$$\mu = 66 - 1.57(1.786) = 63.2$$

We are to find $P(X > 65)$. So we need to change 64 into z-score.

$$z = \frac{X - \mu}{\sigma}$$

$$= \frac{65 - 63.2}{1.786}$$

$$= 1.01$$

$$P(X > 65) = P(z > 1.01)$$

$$= 1 - P(z \leq 1.01)$$

$$= 1 - .8438$$

$$= .1562$$

The correct answer is **A**.

9. The time until the next death in a town is exponentially distributed with mean 1.5 weeks. Find the probability that no deaths occur for 3 weeks from now but at least one death occurs in the 4th week.

A) .006

B) .026

C) .046

D) .066

E) .086

Solution:

Let X be the number of weeks until next death.

$$F(x) = 1 - e^{-\frac{x}{1.5}}$$

No death during next 3 weeks and at least 1 death in the 4th week is equivalent to the statement:

The number of weeks it takes for the 1st death to occur is between 3 and 4.

So, we are to find $P(3 < X < 4)$.

$$P(3 < X < 4) = F(4) - F(3)$$

$$= .066$$

The correct answer is **D**.

10. Annual incomes of full-time working adults in a city are exponentially distributed with mean 40,000. The probability that a randomly selected annual income is between 30,000 and 35,000 is the same as the probability that an annual income is between 50,000 and k. Find k.

A) 58514

B) 58614

C) 58714

D) 58814

E) 58914

Solution:

$$F(x) = 1 - e^{-\frac{x}{40000}}$$

We are given that:

$$P(30000 < X < 35000) = P(50000 < X < k)$$

$$F(35000) - F(30000) = F(k) - F(50000)$$

$$\left(1 - e^{-\frac{35000}{40000}}\right) - \left(1 - e^{-\frac{30000}{40000}}\right) = \left(1 - e^{-\frac{k}{40000}}\right) - \left(1 - e^{-\frac{50000}{40000}}\right)$$

$$.0555 = .2865 - e^{-\frac{k}{40000}}$$

$$e^{-\frac{k}{40000}} = .231$$

$$-\frac{k}{40} = -1.465$$

$$k = 58614$$

The correct answer is **B**.

Tools Needed for Problems 208-218

$$F(k) = P(X \leq k)$$

The binomial pmf is:

$$f(x) = \binom{n}{x} (p)^x (1-p)^{n-x}$$

$$P(A|B) = \frac{P(AB)}{P(B)}$$

The pmf of a Poisson variable *X* with mean m is:

$$f(x) = \frac{m^x e^{-m}}{x!}, x = 0,1,2,3, \ldots$$

The pdf and cdf of an exponential distribution with mean m are:

$$f(x) = \frac{1}{m} e^{-\frac{x}{m}}, \qquad x > 0$$

$$F(x) = 1 - e^{-\frac{x}{m}}$$

$$P(a \leq X \leq b) = F(b) - F(a)$$

All measurements, for example, heights, weights, times, are continuous variables. For continuous variables it makes no difference whether the probability expressions have strict inequalities or non-strict inequalities.

For a discrete random variable,

$$\sum f(x) = 1$$

$$\sum x f(x) = E[X]$$

where the above summations are over all possible values of *X*.

A and B are independent if and only if $P(AB) = P(A)P(B)$

$$\int x e^{ax} dx = \frac{x e^{ax}}{a} - \frac{e^{ax}}{a^2}$$

SOA Sample Question 208 Explanation

Let X be the lifetime of the machine part. Then:

$$f(x) = \frac{1}{5}e^{-\frac{x}{5}}, \qquad x > 0$$

$$F(x) = 1 - e^{-\frac{x}{5}}$$

We are to find $E[X|X < 10]$.

For this we need $f(x|x < 10)$

$$f(x|x < 10) = \frac{f(x \text{ and } x < 10)}{P(X < 10)}$$

$$= \frac{f(x)}{F(10)}, \qquad 0 < x < 10$$

$$= \frac{1}{5}e^{-\frac{x}{5}}\left(\frac{1}{1 - e^{-\frac{10}{5}}}\right), \qquad 0 < x < 10$$

$$= .2313e^{-\frac{x}{5}}, \qquad 0 < x < 10$$

$$E[X|X < 10] = \int_0^{10} x\, f(x|x < 10)\, dx = .2313\int_0^{10} x\, e^{-\frac{x}{5}}\, dx$$

Using our integration by parts shortcut:

$$\int xe^{ax}dx = \frac{xe^{ax}}{a} - \frac{e^{ax}}{a^2}$$

$$E[X|X < 10] = .2313\left[\frac{xe^{-\frac{1}{5}x}}{-1/5} - \frac{e^{-\frac{1}{5}x}}{(-1/5)^2}\right]\Big|_0^{10}$$

$$= .2313[(-50e^{-2} - 25e^{-2}) - (0 - 25e^{0})] = 3.435$$

The correct answer is **E**.

SOA Sample Question 209 Explanation

This is an exponential function with mean 1/2.

So, the cdf is:

$$F(x) = 1 - e^{-2x}$$

$$P(X \le .5|X \le 1) = \frac{P(X \le .5 \text{ and } X \le 1)}{P(X \le 1)} = \frac{P(X \le .5)}{P(X \le 1)} = \frac{F(.5)}{F(1)} = \frac{1 - e^{-1}}{1 - e^{-2}} = .731$$

The correct answer is **D**.

SOA Sample Question 210 Explanation

The independence condition tells us that

$$P[EF] = P[E]P[F]$$

$$= .84(.65)$$

$$= .546$$

We have the following diagram:

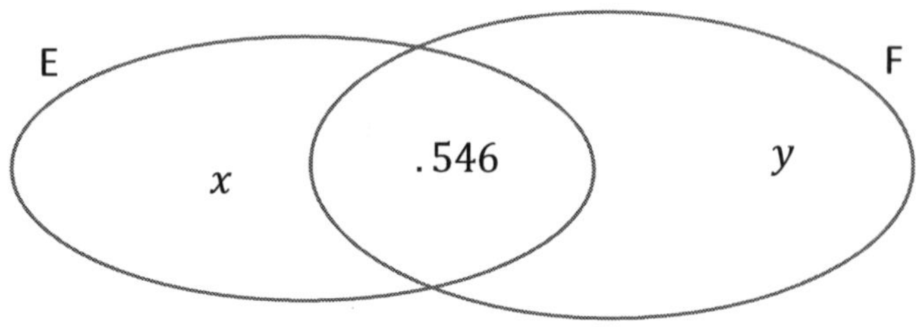

From the diagram:

$$x = P[E] - .546$$

$$= .84 - .546$$

$$= .294$$

$$y = P[F] - .546$$

$$= .65 - .546$$

$$= .104$$

Exactly one event occurring means either only E or only F.

So, we are asked $x + y$

$$x + y = .294 + .104$$

$$= .398$$

The correct answer is **B**.

SOA Sample Question 211 Explanation

Let X be the number of claims in the 1st of the 2 consecutive months.

Let Y be the number of claims in the 2nd of the 2 consecutive months.

We are to find $P(X+Y>3|X<2)$.

We will find $P(X+Y\leq 3|X<2)$ and then take the complement to find the required probability.

$$P(X+Y\leq 3|X<2)=\frac{P(X+Y\leq 3\ and\ X<2)}{P(X<2)} \quad (1)$$

$$P(X<2)=P(N=0)+P(N=1)=\frac{2}{3^{0+1}}+\frac{2}{3^{1+1}}=\frac{8}{9} \quad (2)$$

To find numerator in (1), we tabulate all the (x,y) pairs satisfying this condition:

$$X+Y\leq 3\ and\ X<2$$

Note that since the number of claims are given to be independent over different months, so $X\ and\ Y$ are independent and therefore the probability at each pair of points can be obtained by multiplying the corresponding probabilities for the original variables.

x	0	0	0	0	1	1	1
y	0	1	2	3	0	1	2
$f(x)=\frac{2}{3^{x+1}}$	2/3	2/3	2/3	2/3	2/9	2/9	2/9
$f(y)=\frac{2}{3^{y+1}}$	2/3	2/9	2/27	2/81	2/3	2/9	2/27
$f(x)f(y)$	4/9	4/27	4/81	4/243	4/27	4/81	4/243

$$P(X+Y\leq 3\ and\ X<2)=\sum_{x+y\leq 3,\ x<2} f(x,y)=\sum_{x+y\leq 3,\ x<2} f(x)f(y)$$

$$=\frac{4}{9}+\frac{4}{27}+\frac{4}{81}+\frac{4}{243}+\frac{4}{27}+\frac{4}{81}+\frac{4}{243}$$

$$=.8724 \quad (3)$$

Substituting (2) and (3) in (1) we get:

$$P(X+Y\leq 3|X<2)=\frac{.8724}{\frac{8}{9}}=.9815$$

$$P(X+Y>3|X<2)=1-P(X+Y\leq 3|X<2)$$

$$=1-.9815$$

$$=.0185$$

The correct answer is **E**.

SOA Sample Question 212 Explanation

Let q be the probability of a patient NOT having sleep apnea.

Let X be the number of patients tested until one with disease is found.

We are to find:

$$P(X \geq 12 | X \geq 4) = \frac{P(X \geq 12 \text{ and } X \geq 4)}{P(X \geq 4)}$$

$$= \frac{P(X \geq 12)}{P(X \geq 4)}$$

$$= \frac{P(X \geq 12)}{r} \qquad (1)$$

Now if at least 4 patients are tested, the first 3 do not have the disease. Thus

$$r = P(X \geq 4)$$

$$r = q^3$$

$$\Rightarrow q = r^{1/3} \qquad (2)$$

Similarly, if at least 12 patients are tested, the first 11 do not have the disease.

$$P(X \geq 12) = q^{11}$$

$$P(X \geq 12) = r^{11/3}$$

by using (2).

Thus (1) becomes:

$$P(X \geq 12 | X \geq 4) = \frac{P(X \geq 12)}{r}$$

$$= \frac{r^{\frac{11}{3}}}{r}$$

$$= r^{8/3}$$

The correct answer is **C**.

SOA Sample Question 213 Explanation

Let X be the number of defective bulbs.

So X is binomial with $n = 100, p = .02$.

$$P(X = x) = f(x)$$

$$= \binom{100}{x}(.02)^x(.98)^{100-x}$$

We are to find $P(X = 2|X \leq 2)$

$$P(X = 2|X \leq 2) = \frac{P(X = 2 \; and \; X \leq 2)}{P(X \leq 2)}$$

$$= \frac{f(2)}{f(0) + f(1) + f(2)}$$

$$= \frac{.2734}{.1326 + .27065 + .2734}$$

$$= .404$$

The correct answer is **D**.

SOA Sample Question 214 Explanation

An average of 5 tornadoes in 4 years means an average of 1 tornado in 4/5 years.

So, the time X from now until the next tornado is exponential with mean 4/5 or .8

$$F(x) = 1 - e^{-x/.8}$$

Median is the x value at which the cumulative probability is .5

$$1 - e^{-\frac{x}{.8}} = .5$$

$$e^{-\frac{x}{.8}} = .5$$

$$-\frac{x}{.8} = \ln .5$$

$$x = .55$$

The correct answer is **A**.

SOA Sample Question 215 Explanation

Let X be the loss. If the median m of the loss comes out to be more than the deductible, then the median of the payout equals $m - deductible = m - 1$.

If the median of loss is less than the deductible, then the median of payout is 0.

Median of the loss is the x value at which the cumulative probability is .5.

$$F(x) = 1 - e^{-x/4}$$

$$1 - e^{-\frac{m}{4}} = .5$$

$$e^{-\frac{m}{4}} = .5$$

$$-\frac{m}{4} = \ln .5$$

$$m = 2.77$$

Since median of loss is greater than the deductible of 1, so

$$\text{Median of payout} = m - 1 = 2.77 - 1 = 1.77$$

The correct answer is **A**.

SOA Sample Question 216 Explanation

Let X be the annual number of severe weather events. Let Y be annual payout.

$$f(x) = \frac{m^x e^{-m}}{x!} = \frac{1^x e^{-1}}{x!} = \frac{e^{-1}}{x!}, \qquad x = 0,1,2,3,...$$

$$Y = 1000(X - 2), \qquad X = 3,4,5,...$$

We are to find $E[Y]$.

$$E[Y] = E[1000(X-2)] = 1000E[X-2] = 1000\sum_{x=3}^{\infty}(x-2)f(x)$$

$$= 1000\sum_{x=0}^{\infty}(x-2)f(x) - 1000\sum_{x=0}^{2}(x-2)f(x)$$

$$= 1000\sum_{x=0}^{\infty}xf(x) - 2000\sum_{x=0}^{\infty}f(x) - 1000[-2f(0) - f(1) + 0]$$

$$= 1000E[X] - 2000(1) + 2000f(0) + 1000f(1)$$

$$= 1000(1) - 2000 + 2000e^{-1} + 1000e^{-1} = 104$$

The correct answer is **B**.

SOA Sample Question 217 Explanation

Let X be the number of employee deaths in a year.

$$f(x) = \frac{m^x e^{-m}}{x!} = \frac{2^x e^{-2}}{x!}, \qquad x = 0,1,2,\ldots$$

The annual cost, C, to the company is 100 for 1 death, 200 for 2 deaths, 300 for 3 deaths, and 400 for 4 or more deaths. So,

$$E[C] = 100P(X=1) + 200P(X=2) + 300P(X=3) + 400P(X \geq 4)$$

$$= 100f(1) + 200f(2) + 300f(3) + 400[1 - f(0) - f(1) - f(2) - f(3)]$$

$$= 400 - 400f(0) - 300f(1) - 200f(2) - 100f(3)$$

$$= 400 - 100e^{-2}\left[4 + 3(2) + 2\left(\frac{4}{2}\right) + \frac{8}{6}\right] = 192$$

The correct answer is **C**.

SOA Sample Question 218 Explanation

Let X be the annual number of burglaries.

$$f(x) = \frac{m^x e^{-m}}{x!} = \frac{1^x e^{-1}}{x!} = \frac{e^{-1}}{x!}, \qquad x = 0,1,2,3,\ldots$$

We are to find $E[X|X \geq 2]$. For this, we first find $f(x|x \geq 2)$.

$$f(x|x \geq 2) = P(X = x|x \geq 2)$$

$$= \frac{P(X = x \text{ and } x \geq 2)}{P(X \geq 2)}$$

$$= \frac{f(x)}{1 - f(0) - f(1)}, x = 2,3,4,\ldots$$

$$f(x|x \geq 2) = \frac{f(x)}{1 - e^{-1} - e^{-1}} = 3.78f(x), \qquad x = 2,3,4,\ldots$$

$$E[X|X \geq 2] = \sum_{x=2}^{\infty} xf(x|x \geq 2) = 3.78\sum_{x=2}^{\infty} xf(x)$$

$$= 3.78\sum_{x=0}^{\infty} xf(x) - 3.78\sum_{x=0}^{1} xf(x)$$

$$= 3.78E[X] - 3.78\big(0f(0)\big) - 3.78\big(1f(1)\big)$$

$$= 3.78(1) - 3.78(0) - 3.78e^{-1} = 2.39$$

The correct answer is **B**.

Quiz 19

1. The lifetime of a bulb is exponentially distributed with mean 100 hours. Find the expected lifetime of the bulb (in days) given that it lasts between 80 and 90 hours.
   A) 3.0
   B) 3.5
   C) 4.0
   D) 4.5
   E) 5.0

Solution:

Let X be the lifetime of the bulb. Then:

$$f(x) = \frac{1}{100}e^{-\frac{x}{100}}, \qquad x > 0$$

$$F(x) = 1 - e^{-\frac{x}{100}}$$

We are to find $E[X|80 < X < 90]$. For this we need $f(x|80 < x < 90)$

$$f(x|80 < x < 90) = \frac{f(x \text{ and } 80 < x < 90)}{P(80 < X < 90)}$$

$$= \frac{f(x)}{F(90) - F(80)}, \qquad 80 < x < 90$$

$$= \frac{1}{100}e^{-\frac{x}{100}}\left(\frac{1}{.04276}\right), \qquad 80 < x < 90$$

$$= .2339e^{-\frac{x}{100}}, \qquad 80 < x < 90$$

$$E[X|80 < X < 90] = \int_{80}^{90} x\, f(x|80 < x < 90)\, dx$$

$$= .2339\int_{80}^{90} x\, e^{-\frac{x}{100}}\, dx$$

Recall our integration by parts shortcut:

$$\int xe^{ax}dx = \frac{xe^{ax}}{a} - \frac{e^{ax}}{a^2}$$

$$E[X|80 < X < 90] = .2339\left[\frac{xe^{-\frac{1}{100}x}}{-1/100} - \frac{e^{-\frac{1}{100}x}}{(-1/100)^2}\right]\Bigg|_{80}^{90}$$

$$= .2339[(-9000e^{-.9} - 10000e^{-.9}) - (-8000e^{-.8} - 10000e^{-.8})]$$

$$= 84.9\ hours$$

Changing it into days we get:

$$\frac{84.9}{24} = 3.5\ days$$

The correct answer is **B**.

2. Let X be a random variable with density function

$$f(x) = 5e^{-5x}, \qquad x > 0$$

Find $P(X \geq .2|X \leq .3)$

A) .19
B) .28
C) .36
D) .55
E) .65

Solution:

This is an exponential function with mean 1/5. So, the cdf is:

$$F(x) = 1 - e^{-5x}$$

$$P(X \geq .2|X \leq .3) = \frac{P(.2 \leq X \leq .3)}{P(X \leq .3)}$$

$$= \frac{F(.3) - F(.2)}{F(.3)}$$

$$= \frac{(1 - e^{-1.5}) - (1 - e^{-1})}{(1 - e^{-1.5})}$$

$$= .19$$

The correct answer is **A**.

3. Probability that a randomly chosen college student loves Math is .04. Probability that the student likes chocolate is .95. Liking Math and liking chocolate are independent events. Find the probability that a randomly selected college student likes only Math or only chocolate.

A) .910

B) .912

C) .914

D) .916

E) .918

Solution:

Let M be the event that the student likes Math.

Let C be the event that the student likes Chocolate.

The independence condition tells us that

$$P[MC] = P[M]P[C] = .04(.95) = .038$$

We have the following diagram:

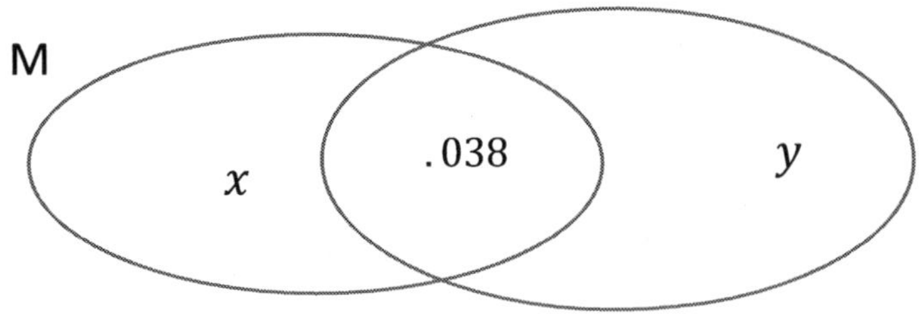

$$x = P[M] - .038$$
$$= .04 - .038$$
$$= .002$$
$$y = P[C] - .038$$
$$= .95 - .038$$
$$= .912$$

We need that either only M or only C occurs.

So, we are asked $x + y$

$$x + y = .002 + .912$$
$$= .914$$

The correct answer is **C**.

4. The number of volcanoes that erupt in a country each month follows a Poisson distribution with mean 1.8. The number of eruptions in different months are mutually independent. Find the probability that more than three eruptions will happen during a consecutive two-month period, given that at most one eruption happened in the first of the two months.

   A) .212

   B) .347

   C) .500

   D) .653

   E) .788

   Solution:

   If N is the number of eruptions in any month, then

$$P(N = n) = f(n) = \frac{1.8^n e^{-1.8}}{n!}, n = 0,1,2,3,...$$

   Let X be the number of eruptions in the 1st of the 2 consecutive months.

Let Y be the number of eruptions in the 2nd of the 2 consecutive months.

We are to find $P(X+Y>3|X\leq 1)$.

We will find $P(X+Y\leq 3|X\leq 1)$ and then take the complement.

$$P(X+Y\leq 3|X\leq 1)=\frac{P(X+Y\leq 3 \text{ } and \text{ } X\leq 1)}{P(X\leq 1)} \quad (1)$$

$$P(X\leq 1)=f(0)+f(1)$$
$$=e^{-1.8}+1.8e^{-1.8}$$
$$=.4628 \quad (2)$$

x	0	0	0	0	1	1	1
y	0	1	2	3	0	1	2
$f(x)=\frac{1.8^x e^{-1.8}}{x!}$	$e^{-1.8}$	$e^{-1.8}$	$e^{-1.8}$	$e^{-1.8}$	.2975	.2975	.2975
$f(y)=\frac{1.8^y e^{-1.8}}{y!}$	$e^{-1.8}$	.2975	.2678	.1607	$e^{-1.8}$	.2975	.2678
$f(x)f(y)$	.0273	.0492	.0443	.0266	.0492	.0885	.0797

To find numerator in (1), we have tabulated all the (x,y) pairs satisfying:

$$X+Y\leq 3 \text{ } and \text{ } X<2$$

Note that since the eruptions are independent over different months, so X *and* Y are independent and therefore the probability at each pair of points can be obtained by multiplying the corresponding probabilities for the original variables.

$$P(X+Y\leq 3 \text{ } and \text{ } X\leq 1)=\sum_{x+y\leq 3,\ x\leq 1} f(x,y)=\sum_{x+y\leq 3,\ x\leq 1} f(x)f(y)$$

$$=.0273+.0492+.0443+.0266+.0492+.0885+.0797$$
$$P(X+Y\leq 3 \text{ } and \text{ } X\leq 1)=.3648 \quad (3)$$

Substituting (2) and (3) in (1) we get:

$$P(X+Y\leq 3|X\leq 1)=\frac{.3648}{.4628}$$

$$=.788$$

$$P(X+Y>3|X\leq 1)=1-P(X+Y\leq 3|X\leq 1)$$

$$=1-.788$$

$$=.212$$

The correct answer is **A**.

5. People in a study are tested, one at a time, for a virus until someone tests positive for the virus. Each person independently has the same probability of having the virus. Probability that at least 3 persons are tested is k. Find the probability that at least 8 persons are tested given that at least 3 persons are tested.

A) $k^{1/2}$

B) $k^{3/2}$

C) $k^{5/2}$

D) $k^{7/2}$

E) $k^{9/2}$

Solution:

Let q be the probability of a person NOT testing positive. Let X be the number of persons tested until one with virus is found. We are to find:

$$P(X \geq 8 | X \geq 3) = \frac{P(X \geq 8 \; and \; X \geq 3)}{P(X \geq 3)}$$

$$= \frac{P(X \geq 8)}{P(X \geq 3)}$$

$$= \frac{P(X \geq 8)}{k}$$

Now if at least 3 persons are tested, the first 2 do not have the virus. Thus

$$k = P(X \geq 3)$$

$$k = q^2$$

$$\Rightarrow q = k^{1/2} \quad (2)$$

Similarly, if at least 8 persons are tested, the first 7 do not have the virus.

$$P(X \geq 8) = q^7$$

$$= k^{7/2}$$

by using (2). Thus (1) becomes:

$$P(X \geq 8 | X \geq 3) = \frac{k^{\frac{7}{2}}}{k}$$

$$= k^{5/2}$$

The correct answer is **C**.

6. In country X, 55% of the newborn children are girls. Among a sample of 8 randomly chosen newborns, what is the probability that exactly half of them are girls, given that at least 3 of them are girls.

A) .288

B) .356

C) .417

D) .500

E) .644

Solution:

Let X be the number of girls. So X is binomial with $n = 8, p = .55$.

$$P(X = x) = f(x) = \binom{8}{x}(.55)^x(.45)^{8-x}$$

We are to find $P(X = 4|X \geq 3)$.

$$P(X = 4|X \geq 3) = \frac{P(X = 4 \text{ and } X \geq 3)}{P(X \geq 3)}$$

$$= \frac{f(4)}{1 - f(0) - f(1) - f(2)}$$

$$= \frac{.2627}{1 - .00168 - .01644 - .07033}$$

$$= .288$$

The correct answer is **A**.

7. A state experiences an average of 4 hurricanes in any 6-year period. The number of years from now until the next hurricane as well as the number of years between hurricanes have identical exponential distributions and all such times are mutually independent. Find 75th percentile of the number of years from now until the state experiences its next hurricane.

A) .19

B) .43

C) .91

D) 1.37

E) 2.08

Solution:

Average of 4 hurricanes in 6 years means an average of 1 hurricane in 6/4 years.

The time X from now until the next hurricane is exponential with mean 6/4 or 1.5

$$F(x) = 1 - e^{-x/1.5}$$

75th percentile is the x value at which the cumulative probability is .75

$$1 - e^{-\frac{x}{1.5}} = .75$$

$$e^{-\frac{x}{1.5}} = .25$$

$$-\frac{x}{1.5} = \ln .25$$

$$x = 2.08$$

The correct answer is **E**.

8. Car repair costs are exponentially distributed with a mean of 400. An auto insurance has a deductible of 200. Find the median insurance payout.

A) 0

B) 77

C) 177

D) 277

E) 477

Solution:

Let X be the cost.

If the median m of the cost comes out to be more than the deductible, then the median of the payout equals $m - deductible = m - 200$.

If the median of cost is less than the deductible, then the median of payout is 0.

Median of the cost is the x value at which the cumulative probability is .5.

$$F(x) = 1 - e^{-x/400}$$

$$1 - e^{-\frac{m}{400}} = .5$$

$$e^{-\frac{m}{400}} = .5$$

$$-\frac{m}{400} = \ln .5$$

$$m = 277$$

Since median of loss is greater than the deductible of 200, so

$$\text{Median of payout} = m - 200$$

$$= 277 - 200$$

$$= 77$$

The correct answer is **B**.

9. An insurance provides each of its clients 200 for each visit to a dentist, up to a maximum of 3 visits per year, and does not provide anything for any more visits. The number of dentist visits per year is Poisson with mean 2.5. Find the expected annual insurance payout per client.

A) 411

B) 413

C) 415

D) 417

E) 419

Solution:

Let X be the number of dental visits in a year for a client.

$$f(x) = \frac{m^x e^{-m}}{x!} = f(x) = \frac{2.5^x e^{-2.5}}{x!}, \qquad x = 0,1,2,\ldots$$

The annual cost, C, to the company is 200 for 1 visit, 400 for 2 visits, and 600 for 3 or more visits. So,

$$E[C] = 200P(X = 1) + 400P(X = 2) + 600P(X \geq 3)$$

$$= 200f(1) + 400f(2) + 600[1 - f(0) - f(1) - f(2)]$$

$$= 600 - 600f(0) - 400f(1) - 200f(2)$$

$$= 600 - 200e^{-2.5}\left[3 + 2(2.5) + \left(\frac{6.25}{2}\right)\right]$$

$$= 417$$

The correct answer is **D**.

10. An insurance on a home does not cover the first flood of a year but pays 3000 for each flood in the year after first flood. Number of floods per year has Poisson distribution with mean 2. Find the expected amount paid to a homeowner by this insurance in one year.

A. 406

B. 1406

C. 1406

D. 2406

E. 3406

Solution:

Let X be the annual number of floods. Let Y be annual payout.

$$f(x) = \frac{m^x e^{-m}}{x!} = \frac{2^x e^{-2}}{x!}, \qquad x = 0,1,2,3,\ldots$$

$$Y = 3000(X-1), \qquad X = 2,3,4,5,\ldots$$

We are to find $E[Y]$.

$$E[Y] = E[3000(X-1)]$$

$$= 3000E[X-1]$$

$$= 3000\sum_{x=2}^{\infty}(x-1)f(x)$$

$$= 3000\sum_{x=0}^{\infty}(x-1)f(x) - 3000\sum_{x=0}^{1}(x-1)f(x)$$

$$= 3000\sum_{x=0}^{\infty}xf(x) - 3000\sum_{x=0}^{\infty}f(x) - 3000[-1f(0) + 0f(1)]$$

$$= 3000E[X] - 3000(1) + 3000f(0)$$

$$= 3000(2) - 3000 + 3000e^{-2}$$

$$= 3406$$

The correct answer is **E**.

The pdf, mean, and variance of uniform $[a, b]$ distribution are:

$$f(x) = \frac{1}{b-a}, \qquad a < x < b$$

$$E[X] = \frac{a+b}{2}$$

$$Var\ X = \frac{(b-a)^2}{12}$$

For a continuous variable:

$$E[X] = \int_{-\infty}^{\infty} x\, f(x)\, dx$$

By law of total expectation, if $A, B, \ldots$are all the possible mutually exclusive events:

$$E[X] = P(A)E[X|A] + P(B)E[X|B] + \cdots$$

If p is the pth percentile of a distribution, then

$$P(X \le m) = p/100$$

Median is the 50th percentile.

The pdf of a Poisson variable with mean m is:

$$f(x) = \frac{m^x e^{-m}}{x!}, \qquad x = 0,1,2, \ldots$$

The variance of a Poisson distribution equals its mean.

The pdf and cdf of exponential distribution of mean m are:

$$f(x) = \frac{1}{m} e^{-\frac{x}{m}}, \qquad x > 0$$

$$F(x) = 1 - e^{-x/m}$$

The standard deviation of an exponential distribution equals its mean.

If

$$X = \begin{cases} A, & with\ probability\ a \\ B, & with\ probability\ b \\ & \vdots \end{cases}$$

Then

$E[X] = aE[A] + bE[B] + \cdots,\qquad E[X^2] = aE[A^2] + bE[B^2] + \cdots$

$$\int (x+k)e^{ax} dx = \frac{(x+k)e^{ax}}{a} - \frac{e^{ax}}{a^2}$$

SOA Sample Question 219 Explanation

Let X be the loss and Y be the unreimbursed portion of loss.

When loss is less than the deductible, all the loss is unreimbursed.

When loss is greater than the deductible, then deductible is the unreimbursed portion of the loss.

$$f(x) = \frac{1}{450}, \qquad 0 < x < 450$$

$$Y = \begin{cases} X, & X \le D \\ D, & X > D \end{cases}$$

$$E[Y] = 56$$

$$\int_{-\infty}^{\infty} y\, f(x)\, dx = 56$$

$$\int_0^D x\left(\frac{1}{450}\right) dx + \int_D^{450} D\left(\frac{1}{450}\right) dx = 56$$

$$\frac{1}{450}\left(\frac{x^2}{2}\right)\Bigg|_0^D + \frac{1}{450} D\, x\Bigg|_D^{450} = 56$$

$$\frac{D^2}{900} + \frac{450D - D^2}{450} = 56$$

$$D^2 + 900D - 2D^2 = 50400$$

$$D^2 - 900D + 50400 = 0$$

$$(D - 60)(D - 840) = 0$$

$$D = 60 \text{ } or \text{ } 840$$

A deductible of 840 makes no sense because the maximum loss is 450. So

$$D = 60$$

The correct answer is **A**.

SOA Sample Question 220 Explanation

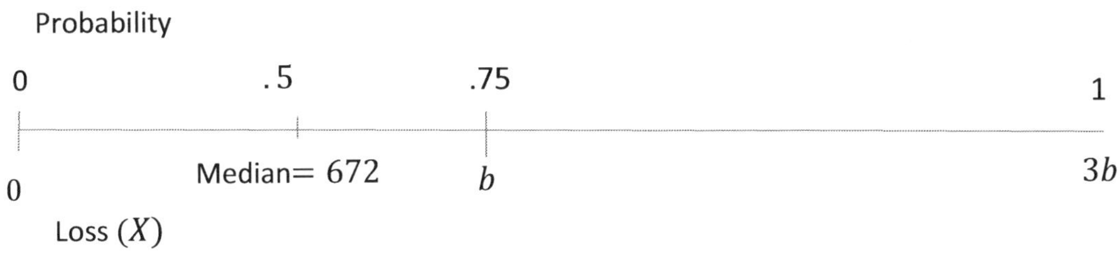

From the picture we see that the median, which corresponds to a cumulative probability of .5, lies in the $[0, b]$ portion.

The median is 672. So,

$$.5 = P(X \leq 672)$$

$$.5 = P(X \; is \; in \; [0, b]) \left(\frac{672 - 0}{b - 0}\right)$$

$$.5 = .75 \left(\frac{672}{b}\right)$$

$$.5 = \frac{504}{b}$$

$$b = \frac{504}{.5}$$

$$b = 1008$$

By law of total probability,

$$E[X] = P(minor)E[X|minor] + P(major)E[X|major]$$

$$= .75E([0, b]) + .25E([b, 3b])$$

Recall that the expected value of a uniform distribution lies at its midpoint. So,

$$E[X] = .75\left(\frac{0 + b}{2}\right) + .25\left(\frac{b + 3b}{2}\right)$$

$$= .875b$$

$$= .875(1008)$$

$$= 882$$

The correct answer is **D**.

SOA Sample Question 221 Explanation

Median claim amount is the claim amount at which the accumulated probability is .5.

Let X be the claim amount and m be the median. Then

$$P(X \leq m) = .5$$

$$P(0 \leq X \leq m) = .5$$

$$P(X = 0) + P(0 < X \leq m) = .5$$

$$.2 + P(0 < X \leq m) = .5$$

$$P(0 < X \leq m) = .3$$

Since only .2 of the probability has accumulated up to a claim amount of 0, the median claim occurs in the region where $X > 0$. So, we need:

$$P(X \leq m | X > 0) = \frac{P(X \leq m \text{ and } X > 0)}{P(X > 0)}$$

$$= \frac{P(0 < X \leq m\,)}{1 - P(X \leq 0)}$$

$$= \frac{.3}{1 - .2}$$

$$= .375$$

We therefore need the cumulative probability corresponding to .375.

Since the table only has cumulative probabilities of .5 or more, we look at the cumulative probability of $1 - .375 = .625$.

From table, $z = .31$ corresponds to cumulative probability of .6217 and $z = .32$ corresponds to .6255. By interpolation,

$$\frac{.625 - .6217}{.6255 - .6217} = .9$$

Thus, $z = .319$ corresponds to .625.

By symmetry of the normal distribution we see that $z = -.319$ corresponds to .375.

$$z = \frac{X - \mu}{\sigma}$$

$$-.319 = \frac{m - 1000}{400}$$

$$-.319(400) = m - 1000$$

$$m = 873$$

The correct answer is **C**.

SOA Sample Question 222 Explanation

Let X be the loss.

We will start by finding the z-score of the deductible.

$$z = \frac{X - \mu}{\sigma}$$

$$= \frac{15000 - 20000}{4500}$$

$$= -1.11$$

$$P(X \geq 15000) = P(z \geq -1.11) = P(z \leq 1.11) = .8665$$

$$P(X < 15000) = 1 - P(X \geq 15000) = 1 - .8665 = .1335$$

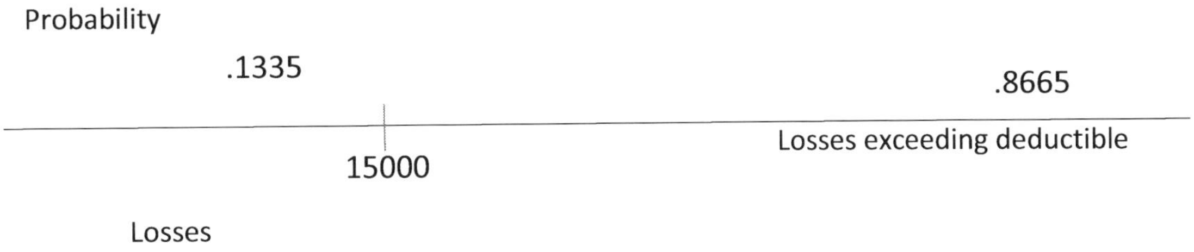

We see from the picture that the 95th percentile of losses exceeding deductible corresponds to a cumulative loss probability of:

$$.1335 + .95(.8665) = .9567$$

From table, $z = 1.71$ corresponds to cumulative probability of .9564 and $z = 1.72$ corresponds to cumulative probability of .9573. By interpolation:

$$\frac{.9567 - .9564}{.9573 - .9564} = .3$$

So, $z = 1.713$ corresponds to cumulative probability of .9567.

So, the required percentile is the loss value corresponding to $z = 1.713$.

$$z = \frac{X - \mu}{\sigma}$$

$$1.713 = \frac{X - 20000}{4500}$$

$$1.713(4500) = X - 20000$$

$$X = 27708$$

This rounds to choice **B**.

SOA Sample Question 223 Explanation

Let be X the monthly demand, and A be the inventory amount.

We need:

$$P(X > A) = .02$$

$$P(X \leq A) = 1 - .02 = .98$$

From tables, a cumulative probability of .9798 corresponds to $z = 2.05$, and a cumulative probability of .9803 corresponds to $z = 2.06$. By interpolation:

$$\frac{.98 - .9798}{.9803 - .9798} = .4$$

So, a cumulative probability of .98 corresponds to $z = 2.054$

Thus, $X = A$ corresponds to $z = 2.054$ in the formula:

$$z = \frac{X - \mu}{\sigma}$$

$$2.054 = \frac{A - 20}{2}$$

$$A = 24.108$$

This rounds to choice **C**.

SOA Sample Question 224 Explanation

Since $0 \le T \le 13, and\ T$ is symmetric about $6.5, and\ T$ is proportional to the given expression in [0,6.5], so half of the total probability lies in [0,6.5], and:

$$0.5 = \int_0^{6.5} f(t)dt = \int_0^{6.5} \frac{c}{1+t} dt = c \ln|1+t| \Big|_0^{6.5} = c\,(\ln 7.5 - \ln 1) = c \ln 7.5$$

$$c = \frac{.5}{\ln 7.5} = .24815$$

If k is the 60th percentile, then $P(T \le k) = .6$.

We would love to use the given expression for $f(t)$ but that is only valid up to an accumulated probability of .5. We therefore use symmetry to get (see figure):

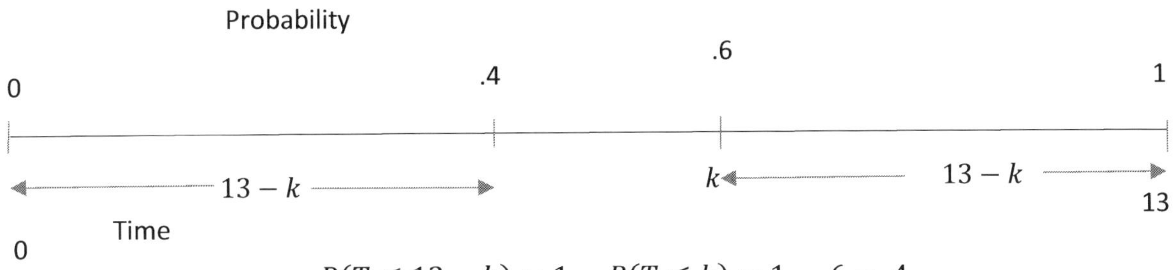

$$P(T \le 13 - k) = 1 - P(T \le k) = 1 - .6 = .4$$

Since this is less than .5, so we can use our known expression for $f(t)$.

$$f(t) = \frac{c}{1+t} = \frac{.24815}{1+t}$$

$$.4 = P(T \le 13 - k)$$

$$= \int_0^{13-k} f(t)dt$$

$$= \int_0^{13-k} \frac{.24815}{1+t} dt$$

$$= .24815 \ln|1+t| \Big|_0^{13-k}$$

$$= .24815\,(\ln(1 + 13 - k) - \ln 1)$$

$$.4 = .24815 \ln(14 - k)$$

$$\ln(14 - k) = 1.612$$

$$14 - k = e^{1.612}$$

$$k = 8.99$$

The correct answer is **C**.

SOA Sample Question 225 Explanation

If m is the mean loss, then the cdf of loss is:

$$F(l) = 1 - e^{-l/m}$$

The loss will be fully covered by policy A if it is less than or equal to 1.

The loss will be fully covered by policy B if it is less than or equal to 2. So,

$$P(L \leq 2) = 1.9P(L \leq 1)$$

$$F(2) = 1.9F(1)$$

$$1 - e^{-\frac{2}{m}} = 1.9\left(1 - e^{-\frac{1}{m}}\right)$$

Let $e^{-\frac{1}{m}} = x$. Then the above equation becomes

$$1 - x^2 = 1.9(1 - x)$$

$$(1 - x)(1 + x) = 1.9(1 - x)$$

$$(1 + x) = 1.9$$

$$x = .9$$

$$e^{-\frac{1}{m}} = .9$$

$$-\frac{1}{m} = \ln .9$$

$$m = -\frac{1}{\ln .9}$$

$$= 9.49$$

The variance of an exponential distribution equals the square of its mean.

$$Var\ L = 9.49^2$$

$$= 90.1$$

The correct answer is **E**.

SOA Sample Question 226 Explanation

$$f(x) = \frac{1}{10}e^{-\frac{x}{10}}, \qquad x > 0$$

$$Y = X - d\,, \qquad X > d$$

$$E[Y] = \int_{-\infty}^{\infty} y f(x)dx = \int_{d}^{\infty} (x-d)\frac{1}{10}e^{-\frac{x}{10}}\,dx$$

We use our shortcut, with $k = -d\,,\ a = -1/10$ to get:

$$E[Y] = \frac{1}{10}\left[\frac{(x-d)e^{-x/10}}{-1/10} - \frac{e^{-x/10}}{(-1/10)^2}\right]_d^{\infty}$$

All terms involving $e^{-\infty}$ will go to 0, no matter what they are multiplied with. So:

$$E[Y] = \frac{1}{10}\left[\frac{e^{-d/10}}{(-1/10)^2}\right] = 10e^{-d/10}$$

$$E[Y^2] = \int_{-\infty}^{\infty} y^2 f(x)dx$$

$$= \int_{d}^{\infty} (x-d)^2\frac{1}{10}e^{-\frac{x}{10}}\,dx$$

$$= (x-d)^2\left(-e^{-\frac{x}{10}}\right)\Big|_d^{\infty} - \int_d^{\infty} -e^{-\frac{x}{10}}\,2(x-d)dx$$

$$= 0 + 2\int_d^{\infty} (x-d)e^{-\frac{x}{10}}\,dx$$

$$= 2\left[\frac{(x-d)e^{-x/10}}{-1/10} - \frac{e^{-x/10}}{(-1/10)^2}\right]_d^{\infty}$$

$$= 2\frac{e^{-d/10}}{(-1/10)^2} = 200e^{-d/10}$$

$$Var\ Y = E[Y^2] - (E[Y])^2$$

$$= 200e^{-d/10} - \left(10e^{-d/10}\right)^2$$

$$= 200e^{-d/10} - 100e^{-2d/10}$$

$$= 100\left(2e^{-d/10} - e^{-d/5}\right)$$

The correct answer is **D**.

SOA Sample Question 227 Explanation

Let $A, B, C,$ be annual number of claims from type A, type B, and type C policies, respectively.

$$X = \begin{cases} A, & prob\ .1 \\ B, & prob\ .5 \\ C, & prob\ .4 \end{cases}$$

$$E[X] = .1E[A] + .5E[B] + .4E[C]$$

$$= .1(1) + .5(2) + .4(10)$$

$$= 5.1$$

$$E[X^2] = .1E[A^2] + .5E[B^2] + .4E[C^2] \quad (1)$$

$$Recall\ that\ variance\ and\ mean\ of\ a\ Poisson\ variable\ are\ the\ same.\ So, from:$$

$$Var\ A = E[A^2] - (E[A])^2$$

$$E[A^2] = Var\ A + (E[A])^2$$

$$= 1 + 1^2$$

$$= 2$$

Similarly,

$$E[B^2] = Var\ B + (E[B])^2$$

$$= 2 + 2^2$$

$$= 6$$

$$E[C^2] = Var\ C + (E[C])^2$$

$$= 10 + 10^2$$

$$= 110$$

$$So, (1)\ becomes:$$

$$E[X^2] = .1(2) + .5(6) + .4(110)$$

$$= 47.2$$

$$Var\ X = E[X^2] - (E[X])^2$$

$$= 47.2 - (5.1)^2$$

$$= 21.19$$

The correct answer is **C**.

SOA Sample Question 228 Explanation

Let X be the annual number of tornadoes.

We are to find $Var[X|X \geq 1]$. For this, we need $f(x|x \geq 1)$.

$$f(x) = \frac{3^x e^{-3}}{x!}, \qquad x = 0,1,2,\ldots$$

$$f(x|x \geq 1) = \frac{P(X = x, and\ X \geq 1)}{P(X \geq 1)}$$

$$= \frac{f(x)}{1 - f(0)}, \qquad x = 1,2,3,\ldots$$

$$= \frac{1}{1-e^{-3}} \frac{3^x e^{-3}}{x!}, \qquad x = 1,2,3,\ldots$$

$$E[X|X \geq 1] = \sum x f(x|x \geq 1) = \sum_{x=1}^{\infty} \frac{x}{1-e^{-3}} \frac{3^x e^{-3}}{x!} = \sum_{x=0}^{\infty} \frac{x}{1-e^{-3}} \frac{3^x e^{-3}}{x!}$$

This last equality is true because for $x = 0$, the expression under the sum is 0 and so we are only adding 0 by changing the index which keeps the equality. So,

$$E[X|X \geq 1] = \frac{1}{1-e^{-3}} \sum_{x=0}^{\infty} x \frac{3^x e^{-3}}{x!} = \frac{1}{1-e^{-3}} \sum_{x=0}^{\infty} x f(x) = \frac{1}{1-e^{-3}} E[X] = \frac{3}{1-e^{-3}}$$

$$E[X^2|X \geq 1] = \sum x^2 f(x|x \geq 1) = \sum_{x=1}^{\infty} \frac{x^2}{1-e^{-3}} \frac{3^x e^{-3}}{x!} = \sum_{x=0}^{\infty} \frac{x^2}{1-e^{-3}} \frac{3^x e^{-3}}{x!}$$

$$= \frac{1}{1-e^{-3}} \sum_{x=0}^{\infty} x^2 \frac{3^x e^{-3}}{x!} = \frac{1}{1-e^{-3}} \sum_{x=0}^{\infty} x^2 f(x) = \frac{1}{1-e^{-3}} E[X^2] \quad (1)$$

Variance of Poisson variable equals mean. So,

$$Var\ X = E[X^2] - (E[X])^2$$

$$E[X^2] = Var\ X + (E[X])^2 = 3 + 3^2 = 12$$

So, eq (1) becomes:

$$E[X^2|X \geq 1] = \frac{12}{1-e^{-3}}$$

$$Var[X|X \geq 1] = E[X^2|X \geq 1] - (E[X|X \geq 1])^2 = \frac{12}{1-e^{-3}} - \left(\frac{3}{1-e^{-3}}\right)^2 = 2.66$$

The correct answer is **C**.

SOA Sample Question 229 Explanation

Let X be the yearly dental expense. Then:

$$f(x) = \frac{1}{1200 - 200} = .001, \qquad 200 \le X \le 1200$$

$$Y = \begin{cases} 0, & X \le 400 \\ X - 400, & 400 < X < 900 \\ 500, & X \ge 900 \end{cases}$$

$$E[Y] = \int_{-\infty}^{\infty} y\, f(x)\, dx$$

$$= \int_{400}^{900} (x - 400)(.001)\, dx + \int_{900}^{1200} 500(.001) dx$$

$$= .001 \frac{(x - 400)^2}{2} \Big|_{400}^{900} + .5x \Big|_{900}^{1200}$$

$$= \frac{.001}{2}(900 - 400)^2 + .5(1200 - 900)$$

$$= 275$$

$$E[Y^2] = \int_{-\infty}^{\infty} y^2\, f(x)\, dx$$

$$= \int_{400}^{900} (x - 400)^2(.001)\, dx + \int_{900}^{1200} 500^2(.001) dx$$

$$= .001 \frac{(x - 400)^3}{3} \Big|_{400}^{900} + 250x \Big|_{900}^{1200}$$

$$= \frac{.001}{3}(900 - 400)^3 + 250(1200 - 900)$$

$$= 116667$$

$$Var\, Y = E[Y^2] - (E[Y])^2$$

$$= 116667 - (275)^2$$

$$= 41042$$

The correct answer is **C**.

SOA Sample Question 230 Explanation

Let X be the damage and Y be the payout. Deductible is $0.5b$.

$$f(x) = \frac{1}{b}, \qquad 0 < x < b$$

$$Var\,X = \frac{(b-0)^2}{12} = .0833b^2$$

$$Y = \begin{cases} 0, & X < 0.5b \\ X - 0.5b, & 0.5b < X < b \end{cases}$$

$$E(Y) = \int_{-\infty}^{\infty} y\, f(x)\, dx = \int_{0.5b}^{b} (x - 0.5b)\left(\frac{1}{b}\right) dx = \int_{0.5b}^{b} \frac{x}{b} - 0.5\, dx$$

$$= \left(\frac{x^2}{2b} - 0.5x\right)\Big|_{x=.5b}^{x=b}$$

$$= \left(\frac{b^2}{2b} - 0.5b\right) - \left(\frac{(.5b)^2}{2b} - 0.5(.5b)\right)$$

$$= \frac{b}{2} - .5b - \frac{.25b}{2} + .25b = .125b$$

$$E(Y^2) = \int_{-\infty}^{\infty} y^2\, f(x)\, dx = \int_{0.5b}^{b} (x - 0.5b)^2\left(\frac{1}{b}\right) dx$$

$$= \frac{1}{b}\left(\frac{(x-.5b)^3}{3}\right)\Big|_{x=.5b}^{x=b}$$

$$= \frac{1}{b}\left(\frac{(b-.5b)^3}{3}\right) = \frac{(.5b)^3}{3b} = \frac{.125}{3}b^2$$

$$Var\,Y = E(Y^2) - (E[Y])^2$$

$$= \frac{.125}{3}b^2 - (.125b)^2$$

$$= .02604b^2$$

$$Var\,Y : Var\,X = \frac{.02604b^2}{.0833b^2}$$

$$= .3125$$

$$= \frac{5}{16}$$

$$= 5:16$$

The correct answer is **D**.

Quiz 20

1. Cost for visiting a dentist is uniformly distributed on [0, 300]. A dental insurance has a deductible of d per visit. The expected value of the uncovered portion of the cost is 85 per visit. Find d.
   A) 103
   B) 113
   C) 123
   D) 133
   E) 143

Solution:

Let X be the cost and Y be the uncovered portion of cost. When cost is less than the deductible, all the cost is uncovered. When cost is greater than the deductible, then deductible is the unreimbursed portion of the cost.

$$f(x) = \frac{1}{300}, \qquad 0 < x < 300$$

$$Y = \begin{cases} X, & X \le d \\ d, & X > d \end{cases}$$

$$E[Y] = 85$$

$$\int_{-\infty}^{\infty} y\, f(x)\, dx = 85$$

$$\int_0^d x\left(\frac{1}{300}\right) dx + \int_d^{300} d\left(\frac{1}{300}\right) dx = 85$$

$$\frac{1}{300}\left(\frac{x^2}{2}\right)\Big|_0^d + \frac{1}{300} d\, x\Big|_d^{300} = 85$$

$$\frac{d^2}{600} + \frac{300d - d^2}{300} = 85$$

$$d^2 + 600D - 2d^2 = 51000$$

$$d^2 - 600d + 51000 = 0$$

$$d = \frac{600 \pm \sqrt{600^2 - 4(1)(51000)}}{2(1)} = 497, 103$$

A deductible of 497 makes no sense because it is greater than max cost of 300.

Hence the deductible is 103

The correct answer is **A**.

2. After a fire in a home, there is a 60% chance that the loss amount follows a uniform distribution on the interval $[0, b]$, and a 40% chance that the loss amount follows a uniform distribution on the interval $[b, 4b]$. The median loss amount due to fire is 950. Calculate the mean loss amount due to fire.
   A) 1182
   B) 1282
   C) 1382
   D) 1482
   E) 1582

Solution:

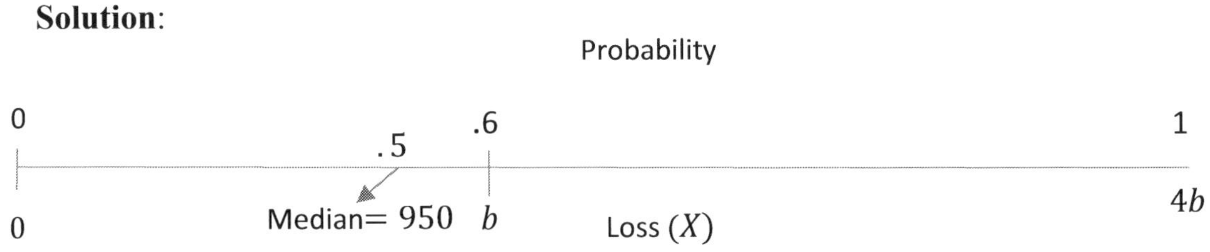

Note that the median, which corresponds to a cumulative probability of .5, lies in $[0, b]$.

The median is 950. So,

$$.5 = P(X \leq 950)$$

$$.5 = P(X \text{ } is \text{ } in \text{ } [0, b])\left(\frac{950 - 0}{b - 0}\right)$$

$$.5 = .6\left(\frac{950}{b}\right)$$

$$.5 = \frac{570}{b}$$

$$b = \frac{570}{.5}$$

$$= 1140$$

By law of total probability,

$$E[X] = P(X \text{ } in \text{ } [0, b])E[X|X \text{ } in \text{ } [0, b]] + P(X \text{ } in \text{ } [b, 4b])E[X|X \text{ } in \text{ } [b, 4b]]$$

$$= .6E([0, b]) + .4E([b, 4b])$$

Recall that the expected value of a uniform distribution lies at its midpoint. So,

$$E[X] = .6\left(\frac{0 + b}{2}\right) + .4\left(\frac{b + 4b}{2}\right)$$

$$= 1.3b$$

$$= 1.3(1140)$$

$$= 1482$$

The correct answer is **D**.

3. A policy will pay for only one fire loss claim per year. For a random policyholder, there is a 70% probability of no fire loss in the next year, in which case the claim amount is 0. If a fire loss occurs in the next year, the claim amount is normally distributed with mean 2000 and standard deviation 900. Find the 75th percentile of the claim amount in the next year for a random policyholder.
A) 1100
B) 1130
C) 1160
D) 1190
E) 1220

Solution:

75th percentile is the claim amount at which the accumulated probability is .75.

Let X be the claim amount and k be the 75th percentile. Then

$$P(X \leq k) = .75$$

$$P(0 \leq X \leq k) = .75$$

$$P(X = 0) + P(0 < X \leq k) = .75$$

$$.7 + P(0 < X \leq k) = .75$$

$$P(0 < X \leq k) = .05$$

Since only .7 of the probability has accumulated up to a claim amount of 0, the 75th percentile of claim amount occurs in the region where $X > 0$. So, we need:

$$P(X \leq k | X > 0) = \frac{P(X \leq k \text{ and } X > 0)}{P(X > 0)}$$

$$= \frac{P(0 < X \leq k)}{1 - P(X \leq 0)}$$

$$= \frac{.05}{1 - .7}$$

$$= .1667$$

We therefore need the cumulative probability corresponding to .1667.

Since the table only has cumulative probabilities of .5 or more, we look at the cumulative probability of $1 - .1667 = .8333$.

From table, $z = .96$ corresponds to cumulative probability of .8315 and $z = .97$ corresponds to .8340. By interpolation,

$$\frac{.8333 - .8315}{.8340 - .8315} = .7$$

Thus, $z = .967$ corresponds to .8333.

By symmetry of the normal distribution we see that $z = -.967$ corresponds to .1667.

$$z = \frac{X - \mu}{\sigma}$$

$$-.967 = \frac{k - 2000}{900}$$

$$-.967(900) = k - 2000$$

$$k = 1130$$

The correct answer is **B**.

4. Costs of doctor visits are normally distributed with mean 300 and standard deviation 100. A medical insurance has a deductible of 50 per visit. Find the median of the costs that exceed the deductible.
A) 293
B) 295
C) 297
D) 299
E) 301

Solution:

Let X be the visit cost. We will start by finding the z-score of the deductible.

$$z = \frac{X - \mu}{\sigma} = \frac{50 - 300}{100} = -2.5$$

$$P(X \geq 50) = P(z \geq -2.5) = P(z \leq 2.5) = .9938$$

$$P(X < 50) = 1 - P(X \geq 50) = 1 - .9938 = .0062$$

We have the following picture:

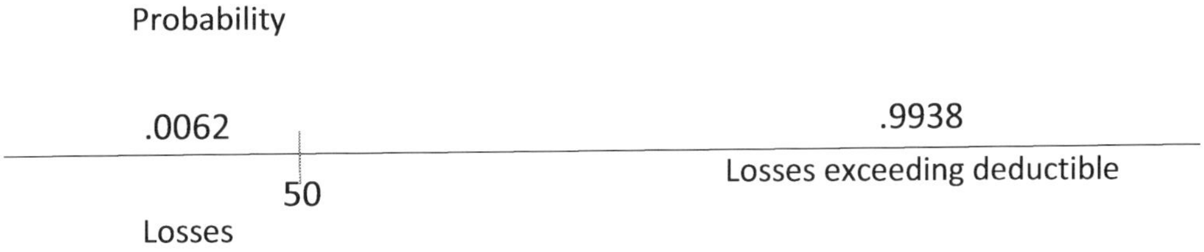

We see from the picture that the median of costs exceeding deductible corresponds to a cumulative loss probability of:

$$.0062 + .5(.9938) = .5031$$

From table, $z = 0$ corresponds to cumulative probability of .5 and $z = .01$ corresponds to cumulative probability of .5040. By interpolation:

$$\frac{.5031 - .5}{.5040 - .5} = .8$$

So, $z = .008$ corresponds to cumulative probability of .5031.

So, the required median is the loss value corresponding to $z = .008$.

$$z = \frac{X - \mu}{\sigma}$$

$$.008 = \frac{X - 300}{100}$$

$$.008(100) = X - 300$$

$$X = 301$$

The correct answer is **E**.

5. Annual home repair costs are uniformly distributed on $[0,9000]$. A home-owner buys a primary home-insurance which covers up to 5000 of the annual repair costs, and a secondary home-insurance which covers up to 3000 of any remaining repair costs in excess of 5000. Let Y be the annual cost covered by secondary insurance. Find $Var\ Y$.
   A) Greater than 1 million but less than 1.5 million
   B) Greater than 1.5 million but less than 2 million
   C) Greater than 2 million but less than 2.5 million
   D) Greater than 2.5 million but less than 3 million
   E) Greater than 3 million
   Solution:

   Let X be the annual repair cost. Then:

$$f(x) = \frac{1}{9000}, \qquad 0 \le X \le 9000$$

$$Y = \begin{cases} 0, & X \le 5000 \\ X - 5000, & 5000 < X < 8000 \\ 3000, & X \ge 8000 \end{cases}$$

$$E[Y] = \int_{-\infty}^{\infty} y\, f(x)\, dx$$

$$= \int_{5000}^{8000} (x - 5000)\left(\frac{1}{9000}\right) dx + \int_{8000}^{9000} 3000\left(\frac{1}{9000}\right) dx$$

$$= \frac{1}{9000} \frac{(x - 5000)^2}{2}\Big|_{5000}^{8000} + \frac{1}{3} x \Big|_{8000}^{9000}$$

$$= \frac{1}{18000}(8000 - 5000)^2 + \frac{1}{3}(9000 - 8000)$$

$$= 833.33$$

$$E[Y^2] = \int_{-\infty}^{\infty} y^2\, f(x)\, dx$$

$$= \int_{5000}^{8000} (x - 5000)^2\left(\frac{1}{9000}\right) dx + \int_{8000}^{9000} 3000^2\left(\frac{1}{9000}\right) dx$$

$$= \frac{1}{9000} \frac{(x - 5000)^3}{3}\Big|_{5000}^{8000} + 1000x\Big|_{8000}^{9000}$$

$$= \frac{1}{27000}(8000 - 5000)^3 + 1000(9000 - 8000)$$

$$= 2000000$$

$$Var\,Y = E[Y^2] - (E[Y])^2$$

$$= 2000000 - (833.33)^2$$

$$= 1305561$$

The correct answer is **A**.

6. The daily cash drawn by customers from a local bank is normally distributed with mean 50,000 and standard deviation 20,000. The bank gets enough cash X at the start of each day so that there is only a 5% chance that it will run out of cash that day. Find X.
A) 79900
B) 80900
C) 81900
D) 82900
E) 83900
Solution:

Let be C the daily cash demand. We need:

$$P(C > X) = .05$$

$$P(C \le X) = 1 - .05 = .95$$

From tables, a cumulative probability of .9495 corresponds to $z = 1.64$, and a cumulative probability of .9505 corresponds to $z = 1.65$.

Since .95 is exactly midway between these 2 probabilities, the same is true for the z-score.

Thus, $C = X$ corresponds to $z = 1.645$ in the formula:

$$z = \frac{C - \mu}{\sigma}$$

$$1.645 = \frac{X - 50000}{20000}$$

$$X = 82900$$

The correct answer is **D**.

7. The number of daily deaths in a city follows a Poisson distribution with mean 1.5. Find the expected number of deaths in a day, given that at least one death occurs that day.
   A) 1.75
   B) 1.82
   C) 1.93
   D) 2.00
   E) 2.06

Solution:

Let X be the daily deaths. We are to find $E[X|X \geq 1]$. We first find $f(x|x \geq 1)$.

$$f(x) = \frac{1.5^x e^{-1.5}}{x!}, \qquad x = 0,1,2,\ldots$$

$$f(x|x \geq 1) = \frac{P(X = x, and\ X \geq 1)}{P(X \geq 1)}$$

$$= \frac{f(x)}{1 - f(0)}, \qquad x = 1,2,3,\ldots$$

$$= \frac{1}{1 - e^{-1.5}} \frac{1.5^x e^{-1.5}}{x!}, \qquad x = 1,2,3,\ldots$$

$$E[X|X \geq 1] = \sum x f(x|x \geq 1)$$

$$= \sum_{x=1}^{\infty} \frac{x}{1 - e^{-1.5}} \frac{1.5^x e^{-1.5}}{x!}$$

$$= \sum_{x=0}^{\infty} \frac{x}{1 - e^{-1.5}} \frac{1.5^x e^{-1.5}}{x!}$$

This last equality is true because for $x = 0$, the expression under the sum is 0 and so we are only adding 0 by changing the index which keeps the equality. So,

$$E[X|X \geq 1] = \frac{1}{1 - e^{-1.5}} \sum_{x=0}^{\infty} x \frac{1.5^x e^{-1.5}}{x!}$$

$$= \frac{1}{1 - e^{-1.5}} \sum_{x=0}^{\infty} x f(x)$$

$$= \frac{1}{1 - e^{-1.5}} E[X]$$

$$= \frac{1.5}{1 - e^{-1.5}}$$

$$= 1.93$$

The correct answer is **C**.

8. Car losses X in an accident are exponentially distributed. Mary's car insurance covers losses up to 3000 for each accident. Ann's car insurance covers losses up to 6000 for each accident. Probability that Ann's car insurance will completely cover a loss is 1.5 times the probability that Mary's car insurance will completely cover a loss. Find $Var\ X$.
A) 18100000
B) 18300000
C) 18500000
D) 18700000
E) 18900000

Solution:

If m is the mean loss, then the cdf of loss is:

$$F(x) = 1 - e^{-x/m}$$

A loss is fully covered by Mary's insurance if it is less than or equal to 3000.

A loss is fully covered by Ann's insurance if it is less than or equal to 6000. So,

$$P(L \le 6000) = 1.5P(L \le 3000)$$

$$F(6000) = 1.5F(3000)$$

$$1 - e^{-\frac{6000}{m}} = 1.5\left(1 - e^{-\frac{3000}{m}}\right)$$

Let $e^{-\frac{3000}{m}} = y$. Then the above equation becomes

$$1 - y^2 = 1.5(1 - y)$$

$$(1 - y)(1 + y) = 1.5(1 - y)$$

$$1 + y = 1.5$$

$$y = .5$$

$$e^{-\frac{3000}{m}} = .5$$

$$-\frac{3000}{m} = \ln .5$$

$$m = -\frac{3000}{\ln .5}$$

$$m = 4328$$

The variance of an exponential distribution equals the square of its mean.

$$Var\ L = 4328^2$$

$$= 18731584$$

This rounds to choice **D**.

9. The number of men who die monthly in a town follows a Poisson distribution with mean 3, while the number of women who die monthly in this town follows a Poisson distribution with mean 2. 45% of town people are men and the remaining are women. Let X represent the number of monthly deaths of the gender of a randomly selected individual in this town. Find Variance of X.
   A) 2.2
   B) 2.7
   C) 3.2
   D) 3.7
   E) 4.2

   Solution:

   Let M be the number of men who die in a month, and W be the number of women who die in a month in this town. Then:

$$X = \begin{cases} M, & prob\ .45 \\ W, & prob\ .55 \end{cases}$$

$$E[X] = .45E[M] + .55E[W]$$

$$= .45(3) + .55(2) = 2.45$$

$$E[X^2] = .45E[M^2] + .55E[W^2] \quad (1)$$

Recall that variance and mean of a Poisson variable are the same. So, from:

$$Var\ M = E[M^2] - (E[M])^2$$

$$E[M^2] = Var\ M + (E[M])^2$$

$$= 3 + 3^2$$

$$= 12$$

Similarly,

$$E[W^2] = Var\ W + (E[W])^2$$

$$= 2 + 2^2$$

$$= 6$$

Equation (1) becomes:

$$E[X^2] = .45(12) + .55(6)$$

$$= 8.7$$

$$Var\ X = E[X^2] - (E[X])^2$$

$$= 8.7 - (2.45)^2$$

$$= 2.7$$

The correct answer is **B**.

Tools Needed for Problems 231-239

$$z = \frac{X - \mu}{\sigma}$$

Loss means negative profit.

Expected value of a constant is that constant.

$$E[aX + bY] = aE[X[+bE[Y]$$

$$SD(X) = \sqrt{E[X^2] - (E[X])^2}$$

$$Var(X|Y = y) = E(X^2|Y = y) - [E(X|Y = y)]^2$$

Pdf of uniform $[a, b]$ is:

$$f(x) = \frac{1}{b - a}, \qquad a < x < b$$

Pmf of Poisson variable with mean m is:

$$f(x) = \frac{m^x e^{-m}}{x!}, \qquad x = 0,1,2, \ldots$$

Mean and variance of a Poisson distribution are equal.

The pdf and cdf of an exponential distribution with mean m are:

$$f(x) = \frac{1}{m} e^{-x/m}, x > 0$$

$$F(x) = 1 - e^{-x/m}$$

$$P(A \cup B) = P(A) + P(B) - P(AB)$$

If two events are independent, then:

$$P(AB) = P(A)P(B)$$

If a probability evaluation of only one variable is done using a joint cdf, then that missing variable is set to its maximum possible value.

$$F(x) = P(X \leq x)$$

SOA Sample Question 231 Explanation

Let X be the annual profit. We are given that:

$$\sigma^2 = \mu^3$$

$$\sigma = \mu^{3/2}$$

Also, loss means negative profit. So, are told that:

$$P(X < 0) = .05 \quad (1)$$

We change 0 into standard score.

$$z = \frac{X-\mu}{\sigma} = \frac{0-\mu}{\mu^{\frac{3}{2}}} = -\frac{1}{\sqrt{\mu}}$$

So, equation (1) becomes:

$$.05 = P(X < 0)$$

$$.05 = P\left(z < -\frac{1}{\sqrt{\mu}}\right)$$

$$.05 = P\left(z > \frac{1}{\sqrt{\mu}}\right)$$

$$.05 = 1 - P\left(z \le \frac{1}{\sqrt{\mu}}\right)$$

$$P\left(z \le \frac{1}{\sqrt{\mu}}\right) = 1 - .05 = .95$$

From table and interpolation, cumulative probability of .95 corresponds to $z = 1.645$. So,

$$\frac{1}{\sqrt{\mu}} = 1.645$$

$$\mu = .37\ billion = 370\ million$$

The correct answer is **A**.

SOA Sample Question 232 Explanation

$$47 = E[(X-1)^2]$$

$$47 = E[X^2 - 2X + 1]$$

$$47 = E[X^2] - 2E[X] + E[1]$$

$$47 = 61 - 2E[X] + 1$$

$$\Rightarrow \quad E[X] = 7.5$$

$$SD(X) = \sqrt{E[X^2] - (E[X])^2} = \sqrt{61 - (7.5)^2} = 2.18$$

The correct answer is **A**.

SOA Sample Question 233 Explanation

Let D be the number of diamonds picked, and S be the number of spades picked.

To find $Var(D|S=0)$, we need to find the corresponding probability function.

There are 7 cards which are not spades.

Not selecting any spade means that both the cards selected are from these 7 non spade cards.

$$P(S=0)=\frac{\#\,of\ ways\ to\ pick\ 2\ non-spades\ from\ 7}{\#\,of\ ways\ to\ pick\ 2\ cards\ from\ 10}=\frac{\binom{7}{2}}{\binom{10}{2}}=\frac{7}{15}$$

$$P(D=0,S=0)=\frac{\#\,of\ ways\ to\ pick\ 2\ hearts\ from\ 5}{\#\,of\ ways\ to\ pick\ 2\ cards\ from\ 10}=\frac{\binom{5}{2}}{\binom{10}{2}}=\frac{2}{9}$$

$$P(D=1,S=0)=\frac{\#\,of\ ways\ to\ pick\ 1\ diamond\ and\ 1\ heart}{\#\,of\ ways\ to\ pick\ 2\ cards\ from\ 10}=\frac{\binom{2}{1}\binom{5}{1}}{\binom{10}{2}}=\frac{2}{9}$$

$$P(D=2,S=0)=\frac{\#\,of\ ways\ to\ pick\ 2\ diamonds\ from\ 2}{\#\,of\ ways\ to\ pick\ 2\ cards\ from\ 10}=\frac{\binom{2}{2}}{\binom{10}{2}}=\frac{1}{45}$$

$$P(D=0|S=0)=\frac{P(D=0,S=0)}{P(S=0)}=\frac{2/9}{7/15}=\frac{10}{21}$$

$$P(D=1|S=0)=\frac{P(D=1,S=0)}{P(S=0)}=\frac{2/9}{7/15}=\frac{10}{21}$$

$$P(D=2|S=0)=\frac{P(D=2,S=0)}{P(S=0)}=\frac{1/45}{7/15}=\frac{1}{21}$$

$$E(D|S=0)=\sum_{d=0}^{2} d\,f(d|s=0)=0P(D=0|S=0)+1P(D=1|S=0)+2P(D=2|S=0)$$

$$=0\left(\frac{10}{21}\right)+1\left(\frac{10}{21}\right)+2\left(\frac{1}{21}\right)=\frac{4}{7}$$

$$E(D^2|S=0)=\sum_{d=0}^{2} d^2\,f(d|s=0)=0+1^2P(D=1|S=0)+2^2P(D=2|S=0)$$

$$=0\left(\frac{10}{21}\right)+1\left(\frac{10}{21}\right)+4\left(\frac{1}{21}\right)$$

$$E(D^2|S=0)=\frac{2}{3}$$

$$Var(D|S=0)=E(D^2|S=0)-[E(D|S=0)]^2=\frac{2}{3}-\left(\frac{4}{7}\right)^2=.34$$

The correct answer is **D**.

SOA Sample Question 237 Explanation (Questions 234-236 are deleted by SOA)

The train will stop the traffic from 7:20 to 7:25.

Let C be the event that the waiting time for car exceeds 3 minutes.

Let B be the event that the waiting time for bus exceeds 3 minutes.

We are to find $P(B \cup C)$

$$P(B \cup C) = P(B) + P(C) - P(BC) \quad (1)$$

Because of independence,:

$$P(BC) = P(B)P(C)$$

So, (1) becomes:

$$P(B \cup C) = P(B) + P(C) - P(B)P(C) \quad (2)$$

The car wait will exceed 3 minutes if the car arrives between 7:20 and 7:22. So,

$$P(C) = \frac{7{:}22 - 7{:}20}{7{:}30 - 7{:}15}$$

$$= \frac{2}{15}$$

Similarly,

$$P(B) = \frac{2}{15}$$

Eq (2) becomes:

$$P(B \cup C) = \frac{2}{15} + \frac{2}{15} - \frac{2}{15}\left(\frac{2}{15}\right)$$

$$= .25$$

The correct answer is **A**.

SOA Sample Question 238 Explanation

$F(2,2)$ is the probability that both A and B make at most 2 attempts.

$$P(A\ makes\ at\ most\ 2) = P(X \le 2) = P(X = 1\ or\ 2) = P(X = 1) + P(X = 2) \quad (1)$$

Only 1 attempt means failing at that attempt (prob p). So

$$P(X = 1) = p$$

Only 2 attempts mean succeeding in 1st (prob $1 - p$)and failing in 2nd (prob p). So

$$P(X = 2) = (1 - p)p$$

Thus, equation (1) becomes:

$$P(X \le 2) = p + (1 - p)p = 2p - p^2 = P(Y \le 2)$$

$$.0441 = F(2,2) = P(X \le 2\ and\ Y \le 2)) = (2p - p^2)(2p - p^2) = (2p - p^2)^2$$

$$(2p - p^2) = \pm\sqrt{.0441} = \pm.21$$

$$p^2 - 2p + .21 = 0\,, \quad p^2 - 2p - .21 = 0$$

$$p = \frac{2 \pm \sqrt{4 - 4(.21)}}{2}\,, \quad \frac{2 \pm \sqrt{4 + 4(.21)}}{2}$$

Since probability is always between 0 and 1, the only valid value among the four is $p = .11118$

$F(1,5)$ is probability that A gets injured in 1st attempt, while B gets injured in at most 5 attempts. Being injured in at most 5 attempts is complement of being uninjured in first 5 attempts.

$$P(Y \le 5) = 1 - P(B\ is\ uininjured\ in\ first\ 5\ attempts) = 1 - (1 - p)^5$$

$$= 1 - (1 - .11118)^5 = .44529$$

Also, $P(X \le 1) = P(X = 1) = p = .11118$. So,

$$F(1,5) = P(X \le 1, and\ Y \le 5) = .11118(.44529) = .0495$$

The correct answer is **C**.

SOA Sample Question 239 Explanation

We are to find $P(X = 3, Y = 3)$

$$F(3,3) = P(X \le 3, Y \le 3)$$

$$P(X = 3, Y = 3) = F(3,3) - F(2,3) - F(3,2) + F(2,2)$$

Note: To better understand the above step, please refer to my youtube video whose link is: https://www.youtube.com/watch?v=gNqmODjYbig

$$= [1 - (.5)^{3+1}][1 - (.2)^{3+1}] - [1 - (.5)^{2+1}][1 - (.2)^{3+1}] - [1 - (.5)^{3+1}][1 - (.2)^{2+1}] + [1 - (.5)^{2+1}][1 - (.2)^{2+1}]$$

$$= .936 - .8736 - .93 + .868 = .0004$$

The correct answer is **B**.

Quiz 21

1. The number of home repairs, X, and the number of car repairs, Y, for a person, this year, has, for non-negative integers x, y, the joint cdf:

$$F(x,y) = [1 - (.5)^{x+1}][1 - (.2)^{y+1}],$$

Calculate the probability that the person has exactly two home repairs and exactly two car repairs this year.

A) .001
B) .002
C) .003
D) .004
E) .005

Solution:

We are to find $P(X = 2, Y = 2)$.

$$P(X = 2, Y = 2) = F(2,2) - F(1,2) - F(2,1) + F(1,1)$$

$$= [1 - (.5)^{2+1}][1 - (.2)^{2+1}] - [1 - (.5)^{1+1}][1 - (.2)^{2+1}]$$
$$- [1 - (.5)^{2+1}][1 - (.2)^{1+1}] + [1 - (.5)^{1+1}][1 - (.2)^{1+1}]$$

$$= .004$$

The correct answer is **D**.

2. A company's weekly profit (in thousands) has a normal distribution with standard deviation equal to the cube of its mean. The probability of a weekly loss is 2.5%. Calculate the company's expected weekly profit.

A) 714
B) 734
C) 754
D) 774
E) 794

Solution:

Let X be the weekly profit. We are given that:

$$\sigma = \mu^3$$

Also, loss means negative profit. So,

$$P(X < 0) = .025$$

We change 0 into standard score.

$$z = \frac{X - \mu}{\sigma} = \frac{0 - \mu}{\mu^3} = -\frac{1}{\mu^2}$$

$$.025 = P(X < 0) = P\left(z < -\frac{1}{\mu^2}\right) = P\left(z > \frac{1}{\mu^2}\right) = 1 - P\left(z \leq \frac{1}{\mu^2}\right)$$

$$P\left(z \le \frac{1}{\mu^2}\right) = 1 - .025 = .975$$

From tables, cumulative probability of .975 corresponds to $z = 1.96$. So,

$$\frac{1}{\mu^2} = 1.96$$

$$\mu = .714\ thousand$$

$$= 714$$

The correct answer is **A**.

3. The expected value of a random variable X is 25 and $E[(X+3)^2] = 900$. Find the standard deviation of X.
   A) 10.17
   B) 10.47
   C) 10.77
   D) 11.07
   E) 11.37

   Solution:

$$900 = E[(X+3)^2]$$

$$900 = E[X^2 + 6X + 9]$$

$$900 = E[X^2] + 6E[X] + E[9]$$

$$900 = E[X^2] + 6(25) + 9$$

We have used the fact that the expected value of a constant is that constant.

$$E[X^2] = 741$$

$$SD(X) = \sqrt{E[X^2] - (E[X])^2}$$

$$= \sqrt{741 - (25)^2}$$

$$= 10.77$$

The correct answer is **C**.

4. There are 2 mathematicians, 3 statisticians, and 4 engineers in a room. Two of these persons are randomly selected. Find the variance of the number of mathematicians selected given that no engineer is selected.
   A) .36
   B) .5
   C) .64
   D) .8
   E) 1

   Solution:

Let M, E be the number of mathematicians and engineers picked, respectively.

To find $Var(M|E = 0)$, we need to find the corresponding probability function.

There are 5 non-engineers.

Not selecting any engineer means that both the persons selected are from these 5 non-engineers.

$$P(E=0)=\frac{\#\,of\ ways\ to\ pick\ 2\ non-engineers\ from\ 5}{\#\,of\ ways\ to\ pick\ 2\ persons\ from\ 9}=\frac{\binom{5}{2}}{\binom{9}{2}}=\frac{5}{18}$$

$$P(M=0,E=0)=\frac{\#\,of\ ways\ to\ pick\ 2\ statisticians\ from\ 3}{\#\,of\ ways\ to\ pick\ 2\ persons\ from\ 9}=\frac{\binom{3}{2}}{\binom{9}{2}}=\frac{1}{12}$$

$$P(M=1,E=0)=\frac{\#\,of\ ways\ to\ pick\ 1\ math\ and\ 1\ stat}{\#\,of\ ways\ to\ pick\ 2\ persons\ from\ 9}=\frac{\binom{2}{1}\binom{3}{1}}{\binom{9}{2}}=\frac{1}{6}$$

$$P(M=2,E=0)=\frac{\#\,of\ ways\ to\ pick\ 2\ math\ from\ 2}{\#\,of\ ways\ to\ pick\ 2\ cards\ from\ 10}=\frac{\binom{2}{2}}{\binom{9}{2}}=\frac{1}{36}$$

$$P(M=0|E=0)=\frac{P(M=0,E=0)}{P(E=0)}=\frac{1/12}{5/18}=.3$$

$$P(M=1|E=0)=\frac{P(M=1,E=0)}{P(E=0)}=\frac{1/6}{5/18}=.6$$

$$P(M=2|E=0)=\frac{P(M=2,E=0)}{P(E=0)}=\frac{1/36}{5/18}=.1$$

$$E(M|E=0)=\sum_{m=0}^{2} m\,f(m|e=0)$$

$$=0P(M=0|E=0)+1P(M=1|E=0)+2P(M=2|E=0)$$

$$=0(.3)+1(.6)+2(.1)$$

$$=.8$$

$$E(M^2|E=0)=\sum_{m=0}^{2} m^2\,f(m|e=0)$$

$$=0^2P(M=0|E=0)+1^2P(M=1|E=0)+2^2P(M=2|E=0)$$

$$=0(.3)+1(.6)+4(.1)=1$$

$$Var(M|E=0)=E(M^2|E=0)-[E(M|E=0)]^2$$

$$=1-(.8)^2=.36$$

The correct answer is **A**.

Tools Needed for Problems 240-245

Variance of an exponential variable is the square of its mean.

$$Var\ X = Var(E[X|S]) + E[Var(X|S)$$

$$Var(aX) = a^2 Var(X)$$

$$E[aX + bY] = aE[X] + bE[Y]$$

$$Var\ X = E[X^2] - (E[X])^2$$

For uniform $[a, b]$ variable,

$$f(x) = \frac{1}{b-a}, \qquad a < x < b, \qquad E[X] = \frac{a+b}{2}, \qquad Var\ (X) = \frac{(b-a)^2}{12}$$

Mean and variance of a binomial variable are:

$$E[X] = np, \quad Var\ X = np(1-p)$$

$$z = \frac{X - \mu}{\sigma}$$

Central Limit Theorem:

If population is normal, or if sample size, $n > 30$, then the sampling distribution of means and sums is approximately normal with mean and standard deviation:

$$\mu_{\bar{X}} = \mu$$

$$\sigma_{\bar{X}} = \frac{\sigma}{\sqrt{n}}$$

$$\mu_{sum} = n\mu$$

$$\sigma_{sum} = \sqrt{n}\,\sigma$$

where μ and σ are the mean and standard deviation of each of the n identically distributed independent normal variables.

Pmf of a Poisson variable with mean λ is:

$$f(x) = \frac{\lambda^x e^{-\lambda}}{x!}, \qquad x = 0,1,2, \ldots$$

Mean and variance of a Poisson variable are the same.

If X, Y are independent, then

$$E[XY] = E[X]E[Y]$$

Expected value of a discrete variable is:

$$E[X] = \sum x\, f(x)$$

SOA Sample Question 240 Explanation

Let X be the number of deaths.

It is binomial with $n = 1000,\ p = .014$. So,

$$E[X] = np = 1000(.014) = 14$$

$$Var\ X = np(1-p) = 14(1-.014) = 13.804$$

Let Y be the payout. Then:

$$Y = 50000X$$

$$E[Y] = 50000E[X] = 50000(14) = 700000$$

$$Var\ Y = 50000^2\ Var\ X = 50000^2(13.804) = 34510000000$$

$$\sigma_Y = \sqrt{Var\ Y} = \sqrt{34510000000} = 185769$$

Let s be the smallest amount of money needed in the fund. We want .99 probability that the total payout is less than this amount. That is:

$$P(Y \le s) = .99 \quad (1)$$

We need the z-score for a cumulative probability of .99.

From table, $z = 2.32$ corresponds to .9898, and $z = 2.33$ corresponds to .9901.

By interpolation:

$$\frac{.99 - .9898}{.9901 - .9898} = .7$$

So, $z = 2.327$ corresponds to a cumulative probability of .99. That is:

$$P(z \le 2.327) = .99 \quad (2)$$

From (1) and (2) we see that $z = 2.327$ corresponds to $Y = s$. Hence,

$$z = \frac{Y - \mu_Y}{\sigma_Y}$$

$$2.327 = \frac{s - 700000}{185769}$$

$$2.327(185769) = s - 700000$$

$$s = 1132284$$

This rounds to 1150000 to the nearest 50 thousand.

The correct answer is **D**.

SOA Sample Question 241 Explanation

Let X_k be the change in month k. Then:

$$X_k = \begin{cases} 1.1\,, & prob\ .5 \\ -.9\,, & prob\ .5 \end{cases}$$

$$E[X_k] = 1.1(.5) - .9(.5) = .1$$

$$E\left[{X_k}^2\right] = 1.1^2(.5) + (-.9)^2(.5) = 1.01$$

$$Var\ X_k = E\left[{X_k}^2\right] - (E[X_k])^2$$

$$= 1.01 - (.1)^2$$

$$= 1$$

Let X be the total change over 100 months. Then:

$$X = \sum_{k=1}^{100} X_k$$

Since 100 > 30, central limit theorem applies and hence the total change is normally distributed with mean and standard deviation:

$$\mu_X = n\mu_{X_k} = 100(.1) = 10$$

$$\sigma_X = \sqrt{n}\,\sigma_{X_k} = \sqrt{100}\sqrt{1} = 10$$

We started with 100 dollars and we are to calculate the probability of the amount being greater than 91 dollars at the end of 100 months.

This means that the total change over the 100 months should be greater than -9 because a final amount of 91 means a total change of exactly $91 - 100 = -9$.

Thus, we need $P(X > -9)$.

We therefore need to change -9 into standard score.

$$z = \frac{X - \mu_X}{\sigma_X} = \frac{-9 - 10}{10} = -1.9$$

$$P(X > -9) = P(z > -1.9)$$

$$= P(z < 1.9)$$

$$= .9713$$

This rounds to choice **E**.

SOA Sample Question 242 Explanation

Note that X is exponential with mean 8, and hence variance $8^2 = 64$.

$$Var\,X = E[X^2] - (E[X])^2$$

$$64 = E[X^2] - (8)^2$$

$$E[X^2] = 128$$

$$P(Z = z) = \begin{cases} .45\,, & z = 1 \\ .55\,, & z = 0 \end{cases}$$

$$E[Z] = 1(.45) + 0(.55) = .45$$

$$E[Z^2] = 1^2(.45) + 0^2(.55) = .45$$

Now since X and Z are independent, so any of their powers are also independent. So:

$$E[ZX] = E[Z]E[X]$$

$$= .45(8)$$

$$= 3.6$$

$$E[(ZX)^2] = E[Z^2X^2]$$

$$= E[Z^2]E[X^2]$$

$$= .45(128)$$

$$= 57.6$$

$$Var\,[ZX] = E[(ZX)^2] - (E[ZX])^2$$

$$= 57.6 - (3.6)^2$$

$$= 44.64$$

This rounds to choice **E**.

SOA Sample Question 243 Explanation

The total number of (x, y) points is $5(5) = 25$.

The benefit could be 0, 50, or 100 according to the situations tabulated below:

Benefit (b)	$Max\ \{x, y\}$	(x, y)	# of Points	Probability $f(b)$
0	0	(0,0)	1	1/25
50	1	(0,1), (1,0), (1,1)	3	3/25
100	2 or more	All the rest	$25 - (3 + 1) = 21$	21/25

The expected total benefit is:

$$E[B] = \sum b\, f(b)$$

$$= 0\left(\frac{1}{25}\right) + 50\left(\frac{3}{25}\right) + 100\left(\frac{21}{25}\right)$$

$$= 90$$

The correct answer is **B**.

SOA Sample Question 244 Explanation

$$E[H] = \sum hf(a, h)$$

$$= 0 + 1(.05 + .02 + .002) + 2(.01 + .002) + 3(.001)$$

$$= .099$$

The correct answer is **B**.

SOA Sample Question 245 Explanation

Let S, X be the speed and loss, respectively.

Since X is exponential with mean $3S$ for a given S, and variance of an exponential variable is the square of its mean, so:

$$E[X|S] = 3S$$

$$Var(X|S) = (3S)^2 = 9S^2$$

By law of total variance:

$$Var\ X = Var(E[X|S]) + E[Var(X|S)]$$

$$= Var\ (3S) + E[9S^2]$$

$$= 3^2 Var\ (S) + 9E[S^2] \quad (1)$$

$$E[S] = \frac{a+b}{2}$$

$$= \frac{5+20}{2}$$

$$= 12.5$$

$$Var\ (S) = \frac{(b-a)^2}{12}$$

$$= \frac{(20-5)^2}{12}$$

$$= 18.75$$

$$Var\ S = E[S^2] - (E[S])^2$$

$$18.75 = E[S^2] - (12.5)^2$$

$$E[S^2] = 175$$

Equation (1) becomes:

$$Var\ (X) = 3^2(18.75) + 9(175)$$

$$= 1743.75$$

This rounds to choice **E**.

Quiz 22

1. The speed just before an accident on a highway is uniformly distributed on [60, 100]. Given the speed, the resulting loss from the accident is exponentially distributed with mean equal to 80 times the speed. Calculate the variance (in millions) of the loss from an accident.

   A) 41
   B) 43
   C) 45
   D) 47
   E) 49

   Solution:

   Let S be the speed and X the loss.

   So X is exponential with mean $80S$ for a given S, and variance of an exponential variable equals square of its mean, so:

$$E[X|S] = 80S$$

$$Var(X|S) = (80S)^2 = 6400S^2$$

By law of total variance:

$$Var\ X = Var(E[X|S]) + E[Var(X|S)]$$

$$= Var\ (80S) + E[6400S^2]$$

$$= 80^2 Var\ (S) + 6400E[S^2] \quad (1)$$

$$E[S] = \frac{a+b}{2} = \frac{60+100}{2} = 80$$

$$Var\ (S) = \frac{(b-a)^2}{12} = \frac{(100-60)^2}{12} = 133.33$$

$$Var\ S = E[S^2] - (E[S])^2$$

$$133.33 = E[S^2] - (80)^2$$

$$E[S^2] = 6533.33$$

Equation (1) becomes:

$$Var\ (X) = 80^2(133.33) + 6400(6533.33)$$

$$= 42666624$$

$$= 42.666624\ million$$

This rounds to choice **B**.

2. A 1-year insurance provides 20000 if a person gets disabled. Each of the 90 insured individuals has 0.8% probability of becoming disabled during the year, independent of any other individual. Find the smallest amount of money that the insurance company must have so that there is at least a 95% chance that it will cover the year's benefits.
A) 42,205
B) 46,205
C) 50, 205
D) 54,205
E) 58,205
Solution:

Let X be the number of disabilities.

It is binomial with $n = 90,\ p = .008$. So,

$$E[X] = np = 90(.008) = .72$$

$$Var\ X = np(1-p) = .72(1 - .008) = .71424$$

Let Y be the payout. Then:

$$Y = 20000X$$

$$E[Y] = 20000E[X] = 20000(.72) = 14400$$

$$Var\ Y = 20000^2\ Var\ X = 20000^2(.71424) = 285696000$$

$$\sigma_Y = \sqrt{Var\ Y}$$

$$= \sqrt{285696000}$$

$$= 16902.5$$

Let s be the smallest amount of money needed in the fund. We want:

$$P(Y \leq s) = .95 \quad (1)$$

From the bottom row of exam table $z = 1.645$ corresponds to .95.

$$P(z \leq 1.645) = .95 \quad (2)$$

From (1) and (2) we see that $z = 1.645$ corresponds to $Y = s$. Hence,

$$z = \frac{Y - \mu_Y}{\sigma_Y}$$

$$1.645 = \frac{s - 14400}{16902.5}$$

$$s = 42205$$

The correct answer is **A**.

3. Bob invests 200 dollars in a stock. Each month, the investment has probability 0.3 of increasing by 2 dollars and probability 0.7 of decreasing by 1.5 dollars. The changes in price in different months are mutually independent. Calculate, using central limit theorem, the probability that the investment has a value greater than 205 dollars at the end of 3 years.

A) .014

B) .033

C) .967

D) .986

E) Not enough information to apply central limit theorem.

Solution:

Let X_k be the change in month k. Then:

$$X_k = \begin{cases} 2\,, & prob\ .3 \\ -1.5\,, & prob\ .7 \end{cases}$$

$$E[X_k] = 2(.3) - 1.5(.7)$$

$$= -.45$$

$$E\left[{X_k}^2\right] = 2^2(.3) + (-1.5)^2(.7)$$

$$= 2.775$$

$$Var\ X_k = E\left[{X_k}^2\right] - (E[X_k])^2$$

$$= 2.775 - (-.45)^2$$

$$= 2.5725$$

Let X be the total change over 36 months. Then:

$$X = \sum_{k=1}^{36} X_k$$

Since 36 > 30, central limit theorem applies and hence the total change is normally distributed with mean and standard deviation:

$$\mu_X = n\mu_{X_k} = 36(-.45) = -16.2$$

$$\sigma_X = \sqrt{n}\,\sigma_{X_k} = \sqrt{36}\sqrt{2.5725} = 9.6234$$

We started with 200 dollars and we are to calculate the probability of the amount being greater than 205 dollars at the end of 36 months.

This means that the total change over the 36 months should be greater than 5 dollars because a final amount of 205 means a total change of exactly:

$$\text{Total change} = 205 - 200 = 5.$$

Thus, we need $P(X > 5)$.

We therefore need to change 5 into standard score.

$$z = \frac{X - \mu_X}{\sigma_X}$$

$$= \frac{5 - (-16.2)}{9.6234}$$

$$= 2.20$$

$$P(X > 5) = P(z > 2.20)$$

$$= 1 - P(z < 2.20)$$

$$= 1 - .9861$$

$$= .0139$$

The correct answer is **A**.

4. Loss X in case of a fire has the pdf:

$$f(x) = 3e^{-3x}, \qquad x > 0$$

The annual number of fires N in city A have the probability function:

$$g(n) = \begin{cases} 0.7, & n = 0 \\ .2, & n = 1 \\ .1, & n = 2 \end{cases}$$

Assume N, X are independent. Find variance of NX, the total annual fire loss in city A.

A) .0556
B) .0756
C) .0956
D) .1156
E) .1356

Solution:

Total annual loss $= (\#\ of\ fires)(Loss\ per\ fire) = NX$

Note that X is exponential with mean 1/3, and hence variance $(1/3)^2 = 1/9$.

$$Var\ X = E[X^2] - (E[X])^2$$

$$1/9 = E[X^2] - (1/3)^2$$

$$E[X^2] = 2/9$$

$$E[N] = 0(.7) + 1(.2) + 2(.1)$$

$$= .4$$

$$E[N^2] = 1^2(.2) + 2^2(.1)$$

$$= .6$$

Now since X and N are independent, so:

$$E[NX] = E[N]E[X]$$

$$= .4\left(\frac{1}{3}\right)$$

$$= .1333$$

$$E[(NX)^2] = E[N^2X^2] = E[N^2]E[X^2]$$

$$= .6(2/9) = .1333$$

$$Var\,[NX] = E[(NX)^2] - (E[NX])^2$$

$$= .1333 - (.1333)^2$$

$$= .1156$$

The correct answer is **D**.

5. A couple gets an insurance policy that reimburses for days of work missed due to illness. Let X, Y denote the number of days missed during a given month by the wife and husband, respectively. The policy pays a monthly benefit of 200 times the sum of X and Y, subject to a benefit limit of 600. X and Y are independent, each with a discrete uniform distribution on the set $\{0,1,2,3\}$. Find expected monthly benefit for missed days of work paid to the couple.

(A) 400

(B) 425

(C) 450

(D) 475

(E) 500

Solution:

The total number of (x, y) points is:

$$4(4) = 16$$

The benefit could be 0, 200, 400 or 600 depending on the situations tabulated below:

Benefit (b)	$x + y$	(x, y)	# of Points	Probability $f(b)$
0	0	(0,0)	1	1/16
200	1	(0,1), (1,0)	2	2/16
400	2	(1,1), (2,0), (0,2)	3	3/16
600	3 or more	All the rest	$16 - (1 + 2 + 3) = 10$	10/16

The expected total benefit is:

$$E[B] = \sum b\,f(b)$$

$$= 0\left(\frac{1}{16}\right) + 200\left(\frac{2}{16}\right) + 400\left(\frac{3}{16}\right) + 600\left(\frac{10}{16}\right)$$

$$= 475$$

The correct answer is **D**.

Tools Needed for Problems 246-255

Coefficient of variation (CV) of a random variable is the ratio of its standard deviation to its mean. That is:

$$CV = \frac{Standard\ Deviation}{Mean}$$

Covariance of 2 variables is:

$$Cov\ (X, Y) = E[XY] - E[X]E[Y]$$

If 2 variables are independent, their covariance is 0.

However, if the covariance of 2 variables is 0, they may or may not be independent.

$$z = \frac{X - \mu}{\sigma}$$

If $W = aX + bY$, then:

$$Var\ W = a^2\ Var\ X + b^2\ Var\ Y + 2ab\ Cov\ (X, Y)$$

$$E[W] = aE[X] + bE[Y]$$

The cdf of an exponential random variable with mean m is:

$$F(x) = 1 - e^{-x/m}$$

$$Var\ X = E[X^2] - (E[X])^2$$

The pmf of a Poisson variable of mean m is:

$$f(x) = \frac{m^x e^{-m}}{x!}, \qquad x = 0,1,2, \ldots$$

Mean and variance of a uniform $[a, b]$ distribution are:

$$E[X] = \frac{a + b}{2}$$

$$Var\ (X) = \frac{(b - a)^2}{12}$$

SOA Sample Question 246 Explanation

$$f(x) = \frac{1.7^x e^{-1.7}}{x!}, \qquad x = 0,1,2,...$$

$$g(y) = \frac{2.3^y e^{-2.3}}{y!}, \qquad y = 0,1,2,...$$

$$h((x,y)|x+y=3) = \frac{h(x,y)\ and\ x+y=3}{P(X+Y=3)}$$

The possible outcomes for which $X + Y = 3$ are tabulated below.

(x,y)	$P(X=x,Y=y) = f(x)g(y) = h(x,y)$	$x-y$	$h((x,y)\|x+y=3)$
(0,3)	$\frac{1.7^0 e^{-1.7}}{0!}\left(\frac{2.3^3 e^{-2.3}}{3!}\right) = .03714$	-3	$\frac{.03714}{.19537} = .1901$
(1,2)	$\frac{1.7^1 e^{-1.7}}{1!}\left(\frac{2.3^2 e^{-2.3}}{2!}\right) = .08236$	-1	$\frac{.08236}{.19537} = .4216$
(2,1)	$\frac{1.7^2 e^{-1.7}}{2!}\left(\frac{2.3^1 e^{-2.3}}{1!}\right) = .06087$	1	$\frac{.06087}{.19537} = .3116$
(3,0)	$\frac{1.7^3 e^{-1.7}}{3!}\left(\frac{2.3^0 e^{-2.3}}{0!}\right) = .01500$	3	$\frac{.15}{.19537} = .0768$
	$P(X+Y=3) = \sum_{x+y=3} f(x)g(y) = .19537$		

$$E(X-Y|X+Y=3) = \sum_{x-y|x+y=3} (x-y)\, h((x,y)|x+y=3)$$

$$= -3(.1901) - 1(.4216) + 1(.3116) + 3(.0768)$$

$$= -.4499$$

$$E([X-Y]^2|X+Y=3) = \sum_{x-y|x+y=3} (x-y)^2\, h((x,y)|x+y=3)$$

$$= (-3)^2(.1901) + (-1)^2(.4216) + 1^2(.3116) + 3^2(.0768)$$

$$= 3.1353$$

$$Var(X-Y|X+Y=3) = E([X-Y]^2|X+Y=3) - [E(X-Y|X+Y=3)]^2$$

$$= 3.1353 - (-.4499)^2$$

$$= 2.93$$

The correct answer is **C**.

SOA Sample Question 247 Explanation

$$E[X] = \sum x f_X(x)$$

$$= 0f_X(0) + 1f_X(1) + 2f_X(2)$$

$$= 0 + 1(a + b + a) + 2\left(\frac{2}{15} + a + \frac{1}{15}\right)$$

$$= 4a + b + 0.4$$

Also, recall that the sum of the marginal probability over all values is 1. That is:

$$\sum f_X(x) = 1$$

$$f_X(0) + f_X(1) + f_X(2) = \left(\frac{1}{15} + a + \frac{2}{15}\right) + (a + b + a) + \left(\frac{2}{15} + a + \frac{1}{15}\right) = 1$$

$$4a + b + .4 = 1$$

$$4a + b = .6 \quad (2)$$

Putting the value of $4a + b$ from (2) in (1) we get:

$$E[X] = .6 + .4 = 1$$

$$Var[X] = E[(x - E[X])^2]$$

$$= \sum_x (x - E[X])^2 f_X(x)$$

$$= \sum_x (x - 1)^2 f_X(x)$$

$$= (0 - 1)^2 f_X(0) + (1 - 1)^2 f_X(1) + (2 - 1)^2 f_X(2)$$

$$= 1\left(\frac{1}{15} + a + \frac{2}{15}\right) + 0 + 1\left(\frac{2}{15} + a + \frac{1}{15}\right)$$

$$= 2a + .4$$

Since $a \geq 0$, the minimum of $Var[X] = 2a + .4$ occurs at $a = 0$. Thus:

$$a = 0$$

$$Var\ X = 2(0) + .4$$

$$= .4$$

The given distribution is completely symmetric in both variables. So, their variances are same.

$$Var\ Y = .4$$

The correct answer is **A**.

SOA Sample Question 248 Explanation

$$Cov(X,Y) = E[XY] - E[X]E[Y]$$
$$= E[XX^2] - E[X]E[X^2]$$
$$= E[X^3] - E[X]E[X^2]$$

So, we need the distribution of $X,\ X^2, and\ X^3$. We tabulate them below:

x	$P(x)$	x^2	x^3
-1	1/3	1	-1
0	1/3	0	0
1	1/3	1	1

$$E[X] = \sum xP(x) = -1\left(\frac{1}{3}\right) + 0\left(\frac{1}{3}\right) + 1\left(\frac{1}{3}\right) = 0$$
$$E[X^2] = \sum x^2P(x) = 1\left(\frac{1}{3}\right) + 0\left(\frac{1}{3}\right) + 1\left(\frac{1}{3}\right) = \frac{2}{3}$$
$$E[X^3] = \sum x^3P(x) = -1\left(\frac{1}{3}\right) + 0\left(\frac{1}{3}\right) + 1\left(\frac{1}{3}\right) = 0$$
$$Cov(X,Y) = E[X^3] - E[X]E[X^2]$$
$$= 0 - 0\left(\frac{2}{3}\right)$$
$$= 0$$

For X and Y to be independent, $P(X = x, Y = y)$ must equal $P(X = x)P(Y = y)$ for all values of X and Y. However,

$$P(X = 0, Y = 0) = P(X = 0, X^2 = 0) = P(X = 0) = 1/3$$
$$P(X = 0)P(Y = 0) = P(X = 0)\ P(X^2 = 0) = \frac{1}{3}\left(\frac{1}{3}\right) = \frac{1}{9} \neq P(X = 0, Y = 0)$$

Hence $X\ and\ Y$ are dependent.

We already saw that $Cov(X,Y) = 0$. So,

The correct answer is **C**.

Note: We know that if $X\ and\ Y$ are independent then $Cov(X,Y) = 0$. The converse, however, is not true. That is, we may have $X\ and\ Y$ being dependent, and yet their covariance may be 0, as we had in this problem.

SOA Sample Question 249 Explanation

Let X, Y be independent losses.

Let $Z = \min\{X, Y\}$.

Loss cdfs are:

$$F(x) = 1 - e^{-x}$$

$$G(y) = 1 - e^{-y}$$

$$P(Z > z) = P(X > z \, and \, Y > z)$$

$$= P(X > z) \, P(\, Y > z)$$

$$= [1 - P(X \leq z)][1 - P(Y \leq z)]$$

$$= [1 - F(z)][1 - G(z)]$$

$$= [e^{-z}][e^{-z}]$$

$$= e^{-2z}$$

$$P(Z \leq z) = 1 - P(Z > z)$$

$$F(z) = 1 - e^{-2z}$$

This is an exponential distribution with mean 1/2

The correct answer is **B**.

SOA Sample Question 250 Explanation

Let X be the daily miles by the car that does 15 mpg.

Then its daily fuel usage is:

$$\frac{X\ miles}{15\dfrac{miles}{gallon}} = \frac{X}{15}\ gallons$$

Let Y be the daily miles by the car that does 30 mpg.

Then its daily fuel usage is:

$$\frac{Y\ miles}{30\dfrac{miles}{gallon}} = \frac{Y}{30}\ gallons$$

Let C be the total daily fuel cost. Then $C = 3(\ total\ daily\ gallons)$. So:

$$C = 3\left(\frac{X}{15} + \frac{Y}{30}\right) = .2X + .1Y$$

We know that if X, Y are normal, then $aX + bY$ is normal. Hence C is normal.

$$\mu_C = .2\mu_X + .1\mu_Y = .2(25) + .1(25) = 7.5$$

$$Var\ C = .2^2\ Var\ X + .1^2\ Var\ Y + 2(.2)(.1)Cov\ (X, Y)$$

But X, Y are independent. So, $Cov\ (X, Y) = 0$. Hence

$$Var\ C = .04(9) + .01(9) = .45$$

$$\sigma_C = \sqrt{Var\ C} = \sqrt{.45}$$

We are to find $P(C < 7)$. So, we need to change 7 into standard score.

$$z = \frac{7 - \mu_C}{\sigma_C}$$

$$= \frac{7 - 7.5}{\sqrt{.45}}$$

$$= -.75$$

$$P(C < 7) = P(z < -.75)$$

$$= P(z > .75)$$

$$= 1 - P(z \le .75)$$

$$= 1 - .7734$$

$$= .23$$

The correct answer is **B**.

SOA Sample Question 251 Explanation

Let X be the first estimate, and Y be the second estimate.

We need $P(X \geq 1.2Y)$.

This is the same as $P(X - 1.2Y \geq 0)$.

Let $W = X - 1.2Y$.

Then, we are to find $P(W \geq 0)$.

We know that if X, Y are normal, then $aX + bY$ is normal.

Hence W is normal.

$$\mu_W = \mu_X - 1.2\,\mu_Y = 10b - 1.2(10b) = -2b$$

$$Var\ W = \ Var\ X + (-1.2)^2\, Var\ Y + 2(1)(-1.2)Cov\ (X, Y) \quad (1)$$

But X, Y are independent. So:

$$Cov\ (X, Y) = 0$$

Hence equation (1) becomes:

$$Var\ W = b^2 + 1.44b^2 = 2.44b^2$$

$$\sigma_W = \sqrt{Var\ W} = \sqrt{2.44b^2} = \sqrt{2.44}\, b$$

We are to find $P(W > 0)$.

So, we need to change 0 into standard score.

$$z = \frac{0 - \mu_W}{\sigma_W}$$

$$= \frac{0 - (-2b)}{\sqrt{2.44}\, b}$$

$$= 1.28$$

$$P(W > 0) = P(z > 1.28)$$

$$= 1 - P(z \leq 1.28)$$

$$= 1 - .8997$$

$$= .1003$$

This rounds to choice **B**.

SOA Sample Question 252 Explanation

Coefficient of variation of a random variable is the ratio of its standard deviation to its mean. Let the common mean of the given variables be μ. So,

$$CV(X) = \frac{\sigma_X}{\mu}$$

$$3 = \frac{\sigma_X}{\mu}$$

$$\sigma_X = 3\mu$$

$$CV(Y) = \frac{\sigma_Y}{\mu}$$

$$4 = \frac{\sigma_Y}{\mu}$$

$$\sigma_Y = 4\mu$$

Let:

$$W = 0.5(X + Y)$$

$$= .5X + .5Y$$

Then:

$$\mu_W = .5\mu_X + .5\mu_Y = .5\mu + .5\mu = \mu$$

$$Var\ W =.5^2\ Var\ X +.5^2\ Var\ Y + 2(.5)(.5)Cov\ (X, Y)$$

But X, Y are independent. So, $Cov\ (X, Y) = 0$. Hence

$$Var\ W = .25(\sigma_X)^2 + .25(\sigma_Y)^2$$

$$= .25(3\mu)^2 + .25(4\mu)^2$$

$$= 6.25\mu^2$$

$$\sigma_W = \sqrt{Var\ W}$$

$$= \sqrt{6.25\mu^2}$$

$$= 2.5\mu$$

$$CV(W) = \frac{\sigma_W}{\mu_W}$$

$$= \frac{2.5\mu}{\mu}$$

$$= 2.5$$

The correct answer is **C**.

SOA Sample Question 253 Explanation

We know that if X, Y are independent random variables, then:

$$Var\ (aX + bY + c) = a^2\ Var\ X + b^2\ Var\ Y$$

$$Var\ Z = Var(3X + 2Y - 5)$$

$$= 3^2\ Var\ X + 2^2\ Var\ Y$$

$$= 9(3) + 4(4)$$

$$= 43$$

The correct answer is **D**.

SOA Sample Question 254 Explanation

Let there be H hurricanes in a high hurricane year.

$$\mu_H = Var\ H = 20$$

Let there be M hurricanes in a medium hurricane year.

$$\mu_M = Var\ M = 15$$

Let there be L hurricanes in a low hurricane year.

$$\mu_L = Var\ L = 10$$

Let there be X hurricanes in a randomly selected year. Then:

$$X = .1H + .3M + .6L$$

$$E[X] = .1E[H] + .3E[M] + .6E[L]$$

$$= .1(20) + .3(15) + .6(10)$$

$$= 12.5$$

$$E[X^2] = .1E[H^2] + .3E[M^2] + .6E[L^2] \qquad (1)$$

$$Var\ H = E[H^2] - (E[H])^2$$

$$E[H^2] = Var\ H + (E[H])^2 = 20 + 20^2 = 420$$

$$E[M^2] = Var\ M + (E[M])^2 = 15 + 15^2 = 240$$

$$E[L^2] = Var\ L + (E[L])^2 = 10 + 10^2 = 110$$

$$E[X^2] = .1E[H^2] + .3E[M^2] + .6E[L^2]$$

$$= .1(420) + .3(240) + .6(110)$$

$$= 180$$

$$Var\ X = E[X^2] - (E[X])^2$$

$$= 180 - 12.5^2$$

$$= 23.75$$

The correct answer is **E**.

SOA Sample Question 255 Explanation

Let F be the annual number of fillings, and R the annual number of root canals.

Payment on each root canal will be:

$$.7(500)$$

$$= 350$$

Total payment, X, will be:

$$X = 50F + 350R$$

$$E[X] = 50E[F] + 350E[R]$$

$$= 50[0(.6) + 1(.2) + 2(.15) + 3(.05)] + 350[0(.8) + 1(.2)]$$

$$= 102.5$$

The correct answer is **B**.

Quiz 23

1. An economist predicts that each year, the probability of the economy being good, moderate, or bad is .3, .5, and .2, respectively. The numbers of new factories that appear in a city in a year have Poisson distribution with mean 8, 4, or 1, depending on whether the economy in the year was good, moderate, or bad, respectively. Find the standard deviation of the number of new factories in the city in a random year.

   A) 3.09

   B) 3.19

   C) 3.29

   D) 3.39

   E) 3.49

   Solution:

   Let there be G new factories in a good year. $\mu_G = Var\ G = 8$

   Let there be M new factories in a moderate year. $\mu_M = Var\ M = 4$

   Let there be B new factories in a bad year. $\mu_B = Var\ B = 1$

   Let there be X new factories in a randomly selected year. Then:

$$X = .3G + .5M + .2B$$

$$E[X] = .3E[G] + .5E[M] + .2E[B]$$

$$= .3(8) + .5(4) + .2(1)$$

$$= 4.6$$

$$Var\ G = E[G^2] - (E[G])^2$$

$$E[G^2] = Var\ G + (E[G])^2 = 8 + 8^2 = 72$$

$$E[M^2] = Var\ M + (E[M])^2 = 4 + 4^2 = 20$$

$$E[B^2] = Var\ B + (E[B])^2 = 1 + 1^2 = 2$$

$$E[X^2] = .3E[G^2] + .5E[M^2] + .2E[B^2]$$

$$= .3(72) + .5(20) + .2(2) = 32$$

$$Var\ X = E[X^2] - (E[X])^2$$

$$= 32 - 4.6^2$$

$$= 10.84$$

$$SD(X)$$

$$= \sqrt{10.84}$$

$$= 3.29$$

   The correct answer is **C**.

2. Let X be the monthly deaths in town A, and let Y be the monthly deaths in town B. X and Y are independent Poisson variables with respective means 1.5 and 2.5. Find $Var(X - Y|X + Y = 2)$

A) 1.58

B) 1.68

C) 1.78

D) 1.88

E) 1.98

Solution:

$$f(x) = \frac{1.5^x e^{-1.5}}{x!}, \qquad x = 0,1,2,\dots$$

$$g(y) = \frac{2.5^y e^{-2.5}}{y!}, \qquad y = 0,1,2,\dots$$

$$h(x,y)|x + y = 2 = \frac{h(x,y) \text{ and } x + y = 2}{P(X + Y = 2)}$$

The possible outcomes for which $X + Y = 2$ are tabulated below.

(x,y)	$P(X = x, Y = y) = f(x)g(y) = h(x,y)$	$x - y$	$h(x,y)\|x + y = 2$
(0,2)	$\frac{1.5^0 e^{-1.5}}{0!}\left(\frac{2.5^2 e^{-2.5}}{2!}\right) = .05724$	-2	$\frac{.05724}{.14653} = .391$
(1,1)	$\frac{1.5^1 e^{-1.5}}{1!}\left(\frac{2.5^1 e^{-2.5}}{1!}\right) = .06868$	0	$\frac{.06868}{.14653} = .469$
(2,0)	$\frac{1.5^2 e^{-1.5}}{2!}\left(\frac{2.5^0 e^{-2.5}}{0!}\right) = .02061$	2	$\frac{.02061}{.14653} = .141$
	$P(X + Y = 2) = \sum_{x+y=2} f(x)g(y) = .14653$		

The standard deviation can be found on calculator as I explain in my youtube video with link:

https://www.youtube.com/watch?v=QNlw_TX-vEI&t=69s

From calculator

$$SD(X - Y|X + Y = 2) = 1.3698$$

$$(X - Y|X + Y = 2) = 1.3698^2$$

$$= 1.88$$

The correct answer is **D**.

3. The severity of an earthquake is measured by a random variable that is uniformly distributed on [1, 9]. The damage from an earthquake with a given intensity y is exponentially distributed with a mean equal to $2y$. Find the variance of the damage from a random earthquake.

A) 143

B) 153

C) 163

D) 173

E) 183

Solution:

Let X be the damage and Y be the earthquake severity.

We are to find $Var\ X$.

We are told that $X|Y = y$ is exponentially distributed with mean $2y$. So:

$$E[X|Y] = 2Y$$

$$Var[X|Y] = (2Y)^2 = 4Y^2$$

Using law of total variance:

$$\begin{aligned} Var\ X &= Var(E[X|Y]) + E[Var(X|Y)] \\ &= Var(2Y) + E[4Y^2] \\ &= 2^2 Var(Y) + 4E[Y^2] \\ &= 4Var(Y) + 4E[Y^2] \end{aligned}$$

Since Y is uniform [1, 9], so:

$$E[Y] = \frac{a+b}{2} = \frac{1+9}{2} = 5$$

$$Var\ (Y) = \frac{(b-a)^2}{12} = \frac{(9-1)^2}{12} = \frac{16}{3}$$

$$Var\ Y = E[Y^2] - (E[Y])^2$$

$$16/3 = E[Y^2] - (5)^2$$

$$E[Y^2] = 30.33$$

$$Var\ X = 4Var(Y) + 4E[Y^2]$$

$$= 4\left(\frac{16}{3}\right) + 4(30.33)$$

$$= 143$$

The correct answer is **A**.

4. Let X be a random variable that takes on the values -1, 0, and 1 with equal probabilities.

Let $Y = X^3$. Which of the following is true?

(A) $\text{Cov}(X, Y) > 0$; the random variables X and Y are dependent.

(B) $\text{Cov}(X, Y) > 0$; the random variables X and Y are independent.

(C) $\text{Cov}(X, Y) = 0$; the random variables X and Y are dependent.

(D) $\text{Cov}(X, Y) = 0$; the random variables X and Y are independent.

(E) $\text{Cov}(X, Y) < 0$; the random variables X and Y are dependent.

Solution:

$$Cov(X,Y) = E[XY] - E[X]E[Y]$$
$$= E[XX^3] - E[X]E[X^3]$$
$$= E[X^4] - E[X]E[X^3]$$

So, we need the distribution of $X,\ X^3, and\ X^4$. We tabulate them below:

x	$P(x)$	x^3	x^4
-1	1/3	-1	1
0	1/3	0	0
1	1/3	1	1

$$E[X] = \sum xP(x) = -1\left(\frac{1}{3}\right) + 0\left(\frac{1}{3}\right) + 1\left(\frac{1}{3}\right) = 0$$

$$E[X^4] = \sum x^4P(x) = 1\left(\frac{1}{3}\right) + 0\left(\frac{1}{3}\right) + 1\left(\frac{1}{3}\right) = \frac{2}{3}$$

$$E[X^3] = \sum x^3P(x) = -1\left(\frac{1}{3}\right) + 0\left(\frac{1}{3}\right) + 1\left(\frac{1}{3}\right) = 0$$

$$Cov(X,Y) = E[X^4] - E[X]E[X^3]$$
$$= \frac{2}{3} - 0(0)$$
$$= \frac{2}{3}$$

If covariance of 2 variables is non-zero, they must be dependent because the covariance of independent variables is 0.

Hence X, Y are dependent.

The correct answer is **A**.

5. Fire losses follow an exponential distribution with mean 2000. Find the expected value of the smallest of three independent fire losses.

A) 167

B) 300

C) 500

D) 575

E) 667

Solution:

Let X, Y, W be the 3 losses.

Let $Z = \min\{X, Y, W\}$.

Loss cdfs are:

$$F(x) = 1 - e^{-x/2000}$$

$$G(y) = 1 - e^{-y/2000}$$

$$H(w) = 1 - e^{-w/2000}$$

$$P(Z > z) = P(X > z, Y > z, and\ W > z)$$

$$= P(X > z)\ P(\ Y > z)P(W > z)$$

$$= [1 - P(X \leq z)][1 - P(Y \leq z)][1 - P(W \leq z)]$$

$$= [1 - F(z)][1 - G(z)][1 - H(z)]$$

$$= \left[e^{-z/2000}\right]\left[e^{-z/2000}\right]\left[e^{-z/2000}\right]$$

$$= e^{-3z/2000}$$

$$P(Z \leq z) = 1 - P(Z > z)$$

$$F(z) = 1 - e^{-3z/2000}$$

This is an exponential distribution with mean:

$$\frac{2000}{3} = 667$$

The correct answer is **E**.

6. A company owns two cars that consume 25 and 32 miles per gallon. Fuel costs 2.5 per gallon. On any business day, each car travels a number of miles that is independent of the other and is normally distributed with mean 40 miles and standard deviation 6 miles. Find the probability that on any given business day, the total fuel cost to the company will be more than 8.

A) .055

B) .080

C) .125

D) .920

E) .945

Solution:

Let X be the daily miles by the car that does 25 mpg. Then its daily fuel usage is:

$$\frac{X\ miles}{25\frac{miles}{gallon}} = \frac{X}{25}\ gallons$$

Let Y be the daily miles by the car that does 32 mpg. Then its daily fuel usage is:

$$\frac{Y\ miles}{32\frac{miles}{gallon}} = \frac{Y}{32}\ gallons$$

Let C be the total daily fuel cost. Then $C = 2.5(\ total\ daily\ gallons)$. So:

$$C = 2.5\left(\frac{X}{25} + \frac{Y}{32}\right) = .1X + .078125Y$$

We know that if X, Y are normal, then $aX + bY$ is normal. Hence C is normal.

$$\mu_C = .1\mu_X + .078125\mu_Y = .1(40) + .078125(40) = 7.125$$

$$Var\ C = .1^2\ Var\ X + .078125^2\ Var\ Y + 2(.1)(.078125)Cov\ (X, Y)$$

But X, Y are independent. So, $Cov\ (X, Y) = 0$. Hence

$$Var\ C = .01(36) + .0061(36) = .5796$$

$$\sigma_C = \sqrt{Var\ C} = \sqrt{.5796} = .7613$$

We are to find $P(C > 8)$. So, we need to change 8 into standard score.

$$z = \frac{8 - \mu_C}{\sigma_C} = \frac{8 - 7.125}{.7613} = 1.15$$

$$P(C > 8) = P(z > 1.15) = 1 - P(z \leq 1.15)$$

$$= 1 - .8749 = .125$$

The correct answer is **C**.

7. Two independent quotes are made on a project. Each quote is normally distributed with mean $5b$ and variance $4b^2$. Find the probability that the 1st quote is at least 30% higher than the 2nd.

A) .30

B) .32

C) .34

D) .36

E) .38

Solution:

Let X be the first quote, and Y be the second quote.

We need $P(X \geq 1.3Y)$.

This is the same as $P(X - 1.3Y \geq 0)$.

Let $W = X - 1.3Y$.

Then, we are to find $P(W \geq 0)$.

We know that if X, Y are normal, then $aX + bY$ is normal.

Hence W is normal.

$$\mu_W = \mu_X - 1.3\mu_Y = 5b - 1.3(5b) = -1.5b$$

$$Var\ W = Var\ X + (-1.3)^2\ Var\ Y + 2(1)(-1.3)Cov\ (X, Y)$$

But X, Y are independent. So, $Cov\ (X, Y) = 0$. Hence

$$Var\ W = 4b^2 + 1.69(4b^2) = 10.76b^2$$

$$\sigma_W = \sqrt{Var\ W} = \sqrt{10.76b^2} = \sqrt{10.76}\ b$$

We are to find $P(W > 0)$.

So, we need to change 0 into standard score.

$$z = \frac{0 - \mu_W}{\sigma_W} = \frac{0 - (-1.5b)}{\sqrt{10.76}\ b} = .46$$

$$P(W > 0) = P(z > .46)$$

$$= 1 - P(z \leq .46)$$

$$= 1 - .6772$$

$$= .32$$

This rounds to choice **B**.

8. The independent random variables X and Y have the same variance. The coefficients of variation of X and Y are 5 and 6 respectively. Calculate the coefficient of variation of $0.25(X+Y)$.

A) 3.56

B) 3.66

C) 3.76

D) 3.86

E) 3.96

Solution:

Variances are the same for both variables, so the standard deviations are also the same, say, σ.

$$CV(X) = \frac{\sigma_X}{\mu_X} = \frac{\sigma}{\mu_X}$$

$$5 = \frac{\sigma}{\mu_X}$$

$$\mu_X = \frac{\sigma}{5}$$

$$CV(Y) = \frac{\sigma_Y}{\mu_Y} = \frac{\sigma}{\mu_Y}$$

$$6 = \frac{\sigma}{\mu_Y}$$

$$\mu_Y = \frac{\sigma}{6}$$

Let $W = 0.25(X+Y) = .25X + .25Y$. Then:

$$\mu_W = .25\mu_X + .25\mu_Y = .25\left(\frac{\sigma}{5}\right) + .25\left(\frac{\sigma}{6}\right) = \frac{11\sigma}{120}$$

$$Var\ W = .25^2\ Var\ X + .25^2\ Var\ Y + 2(.25)(.25)Cov\ (X,Y)$$

But X, Y are independent. So, $Cov\ (X,Y) = 0$. Hence

$$Var\ W = .0625(\sigma)^2 + .0625(\sigma)^2 = .125\sigma^2$$

$$\sigma_W = \sqrt{Var\ W} = \sqrt{.125\sigma^2} = \sqrt{.125}\sigma$$

$$CV(W) = \frac{\sigma_W}{\mu_W} = \frac{\sqrt{.125}\sigma}{\frac{11\sigma}{120}}$$

$$= 3.86$$

The correct answer is **D**.

Tools needed for problems 256-287

The pmf of a Poisson random variable with mean m is:

$$f(x) = \frac{m^x e^{-m}}{m!}$$

For a uniform $[a, b]$ distribution,

$$E[X] = \frac{a+b}{2}$$

$$Var[X] = \frac{(b-a)^2}{12}$$

For any distribution we have:

$$Var[X] = E[X^2] - (E[X])^2$$

$$P(A|B) = \frac{P(AB)}{P(B)}$$

For a binomial distribution, the pmf is:

$$f(x) = \binom{n}{x} p^x (1-p)^{n-x}$$

When $n > 20,$ and either $np < 5$ or $n(1-p) < 5$, then binomial distribution can be approximated by Poisson distribution. We use the binomial mean, that is, np to do this.

The pdf of exponential distribution with mean m is:

$$f(x) = \frac{1}{m} e^{-x/m}$$

The variance of an exponential distribution with mean m is m^2

The cdf of exponential distribution with mean m is:

$$F(x) = 1 - e^{-x/m}$$

If X is a continuous random variable with pdf $f(x)$ then:

$$P(X < a) = \int_{-\infty}^{a} f(x)\, dx$$

For a continuous random variable X,

$$E[X] = \int_{-\infty}^{\infty} x\, f(x)\, dx$$

$$E[X^2] = \int_{-\infty}^{\infty} x^2\, f(x)\, dx$$

$$Var\,(X+Y) = Var\,X + Var\,Y + 2\,COV(X,Y)$$

The correlation coefficient r is given by:

$$r = \frac{COV(X,Y)}{\sqrt{(Var\ X)\ (Var\ Y)}}$$

If the joint pdf of 2 variables can be written as a product of individual variables and the region of integration is a rectangle, then the variables are independent.

If 2 variables are independent, then their covariance and correlation are both 0.

If X, Y are normal variables with means μ_X, μ_Y, respectively, and standard deviations σ_X , σ_Y, respectively, then the mean and variance of the sum are:

$$\mu_{X+Y} = \mu_X + \mu_Y$$

$$\sigma_X = \sqrt{\sigma_X{}^2 + \sigma_Y{}^2}$$

If X and Y are independent random variables, then $Var\ (X + Y) = Var\ X + Var\ Y$

SOA Sample Question 256 Explanation

Let X be the loss.

Let Y be reimbursement given that the loss exceeds deductible.

By memoryless property of the exponential distribution, Y has the same distribution as X.

We are given that:

$$P(Y < 6000) = .5$$

We are to find $P(3000 < Y < 9000)$.

$$G(y) = 1 - e^{-ky}$$

$$G(6000) = 1 - e^{-6000k}$$

$$P(Y < 6000) = 1 - e^{-6000k}$$

$$.5 = 1 - e^{-6000k}$$

$$e^{-6000k} = .5$$

$$\sqrt{e^{-6000k}} = \sqrt{.5}$$

$$e^{-3000k} = .707$$

$$P(3000 < Y < 9000) = G(9000) - G(3000)$$

$$= (1 - e^{-9000k}) - (1 - e^{-3000k})$$

$$= e^{-3000k} - e^{-9000k}$$

$$= e^{-3000k} - (e^{-3000k})^3$$

$$= .707 - (.707)^3$$

$$= .35$$

The correct answer is **B**.

SOA Sample Question 257 Explanation

The first target is to find a. For this, we will need to work with the distribution of X.

We know that for a uniform $[a, b]$ distribution,

$$E[X] = \frac{a+b}{2}$$

$$Var[X] = \frac{(b-a)^2}{12}$$

So, using the given distribution of X, we have

$$E[X] = \frac{a+100}{2}$$

$$Var[X] = \frac{(100-a)^2}{12}$$

We also know that $Var[X] = E[X^2] - (E[X])^2$. From this we get:

$$E[X^2] = Var[X] + (E[X])^2$$

Using the given value of $E[X^2]$, the above equation becomes:

$$\frac{19600}{3} = \frac{(100-a)^2}{12} + \left(\frac{a+100}{2}\right)^2$$

$$\frac{19600}{3} = \frac{10000 - 200a + a^2}{12} + \frac{a^2 + 200a + 10000}{4}$$

Multiplying throughout by 12 to clear the denominators, we get:

$$78400 = 10000 - 200a + a^2 + 3a^2 + 600a + 30000$$

$$0 = 4a^2 + 400a - 38400$$

$$0 = a^2 + 100a - 9600$$

$$0 = (a + 160)(a - 60)$$

$$a = -160, 60$$

But a is the lower limit of a percentage Exam score, so it cannot be negative. Thus $a = 60$.

The distribution of Y is therefore uniform on $[1.25(60), 100] = [75,100]$.

Let the 80th percentile of this distribution be k. Then we have:

$$P(X < k) = .80$$

$$\frac{k - 75}{100 - 75} = .8$$

$$k - 75 = 20$$

$$k = 95$$

The correct answer is **E**.

SOA Sample Question 258 Explanation

Let the 3 circles represent the number of people having each of the 3 risk factors.

Let the outer rectangle represent the total number of people in the study.

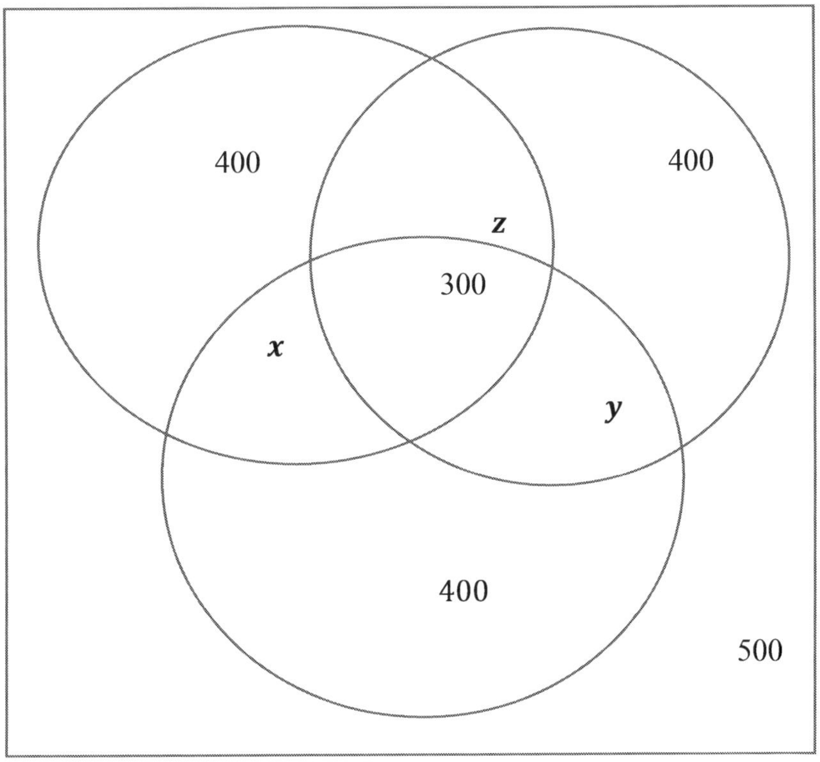

From the given conditions we have:

$$x + z + 400 + 300 = 1000$$

This gives:

$$x + z = 300 \qquad (1)$$

Similarly,

$$y + z = 300 \qquad (2)$$

$$x + y = 300 \qquad (3)$$

From (1) and (2) we get $x = y$. Substituting this in (3) we get:

$$x + x = 300$$

$$x = 150$$

$$y = 150$$

$$z = 150$$

$$Total\ \# = 400 + 400 + 400 + 150 + 150 + 150 + 300 + 500 = 2450$$

The correct answer is **C.**

SOA Sample Question 259 Explanation

	1 Car = 100% − 64% = 36%	**More than 1 Car** = 64%	Total
Sports Car	20% − 9.6% = 10.4%	.15(64%) = 9.6%	20%
Not Sports Car	36% − 10.4% = 25.6%		

From the above table we see that the required probability is .256

This rounds to choice **C**.

SOA Sample Question 260 Explanation

This is a binomial experiment with $n = 200,\ p = .01$.

We are to find $P(X \leq 5)$.

For a binomial distribution, the pmf is:

$$f(x) = \binom{n}{x} p^x (1-p)^{n-x}$$

$$= \binom{200}{x} .01^x (.99)^{200-x}$$

$$P(X \leq 5) = f(0) + f(1) + f(2) + f(3) + f(4) + f(5)$$

$$= \binom{200}{0} .01^0 (.99)^{200} + \binom{200}{1} .01^1 (.99)^{199} + \binom{200}{2} .01^2 (.99)^{198}$$
$$+ \binom{200}{3} .01^3 (.99)^{197} + \binom{200}{4} .01^4 (.99)^{196} + \binom{200}{5} .01^5 (.99)^{195}$$

$$= .98$$

Note that when $n > 20$, and either $np < 5$ or $n(1-p) < 5$, then binomial distribution can be approximated by Poisson distribution and the resulting calculations are less tedious. So here, the mean m is given by:

$$m = np$$
$$= 200(.01)$$
$$= 2 < 5$$

So, using Poisson formula:

$$f(x) = \frac{m^x e^{-m}}{x!}$$

$$P(X \leq 5) = f(0) + f(1) + f(2) + f(3) + f(4) + f(5)$$

$$= e^{-2}\left(\frac{2^0}{0!} + \frac{2^1}{1!} + \frac{2^2}{2!} + \frac{2^3}{3!} + \frac{2^4}{4!} + \frac{2^5}{5!}\right)$$

$$= .98$$

We can see that the Poisson calculations are less tedious than the Binomial ones.

If such a question appears in the exam, you can do it the Poisson way as long as there are sufficient differences in the answer choices which is the case here because the answer choices differ by at least 3 in the 2nd decimal place. If the difference had been only 1 in the 2nd place, for example, having choices of .97, .98, .99, then it would be safer to stick to the exact form which is the binomial form.

The correct answer is **E**.

SOA Sample Question 261 Explanation

This is a binomial experiment with $n = 5,\ p = .2$.

We are to find $P(X \geq 2)$.

For a binomial distribution, the pmf is:

$$f(x) = \binom{n}{x} p^x (1-p)^{n-x}$$

$$= \binom{5}{x} .2^x (.8)^{5-x}$$

$$P(X \geq 2) = 1 - P(X \leq 1)$$

$$= 1 - [f(0) + f(1)]$$

$$= 1 - \left[\binom{5}{0} .2^0 (.8)^{5-0} + \binom{5}{1} .2^1 (.8)^{5-1}\right]$$

$$= .26$$

The correct answer is **C**.

SOA Sample Question 262 Explanation

Let p be the probability that a random computer is defective. This is binomial with $n = 100$.

Let X be the number of defective computers. The binomial pmf is:

$$f(x) = \binom{100}{x} p^x (1-p)^{100-x}$$

We are given that:

$$f(3) = 2f(2)$$

$$\binom{100}{3} p^3 (1-p)^{100-3} = 2\binom{100}{2} p^2 (1-p)^{100-2}$$

$$161700p^3(1-p)^{97} = 9900p^2(1-p)^{98}$$

Dividing both sides by $9900p^2(1-p)^{97}$ we get:

$$16.333p = 1 - p$$

$$17.333p = 1$$

$$p = .058$$

The correct answer is **C**.

SOA Sample Question 263 Explanation

$$P(Fire) = .2$$

$$P(Theft) = .3$$

$$P(either\ fire\ or\ theft, but\ not\ both) = P[(Fire, not\ theft)\ OR\ (theft, not\ fire)]$$

$$= P(Fire, not\ theft) + P(theft, not\ Fire)$$

$$.2(1 - .3) + .3(1 - .2)$$

$$= .38$$

The correct answer is **B**.

SOA Sample Question 264 Explanation

Let M be the event that a person is male.

Let F be the event that a person is female.

Let C be the event a person contributes to a supplemental retirement plan.

We are to find $P(F|C)$.

We are given that:

$$P(F) = .45$$

$$P(M) = 1 - .45 = .55$$

$$P(F|C) = \frac{P(F\ and\ C)}{P(C)} \quad (1)$$

$$P(F\ and\ C) = .45(.2)$$

$$= .09 \quad (2)$$

$$P(C) = P(Male\ contributes\ or\ Female\ contributes)$$

$$= P(M\ and\ C) + P(F\ and\ C)$$

$$= .55(.3) += .45(.2)$$

$$= .255 \quad (3)$$

Using (2) and (3), equation (1) becomes:

$$P(F|C) = \frac{.09}{.255}$$

$$= .35$$

The correct answer is **C**.

SOA Sample Question 265 Explanation

Let p be the probability that a policy holder is from territory X.

Then $1 - p$ is the probability that a policy holder is from territory Y.

$$P(no\ claim) = P(from\ X\ and\ no\ claim, or\ from\ Y\ and\ no\ claim)$$

$$P(no\ claim) = P(from\ X\ and\ no\ claim) + P(\ from\ Y\ and\ no\ claim)$$

$$.2 = p(.15) + (1 - p).4$$

$$.2 = .15p + .4 - .4p$$

$$.25p = .2$$

$$p = .8$$

$$P(from\ X\ and\ no\ claim) = .8(.15) = .12$$

$$P(X|no\ claim) = \frac{P(X\ and\ no\ claim)}{P(no\ claim)}$$

$$= \frac{.12}{.2}$$

$$= .6$$

The correct answer is **D**.

SOA Sample Question 266 Explanation

The largest claim will be less than 25 if and only if each of the claims is less than 25.

The probability of each claim being less than 25 is given by:

$$P(X < 25) = \int_{-\infty}^{25} f(x)\,dx$$

$$= \int_{10}^{25} \frac{10}{x^2}\,dx$$

$$= -\frac{10}{x}\Big|_{10}^{25}$$

$$= -\frac{10}{25} + \frac{10}{10}$$

$$= 3/5$$

So, the probability that each of the 3 claims is less than 25 is:

$$\left(\frac{3}{5}\right)\left(\frac{3}{5}\right)\left(\frac{3}{5}\right) = \frac{27}{125}$$

The correct answer is **C**.

SOA Sample Question 267 Explanation

The cdf of exponential distribution with mean .5 is:

$$F(x) = 1 - e^{-x/.5}$$

The lifetime being greater than .7, given that is is greater than .4 means that it lives at least another .3 after living the first .4. By memoryless property of exponential distribution we know that the probability of living another .3 is independent of how much it has lived before.

Thus, all we need is $P(X > .3)$.

$$P(X > .3) = 1 - F(.3)$$

$$= 1 - \left(1 - e^{-.3/.5}\right)$$

$$= .549$$

The correct answer is **D**.

SOA Sample Question 268 Explanation

The number of crop destructions X during 5 years is binomial with:

$$n = 5, \ \ p = .5$$

$$f(x) = \binom{n}{x} p^x (1-p)^{n-x}$$

$$= \binom{5}{x} .5^x (.5)^{5-x}$$

$$= \binom{5}{x} .5^5$$

The possible benefits amount and their probabilities are tabulated below:

Benefit	When X is	Probability
20	1	$f(1) = \binom{5}{1} .5^5 = .15625$
40	2	$f(2) = \binom{5}{2} .5^5 = .3125$
60	≥ 3	$1 - f(0) - f(1) - f(2) = .5$

So, the expected benefit is:

$$20(.15625) + 40(.3125) + 60(.5) = 45.625$$

This rounds to choice **D**.

SOA Sample Question 269 Explanation

If X, Y are normal variables with means μ_X, μ_Y, respectively, and standard deviations σ_X , σ_Y, respectively, then the mean and variance of the sum are:

$$\mu_{X+Y} = \mu_X + \mu_Y$$

$$\sigma_{X+Y} = \sqrt{\sigma_X{}^2 + \sigma_Y{}^2}$$

So, for this problem,

$$\mu_{X+Y} = 10 + 12$$

$$= 22$$

$$\sigma_{X+Y} = \sqrt{3^2 + 4^2}$$

$$= 5$$

We need $P(X + Y \leq 29)$. We next change 29 in standard score so that we can use the tables.

$$z = \frac{29 - \mu_{X+Y}}{\sigma_{X+Y}}$$

$$= \frac{29 - 22}{5}$$

$$= 1.4$$

$$P(X + Y \leq 29) = P(z \leq 1.4)$$

$$= .9192$$

This rounds to choice **E**.

SOA Sample Question 270 Explanation

We know that the variance of a sum of independent random variables equals the sum of individual variances. So, variance of the total cost in this case is:

$$Var = 1^2 + 1^2 + 1.5^2 + 2^2$$

$$= 8.25$$

$$SD = \sqrt{Var}$$

$$= \sqrt{8.25}$$

$$= 2.87$$

The correct answer is **C**.

Next several problems in the SOA set are duplicates as explained below:

271 is duplicate of 264

272 is duplicate of 260

273 is duplicate of 270

274 is duplicate of 259

275 is duplicate of 259

276 is duplicate of 269

277 is duplicate of 258

278 is duplicate of 268

279 is duplicate of 267

280 is duplicate of 261

281 is duplicate of 265

282 is duplicate of 266

283 is duplicate of 263

SOA Sample Question 284 Explanation

The total expenditure is $X + Y$. So, we need $Var\ (X + Y)$.

$$Var\ (X + Y) = Var\ X + Var\ Y + 2\ COV(X, Y) \quad (1)$$

$Var\ Y$ is given to be 12500.

$Var\ X$ can be found by noting that X is exponentially distributed with mean $20\sqrt{5}$. So,

$$Var\ X = \left(20\sqrt{5}\right)^2$$

$$= 2000$$

We also know that the correlation coefficient r is given by:

$$r = \frac{COV(X, Y)}{\sqrt{(Var\ X)\ (Var\ Y)}}$$

$$.2 = \frac{COV(X, Y)}{\sqrt{2000\ (12500)}}$$

$$COV(X, Y) = 1000$$

So, (1) becomes:

$$Var\ (X + Y) = 2000 + 12500 + 2(1000)$$

$$= 16500$$

The correct answer is **D**.

SOA Sample Question 285 Explanation

Let N be the number of appraisals and let us call an appraisal being less than the price as a success. Let Y be the amount of appraisal which is given to be uniformly distributed on $[\theta - 3,\ \theta + 1]$. Then N is binomially distributed with $n = 4$, and the probability of success:

$$p = P(Y < \theta)$$

$$= \frac{\theta - (\theta - 3)}{(\theta + 1) - (\theta - 3)}$$

$$= \frac{3}{4}$$

$$= .75$$

We need $P(L < \theta < H)$ which is the probability that the lowest of the 4 appraisals is below the actual price and the highest appraisal is above the actual price. This will happen if exactly 1, 2, or 3 appraisals are below the actual price, that is, the number of binomial successes is 1,2, or 3. So, using the binomial pmf:

$$f(x) = \binom{4}{x}.75^x(.25^{4-x})$$

$$P(X = 1,2, or\ 3) = f(1) + f(2) + f(3)$$

$$= \binom{4}{1}.75^1(.25^{4-1}) + \binom{4}{2}.75^2(.25^{4-2}) + \binom{4}{3}.75^3(.25^{4-3})$$

$$= .680$$

The correct answer is **D**.

SOA Sample Question 286 Explanation

Let the 2 observed losses be X and Y. We are to find $P(Y > 2X \text{ or } X > 2Y)$.

$$P(Y > 2X) = 1 - P(Y < 2X)$$

$$f(x) = e^{-x}$$

$$f(y) = e^{-y}$$

$$f(x, y) = e^{-x}e^{-y}, \qquad x > 0, \qquad y > 0$$

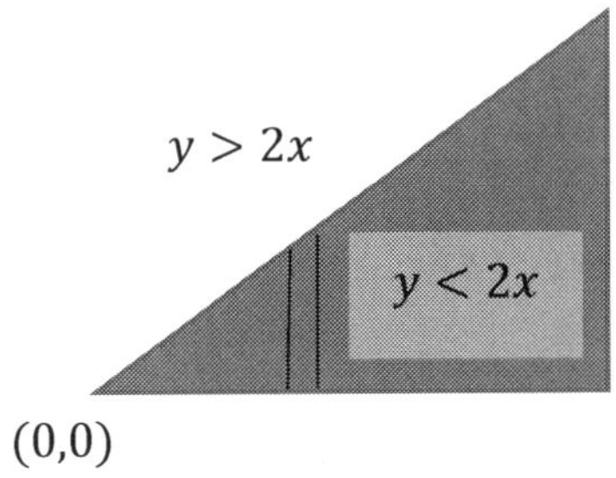

$$P(Y < 2X) = \int_0^{\infty}\int_0^{2x} e^{-x}e^{-y}\, dy\, dx$$

$$= \int_0^{\infty} e^{-x}(-e^{-y})|_{y=0}^{y=2x}\, dx$$

$$= \int_0^{\infty} e^{-x}(-e^{-2x} + 1)\, dx$$

$$= \int_0^{\infty} (-e^{-3x} + e^{-x})\, dx$$

$$= \left(\frac{e^{-3x}}{3} - e^{-x}\right)|_0^{\infty}$$

$$= \left(\frac{e^{-\infty}}{3} - e^{-\infty}\right) - \left(\frac{1}{3} - 1\right) = \frac{2}{3}$$

$$P(Y > 2X) = 1 - \frac{2}{3} = \frac{1}{3} = P(X > 2Y)$$

$$P(Y > 2X \text{ or } X > 2Y) = P(Y > 2X) + P(X > 2Y)$$

$$= \frac{1}{3} + \frac{1}{3} = \frac{2}{3}$$

The correct answer is **E**.

Note that SOA Problem 287 is a duplication of problem 262

Quiz 24

1. Auto loss is modelled by an exponential distribution. An insurance company will cover the amount of that exceeds a deductible of 300. The probability that the reimbursement is less than 400, given that the loss exceeds the deductible, is 0.2. Calculate the probability that the reimbursement is greater than 800, given that the loss exceeds the deductible.
   A) .36

   B) .44

   C) .50

   D) .56

   E) .64

   Solution:

   Let X be the loss, Y be reimbursement given that the loss exceeds deductible.

   By memoryless property of the exponential distribution, Y has the same distribution as X.

   We are to find $P(Y > 800)$.

$$G(y) = 1 - e^{-ky}$$

$$G(400) = 1 - e^{-400k}$$

$$P(Y < 400) = 1 - e^{-400k}$$

$$.2 = 1 - e^{-400k}$$

$$e^{-400k} = .8$$

$$\begin{aligned} P(Y < 800) &= G(800) \\ &= 1 - e^{-800k} \\ &= 1 - (e^{-400k})^2 \\ &= 1 - (.8)^2 \\ &= .36 \\ P(Y > 800) &= 1 - .36 \\ &= .64 \end{aligned}$$

The correct answer is **E**.

2. In a test, 30% of the students in the class got an A. 40% of the girls in the class got an A, while 25% of the boys in the class got an A. Find the probability that a randomly selected student in that class is a girl, given that the student got an A.
   A) .111
   B) .222
   C) .333
   D) .444
   E) .555

   Solution:

Let p be the probability that a student is a girl.

Then $1 - p$ is the probability that the student is a boy.

$$P(A) = P(girl\ and\ A, or\ boy\ and\ A)$$

$$P(A) = P(girl\ and\ A) + P(\ Boy\ and\ A)$$

$$.3 = p(.4) + (1 - p).25$$

$$.3 = .4p + .25 - .25p$$

$$.05 = .15p$$

$$p = \frac{1}{3}$$

$$P(girl\ and\ A) = \frac{1}{3}(.4) = .133$$

$$P(girl|A) = \frac{P(girl\ and\ A)}{P(A)}$$

$$= \frac{.133}{.3}$$

$$= .444$$

The correct answer is **D**.

3. In College X, 15% students like Math, while 20% students like English. Find the probability that a randomly selected student likes exactly one of the two subjects.
A) .10
B) .18
C) .22
D) .29
E) .35

Solution:

Let M be the event that a student likes Math.

Let E be the event that a students likes English

$$P(M) = .15$$

$$P(E) = .2$$

$$P(exacly\ one) = P[(M, not\ E)\ OR\ (E, not\ M)]$$

$$= P(M, not\ E) + P(E, not\ M)$$

$$.15(1 - .2) + .2(1 - .15)$$

$$= .38$$

The correct answer is **D**.

4. A student has the same probability of guessing an answer correctly in a 30-question multiple choice exam (we don't know how many answer choices are available for each question). The probability that he guesses a total of 3 questions correctly is 1.5 times the probability that he guesses a total of 4 questions correctly. What is the probability that he guesses 5 questions correctly?
   A) .05
   B) .06
   C) .07
   D) .08
   E) .09

Solution:

Let p be the probability of correctly guessing a question. This is binomial with $n = 30$.

Let X be the number of defective computers. The binomial pmf is:

$$f(x) = \binom{30}{x} p^x (1-p)^{30-x}$$

We are to find $f(5)$. We are given that:

$$f(3) = 1.5f(4)$$

$$\binom{30}{3} p^3 (1-p)^{30-3} = 1.5 \binom{30}{4} p^4 (1-p)^{30-4}$$

$$4060p^3(1-p)^{27} = 41107.5p^4(1-p)^{26}$$

Dividing both sides by $4060p^3(1-p)^{26}$ we get:

$$1 - p = 10.125p$$

$$11.125p = 1$$

$$p = .09$$

$$f(5) = \binom{30}{5} .09^5 (1 - .09)^{30-5}$$

$$= .08$$

The correct answer is **D**.

5. There is 0.2% probability that a dog will catch rabies at some point. Find, using Poisson approximation, the probability that out of 300 randomly selected dogs, fewer than 7 will catch rabies.
   A) .992
   B) .994
   C) .996
   D) .998
   E) 1.000

Solution:

This is a binomial experiment with $n = 300$, $p = .01$.

We are to find $P(X < 7)$. This is the same as finding $P(X \leq 6)$.

The mean m is given by:

$$m = np$$
$$= 300(.002)$$
$$= .06$$

So, we approximate it with the Poisson formula:

$$f(x) = \frac{m^x e^{-m}}{m!}$$

$$P(X \leq 6) = f(0) + f(1) + f(2) + f(3) + f(4) + f(5) + f(6)$$

$$= e^{-.6}\left(\frac{.6^0}{0!} + \frac{.6^1}{1!} + \frac{.6^2}{2!} + \frac{.6^3}{3!} + \frac{.6^4}{4!} + \frac{.6^5}{5!} + \frac{.6^6}{6!}\right)$$

$$= 1$$

The correct answer is **E**.

6. The number of students in a class who like apples is 20, the number who likes oranges is 20, and the number who likes bananas is also 20. The number of students who liked only apples is 8, those who like only oranges is 8, and those who like only bananas is also 8. Exactly 6 students liked all the 3 fruits. Exactly 10 students liked none of the 3. How many students are in this class?
   A) 45
   B) 49
   C) 53
   D) 57
   E) 60

   Solution:

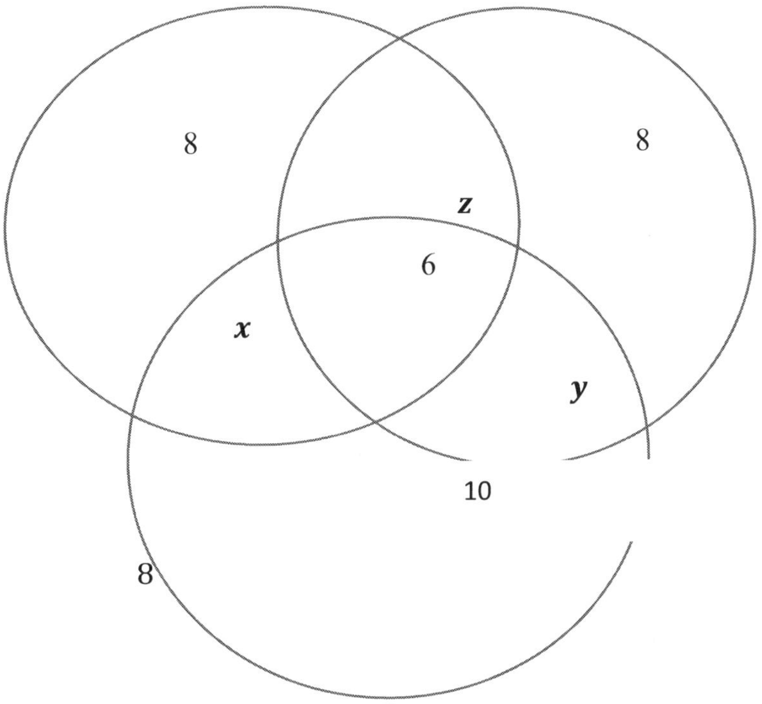

From the given conditions we have:

$$x + z + 8 + 6 = 20$$

This gives:

$$x + z = 6 \quad (1)$$

Similarly,

$$y + z = 6 \quad (2)$$

$$x + y = 6 \quad (3)$$

From (1) and (2) we get $x = y$. Substituting this in (3) we get:

$$x + x = 6$$

$$x = 3$$

$$y = 3$$

$$z = 3$$

$$Total\ \# = 8 + 8 + 8 + 3 + 3 + 3 + 6 + 10 = 49$$

The correct answer is **B.**

7. In a survey on couples, 40% of the couples had one or more child, and among these child possessing couples 35% usually ate home-cooked food. Overall, 24% couples usually ate home-cooked food. Find the probability that a randomly selected couple does not have a child and they do not usually eat at home.
   A) .1
   B) .2
   C) .3
   D) .4
   E) .5

Solution:

	No Child = 100% − 40% = 60%	1 or more child = 40%	Total
Usually home	$24\% - 14\% = 10\%$	$.35(40\%) = 14\%$	24%
Not usually home	60% − 10% = 50%		

From the above table we see that the required probability is $.5$

The correct answer is **E**.

8. In fall semester, a professor did not use online HW and the student grades were uniformly distributed on $[a, 100]$. In the spring semester, he used online HW and the student grades were distributed uniformly on $[2a, 100]$. The variance of the grades in fall semester was 588. Find the median of the spring semester grades.
   A) 66
   B) 69
   C) 72
   D) 75
   E) 78

Solution

Let X represent the fall grades, and Y represent the spring grades.

The first target is to find a. For this, we will need to work with the distribution of X.

We know that for a uniform $[a, b]$ distribution,

$$Var[X] = \frac{(b-a)^2}{12}$$

$$588 = \frac{(100-a)^2}{12}$$

$$7056 = (100-a)^2$$

Taking square roots of both sides we get:

$$\pm 84 = 100 - a$$

$$a = 16, 184$$

But a has to be less than 100. Thus $a = 16$.

The distribution of Y is therefore uniform on $[2(16), 100] = [32,100]$.

Let the median, or 50th percentile of this distribution be k. Then we have:

$$P(X < k) = .5$$

$$\frac{k-32}{100-32} = .5$$

$$k - 32 = 34$$

$$k = 66$$

The correct answer is **A**.

Tools Needed for Problems 288-319

If population is normal, or if sample size, $n > 30$, then the sampling distribution of means and sums is approximately normal with mean and standard deviation:

$$\mu_{\bar{X}} = \mu$$

$$\sigma_{\bar{X}} = \frac{\sigma}{\sqrt{n}}$$

$$\mu_{sum} = n\mu$$

$$\sigma_{sum} = \sqrt{n}\,\sigma$$

where μ and σ are mean and standard deviation of each of n identical variables.

$$Var\,X = E[X^2] - (E[X])^2$$

For a discrete random variable,

$$E[X] = \sum_x x\,f(x)$$

$$E[X^2] = \sum_x x^2\,f(x)$$

$$E[XY] = \sum_{x,y} xy\,f(x,y)$$

$$f_X(x) = \sum_y f(x,y)$$

$$z = \frac{X - mean}{SD}$$

$$Cov\,(X,Y) = E[XY] - E[X]E[Y]$$

$$Corr\,(X,Y) = \frac{Cov(X,Y)}{\sqrt{(Var\,X)(\,Var\,Y)}}$$

The pmf of Poisson with mean m is:

$$f(x) = \frac{m^x e^{-m}}{x!}$$

$$Var(X+Y) = Var\,X + Var\,Y + 2Cov(X,Y)$$

The pmf of geometric distribution is:

$$f(n) = p(1-p)^{n-1}$$

where $n =$ number of trials for the first success, and

$p =$ probability of success in each trial

The cdf of exponential distribution is:

$$F(x) = 1 - e^{x/4}$$

If $f(x)$ is the pdf of X, and $g(x)$ is any function, then:

$$E[g(x)] = \int_{-\infty}^{\infty} g(x)\, f(x)\, dx$$

Partition rule says:

$$P(A) = P(AB) + P(AB^C)$$

From this we get:

$$P(AB^C) = P(A) - P(AB)$$

If A and B are independent events then:

$$P(AB) = P(A)P(B)$$

$$z = \frac{X - mean}{SD}$$

$$P(A|B) = \frac{P(AB)}{P(B)}$$

Cdf of an exponential distribution with mean m is:

$$F(x) = 1 - e^{-x/m}$$

SOA Sample Question 288 Explanation

Let A be the event that a woman is pregnant.

Let B be the event that a woman is not pregnant. Since 20% are pregnant, so:

$$P(A) = .2$$

$$P(B) = 1 - P(A)$$

$$= 1 - .2$$

$$= .8$$

Let "X" be the event that the test says that a woman is pregnant.

Let "Y" be the event that the test says that a woman is not pregnant. Then:

$$P(Y|A) = .1$$

$$P(X|A) = 1 - P(Y|A)$$

$$= 1 - .1$$

$$= .9$$

$$P(X|B) = .2$$

$$P(Y|B) = 1 - P(X|B)$$

$$= 1 - .2$$

$$= .8$$

We are to find $P(A|X)$.

$$P(A|X) = \frac{P(A \text{ } and \text{ } X)}{P(X)}$$

$$= \frac{P(A \text{ } and \text{ } X)}{P(A \text{ } and \text{ } X) + P(B \text{ } and \text{ } X)}$$

$$= \frac{P(A)P(X|A)}{P(A)P(X|A) + P(B)P(X|B)}$$

$$= \frac{.2(.9)}{.2(.9) + .8(.2)}$$

$$= .53$$

The correct answer is **D**.

SOA Sample Question 289 Explanation

Let Y be the amount paid. First payment happens 10 inches in excess of 40 inches, that is, at 50 inches.

x	$p(x)$	Y
$0 \le x < 50$	$.06 + .18 + .26 + .22 = .72$	0
$50 \le x < 60$	$.14$	200
$60 \le x < 70$	$.06$	400
$x \ge 70$	$.04 + .04 = .08$	500

Note that if we were finding SD by hand, we can omit the 0-payment entry but we must include it if we are doing it on calculator, which I am as I explain in my youtube video whose link is:

https://www.youtube.com/watch?v=FEJ-UZwfdls

We get from calculator:

$$SD = 163.5$$

The correct answer is **A**.

SOA Sample Question 290 Explanation

$$p(x) = \begin{cases} 0.5, & x = 0 \\ 0.5, & x = 2 \end{cases}$$

$$\mu = E[X] = \sum_x x\,p(x) = 0(.5) + 2(.5) = 1$$

$$E[X^2] = \sum_x x^2\,p(x) = 0^2(.5) + 2^2(.5) = 2$$

$$Var\,X = E[X^2] - (E[X])^2$$

$$= 2 - 1^2$$

$$= 1$$

$$\sigma = \sqrt{Var\,X}$$

$$= \sqrt{1}$$

$$= 1$$

By central limit theorem,

$$\mu_{sum} = n\mu = 100(1) = 100$$

$$\sigma_{sum} = \sqrt{n}\,\sigma = \sqrt{100}\,(1) = 10$$

We need to change 115 into standard score.

$$z = \frac{115 - \mu_{sum}}{\sigma_{sum}}$$

$$= \frac{115 - 100}{10}$$

$$= 1.5$$

$$P(S > 115) = P(z > 1.5)$$

$$= 1 - P(z \leq 1.5)$$

$$= 1 - .9332$$

$$= .0668$$

This rounds to choice **B**.

SOA Sample Question 291 Explanation

$$p(x,y)=\begin{cases}.25, & x=0,\ y=0\\ .25, & x=1, y=0\\ .125, & x=0,\ y=1\\ .375, & x=1,\ y=1\end{cases}$$

$$f_X(x)=\begin{cases}.25+.125=.375, & x=0\\ .25+.375=.625, & x=1\end{cases}$$

$$f_Y(y)=\begin{cases}.25+.25=.5, & y=0\\ .125+.375=.5, & y=1\end{cases}$$

$$E[X]=\sum_x x\,f_X(x)=0(.375)+1(.625)=.625$$

$$E[Y]=\sum_y y\,f_Y(y)=0(.5)+1(.5)=.5$$

$$E[XY]=\sum_{x,y} xy\,p(x,y)=0(0).25+1(0).25+0(1).125+1(1).375=.375$$

$$E[X^2]=\sum_x x^2 f_X(x)=0^2(.375)+1^2(.625)=.625$$

$$E[Y^2]=\sum_y y^2 f_Y(y)=0^2(.5)+1^2(.5)=.5$$

$$Var\ X=E[X^2]-(E[X])^2=.625-.625^2=.234$$

$$Var\ Y=E[Y^2]-(E[Y])^2=.5-.5^2=.25$$

$$Cov\ (X,Y)=E[XY]-E[X]E[Y]=.375-.625(.5)=.0625$$

$$Corr\ (X,Y)=\frac{Cov(X,Y)}{\sqrt{(Var\ X)(\ Var\ Y)}}$$

$$=\frac{.0625}{\sqrt{(.234)(.25)}}$$

$$=.26$$

The correct answer is **C**.

SOA Sample Question 292 Explanation

$$f_Y(y) = \sum_x p(x,y), \qquad x = 0,1,2,3,4,5, \ \ y = 0, \dots, x$$

According to the given condition, y takes integer values less than or equal to x. So,

$$f_Y(0) = p(0,0) + p(1,0) + p(2,0) + p(3,0) + p(4,0) + p(5,0) = 6\left(\frac{1}{21}\right) = \frac{6}{21}$$

$$f_Y(1) = p(1,1) + p(2,1) + p(3,1) + p(4,1) + p(5,1) = 5\left(\frac{1}{21}\right) = \frac{5}{21}$$

$$f_Y(2) = p(2,2) + p(3,2) + p(4,2) + p(5,2) = 4\left(\frac{1}{21}\right) = \frac{4}{21}$$

$$f_Y(3) = p(3,3) + p(4,3) + p(5,3) = 3\left(\frac{1}{21}\right) = \frac{3}{21}$$

$$f_Y(4) = p(4,4) + p(5,4) = 2\left(\frac{1}{21}\right) = \frac{2}{21}$$

$$f_Y(5) = p(5,5) = \frac{1}{21}$$

$$E[Y] = \sum_y y f_Y(y) = 0\left(\frac{6}{21}\right) + 1\left(\frac{5}{21}\right) + 2\left(\frac{4}{21}\right) + 3\left(\frac{3}{21}\right) + 4\left(\frac{2}{21}\right) + 5\left(\frac{1}{21}\right) = \frac{5}{3}$$

$$E[Y^2] = \sum_y y^2 f_Y(y) = 0\left(\frac{6}{21}\right) + 1\left(\frac{5}{21}\right) + 4\left(\frac{4}{21}\right) + 9\left(\frac{3}{21}\right) + 16\left(\frac{2}{21}\right) + 25\left(\frac{1}{21}\right) = 5$$

$$Var\,Y = E[Y^2] - (E[Y])^2$$

$$= 5 - \left(\frac{5}{3}\right)^2$$

$$= 2.22$$

The correct answer is **B**.

SOA Sample Question 293 Explanation

(x,y)	$w=x+y$	$p(w)$
$(0,0)$	0	$.9729$
$(0,40),(40,0)$	40	$.01+.01=.02$
$(0,200),(200,0)$	200	$.002+.002=.004$
$(40,40)$	80	$.002$
$(40,200),(200,40)$	240	$.0005+.0005=.001$
$(200,200)$	400	$.0001$

From Calculator,

$$SD = 16.56$$

This rounds to choice **D**.

SOA Sample Question 294 Explanation

Let *X* be the relative change in value of stock X.

Let *Y* be the relative change in value of stock Y.

$$E[X] = .3(.18) + .5(.08) - .2(.13) = .068$$

$$E[Y] = .3(.15) + .5(.07) - .2(.06) = .068$$

$$E[X^2] = .3(.18)^2 + .5(.08)^2 + .2(.13)^2 = .0163$$

$$E[Y^2] = .3(.15)^2 + .5(.07)^2 + .2(.06)^2 = .00992$$

$$Var\ X = E[X^2] - (E[X])^2 = .0163 - (.068)^2 = .011676$$

$$Var\ Y = E[Y^2] - (E[Y])^2 = .00992 - (.068)^2 = .005296$$

So, the expected values, or means, of *X* and *Y* are equal, but *X* has a larger variance.

The correct answer is **B**.

SOA Sample Question 295 Explanation

Let X be the number of purchases.

We are to find $P(X \leq 2)$.

$$P(X \leq 2) = 1 - P(X > 2)$$

$$= 1 - P(3) - P(4) \quad (1)$$

Now 3 purchases can happen in the following ways:

(i) All the first 3 purchase, while the 4th does not. Probability of this case is:

$$.5(.5)(.5)(1 - .1) = .1125$$

(ii) 2 of the first 3 purchase, and the 4th purchases. Probability of this case is:

$$\binom{3}{2} .5^2(1 - .5)^{3-2}(.1) = .0375$$

The probability of 3 purchases is the sum of the probabilities of these 2 cases. So,

$$P(3) = .1125 + .0375$$

$$= .15$$

$$P(4) = .5(.5)(.5)(.1)$$

$$= .0125$$

So, equation (1) becomes:

$$P(X \leq 2) = 1 - .15 - .0125$$

$$= .84$$

The correct answer is **D**.

SOA Sample Question 296 Explanation

Let x be the number of policies on female smokers.

Let w be the number of policies on male smokers.

Let y be the number of policies on male non- smokers.

Then $y + 100$ is the number of policies on female non-smokers, by condition (ii).

By condition (iii),

$$w + x = 350 \quad (1)$$

By condition (i), total policies on males $= 150 +$ total policies on females. That is:

$$w + y = 150 + x + (y + 100)$$

This simplifies to:

$$w - x = 250 \quad (2)$$

Subtracting equation (2) from equation (1), we get:

$$2x = 100$$

$$x = 50$$

The correct answer is **A**.

SOA Sample Question 297 Explanation

$$f(x) = k(10+x)^{-2}, \qquad 0 < x < 40$$

We first need to find k. For this, we set the integral of the pdf to 1.

$$\int_{-\infty}^{\infty} f(x)\,dx = 1$$

$$\int_{0}^{40} k(10+x)^{-2}\,dx = 1$$

$$k\frac{(10+x)^{-1}}{-1}\Big|_0^{40} = 1$$

$$-k\left(\frac{1}{50} - \frac{1}{10}\right) = 1$$

$$\frac{2k}{25} = 1$$

$$k = 12.5$$

$$P(X < 5) = \int_{-\infty}^{5} f(x)\,dx$$

$$= \int_{0}^{5} 12.5(10+x)^{-2}\,dx$$

$$= 12.5\frac{(10+x)^{-1}}{-1}\Big|_0^{5}$$

$$= -12.5\left(\frac{1}{15} - \frac{1}{10}\right)$$

$$= .42$$

The correct answer is **C**.

SOA Sample Question 298 Explanation

x	$P(x)$
0	.5
1	.2
2	.3

$$E[X] = 0(.5) + 1(.2) + 2(.3) = .8$$

Expected claim on 76 policies, by central limit theorem, will be:

$$\mu_{sum} = nE[X]$$
$$= 76(.8)$$
$$= 60.8$$

Thus, expected premium on 76 policies will be:

$$1.25(60.8) = 76$$

$$E[X^2] = 0(.5) + 1(.2) + 4(.3) = 1.4$$
$$Var\ X = E[X^2] - (E[X])^2$$
$$= 1.4 - .8^2$$
$$= .76$$

If S is the total claim on 76 policies, then, by central limit theorem,

$$\sigma_{sum} = \sqrt{n}\,\sigma$$
$$= \sqrt{76}\,\sqrt{.76}$$
$$= 7.6$$

We need $P(S > 76)$. We thus need to change 76 into standard score.

$$z = \frac{76 - 60.8}{7.6}$$
$$= 2$$

$$P(S > 76) = P(z > 2)$$
$$= 1 - P(z \le 2)$$
$$= 1 - .9772$$
$$= .0228$$

The correct answer is **A**.

SOA Sample Question 299 Explanation

The pmf of Poisson with mean m is:

$$f(x) = \frac{m^x e^{-m}}{x!}$$

So, the probability of no successes is:

$$f(0) = \frac{m^0 e^{-m}}{0!}$$

$$= e^{-m}$$

So, the mean can be calculated by taking natural log of both sides:

$$\ln f(0) = -m$$

$$m = -\ln f(0)$$

Total # of policies $= 20000 + 45000 + 35000 = 100000$

Group	# of policies	$f(0)$	$m = -\ln f(0)$	Total Expected Claims in Group $= nm$
A	20000	.7	.3567	7134
B	45000	.9	.1054	4743
C	35000	.5	.6931	24259

$$Total\ Expected\ Claims = \sum nm$$

$$= 7134 + 4743 + 24259$$

$$= 36136$$

$$= 36.136\ thousand$$

The correct answer is **C**.

SOA Sample Question 300 Explanation

Annual Poisson mean= .288

So, the 3-year Poisson mean is:

$$m = 3(.288)$$
$$= .864$$

The pmf of Poisson with mean m is:

$$f(x) = \frac{m^x e^{-m}}{x!}$$

$$P(divident) = P(no\ more\ than\ 1\ claim)$$
$$= f(0) + f(1)$$
$$= e^{-.864} + .864e^{-.864}$$
$$= .79$$

The correct answer is **E**.

SOA Sample Question 301 Explanation

Let F be the number of fire losses.

Let T be the number of theft losses losses.

$$Var(F + T) = Var\ F + Var\ T + 2Cov(F, T)$$
$$= 5 + 8 + 2(3)$$
$$= 19$$

The correct answer is **E**.

SOA Sample Question 302 Explanation

Daily mean = 4

So, the 3-day Poisson mean is:

$$m = 3(4)$$
$$= 12$$

The pmf of Poisson with mean m is:

$$f(x) = \frac{m^x e^{-m}}{x!}$$

$$P(at\ most\ 1\ accident)$$
$$= f(0) + f(1)$$
$$= e^{-12} + 12e^{-12}$$
$$= 13e^{-12}$$

The correct answer is **A**.

SOA Sample Question 303 Explanation

Since the probability of a head/tail is 0.5, so:

$$P(3\ heads\ in\ 3\ tosses) = .5(.5)(.5) = .125$$

Similarly,

$$P(3\ tails\ in\ 3\ tosses) = .5(.5)(.5) = .125$$

$$p = P(success) = P(3\ heads\ in\ 3\ tosses\ or\ 3\ tails\ in\ 3\ tosses\ )$$
$$= P(3\ heads\ in\ 3\ tosses) + P\ (3\ tails\ in\ 3\ tosses\ )$$
$$= .125 + .125$$
$$= .25$$

This is a geometric distribution with $n = 3$ because we are talking about the number of trials for the first success. We know that the pmf of geometric distribution is:

$$f(n) = p(1-p)^{n-1}$$
$$f(3) = .25(1-.25)^{3-1}$$
$$= .141$$

The correct answer is **C**.

SOA Sample Question 304 Explanation

Company	# of Trucks
P	4
Q	3
R	2
Total	9

$$P(\text{at least } 1 \text{ of } 2 \text{ from } P) = P(\text{exactly } 1 \text{ from } P) + P(\text{both from } P) \quad (1)$$

$$P(\text{exactly } 1 \text{ from } P) = P(1st \text{ from } P \text{ and } 2nd \text{ not}) + P(1st \text{ not but } 2nd \text{ from } P)$$

$$= \frac{4}{9}\left(\frac{5}{8}\right) + \frac{5}{9}\left(\frac{4}{8}\right)$$

$$= \frac{40}{72}$$

$$P(\text{both from } P) = \frac{4}{9}\left(\frac{3}{8}\right) = \frac{12}{72}$$

So, equation (1) becomes:

$$P(\text{at least } 1 \text{ of } 2 \text{ from } P) = \frac{40}{72} + \frac{12}{72}$$

$$= .72$$

The correct answer is **E**.

SOA Sample Question 305 Explanation

To pass the test, the candidate:

(i) must have at most one error, and
(ii) should complete the test in less than or equal to 50 minutes.
We will calculate the probabilities of these 2 independent events separately and then multiply to get the required answer. The pmf of Poission with mean m is:

$$f(x) = \frac{3^x e^{-3}}{x!}$$

$$P(at\ most\ 1\ error) = f(0) + f(1)$$

$$= .199$$

We next change 50 into standard score.

$$z = \frac{50 - mean}{SD}$$

$$= \frac{50 - 45}{10}$$

$$= .5$$

$$P(time \leq 50) = P(z \leq .5)$$

$$= .6915$$

$$P(pass) = P(at\ most\ 1\ error)P(time \leq 50)$$

$$= .199(.6915)$$

$$= .14$$

The correct answer is **B**.

SOA Sample Question 306 Explanation

Let H be the event that a person is home renter.

Let A be the event that a person is apartment renter.

$$P(H) = .4$$

$$P(A) = .6$$

Let X be the policy duration time for home renters.

Let Y be the policy duration time for apartment renters.

The respective cdfs of the two exponential distributions are thus:

$$F(x) = 1 - e^{-x/4}$$

$$G(y) = 1 - e^{-y/2}$$

Probability that a home renter will still have the policy after 1 year is:

$$P(X > 1) = 1 - P(X \leq 1)$$

$$= 1 - F(1)$$

$$= .7788$$

Probability that an apartment renter will still have the policy after 1 year is:

$$P(Y > 1) = 1 - P(Y \leq 1)$$

$$= 1 - G(1)$$

$$= .6065$$

Let S be the event that a renter still has policy after 1 year. We are to find $P(H|S)$

$$P(H|S) = \frac{P(H \text{ and } S)}{P(S)}$$

$$= \frac{P(H \text{ and } S)}{P(H \text{ and } S) + P(A \text{ and } S)}$$

$$= \frac{P(H)P(X > 1)}{P(H)P(X > 1) + P(A)P(Y > 1)}$$

$$= \frac{.4(.7788)}{.4(.7788) + .6(.6065)}$$

$$= .46$$

The correct answer is **C**.

SOA Sample Question 307 Explanation

By central limit theorem

$$\mu_{\bar{X}} = \mu$$

$$\sigma_{\bar{X}} = \frac{\sigma}{\sqrt{n}}$$

where μ and σ are mean and standard deviation of each of n identical variables.

If n policies are sold, and S is the average benefit per policy, then:

$$\mu_S = 2475$$

$$\sigma_S = \frac{250}{\sqrt{n}}$$

Thus, we are looking for $P(S < 2500)$.

A cumulative probability of .99 corresponds to $z = 2.326$. Thus, our z −score equation is:

$$2.326 = \frac{2500 - 2475}{\frac{250}{\sqrt{n}}}$$

$$\frac{250}{\sqrt{n}} = \frac{25}{2.326}$$

$$\sqrt{n} = 23.26$$

$$n = 541.03$$

This corresponds to 99% probability of average benefit being in the desired range. We need the probability to be at least 99%. So, our sample size should be at greater than or equal to 541.03. Since sample size is an integer. So, the minimum size needed is 542.

The correct answer is **B**.

SOA Sample Question 308 Explanation

Let Y be the payment. A payment of 1000 happens for $1 \leq X < 5$, and no payment happens otherwise. From the given table we see that:

$$P(X < 1) = .05$$

$$P(X \geq 5) = 1 - P(X < 5)$$

$$= 1 - .48$$

$$= .52$$

X	$Probability\ (p)$	Payment(y)	yp	y^2	y^2p
$X < 1\ or\ X \geq 5$	$.05 + .52 = .57$	0	0	0	0
$1 \leq X < 5$	$1 - .57 = .43$	1000	430	1000000	430000
Sum			430		430000

$$E[Y] = \sum yp = 430$$

$$E[Y^2] = \sum y^2p = 430000$$

$$SD(Y) = \sqrt{E[Y^2] - (E[Y])^2}$$

$$= \sqrt{430000 - (430)^2}$$

$$= 495$$

The correct answer is **D**.

SOA Sample Question 309 Explanation

Let L be the probability of a loss. We are to find $P(A|L)$.

$$P(A|L) = \frac{P(A\ and\ L)}{P(L)}$$

$$= \frac{P(A\ and\ L)}{P(A\ and\ L) + P(B\ and\ L) + P(C\ and\ L)}$$

$$= \frac{.4(.015)}{.4(.015) + .35(.011) + .25(.008)}$$

$$= .506$$

The correct answer is **E**.

SOA Sample Question 310 Explanation

$$f(x) = \frac{x}{50}, \quad 0 < x < 10$$

Let Y be the claim amount under policy 1.

Let Z be the claim amount under policy 2.

$$Y = \begin{cases} X, & X < 4 \\ 4, & X \geq 4 \end{cases}$$

$$Z = \begin{cases} 0, & X < 4 \\ X - 4, & X \geq 4 \end{cases}$$

$$E[Y] = \int_{-\infty}^{\infty} y\, f(x)\, dx$$

$$= \int_0^4 x \frac{x}{50}\, dx + \int_4^{10} 4 \frac{x}{50}\, dx$$

$$= \frac{x^3}{150} \Big|_0^4 + 4 \frac{x^2}{100} \Big|_4^{10}$$

$$= \frac{4^3}{150} + .04(100 - 16)$$

$$= 3.79$$

$$E[Z] = \int_{-\infty}^{\infty} z\, f(x)\, dx$$

$$= \int_4^{10} \frac{(x-4)x}{50}\, dx$$

$$= \frac{1}{50} \int_4^{10} x^2 - 4x\, dx$$

$$= \frac{1}{50} \left(\frac{x^3}{3} - 2x^2 \right) \Big|_4^{10}$$

$$= \frac{1}{50} \left(\frac{10^3}{3} - 2(10)^2 \right) - \frac{1}{50} \left(\frac{4^3}{3} - 2(4)^2 \right)$$

$$= 2.88$$

$$E[Y] - E[Z] = 3.79 - 2.88$$

$$= .91$$

The correct answer is **D**.

SOA Sample Question 311 Explanation

Let $Z = X - Y$. We are to find $Var\ Z$.

Since X is the premium and Y is the discount, so $Y \le X$, because discount can never be greater than the premium. We thus have the following table:

(x, y)	Probability (p)	$z = x - y$	zp	z^2p
(1,1)	$\frac{2}{31}$	0	0	0
(1,0), (2,1)	$\frac{1}{31} + \frac{5}{31} = \frac{6}{31}$	1	$\frac{6}{31}$	$\frac{6}{31}$
(2,0), (3,1)	$\frac{4}{31} + \frac{10}{31} = \frac{14}{31}$	2	$\frac{28}{31}$	$\frac{56}{31}$
(3,0)	$\frac{9}{31}$	3	$\frac{27}{31}$	$\frac{81}{31}$
Sum			$E[Z] = \frac{61}{31}$	$E[Z^2] = \frac{143}{31}$

$$Var\ Z = E[Z^2] - (E[Z])^2$$

$$= \frac{143}{31} - \left(\frac{61}{31}\right)^2$$

$$= .74$$

The correct answer is **C**.

SOA Sample Question 312 Explanation

Let X be the event of filing a medical claim.

Let Y be the event of filing a property claim.

$$P(X) = .3$$

$$P(Y) = .42$$

$$P(X \cup Y) = .6$$

By addition rule:

$$P(X \cup Y) = P(X) + P(Y) - P(XY)$$

$$.6 = .3 + .42 - P(XY)$$

$$P(XY) = .12 = P(both)$$

Let N be the event that the policy holder will not file both types of claims.

$$P(N) = 1 - P(both)$$

$$= 1 - .12$$

$$= .88$$

$$P(exactly\ one, given\ not\ both) = \frac{P(exactly\ one\ and\ not\ both)}{P(not\ both)}$$

$$= \frac{P(exactly\ one)}{P(N)} \quad (1)$$

$$P(exactly\ one) = P(X\ and\ not\ Y) + P(Y\ and\ not\ X) \quad (2)$$

As a consequence of partition rule we have:

$$P(X\ and\ not\ Y) = P(X) - P(XY)$$

$$= .3 - .12$$

$$= .18$$

$$P(Y\ and\ not\ X) = P(Y) - P(YX)$$

$$= .42 - .12$$

$$= .3$$

So, equation (2) becomes:

$$P(exactly\ one) = .18 + .3 = .48$$

Substituting this in equation (1) we get:

$$P(exactly\ one, given\ not\ both) = \frac{.48}{.88} = .55$$

The correct answer is **D**.

SOA Sample Question 313 Explanation

Let A_k be the event that a property claim is reported in year k.

Let B_k be the event that a liability claim is reported in year k.

$$P(A_9) = P(A_1)\,(1.25)^8$$

$$P(B_9) = P(B_1)\,(.75)^8$$

$$P(both\ claims\ in\ year\ 9) = P(A_9)P(B_9)\ (by\ independence)$$

$$= P(A_1)\,(1.25)^8 P(B_1)\,(.75)^8$$

$$= .5967P(A_1)P(B_1) \quad (1)$$

We are given that:

$$P(A_1B_1) = .01$$

$$P(A_1)P(B_1) = .01$$

Substituting this in equation (1) we get:

$$P(both\ claims\ in\ year\ 9) = .01(.5967)$$

$$= .006$$

The correct answer is **B**.

SOA Sample Question 314 Explanation

We are given that 1st year policy-holders account for 15% business.

So, multi-year policy-holders account for 85% business.

Let X be the number of claims by a 1st year policy-holder.

Let Y be the number of claims by a multi-year policy-holder.

Then, by the Poisson formula, we get:

$$f(x) = \frac{.5^x e^{-.5}}{x!}$$

$$g(y) = \frac{.2^y e^{-.2}}{y!}$$

Let F be the event that the filer is a 1st year policy-holder.

Let M be the event that the filer is a multi-year policy-holder.

Let N be the number of claims.

We are to find $P(F|N \geq 1)$.

$$P(F|N \geq 1) = \frac{P(F, and\ N \geq 1)}{P(N \geq 1)}$$

$$= \frac{P(F)\ P(\ X \geq 1)}{P(F)P(\ X \geq 1) + P(M)\ P(\ Y \geq 1)}$$

$$= \frac{.15(1 - f(0))}{.15(1 - f(0)) + .85(1 - g(0))}$$

$$= \frac{.15(1 - e^{-.5})}{.15(1 - e^{-.5}) + .85(1 - e^{-.2})}$$

$$= .277$$

The correct answer is **B**.

SOA Sample Question 315 Explanation

Let $Z = \min\{Y_1, Y_2\}$.

We are to find $P(Z > e^{16})$

$$P(Z > e^{16}) = P(Y_1 > e^{16} \; and \; Y_2 > e^{16})$$

$$= P(Y_1 > e^{16})P(Y_2 > e^{16})$$

Last equation is true because of independence that is given. Thus:

$$P(Z > e^{16}) = P(e^{X_1} > e^{16})P(e^{X_2} > e^{16})$$

$$= P(X_1 > 16)P(X_2 > 16) \quad (1)$$

We need to change 16 into standard score for each of the two normal variables.

$$z = \frac{X - mean}{SD}$$

$$z_1 = \frac{16 - 16}{1.5} = 0$$

$$z_1 = \frac{16 - 15}{2} = .5$$

So, equation (1) becomes:

$$P(Z > e^{16}) = P(z_1 > 0)P(z_2 > .5)$$

$$= [1 - P(z_1 \leq 0)][1 - P(z_1 \leq .5)]$$

$$= (1 - .5)(1 - .6915)$$

$$= .154$$

The correct answer is **B**.

SOA Sample Question 316 Explanation

By law basic probability:

$$P(A) + P(B) + P(C) = 1$$

Substituting conditions (i) and (ii) in the above equation we get:

$$5P(C) + 4(C) + P(C) = 1$$

$$10P(C) = 1$$

$$P(C) = \frac{1}{10} = .1$$

$$P(A) = 5P(C) = .5$$

$$P(B) = 4P(C) = .4$$

We are to find $P(C|0\ claims)$

$$P(C|0\ claims) = \frac{P(C\ and\ 0\ claims)}{P(0\ claims)}$$

$$= \frac{P(C\ and\ 0\ claims)}{P(C\ and\ 0\ claims) + P(B\ and\ 0\ claims) + P(A\ and\ 0\ claims)}$$

$$= \frac{P(C)\,P(\,0\ claims|C)}{P(C)P(\,0\ claims|C) + P(B)P(\,0\ claims|B) + P(A)P(\,0\ claims|A)}$$

$$= \frac{.1(.4)}{.1(.4) + .4(.2) + .5(.1)}$$

$$= .235$$

The correct answer is **C**.

SOA Sample Question 317 Explanation

$$P(death\ in\ year\ 1) = .01$$

$$P(death\ in\ year\ 2) = P(lives\ through\ year\ 1\ and\ dies\ in\ year\ 2)$$

$$= .99(.01)$$

$$= .0099$$

$$P(death\ in\ year\ 3) = P(lives\ through\ years\ 1,2, and\ dies\ in\ year\ 3)$$

$$=.99^2(.01)$$

$$= .0098$$

$$P(death\ in\ year\ 4) = P(lives\ through\ years\ 1,2,3, and\ dies\ in\ year\ 4)$$

$$=.99^3(.01)$$

$$= .0097$$

$$P(death\ in\ year\ 5) = P(lives\ through\ years\ 1,2,3,4, and\ dies\ in\ year\ 5)$$

$$=.99^4(.01)$$

$$= .0096$$

If Y is the benefit then:

$$E[Y] = \sum (benefit\ if\ death\ in\ year\ k)P(death\ in\ year\ k)$$

$$= (ben. if\ death\ yr\ 1)P(death\ yr\ 1) + \cdots + (ben. if\ death\ yr\ k)P(death\ yr\ k)$$

$$= 25000(.01) + 20000(.0099) + 15000(.0098) + 10000(.0097) + 5000(.0096)$$

$$= 740$$

The correct answer is **B**.

SOA Sample Question 318 Explanation

Let A be the event that a woman is pregnant.

Let B be the event that a woman is not pregnant. Since 30% are pregnant, so:

$$P(A) = .3$$

$$P(B) = 1 - P(A)$$

$$= 1 - .3$$

$$= .7$$

Let "X" be the event that the test says that a woman is pregnant.

Let "Y" be the event that the test says that a woman is not pregnant. Then:

$$P(Y|A) = .1$$

$$P(X|A) = 1 - P(Y|A)$$

$$= 1 - .1$$

$$= .9$$

$$P(X|B) = .2$$

$$P(Y|B) = 1 - P(X|B)$$

$$= 1 - .2$$

$$= .8$$

We are to find $P(A|X)$.

$$P(A|X) = \frac{P(A \text{ } and \text{ } X)}{P(X)}$$

$$= \frac{P(A \text{ } and \text{ } X)}{P(A \text{ } and \text{ } X) + P(B \text{ } and \text{ } X)}$$

$$= \frac{P(A)P(X|A)}{P(A)P(X|A) + P(B)P(X|B)}$$

$$= \frac{.3(.9)}{.3(.9) + .7(.2)}$$

$$= .66$$

The correct answer is **C**.

SOA Sample Question 319 Explanation

Let X be the number of purchases.

We are to find $P(X \leq 2)$.

$$P(X \leq 2) = 1 - P(X > 2)$$

$$= 1 - P(3) - P(4) \quad (1)$$

Now 3 purchases can happen in the following ways:

(iii) All the first 3 purchase, while the 4th does not. Probability of this case is:

$$.7(.7)(.7)(1 - .2) = .2744$$

(iv) 2 of the first 3 purchase, and the 4th purchases. Probability of this case is:

$$\binom{3}{2}.7^2(1 - .7)^{3-2}(.2) = .0882$$

The probability of 3 purchases is the sum of the probabilities of these 2 cases. So,

$$P(3) = .2744 + .0882$$

$$= .3626$$

$$P(4) = .7(.7)(.7)(.2)$$

$$= .0686$$

So, equation (1) becomes:

$$P(X \leq 2) = 1 - .3626 - .0686$$

$$= .57$$

The correct answer is **C**.

Quiz 25

1. Consider 50 independent throws of a loaded 2-sided die. In each throw, the probability of getting a 1 is .6, and the probability of getting a 2 is .4. Find the probability that the average of the 50 throws is less than 1.5

A) .075

B) .147

C) .500

D) .853

E) .925

Solution:

Let $X_1, \ldots, X_{50}$ be the variables representing the results of the 50 throws. For each:

$$p(x) = \begin{cases} 0.6, & x = 1 \\ 0.4, & x = 2 \end{cases}$$

$$\mu = E[X] = \sum_x x\, p(x) = 1(.6) + 2(.4) = 1.4$$

$$E[X^2] = \sum_x x^2\, p(x) = 1^2(.6) + 2^2(.4) = 2.2$$

$$Var\ X = E[X^2] - (E[X])^2$$

$$= 2.2 - 1.4^2$$

$$= .24$$

$$\sigma = \sqrt{.24}$$

$$\bar{X} = \frac{X_1 + \cdots + X_{50}}{50}$$

By central limit theorem,

$$\mu_{\bar{X}} = \mu = 1.4$$

$$\sigma_{\bar{X}} = \frac{\sigma}{\sqrt{n}} = \frac{\sqrt{.24}}{\sqrt{50}} = .0693$$

We need to change 1.5 into standard score.

$$z = \frac{1.5 - \mu_{\bar{X}}}{\sigma_{\bar{X}}} = \frac{1.5 - 1.4}{.0693} = 1.44$$

$$P(\bar{X} < 1.5) = P(z < 1.44)$$

$$= .9251$$

The correct answer is **E**.

2. In a small town:

(i) There are 30 more adults than children.

(ii) The number of children who go to park daily is 20 more than the number of adults who go to park daily.

(iii) There are 80 persons who do not go to park daily.

Find the number of children who do not go to park daily.

A) 10

B) 15

C) 20

D) 25

E) 30

Solution:

Let x be the number of children who do not go to park daily.

Let w be the number of adults who do not go to park daily.

Let y be the number of adults who go to park daily.

Then $y + 20$ is the number of children who go to park daily, by condition (ii).

By condition (iii),

$$w + x = 80 \quad (1)$$

By condition (i), total adults $=$ 30 $+$ total children. That is:

$$w + y = 30 + x + (y + 20)$$

This simplifies to:

$$w - x = 50 \quad (2)$$

Subtracting equation (2) from equation (1), we get:

$$2x = 30$$

$$x = 15$$

The correct answer is **B**.

3. To pass, a test must be completed in 180 minutes with no more than 4 errors. From past experience, it is known that the number of test errors for an applicant follows Poisson distribution with mean 5, and the time needed for the test follows a normal distribution with mean 170 minutes and variance 150. Assume the number of errors and time needed for test are independent. Find the probability that a randomly chosen applicant will fail the test.

A) .35

B) .45

C) .50

D) .55

E) .65

Solution:

To pass the test, the candidate:

(i) must have at most 4 errors, and

(ii) should complete the test in less than or equal to 180 minutes.

We will calculate the probabilities of these 2 independent events separately and then multiply to get the required answer. The pmf of Poission with mean m is:

$$f(x) = \frac{5^x e^{-5}}{x!}$$

$$P(at\ most\ 4\ errors) = f(0) + f(1) + f(2) + f(3) + f(4) = .4405$$

We next change 180 into standard score.

$$z = \frac{180 - mean}{SD}$$

$$= \frac{180 - 170}{\sqrt{150}}$$

$$= .82$$

$$P(time \leq 180) = P(z \leq .82)$$

$$= .7939$$

$$P(pass) = P(at\ most\ 4\ errors)P(time \leq 180)$$

$$= .4405(.7939)$$

$$= .35$$

$$P(fail) = 1 - P(pass)$$

$$= 1 - .35$$

$$= .65$$

The correct answer is **E**.

4. An insurance pays 5000 upon death if the buyer survives at least one year but less than 3 years after purchase. Let X be the number of years the buyer survives after buying the policy.

x	$P(X < x)$
1	.01
2	.03
3	.07

Find the variance of the payment made under this policy.

A) 1,410,000

B) 1,430,000

C) 1,450,000

D) 1,470,000

E) 1,490,000

Solution:

Let Y be the payment. A payment of 5000 happens for $1 \leq X < 3$, and no payment happens otherwise. From the given table we see that:

$$P(X < 1) = .01$$

$$P(X \geq 3) = 1 - P(X < 3)$$

$$= 1 - .07$$

$$= .93$$

X	$Probability\ (p)$	Payment(y)	yp	y^2	y^2p
$X < 1\ or\ X \geq 3$	$.01 + .93 = .94$	0	0	0	0
$1 \leq X < 3$	$1 - .94 = .06$	5000	300	25000000	1500000
Sum			300		1500000

$$E[Y] = \sum yp = 300$$

$$E[Y^2] = \sum y^2p = 1500000$$

$$Var\ Y = E[Y^2] - (E[Y])^2$$

$$= 1500000 - (300)^2$$

$$= 1,410,000$$

The correct answer is **A**.

5. At a certain university,

(i) probability that a student needs remedial Math is .25.

(ii) probability that a student needs remedial English is .15.

(iii) probability that a student needs remedial Math or remedial English is .3.

Find the probability that a randomly chosen student at this university will need exactly one of these remedial subjects given that the student does not need both.

A) 1/9

B) 2/9

C) 3/9

D) 4/9

E) 5/9

Solution:

Let X be the event of needing remedial Math and Y be the event of needing English.

$$P(X) = .25$$

$$P(Y) = .15$$

$$P(X \cup Y) = .3$$

$$P(X \cup Y) = P(X) + P(Y) - P(XY)$$

$$.3 = .25 + .15 - P(XY)$$

$$P(XY) = .1 = P(both)$$

Let N be the event that the student does not need both.

$$P(N) = 1 - P(both) = 1 - .1 = .9$$

$$P(exactly\ one, given\ not\ both) = \frac{P(exactly\ one\ and\ not\ both)}{P(not\ both)} = \frac{P(exactly\ one)}{P(N)} \quad (1)$$

$$P(exactly\ one) = P(X\ and\ not\ Y) + P(Y\ and\ not\ X) \quad (2)$$

As a consequence of partition rule we have:

$$P(X\ and\ not\ Y) = P(X) - P(XY) = .25 - .1 = .15$$

$$P(Y\ and\ not\ X) = P(Y) - P(YX) = .15 - .1 = .05$$

So, equation (2) becomes:

$$P(exactly\ one) = .15 + .05 = .2$$

Substituting this in equation (1) we get:

$$P(exactly\ one, given\ not\ both) = \frac{.2}{.9} = \frac{2}{9}$$

The correct answer is **B**.

Tools needed for problems 320-332

By Central limit theorem, if population is normal, or if sample size, $n > 30$, then the sampling distribution of means and sums is approximately normal with mean and standard deviation:

$$\mu_{\bar{X}} = \mu$$

$$\sigma_{\bar{X}} = \frac{\sigma}{\sqrt{n}}$$

$$\mu_{sum} = n\mu$$

$$\sigma_{sum} = \sqrt{n}\,\sigma$$

where μ and σ are mean and standard deviation of each of n identical variables.

Thus, the binomial probability function is:

$$f(x) = \binom{n}{x} (success\ probability)^x\ (failure\ probability)^{n-x}$$

Here, $x = number\ of\ successes,\ \ n = number\ of\ trials$

$$\binom{n}{r} = \frac{n!}{r!\,(n-r)!}$$

The variance of a negative binomial distribution:

$$Var\ X = \frac{r(1-p)}{p^2}$$

$$X = \#\ of\ trial\ needed\ for\ r\ successes$$

$$p = probability\ of\ success\ in\ each\ trial$$

For a Poisson random variable, variance equals mean.

The cdf of an exponential distribution with mean k is:

$$F(x) = 1 - e^{-\frac{x}{k}}$$

The standard deviation of an exponential variable equals its mean.

If X is a random variable and a, b are constants, then:

$$Var(aX + b) = a^2\ Var\ X$$

If X, Y are random variables and a, b, c are constants, then:

$$Var(aX + bY + c) = a^2\ Var\ X + b^2\ Var\ Y + 2ab\ Cov(X, Y)$$

If X, Y are independent then $Cov(X, Y) = 0$

SOA Sample Question 320 Explanation

Central Limit Theorem tells us that the distribution of the sum of more than 30 identically distributed variables (100 here) is approximately normal.

Also, if there are n such variables, then the mean and standard deviation of the sum are:

$$\mu = n(mean\ of\ each)$$

$$= 100(1000)$$

$$= 100000$$

$$\sigma = \sqrt{n}\,(SD\ of\ each)$$

$$= \sqrt{100}\,400$$

$$= 4000$$

We need $P(S < 92000)$.

Thus, we need to change 92000 into standard score.

$$z = \frac{92000 - \mu}{\sigma}$$

$$= \frac{92000 - 100000}{4000}$$

$$= -2$$

$$P(S < 92000) = P(z < -2)$$

$$= P(z > 2)$$

$$= 1 - P(z \leq 2)$$

$$= 1 - .9772$$

$$= .0228$$

This rounds to choice **A**.

SOA Sample Question 321 Explanation

The number of non-defective bulbs, X, in a batch of 50 total bulbs is a binomial random variable with probability of success $1-p$. Note that we usually call the success probability as p but the notation given in the problem is forcing this success probability to be $1-p$. So, the failure probability is p. Thus, the binomial probability function in this case will be:

$$f(x) = \binom{50}{x}(1-p)^x\, p^{50-x}$$

This is because the success probability needs to have the power x while the failure probability needs to have the complement of this power.

$$P(X \geq n) = f(n) + f(n+1) + f(n+2) + \cdots + f(50)$$

$$= \sum_{k=n}^{50} f(k)$$

$$= \sum_{k=n}^{50} \binom{50}{k}(1-p)^k\, p^{50-k}$$

$$= \sum_{k=n}^{50} \frac{50!}{k!\,(50-k)!}(1-p)^k\, p^{50-k}$$

Thus $P(X \geq n) \geq .95$ can be written as:

$$\sum_{k=n}^{50} \frac{50!}{k!\,(50-k)!}(1-p)^k\, p^{50-k} \geq .95$$

The correct answer is **A**.

SOA Sample Question 322 Explanation

Let getting a 6 be a success.

The number of rolls required for r successes has a negative binomial distribution.

The variance of a negative binomial distribution with success probability p is:

$$Var\ X = \frac{r(1-p)}{p^2}$$

$$r = 3$$

$$p = 1/6$$

$$Var\ X = \frac{3\left(1-\frac{1}{6}\right)}{\left(\frac{1}{6}\right)^2}$$

$$= 90$$

The correct answer is **E**.

SOA Sample Question 323 Explanation

Let $A, B, C, D,$ be the events of selling auto, home, health, and life insurances, respectively.

We are given that:

$$P(A) = .45$$

$$P(B) = .55$$

$$P(C) = .6$$

$$P(D) = .6$$

$$P(more\ than\ 2\ products) = P(3\ or\ 4\ products)$$

$$P(3\ products) = P(A\ B\ C\ D^c) + P(A\ B\ C^c\ D) + P(A\ B^c\ C\ D) + P(A^c\ B\ C\ D)$$

$$= .45(.55)(.6)(.4) + .45(.55)(.4)(.6) + .45(.45)(.6)(.6) + .55(.45)(.6)(.6) = .3006$$

$$P(4\ products) = P(A\ B\ C\ D) = .45(.55)(.6)(.6) = .0891$$

$$P(3\ or\ 4\ products) = P(3\ products) + P(4\ products) = .3006 + .0891 = .3897$$

The correct answer is **C**.

SOA Sample Question 324 Explanation

For a Poisson random variable, variance equals mean.

Central Limit Theorem tells us that the distribution of the sum of more than 30 identically distributed variables (1600 here) is approximately normal.

Also, if there are n such variables, then the mean and standard deviation of the sum are:

$$\mu = n(mean\ of\ each) = 1600(4) = 6400$$

$$\sigma = \sqrt{n}\ (SD\ of\ each) = \sqrt{1600}\ \sqrt{4} = 80$$

We need $P(S \geq 6496)$. Thus, we need to change 6496 into standard score.

$$z = \frac{6496 - \mu}{\sigma}$$

$$= \frac{6496 - 6400}{80}$$

$$= 1.2$$

$$P(S \geq 6496) = P(z \geq 1.2)$$

$$= 1 - P(z < 1.2)$$

$$= 1 - .8849$$

$$= .1151$$

This rounds to choice **B**.

SOA Sample Question 325 Explanation

See the figure. Since only exactly 2 coverages are possible, so the only non-zero portions are the intersections of two of H, L, R, and the part outside of all 3 which indicates no coverage.

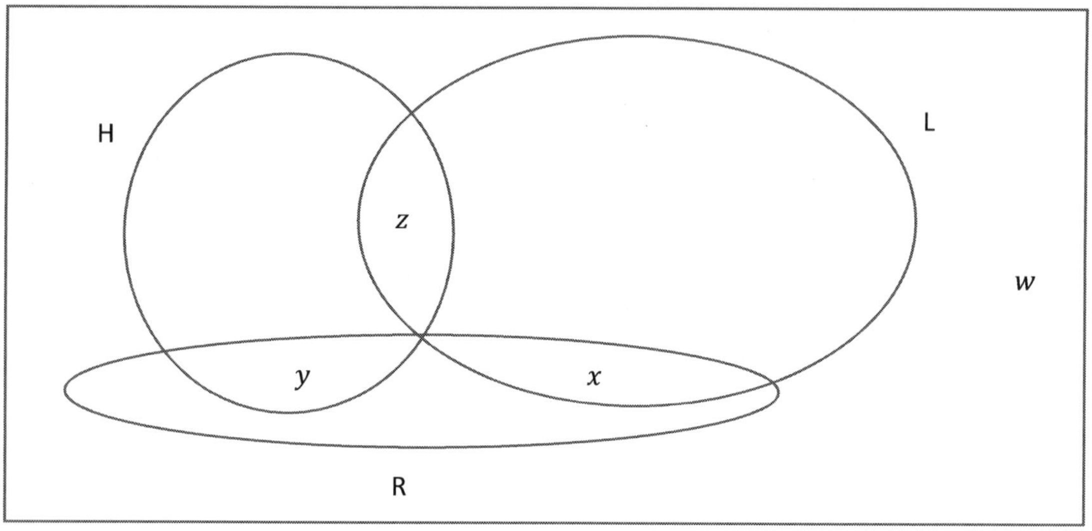

By the given conditions:

$$y + z = .625 \quad (1)$$

$$x + z = .375 \quad (2)$$

$$x + y = .5 \quad (3)$$

We need to find x. If we add equations (2) and (3) and subtract (1) we get:

$$(x + z) + (x + y) - (y + z) = .375 + .5 - .625$$

$$2x = .25$$

$$x = .125 = 12.5\%$$

The correct answer is **A**.

SOA Sample Question 326 Explanation

The given variable is exponential with cdf and mean given by:

$$F(x) = 1 - e^{-\frac{x}{20}}$$

$$E[X] = 20$$

We also know that the standard deviation of an exponential variable equals its mean.

$$SD = 20$$

$$P(E[X] - .5SD \le X \le E[X] + .5SD) = P(20 - .5(20) \le X \le 20 + .5(20)$$

$$= P(10 \le X \le 30) = F(30) - F(10) = \left(1 - e^{-\frac{30}{20}}\right) - \left(1 - e^{-\frac{10}{20}}\right) = .38$$

The correct answer is **B**.

SOA Sample Question 327 Explanation

Let X represent individual claim amounts.

By Central Limit Theorem, if sample size, $n > 30$ (100 in this case), then the sampling distribution of means is approximately normal with mean and standard deviation:

$$\mu_{\bar{X}} = \mu$$

$$\sigma_{\bar{X}} = \frac{\sigma}{\sqrt{n}}$$

where μ and σ are mean and standard deviation of each of n identical variables. So:

$$\mu_{\bar{X}} = 2500$$

$$\sigma_{\bar{X}} = \frac{500}{\sqrt{100}}$$

$$= 50$$

We are given that $P(\bar{X} > K) = .01$. This implies:

$$P(\bar{X} \leq K) = .99$$

We first need to find z corresponding to a cumulative probability of .99.

From the little table given at the bottom of the exam table we get $z = 2.326$

$$z = \frac{K - \mu_{\bar{X}}}{\sigma_{\bar{X}}}$$

$$2.326 = \frac{K - 2500}{50}$$

$$K = 2616$$

The correct answer is **C**.

SOA Sample Question 328 Explanation

Let C be the cost in the 2nd year. Then:

$$C = 1.03X + 2.5$$

We know that if X is a random variable and a, b are constants, then:

$$Var(aX + b) = a^2\, Var\, X$$

Thus:

$$Var\, C = 1.03^2\, Var\, X$$

$$= 1.03^2(50)$$

$$= 53.045$$

The correct answer is **B**.

SOA Sample Question 329 Explanation

Consider the following table:

# of LH Parents	Prob. of LH Parents	Prob of LH Child	Prob of Parent & Child
2	$\frac{1}{50}$	$\frac{1}{2}$	$\left(\frac{1}{50}\right)\left(\frac{1}{2}\right)=\frac{1}{100}$
1	$\frac{1}{5}$	$\frac{1}{6}$	$\left(\frac{1}{5}\right)\left(\frac{1}{6}\right)=\frac{1}{30}$
0	$1-\frac{1}{50}-\frac{1}{5}=\frac{39}{50}$	$\frac{1}{16}$	$\left(\frac{39}{50}\right)\left(\frac{1}{16}\right)=\frac{39}{800}$

$$P(0\ LH\ Parents \mid LH\ Child)=\frac{P(\ 0\ LH\ Parents\ \&\ LH\ Child)}{P(LH\ Child)}$$

$$=\frac{\frac{39}{800}}{\frac{1}{100}+\frac{1}{30}+\frac{39}{800}}$$

$$=.53$$

The correct answer is **C**.

SOA Sample Question 330 Explanation

$$Z=4X-Y-3$$

$$Var\ X=2$$

$$VarY=3$$

We know that if X, Y are random variables and a, b, c are constants, then:

$$Var(aX+bY+c)=a^2\ Var\ X+b^2\ Var\ Y+2ab\ Cov(X,Y)$$

Since X, Y are independent, so

$$Cov(X,Y)=0$$

Thus,

$$Var\ Z=4^2\ (2)+(-1)^2\ (3)$$

$$=35$$

The correct answer is **E**.

SOA Sample Question 331 Explanation

Suppose the total size of the group is 100. Then we have the following diagram:

The problem is captured by the following Venn diagram:

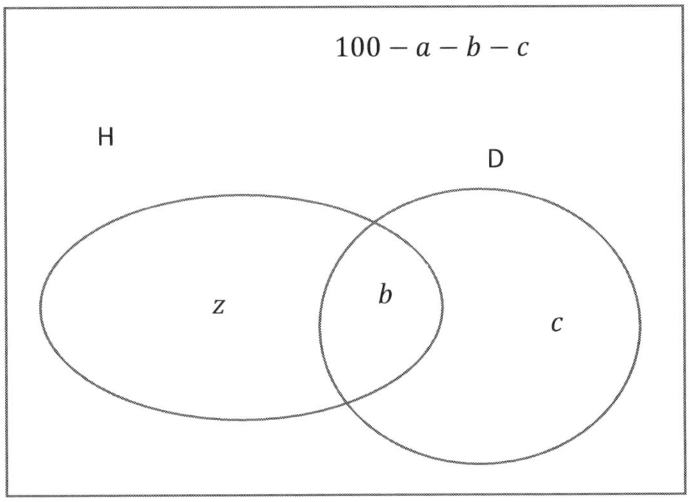

We are given that:

$$x = z + b$$

$$y = b + c$$

We need to find c, which gives the number of persons with only disability insurance.

If we subtract these equations we get:

$$x - y = (z + b) - (b + c)$$

$$x - y = z - c$$

$$c = y - x + z$$

Since the total number is 100, the required probability is:

$$\frac{y - x + z}{100}$$

The correct answer is **A**.

SOA Sample Question 332 Explanation

Total number of outcomes for rolling 3 dice is $6^3 = 216$.

Exactly 2 matches can occur in the following ways:

Case 1: Second matches with the First, and Third is different

1st die can have any of the 6 numbers. (6 ways)

2nd should have exactly the number which the 1st has. (1 way)

3rd should have any of the other 5 numbers. (5 ways)

Thus, the total number of ways in which this case can happen is:

$$6(1)(5) = 30 \qquad (1)$$

Case II: Second doesn't match with the 1st, and 3rd matches with either the 1st or 2nd

1st die can have any of the 6 numbers. (6 ways)

2nd should have any of the other 5 numbers. (5 ways)

3rd should match with either the 1st or 2nd. (2 ways)

Thus, the total number of ways in which this case can happen is:

$$6(5)(2) = 60 \qquad (2)$$

Overall the total number of ways in which exactly 2 matches happen is found by adding (1) and (2) which gives:

$$30 + 60 = 90.$$

Thus, the required probability is:

$$\frac{90}{216} = .417$$

The correct answer is **B**.

Tools needed for problems 333-346

Hypergeometric Formula:

If we have N items, of which a items are of type A, b items are of type $B,$ then the probability of selecting n items, of which x items are of type A is:

$$\frac{\binom{a}{x}\binom{b}{n-x}}{\binom{N}{n}}$$

For a uniform $[a, b]$ distribution, the pdf is given as:

$$f(x) = \frac{1}{b-a}, \qquad a \le x \le b$$

The formula for the pdf of an exponential distribution with mean m is:

$$f(x) = \frac{1}{m}e^{-\frac{x}{m}}, \ x \ge 0$$

Integration by parts shortcut:

$$\int (x+k)e^{ax}dx = \frac{(x+k)e^{ax}}{a} - \frac{e^{ax}}{a^2}$$

Standard deviation of binomial distribution is:

$$SD = \sqrt{np(1-p)}$$

$$E(X \mid Y = y) = \sum_x x\, P(X = x \mid Y = y)$$

The pdf of a Poisson distribution with mean m is:

$$f(x) = \frac{m^x e^{-m}}{x!}, \qquad x = 0,1,2,3,\ldots,$$

If $X_1, X_2, X_3, \ldots, X_n$ are n independent and identically distributed random variables, and $X_{(1)}, X_{(2)}, X_{(3)}, \ldots$ are these random variables in ascending order, then the cdf of $X_{(r)}$ is:

$$F_{X_{(r)}}(y) = \sum_{j=r}^{n} \binom{n}{j} [F_X(y)]^j \, [1 - F_X(y)]^{n-j}$$

If X, Y are independent normal random variables, then so it $Z = aX + bY$, where a, b are constants. The mean and variance of Z are:

$$\mu_Z = a\mu_X + b\mu_Y$$

$$Var\ Z = a^2 Var\ X + b^2 Var\ Y$$

SOA Sample Question 333 Explanation

By hypergeometric formula, if we have N items, of which a items are of type A, b items are of type B, then the probability of selecting n items, of which x items are of type A is:

$$\frac{\binom{a}{x}\binom{b}{n-x}}{\binom{N}{n}}$$

$$N = 17$$

$$n = 6$$

$$a = 10\ (total\ non-smokers)$$

$$b = 7\ (total\ smokers)$$

$$x = 3\ (\#\ of\ non-smokers\ picked)$$

So, the required probability is:

$$\frac{\binom{10}{3}\binom{7}{6-3}}{\binom{17}{6}} = .339$$

The correct answer is **D**.

SOA Sample Question 334 Explanation

$$P(M) = .6$$

$$P(F) = .4$$

$$P(S|M) = .2$$

$$P(F|S) = .2$$

$$P(S|F) = x = ?$$

Using Bayes' Theorem:

$$P(F|S) = \frac{P(S|F)P(F)}{P(S|F)P(F) + P(S|M)P(M)}$$

$$.2 = \frac{x(.4)}{x(.4) + .2(.6)}$$

$$.2(.4x + .12) = .4x$$

$$.08x + .024 = .4x$$

$$.024 = .32x$$

$$x = .075 = 7.5\%$$

The correct answer is **A**.

SOA Sample Question 335 Explanation

By hypergeometric formula:

$$f(x) = \frac{\binom{a}{x}\binom{b}{n-x}}{\binom{N}{n}}$$

$$N = 10\ (total\ glasses\ in\ the\ box)$$

$$n = 3\ (\#\ of\ glasses\ inspected)$$

$$a = 8\ (\#of\ total\ glasses\ in\ good\ condition)$$

$$b = 2\ (\#of\ total\ glasses\ in\ bad\ condition)$$

$$x = \#\ of\ inspected\ glasses\ in\ good\ condition$$

We need the probability that at least 2 of the 3 picked are good. Thus, $x = 2\ or\ 3$.

$$P(\,At\ least\ 2\ in\ good\ condition) = f(2) + f(3) = \frac{\binom{8}{2}\binom{2}{1}}{\binom{10}{3}} + \frac{\binom{8}{3}\binom{2}{0}}{\binom{10}{3}} = .93$$

The correct answer is **E**.

SOA Sample Question 336 Explanation

For the loss distribution of this problem, since $a = 0,\ \ b = 100$, we have:

$$f(x) = \frac{1}{100}, \qquad 0 \le x \le 100$$

Let Y be a random variable representing the payment under the deductible d. Then:

$$Y = \begin{cases} 0, & X < d \\ X - d, & X > d \end{cases}$$

$$E[Y] = \int_{-\infty}^{\infty} y\, f(x)\, dx = \int_{d}^{100} (x-d)\left(\frac{1}{100}\right) dx = \frac{(x-d)^2}{200}\Big|_{d}^{100}$$

$$32 = \frac{(100-d)^2}{200}$$

$$(100-d)^2 = 6400$$

$$100 - d = \pm 80$$

$$d = 20, 180$$

But maximum loss is 100, so a deductible of 180 makes no sense. Thus:

$$d = 20$$

The correct answer is **C**.

SOA Sample Question 337 Explanation

Let X be the random variable representing losses.

The formula for the pdf of an exponential distribution with mean 10 is:

$$f(x) = \frac{1}{10} e^{-\frac{x}{10}}, \quad x \geq 0$$

Let Y be a random variable representing the payment under the deductible of 3. Then:

$$Y = \begin{cases} 0, & X < 3 \\ X - 3, & X > 3 \end{cases}$$

$$E[Y] = \int_{-\infty}^{\infty} y\, f(x)\, dx$$

$$= \int_{3}^{\infty} (x - 3) \left(\frac{1}{10} e^{-\frac{x}{10}} \right) dx$$

Recall the integration by parts shortcut:

$$\int (x + k) e^{ax} dx = \frac{(x + k)e^{ax}}{a} - \frac{e^{ax}}{a^2}$$

Here, after factoring out the 1/10 we have:

$$k = -3, \qquad a = -\frac{1}{10}$$

$$E[Y] = \frac{1}{10} \left[\frac{(x - 3)e^{-\frac{x}{10}}}{-1/10} - \frac{e^{-\frac{x}{10}}}{(-1/10)^2} \right]_3^{\infty}$$

$$= \frac{1}{10} (100) e^{-\frac{3}{10}}$$

$$= 7.41$$

The correct answer is **D**.

SOA Sample Question 338 Explanation

At most one filling means 0 or 1 filling.

Let R = Number of Root Canals.

Let F = Number of fillings.

Thus, we need to find $E(R \mid F = 0 \; or \; 1)$.

$$P(R = r \mid F = 0 \; or \; 1) = \frac{P(R = r \; and \; F = 0 \; or \; 1)}{P(F = 0 \; or \; 1)}$$

$$= \frac{P(R = r \; and \; F = 0) or \; P(R = r \; and \; F = 1)}{P(F = 0 \; or \; 1)}$$

$$= \frac{f(r,0) + f(r,1)}{f(0) + f(1)} \qquad (1)$$

Let us first find the two components of the denominator of (1).

$$f(0) = .4 + .04 + .01 = .45$$

$$f(1) = .26 + .03 + .01 = .3$$

$$f(0) + f(1) = .45 + .3 = .75$$

R	$f(r,0) + f(r,1)$	$P(R = r \mid F = 0 \; or \; 1) = \frac{f(r,0)+f(r,1)}{.75}$
0	$.4 + .26 = .66$	$.88$
1	$.04 + .03 = .07$	$.0933$
2	$.01 + .01 = .02$	$.0267$

$$E(R \mid F = 0 \; or \; 1) = \sum_r r \, P(R = r \mid F = 0 \; or \; 1)$$

$$= 0(.88) + 1(.0933) + 2(.0267)$$

$$= .15$$

The correct answer is **B**.

SOA Sample Question 339 Explanation

N is binomial with $n = 500, \; p = .12$

We know that the standard deviation of binomial distribution is:

$$SD = \sqrt{np(1-p)}$$

$$= \sqrt{500(.12)(1 - .12)}$$

$$= 7.27$$

The correct answer is **A**.

SOA Sample Question 340 Explanation

$$P(X < 4 \mid X \geq 3) = \frac{P(X < 4 \,\&\, X \geq 3)}{P(X \geq 3)}$$

$$= \frac{P(3 \leq X < 4)}{P(X \geq 3)} \qquad (1)$$

Let us find numerator and denominator of (1) separately.

$$P(3 \leq X < 4) = \int_3^4 f(x)\,dx$$

$$= \int_3^4 \frac{2}{x^3}\,dx$$

$$= 2\frac{x^{-2}}{-2}\Big|_3^4$$

$$= -\frac{1}{4^2} + \frac{1}{3^2}$$

$$= \frac{7}{144} \qquad (2)$$

$$P(X \geq 3) = \int_3^\infty f(x)\,dx$$

$$= \int_3^\infty \frac{2}{x^3}\,dx$$

$$= 2\frac{x^{-2}}{-2}\Big|_3^\infty$$

$$= -\frac{1}{\infty^2} + \frac{1}{3^2}$$

$$= \frac{1}{9} \qquad (3)$$

Substituting (2) and (3) in (1) we get:

$$P(X < 4 \mid X \geq 3) = \frac{7/144}{1/9}$$

$$= .44$$

The correct answer is **E**.

SOA Sample Question 341 Explanation

We first need to find k. For any pdf:

$$\int_{-\infty}^{\infty} f(x)\,dx = 1$$

$$\int_{0}^{30} \frac{k}{(x+5)^2}\,dx = 1$$

$$k\frac{(x+5)^{-1}}{-1}\Big|_{0}^{30} = 1$$

$$-k\left(\frac{1}{35}-\frac{1}{5}\right) = 1$$

$$k = \frac{35}{6}$$

So, the pdf is:

$$f(x) = \frac{35(x+5)^{-2}}{6}, \qquad 0 < x < 30$$

We need $P(5 < X < 10)$.

$$P(5 < X < 10) = \int_{5}^{10} f(x)\,dx$$

$$= \int_{5}^{10} \frac{35(x+5)^{-2}}{6}\,dx$$

$$= \frac{35}{6}\frac{(x+5)^{-1}}{-1}\Big|_{5}^{10}$$

$$= -\frac{35}{6}\left(\frac{1}{15}-\frac{1}{10}\right)$$

$$= .194$$

The correct answer is **B**.

SOA Sample Question 342 Explanation

The pdf of a Poisson distribution with mean m is:

$$f(x) = \frac{m^x e^{-m}}{x!}, \qquad x = 0,1,2,3,...,$$

$$F(1) = P(X \leq 1) = f(0) + f(1) = e^{-m} + me^{-m} = e^{-m}(1+m)$$

$$F(2) = P(X \leq 2) = f(0) + f(1) + f(2) = e^{-m} + me^{-m} + \frac{m^2 e^{-m}}{2!} = e^{-m}(1 + m + \frac{m^2}{2})$$

Dividing the two equations we get:

$$\frac{F(2)}{F(1)} = \frac{e^{-m}(1 + m + \frac{m^2}{2})}{e^{-m}(1+m)}$$

$$2.6 = \frac{1 + m + \frac{m^2}{2}}{1+m}$$

$$2.6 + 2.6m = 1 + m + .5m^2$$

$$.5m^2 - 1.6m - 1.6 = 0$$

$$m = \frac{-b \pm \sqrt{b^2 - 4ac}}{2a} = \frac{1.6 \pm \sqrt{1.6^2 - 4(.5)(-1.6)}}{2(.5)} = 1.6 \pm 2.4 = 4$$

We ignore the negative value because mean of a Poisson distribution is positive.

The correct answer is **B**.

SOA Sample Question 343 Explanation

x	$P(X \geq x) = \frac{1}{2}\left(1 - \sqrt{\frac{x-1}{5}}\right)$	$f(x) = P(X = x) = P(X \geq x) - P(X \geq x+1)$
0	1	$1 - .5 = .5$
1	$.5$	$.5 - .2764 = .2236$
2	$.2764$	$.2764 - .1838 = .0926$
3	$.1838$	$.1838 - .1127 = .0711$
4	$.1127$	$.1127 - .0528 = .0599$
5	$.0528$	$.0528 - 0 = .0528$

$$E[X] = \sum_x x\, f(x)$$

$$= 0(.5) + 1(.2236) + 2(.0926) + \cdots + 5(.0528)$$

$$= 1.1$$

The correct answer is **B**.

SOA Sample Question 344 Explanation

If X_1, X_2, X_3 are n independent and identically distributed random variables, and $X_{(1)}, X_{(2)}, X_{(3)}, \ldots$ are these random variables in ascending order, then the cdf of $X_{(r)}$ is:

$$F_{X_{(r)}}(y) = \sum_{j=r}^{n} \binom{n}{j} [F_X(y)]^j \, [1 - F_X(y)]^{n-j} \quad (1)$$

Here, $n = 3, \; r = 2$

This is because we pick a sample of 3, and if we arrange 3 variables in ascending order, then the median is the 2nd one. We now find the cdf of the given function:

$$F_X(y) = \int_{-\infty}^{y} f(x)dx$$

$$= \int_{0}^{y} 2x \, dx$$

$$= y^2$$

So, using (1), the cdf of the median is:

$$F_{X_{(2)}}(y) = \sum_{j=2}^{3} \binom{3}{j} [y^2]^j \, [1 - y^2]^{3-j}$$

$$= \binom{3}{2} y^4 (1 - y^2)^{3-2} + \binom{3}{3} y^6 (1 - y^2)^{3-3}$$

$$= 3y^4(1 - y^2) + y^6$$

$$= 3y^4 - 2y^6$$

The pdf $g(y)$ of the median is found by taking the derivative of its cdf:

$$g(y) = 12y^3 - 12y^5, \qquad 0 < y < 1$$

$$E[Y] = \int_{-\infty}^{\infty} y \, g(y)dy = \int_{0}^{1} 12y^4 - 12y^6 \; dy = \frac{24}{35}$$

$$E[Y^2] = \int_{-\infty}^{\infty} y^2 \, g(y)dy = \int_{0}^{1} 12y^5 - 12y^7 \; dy = .5$$

$$Var\,Y = E[Y^2] - (E[Y])^2 = .5 - \left(\frac{24}{35}\right)^2 = .03$$

The correct answer is **B**.

SOA Sample Question 345 Explanation

We know that if W, T are independent normal random variables, then so it $X = aW + bT$, where a, b are constants. The mean and variance of X are:

$$\mu_X = a\mu_W + b\mu_T$$

$$Var\ X = a^2 Var\ W + b^2 Var\ T$$

Let $X = W - T$.

Since W, T are normal, so is X, and since W, T have same mean, so:

$$\mu_X = \mu_W - \mu_T$$

$$= 0$$

$$Var\ X = Var\ W + Var\ T$$

$$= 4 + 12$$

$$= 16$$

$$P(|W - T| < 1) = P(|X| < 1)$$

$$= P(-1 < X < 1)$$

So, we need to change -1 and 1 in standard scores.

$$z = \frac{X - \mu}{\sigma}$$

$$z_{-1} = \frac{-1 - 0}{\sqrt{16}} = -.25$$

$$z_1 = \frac{1 - 0}{\sqrt{16}} = .25$$

$$P(-1 < X < 1) = P(-.25 < z < .25)$$

$$= P(z < .25) - P(z < -.25)$$

$$= P(z < .25) - P(z > .25)$$

$$= P(z < .25) - [1 - P(z < .25)]$$

$$= 2P(z < .25) - 1$$

$$= 2(.5987) - 1$$

$$= .1974$$

The correct answer is **A**.

SOA Sample Question 346 Explanation

See the figure. The only way exactly two events can occur is if both A and B occur. Hence the intersection of A and B is .06.

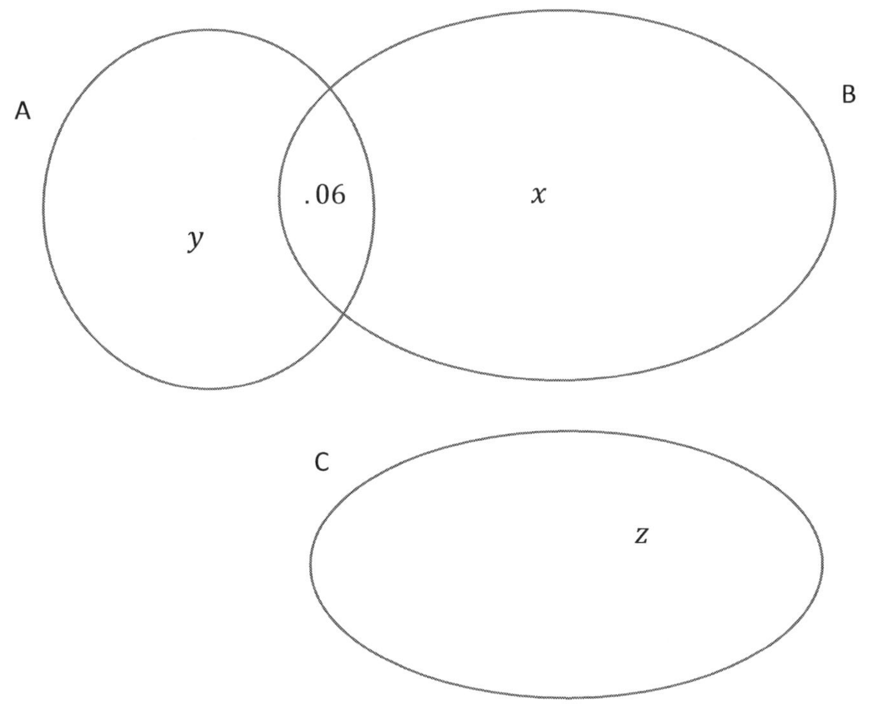

According to the first condition:

$$x + y + z + .06 = .9$$

$$x + y + z = .84 \quad (1)$$

According to the last condition:

$$x + y = .38 \quad (2)$$

Substituting (2) in (1) we get:

$$.38 + z = .84$$

$$z = .46$$

$$P[C] = .46$$

The correct answer is **B**.

Tools needed for problems 347-367

$$Coefficient\ of\ Variation = \frac{Standard\ Deviation}{Mean}$$

$$SD(X) = \sqrt{E[X^2] - (E[X])^2}$$

Pdf of a binomial distribution is:

$$f(x) = \binom{n}{x} p^x (1-p)^{n-x}, \quad x = 0,1,2,3, \dots, n$$

Poisson Distribution:

$$f(x) = \frac{m^x e^{-m}}{x!}, \qquad x = 0,1,2,3, \dots$$

where m = mean.

The variance of a Poisson distribution equals its mean.

Geometric distribution gives the probability of the 1st success requiring K independent trials, each with success probability p. The pmf and expected value are:

$$f(k) = p(1-p)^{k-1}$$

$$E[K] = \frac{1}{p}$$

Geometric distribution is memoryless. This means that:

$$E[K|K > a] = a + E[K]$$

Mean and standard deviation of a binomial distribution are:

$$Mean = np$$

$$SD = \sqrt{np(1-p)}$$

Continuity Correction:

$$P(X > n) = P(X \geq n + .5)$$

$$P(X < n) = P(X \leq n - .5)$$

This correction is used when a discrete variable is approximated by a continuous variable.

The cdf of an exponential distribution with mean m is

$$F(x) = 1 - e^{-x/m}$$

By hypergeometric formula, if we have N items, of which a items are of type A, b items are of type B, then the probability of selecting n items, of which x items are of type A is:

$$\frac{\binom{a}{x}\binom{b}{n-x}}{\binom{N}{n}}$$

SOA Sample Question 347 Explanation

We know that coefficient of variation is the ration of standard deviation to mean. So,

$$CV(Y) = \frac{SD(Y)}{E(Y)}$$

To get $E(Y)$ we need the marginal distribution function $p(y)$. We get:

$$p(0) = P[Y = 0] = f(0,0) + f(1,0) = .90 + .01 = .91$$

$$p(1) = P[Y = 1] = f(0,1) + f(1,1) = .05 + .04 = .09$$

$$E(Y) = \sum y\, p(y) = 0\, p(0) + 1\, p(1) = .09$$

$$E(Y^2) = \sum y^2\, p(y) = 0^2\, p(0) + 1^2\, p(1) = .09$$

$$SD(Y) = \sqrt{E[Y^2] - (E[Y])^2} = \sqrt{.09 - (.09)^2} = .286$$

$$CV(Y) = \frac{.286}{.09} = 3.18$$

The correct answer is **D**.

SOA Sample Question 348 Explanation

Benefit will be received if and only if at least one of the 3 losses is greater than the deductible.

Let X be the loss amount in a single loss. Since X is uniform [0, 100], so:

$$P(X > 30) = \frac{100 - 30}{100 - 0} = .7$$

Let Y be the event that a loss is greater than 30.

The Y is binomial with $n = 3,\ \ p = .7$

$$f(y) = \binom{n}{y} p^y (1 - p)^{n-y} = \binom{3}{y} .7^y (.3)^{3-y}$$

$$P(Y \geq 1) = 1 - P(Y = 0) = 1 - f(0) = 1 - (.3)^3 = .973$$

The correct answer is **E**.

SOA Sample Question 349 Explanation

Suppose there are 100 students in the group.

Then 70 will pass and 30 will fail In January.

Suppose a student who fails in January has probability x of passing in February.

Thus, a student who passes in January has probability $2x$ of passing in February.

So, the # of February passes among the 30 January failures is $30x$.

And the # of February passes among the 70 January passes is $70(2x) = 140x$.

Since the total # of Passes in February is 50, so:

$$30x + 140x = 50$$

$$x = .2941$$

Thus, a January passer has probability $2(.2941) = .5882$ of passing in February.

Let J be the event that a student passes in January.

Let F be the event that a student passes in February. Then we have:

$$P(J) = .7$$

$$P(F|J) = .5882$$

$$P(Pass\ Both) = P(J) \cdot P(F|J) = .7(.5882) = .41$$

The correct answer is **B**.

SOA Sample Question 350 Explanation

Let X be the loss.

Cdf of an exponential function with mean 2000 is

$$F(x) = 1 - e^{-x/2000}$$

Since the maximum payment is 3000, so exactly 3000 will be paid if the loss is 3000 or greater.

Thus, we need $P(X \geq 3000)$.

$$P(X \geq 3000) = 1 - P(X < 3000)$$

$$= 1 - F(3000)$$

$$= 1 - \left(1 - e^{-\frac{3000}{2000}}\right)$$

$$= .223$$

The correct answer is **B**.

SOA Sample Question 351 Explanation

Let H be the # of high-risk persons having accidents.

Let L be the # of low-risk persons having accidents.

Then H is binomial with:

$$n = 2,$$

$$p = 1 - .6 = .4$$

And L is binomial with:

$$n = 2,$$

$$p = 1 - .9 = .1$$

$$P(0\ accident) = none\ of\ the\ 4\ have\ accidents = .6(.6)(.9)(.9) = .2916$$

$$P(1\ accident) = P(H = 1\ \&\ L = 0) + P(H = 0\ \&\ L = 1)$$

$$= P(H = 1)\ P(L = 0) + P(H = 0)\ P(L = 1)$$

$$= \binom{2}{1}.4^1(1 - .4)^{2-1}(.9)^2 + (.6)^2\binom{2}{1}.1^1(1 - .1)^{2-1} = .4536$$

$$P(at\ most\ 1\ accident) = P(0\ accident) + P(1\ accident) = .2916 + .4536 = .7452$$

The correct answer is **E**.

SOA Sample Question 352 Explanation

Let Y be the amount paid.

First payment happens at 2 inches in excess of 12 inches, that is, at 14 inches.

x	$p(x)$	Y
$0 \le x < 14$	$.04 + .06 + .07 + .09 + .12 + .14 + .18 = .7$	0
$14 \le x < 16$	$.11$	5000
$16 \le x < 18$	$.08$	10000
$18 \le x < 20$	$.07$	15000
$x \ge 20$	$.04$	18000

Note that if we were finding SD by hand, we can omit the 0-payment entry but we must include it if we are doing it on calculator, which I am, as I explain in my YouTube video about a similar problem whose link is:

https://www.youtube.com/watch?v=FEJ-UZwfdls

If you are using Multiview calculator emember to put payments in the first column and probabilities in the 2nd column. We get from calculator:

$$SD = 5452$$

The correct answer is **D**.

SOA Sample Question 353 Explanation

We are to find $P(X \leq 3|X \geq 2.5$. This is because the amount is measured in tens of thousands.

$$P(X \leq 3|X \geq 2.5) = \frac{P(X \leq 3 \,\&\, X \geq 2.5)}{P(X \geq 2.5)} = \frac{P(2.5 \leq X \leq 3)}{P(X \geq 2.5)}$$

$$P(2.5 \leq X \leq 3) = \int_{1.5}^{2} f(x)dx = \int_{2.5}^{3} 8x^{-3}dx = 8\frac{x^{-2}}{-2}\Big|_{2.5}^{3} = .1956$$

$$P(X \geq 2.5) = \int_{2.5}^{\infty} 8x^{-3}dx = 8\frac{x^{-2}}{-2}\Big|_{2.5}^{\infty} = -4(\infty^{-2} - 2.5^{-2}) = .64$$

We have used the fact that:

$$\infty^{-2} = \frac{1}{\infty^2} = 0$$

$$P(X \leq 3|X \geq 2.5) = \frac{.1956}{.64} = .31$$

The correct answer is **B**.

SOA Sample Question 354 Explanation

Let A be the event that an accident happens.

Let M be the event that an insured driver is male.

Let F be the event that an insured driver is female.

We are given that:

$$P(M \text{ } and \text{ } A) = .3$$

$$P(A|M) = .5$$

Using Bayes' Theorem:

$$P(A|M) = \frac{P(A \text{ } and \text{ } M)}{P(M)}$$

$$.5 = \frac{.3}{P(M)}$$

$$P(M) = .6$$

$$P(F) = 1 - P(M) = 1 - .6 = .4$$

The correct answer is **B**.

SOA Sample Question 355 Explanation

Since mean m of a Poisson distribution equals its variance we have:

$$m = Var = (SD)^2 = (2)^2 = 4$$

$$f(x) = \frac{m^x e^{-m}}{x!} = \frac{4^x e^{-4}}{x!}$$

$$P(X \geq 2) = 1 - P(X < 2) = 1 - [f(0) + f(1)]$$

$$f(0) = \frac{4^0 e^{-4}}{0!} = e^{-4}$$

$$f(1) = \frac{4^1 e^{-4}}{1!} = 4e^{-4}$$

$$P(X \geq 2) = 1 - [e^{-4} + 4e^{-4}] = .908$$

The correct answer is **E**.

SOA Sample Question 356 Explanation

The number of independent trials K needed for first success form a geometric distribution with:

$$f(k) = p(1-p)^{k-1}, \quad k = 1,2,3,\ldots,$$

where p is the probability of success in each trial. Here, $p = .25$.

$$P(k > 3) = 1 - P(k \leq 3) = 1 - [f(1) + f(2) + f(3)]$$

$$f(1) = .25(1 - .25)^{1-1} = .25$$

$$f(2) = .25(1 - .25)^{2-1} = .1875$$

$$f(3) = .25(1 - .25)^{3-1} = .1406$$

$$P(k > 3) = 1 - [.25 + .1875 + .1406] = .422$$

The correct answer is **C**.

SOA Sample Question 357 Explanation

X rolls needed for the first 5, and Y rolls are needed for the first 6.

X has a geometric distribution with $p = 1/6$

We are given that $Y = 1$. Thus one roll is needed for the first 6, i.e., the first roll is a 6.

So, the first roll is NOT a 5. In other words, we need more than one roll to get the first 5.

Geometric distribution is memoryless. This means that:

$$E[X|Y = 1] = E[X|X > 1] = 1 + E[X] = 1 + \frac{1}{p} = 1 + \frac{1}{\left(\frac{1}{6}\right)} = 7$$

The correct answer is **E**.

SOA Sample Question 358 Explanation

Let X be the number of accidents. Then its pmf is:

$$f(x) = \frac{2.5^x e^{-2.5}}{x!}, \qquad x = 0,1,2,3,\ldots$$

Consider the following table:

x	Probability $f(x)$	Cumulative Probability	Remaining Probability
0	.0821	.0821	$1 - .0821 = .9179$
1	.2052	.2973	$1 - .2973 = .7027$
2	.2565	.5538	$1 - .5538 = .4462$
3	.2138	.7676	$1 - .7676 = .2324$

Mode is the value of x with the highest probability.

We see that the probability at $x = 2$ is .2565 which is the highest among the tabulated ones.

The remaining probability in the table after the listed values is .2324 which is less than .2565.

Thus, no other probability can exceed .2324.

Hence, the highest possible probability is .2565. Therefore, the mode is 2.

The correct answer is **C**.

SOA Sample Question 359 Explanation

We are given that:

$$P[M|X] = .3 \quad (1)$$

$$P[F|Y] = .4 \quad (2)$$

$$P[Y] = .6 \quad (3)$$

We are to find $P[Y|M]$.

Taking complements of (1), (2), and (3) we get:

$$P[F|X] = 1 - P[M|X] = 1 - .3 = .7$$

$$P[M|Y] = 1 - P[F|Y] = 1 - .4 = .6$$

$$P[X] = 1 - P[Y] = 1 - .6 = .4$$

Using Bayes' Theorem:

$$P[Y|M] = \frac{P[M|Y]\,P[Y]}{P[M|X]\,P[X] + P[M|Y]\,P[Y]} = \frac{.6\,(.6)}{.3(.4) + .6(.6)} = .75$$

The correct answer is **E**.

SOA Sample Question 360 Explanation

Note that only one surcharge happens per driver, depending on the last accident. That last accident could have happened last year, or the year before that, or the year before that, etc.

Year of Last Accident	Surcharge (x)	Probability $f(x)$ of last accident in year = Probability accident in the year but No accident in later years	$xf(x)$
$t-1$	.2	$.1$	.02
$t-2$	.15	$.1(.9) = .09$	.0135
$t-3$	.1	$.1(.9)(.9) = .081$	.0081
$t-4$	.05	$.1(.9)(.9).9) = .0729$	.003645

$$E[X] = \sum x\,f(x) = .02 + .0135 + .0081 + .003645 = .045 = 4.5\%$$

The correct answer is **A**.

SOA Sample Question 361 Explanation

Loss	Insurance pay after deductible of 500 x	Probability $f(x)$	$xf(x)$
0	0	.75	0
1000	500	.12	60
5000	4500	.08	360
10000	9500	.04	380
15000	14500	.01	145

$$Premium = 75 + E[X] = 75 + (0 + 60 + 360 + 380 + 145) = 1020$$

The correct answer is **C**.

SOA Sample Question 362 Explanation

Let X be the number of flights delayed. Then X is binomial with:$n = 180, \quad p = 1/6$

Mean and standard deviation of a binomial distribution are:

$$Mean = np = 180\left(\frac{1}{6}\right) = 30$$

$$SD = \sqrt{np(1-p)} = \sqrt{30\left(1 - \frac{1}{6}\right)} = 5$$

$$P(X \geq 40) = P(X > 39) = P(X \geq 39.5)\ (Continuity\ Correction)$$

We need to change 39.5 into standard score:

$$z = \frac{X - mean}{SD} = \frac{39.5 - 30}{5} = 1.9$$

$$P(X \geq 39.5) = P(z \geq 1.9) = 1 - P(z < 1.9) = 1 - .9713 = .029$$

The correct answer is **E**.

SOA Sample Question 363 Explanation

Class	Probability	Prob. Of Hospital	P (Class & Hospital)
A	$\frac{12000}{30000} = .4$	$1 - .98 = .02$	$.4(.02) = .008$
B	$\frac{18000}{30000} = .6$	$1 - .995 = .005$	$.6(.005) = .003$

$$P(A|H) = \frac{P(H\,\&\,A)}{P(H)} = \frac{.008}{.008 + .003} = .727$$

The correct answer is **E**.

SOA Sample Question 364 Explanation

Let X be the lifetime of a part. Then lifetimes of both parts have the cdf:

$$F(x) = 1 - e^{-x/5}$$

We are given that the machine functions 1 year from now. This means at least 1 part is working one year from now. So, we need $P(Both\ part\ work\ 1\ year\ from\ now|at\ least\ 1\ working)$.

$$P(Both\ working\ in\ 1\ year|at\ least\ 1\ works) = \frac{P(Both\ Working)}{P(At\ least\ 1\ working)}$$

$$= \frac{P(X_1 \geq 1, \& X_2 \geq 1)}{1 - P\ (none\ working\ in\ 1\ year)}$$

$$= \frac{P(X_1 \geq 1)\ P(\ X_2 \geq 1)}{1 - P\ (X_1 \leq 1, \& X_2 \leq 1)}$$

$$= \frac{\big(1 - F(1)\big)\big(1 - F(1)\big)}{1 - F(1)F(1)}$$

$$= \frac{e^{-\frac{1}{5}} e^{-\frac{1}{5}}}{1 - \left(1 - e^{-\frac{1}{5}}\right)\left(1 - e^{-\frac{1}{5}}\right)}$$

$$= .693$$

The correct answer is **D**.

SOA Sample Question 365 Explanation

Let R be the event of having a root canal, and F be the event of having a filling.

$$P(0\ R\ |0\ F) = \frac{P(\ 0\ R\ and\ 0\ F)}{P(\ 0\ F)} = \frac{1 - P(at\ least\ 1\ R\ or\ F)}{P(\ 0\ F)} = \frac{1 - .35}{.7} = .93$$

The correct answer is **E**.

SOA Sample Question 366 Explanation

By hypergeometric formula:

$$f(x) = \frac{\binom{a}{x}\binom{b}{n-x}}{\binom{N}{n}}$$

$$N = Total\ boxes = 10$$

$$n = Selected\ boxes = 5$$

$$a = Total\ Intact\ boxes = 7$$

$$b = Total\ Broken\ boxes = 10 - 7 = 3$$

$$P(3\ intact\ boxes\ among\ the\ selected) = f(3)$$

$$= \frac{\binom{7}{3}\binom{3}{5-3}}{\binom{10}{5}}$$

$$= .417$$

The correct answer is **D**.

SOA Sample Question 367 Explanation

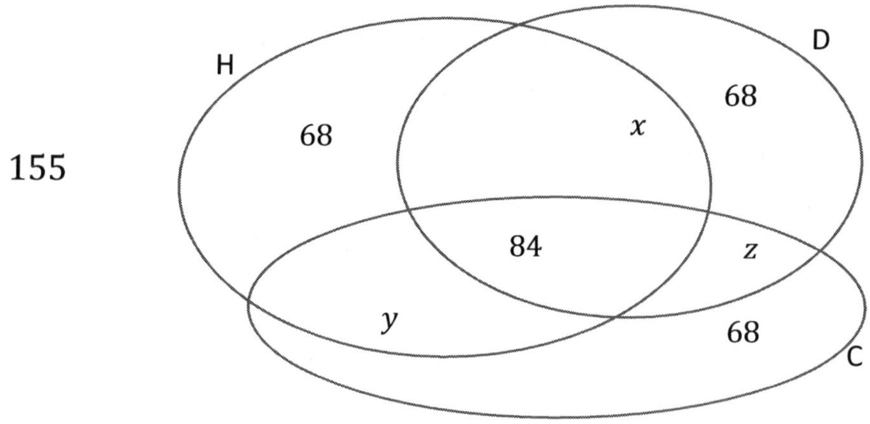

By the given conditions:

$$Total\ Heart: \quad 268 = 68 + x + y + 84 \quad (1)$$

$$Total\ Diabetes: \quad 268 = 68 + x + z + 84 \quad (2)$$

$$Total\ Cholestrol: \quad 268 = 68 + z + y + 84 \quad (3)$$

Simplifying (1), (2), and (3) we get:

$$x + y = 116 \quad (4)$$

$$x + z = 116 \quad (5)$$

$$z + y = 116 \quad (6)$$

Adding (4), (5), and (6) we get:

$$2x + 2y + 2z = 348$$

$$x + y + z = 174 \quad (7)$$

Substituting (4) in (7) we get:

$$116 + z = 174$$

$$z = 58$$

Substituting z in (5), and then in (6) we get:

$$x = 58$$

$$y = 58$$

$$Total = 155 + 68 + 68 + 68 + 84 + x + y + z$$

$$= 155 + 68 + 68 + 68 + 84 + 58 + 58 + 58$$

$$= 617$$

The correct answer is **C**.

Tools needed for problems 368-389

$$\textit{Addition Rule}: \quad P(A \cup B) = P(A) + P(B) - P(A \cap B)$$

$$\textit{Multiplication Rule}: \quad P(A \cap B) = P(A|B)\, P(B) = P(B|A)\, P(A)$$

If A and B are independent events then multiplication rule becomes:

$$P(A \cap B) = P(A)\, P(B)$$

If a distribution is symmetric about its mean, then its mean and median are equal.

Normal and uniform distributions are symmetric about their means.

The cdf of an exponential distribution with mean λ is:

$$F(x) = 1 - e^{-x/\lambda}$$

To get the mode of X, we need the value at which probability is maximum.

Absolute maximum of a function occurs either at end points of the domain, or at critical points.

Critical points of a function are those where the derivative is 0 or undefined.

By *hypergeometric formula*, if we have N items, of which a items are of type A, b items are of type B, then the probability of selecting n items, of which x items are of type A is:

$$f(x) = \frac{\binom{a}{x}\binom{b}{n-x}}{\binom{N}{n}}$$

If X, Y, Z are normal and a, b, c, k are constants, then $aX + bY + cZ + k$ is normal.

$$E[aX + bY + cZ + k] = a\, E[X] + b\, E[Y] + c\, E[Z] + k$$

$$Var[aX + bY + cZ + k] = a^2\, Var[X] + b^2\, Var\,[Y] + c^2\, Var\,[Z]$$

Sum of the first n integers is:

$$\frac{n(n+1)}{2}$$

$$\binom{n}{r} = \frac{n!}{r!\,(n-r)!} = n(n-1)(n-2)\,....\,(n-r+1)$$

$$Var\,(X) = Var(E[X|N]) + E[Var(X|N)]$$

Variance of exponential distribution equals the square of its mean.

The pdf and cdf of an exponential distribution with mean m are:

$$f(x) = \frac{1}{m} e^{-\frac{x}{m}}, \;\; x > 0$$

$$F(x) = 1 - e^{-\frac{x}{m}}$$

Variance of a Poisson variable equals its mean.

$$E[X^2] = Var[X] + (E[X])^2$$

SOA Sample Question 368 Explanation

Let S be the event that someone is a smoker.

Let B be the event that someone has a below normal lung function.

We are given that:

$$P(S \cup B) = .4$$

$$P(S) = .25$$

$$P(B|S) = .7$$

Using the addition and multiplication rules:

$$P(S \cup B) = P(S) + P(B) - P(S \cap B)$$

$$P(S \cup B) = P(S) + P(B) - P(B|S)\,P(S)$$

$$.4 = .25 + P(B) - .7(.25)$$

$$P(B) = .325 = 32.5\%$$

The correct answer is **C**.

SOA Sample Question 369 Explanation

Let H be the event that husband survives the next 2 years.

Let W be the event that wife survives the next 2 years.

$$P(H) = 1 - .1$$

$$= .9$$

$$P(H \cap W) = .7$$

Since H and B are independent events we have:

$$P(H \cap W) = P(H)\,P(W)$$

$$.7 = .9\,P(W)$$

$$P(W) = .778$$

$$P(Wife\ Dies) = 1 - P(Wife\ Lives)$$

$$= 1 - P(W)$$

$$= 1 - .778$$

$$= .222$$

The correct answer is **E**.

SOA Sample Question 370 Explanation

Business	**Probability Type**	**Probability Bankrupt**	**Probability Type & Bankrupt**
Retail	.6	.12	$.6(.12) = .072$
Service	.25	.08	$.25(.08) = .02$
Transportation	.1	.06	$.1(.06) = .006$
Other	.05	0	$.05(0) = 0$

$$P(Service\ |Bankrupt) = \frac{P(Service\ and\ Bankrupt)}{P(Bankrupt)} = \frac{.02}{.072 + .02 + .006 + 0} = .204$$

The Correct answer is **C**.

SOA Sample Question 371 Explanation

$$X^2 - 8X + 1 > 0 \quad (1)$$

Roots of the corresponding equality can be found by quadratic formula:

$$\frac{-b \pm \sqrt{b^2 - 4ac}}{2a} = \frac{8 \pm \sqrt{8^2 - 4(1)(1)}}{2(1)} = 7.873, \qquad .127$$

So, (1) can be written in factored form as:

$$(X - 7.873)(X - .127) > 0$$

If product of 2 factors is positive, then both are positive or both negative. If both positive, then:

$$X > 7.873, \qquad and\ \ X > .127$$

$$\Rightarrow X > 7.873$$

If both factors are negative, we get:

$$X < 7.873, \qquad and\ \ X < .127$$

$$\Rightarrow X < .127$$

Thus, $X^2 - 8X + 1 > 0$ implies that either $X > 7.873$ or $X < .127$. So:

$$P(X^2 - 8X + 1) > 0 = P(X > 7.873) + P(X < .127)$$

$$z_{7.873} = \frac{7.873 - 5}{2} = 1.44$$

$$z_{.127} = \frac{.127 - 5}{2} = 2.44$$

$$P(X > 7.873) + P(X < .127) = P(z > 1.44) + P(z < -2.44)$$
$$= 1 - P(z \leq 1.44) + 1 - P(z \leq 2.44)$$

$$= 1 - .9251 + 1 - .9927 = .0822$$

The correct answer is **C**.

SOA Sample Question 372 Explanation

If a distribution is symmetric about its mean, then its mean and median are equal.

So, for symmetric distributions, doubling the mean implies doubling the median.

Normal and uniform distributions are symmetric about their means.

Thus, for normal and uniform distributions, doubling the mean will double the median.

Exponential distribution is not symmetric about its mean. However, it is still not impossible for a non-symmetric distribution's median to double if its mean is doubled.

Let us find the median of an exponential distribution of mean λ. The cdf is:

$$F(x) = 1 - e^{-x/\lambda}$$

The median is found by setting the cdf equal to .5:

$$1 - e^{-\frac{x}{\lambda}} = .5$$

$$e^{-\frac{x}{\lambda}} = .5$$

$$x = -\lambda \ln .5$$

Thus, the median of an exponential distribution with mean λ is $-\lambda \ln(.5)$.

If we double the mean, that is, if mean becomes 2λ, then the median is $-2\lambda \ln(.5)$.

Thus, we see that the median is doubled by doubling the mean.

Hence, for all 3 given distributions, doubling the mean doubles the median.

The correct answer is **A**.

SOA Sample Question 373 Explanation

To get the variance of X, we first need the marginal distribution of X.

$$p(x,y) = \frac{x+y+2}{36}, \quad x = 0,1,2, \quad y = 0,1,2$$

$$P(X=0) = p(0,0) + p(0,1) + p(0,2) = \frac{2}{36} + \frac{3}{36} + \frac{4}{36} = \frac{1}{4}$$

$$P(X=1) = p(1,0) + p(1,1) + p(1,2) = \frac{3}{36} + \frac{4}{36} + \frac{5}{36} = \frac{1}{3}$$

$$P(X=2) = p(2,0) + p(2,1) + p(2,2) = \frac{4}{36} + \frac{5}{36} + \frac{6}{36} = \frac{5}{12}$$

We find standard deviation by calculator, and then square it to get variance:

$$Var\ X = (\sigma_X)^2 = (.7993)^2 = .64$$

The correct answer is **B**.

SOA Sample Question 374 Explanation

To get the mode of X, we need the value at which probability is maximum.

In other words, we need to find the absolute maximum of $f(x)$.

From calculus we know that absolute maximum of a function occurs either at the end points of the domain, or at critical points.

Critical points of a polynomial are those where the derivative is 0.

$$f(x) = \frac{5}{72}[3(x-2)^2 - (x-2)^4 + 4], \qquad 0 < x < 3$$

$$f'(x) = \frac{5}{72}[6(x-2)^1 - 4(x-2)^3] = 0$$

$$(x-2)[6 - 4(x-2)^2] = 0$$

$$If \;\; x - 2 = 0$$

$$Then \;\; x = 2$$

$$If \;\; 6 - 4(x-2)^2 = 0$$

$$Then \;\; 4(x-2)^2 = 6$$

$$(x-2)^2 = 1.5$$

$$x - 2 = \pm 1.225$$

$$x = 3.225, \;\; .775$$

3.225 is outside the domain of the main function and hence not a candidate.

We now evaluate the density function at all the candidate values to find max.

x	$f(x)$
0 (left end point)	0
3 (right end point)	0
2	.278
.775	.434

Among the listed function values, the highest is .434, and so the mode is the corresponding variable value of $x = .775$.

The correct answer is **B**.

SOA Sample Question 375 Explanation

The person died 3 months ago. So, 4 months from now, we will be 7 months from death. Therefore, we are to find $P(T > 7 \mid T > 3)$.

$$P(T > 7 \mid T > 3) = \frac{P(T > 7 \,\&\, T > 3)}{P(T > 3)}$$

$$= \frac{P(T > 7)}{P(T > 3)} \quad (1)$$

$$f(t) = \frac{4\beta^4}{t^5}, \quad t > \beta$$

$$P(T > 7) = \int_7^\infty f(t)\,dt$$

$$= \int_7^\infty \frac{4\beta^4}{t^5}\,dt$$

$$= \int_7^\infty 4\beta^4 t^{-5}\,dt$$

$$= 4\beta^4 \frac{t^{-4}}{-4} \Big|_7^\infty$$

$$= -\beta^4(0 - 7^{-4})$$

$$= \frac{\beta^4}{7^4} \quad (2)$$

Similarly, we get:

$$P(T > 3) = \frac{\beta^4}{3^4} \quad (3)$$

Substituting (2) and (3) in (1) we get:

$$P(T > 7 \mid T > 3) = \frac{\frac{\beta^4}{7^4}}{\frac{\beta^4}{3^4}}$$

$$= \frac{3^4}{7^4}$$

$$= \frac{81}{2401}$$

The correct answer is **A**.

SOA Sample Question 376 Explanation

By hypergeometric formula:

$$f(x) = \frac{\binom{a}{x}\binom{b}{n-x}}{\binom{N}{n}}$$

$$N = Total\ employees = 15$$

$$n = Selected\ employees = 4$$

$$a = Total\ Seniors = 5$$

$$b = Juniors = 10$$

$$P(at\ least\ 3\ seniors\ among\ the\ 4\ selected) = f(3) + f(4)$$

$$= \frac{\binom{5}{3}\binom{10}{4-3}}{\binom{15}{4}} + \frac{\binom{5}{4}\binom{10}{4-4}}{\binom{15}{4}} = .077$$

The correct answer is **C**.

SOA Sample Question 377 Explanation

Let H be the event of having high heart rate.

Let L be the event of having low or normal heart rate.

Let S be the event of having a stroke.

From the given information we have:

$$P(H) = \frac{1100}{3000}$$

$$P(L) = \frac{1900}{3000}$$

$$P(S|H) = \frac{60}{1100}$$

$$P(S|L) = \frac{28}{1900}$$

By Bayes' Theorem:

$$P(L|S) = \frac{P(S|L)\,P(L)}{P(S|L)\,P(L) + P(S|H)\,P(H)} = \frac{\left(\frac{28}{1900}\right)\left(\frac{1900}{3000}\right)}{\left(\frac{28}{1900}\right)\left(\frac{1900}{3000}\right) + \left(\frac{60}{1100}\right)\left(\frac{1100}{3000}\right)} = .318$$

The correct answer is **C**.

SOA Sample Question 378 Explanation

80th percentile means a cumulative probability of .8.

From the bottom row of the table provided in the exam, we see that the standard score corresponding to a cumulative probability of .8 is $z = .842$. Using z −score formula:

$$z = \frac{X - \mu}{\sigma}$$

$$.842 = \frac{8.40 - 6.72}{\sigma}$$

$$\sigma = 1.995$$

90th percentile means a cumulative probability of .9.

From the bottom row of the table provided in the exam, we see that the standard score corresponding to a cumulative probability of .9 is $z = 1.282$. Using z −score formula:

$$z = \frac{X - \mu}{\sigma}$$

$$1.282 = \frac{X - 6.72}{1.995}$$

$$X = 9.28$$

The correct answer is **C**.

SOA Sample Question 379 Explanation

Median m is the value at which cumulative probability is .5.

$$\int_0^m \frac{(4-x)^3}{64}\,dx = .5$$

$$-\frac{1}{64}\frac{(4-x)^4}{4}\Big|_0^m = .5$$

$$-\frac{1}{256}[(4-m)^4 - (4)^4] = .5$$

$$(4-m)^4 - 256 = -128$$

$$(4-m)^4 = 128$$

$$4 - m = \pm\sqrt[4]{128}$$

$$m = 4 \pm \sqrt[4]{128}$$

Since the pdf is non-zero for $0 < x < 4$, the median has to be less than 4. Thus:

$$m = 4 - \sqrt[4]{128}$$

The correct answer is **B**.

SOA Sample Question 380 Explanation

Let X be the length of the finished product.

Let L be the total original length from the spool.

Let T_1 and T_2 be the lengths of the 2 trim cuts.

Total extension provided by the 2 guards is $1 + 1 = 2$. So,

$$X = L - T_1 - T_2 + 2$$

Since $L,\ T_1,\ T_2$ are normal, so X is also normal and:

$$\mu_X = E[L] - E[T_1] - E[T_2] + 2 = 1205 - 2 - 2 + 2 = 1203$$

$$Var[X] = Var[L] + (-1)^2\,Var\,[T_1] + (-1)^2\,Var\,[T_2] = 5 + .5 + .5 = 6$$

We are to find $P(X \geq 1200)$. So, we need to change 1200 in standard score.

$$z = \frac{X - \mu}{\sigma} = \frac{1200 - 1203}{\sqrt{6}} = -1.225$$

$$P(X \geq 1200) = P(z \geq -1.225) = P(z \leq 1.225)$$

1.225 is the midpoint of 1.22 and 1.23.

In the table, the cumulative probability corresponding to $z = 1.22$ is .8888, while that corresponding to $z = 1.23$ is .8903. The midpoint of these probabilities is .88975.

The correct answer is **B**.

SOA Sample Question 381 Explanation

The pdf and cdf of an exponential distribution with mean m are:

$$f(x) = \frac{1}{m}e^{-\frac{x}{m}},\ \ x > 0$$

$$F(x) = 1 - e^{-\frac{x}{m}}$$

So, we recognize the given function as the pdf of an exponential distribution with mean:

$$m = \frac{1}{.0625} = 16$$

$$P(X < 20 | X \geq 5) = \frac{P(X < 20\ \&\ X \geq 5)}{P(X \geq 5)} = \frac{P(5 \leq X < 20\,)}{1 - P(X < 5)}$$

$$= \frac{F(20) - F(5)}{1 - F(5)} = \frac{\left(1 - e^{-\frac{20}{16}}\right) - \left(1 - e^{-\frac{5}{16}}\right)}{1 - \left(1 - e^{-\frac{5}{16}}\right)} = .608$$

The correct answer is **C**.

SOA Sample Question 382 Explanation

To find the conditional variance of $Y|X=3$ we need to find distribution of $Y|X=3$.

Let L be the number of pages with low graphical content. Since 4 pages are selected, so:

$$X+L+Y=4$$

This means that if $X=3$, then $Y=0\ or\ 1$.

$$P(Y=0|X=3)=\frac{P(Y=0\ \&\ X=3)}{P(X=3)}$$

$$=\frac{P(Y=0,\ X=3,\ L=1)}{P(X=3)}\qquad (\because X+Y+L=4)\qquad (1)$$

Let us examine the denominator. When $X=3$, then the sum of the other 2 variables is 1 because the total picked is 4.

For X we have a total of 10 choices, while for other 2 variables we have $5+15=20$ choices.

So, by hypergeometric formula:

$$P(X=3)=\frac{\binom{10}{3}\binom{20}{1}}{\binom{30}{4}}=.0876$$

Also, since there are a total of 15 choices for Y, 10 for X, and 5 for L we have:

$$P(Y=0,X=3,L=1)=\frac{\binom{15}{0}\binom{10}{3}\binom{5}{1}}{\binom{30}{4}}=.0219$$

Substituting these values in (1) we get:

$$P(Y=0|X=3)=\frac{.0219}{.0876}=.25$$

$$P(Y=1|X=3)=\frac{P(Y=1\ \&\ X=3)}{P(X=3)}$$

$$=\frac{P(Y=1,\ X=3,\ L=0)}{P(X=3)}\qquad (\because X+Y+L=4)$$

$$=\frac{\frac{\binom{15}{1}\binom{10}{3}\binom{5}{0}}{\binom{30}{4}}}{.0876}=.75$$

We can now use calculator with Y values of 0 & 1 and probabilities of .25 & .75.

$$Var(Y|X=3)=(.433)^2=.1875$$

The correct answer is **A**.

SOA Sample Question 383 Explanation

Let X be the size of the claim.

The pdf is:

$$f(x) = cx^{\frac{1}{n}}, \quad 0 < x < 1$$

The 30th percentile, x_{30} is the value at which the cumulative probability is .3.

$$\int_0^{x_{30}} cx^{\frac{1}{n}}\, dx = .3$$

$$c\frac{x^{\frac{1}{n}+1}}{\frac{1}{n}+1}\Big|_0^{x_{30}} = .3$$

$$x_{30}^{\frac{1}{n}+1} = \frac{.3}{c}\left(\frac{1}{n}+1\right)$$

$$x_{30}^{\frac{1+n}{n}} = \frac{.3}{c}\left(\frac{1}{n}+1\right)$$

$$x_{30} = \left[\frac{.3}{c}\left(\frac{1}{n}+1\right)\right]^{\frac{n}{n+1}} \qquad (1)$$

Similarly, the 20th percentile, x_{20} is:

$$x_{20} = \left[\frac{.2}{c}\left(\frac{1}{n}+1\right)\right]^{\frac{n}{n+1}} \qquad (2)$$

Dividing (1) by (2) we get:

$$\frac{x_{30}}{x_{20}} = \left(\frac{.3}{.2}\right)^{\frac{n}{n+1}}$$

$$= (1.5)^{\frac{n}{n+1}}$$

$$= \sqrt[n+1]{1.5^n}$$

The correct answer is **D**.

SOA Sample Question 384 Explanation

Let X be the size of the claim.

The pdf of the 1st plan is:

$$f(x) = cx^2, \ \ 0 < x < 1$$

The integral of any pdf is 1. We will use this fact to find c:

$$\int_0^1 cx^2 \ dx = 1$$

$$c\frac{x^3}{3}\Big|_0^1 = 1$$

$$c = 3$$

So, the pdf of the 1st plan is:

$$f(x) = 3x^2, \ \ 0 < x < 1$$

The pth percentile, is the $x -$ value at which the cumulative probability is p.

$$F(x) = \int_0^x 3x^2 \ dx = p$$

$$3\frac{x^{\ 3}}{3}\Big|_0^1 = p$$

$$x = p^{\frac{1}{3}}$$

$$p = x^3 \ \ (1)$$

This $x -$ value is also the p^2 percentile of the 2nd plan. So, the cdf of the 2nd plan is:

$$G(x) = p^2 \ \ (2)$$

Substituting (1) in (2) we get:

$$G(x) = (x^3)^2$$

$$= x^6$$

Pdf is the derivative of cdf. So,

$$g(x) = G^{\prime(x)}$$

$$= 6x^5$$

The correct answer is **B**.

SOA Sample Question 385 Explanation

Let X be the time to failure. Cdf of an exponential distribution with mean m is:

$$F(x) = 1 - e^{-\frac{x}{m}} \quad (1)$$

Since 20% fail within 2 years, we have:

$$P(X \leq 2) = F(2) = .2$$

Substituting this in (1) we get:

$$.2 = 1 - e^{-\frac{2}{m}}$$

$$e^{-\frac{2}{m}} = .8$$

$$m = \frac{2}{\ln .8} = 8.963$$

We need to find t such that $F(t) = .8$

$$F(t) = 1 - e^{-\frac{t}{8.963}}$$

$$.8 = 1 - e^{-\frac{t}{8.963}}$$

$$e^{-\frac{t}{8.963}} = .2$$

$$t = 14.4$$

The correct answer is **D**.

SOA Sample Question 386 Explanation

Let N be the number of tickets received by a driver. Then, the fine paid by the driver will be:

$$F = 1 + 2 + 3 + \cdots + N = \frac{N(N+1)}{2}$$

$$E[F] = E\left[\frac{N(N+1)}{2}\right] = \frac{1}{2}E[N^2 + N] = \frac{1}{2}(E[N^2] + E[N]) \quad (1)$$

But N is Poisson with mean 4. So:

$$E[N] = 4, \qquad Var[N] = 4$$

Also, for any random variable:

$$E[N^2] = Var[N] + (E[N])^2 = 4 + (4)^2 = 20$$

Substituting these values in (1) we get:

$$E[F] = \frac{1}{2}(20 + 4) = 12$$

The correct answer is **D**.

SOA Sample Question 387 Explanation

Number of total Files = d

Total number of files other than the 2 most recent files = $d - 2$.

Let X be the number of corrupted files among the 2 most recent files. Then X has a hypergeometric distribution and we have:

$$f(x) = \frac{\binom{2}{x}\binom{d-2}{n-x}}{\binom{d}{n}} \qquad (1)$$

To get the probability that neither of the 2 most recent files are corrupted, we see that we are selecting 2 files ($n = 2$) so that none of the 2 recent files are corrupted ($x = 0$). Thus the 2 corrupted files need to be among the $d - 2$ files that are not recent. So, (1) gives:

$$f(0) = \frac{\binom{2}{0}\binom{d-2}{2-0}}{\binom{d}{2}}$$

$$\frac{40}{51} = \frac{(d-2)(d-3)}{d(d-1)} \qquad \left(\because \binom{n}{r} = n(n-1)(n-2)\ldots.(n-r+1)\right)$$

$$40(d^2 - d) = 51(d^2 - 5d + 6)$$

$$11d^2 - 215d + 306 = 0$$

$$d = \frac{215 \pm \sqrt{215^2 - 4(11)(306)}}{2(11)}$$

$$d = 18, \quad \frac{17}{11}$$

Since d is the total number of files, so it has to be an integer. Thus, $d = 18$.

The probability that none of the 3 most recent files are corrupted, given that exactly 2 files are corrupted is by hypergeometric formula by noting that now we select 2 corrupted files which both have to be among the $d - 3$ files that are not recent

$$f(0) = \frac{\binom{3}{0}\binom{d-3}{2}}{\binom{d}{2}}$$

$$= \frac{\binom{3}{0}\binom{18-3}{2}}{\binom{18}{2}}$$

$$= .686$$

The correct answer is **C**.

SOA Sample Question 388 Explanation

Let N be the number of claims in a random claim on which benefit is paid. Thus $N = 0 \text{ } or \text{ } 1$.

$$P(N = 0) = .75$$

$$P(N = 1) = 1 - .75 = .25$$

Let X be the benefit paid for a randomly selected claim.

We are to find $Var\ (X)$. We know that:

$$Var\ (X) = Var(E[X|N]) + E[Var(X|N)] \quad (1)$$

If benefit is not paid on a claim, then the expected value and variance of benefit are 0.

$$E[X|N = 0] = 0 \quad (2)$$

$$Var[X|N = 0] = 0 \quad (3)$$

If benefit is paid on a claim, then $N = 1$ and benefit is exponential with mean 8. Since the variance of exponential distribution equals the square of its mean we have:

$$E[X|N = 1] = 8 \quad (4)$$

$$Var[X|N = 1] = 8^2 = 64 \quad (5)$$

Note from (2) and (4) that $E[X|N]$ takes two possible values, 0 and 8.

N	Probability	$E[X\|N]$
0	.75	0
1	.25	8

In calculator if we put 0, 8 for variable, and .75, .25 for the probabilities we get:

$$Var(E[X|N]) = 3.464^2 = 12 \quad (6)$$

Also, note from (3) and (5) that $Var[X|N]$ takes two possible values, 0 and 64.

N	Probability	$Var[X\|N]$
0	.75	0
1	.25	64

$$E(Var[X|N]) = 0(.75) + 64(.25) = 16 \quad (7)$$

Substituting (6) and (7) in (1) we get:

$$Var\ (X) = 12 + 16$$

$$= 28$$

The correct answer is **D**.

SOA Sample Question 389 Explanation

Suppose hats are in the box. Let us first find the total possibilities of re-wearing the hats:

First man can pick any of the 4 hats.

Second man can pick any of the remaining 3 hats.

Third man can pick any of the remaining 2 hats.

Fourth man will pick the remaining 1 hat. So

$$Total\ Possibilites = 4(3)(2)(1) = \mathbf{24}$$

We are to find the probability that none of them wears the correct hat.

It is easier to find the complementary event, that is, at least one wears correct hat. This can be broken down into the following cases.

Case I: First drawer wears the correct hat.

In this case, the first drawer has only **1** possibility, that is, to choose the correct hat.

Second drawer can choose any of the remaining **3** hats.

Third drawer can choose any of the remaining **2** hats.

Fourth drawer gets the remaining **1** hat.

Total possibilities in this case $= 1(3)(2)(1) = \mathbf{6}$

Case II: First drawer wears wrong hat, but one of the remaining drawers wears the correct hat.

In this case, the first drawer can choose any of the **3** wrong hats.

Now, if the first drawer wears a wrong hat, someone else will also wear a wrong hat because he will wear the hat which belonged to the first drawer.

Any of the **3** remaining drawers can wear the hat belonging to the first drawer.

So, after we have dealt with the two people wearing wrong hats, suppose the two remaining people are X and Y. There is one **1** way in which someone wears the correct hat, that is, X wears his own hat, which means that Y will also wear hit own hat.

Total possibilities in this case $= 3(3)(1) = \mathbf{9}$

From cases I and II we see that total ways in which at least one wears correct hat is $6 + 9 = \mathbf{15}$.

$$P(at\ least\ 1\ correct) = \frac{15}{24}$$

$$P(none\ correct) = 1 - \frac{15}{24}$$

$$= .375$$

The correct answer is **D**.

Tools needed for problems 390-412

A random variable X is said to have gamma distribution with parameters α, θ if its pdf is:

$$f(x) = \frac{1}{\theta^\alpha \Gamma(\alpha)} x^{\alpha-1} e^{-\frac{x}{\theta}}, \ x > 0$$

Mean and variance of a gamma distribution are:

$$Mean = \alpha\theta$$

$$Variance = \alpha\theta^2$$

If n is an integer then $\Gamma(n) = (n-1)!$

Integration by parts shortcut:

$$\int (x+k)e^{ax}dx = \frac{(x+k)e^{ax}}{a} - \frac{e^{ax}}{a^2}$$

$$\lim_{x\to\infty} x^n e^{-x} = 0, \qquad n > 0$$

Sum of independent Poisson distributions is also Poisson with mean equal to the sum of the individual means. Pmf of a Poisson distribution with mean λ is:

$$f(x) = \frac{\lambda^x e^{-\lambda}}{x!}, \ x = 0,1,2,3,\ldots$$

If the mean λ of a Poisson distribution is non-integer, then its mode is the greatest integer less than λ. If λ is an integer, then the modes are λ and $\lambda - 1$.

For a Poisson distribution, variance = mean.

If the derivative of a function is always negative, the function is monotonically decreasing.

$$\int e^{ax+b}dx = \frac{1}{a}e^{ax+b}$$

For a distribution that is symmetric with respect to the center, mean = median.

$$Var\ X = E[X^2] - (E[X])^2$$

Cdf and median of an exponential distribution with mean m are given as:

$$F(x) = 1 - e^{-\frac{x}{m}}$$

$$Median = m \ln 2$$

Variance of an exponential distribution equals the square of its mean.

Since exponential distribution is memoryless, so for any positive k:

$$Var(X|X > k) = Var\ X$$

SOA Sample Question 390 Explanation

A random variable X is said to have gamma distribution with parameters α, θ if its pdf is:

$$f(x) = \frac{1}{\theta^\alpha \Gamma(\alpha)} x^{\alpha-1} e^{-\frac{x}{\theta}}, \; x > 0$$

Mean and variance of a gamma distribution are:

$$Mean = \alpha\theta$$

$$Variance = \alpha\theta^2$$

$$\alpha\theta = 6 \quad (1)$$

$$\alpha\theta^2 = 18 \quad (2)$$

Diving (2) by (1) we get:

$$\theta = 3$$

Substituting (2) in (1) we get:

$$\alpha = 2$$

So, noting that $\Gamma(2) = 1! = 1$, the pdf is:

$$f(x) = \frac{1}{3^2\Gamma(2)} x^{2-1} e^{-\frac{x}{3}}, \; x > 0$$

$$= \frac{1}{9} x e^{-\frac{x}{3}}, \; x > 0$$

$$P(X > 4) = \int_4^\infty \frac{1}{9} x e^{-\frac{x}{3}} \, dx$$

Our integration by parts shortcut gives:

$$\int x e^{ax} dx = \frac{x e^{ax}}{a} - \frac{e^{ax}}{a^2}$$

$$P(X > 4) = \frac{1}{9}\left[\frac{x e^{-x/3}}{-1/3} - \frac{e^{-x/3}}{(-1/3)^2}\right]_4^\infty$$

$$= \frac{1}{9}\left[0 - \frac{4e^{-\frac{4}{3}}}{-\frac{1}{3}} + \frac{e^{-\frac{4}{3}}}{\left(-\frac{1}{3}\right)^2}\right]$$

$$= .62$$

The correct answer is **E**.

SOA Sample Question 391 Explanation

96th percentile corresponds to a cumulative probability of .96. This is almost equal to the table value of .9599 which corresponds to $z = 1.75$. Using the information for company A we get:

$$z = \frac{X - 30}{\sigma}$$

$$1.75 = \frac{214 - 30}{\sigma}$$

$$\sigma = 105.143$$

90th percentile corresponds to a cumulative probability of .9. From the bottom area of the exam table, we see that the corresponding standard score is $z = 1.282$.

Using the information for company B we get:

$$1.282 = \frac{214 - \mu_B}{105.143}$$

$$\mu_B = 79$$

The correct answer is **D**.

SOA Sample Question 392 Explanation

We first find c by setting the integral of the pdf equal to 1:

$$\int_{-\infty}^{\infty} f(x)\,dx = 1$$

$$\int_{5}^{8} c(x-5)\,dx + \int_{8}^{11} c(11-x)\,dx = 1$$

$$c\frac{(x-5)^2}{2}\Big|_5^8 - c\frac{(11-x)^2}{2}\Big|_8^{11} = 1$$

$$c = \frac{1}{9}$$

$$f(x) = \begin{cases} \dfrac{x-5}{9}, & 5 \le x \le 8 \\ \dfrac{11-x}{9}, & 8 < x \le 11 \end{cases}$$

We are to find $P(6 < X < 8)$. For this range the first piece of the function applies.

$$P(6 < X < 8) = \int_6^8 \frac{x-5}{9}\,dx = \frac{1}{9}\left[\frac{(x-5)^2}{2}\right]_6^8 = \frac{1}{18}(9-1) = .444$$

The correct answer is **E**.

SOA Sample Question 393 Explanation

Since 1 hurricane happens in 10 years, mean number of hurricanes in 1 year = $1/10$.

Since 1 fire happens in 50 years, mean number of hurricanes in 1 year = $1/50$.

We know that the sum of independent Poisson distributions is also Poisson with mean equal to the sum of the individual means.

So, if Y is the total hurricanes plus fires per year, then Y is Poisson with mean:

$$m = \frac{1}{10} + \frac{1}{50} = .12$$

Total hurricanes plus fires in 40 years is also Poisson with mean:

$$\lambda = .12(40) = 4.8$$

We first find the mode of X. We can do it by tabulating the values like we did in some of the earlier problems. However, for a Poisson distribution we have the following shortcut:

If the mean λ of a Poisson distribution is non-integer, then its mode is the greatest integer less than λ. If λ is an integer, then the modes are λ and $\lambda - 1$.

Here, $\lambda = 4.8$ which is not an integer. So, the mode of X is 4.

$$Mode\ of\ payout = 1000(Mode\ of\ X)$$

$$= 1000(4)$$

$$= 4000$$

The correct answer is **C**.

SOA Sample Question 394 Explanation

$$f(x) = \frac{1}{\beta} e^{-\frac{(x-d)}{\beta}}, \quad x \geq d$$

Mode is the value of x at which the pdf is maximum.

$$f'(x) = \frac{-1}{\beta^2} e^{-\frac{(x-d)}{\beta}} < 0$$

Since the derivative is always negative, so the function is monotonically decreasing. Hence the mode happens at the lowest value of the independent variable, that is, at $x = d$.

10th percentile, x_{10} is the value at which the cumulative probability is .1.

$$\int_{d}^{x_{10}} \frac{1}{\beta} e^{-\frac{(x-d)}{\beta}} dx = .1$$

$$-e^{-\frac{(x-d)}{\beta}} \Big|_{x=d}^{x=x_{10}} = .1$$

$$-e^{-\frac{(x_{10}-d)}{\beta}} + e^{-\frac{(d-d)}{\beta}} = .1$$

$$-e^{-\frac{(x_{10}-d)}{\beta}} + e^{0} = .1$$

$$-e^{-\frac{(x_{10}-d)}{\beta}} + 1 = .1$$

$$e^{-\frac{(x_{10}-d)}{\beta}} = .9$$

$$-\frac{(x_{10}-d)}{\beta} = \ln .9$$

$$x_{10} - d = -\beta \ln \frac{9}{10}$$

$$x_{10} - mode = -\beta \ln \frac{9}{10} \quad (\because mode = d)$$

$$= \beta \ln \frac{10}{9}$$

The correct answer is **B**.

SOA Sample Question 395 Explanation

$$f(x) = \frac{c}{x^2}, \quad x > 100$$

We first find the constant by setting the integral of pdf equal to 1.

$$\int_{-\infty}^{\infty} f(x)\,dx = 1$$

$$\int_{100}^{\infty} \frac{c}{x^2} dx = 1$$

$$\int_{100}^{\infty} cx^{-2} dx = 1$$

$$c\frac{x^{-1}}{-1}\Big|_{100}^{\infty} = 1$$

$$-\frac{c}{x}\Big|_{100}^{\infty} = 1$$

$$-\frac{c}{\infty} + \frac{c}{100} = 1$$

$$0 + \frac{c}{100} = 1$$

$$c = 100$$

$$f(x) = \frac{100}{x^2}, \quad x > 100$$

Median is the value m at which cumulative probability is .5

$$\int_{100}^{m} 100x^{-2} dx = .5$$

$$100\frac{x^{-1}}{-1}\Big|_{100}^{m} = .5$$

$$-\frac{100}{m} + \frac{100}{100} = .5$$

$$\frac{100}{m} = .5$$

$$m = 200$$

The correct answer is **D**.

SOA Sample Question 396 Explanation

$$f(x) = kx^{.25}, \qquad 0 < x < 100$$

We first find the constant by setting the integral of pdf equal to 1.

$$\int_0^{100} kx^{.25}dx = 1$$

$$k\frac{x^{1.25}}{1.25}\Big|_0^{100} = 1$$

$$k\frac{100^{1.25}}{1.25} = 1$$

$$k = \frac{1.25}{100^{1.25}}$$

90th percentile p is the value at which the accumulated conditional probability is .9. That is:

$$P(X \le p|X > 20) = .9$$

$$\frac{P(X \le p \,\&\, X > 20)}{P(X > 20} = .9$$

$$\frac{P(20 < X \le p\,)}{1 - P(X < 20)} = .9$$

$$\frac{P(20 < X \le p\,)}{1 - P(X < 20)} = .9$$

$$\frac{F(p) - F(20)}{1 - F(20)} = .9 \quad (1)$$

$$F(p) = \int_0^p kx^{.25}dx = k\frac{x^{1.25}}{1.25}\Big|_0^p = k\frac{p^{1.25}}{1.25} = \frac{1.25}{100^{1.25}}\frac{p^{1.25}}{1.25} = \frac{p^{1.25}}{100^{1.25}}$$

$$F(20) = \frac{20^{1.25}}{100^{1.25}}$$

Substituting these values of $F(p)$ and $F(20)$ in (1) we get:

$$\frac{\frac{p^{1.25}}{100^{1.25}} - \frac{20^{1.25}}{100^{1.25}}}{1 - \frac{20^{1.25}}{100^{1.25}}} = .9$$

$$p = 93$$

The correct answer is **E**.

SOA Sample Question 397 Explanation

Consider the table:

Satisfaction	Combined Frequency of A and B	Frequency of A
0	9	8
1	6	
2	12	8
3	6	
4	6	
5	9	8

Mode is the satisfaction value with the highest frequency.

We are given that A has 3 modes, each with a frequency of 8.

So, these modes must be 0, 2, and 5 because these are the only satisfaction values that have a combined frequency of 8 or more.

We are also given the all frequencies of A are at least 4. So, the table becomes:

Satisfaction	Combined Frequency of A and B	Frequency of A	Frequency of B
0	9	8	$9-8=1$
1	6	≥ 4	0, 1, or 2
2	12	8	$12-8=4$
3	6	≥ 4	0, 1, or 2
4	6	≥ 4	0, 1, or 2
5	9	8	$9-8=1$

From the last column above, we see that the highest possible frequency of B is 4, occurring at a satisfaction level of 2. All other satisfaction levels must have a lower frequency than 4.

Thus, the only mode of B is 2.

Hence, B has only **1** mode.

The correct answer is **B**.

SOA Sample Question 398 Explanation

Consider the following table:

Class	Probability of Class	Probability of No Fire in Years 1,2	P(Class & no fire in Years 1,2)
High-Risk	.1	$.8^2 = .64$	$.1(.64) = .064$
Low-Risk	.9	$.99^2 = .9801$	$.9(.9801) = .8821$

Let H be the event of being high-risk.

Let L be the event of being low-risk.

Let N be the event of no fires in Years 1,2.

$$P(H|N) = \frac{P(H \,\&\, N)}{P(N)}$$

$$= \frac{.064}{.064 + .8821}$$

$$= .0676$$

$$P(L|N) = 1 - P(H|N)$$

$$= 1 - .0676$$

$$= .9324$$

Thus, there is .0676 probability that the chosen owner with no fire in Years 1,2 was High-Risk.

And there is .9324 probability that the chosen owner with no fire in Years 1,2 was Low-Risk.

So, we have the following up-dated table.

Class	$P(Class|N)$	Probability of No Fire in Years 3,4	P(Class & no fire in Years 3,4)
H	.0676	$.8^2 = .64$	$.0676(.64) = .0433$
L	.9324	$.99^2 = .9801$	$.9324(.9801)) = .9138$

Probability that selected owner will have no fires in Years 3,4 is found by adding the last column:

$$.0433 + .9138 = .9571$$

The correct answer is **E**.

SOA Sample Question 399 Explanation

N is the number of patients tested until 5 stage IV patients are found.

We are told that in the n patients, c have cancer.

This means that in the c patients, $n-c$ do not have cancer.

Since the nth patient has cancer, so in the first $n-1$ patients, $n-c$ don't have cancer.

Since c patients have cancer in the n patients, and the nth patient has cancer, so among the first $n-1$ patients, $c-1$ have cancer.

Since the nth patient is the 5th one to have stage IV cancer, so in the first $n-1$ patients, 4 have stage IV cancer.

Out of the $c-1$ cancer patients among the first $n-1$ patients , since 4 are stage IV, therefore $c-1-4=c-5$ are non-stage IV cancer patients.

From the above discussion, the first $n-1$ patients are comprised of:

(1) $n-c$ with no cancer,
(2) $c-5$ non-stage IV cancer patients, and
(3) 4 stage IV cancer patients

Let us find the respective probabilities:

$$P(\, no\ cancer) = 1 - P(cancer) = 1 - .2 = .8$$

$$P(stage\ IV\ cancer) = .2(.08) = .016$$

$$P(non\ stage\ IV\ cancer) = P(cancer) - P(stage\ IV) = .2 - .016 = .184$$

Using the pmf of multinomial distribution, the probability of the numbers mentioned in (1), (2), and (3) among the first $n-1$ patients is given as:

$$f(n-c, c-5, 4) = \frac{(n-1)!}{(n-c)!\,(c-5)!\,4!}(.8)^{n-c}(.184)^{c-5}(.016)^4$$

$$p_{N,C}(n,c) = P(numbers\ in\ (1),(2),(3)\ in\ first\ n-1) * P(nth\ is\ stage\ IV)$$

$$= f(n-c, c-5, 4) * .016$$

$$= \frac{(n-1)!}{(n-c)!\,(c-5)!\,4!}(.8)^{n-c}(.184)^{c-5}(.016)^4 * .016$$

$$= \frac{(n-1)!}{(n-c)!\,(c-5)!\,4!}(.8)^{n-c}(.184)^{c-5}(.016)^5$$

The correct answer is **A**.

SOA Sample Question 400 Explanation

We are to find $P(X+Y \geq 2)$. It is lesser work to find the complement $P(X+Y<2)$. Values satisfying this condition are tabulated below:

(x,y)	$p(x,y) = \frac{8-2x-y}{54}$
(0,0)	$\frac{8}{54}$
(0,1)	$\frac{7}{54}$
(1,0)	$\frac{6}{54}$

$$P(X+Y<2) = \frac{8}{54} + \frac{7}{54} + \frac{6}{54} = \frac{21}{54}$$

$$P(X+Y \geq 2) = 1 - P(X+Y<2) = 1 - \frac{21}{54} = .61$$

The correct answer is **E**.

SOA Sample Question 401 Explanation

Cumulative probability of .3446 is not found in the table because it corresponds to a negative standard score. To work around this we look at the cumulative probability $1 - .3446 = .6554$.

This corresponds to $z = .4$. Thus, cumulative probability of .3446 corresponds to $z = -.4$.

$$z = \frac{X-\mu}{\sigma}$$

$$-.4 = \frac{1000-\mu}{\sqrt{250000}}$$

$$\mu = 1200$$

90th percentile corresponds to a cumulative probability of .9.

From the bottom of the exam table this corresponds to $z = 1.2816$.

So, the 90th percentile p is given by the equation:

$$1.2816 = \frac{p-1200}{\sqrt{250000}}$$

$$p = 1840.8$$

A normal distribution is symmetric about the mean. Thus, its median equals mean.

$$Median = 1200$$

$$p - median = 1840.8 - 1200 = 640.8$$

The correct answer is **C**.

SOA Sample Question 402 Explanation

Let X be the number of phone calls per minute. We are given that:

$$E[X^2] = .2756$$

We know that for any random variable:

$$Var\,X = E[X^2] - (E[X])^2$$

Also, for Poisson, mean and variance are equal. So, if the mean is m then above equation gives:

$$m = .2756 - m^2$$

$$m^2 + m - .2756 = 0$$

$$m = \frac{-1 \pm \sqrt{1^2 - 4(1)(-.2756)}}{2(1)}$$

$$= .225, -1.225$$

Mean of a Poisson distribution is always positive. So, $m = .225$.

This is a 1-minute mean. We need mean over a 15-minute period which is given as:

$$\lambda = .225(15) = 3.375$$

Pmf of a Poisson distribution with mean λ is:

$$f(x) = \frac{\lambda^x e^{-\lambda}}{x!}, \quad x = 0,1,2,3, \ldots$$

$$= \frac{3.375^x e^{-3.375}}{x!}$$

$$P(X > 2) = 1 - P(X \leq 2)$$

$$= 1 - f(0) - f(1) - f(2)$$

$$= 1 - \frac{3.375^0 e^{-3.375}}{0!} - \frac{3.375^1 e^{-3.375}}{1!} - \frac{3.375^2 e^{-3.375}}{2!}$$

$$= .655$$

The correct answer is **A**.

SOA Sample Question 403 Explanation

This is hypergeometric. The required probability is:

$$P(1W, 3H, 1A) = \frac{\binom{5}{1}\binom{4}{3}\binom{6}{1}}{\binom{15}{5}}$$

$$= .04$$

The correct answer is **C**.

SOA Sample Question 404 Explanation

$$p(x,y) = \frac{24 - 7x - 3y}{126}, \quad x = 0,1,2, \quad y = 0,1,2$$

To get the variance of Y, we first need the marginal distribution of Y.

$$P(Y=0) = p(0,0) + p(1,0) + p(2,0) = \frac{24}{126} + \frac{17}{126} + \frac{10}{126} = \frac{51}{126}$$

$$P(Y=1) = p(0,1) + p(1,1) + p(2,1) = \frac{21}{126} + \frac{14}{126} + \frac{7}{126} = \frac{42}{126}$$

$$P(Y=2) = 1 - P(Y=0) - P(Y=1) = 1 - \frac{51}{126} - \frac{42}{126} = \frac{33}{126}$$

We can now use calculator to find the variance, by putting the Y values in 1st column and the probability values in the 2nd column. Calculator gives us SD which we square to get variance:

$$Var\ X = (\sigma_X)^2 = (.8039)^2 = .65$$

The correct answer is **B**.

SOA Sample Question 405 Explanation

Let us first focus on the expected gain from a single entry.

Total Number of ways in which 5 numbers can be selected from 30 is $\binom{30}{5}$.

Of these, only one is winning.

Also, only 1 of the 5 winning numbers is a bonus number, and other 4 are not. So,

$$P(win\ \&\ bonus) = \frac{1}{\binom{30}{5}}\left(\frac{1}{5}\right)$$

$$P(win\ and\ no\ bonus) = \frac{1}{\binom{30}{5}}\left(\frac{4}{5}\right)$$

Base winning amount without bonus $= 50000$

Winning amount with bonus $= 50000 + 250000 = 300000$

So, the expected gain $E[X]$ from each entry is:

$$E[X] = 50000\frac{1}{\binom{30}{5}}\left(\frac{4}{5}\right) + 300000\frac{1}{\binom{30}{5}}\left(\frac{1}{5}\right) = .70172$$

Expected gain from 100,000 entries is:

$$100000E[X] = 100000(.70712) = 70712$$

The correct answer is **A**.

SOA Sample Question 406 Explanation

Y = Number of policies from the selected 5 with fewer than 2 claims.

$$P(fewer\ than\ 2\ claims) = P(0) + P(1) = s + t$$

c represents the probability that all 5 selected policies have fewer than 2 claims.

$$c = P(Y = 5)$$

$$c = (s + t)^5$$

$$c^{\frac{1}{5}} = s + t$$

$$s = c^{\frac{1}{5}} - t \quad (1)$$

Also, sum of all the probabilities in the table must equal 1. So:

$$s + t + .75s + 0 = 1$$

$$t = 1 - 1.75s \quad (2)$$

Substituting s from (1) in (2) we get:

$$t = 1 - 1.75\left(c^{\frac{1}{5}} - t\right)$$

$$t = 1 - 1.75c^{\frac{1}{5}} + 1.75t$$

$$.75t = 1.75c^{\frac{1}{5}} - 1$$

$$t = \frac{1.75c^{\frac{1}{5}} - 1}{.75} = \frac{\frac{7}{4}c^{0.2} - 1}{\frac{3}{4}} = \frac{\frac{7c^{0.2} - 4}{4}}{\frac{3}{4}} = \frac{7c^{0.2} - 4}{3}$$

The correct answer is **E**.

SOA Sample Question 407 Explanation

Median of an exponential distribution with mean m is:

$$Median = m \ln 2$$

$$3 = m \ln 2$$

$$m = 4.328$$

Variance of an exponential distribution equals the square of its mean.

Since exponential distribution is memoryless, so:

$$Var(X|X > k) = Var\ X = m^2 = 4.328^2 = 18.7$$

The correct answer is **E**.

SOA Sample Question 408 Explanation

Consider the following table:

Coin	Probability of head	Probability of 2 heads in 2 tosses
Fair	.5	$.5^2 = .25$
2-Headed	1	$1^2 = 1$

Let F be the event of selecting the fair coin.

Let B be the event of selecting the 2-headed coin.

Let H be the event of getting a head.

Since initially the 2-coins are equally likely to be selected, so

$$P(HH|F) = \frac{.25}{1 + .25}$$

$$= .2$$

$$P(HH|B) = \frac{1}{1 + .25}$$

$$= .8$$

Thus, there is .2 probability that the chosen coin that gave 2 heads was fair.

And there is .8 probability that the chosen coin that gave 2 heads was 2-headed.

So, we have the following up-dated table.

Coin	$P(Coin\|HH)$	Probability of Head on Toss 3	P(Coin & Head on Toss 3)
F	.2	$.5$	$.2(.5) = .1$
B	.8	1	$.8(1)) = .8$

Probability or a head on 3rd toss is found by adding the last column:

$$.1 + .8 = .9$$

$$= \frac{9}{10}$$

The correct answer is **E**.

SOA Sample Question 409 Explanation

Let X be the loss.

Since the cdf becomes 1 after $x = 10$, so by continuity:

$$F(10) = 1$$

$$c\left(\frac{10}{15}\right)^{\frac{4}{3}} = 1$$

$$c = 1.7171$$

$$F(x) = 1.717\left(\frac{x}{15}\right)^{\frac{4}{3}}, \quad 0 \le x \le 10$$

If the loss is less than or equal to m, it is completely reimbursed.

If the loss is greater than m, it is partially reimbursed (for an amount m). So:

$$P(X > m) = .56$$

$$1 - P(X \le m) = .56$$

$$1 - F(m) = .56$$

$$1 - 1.7171\left(\frac{m}{15}\right)^{\frac{4}{3}} = .56$$

$$.44 = 1.7171\left(\frac{x}{15}\right)^{\frac{4}{3}}$$

$$\left(\frac{x}{15}\right)^{\frac{4}{3}} = .2562$$

$$\frac{x}{15} = .36$$

$$x = 5.4$$

The correct answer is **A**.

SOA Sample Question 410 Explanation

$X =$ Number of tornadoes.

$Y =$ Total loss due to all tornadoes.

$$F(2,3) = P(X \leq 2, Y \leq 3)$$

$$= P(at\ most\ 2\ tornadoes\ and\ total\ loss\ at\ most\ 3)$$

Let us consider the cases in which we have at most 2 tornadoes such that total loss is at most 3.

Case 1: X = 0 or 1

If there is no tornado, then of course there is no loss and thus the maximum loss condition is true.

If there is 1 tornado, then the maximum loss is 2.

Thus, whether $X = 0\ or\ 1$, the total loss is at most 3 (actually, less than 3). Thus:

$$P(X = 0\ or\ 1, Y \leq 3) = P(X = 0\ or\ 1)$$

$$= P(X = 0) + P(X = 1)$$

$$= .8 + .12$$

$$= .92 \quad (1)$$

Case 2: X = 2

In this case, there are 2 tornadoes. So, total loss will be at most 3 unless both losses are 2 each.

$$P(both\ losses\ 2\ each) = .5(.5)$$

$$= .25$$

$$P(total\ loss\ at\ most\ 3\ given\ 2\ losses) = 1 - P(Both\ losses\ 2\ each)$$

$$= 1 - .25$$

$$= .75$$

$$P(X = 2, Y \leq 3) = P(X = 2)\ P(Y \leq 3 | X = 2)$$

$$= .05(.75)$$

$$= .0375 \quad (2)$$

From (1) and (2):

$$F(2,3) = P(X = 0\ or\ 1, Y \leq 3) + P(X = 2, Y \leq 3)$$

$$= .92 + .0375$$

$$= .9575$$

The correct answer is **E**.

SOA Sample Question 411 Explanation

$$p(x,y)=\frac{(4-x)(3-y)}{60},\quad x=0,1,2,3,\ \ y=0,1,2$$

To get the variance of Y, we first need the marginal distribution of Y.

$$P(Y=0)=p(0,0)+p(1,0)+p(2,0)+p(3,0)=\frac{12}{60}+\frac{9}{60}+\frac{6}{60}+\frac{3}{60}=\frac{1}{2}$$

$$P(Y=1)=p(0,1)+p(1,1)+p(2,1)+p(3,1)=\frac{8}{60}+\frac{6}{60}+\frac{4}{60}+\frac{2}{60}=\frac{1}{3}$$

$$P(Y=2)=1-P(Y=0)-P(Y=1)=1-\frac{1}{2}-\frac{1}{3}=\frac{1}{6}$$

We can now use calculator to find the variance, by putting the Y values in 1st column and the probability values in the 2nd column. Calculator gives us SD which we square to get variance:

$$Var\ X=(\sigma_X)^2$$

$$=(.745)^2$$

$$=.56$$

The correct answer is **A**.

SOA Sample Question 412 Explanation

Maximum of 3 will be less than 7 if and only if all 3 claims are less than 7.

Let the 3 claims be X_1, X_2, X_3. Then, for each $i=1,2,3$:

$$P(X_i)<7=\frac{7-0}{10-0}$$

$$=.7$$

$$P(Max<7)=P(X_1<7)\cdot P(X_2<7)\cdot P(X_3<7)$$

$$=.7(.7)(.7)$$

$$=.343$$

The correct answer is **D**.

Tools needed for problems 413-430

Negative binomial distribution

N has negative binomial distribution if the probability of needing n trials to get r successes is:

$$P(N = n) = \binom{n-1}{r-1} p^r (1-p)^{n-r}$$

where p is the probability of success in each trial.

If n is a positive integer, then:

$$\binom{n}{1} = 1$$

Hypergeometric Formula:

If we have N items, of which a items are of type A, b items are of type B, then the probability of selecting n items, of which x items are of type A is:

$$\frac{\binom{a}{x}\binom{b}{n-x}}{\binom{N}{n}}$$

Variance of a Poisson variable equals its mean.

Integration by parts shortcut:

$$\int (x+k)e^{ax}dx = \frac{(x+k)e^{ax}}{a} - \frac{e^{ax}}{a^2}$$

Median of an exponential distribution with mean λ is $\lambda \ln 2$.

Variance of an exponential distribution equals square of its mean.

Cdf of an exponential distribution with mean λ is

$$F(x) = 1 - e^{-x/\lambda}$$

Addition Rule:

$$P[A \cup B] = P[A] + P[B] - P[A \cap B]$$

Pmf of a Poisson distribution with mean λ is:

$$f(x) = \frac{\lambda^x e^{-\lambda}}{x!}, \quad x = 0,1,2,3, \ldots$$

If the mean λ of a Poisson distribution is non-integer, then its mode is the greatest integer less than λ. If λ is an integer, then the modes are λ and $\lambda - 1$.

SOA Sample Question 413 Explanation

Let N be the number of policies examined.

If he continues forever until 2 frauds are found, then N has a negative binomial distribution.

In negative binomial, the probability of needing n trials to get r successes is:

$$P(N = n) = \binom{n-1}{r-1} p^r (1-p)^{n-r}$$

where p is the probability of success in each trial.

In this case, p is the probability that a selected policy has a claim and a fraud. So:

$$p = P(Claim\ and\ Fraud)$$

$$= .9(.2)$$

$$= .18$$

Also, $r = 2$. So:

$$P(N = n) = \binom{n-1}{2-1} .18^r (1 - .18)^{n-2}$$

$$= (n-1)(.18)^2(.82)^{n-2} \quad (1)$$

However, since he does not go on forever but stops after 5 policies, so we can use equation (1) only for the probabilities of examining 1,2,3, or 4 policies. 5th policy is handled differently.

There is no way that 2 fraudulent claims can be found be examining only 1 policy. So:

$$P(1) = 0$$

Using (1) repeatedly, we get the other probabilities:

$$P(2) = (2-1)(.18)^2(.82)^{2-2} = .0324$$

$$P(3) = (3-1)(.18)^2(.82)^{3-2} = .0531$$

$$P(4) = (4-1)(.18)^2(.82)^{4-2} = .0654$$

Since he stops after 5 policies, so $P(5)$ cannot be found from equation (1) but through:

$$P(1) + P(2) + P(3) + P(4) + P(5) = 1$$

$$0 + .0324 + .0531 + .0654 + P(5) = 1$$

$$P(5) = .8491$$

$$E[N] = \sum n\, p(n)$$

$$= 1(0) + 2(.0324) + 3(.0531) + 4(.0654) + 5(.8491)$$

$$= 4.73$$

The correct answer is **B**.

SOA Sample Question 414 Explanation

This is hypergeometric, which says that if we have N items, of which a items are of type A, b items are of type $B,$ then the probability of selecting n items, of which x items are of type A is:

$$f(x) = \frac{\binom{a}{x}\binom{b}{n-x}}{\binom{N}{n}}, \qquad x = 0,1,2,\dots,n$$

Here:

$$N = 9$$

$$n = 4$$

$$a = 6$$

$$b = N - a$$

$$= 9 - 6$$

$$= 3$$

$$f(x) = \frac{\binom{6}{x}\binom{3}{4-x}}{\binom{9}{4}}$$

We are to find $P(X \geq 3)$.

$$P(X \geq 3) = f(3) + f(4)$$

$$= \frac{\binom{6}{3}\binom{3}{4-3}}{\binom{9}{4}} + \frac{\binom{6}{4}\binom{3}{4-4}}{\binom{9}{4}}$$

$$= .6$$

The correct answer is **E**.

SOA Sample Question 415 Explanation

Total people $= 200$, of which 60% buy nothing.

$$\# \; buying \; nothing = .6(200) = 120$$

Let C be the number of people buying carriage only.

Let S be the number of people buying seat only.

Let B be the number of people buying both carriage and seat.

$$Total \; people = C + S + B + 120$$

$$200 = C + S + B + 120$$

$$C + S + B = 80 \quad (1)$$

We are given that 20% people buy a carriage. That is:

$$C + B = .2(200)$$

$$= 40 \quad (2)$$

Also, 35% people buy a car seat. That is:

$$S + B = .35(200)$$

$$= 70 \quad (3)$$

Adding (2) and (3) we get:

$$C + B + S + B = 40 + 70$$

$$C + S = 110 - 2B \quad (4)$$

Substituting the value of $C + S$ from (4) in (1)

$$110 - 2B + B = 80$$

$$B = 30$$

Substituting the value of B in (2) and (3) we get:

$$C = 10$$

$$S = 40$$

10% discount on buying both carriage and seat means paying 90% of total price of both.

Expected revenue is given as:

$$R = 300C + 100S + .9(300 + 100)B$$

$$= 300(10) + 100(40) + 360(30)$$

$$= 17800$$

The correct answer is **B**.

SOA Sample Question 416 Explanation

We know that mean and variance of a Poisson variable are equal. So:

Expected claims by a single policy holder $= mean = variance = 1$.

Expected claims by 1000 policy holders $= 1000(1) = 1000$.

Expected payment to 1000 policy holders $= 100(1000) = 100000$.

Expected premium from 1000 policy holders $= 1.03(100000) = 103000$.

Let X_i be the number of claims made by policy holder i.

Let S be the total claim payment. Then:

$$E[X_i] = Var[X_i] = 1$$

$$S = 100(X_1 + X_2 + X_3 + \cdots + X_{1000}) \quad (1)$$

$$E[S] = 100(E[X_i] + E[X_i] + \cdots + E[X_i]) = 100(1000) = 100000$$

$$Var[S] = 100^2(Var[X_i] + Var[X_i] + \cdots + Var[X_i]) = 10000(1000) = 10000000$$

We are to find $P(S > 103000)$. So, we need to change 103000 to standard score:

$$z = \frac{103000 - 100000}{\sqrt{10000000}} = .95$$

$$P(z > .95) = 1 - P(z \leq .95) = 1 - .8289 = .171$$

This is closest to choice C. The difference is because they are using a "continuity correction" which makes no sense here. Continuity correction is used when we treat a discrete variable as a continuous variable. However, in this problem, everything is already continuous. Note that even though a Poisson distribution is discrete, the mean of a Poisson distribution is continuous. Similarly, the payout is continuous. So, continuity correction does not apply.

The correct answer is **C**.

SOA Sample Question 417 Explanation

This is negative binomial. So, the probability of needing n trials to get r successes is:

$$P(N = n) = \binom{n-1}{r-1} p^r (1-p)^{n-r}$$

where p is the probability of success in each trial.

In this case, p is the probability of a fatal crash is a single instance of saving a documuent. So:

$$p = \frac{1}{50}, \qquad r = 2, \qquad n = 4$$

$$P(N = 4) = \binom{4-1}{2-1}\left(\frac{1}{50}\right)^2\left(1 - \frac{1}{50}\right)^{4-2} = .00115$$

The correct answer is **B**.

SOA Sample Question 418 Explanation

$$P(1\ accident\ in\ a\ year) = .08$$

$$P(2\ accident\ in\ a\ year) = .02$$

$$P(2\ accidents\ in\ 2\ yrs) = P(0\ in\ 1st, 2\ in\ 2nd) + P(2\ in\ 1st, 0\ in\ 2nd) + P(1\ in\ each\ yr)$$

$$= .9(.02) + .02(.9) + .08(.08) = .0424$$

$$P(1\ in\ each\ yr|2\ in\ 2\ yrs) = \frac{P(1\ in\ each\ yr\ \&\ 2\ in\ 2\ yrs)}{P(2\ in\ 2\ yrs)} = \frac{P(1\ in\ each\ yr)}{P(2\ in\ 2\ yrs)}$$

$$= \frac{.08(.08)}{.0424} = .151$$

The correct answer is **C**.

SOA Sample Question 419 Explanation

Let X be the number of years before repair is needed.

Since the warranty is 2 years, 2e are to find $P(X > 4.5|X>2)$.

$$P(X > 4.5|X > 2) = \frac{P(X > 4.5\ and\ X > 2)}{P(X > 2)} = \frac{P(X > 4.5)}{P(X > 2)} = \frac{\frac{5-4.5}{5-0}}{\frac{5-2}{5-0}} = \frac{.5}{3} = .17$$

The correct answer is **B**.

SOA Sample Question 420 Explanation

$$f(x) = xe^{-x},\ \ x > 0$$

Since X is in tens of millions of years, we are to find $P(1 < X < 2)$.

$$P(1 < X < 2) = \int_1^2 f(x)\,dx = \int_1^2 xe^{-x}\,dx$$

Recall the integration by parts shortcut:

$$\int xe^{ax}dx = \frac{xe^{ax}}{a} - \frac{e^{ax}}{a^2}$$

Here, $a = -1$.

$$P(1 < X < 2) = \frac{xe^{-x}}{-1} - \frac{e^{-x}}{(-1)^2}\Big|_1^2 = -2e^{-2} - e^{-2} - (-e^{-1} - e^{-1}) = -3e^{-2} + 2e^{-1} = .3298$$

The correct answer is **C**.

SOA Sample Question 421 Explanation

We know that the median of an exponential distribution with mean λ is $\lambda \ln 2$.

$$2.7 = \lambda \ln 2$$

$$\lambda = 3.8953$$

Also, cdf of the exponential distribution is:

$$F(x) = 1 - e^{-x/\lambda}$$

$$F(x) = 1 - e^{-x/3.8953}$$

87.5th percentile p is the value at which the cumulative probability is .875.

$$F(p) = .875$$

$$1 - e^{-\frac{p}{3.8953}} = .875$$

$$e^{-\frac{p}{3.8953}} = .125$$

$$-\frac{p}{3.8953} = \ln .125$$

$$p = 8.1$$

The correct answer is **C**.

SOA Sample Question 422 Explanation

If an event is certain to occur, its probability is 1. Thus, we are given that:

$$P[A \cap B] = 0$$

$$P[A \cup B] = 1$$

$$P[C \cap D] = 0$$

$$P[C \cup D] = 1$$

By addition rule:

$$P[A \cup B] = P[A] + P[B] - P[A \cap B]$$

$$0 = P[A] + P[B] - 1$$

$$P[A] + P[B] = 1 \qquad (1)$$

We are given that $P[A] = .75$.

So, from equation (1), $P[B] = .25$.

Also, by addition rule:

$$P[C \cup D] = P[C] + P[D] - P[C \cap D]$$

$$0 = P[C] + P[D] - 1$$

$$P[C] + P[D] = 1 \qquad (2)$$

We are given that $P[D] = .2$.

So, from equation (2), $P[C] = .8$.

Again, by addition rule:

$$P[A \cup C] = P[A] + P[C] - P[A \cap C]$$

$$= .75 + .8 - .55$$

$$= 1$$

This means that At least one of $A\ or\ C$ is certain to occur.

That is, either $A\ or\ C$ (or both) must occur. (3)

If A occurs, then B cannot occur (given that A and B are mutually exclusive). (4)

If C occurs, then D cannot occur (given that C and D are mutually exclusive). (5)

Statements (3), (4) and (5) show that at least one of B and D does not occur.

In other words, both B and D can never occur at the same time.

That is the same as saying that $P[B \cap D] = 0$

The correct answer is **A**.

SOA Sample Question 423 Explanation

In the table below, bold entries are calculations resulting from the given information (un-bold).

Note that the last entry in table has to be 1 because that is the total of all possible probabilities.

	Overstated	Not Overstated	Total
Claimed at least 1000	.45	$\mathbf{.7 - .45 = .25}$	.7
Claimed less than 1000	$\mathbf{.5 - .45 = .05}$		$\mathbf{1 - .7 = .3}$
Total	.5	$\mathbf{1 - .5 = .5}$	1

$$P(Overstated|Claimed\ less\ than\ 1000) = \frac{P(Overstated\ \&\ Claimed\ less\ than\ 1000)}{P(Claimed\ less\ than\ 1000)}$$

$$= \frac{.05}{.3}$$

$$= \frac{1}{6}$$

The correct answer is **C**.

SOA Sample Question 424 Explanation

There are $\binom{26}{3} = 2600$ ways to choose 3 distinct letters of the alphabet.

Since any of these 3 distinct letters can be put in the 1st spot, so there are:

$2600(3) = 7800$ ways to choose 3 distinct letters and put one of them in 1st spot.

For each of these ways, there are $4\ P\ 2 = 12$ ways to put 2 of the remaining letters in any of the 4 remaining spots.

So, there are $7800(12) = 93600$ ways to put the letters according to the given conditions.

For each of these, there are $10(10) = 100$ ways to put the two digits, because there are 10 digits $(0,1,2,\ldots,9)$, and repetitions are allowed.

So, there are a total of $93600(100) = 9360000 = 9.36$ million ways.

The correct answer is **E**.

SOA Sample Question 425 Explanation

Let X be the number of fillings per year.

The pmf of a Poisson distribution with mean λ is:

$$f(x) = \frac{\lambda^x e^{-\lambda}}{x!}, \quad x = 0,1,2,3,\ldots$$

$$f(0) = \frac{\lambda^0 e^{-\lambda}}{0!}$$

$$.18 = e^{-\lambda}$$

$$\ln .18 = -\lambda$$

$$\lambda = 1.7148$$

We also know that If the mean λ of a Poisson distribution is non-integer, then its mode is the greatest integer less than λ. If λ is an integer, then the modes are λ and $\lambda - 1$.

Here, λ is a non-integer. Therefore, mode is the greatest integer less than λ.

So, the mode is 1.

The correct answer is **B**.

SOA Sample Question 426 Explanation

$$f(t) = kt, \quad 0 < t < 50$$

We are to find $P(T \le 25|T > 20)$.

$$P(T \le 25|T > 20) = \frac{P(T \le 25 \; and \; T > 20}{P(T > 20)}$$

$$= \frac{P(20 < T \le 25)}{P(T > 20)} \quad (1)$$

$$P(20 < T \le 25) = \int_{20}^{25} f(t)\, dt$$

$$= \int_{20}^{25} kt\, dt$$

$$= k\frac{t^2}{2}\Big|_{20}^{25}$$

$$= k\left(\frac{25^2}{2} - \frac{20^2}{2}\right)$$

$$= 112.5k \quad (2)$$

$$P(T > 20) = \int_{20}^{\infty} f(t)\, dt$$

$$= \int_{20}^{50} kt\, dt$$

$$= k\frac{t^2}{2}\Big|_{20}^{50}$$

$$= k\left(\frac{50^2}{2} - \frac{20^2}{2}\right)$$

$$= 1050k \quad (3)$$

Substituting (2) and (3) in (1) we get:

$$P(T \le 25|T > 20) = \frac{112.5k}{1050k}$$

$$= .11$$

The correct answer is **B**.

SOA Sample Question 427 Explanation

Let probability of death of a low-risk policy holder be x.

Then, probability of death of a medium-risk policy holder is $3x$.

And, probability of death of a high-risk policy holder is $2(3x) = 6x$.

Let L be the event that a policy-holder is low-risk.

Let M be the event that a policy-holder is medium-risk.

Let H be the event that a policy-holder is high-risk.

Then, $P(L) = .45$.

And, $P(M) = .35$.

This gives, $P(H) = 1 - .45 - .35 = .2$.

Let D be the event that a policy-holder dies next year.

$$P(D) = P(D|L)P(L) + P(D|M)P(M) + P(D|H)P(H)$$

$$.009 = x(.45) + 3x(.35) + 6x(.2)$$

$$.009 = 2.7x$$

$$x = \frac{1}{300}$$

$$P(Death\ of\ a\ high - risk\ person) = 6x = 6\left(\frac{1}{300}\right) = .02$$

The correct answer is **B**.

SOA Sample Question 428 Explanation

Let the time for chip replacement be X.

Then X is exponential with mean 7.2.

$$F(x) = 1 - e^{-x/7.2}$$

$$.05 = 1 - e^{-t/7.2}$$

$$e^{-\frac{t}{7.2}} = .95$$

$$-\frac{t}{7.2} = \ln .95$$

$$t = .369$$

The correct answer is **B**.

SOA Sample Question 429 Explanation

$$f(x) = kx, \quad 0 < x < 2$$

We first find the constant by setting the pdf equal to 1:

$$\int_{-\infty}^{\infty} f(x) = 1$$

$$\int_{0}^{2} kx = 1$$

$$k\frac{x^2}{2}|_0^2 = 1$$

$$k\left(\frac{2^2}{2} - \frac{0^2}{2}\right) = 1$$

$$2k = 1$$

$$k = .5$$

$$f(x) = .5x, \quad 0 < x < 2$$

80th percentile p is the value at which the cumulative probability is .8.

$$\int_{-\infty}^{p} f(x) = .8$$

$$\int_{0}^{p} .5x = .8$$

$$.5\frac{x^2}{2}|_0^p = .8$$

$$.5\left(\frac{p^2}{2} - \frac{0^2}{2}\right) = .8$$

$$.25p^2 = .8$$

$$p^2 = 3.2$$

$$p = \sqrt{3.2}$$

$$= 1.79$$

The correct answer is **E**.

SOA Sample Question 430 Explanation

Let X be the lifespan of TV A.

Let Y be the lifespan of TV B.

Cdfs of the two lifespans are:

$$F(x) = 1 - e^{-x/m_A}$$

$$G(y) = 1 - e^{-y/m_B}$$

Mean of an exponential distribution equals square root of its variance.

$$Var\ X = 5.6$$

$$m_A = \sqrt{5.6}$$

$$= 2.3664$$

We are given that $P(X > T) = .49$.

$$1 - P(X \leq T) = .49$$

$$1 - F(T) = .49$$

$$e^{-T/2.3664} = .49$$

$$-\frac{T}{2.3664} = \ln .49$$

$$T = 1.688$$

We are also given that $P(Y > T) = .7$

$$1 - P(Y \leq T) = .7$$

$$1 - G(T) = .7$$

$$e^{-T/m_B} = .7$$

$$-\frac{1.688}{m_B} = \ln .7$$

$$m_B = 4.733$$

$$Var\ Y = {m_B}^2$$

$$= 4.733^2$$

$$= 22.4$$

The correct answer is **E**.

Tools needed for problems 431-446

Sum of independent normal variables is normal.

If X, Y are random variables, and a, b are any real numbers, then:

$$E[aX + bY] = aE[X] + bE[Y]$$

$$Var[aX + bY] = a^2Var[X] + b^2Var[Y]$$

The above formulas are generalized in the natural way for more than 2 random variables.

In the standard normal distribution:

$$P(-a < Z < a) = 2P(z < a) - 1$$

$$P(Z > b) = P(Z < -b)$$

$$P(Z < c) = P(Z > -c)$$

Sum of independent normal distributions is normal.

Pmf of Poisson distribution with mean m is:

$$f(x) = \frac{m^x e^{-m}}{x!}, \qquad x = 0,1,2,3, \dots$$

Median of an exponential distribution with mean λ is $\lambda \ln 2$.

Variance of an exponential distribution equals square of its mean.

Hypergeometric Formula:

If we have N items, of which a items are of type A, b items are of type B, then the probability of selecting n items, of which x items are of type A is:

$$\frac{\binom{a}{x}\binom{b}{n-x}}{\binom{N}{n}}$$

Variance of uniform $[a, b]$ distribution is:

$$Var\ X = \frac{(b-a)^2}{12}$$

If X is a continuous random variable, f is the pdf of X, and g is any function of X, then:

$$E[g(X)] = \int_{-\infty}^{\infty} g(x)\, f(x)\, dx$$

SOA Sample Question 431 Explanation

Let A, B, C, D be the profits in 1st, 2nd, 3rd, and 4th quarters, respectively. Let:

$$\mu_A = \mu_B = \mu_C = \mu_D = \mu$$

$$\sigma_A = \sigma_B = \sigma_C = \sigma_D = \sigma$$

Sum of independent normal variables is normal. Let:

$$X = A + B + C + D$$

$$\mu_X = \mu_A + \mu_B + \mu_C + \mu_D = 4\mu$$

$$Var\ X = Var\ A + Var\ B + Var\ C + Var\ D = 4\sigma^2$$

We are given that:

$$P(A > 0) = .8 \quad (1)$$

From the bottom of the exam table, we get that:

$$P(Z < .8416) = .8$$

By symmetry of the normal distribution, this implies that:

$$P(Z > -.8416) = .8 \quad (2)$$

From (1) and (2) we see that $A = 0$ corresponds to $Z = -.8416$. Thus we have:

$$z = \frac{A - \mu_A}{\sigma_A}$$

$$-.8416 = \frac{0 - \mu}{\sigma}$$

$$\frac{\mu}{\sigma} = .8416$$

We are to find $P(X > 0)$. So, we need to change 0 in standard score:

$$z = \frac{X - \mu_X}{\sigma_X} = \frac{0 - 4\mu}{\sqrt{4\sigma^2}} = \frac{-4\mu}{2\sigma} = -2\left(\frac{\mu}{\sigma}\right) = -2(.8416) = -1.6832$$

$$P(X > 0) = P(Z > -1.68)$$

$$= P(Z < 1.68)$$

$$= .9535$$

The correct answer is **D**.

SOA Sample Question 432 Explanation

Cumulative probability of .1056 is not present in the table, so we look at its complement:

$$1 - .1056 = .8944$$

This correspond to a z-value of 1.25.

Hence, the z-value corresponding to a cumulative probability of .1056 is -1.25.

Thus $z = -1.25$ corresponds to $X = 400$ in the equation:

$$z = \frac{X - \mu}{\sigma}$$

$$-1.25 = \frac{400 - 500}{\sigma}$$

$$\sigma = 80$$

To find $P[370 < N_f < 730$, we need to change 370 and 730 in standard scores:

$$z_{370} = \frac{370 - 550}{1.25\sigma} = \frac{-180}{1.25(80)} = -1.8$$

$$z_{730} = \frac{730 - 550}{1.25\sigma} = \frac{180}{1.25(80)} = 1.8$$

$$P[370 < N_f < 730] = P(-1.8 < Z < 1.8)$$

$$= 2P(Z < 1.8) - 1$$

$$P[370 < N_f < 730] = 2(.9641) - 1$$

$$= .928$$

The correct answer is **B**.

SOA Sample Question 433 Explanation

Let X be the profit from selling flood insurance.

Let Y be the profit from selling fire insurance.

We are given that:

$$P(X > 0) = .67 \quad (1)$$

A cumulative probability of .6700 corresponds to $z = 0.44$

$$P(Z < .44) = .67$$

$$P(Z > -.44) = .67 \quad (2)$$

The last equation results from the fact that in standard normal distribution:

$$P(Z < c) = P(Z > -c)$$

Comparing (1) and (2) we see that $X = 0$ corresponds to $Z = -.44$.

$$z = \frac{X - \mu}{\sigma}$$

$$-.44 = \frac{0 - \mu_X}{\sigma_X}$$

$$\frac{\mu_X}{\sigma_X} = .44 \quad (3)$$

Let $T = X + Y$. We know that sum of independent normal variables is normal.

$$\mu_T = \mu_X + \mu_Y = \mu_X + 3\mu_X = 4\mu_X$$

$$Var\ T = Var\ X + Var\ Y = {\sigma_X}^2 + {\sigma_Y}^2 = {\sigma_X}^2 + (3\sigma_X)^2 = 10{\sigma_X}^2$$

We are to find $P(T > 0)$. So, we need to change 0 into standard score:

$$z = \frac{T - \mu_T}{\sigma_T} = \frac{0 - 4\mu_X}{\sqrt{10{\sigma_X}^2}} = \frac{-4}{\sqrt{10}}\left(\frac{\mu_X}{\sigma_X}\right) = \frac{-4}{\sqrt{10}}(.44) = -.56$$

$$P(T > 0) = P(Z > -.56)$$

$$= P(Z < .56)$$

$$= .7123$$

The correct answer is **A**.

SOA Sample Question 434 Explanation

Let number of accidents resulting from 1st coaster be X.

Let number of accidents resulting from 2nd coaster be Y.

Then, the probability functions of the two variables are:

$$f(x) = \frac{.5^x e^{-.5}}{x!}, \qquad x = 0,1,2,3,\ldots$$

$$g(y) = \frac{{\lambda_2}^y e^{-\lambda_2}}{y!}, \qquad y = 0,1,2,3,\ldots$$

We are given that:

$$P(Y \geq 1) = 2P(X \geq 1)$$

Writing the probabilities as complements we get:

$$1 - g(0) = 2[1 - f(0)]$$

$$1 - e^{-\lambda_2} = 2[1 - e^{-.5}]$$

$$e^{-\lambda_2} = .2131$$

$$-\lambda_2 = \ln .2131$$

$$\lambda_2 = 1.55$$

The correct answer is **D**.

SOA Sample Question 435 Explanation

Let number of accidents be X.

Variance of an exponential distribution equals square of its mean λ.

Therefore, mean will be the square root of the variance.

$$\lambda = \sqrt{7225} = 85$$

We know that median m of an exponential distribution with mean λ is $\lambda \ln 2$.

$$m = 85 \ln 2 = 59$$

We are to find $m - \lambda$.

$$m - \lambda = 59 - 85 = -26$$

The correct answer is **B**.

SOA Sample Question 436 Explanation

Let a random loss be X. Cdf of an exponential distribution with mean λ is

$$F(x) = 1 - e^{-x/\lambda}$$

Standard deviation of an exponential distribution equals its mean λ. Therefore, $\lambda = 1000$.

$$F(x) = 1 - e^{-x/1000}$$

$$P[X > 1500|X > 1000] = \frac{P[X > 1500 \text{ and } X > 1000]}{P[X > 1000]} = \frac{P[X > 1500]}{P[X > 1000]} = \frac{1 - P[X \le 1500]}{1 - P[X \le 1000]}$$

$$= \frac{1 - F(1500]}{1 - F(1000)} = \frac{e^{-\frac{1500}{1000}}}{e^{-\frac{1000}{1000}}} = .61$$

The correct answer is **D**.

SOA Sample Question 437 Explanation

Let number of injuries be X. According to the given conditions:

$$f(1) + f(2) = .25 \quad (1)$$

$$f(2) + f(3) = .036 \quad (2)$$

$$f(0) = 1 - P(X \ge 1) = 1 - .26 = .74$$

$$f(0) + f(1) + f(2) + f(3) = 1 - P(X \ge 4) = 1 - .002 = .998$$

$$.74 + f(1) + f(2) + f(3) = .998$$

$$f(1) + f(2) + f(3) = .258 \quad (3)$$

Adding (1) and (2) we get:

$$f(1) + 2f(2) + f(3) = .286 \quad (4)$$

Subtracting (3) from (4) we get:

$$f(2) = .028$$

The correct answer is **D**.

SOA Sample Question 438 Explanation

First 5 items will fill the truck to capacity if and only if 3 are Type A and 2 are Type B are chosen from the 10 available items (of which 6 are Type A and 4 are Type B).

Thus, this is hypergeometric. Required probability is:

$$\frac{\binom{6}{3}\binom{4}{2}}{\binom{10}{5}} = \frac{(20)(6)}{252} = \frac{10}{21}$$

The correct answer is **E**.

SOA Sample Question 439 Explanation

Let profit in 1st year be X, and profit in 2nd year be Y.

$$P(X > 0) = .8531 \quad (1)$$

A cumulative probability of .8531 corresponds to $z = 1.05$. So:

$$P(Z \leq 1.05) = .8531$$

$$P(Z \geq -1.05)) = .8531 \quad (2)$$

Comparing (1) and (2) we see that $X = 0$ corresponds to $Z = -1.05$.

So, if the common mean of both years is μ, then:

$$z = \frac{X - \mu}{\sigma_X}$$

$$-1.05 = \frac{0 - \mu}{\sigma_X}$$

$$\sigma_X = .9524\mu$$

$$P(Y > 0) = .9192 \quad (3)$$

A cumulative probability of .9192 corresponds to $z = 1.4$. So:

$$P(Z \leq 1.4) = .9192$$

$$P(Z \geq -1.4)) = .9192 \quad (4)$$

Comparing (3) and (4) we see that $X = 0$ corresponds to $Z = -1.4$.

$$-1.4 = \frac{0 - \mu}{\sigma_Y}$$

$$\sigma_Y = .7143\mu$$

Let $T = X + Y$. Then T is normal with mean $\mu + \mu = 2\mu$, and variance:

${\sigma_X}^2 + {\sigma_Y}^2 = (.9524\mu)^2 + (.7143\mu)^2 = 1.4173\mu^2$.

We are to find $P(T > 0)$. So, we need to change 0 in standard score:

$$z = \frac{0 - 2\mu}{\sqrt{1.4173\mu^2}} = -1.68$$

$$P(T > 0) = P(Z > -1.68) = P(Z < 1.68) = .9535$$

The correct answer is **D**.

SOA Sample Question 440 Explanation

Median of an exponential distribution with mean λ is $\lambda \ln 2$.

$$400 = \lambda \ln 2$$

$$\lambda = 577$$

The correct answer is **E**.

SOA Sample Question 441 Explanation

We know the if X is uniformly distributed on $[a, b]$, then

$$Var\ X = \frac{(b-a)^2}{12}$$

Let H be the hospital charges. Then H is uniform $[0, b]$.

$$SD(H) = \sqrt{\frac{(b-0)^2}{12}}$$

$$9.6 = \sqrt{\frac{(b)^2}{12}}$$

$$92.16 = \frac{b^2}{12}$$

$$b = 33.26$$

Let S be surgery charges. Then S is uniform $[0, 2b-6] = [0, 2(33.26) - 6] = [0, 60.52]$.

$$SD(H) = \sqrt{\frac{(60.52-0)^2}{12}}$$

$$= 17.5$$

The correct answer is **C**.

SOA Sample Question 442 Explanation

X is uniform on $[a, b]$.

$$P(X > 8) = \frac{b-8}{b-a}$$

$$.6 = \frac{b-8}{b-a} \quad (1)$$

$$P(X > 8) = \frac{b-11}{b-a}$$

$$.2 = \frac{b-11}{b-a} \quad (2)$$

Dividing (1) by (2) we get:

$$3 = \frac{b-8}{b-11}$$

$$b = 12.5$$

Substituting this value in (2) we get:

$$.2 = \frac{12.5-11}{12.5-a}$$

$$a = 5$$

$$Var\,X = \frac{(b-a)^2}{12} = \frac{(12.5-5)^2}{12} = 4.69$$

The correct answer is **B**.

SOA Sample Question 443 Explanation

$$E(|X-2|) = \int_{-\infty}^{\infty} |x-2|\, f(x)\, dx$$

$$|X-2| = \begin{cases} X-2, & if\ X > 2 \\ 2-X, & if\ X < 2 \end{cases}$$

$$E(|X-2|) = \int_{-\infty}^{2} (2-x) f(x)\, dx + \int_{2}^{\infty} (x-2)\, f(x)\, dx$$

$$= \int_{1}^{2} (2-x)\left(\frac{x-1}{4}\right) dx + \int_{2}^{3} (x-2)\left(\frac{x-1}{4}\right) dx + \int_{3}^{5} (x-2)\left(\frac{5-x}{4}\right) dx$$

$$= \frac{1}{4}\int_{1}^{2} (2-x)(x-1)\, dx + \frac{1}{4}\int_{2}^{3} (x-2)(x-1)\, dx + \frac{1}{4}\int_{1}^{2} (x-2)(5-x)\, dx$$

The correct answer is **E**.

SOA Sample Question 444 Explanation

$$p(x,y) = \frac{-2x - 4y + xy + 8}{18}, \quad x = 1,2,3, \quad y = 0,1$$

$$E\left(\frac{Y}{X}\right) = \sum_{x,y} \left(\frac{y}{x}\right) p(x,y)$$

$$= \left(\frac{0}{1}\right) p(1,0) + \left(\frac{0}{2}\right) p(2,0) + \left(\frac{0}{3}\right) p(3,0) + \left(\frac{1}{1}\right) p(1,1) + \left(\frac{1}{2}\right) p(2,1) + \left(\frac{1}{3}\right) p(3,1)$$

$$= 0 + 0 + 0 + 1\left(\frac{3}{18}\right) + \frac{1}{2}\left(\frac{2}{18}\right) + \frac{1}{3}\left(\frac{1}{18}\right)$$

$$= .241$$

The correct answer is **C**.

SOA Sample Question 445 Explanation

Let the 3 risk factors be A, B, C which are represented by the ellipses below:

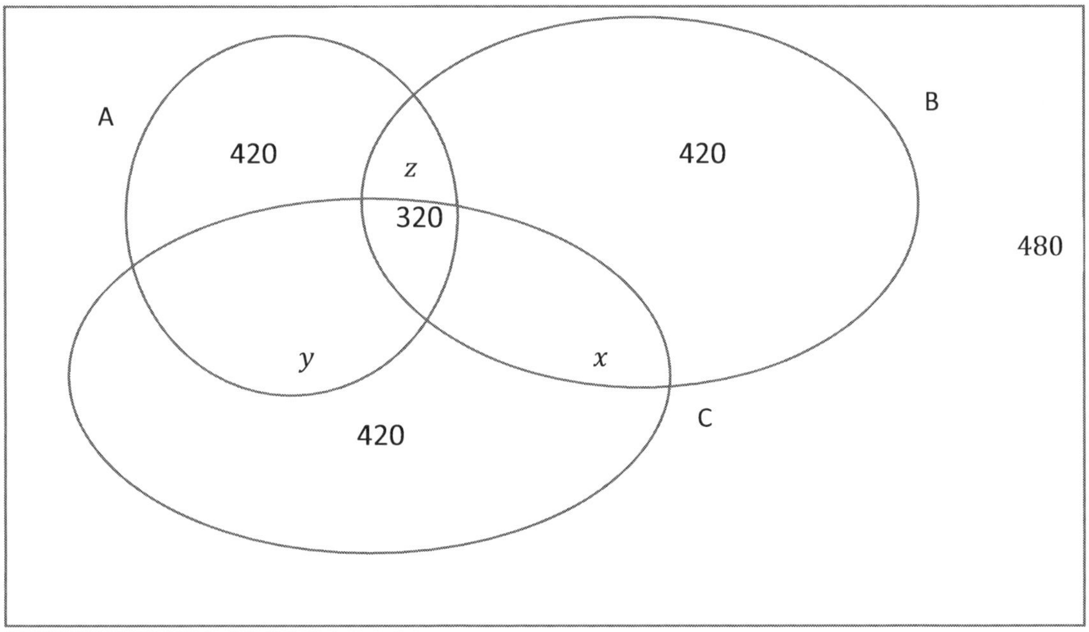

By the given conditions:

$$y + z + 420 + 320 = 1200$$

$$x + z + 420 + 320 = 1200$$

$$x + y + 420 + 320 = 1200$$

These equations simplify to:

$$y + z = 460 \quad (1)$$

$$x + z = 460 \quad (2)$$

$$x + y = 460 \quad (3)$$

Adding (1), (2), and (3) we get:

$$2x + 2y + 2z = 1380$$

$$x + y + z = 690$$

$$Total = x + y + z + 3(420) + 320 + 480 = 690 + 3(420) + 320 + 480$$

$$= 2750$$

The correct answer is **C**.

SOA Sample Question 446 Explanation

Let M be the length of the morning route.

Let A be the length of the afternoon route.

$$E[A] = \sum a\, f(a)$$

$$E[A] = 0(0+0+y) + 5(2x+2x+0) + 30(3x+0+0)$$

$$E[A] = 110x$$

$$11 = 110x$$

$$x = .1$$

Also, sum of all the 9 probabilities in the table must be 1.

$$0 + 2x + 3x + 0 + 2x + 0 + y + 0 + 0 = 1$$

$$7x + y = 1$$

$$y = 1 - 7x$$

$$= 1 - 7(.1)$$

$$= .3$$

So, the marginal density of A is tabulated below:

A	$f(A)$
0	$0 + 0 + y = .3$
5	$2x + 2x + 0 = 4x = 4(.1) = .4$
30	$3x + 0 + 0 = 3x = 3(.1) = .3$

From calculator:

$$SD(A) = 12.6095$$

$$Var\ A = 12.6095^2$$

$$= 159$$

The correct answer is **A**.

Tools needed for problems 447-458

Pdf of a uniform $[a,b]$ distribution is:

$$f(x) = \frac{1}{b-a}, \quad a < x < b$$

For a uniform $[a,b]$ distribution, if $a < c < d < b$, then:

$$P(X \le c) = \frac{c-a}{b-a}, \quad and \quad P(c \le X \le d) = \frac{d-c}{b-a}$$

If Y is a function of X, then the expected value of Y is:

$$E[Y] = \int_{-\infty}^{\infty} y\, f(x)\, dx$$

If X and Y are random variables, their joint probability function is defined as:

$$F(a,b) = P(X \le a, Y \le b)$$

$$Coefficient\ of\ Variation = \frac{SD}{Mean}$$

Variance of a Poisson variable equals its mean.

For any random variables X, Y, Z:

$$E(aX + bY + cZ) = aE[X] + bE[Y] + cE[Z]$$

Also, if X, Y, Z are independent random variables then for any constants a, b, c:

$$Var(aX + bY + cZ) = a^2 VarX + b^2 VarY + c^2 VarZ$$

If $a > 0$, $\lim_{x\to\infty} e^{-ax} = 0$ and $\lim_{x\to\infty} xe^{-ax} = 0$

$$Integration\ by\ parts\ shortcut: \quad \int (x+k)e^{ax}dx = \frac{(x+k)e^{ax}}{a} - \frac{e^{ax}}{a^2}$$

Central Limit Theorem

If population is normal, or if sample size, $n > 30$, then the sampling distribution of means and sums is approximately normal with mean and standard deviation:

$$\mu_{sum} = n\mu$$

$$\sigma_{sum} = \sqrt{n}\,\sigma$$

where μ and σ are mean and standard deviation of each of n identical variables.

$$Var\ X = E[X^2] - [E(X)]^2$$

Pmf of a Poisson variable with mean m is:

$$f(x) = \frac{m^x e^{-m}}{x!}, \quad x = 0,1,2,\ldots$$

SOA Sample Question 447 Explanation

Let X be the amount of money stolen. The pdf of X is:

$$f(x) = \frac{1}{1000}, \quad 0 < x < 1000$$

Let Y be the claim payment. Then:

$$Y = \begin{cases} 0, & X \leq 400 \\ p(X - 400), & X > 400 \end{cases}$$

The expected value of the claim payment is:

$$E[Y] = \int_{-\infty}^{\infty} y\, f(x)\, dx$$

$$90 = \int_{400}^{1000} p(x - 400)\left(\frac{1}{1000}\right) dx$$

$$90000 = p \int_{400}^{1000} (x - 400)\ dx$$

$$90000 = p\frac{(x - 400)^2}{2}\Big|_{400}^{1000}$$

$$180000 = p[(1000 - 400)^2 - (400 - 400)^2]$$

$$p = .5$$

$$= 50\%$$

The correct answer is **D**.

SOA Sample Question 448 Explanation

Let X be the loss amount for each of the 2 losses. The pdf of each loss is:

$$f(x) = \frac{1}{10}, \quad 0 < x < 10$$

Let A be the claim payment under policy A.

Let B be the claim payment under policy B.

$$A = X - 5, \;\; 5 \le X \le 10$$

$$B = X - 5, \;\; 5 \le X \le 10$$

$$M = Maximum\,\{A, B\}$$

We are to find $P(M \le t)$.

Now the maximum of 2 numbers is less than t if both numbers are less than t. So:

$$P(M \le t) = P(A \le t \; and \; B \le t)$$

$$= P(A \le t) \cdot P(B \le t)$$

$$= P(X - 5 \le t) \cdot P(X - 5 \le t)$$

$$= P(X \le t + 5) \cdot P(X \le t + 5)$$

$$= \frac{t + 5 - 0}{10 - 0} \cdot \frac{t + 5 - 0}{10 - 0}$$

$$= \left(\frac{t + 5}{10}\right)^2$$

The correct answer is **D**.

SOA Sample Question 449 Explanation

We are given the cumulative probabilities. Note that:

$$F(a,b) = P(X \leq a, Y \leq b)$$

$$F(5,9) = p(3,8) + p(4,8) + p(5,8) + p(3,9) + p(4,9) + p(5,9)$$

$$F(5,8) = p(3,8) + p(4,8) + p(5,8)$$

If we subtract these we get:

$$F(5,9) - F(5,8) = p(3,9) + p(4,9) + p(5,9) \qquad (1)$$

The right side of (1) is almost what we are to find, except that it has an extra term $p(3,9)$.

$$F(3,9) = p(3,8) + p(3,9) \qquad (2)$$

Subtracting (1) and (2) we get:

$$F(5,9) - F(5,8) - F(3,9) = p(4,9) + p(5,9) - P(3,8) \qquad (3)$$

So, although we were able to remove the unwanted term $p(3,9)$, we ended up having another unwanted term $p(3,8)$. However, this is easy to remove because:

$$F(3,8) = p(3,8) \qquad (4)$$

Adding (3) and (4) we get:

$$F(5,9) - F(5,8) - F(3,9) + F(3,8) = p(4,9) + p(5,9)$$

$$.84 - .67 - .65 + .53 = p(4,9) + p(5,9)$$

$$.05 = p(4,9) + p(5,9)$$

The correct answer is **E**.

SOA Sample Question 450 Explanation

Variance of a Poisson variable equals its mean.

$$Coefficient\ of\ Variation = \frac{SD}{Mean} \quad (1)$$

$$E[U] = E(100X + 150Y + 200Z)$$

$$Mean\ (U) = 100E[X] + 150E[Y] + 200E[Z]$$

$$= 100\lambda + 150\lambda + 200\lambda$$

$$= 450\lambda \quad (2)$$

$$Var[U] = Var(100X + 150Y + 200Z)$$

$$= 100^2 VarX + 150^2 VarY + 200^2 VarZ$$

$$= 10000\lambda + 22500\lambda + 40000\lambda$$

$$= 72500\lambda$$

$$SD(U) = \sqrt{Var\ (U)}$$

$$= \sqrt{72500\lambda} \quad (3)$$

Substituting (2) and (3) in (1) we get:

$$CV(U) = \frac{\sqrt{72500\lambda}}{450\lambda}$$

$$.9 = \frac{\sqrt{72500\lambda}}{450\lambda}$$

$$.81 = \frac{72500\lambda}{202500\lambda^2}$$

$$\lambda = .44$$

The correct answer is **A**.

SOA Sample Question 451 Explanation

Let the 3 lifetimes be Y_1, Y_2, Y_3. We will need to find the cdf of any of these.

$$F(x) = P(Y \le x)$$

$$= \int_{-\infty}^{x} f(y)\, dy$$

$$= \int_{5}^{x} e^{-(y-5)}\, dy$$

$$= -e^{-(y-5)}\Big|_5^x$$

$$= -e^{-(x-5)} + e^{-(5-5)}$$

$$= 1 - e^{-(x-5)} \qquad (1)$$

We are to find the expected value of the minimum of these lifetimes. Let:

$$X = \min\{Y_1, Y_2, Y_3\}$$

So, we are to find $E[X]$. We next find the cdf of X.

$$G(x) = P(X \le x)$$

$$= 1 - P(X > x)$$

$$= 1 - P(Y_1 > x, Y_2 > x, Y_3 > x)$$

$$= 1 - [1 - P(Y_1 \le x)] \cdot [1 - P(Y_2 \le x)] \cdot [1 - P(Y_3 \le x)]$$

$$= 1 - [1 - F(x)] \cdot [1 - F(x)] \cdot [1 - F(x)]$$

$$= 1 - \left[1 - 1 + e^{-(x-5)}\right]^3$$

$$= 1 - e^{-3(x-5)}$$

Pdf of X is found by taking the derivative of its cdf. So:

$$g(x) = G'(x) = 3e^{-3(x-5)}, \qquad x > 5$$

$$E[X] = \int_{-\infty}^{\infty} x\, g(x)\, dx = 3\int_{5}^{\infty} x\, e^{-3(x-5)} dx = 3e^{15}\int_{5}^{\infty} x\, e^{-3x} dx$$

Using integration by parts, or the shortcut we have already used so many times we get:

$$E[X] = 3e^{15}\left[\frac{x\, e^{-3x}}{-3} - \frac{e^{-3x}}{9}\right]_5^{\infty} = 3e^{15}\left[\frac{5\, e^{-15}}{3} + \frac{e^{-15}}{9}\right] = 3e^{15}\,\frac{16e^{-15}}{9} = \frac{16}{3} = 5.33$$

The correct answer is **B**.

SOA Sample Question 452 Explanation

Let each claim amount be X. By Central Limit Theorem:

$$\mu_{sum} = n\mu$$

$$= 25(1000)$$

$$= 25000$$

$$\sigma_{sum} = \sqrt{n}\,\sigma$$

$$= \sqrt{25}\,(625)$$

$$= 3125$$

We are to find $P(Sum > 27500)$.

So, we change 27500 into standard score:

$$z = \frac{27500 - 25000}{3125}$$

$$= .8$$

$$P(Sum > 27500) = P(z > .8)$$

$$= 1 - P(z \leq .8)$$

$$= 1 - .7881$$

$$= .2119$$

The correct answer is **D**.

SOA Sample Question 453 Explanation

Let X be the amount of each loss. The pdf of X is:

$$f(x) = \frac{1}{480}, \quad 0 < x < 480$$

Let Y be the claim payment, and p be the constant percentage mentioned. Then:

$$Y = \begin{cases} 0, & X \le 240 \\ p(X-240), & X > 240 \end{cases}$$

The expected value of the claim payment is:

$$E[Y] = \int_{-\infty}^{\infty} y\, f(x)\, dx$$

$$= \int_{240}^{480} p(x-240)\left(\frac{1}{480}\right) dx$$

$$= \frac{p}{480} \frac{(x-240)^2}{2} \Big|_{240}^{480}$$

$$= 60p$$

$$E[Y^2] = \int_{-\infty}^{\infty} y^2 f(x)\, dx$$

$$= \int_{240}^{480} p^2(x-240)^2\left(\frac{1}{480}\right) dx$$

$$= \frac{p^2}{480} \frac{(x-240)^3}{3} \Big|_{240}^{480}$$

$$= 9600p^2$$

$$Var\, Y = E[Y^2] - [E(Y)]^2$$

$$2000 = 9600p^2 - [60p]^2$$

$$2000 = 6000p^2$$

$$p = .577$$

$$= 57.7\%$$

The correct answer is **C**.

SOA Sample Question 454 Explanation

Let X be the amount of each loss. The pdf of X is:

$$f(x) = \frac{1}{1000}\,, \quad 0 < x < 10000$$

Let Y be the claim payment. Then:

$$Y = X - 400, \;\; X > 400$$

$$P(Y > 300 \mid Y < 400) = P(X - 400 > 300 \mid X - 400 < 400)$$

$$= P(X > 700 \mid X < 800) = \frac{P(X > 700 \; and \; X < 800)}{P(X < 800)}$$

$$= \frac{P(700 < X < 800)}{P(X < 800)} = \frac{\frac{800-700}{1000-0}}{\frac{800-0}{1000-0}} = .125$$

The correct answer is **B**.

SOA Sample Question 455 Explanation

Let L be the event that a policy-holder is low-risk.

Let H be the event that a policy-holder is high-risk.

Let X be the number of hospitalizations, which is Poisson.

Pmf of a Poisson variable with mean m is:

$$f(x) = \frac{m^x e^{-m}}{x!}\,, \quad x = 0,1,2, \ldots$$

Thus, the probability of no hospitalization is:

$$f(0) = e^{-m}$$

$$P(\,X = 0|L) = f(0 \mid L) = e^{-.05}$$

$$P(\,X = 0|H) = f(0 \mid H) = e^{-.3}$$

We are to find $P(L \mid X = 0)$. By Baye's theorem:

$$P(L \mid X = 0) = \frac{P\,(L \,\&\, X = 0|L)}{P\,(L \,\&\, X = 0|L) + P\,(H \,\&\, X = 0|H)}$$

$$= \frac{P\,(L\,)\,P\,(X = 0|L)}{P\,(L\,)\,P(\,X = 0|L) + P\,(H)\;\,P(\,X = 0|H)}$$

$$= \frac{.7e^{-.05}}{.7e^{-.05} + .3e^{-.3}}$$

$$= .75$$

The correct answer is **D**.

SOA Sample Question 456 Explanation

This is hypergeometric. The 3 types given can be collapsed to 2 types: normal and not normal.

We have a total of **6 normal**, and $3 + 1 =$ **4 not normal**.

$$P(2\ normal\ out\ of\ 4) = \frac{(\#\ of\ ways\ to\ get\ 2\ normal)(\#\ of\ ways\ to\ get\ 2\ not\ normal)}{(\#\ of\ ways\ to\ get\ 4\ total)}$$

$$= \frac{\binom{6}{2}\binom{4}{2}}{\binom{10}{4}} = .429$$

The correct answer is **E**.

SOA Sample Question 457 Explanation

Let Y be the number of doctor's visits. Pmf of a Poisson variable with mean k is:

$$f(y) = \frac{k^y e^{-k}}{y!}, \quad y = 0,1,2, \ldots$$

The probability of no visit given $X = k$ is:

$$f(0 \mid X = k) = e^{-k}$$

To find the probability of at least one visit, we find the probability of no visit and complement it.

$$f(0) = \sum_{k=0}^{3} P(X = k)\, f(0|X = k) = .28(1) + .12e^{-1} + .42e^{-2} + .18e^{-3} = .39$$

$$P(\,at\ least\ 1\ visit) = 1 - f(0) = 1 - .39 = .61$$

The correct answer is **C**.

SOA Sample Question 458 Explanation

Let a be the number of units of Asset A.

Then the number of units of Asset B will be $10 - a$.

Let T be the total payoff.

$$T = aX + (10 - a)Y$$

Since X and Y are independent, so:

$$Var\ T = a^2\ Var\ X + (10 - a)^2\ Var\ Y = a^2\ (30) + (10 - a)^2\ (20)$$

$$= 30a^2 + 20(100 - 20a + a^2) = 50a^2 - 400a + 2000$$

This is the equation of a parabola, so the required minimum will be the vertex:

$$a = -\frac{-400}{2(50)} = 4$$

The correct answer is **C**.

Tools needed for problems 459-469

Central Limit Theorem

If population is normal, or if sample size, $n > 30$, then the sampling distribution of means and sums is approximately normal with mean and standard deviation:

$$\mu_{\bar{X}} = \mu$$

$$\sigma_{\bar{X}} = \frac{\sigma}{\sqrt{n}}$$

where μ and σ are mean and standard deviation of each of n identical variables.

For Poisson, standard deviation is square root of the mean.

Pmf of a Poisson variable with mean m is:

$$f(x) = \frac{m^x e^{-m}}{x!}, \quad x = 0,1,2, \dots$$

Geometric distribution gives the probability of the 1st success requiring k independent trials, each with success probability p. The pmf is:

$$f(k) = p(1-p)^{k-1}, \qquad k = 1,2,3, \dots$$

The geometric sum of n terms, with first term a, and common ratio r equals:

$$\frac{a(1-r^n)}{1-r}$$

Mean and variance of a uniform (a, b) distribution is:

$$E[X] = \frac{b+a}{2}, \qquad Var\ X = \frac{(b-a)^2}{12}$$

For an exponential distribution, standard deviation and mean are equal.

The cdf of an exponential distribution with mean m is:

$$F(x) = 1 - e^{-x/m}$$

Mean and variance of a binomial distribution are:

$$E[X] = np, \qquad Var\ X = np(1-p)$$

Correlation coefficient between 2 variables is:

$$\rho = \frac{Cov\ (X, Y)}{\sigma_X \sigma_Y}$$

For discrete random variables:

$$E[XY] = \sum_{x,y} x\, y\, P(X = x,\ Y = y)$$

pth percentile is the variable value p such that $P(X \leq p) = p/100$

SOA Sample Question 459 Explanation

For Poisson, standard deviation is square root of the mean.

By Central Limit Theorem:

$$\mu_{\bar{X}} = \mu = 16$$

$$\sigma_{\bar{X}} = \frac{\sigma}{\sqrt{n}} = \frac{\sqrt{16}}{\sqrt{64}} = .5$$

We are to find $P(15 < \bar{X} < 18)$. So, we need to change 15 and 18 to standard scores:

$$z_{15} = \frac{15 - 16}{.5} = -2$$

$$z_{18} = \frac{18 - 16}{.5} = 4$$

$$P(15 < \bar{X} < 18) = P(-2 < z < 4) = P(z < 4) - P(z < -2) = P(z < 4) - P(z > 2)$$

$$= P(z < 4) - [1 - P(z \le 2)] = 1 - [1 - .9772] = .9772$$

This rounds to Choice **D**.

SOA Sample Question 460 Explanation

$$P(N = 1 \mid N \ge 1 \,\&\, X \ \le 2000) = \frac{P(N = 1 \,\&\, N \ge 1 \,\&\, X \le 2000)}{P(N \ge 1 \ and \ X \le 2000)}$$

$$= \frac{P(N = 1 \,\&\, X \le 2000)}{P(N \ge 1 \,\&\, X \le 2000)} \quad (1)$$

$$F(x) = 1 - \frac{500n}{x}, \quad X \ge 500n$$

This means that

$$P(X \le 2000 \mid N = 1) = 1 - \frac{500(1)}{2000} = .75$$

$$P(X \le 2000 \mid N = 2) = 1 - \frac{500(2)}{2000} = .5$$

$$P(N = 1 \ and \ X \le 2000) = P(N = 1)\, P(X \le 2000 \mid N = 1) = .08(.75) = .06 \quad (2)$$

$$P(N = 2 \ and \ X \le 2000) = P(N = 2)\, P(X \le 2000 \mid N = 1) = .02(.5) = .01$$

$$P(N \ge 1 \ and \ X \le 2000) = P(N = 1 \ and \ X \le 2000) + P(N = 2 \ and \ X \le 2000)$$

$$= .06 + .01 = .07 \quad (3)$$

Substituting (2) and (3) in (1) we get:

$$P(N = 1 \mid N \ge 1 \,\&\, X \ \le 2000) = \frac{.06}{.07} = \frac{6}{7}$$

The correct answer is **E**.

SOA Sample Question 461 Explanation

Pmf of a Poisson variable with mean m is:

$$f(x) = \frac{m^x e^{-m}}{x!}, \quad x = 0,1,2,\ldots$$

$$f(0) = e^{-m} = e^{-1.5}$$

Hence the mean of this distribution is $m = 1.5$

$$f(x) = \frac{1.5^x e^{-1.5}}{x!}$$

$$P(X \geq 4 \mid X \geq 1) = \frac{P(X \geq 4 \text{ and } X \geq 1)}{P(X \geq 1)} = \frac{P(X \geq 4)}{P(X \geq 1)}$$

$$= \frac{1 - P(X < 4)}{1 - P(X < 1)} = \frac{1 - [f(0) + f(1) + f(2) + f(3)]}{1 - f(0)}$$

$$= \frac{1 - e^{-1.5} - \frac{1.5^1 e^{-1.5}}{1!} - \frac{1.5^2 e^{-1.5}}{2!} - \frac{1.5^3 e^{-1.5}}{3!}}{1 - e^{-1.5}} = .084$$

The correct answer is **B**.

SOA Sample Question 462 Explanation

If X be the number of people tested until positive, X is geometric with success parameter p.

So, the probability of the 1st success requiring k independent trials is:

$$f(X = k) = p(1-p)^{k-1}, \qquad k = 1,2,3,\ldots$$

$$P(X \leq m \mid X \leq n) = \frac{P(X \leq m \text{ and } X \leq n)}{P(X \leq n)} = \frac{P(X \leq m)}{P(X \leq n)}$$

$$= \frac{f(1) + f(2) + f(3) + \cdots + f(m)}{f(1) + f(2) + f(3) + \cdots + f(m)} = \frac{\sum_{k=1}^{m} p(1-p)^{k-1}}{\sum_{k=1}^{n} p(1-p)^{k-1}} \qquad (1)$$

The geometric sum of n terms, with first term a, and common ratio r equals:

$$\frac{a(1 - r^n)}{1 - r}$$

In each of the above sums, $1st\ term = p, \quad ratio = 1 - p$

So, using the geometric sum formula for both the numerator and denominator, (1) becomes:

$$P(X \leq m \mid X \leq n) = \frac{\frac{p(1-(1-p)^m)}{1-(1-p)}}{\frac{p(1-(1-p)^n)}{1-(1-p)}} = \frac{1-(1-p)^m}{1-(1-p)^n}$$

The correct answer is **E**.

SOA Sample Question 462 Explanation

Let X be the number of repair jobs. Pmf of a Poisson variable with mean m is:

$$f(x) = \frac{m^x e^{-m}}{x!}\ ,\ \ x = 0,1,2,\ldots$$

$$P(X \geq 1) = 1 - P(X < 1)$$

$$0.10 = 1 - f(0)$$

$$.1 = 1 - e^{-m}$$

$$e^{-m} = .9$$

$$m = -\ln .9 = .1054$$

The pmf then becomes:

$$f(x) = \frac{.1054^x(.9)}{x!}$$

$$P(X \geq 2) = 1 - P(X < 2) = 1 - f(0) - f(1) = 1 - .9 - .1054(.9) = .0052$$

The correct answer is **A**.

SOA Sample Question 464 Explanation

Variance of a uniform (a, b) distribution is:

$$Var = \frac{(b-a)^2}{12}$$

$$SD = \sqrt{\frac{(b-a)^2}{12}} = \frac{b-a}{2\sqrt{3}} \quad (1)$$

Interquartile range is the range of the middle 50% of the data. Since the distribution is uniform, the middle 50% means the length of the middle half of the interval, or simply half the length:

$$IQR = \frac{b-a}{2} \quad (2)$$

Dividing (1) by (2) we get:

$$\frac{SD}{IQR} = \frac{\frac{b-a}{2\sqrt{3}}}{\frac{b-a}{2}}$$

$$= \frac{1}{\sqrt{3}}$$

The correct answer is **A**.

SOA Sample Question 465 Explanation

Let X be the loss, and d be the deductible.

For an exponential distribution, standard deviation and mean are equal.

Hence, the cdf in this case is:

$$F(x) = 1 - e^{-x/\sigma}$$

We are given that:

$$P(X > d + \sigma) = .2$$

$$1 - P(X \leq d + \sigma) = .2$$

$$1 - F(d + \sigma) = .2$$

$$e^{-(d+\sigma)/\sigma} = .2$$

$$e^{-\frac{d}{\sigma}-1} = .2$$

$$e^{-\frac{d}{\sigma}}e^{-1} = .2$$

$$e^{-\frac{d}{\sigma}} = .2e \quad (1)$$

We are to find $P(X > d + .5\sigma)$.

$$P(X > d + .5\sigma) = 1 - P(X \leq d + .5\sigma)$$

$$= 1 - F(d + .5\sigma)$$

$$= e^{-(d+.5\sigma)/\sigma}$$

$$= e^{-\frac{d}{\sigma}-.5}$$

$$= e^{-\frac{d}{\sigma}}e^{-.5} \quad (2)$$

Substituting (1) in (2) we get:

$$P(X > d + .5\sigma) = .2e(e^{-.5})$$

$$= .33$$

The correct answer is **A**.

SOA Sample Question 466 Explanation

Let X be the number of auto claims in a year.

Let Y be the number of homeowners claims in a year.

Then X is binomial with $n = 1,\ p = .1$

$$E[X] = np = 1(.1) = .1$$

$$\sigma_X = \sqrt{np(1-p)} = \sqrt{1(.1)(1-.1)} = .3$$

And Y is binomial with $n = 1,\ p = .05$

$$E[Y] = np = 1(.05) = .05$$

$$\sigma_Y = \sqrt{np(1-p)} = \sqrt{1(.05)(1-.05)} = .218$$

We are to find $P(X = 1, Y = 1)$. For this, note that:

$$E[XY] = \sum_{x,y=0,1} x\, y\, P(X = x,\ Y = y)$$

$$= 1(1)\, P(X = 1, Y = 1) + 0 + 0 + 0$$

$$= P(X = 1, Y = 1)$$

Thus, we need to find $E[XY]$. For this, we use the definition of the correlation coefficient:

$$\rho = \frac{E[XY] - E[X]E[Y]}{\sigma_X \sigma_Y}$$

$$.3 = \frac{E[XY] - .1(.05)}{.3(.218)}$$

$$E[XY] = .025$$

The correct answer is **C**.

SOA Sample Question 467 Explanation

$$p(x,y) = \frac{x - 2y - xy + 3}{18}, \quad x = 1,2,3,\ \ y = 0,1$$

$$E\left[\frac{Y}{X}\right] = \sum_{x,y} \frac{y}{x}\, p(x,y)$$

$$= 0 + 0 + 0 + \frac{1}{1}p(1,1) + \frac{1}{2}p(2,1) + \frac{1}{3}p(3,1) = \frac{1}{18} + \frac{1}{2}\left(\frac{1}{18}\right) + \frac{1}{3}\left(\frac{1}{18}\right)$$

$$= \frac{11}{108}$$

The correct answer is **B**.

SOA Sample Question 468 Explanation

Let H be the event of being high-risk, and L be the event of being low-risk.

$$P(H) = .1$$

$$P(L) = 1 - .1$$

$$= .9$$

Let T be the event of having accident this year, and N be the event of having accident next year.

We are to find $P(N|T)$.

$$P(N|T) = \frac{P(N \,\&\, T)}{P(T)} \quad (1)$$

We first evaluate the numerator using the Law of Total Probability.

$$P(N \,\&\, T) = P(N \,\&T|H)P(H) + P(N \,\&T|L)P(L)$$

$$= .12(.12).1 + .05(.05).9$$

$$= .00369 \quad (2)$$

Denominator of (1), by Law of total probability, is:

$$P(T) = P(T|H)P(H) + P(T|L)P(L)$$

$$= .12(.1) + .05(.9)$$

$$= .057 \quad (3)$$

Substituting (2) and (3) in (1) we get:

$$P(N|T) = \frac{.00369}{.057}$$

$$= .065$$

The correct answer is **D**.

SOA Sample Question 469 Explanation

Mean and variance of a uniform (a, b) distribution is:

$$E[X] = \frac{b+a}{2}$$

$$12 = \frac{b+a}{2}$$

$$24 = b + a$$

$$b = 24 - a \quad (1)$$

75th percentile it the variable value p such that:

$$P(X \leq p) = .75$$

So here, since the 75th percentile is 18, so:

$$P(X \leq 18) = .75$$

$$\frac{18 - a}{b - a} = .75$$

Using (1), the above equation becomes:

$$\frac{18 - a}{24 - a - a} = .75$$

$$18 - a = .75(24 - 2a)$$

$$18 - a = 18 - 1.5a$$

$$a = 0$$

Substituting in (1) we get:

$$b = 24$$

Variance of the uniform distribution is:

$$Var\ X = \frac{(b-a)^2}{12}$$

$$= \frac{(24-0)^2}{12}$$

$$= 48$$

The correct answer is **C**.

Tools needed for problems 470-485

Geometric distribution with success probability p can also be characterized as the number of failures x before the first success. In this case the pmf is:

$$f(x) = p(1-p)^x, \qquad x = 0,1,2,3,\ldots$$

Variance of geometric distribution with this characterization is:

$$Var\ X = \frac{1-p}{p^2}$$

Also, geometric distribution is memoryless. Thus, if a geometric distribution is shifted to the right, its variance is the same as that of the original distribution. In other words:

$$Var\ (X \mid X > k) = Var\ X.$$

Pmf of Binomial is:

$$f(x) = \binom{n}{x} p^x (1-p)^{n-x}, \ x = 0,1,2,\ldots$$

$$\binom{n}{r} = \frac{n!}{r!\,(n-r)!}$$

For a uniform $[a, b]$ distribution, the pdf, mean, and variance are:

$$f(x) = \frac{1}{b-a}, \qquad a \le x \le b, \quad E[X] = \frac{a+b}{2}, \quad Var\ X = \frac{(b-a)^2}{12}$$

$$Var\ Y = E[Y^2] - [E(Y)]^2$$

Variance of an exponential distribution equals square of it is mean.

If X, Y are independent, then:

$$Var(X+Y) = Var\ X + Var\ Y$$

If X has a discrete uniform distribution over n points, then the probability of each point is:

$$f(x) = \frac{1}{n}$$

Variance of binomial is $np(1-p)$.

pth percentile, x_p, is the variable value up to which the cumulative probability is p.

For a uniform $[a, b]$ distribution, the pth percentile follows the equation:

$$\frac{x_p - a}{b-a} = p$$

SOA Sample Question 470 Explanation

$$p(x) = \frac{1}{5}\left(\frac{4}{5}\right)^x, x = 0,1,2,3,...$$

We know that this is a geometric distribution of the form :

$$f(x) = p(1-p)^x, \qquad k = 0,1,2,3,...$$

Variance of geometric distribution with this characterization is:

$$Var\ X = \frac{1-p}{p^2} = \frac{1-\frac{1}{5}}{\left(\frac{1}{5}\right)^2} = 20$$

Using the memoryless property of geometric distribution we have:

$$Var\ (X|X > 1) = Var\ X$$

$$= 20$$

The correct answer is **C**.

SOA Sample Question 471 Explanation

$$p(x,y) = \frac{2x+y+1}{36}, \qquad x = 0,1,2, \ \ y = 0,1,2$$

To find variance of marginal distribution, we first need to find the marginal distribution $f(x)$.

$$f(0) = p(0,0) + p(0,1) + p(0,2) = \frac{1}{36} + \frac{2}{36} + \frac{3}{36} = \frac{1}{6}$$

$$f(1) = p(1,0) + p(1,1) + p(1,2) = \frac{3}{36} + \frac{4}{36} + \frac{5}{36} = \frac{1}{3}$$

$$f(2) = p(2,0) + p(2,1) + p(2,2) = \frac{5}{36} + \frac{6}{36} + \frac{7}{36} = \frac{1}{2}$$

We can now use calculator to find the standard deviation.

In the first column of the Multiview calculator enter the x values: 0,1,2.

In the second column enter the corresponding $f(x)$ values. We get:

$$SD = .745356$$

$$Var = SD^2$$

$$= .56$$

The correct answer is **A**.

SOA Sample Question 472 Explanation

Let X be the number of games won. Then X is binomial with $p = .6$. So, the pmf is:

$$f(x) = \binom{n}{x}.6^x(.4)^{n-x}$$

We are given that:

$$f(3) = 5f(2)$$

$$\binom{n}{3}.6^3(.4)^{n-3} = 5\binom{n}{2}.6^2(.4)^{n-2}$$

Dividing both sides by $.6^2(.4)^{n-3}$ we get:

$$\binom{n}{3}(.6) = 5\binom{n}{2}(.4)$$

$$\frac{n!}{3!\,(n-3)!}(.6) = \frac{n!}{2!\,(n-2)!}(2)$$

$$(n-2)!\,(.6) = 6(n-3)!$$

$$(n-2)(n-3)!\,(.6) = 6(n-3)!$$

$$n - 2 = 10$$

$$n = 12$$

The correct answer is **D**.

SOA Sample Question 473 Explanation

Let X be the loss. Then:

$$f(x) = 1, \quad 0 < x < 1.$$

Let Y be a random variable representing the payment under the deductible d. Then:

$$Y = \begin{cases} 0, & X < d \\ X - d, & X > d \end{cases}$$

$$E[Y] = \int_{-\infty}^{\infty} y\, f(x)\, dx$$

$$.245 = \int_{d}^{1} (x - d)\,(1) dx$$

$$.245 = \frac{(x-d)^2}{2} \Big|_d^1$$

$$.245 = \frac{(1-d)^2}{2}$$

$$1 - d = \pm .7$$

$$d = .3, \qquad 1.7$$

But maximum loss is 1, so a deductible of 1.7 makes no sense. Thus:

$$d = .3$$

$$E[Y^2] = \int_{-\infty}^{\infty} y^2\, f(x)\, dx$$

$$= \int_{.3}^{1} (x - .3)^2\,(1) dx$$

$$= \frac{(x-.3)^3}{3} \Big|_{.3}^1$$

$$= .1143$$

$$Var\, Y = E[Y^2] - [E(Y)]^2$$

$$= .1143 - .245^2$$

$$= .054$$

The correct answer is **B**.

SOA Sample Question 474 Explanation

Let X be the number of years between now and the 1st ticket.

Let Y be the number of years between the 1st ticket and 2nd ticket. Then:

X is exponentially distributed with mean .8

Y is exponentially distributed with mean $m > .8$

Since variance of an exponential distribution equals square of it is mean, so:

$$Var\ X = .8^2$$

$$= .64$$

$$Var\ Y = m^2$$

We are given that X, Y are independent.

We are also given that:

$$Var\ (X + Y) = 2.65$$

We know that if X, Y are independent then:

$$Var(X + Y) = Var\ X + Var\ Y$$

$$2.65 = .64 + m^2$$

$$m = 1.42$$

The correct answer is **C**.

SOA Sample Question 475 Explanation

$$P(X \geq x) = \frac{1}{4}\left(1 - \frac{x-2}{3}\right)^2 \quad , \quad x = 1,2,3,4$$

Putting in the given values we get:

$$P(X \geq 1) = .4444$$

$$P(X \geq 2) = .25$$

$$P(X \geq 3) = .1111$$

$$P(X \geq 4) = .0278$$

Since X is the number of defectives in a shipment of 4, so X can be 0,1,2,3, or 4. Let:

$$p(X = k) = p(k), \quad k = 0,1,2,3,4$$

Then we have:

$$p(0) = 1 - P(X \geq 1)$$

$$= 1 - .4444$$

$$= .5556$$

$$p(1) = P(X \geq 1) - P(X \geq 2)$$

$$= .4444 - .25$$

$$= .1944$$

$$p(2) = P(X \geq 2) - P(X \geq 3)$$

$$= .25 - .1111$$

$$= .1389$$

$$p(3) = P(X \geq 3) - P(X \geq 4)$$

$$= .1111 - .0278$$

$$= .0833$$

$$p(4) = P(X \geq 4)$$

$$= .0278$$

$$E[X] = \sum x\, p(x)$$

$$= 0(.5556) + 1(.1944) + 2(.1389) + 3(.0833) + 4(.0278)$$

$$= .83$$

The correct answer is **A**.

SOA Sample Question 476 Explanation

$$P(\geq\ 2\ disabilities|\leq\ 1\ death) = \frac{P(\geq\ 2\ disabilities\ and\ \leq\ 1\ death)}{P(\leq\ 1\ death)}$$

$$= \frac{P(2\ or\ 3\ disabilities\ and\ 0\ or\ 1\ death)}{P(0\ or\ 1\ death)}$$

$$= \frac{P(2\ disabilities\ and\ 0\ or\ 1\ death) + P(3\ disabilities\ and\ 0\ or\ 1\ death)}{P(0\ death) + P(1\ death)}$$

$$= \frac{(.07 + .05) + (.04 + .02)}{(.45 + .08 + .07 + .04) + (.09 + .06 + .05 + .02)}$$

$$= .21$$

The correct answer is **D**.

SOA Sample Question 477 Explanation

$$f(t) = kt,\ \ 0 < t < 20$$

$$P(T < 10\,|\,T > 5) = \frac{P(T < 10\ and\ T > 5)}{P(T > 5)} = \frac{P(5 < T < 10)}{P(T > 5)} \qquad (1)$$

$$P(5 < T < 10) = \int_5^{10} f(t)\,dt = \int_5^{10} kt\,dt = k\frac{t^2}{2}\Big|_5^{10} = k\left(\frac{10^2}{2} - \frac{5^2}{2}\right) = 37.5k \qquad (2)$$

$$P(T > 5) = \int_5^{\infty} f(t)\,dt = \int_5^{20} kt\,dt = k\frac{t^2}{2}\Big|_5^{20} = k\left(\frac{20^2}{2} - \frac{5^2}{2}\right) = 187.5k \qquad (3)$$

Substituting (2) and (3) in (1) we get:

$$P(T < 10\,|\,T > 5) = \frac{37.5k}{187.5k} = .2$$

The correct answer is **B**.

SOA Sample Question 478 Explanation

Because of independence, the variance of the total cost C will equal the sum of the variances of the individual costs.

$$Var\ C = 1^2 + 2^2 + 3^2 + 4^2 = 30$$

$$SD\ (C) = \sqrt{30} = 5.5$$

The correct answer is **B**.

SOA Sample Question 479 Explanation

Let H be the hospitalization charges and S be the surgery charges.

We are given that H is uniform $[0, c]$. So, its standard deviation is.:

$$SD(H) = \sqrt{\frac{(c-0)^2}{12}}$$

$$4\sqrt{3} = \frac{c}{\sqrt{12}}$$

$$c = 24$$

We are also given that S is uniform $[0, 3c - 18]$.

Substituting the value of c we get $[0, 3(24) - 18] = [0, 54]$. Thus, its standard deviation is:

$$SD(S) = \sqrt{\frac{(54-0)^2}{12}}$$

$$= 15.6$$

The correct answer is **D**.

SOA Sample Question 480 Explanation

Let X be the number of accidents of one policy holder. We have the following table:

x	$f(x)$	$xf(x)$	$x^2 f(x)$
0	$.8$	0	0
1	$.16$	$.16$	$.16$
2	$.04$	$.08$	$.16$
		$E[X] = \sum x\, f(x) = .24$	$E[X^2] = \sum x^2\, f(x) = .32$

$$Var\ X = E[X^2] - [E(X)]^2$$

$$= .32 - .24^2$$

$$= .2624$$

Since the variances of the policyholders are independent, so the total variance T of all 144 policyholders will be the sum of the individual ones.

$$Var\ T = 144(.2624)$$

$$= 37.79$$

The correct answer is **C**.

SOA Sample Question 481 Explanation

Let N be the number of days to repair, and C be the repair cost. We have the following table:

n	$f(n)$	$C(n) = n^2 + n + 1$
1	$.2$	3
2	$.2$	7
3	$.2$	13
4	$.2$	21
5	$.2$	31

$$E[C] = E[N^2 + N + 1] = \sum (n^2 + n + 1)\, f(n) = 15$$

The correct answer is **E**.

SOA Sample Question 482 Explanation

Let X be the delay time. It is uniformly distributed. So:

$$f(x) = \frac{1}{b-a}, \qquad a \le x \le b$$

$$E[X] = \frac{a+b}{2}$$

$$3 = \frac{a+b}{2}$$

$$b = 6 - a \quad (1)$$

$$Var\ X = \frac{(b-a)^2}{12}$$

$$1 = \frac{(b-a)^2}{12} \quad (2)$$

Substituting (1) in (2) we get:

$$1 = \frac{(6-a-a)^2}{12}$$

$$12 = (6-2a)^2$$

$$6 - 2a = \pm\sqrt{12}$$

$$a = 1.27,\ \ 4.73$$

If $a = 1.27$, then (1) gives $b = 4.73$

If $a = 4.73$, then (1) gives $b = 1.27$

Looking at the pdf, we know that a should be less than b. Thus $a = 1.27$

Again looking at the pdf, we see that a is the smallest possible value of delay.

The correct answer is **B**.

SOA Sample Question 483 Explanation

Let X be the number of patients having disease A. Then X is binomial.

$$Var\ X = np(1-p)$$

$$9 = 100p(1-p)$$

$$.09 = p(1-p)$$

We can solve this as a quadratic equation but we can also see by inspection that $p = .1\ or\ .9$.

But since we are given that $p < .5$, so we have $p = .1$

This is probability that a patient will have disease A, and also probability of having disease B.

$$P(patient\ has\ at\ least\ one\ disease) = 1 - P(none\ of\ the\ 2\ diseases) = 1 - .9(.9) = .19$$

Let Y be the number of patients having at least one disease. This is binomial $n = 100,\ q = .19$

$$Var\ Y = nq(1-q) = 100(.19)(1-.19) = 15.39$$

The correct answer is **A**.

SOA Sample Question 484 Explanation

Let X be the Denver salaries which are uniform $[25, 90]$.

Let Y be the Philadelphia salaries which are uniform $[45, x]$.

Let Z be the Salt Lake City salaries which are uniform $[10, x/3]$.

40th percentile, p_{40}, of X is the point up to which the cumulative probability is .4. So:

$$\frac{p_{40} - 25}{90 - 25} = .4$$

$$p_{40} = 51$$

20th percentile, p_{20}, of Y is the point up to which the cumulative probability is .2.

$$\frac{p_{20} - 45}{x - 45} = .2$$

$$\frac{51 - 45}{x - 45} = .2$$

$$x = 75$$

Median, m, of Z is the point up to which the cumulative probability is .5. So:

$$\frac{m - 10}{\frac{x}{3} - 10} = .5$$

$$\frac{m - 10}{\frac{75}{3} - 10} = .5$$

$$m = 17.5$$

The correct answer is **B**.

SOA Sample Question 485 Explanation

Let X be the loss which is uniform $[a, 2a]$.

40th percentile, p_{40}, of X is the point up to which the cumulative probability is .4. So:

$$\frac{p_{40} - a}{2a - a} = .4$$

$$p_{40} - a = .4a$$

$$p_{40} = 1.4a \quad (1)$$

80th percentile, p_{80}, of X is the point up to which the cumulative probability is .8.

$$\frac{p_{80} - a}{2a - a} = .8$$

$$p_{80} - a = .8a$$

$$p_{80} = 1.8a \quad (2)$$

pth percentile, x_p, is the variable value up to which the cumulative probability is p.

$$\frac{x_p - a}{2a - a} = p$$

$$x_p - a = ap$$

$$x_p = a(p + 1) \quad (3)$$

We are given that:

$$\frac{p_{40}}{x_p} = \frac{x_p}{p_{80}} \quad (4)$$

Substituting (1), (2), and (3) in (4) we get:

$$\frac{1.4a}{a(p + 1)} = \frac{a(p + 1)}{1.8a}$$

$$(p + 1)^2 = 2.52$$

$$p + 1 = \pm 1.587$$

$$p = .587 \; or - 2.587$$

Probability cannot be negative. So,

$$p = .587$$

$$= 58.7\%$$

The correct answer is **B**.

Tools needed for problems 486-505

N has ***negative binomial distribution*** if the probability of needing n trials to get r successes is:

$$P(N = n) = \binom{n-1}{r-1} p^r (1-p)^{n-r}$$

where p is the probability of success in each trial.

The pdf, and pth percentile, x_p of a of uniform $[a, b]$ distribution are given as follows:

$$f(x) = \frac{1}{b-a}, \quad a < x < b, \qquad \frac{x_p - a}{b-a} = \frac{p}{100}$$

If X is a continuous random variable with pdf $f(x)$, then the expected value of a function $h(x)$ is

$$E[h(X)] = \int_{-\infty}^{\infty} h(x)\, f(x)\, dx$$

The pmf, expected value, and variance of binomial are:

$$f(x) = \binom{n}{x} p^x (1-p)^{n-x}, \qquad E[X] = np, \qquad Var\ X = np(1-p)$$

For a continuous random variable, pdf is the derivative of cdf.

Cdf of an exponential distribution with mean m is:

$$F(x) = 1 - e^{-\frac{x}{m}}$$

$$Var\ X = E[X^2] - (E[X])^2$$

The pdf and cdf of exponential distribution with mean m are:

$$f(x) = \frac{1}{m} e^{-x/m}, \quad x > 0, \qquad F(x) = 1 - e^{-x/m}$$

Pmf of Poisson with mean m is:

$$f(x) = \frac{m^x e^{-m}}{x!}, \qquad x = 0,1,2,3, \ldots$$

By ***hypergeometric***, if we have N items, of which a items are of type A, b items are of type B, then the probability of selecting n items, of which x items are of type A is:

$$\frac{\binom{a}{x}\binom{b}{n-x}}{\binom{N}{n}}$$

Geometric distribution gives the probability of the 1st success requiring k independent trials, each with success probability p. The pmf is:

$$f(k) = p(1-p)^{k-1}$$

The sum of N independent Poisson variables with means $k_1, k_2, \ldots, k_N$, is also Poisson with mean $k_1 + k_2 + \cdots + k_N$

SOA Sample Question 486 Explanation

$$P(a\ claim\ deos\ not\ exceed\ 1000) = 1 - .2 = .8$$

$$P(none\ of\ the\ 3\ claims\ exceed\ 1000) = .8(.8)(.8) = .512$$

$$P(\ at\ least\ one\ of\ the\ claims\ exceeds\ 1000) = 1 - P(none\ of\ the\ 3\ exceeds\ 1000)$$

$$= 1 - .512$$

$$= .488$$

The correct answer is **B**.

SOA Sample Question 487 Explanation

$$P(does\ not\ pass\ all\ 3) = 1 - P(passes\ all\ 3)$$

$$= 1 - .36$$

$$= .64$$

$$P(passes\ 2\ |does\ not\ pass\ all\ 3) = \frac{P(passes\ 2\ \&\ deos\ not\ pass\ all\ 3)}{P(does\ not\ pass\ all\ 3)}$$

$$= \frac{.48 - .36}{.64}$$

$$= .19$$

The correct answer is **B**.

SOA Sample Question 488 Explanation

This is a negative binomial distribution. The probability of rth success on nth trial is:

$$f(n) = \binom{n-1}{r-1} p^r (1-p)^{n-r}$$

$$f(8) = \binom{8-1}{3-1} .25^3 (1 - .25)^{8-3}$$

$$= .08$$

The correct answer is **B**.

SOA Sample Question 489 Explanation

Let X be the loss, Y be the benefit, and M be the maximum benefit.

Since X is uniform [0, 60], its pdf is:

$$f(x) = \frac{1}{60-10} = \frac{1}{50}, \qquad 10 < x < 60$$

$$Y = \begin{cases} X, & X \leq M \\ M, & X > M \end{cases}$$

$$E[Y] = \int_{-\infty}^{\infty} y\, f(x)\, dx$$

$$31 = \int_{-\infty}^{M} x\, f(x)\, dx + \int_{M}^{\infty} M\, f(x)\, dx = \int_{10}^{M} x \frac{1}{50}\, dx + \int_{M}^{60} \frac{M}{50}\, dx = \frac{x^2}{100}\Big|_{10}^{M} + \frac{M\,x}{50}\Big|_{M}^{60}$$

$$31 = \frac{M^2}{100} - \frac{10^2}{100} + \frac{60M}{50} - \frac{M^2}{50} = -.01M^2 + 1.2M - 1$$

$$.01M^2 - 1.2M + 32 = 0$$

$$M = \frac{1.2 \pm \sqrt{1.2^2 - 4(.01)(32)}}{2(.01)} = 80 \;\; or \;\; 40$$

Maximum benefit cannot be more than the maximum loss, which is 60. Hence $M = 40$

The correct answer is **C**.

SOA Sample Question 490 Explanation

Let X be the # of fragile packages that break, and Y be the # of non-fragile packages that break.

Since we are given that 2 packages break from the 4, we are to find $P(X = 2 \; given \; X + Y = 2)$.

$$P(X = 2 \mid X + Y = 2) = \frac{P(X = 2 \; and \; X + Y = 2)}{P(X + Y = 2)} = \frac{P(X = 2, Y = 0)}{P(X + Y = 2)} \qquad (1)$$

X is binomial with $n = 2,\ p = .1,$ and Y is binomial with $n = 2,\ p = .2$.

Numerator of (1) is the probability that both fragile packages break, and both non-fragiles don't.

$$P(X = 2, Y = 0) = .2(.2)(.9)(.9) = .0324 \qquad (2)$$

$$P(X + Y = 2) = P(X = 2, Y = 0) + P(X = 0, Y = 2) + P(X = 1, Y = 1)$$

$$= .0324 + .8(.8)(.1)(.1) + \binom{2}{1}.1^1(.9)^{2-1}\binom{2}{1}.2^1(.8)^{2-1} = .0964 \qquad (3)$$

Substituting (2) and (3) in (1) we get:

$$P(X = 2 \mid X + Y = 2) = \frac{.0324}{.0964} = .336$$

The correct answer is **D**.

SOA Sample Question 491 Explanation

This function is continuous in each portion as well as at the end points. So, the pdf in each interval is found by taking the derivative of the cdf:

$$f(x) = F'(x) = \begin{cases} 0, & x < 0 \\ \frac{3}{2}x^2, & 0 < x < 1 \\ 2 - x, & 1 < x < 2 \\ 0, & x > 2 \end{cases}$$

$$E[X] = \int_{-\infty}^{\infty} x\, f(x)\, dx = \int_0^1 x\, \frac{3}{2}x^2\, dx + \int_1^2 x(2-x) = \int_0^1 \frac{3}{2}x^3\, dx + \int_1^2 2x - x^2\, dx$$

$$= \frac{3}{8}x^4 \Big|_0^1 + \left(x^2 - \frac{x^3}{3}\right)\Big|_1^2$$

$$= \frac{3}{8} + \left(4 - \frac{8}{3}\right) - \left(1 - \frac{1}{3}\right) = \frac{25}{24}$$

The correct answer is **E**.

SOA Sample Question 492 Explanation

Cdf of an exponential distribution with mean m is:

$$F(x) = 1 - e^{-\frac{x}{m}} \quad (1)$$

$$P(X > 1) = 1 - P(X \leq 1)$$

$$.8 = 1 - F(1) = 1 - \left(1 - e^{-\frac{1}{m}}\right) = e^{-\frac{1}{m}}$$

$$-\frac{1}{m} = \ln .8$$

Substituting this in (1) we get:

$$F(x) = 1 - e^{x \ln .8} = 1 - e^{\ln(.8^x)} = 1 - .8^x$$

The correct answer is **C**.

SOA Sample Question 493 Explanation

$$P(Dis \geq 2 | Death \leq 1) = \frac{P(Dis \geq 2 \text{ and } Death \leq 1)}{P(Death \leq 1)}$$

$$= \frac{.04 + .03 + .03 + .02}{.51 + .08 + .04 + .03 + .09 + .06 + .03 + .02} = .14$$

The correct answer is **B.**

SOA Sample Question 494 Explanation

Being accident-free is binomial with $n = 12$. For binomial:

$$E[X] = np$$

$$9 = 12p$$

$$p = .75$$

$$Var\ X = np(1-p) = 9(1-.75) = 2.25$$

The correct answer is **C**.

SOA Sample Question 495 Explanation

$$E[X] = \int_{-\infty}^{\infty} x\, f(x)\, dx = \frac{3}{2}\int_{5}^{7} x(x-6)^2\ dx = \frac{3}{2}\int_{5}^{7} x^3 - 12x^2 + 36x\ dx$$

$$= \frac{3}{2}\left(\frac{x^4}{4} - 4x^3 + 18x^2\right)\Big|_5^7 = 6$$

$$E[X^2] = \int_{-\infty}^{\infty} x^2\, f(x)\, dx = \frac{3}{2}\int_{5}^{7} x^2(x-6)^2\ dx = \frac{3}{2}\int_{5}^{7} x^4 - 12x^3 + 36x^2\ dx$$

$$= \frac{3}{2}\left(\frac{x^5}{5} - 3x^4 + 12x^3\right)\Big|_5^7 = 36.6$$

$$Var\ X = E[X^2] - (E[X])^2 = 36.6 - 36 = .6$$

The correct answer is **B**.

SOA Sample Question 496 Explanation

$$P(a\ machine\ fails\ during\ 2nd\ year) = P(1 \le X \le 2) = F(2) - F(1)$$

$$= \left[1 - \left(\frac{1}{2}\right)^{\frac{1}{4}}\right] - \left[1 - \left(\frac{1}{1}\right)^{\frac{1}{4}}\right] = .1591$$

$$P(a\ machine\ does\ not\ fail\ during\ 2nd\ year) = 1 - .1591 = .8409$$

$$P(at\ least\ one\ fails\ during\ 2nd\ year) = 1 - P(none\ of\ the\ 3\ fail)$$

$$= 1 -.8409^3 = .4054$$

The payment of 1000 occurs if at least one of the 3 machines fail during 2nd year. So:

$$Expected\ pmt = 1000(.4054) = 405$$

The correct answer is **C**.

SOA Sample Question 497 Explanation

The given pdf is exponential with mean 6. So, the cdf is:

$$F(x) = 1 - e^{-x/6}$$

Let G be the cumulative distribution function of W.

Minimum of 3 losses will be greater than a number if and only if each of the 3 losses is greater than that number. You can verify this by taking some example numbers. So:

$$P(W > x) = P(X > x \,\&\, Y > x \,\&\, Z > x) = P(X > x) \cdot P(Y > x) \cdot P(X > x)$$

$$1 - P(W \le x) = [1 - P(X \le x)]\,[1 - P(Y \le x)]\,[1 - P(X \le x)]$$

$$1 - G(x) = [1 - F(x)]\,[1 - F(x)][1 - F(x)]$$

$$1 - G(x) = e^{-\frac{x}{6}} \cdot e^{-\frac{x}{6}} \cdot e^{-\frac{x}{6}}$$

$$1 - G(x) = e^{-x/2}$$

$$G(x) = 1 - e^{-x/2}$$

Thus, the cdf of W is the cdf of an exponential distribution with mean 2.

Hence W has an exponential distribution with expected value of 2.

The correct answer is **D**.

SOA Sample Question 498 Explanation

We are given that:

$$P(Under\ 25) = .55$$

$$P(Over\ 65) = .15$$

$$\Rightarrow P(25 - 65) = 1 - .55 - .15 = .3$$

$$P(Under\ 25 \mid Suburban) = \frac{P(Under\ 25\ and\ Suburban)}{P(Suburban)}$$

$$= \frac{P(Under\ 25\ and\ Suburban)}{P(Under\ 25\ and\ Suburban) + P(25 - 65\ and\ Suburban) + P(Over\ 65\ and\ Suburban)}$$

$$= \frac{.55\left(\frac{1}{5}\right)}{.55\left(\frac{1}{5}\right) + .3\left(\frac{3}{5}\right) + .15\left(\frac{7}{20}\right)}$$

$$= .32$$

The correct answer is **C**.

.

SOA Sample Question 499 Explanation

Pmf of Poisson with mean 4 is:

$$f(x) = \frac{4^x e^{-4}}{x!}, \qquad x = 0,1,2,3,\ldots$$

$$P(X > 3 \mid X \geq 1) = \frac{P(X > 3 \; and \; X \geq 1)}{P(X \geq 1)} = \frac{P(X > 3)}{P(X \geq 1)} = \frac{1 - P(X \leq 3)}{1 - P(X < 1)}$$

$$= \frac{1 - f(0) - f(1) - f(2) - f(3)}{1 - f(0)}$$

$$= \frac{1 - e^{-4} - 4e^{-4} - \frac{4^2 e^{-4}}{2!} - \frac{4^3 e^{-4}}{3!}}{1 - e^{-4}}$$

$$= .577$$

The correct answer is **B**.

SOA Sample Question 500 Explanation

Let p be the probability of being injury free in a season.

$$P(no \; injury \; in \; exactly \; 1 \; of \; 2) = P(injury \; in \; 1 \; not \; in \; 2) + P(injury \; in \; 2 \; and \; not \; in \; 1)$$

$$x = (1 - p)p + (1 - p)p$$

$$= 2p(1 - p)$$

$$p(1 - p) = \frac{x}{2} \qquad (1)$$

Let the event of being injury free in a year be Y. This is binomial with $n = 4$.

$$f(y) = \binom{4}{y} p^y (1 - p)^{4-y}$$

$$P(injury \; free \; in \; exactly \; 2 \; of \; next \; 4 \; seasons) = f(2) = \binom{4}{2} p^2 (1 - p)^{4-2}$$

$$= 6p^2(1 - p)^2$$

$$= 6[p(1 - p)]^2 \qquad (2)$$

Substituting (1) in (2) we get:

$$P(injury \; free \; in \; exactly \; 2 \; of \; next \; 4 \; seasons) = 6\left(\frac{x}{2}\right)^2 = 1.5x^2$$

The correct answer is **D**.

SOA Sample Question 501 Explanation

By hypergeometric, if we have N items, of which a items are of type A, b items are of type $B,$ then the probability of selecting n items, of which x items are of type A is:

$$f(x)=\frac{\binom{a}{x}\binom{b}{n-x}}{\binom{N}{n}}$$

Here, $N=$ Total homeowners $=$ 10

$$a=total\ insured=8$$

$$b=total\ uninsured=10-8=2$$

$$n=selected=3$$

$$P(at\ least\ 2\ insured\ in\ the\ 3\ selected)=f(2)+f(3)$$

$$=\frac{\binom{8}{2}\binom{2}{3-2}}{\binom{10}{3}}+\frac{\binom{8}{3}\binom{2}{3-3}}{\binom{10}{3}}=.933$$

The correct answer is **E**.

SOA Sample Question 502 Explanation

Let X be the loss which is given to be exponential. If the mean loss is m its cdf is:

$$F(x)=1-e^{-x/m}$$

Since plan A reimburses a loss up to 2, this plan will completely cover the hospitalization if the loss is less than or equal to 2. So:

$$P(plan\ A\ completely\ covers\ loss)=P(X\leq 2)$$

$$.15=F(2)$$

$$.15=1-e^{-2/m}$$

$$e^{-\frac{2}{m}}=.85$$

$$m=12.30626$$

Since plan A reimburses a loss up to 10, this plan will completely cover the hospitalization if the loss is less than or equal to 10. So:

$$P(plan\ B\ completely\ covers\ loss)=P(X\leq 10)=F(10)$$

$$=1-e^{-\frac{10}{12.30626}}=.556$$

The correct answer is **D**.

SOA Sample Question 503 Explanation

This is geometric. If 1st success requires k trials, each with success probability p the pmf is:

$$f(k) = p(1-p)^{k-1}$$

$$f(2) = p(1-p)^{2-1}$$

$$.16 = p(1-p)$$

We can solve this by arranging it as a standard quadratic equation, but we can also easily see by inspection that this equation is satisfied by $p = .2 \; or \; .8$.

But we are given that that success probability is less than .5. So, $p = .2$.

$$f(4) = .2(1-.2)^{4-1} = .1024$$

The correct answer is **D**.

SOA Sample Question 504 Explanation

pth percentile, x_p of a of uniform $[a, b]$ distribution is given as follows:

$$\frac{x_p - a}{b - a} = \frac{p}{100}$$

Thus, the 30th percentile of the loss is:

$$\frac{x_{30} - 2}{10 - 2} = \frac{30}{100}$$

$$x_{30} = 4.4$$

If 60% of loss is reimbursed, then 40% is not reimbursed. So:

$$30th\ percentile\ of\ unreimbursed\ loss = .4x_{30} = .4(4.4) = 1.76$$

The correct answer is **A**.

SOA Sample Question 505 Explanation

Sum of 7 independent Poisson variables each with mean .2 is Poisson with mean $.2(7) = 1.4$.

$$f(x) = \frac{1.4^x e^{-1.4}}{x!}$$

$$f(3) = \frac{1.4^3 e^{-1.4}}{3!}$$

$$= .113$$

The correct answer is **C**.

Tools needed for problems 506-530

The pdf, mean and variance of a **gamma** distribution with parameters α, θ are:

$$f(x) = cx^{\alpha-1}e^{-\frac{x}{\theta}}, \; x > 0, \qquad E[X] = \alpha\theta, \qquad Var\,(X) = \alpha\theta^2$$

The pth percentile of a random variable X is the value x_p such that:

$$F(x_p) = \frac{p}{100}$$

By Central Limit Theorem if a population is normal, or if sample size, $n > 30$, then the sampling distribution of means and sums is approximately normal with mean and standard deviation:

$$\mu_{\bar{X}} = \mu \qquad \sigma_{\bar{X}} = \frac{\sigma}{\sqrt{n}} \qquad \mu_{sum} = n\mu \qquad \sigma_{sum} = \sqrt{n}\,\sigma$$

where μ and σ are mean and standard deviation of each of n identical variables.

$$z = \frac{X-\mu}{\sigma}$$

$$Var\,Y = E[Y^2] - (E[Y])^2$$

Variance of an exponential distribution equals square of its mean

For Poisson, mean equals variance. The pmf of Poisson with mean m is:

$$f(x) = \frac{m^x e^{-m}}{x!}, \qquad x = 0,1,2,3,\ldots$$

If X, Y are discrete random variables with joint probability function $f(x)$, then:

$$E[X,Y] = \sum_{x,y} xy\, f(x,y)$$

A random variable X is said to have beta distribution with parameters a, b if its pdf is:

$$f(x) = \frac{\Gamma(a+b)}{\Gamma(a)\Gamma(b)} x^{a-1}(1-x)^{b-1}, \quad 0 < x < 1$$

If X, Y are random variables and a, b are constants then:

$$Var\,(aX + bY) = a^2 Var\,X + b^2 Var\,Y + 2ab\,Cov\,(X,Y)$$

If X, Y are independent random variables then $Cov\,(X,Y) = 0$.

The sum of 2 independent normal variables is also normal.

Cdf of an exponential distribution with mean k is:

$$F(x) = 1 - e^{-x/k}$$

$$P(A|B) = \frac{P(AB)}{P(B)}$$

By **addition rule**, $P(A \cup B) = P(A) + P(B) - P(AB)$

SOA Sample Question 506 Explanation

There are a total of 4 assignments: 1 outdoor and 3 indoors.

$$P(Bob\ gets\ 1\ out, 1\ in) = P(1st\ out, 2nd\ in) + P(1st\ in, 2nd\ out)$$

$$= \frac{1}{4}\left(\frac{3}{4}\right) + \frac{3}{4}\left(\frac{1}{4}\right)$$

$$= \frac{3}{8}$$

Since Ann does without replacement, so her distribution is hypergeometric.

$$P(Ann\ gets\ 1\ out\ 1\ in) = \frac{\binom{1}{1}\binom{3}{1}}{\binom{4}{2}}$$

$$= \frac{1}{2}$$

$$P(Bob\ |1\ in\ 1\ out) = \frac{P(Bob\ and\ 1\ in\ 1\ out)}{P(1\ in\ 1\ out)}$$

$$= \frac{P(Bob\ and\ 1\ in\ 1\ out)}{P(Bob\ and\ 1\ in\ 1\ out) + P(Ann\ and\ 1\ in\ 1\ out)}$$

$$= \frac{\frac{3}{8}}{\frac{3}{8} + \frac{1}{2}}$$

$$= \frac{3}{7}$$

The correct answer is **C**.

SOA Sample Question 507 Explanation

A random variable X is said to have gamma distribution with parameters α, θ if its pdf is:

$$f(x) = cx^{\alpha-1}e^{-\frac{x}{\theta}},\ \ x > 0$$

Hence, we are given a gamma distribution with $\alpha = 6,\ \ \theta = 1/.01$

$$E[X] = \alpha\theta$$

$$= \frac{6}{.01}$$

$$= 600$$

The correct answer is **E**.

SOA Sample Question 508 Explanation

$$f(x) = kx(1 + x^2)^{-9}, \qquad x \geq 0$$

We first find the constant by setting the integral to 1 on its entire range:

$$\int_0^\infty kx(1 + x^2)^{-9} dx = 1$$

$$\frac{k}{2}\frac{(1 + x^2)^{-8}}{-8}\Big|_0^\infty = 1$$

$$k = 16$$

The 2nd percentile of a random variable X is the value p such that:

$$F(p) = .02$$

$$\int_{-\infty}^p f(x)\, dx = .02$$

$$\int_0^p 16x(1 + x^2)^{-9} dx = .02$$

$$\frac{16}{2}\frac{(1 + x^2)^{-8}}{-8}\Big|_0^p = .02$$

$$-(1 + p^2)^{-8} + 1 = .02$$

$$(1 + p^2)^{-8} = .98$$

$$1 + p^2 = .98^{-1/8}$$

$$p^2 = .98^{-\frac{1}{8}} - 1$$

$$p = \sqrt{.98^{-1/8} - 1}$$

$$= .05$$

The correct answer is **D**.

SOA Sample Question 509 Explanation

There are 12 months in a year. So, if μ is the monthly mean, and σ is the monthly standard deviation of the profit, then by Central Limit Theorem:

$$\mu_{year} = 12\mu$$

$$\sigma_{year} = \sqrt{12}\,\sigma$$

where μ and σ are mean and standard deviation of each of n identical variables.

If Y is the yearly profit, we are given that. $P(Y > 0) = .6$.

Thus, we need to change 0 into z score.

$$z = \frac{0 - 12\mu}{\sqrt{12}\sigma} = \frac{-\sqrt{12}\mu}{\sigma}$$

$$P\left(z > \frac{-\sqrt{12}\mu}{\sigma}\right) = .6$$

$$P\left(z < \frac{\sqrt{12}\mu}{\sigma}\right) = .6$$

In table .5987 corresponds to $z = .25$, and .6026 corresponds to $z = .26$.

$$\frac{.6 - .5987}{.6026 - .5987} = .33$$

Thus, by interpolation, a cumulative probability of .6 corresponds to $z = .2533$. This gives:

$$\sqrt{12}\frac{\mu}{\sigma} = .2533$$

$$\frac{\mu}{\sigma} = .07$$

Let the monthly profit be X. We are to find $P(X > 0)$. Changing 0 in z-score we get:

$$z = \frac{0 - \mu}{\sigma} = -\frac{\mu}{\sigma} = -.07$$

$$P(X > 0) = P(z > -.07)$$

$$= P(z < .07)$$

$$= .5279$$

The correct answer is **B**.

SOA Sample Question 510 Explanation

There possible maximum values and their probabilities are tabulated below:

(x,y)	$Max\{x,y\}$	Probability
(0,0)	0	$.38$
(0,1),(1,0),(1,1)	1	$.16 + .10 + .11 = .37$
(0,2),(1,2),(2,2),(2,0),(2,1)	2	$.06 + .09 + .05 + .02 + .03 = .25$

$$E[Max\{X,Y\}] = 0(.38) + 1(.37) + 2(.25) = .87$$

The correct answer is **C**.

SOA Sample Question 511 Explanation

Let X be one of the losses. Then for some constant k:

$$f(x) = kx^5, \quad 0 < x < 1$$

We first find the constant by setting the integral to 1 on its entire range:

$$\int_0^1 kx^5 dx = 1$$

$$k\frac{x^6}{6}\Big|_0^1 = 1$$

$$k = 6$$

A loss will result in a payment if and only if it exceeds the deductible.

$$P(X \leq d) = \int_0^d 6x^5 dx = x^6\Big|_0^d = d^6$$

$$P(none\ of\ the\ losses\ pay) = P(both\ losses\ are\ less\ than\ or\ equal\ to\ deductible)$$

$$= P(X \leq d) \cdot P(X \leq d) = d^6 d^6 = d^{12}$$

$$P(at\ least\ 1\ loss\ pays) = 1 - P(none\ pays)$$

$$P = 1 - d^{12}$$

$$d^{12} = 1 - P$$

$$d = \sqrt[12]{1 - P}$$

The correct answer is **E**.

SOA Sample Question 512 Explanation

For Poisson, mean equals variance. So, variance is also 20.

$$Var\ X = E[X^2] - (E[X])^2$$

$$20 = E[X^2] - (20)^2$$

$$E[X^2] = 420$$

$$E[X^2] + E[X] = 420 + 20 = 440$$

The correct answer is **D**.

SOA Sample Question 513 Explanation

Let the distance of P from origin be X.

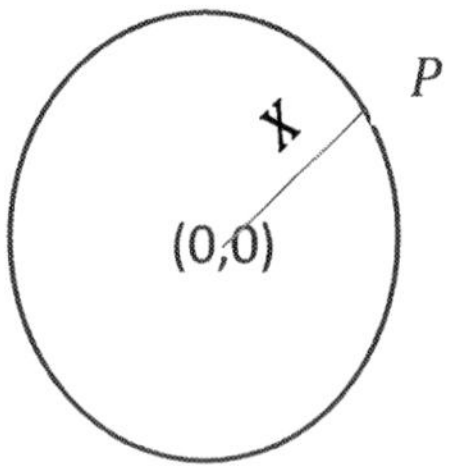

Let A be the area of the circle. Then:

$$A = \pi X^2$$

$$Var\ A = \pi^2 Var(X^2)$$

$$Var(X^2) = E[X^2]^2 - (E[X^2])^2 = E[X^4] - (E[X^2])^2$$

Since X is uniform [0,3], so:

$$f(x) = \frac{1}{3}, \quad 0 < x < 3$$

$$E[X^2] = \int_{-\infty}^{\infty} x^2 f(x) = \int_0^3 x^2 \left(\frac{1}{3}\right) dx = \frac{x^3}{9}\Big|_0^3 = 3$$

$$E[X^4] = \int_{-\infty}^{\infty} x^4 f(x) = \int_0^3 x^4 \left(\frac{1}{3}\right) dx = \frac{x^5}{15}\Big|_0^3 = \frac{81}{5}$$

$$Var(X^2) = E[X^4] - (E[X^2])^2 = \frac{81}{5} - 9 = \frac{36}{5}$$

$$Var\ A = \pi^2 Var(X^2) = \pi^2 \left(\frac{36}{5}\right)$$

The correct answer is **D**.

SOA Sample Question 514 Explanation

$$E[X,Y] = \sum_{x,y} xy\, f(x,y)$$

$$= 1(10)\frac{|10-6-2|}{18} + 2(10)\frac{|10-12-2|}{18} + 1(12)\frac{|12-6-2|}{18} + 2(12)\frac{|12-12-2|}{18}$$

$$+1(14)\frac{|14-6-2|}{18} + 2(14)\frac{|14-12-2|}{18} = \frac{280}{18} = \frac{140}{9}$$

The correct answer is **A**.

SOA Sample Question 515 Explanation

We first need to find k by setting the integral of pdf over its entire range equal to 1:

$$\int_0^1 k(1-x)^3 dx = 1$$

$$-k\frac{(1-x)^4}{4}\Big|_0^1 = 1$$

$$-k\left(0-\frac{1}{4}\right) = 1$$

$$k = 4$$

Median loss m is found by setting cumulative probability up to m equal to .5:

$$\int_0^m 4(1-x)^3 dx = .5$$

$$-4\frac{(1-x)^4}{4}\Big|_0^m = .5$$

$$-(1-m)^4 + 1 = .5$$

$$(1-m)^4 = .5$$

$$m = .1591\ millions = 159100$$

This rounds to 159000 to the nearest 1000.

Since median loss is less than the maximum benefit of 225000, it is also the median benefit.

Note that if this median had exceeded 225000, then the median benefit would be 225000.

The correct answer is **A**.

SOA Sample Question 516 Explanation

By Appendix 2 we recognize this as a beta distribution with:

$$k = \frac{\Gamma(13+2)}{\Gamma(13)\Gamma(2)} = \frac{\Gamma(15)}{\Gamma(13)\Gamma(2)} = \frac{14\,!}{12!\,1!} = 182$$

$$f(r) = 182r^{12}\,(1-r)\,, \quad 0 < r < 1$$

$$P(R > .9) = \int_{.9}^{1} 182r^{12}\,(1-r)\,dr = 182\int_{.9}^{1} r^{12} - r^{13}dr = 182\left[\frac{r^{13}}{13} - \frac{r^{14}}{14}\right]\Big|_{.9}^{1} = .415$$

The correct answer is **C**.

SOA Sample Question 517 Explanation

All the table probabilities should add up to 1:

$$.31 + p + .05 + .21 + .13 + q = 1$$

$$p + q = .3 \quad (1)$$

Marginal distributions are:

$$f_X(0) = .31 + p + .05 = p + .36$$

$$f_X(1) = .21 + .13 + q = .34 + q$$

$$f_Y(0) = .31 + .21 = .52$$

$$f_Y(1) = p + .13$$

$$f_Y(2) = q + .05$$

$$Expected\ Type\ I\ Cost = 0f_X(0) + 750f_X(1)$$

$$345 = 750(.34 + q)$$

$$q = .12$$

Substituting this in (1) we get $p = .18$.

$$E[Y] = \sum_y y\,f_Y(y) = 0f_Y(0) + 1f_Y(1) + 2f_Y(2) = 0 + 1(.18 + .13) + 2(.12 + .05) = .65$$

$$E[Y^2] = \sum_y y^2\,f_Y(y) = 0 + 1^2f_Y(1) + 2^2f_Y(2) = 0 + 1(.18 + .13) + 4(.12 + .05) = .99$$

$$Var\ Y = E[Y^2] - (E[Y])^2 = .99 - .65^2 = .57$$

The correct answer is **B**.

SOA Sample Question 518 Explanation

Let X be the number of earthquakes in the next decade. The pmf of Poisson with mean m is:

$$f(x) = \frac{m^x e^{-m}}{x!}$$

We are given that:

$$f(2) = .43f(1)$$

$$\frac{m^2 e^{-m}}{2!} = .43\frac{m^1 e^{-m}}{1!}$$

$$m = .86$$

$$P(X \geq 3) = 1 - P(X < 3)$$

$$= 1 - f(0) - f(1) - f(2)$$

$$= 1 - \frac{.86^0 e^{-.86}}{0!} - \frac{.86^1 e^{-.86}}{1!} - \frac{.86^2 e^{-.86}}{2!}$$

$$= .056$$

The correct answer is **D**.

SOA Sample Question 519 Explanation

Let X *and* Y be the durations of tornadoes in cities A and B respectively.

Since variance of an exponential distribution equals square of its mean, so:

$$Var\ X = 5^2 = 25$$

$$Var\ Y = 4^2 = 16$$

Let the total damage caused in both cities be T. Then:

$$T = damage\ in\ A + damage\ in\ B$$

$$= 1(X) + c(Y)$$

$$= X + cY$$

$$Var\ T = Var\ X + c^2 Var\ Y$$

$$5.2^2 = 25 + 16c^2$$

$$c = .36$$

The correct answer is **C**.

SOA Sample Question 520 Explanation

All possible values of variables and their probabilities are tabulated below:

(w,x,y)	$f(w,x,y)=k(x+y-w)$
(0,1,1)	$2k$
(0,1,2)	$3k$
(0,2,1)	$3k$
(0,2,2)	$4k$
(1,1,1)	k
(1,1,2)	$2k$
(1,2,1)	$2k$
(1,2,2)	$3k$

Sum of all these probabilities should be 1. So:

$$20k = 1$$

$$k = \frac{1}{20}$$

$$P(W=0,Y=1) = 2k+3k = 5k = \frac{5}{20} = .25$$

$$P(W=1,Y=1) = k+2k = 3k = \frac{3}{20} = .15$$

$$P(Y=1) = .25 + .15 = .4$$

$$P(W=0|Y=1) = \frac{P(W=0,Y=1)}{P(Y=1)} = \frac{.25}{.4} = \frac{5}{8}$$

$$P(W=1|Y=1) = \frac{P(W=1,Y=1)}{P(Y=1)} = \frac{.15}{.4} = \frac{3}{8}$$

$$E(W|Y=1) = \sum_w wf(w|y=1) = 0 + 1f(1|y=1) = \frac{3}{8}$$

$$E(W^2|Y=1) = \sum_w w^2 f(w|y=1) = 0 + 1^2 f(1|y=1) = \frac{3}{8}$$

$$Var(W|Y=1) = E(W^2|Y=1) - [E(W|Y=1)]^2$$

$$= \frac{3}{8} - \left(\frac{3}{8}\right)^2$$

$$= \frac{3}{8} - \frac{9}{64}$$

$$= \frac{15}{64}$$

The correct answer is **B**.

SOA Sample Question 521 Explanation

The sum of 2 independent normal variables is also normal with mean equal to the sum of two means, and variance equal to the sum of the two variances. Let $W = X + Y$.

$$E[W] = E[X] + E[Y] = 15 + 20 = 35$$

$$Var\ (W) = Var\ X + Var\ Y = 4^2 + 5^2 = 41$$

We need $P(W < 45)$. So, we need to change 45 into z-score.

$$z = \frac{45 - 35}{\sqrt{41}} = 1.56$$

$$P(W < 45) = P(z < 1.56)$$

$$= .9406$$

The correct answer is **D**.

SOA Sample Question 522 Explanation

Let X be the time in months until charged. Cdf of an exponential distribution with mean k is:

$$F(x) = 1 - e^{-x/k}$$

Median is the x-value that corresponds to a cumulative probability of .5. So:

$$.5 = 1 - e^{-\frac{1.733}{k}}$$

$$k = 2.5$$

$$P(median < X < mean) = P(1.733 < X < 2.5) = F(2.5) - F(1.733)$$

$$= \left(1 - e^{-\frac{2.5}{2.5}}\right) - \left(1 - e^{-\frac{1.733}{2.5}}\right)$$

$$= e^{-.6932} - e^{-1}$$

$$= .5 - e^{-1}$$

The correct answer is **A**.

SOA Sample Question 523 Explanation

81st percentile corresponds to a cumulative probability of .81.

In the exam table, $z = .87$ corresponds to a cumulative probability of .8078, and $z = .88$ corresponds to a cumulative probability of .8106. By interpolation:

$$\frac{.8 - .8078}{.8106 - .8078} = .8$$

So, the z-score for a cumulative probability of .81 is .878. So, 81st percentile of Policy II is:

$$.878 = \frac{x_{81} - 8000}{1.5k}$$

$$x_{81} = 1.317k + 8000$$

This is also the pth percentile of policy I. So the z-score for the pth percentile of Policy I is:

$$z = \frac{(1.317k + 8000) - 8000}{k} = 1.317$$

In the exam table, $z = 1.31$ corresponds to a cumulative probability of .9049, and $z = 1.32$ corresponds to a cumulative probability of .9066. Since $z = 1.317$ is .7 of the distance from the smaller of the two z values, so, by interpolation, the cumulative probability should also be .7 of the distance from the smaller of the two cumulative probabilities:

$$.9049 + .7(.9066 - .9049) = .906 = 90.6\%$$

The correct answer is **D**.

SOA Sample Question 524 Explanation

Since 15 out of a total of 35 have at least one of the two issues, so, by complement:

$$Number\ of\ people\ with\ neither\ blood\ pressure\ nor\ cholestrol = 35 - 15 = \mathbf{20}$$

Similar to the well-known formula $P(A\ or\ B) = P(A) + P(B) - P(A\ and\ B)$ we have:

$$\#\ with\ at\ least\ 1\ issue = \#\ of\ High\ blood + \#\ of\ High\ Cholestrol - \#\ with\ both\ issues$$

$$15 = 9 + 9 - \#\ with\ both\ issues$$

$$\#\ with\ both\ issues = \mathbf{3}$$

$$\#\ with\ only\ high\ blood = \#\ with\ high\ blood - \#\ with\ both\ issues = 9 - 3 = \mathbf{6}$$

$$\#\ with\ only\ high\ cholestrol = \#\ with\ high\ cholestrol - \#\ with\ both\ issues = 9 - 3 = \mathbf{6}$$

So, the total of 8 should have 4 high blood out of 6 high blood, 1 high cholesterol out of 6 high cholesterol, 2 both out of 3 both, and 1 neither out of 20 neither. So, the required number is:

$$\binom{6}{4}\binom{6}{1}\binom{3}{2}\binom{20}{1} = 5400$$

The correct answer is **C**.

SOA Sample Question 525 Explanation

We are only interested in viewers who regularly watch news.

Of these news watchers, .08 watch sports but not movies, and .22 watch movies but not sports.

Thus, from the regular news watchers, $.08 + .22 = .3$ watch exactly 1 of the entertainments.

Also, from the news watchers, .35 watch both sports and movies, that is, they watch 2 categories.

Finally, from the news watchers, .05 watch neither sports nor movies.

If we use the Multiview calculator, we don't need to change these into conditional probabilities.

In L1 column, enter the number of categories watched, that is, 0,1, and 2.

In L2, enter the corresponding probabilities, that is, .05, .3, and .35.

Find the population standard deviation using 1-var statistics:

$$\sigma = .6227$$

$$Var = \sigma^2$$

$$= .6227^2$$

$$= .388$$

The correct answer is **B**.

SOA Sample Question 526 Explanation

Let T be the total losses over the 50 territories.

For exponential distribution, standard deviation equals mean. By central limit theorem:

$$\mu_{sum} = n\mu \qquad \sigma_{sum} = \sqrt{n}\,\sigma$$

$$\mu_T = 50(100000) = 5000000$$

$$\sigma_T = \sqrt{50}\,(1-0000) = 707107$$

We need $P(T > 5.5\ M)$. So we need to change 5500000 into z score:

$$z = \frac{5500000 - 5000000}{707107} = .71$$

$$P(T > 5.5\ M) = P(z > .71)$$

$$= 1 - P(z \leq .71)$$

$$= 1 - .758$$

$$= .24$$

The correct answer is **C**.

SOA Sample Question 527 Explanation

$$Var\ (X+Y) = Var\ X + Var\ Y + 2Cov(X,Y)$$

$$10 = Var\ X + Var\ X + 2Cov(X,Y)$$

$$10 = 2Var\ X + 2Cov(X,Y)$$

$$Var\ X = 5 - Cov(X,Y) \quad (1)$$

$$Var\ (X-2Y) = (1)^2 Var\ X + (-2)^2 Var\ Y + 2(1)(-2)\ Cov\ (X,Y)$$

$$16 = Var\ X + 4Var\ X - 4\ Cov\ (X,Y)$$

$$16 = 5Var\ X - 4\ Cov\ (X,Y) \qquad (2)$$

Substituting (1) in (2) we get:

$$16 = 5[5 - Cov(X,Y)] - 4\ Cov\ (X,Y)$$

$$16 = 25 - 5Cov(X,Y) - 4\ Cov\ (X,Y)$$

$$Cov\ (X,Y) = 1$$

The correct answer is **D**.

SOA Sample Question 528 Explanation

Let A be the event of purchasing fire, and B be the event of purchasing flood policy.

By condition (i):

$$P(A \cup B)^C = .2 + P(AB)$$

$$1 - P(A \cup B) = .2 + P(AB)$$

$$P(A \cup B) = .8 - P(AB)$$

$$P(A) + P(B) - P(AB) = .8 - P(AB)$$

$$P(A) + P(B) = .8 \quad (1)$$

By condition (iii):

$$P(A|B) = 2P(B|A)$$

$$\Rightarrow \frac{P(AB)}{P(B)} = 2\frac{P(AB)}{P(A)}$$

$$\Rightarrow P(A) = 2P(B)$$

Substituting this in (1) we get:

$$2P(B) + P(B) = .8$$

$$P(B) = .27$$

The correct answer is **A**.

SOA Sample Question 529 Explanation

For Poisson, mean equals variance. Hence, the mean of 1 application is .25.

The mean of 2 applications will be $.25(2) = .5$

Let X be the number of errors in 2 applications. Then X is Poisson with mean .5.

$$f(x) = \frac{.5^x e^{-.5}}{x!}$$

$$P(X > 1) = 1 - P(X \leq 1)$$

$$= 1 - f(0) - f(1)$$

$$= 1 - \frac{.5^0 e^{-.5}}{0!} - \frac{.5^1 e^{-.5}}{1!}$$

$$= .09$$

The correct answer is **B**.

SOA Sample Question 530 Explanation

Sum will be 11 if one die shows 5 and the other one shows 6.

Let the 3 dice be called A, B, and C in the order that they are given.

Only A has a 5. So, the sum of 11 can occur if either A and B are chosen, or A and C are chosen. There are 3 possible pairs in 3 dice, so each pair has 1/3 probability of being picked.

If A and B are chosen, then 11 occurs if A shows 5 and B shows 6. The probability of this is:

$$p_1 = P(A, B \text{ are chosen}, \& \text{ A shows } 5 \text{ \& B shows } 6) = \frac{1}{3}\left(\frac{1}{6}\right)\left(\frac{2}{6}\right) = \frac{1}{54}$$

If A and C are chosen, then 11 occurs if A shows 5 and B shows 6. The probability of this is:

$$p_2 = P(A, C \text{ are chosen}, \& \text{ A shows } 5 \text{ \& C shows } 6) = \frac{1}{3}\left(\frac{1}{6}\right)\left(\frac{6}{6}\right) = \frac{1}{18}$$

The required probability is the sum of these 2:

$$p_1 + p_2 = \frac{1}{54} + \frac{1}{18}$$

$$= .074$$

The correct answer is **C**.

Tools needed for problems 531-554

If A, B are independent events then $P(AB) = P(A)\,P(B)$

By **hypergeometric,** if we have N items, of which a items are of type A, b items are of type B, then the probability of selecting n items, of which x items are of type A is:

$$\frac{\binom{a}{x}\binom{b}{n-x}}{\binom{N}{n}}$$

The pmf of Poisson with mean k is:

$$f(x) = \frac{k^x e^{-k}}{x!}$$

$$Var\,(aX + bY) = a^2 Var\,X + b^2 Var\,Y + 2ab\,Cov\,(X,Y)$$

If X, Y are independent, then $Cov\,(X,Y) = 0$.

By addition rule, $P(A \cup B) = P(A) + P(B) - P(AB)$.

Pmf of binomial is:

$$f(x) = \binom{n}{x} p^x (1-p)^{n-x}$$

If success probability of each trial in a **geometric distribution** is between 0 and 1, its **mode** is 1.

$$E[aX + bY + cZ] = aE[X] + bE[Y] + cE[Z]$$

If X, Y, Z are independent, then:

$$Var\,(aX + bY + cZ) = a^2 Var\,X + b^2 Var\,Y + c^2 Var\,Z$$

Pdf and cdf of an exponential distribution with mean m are:

$$f(x) = \frac{1}{m} e^{-x/m}, \qquad x > 0, \qquad F(x) = 1 - e^{-x/m}$$

Since exponential distribution is memoryless, so:

$$P(X \geq a + k | X \geq a) = P(X \geq k)$$

If $X_1, X_2, X_3, \ldots$are independent, then $Var(X_1 + X_2 + X_3 + \cdots) = Var\,X_1 + Var\,X_2 + \cdots$

Number of ways n people can be seated on a **round table** is $(n-1)!$

The rth percentile of a random variable with cdf $F(x)$ is the number p such that:

$$F(p) = \frac{r}{100}$$

For uniform $[a, b]$, the pdf, variance, and the rth percentile p are given by:

$$f(x) = \frac{1}{b-a}, \qquad a < x < b, \quad Var\,X = \frac{(b-a)^2}{12}, \qquad \frac{p-a}{b-a} = \frac{r}{100}$$

SOA Sample Question 531 Explanation

Let F be the event of a fire claim, and T be the event of a theft claim.

$$P(neither\ F\ nor\ T) = 1 - P(F \cup T) = 1 - [P(F) + P(T) - P(FT)] \quad (1)$$

Independence means $P(FT) = P(F)\,P(T)$, and then $P(neither\ F\ nor\ T) = p$. So (1) gives:

$$p = 1 - [P(F) + P(T) - P(F)\,P(T)]$$
$$= 1 - [.1 + .3 - .1(.3)]$$
$$= .63$$

Mutually exclusive means $P(FT) = 0$, and then $P(neither\ F\ nor\ T) = r$. So (1) gives:

$$r = 1 - [.1 + .3 - 0]$$
$$= .6$$
$$p - r = .63 - .6$$
$$= .03$$

The correct answer is **D**.

SOA Sample Question 532 Explanation

$$P(insured|fails) = \frac{P(insured\ and\ fails)}{P(fails)} = \frac{.8(.03)}{.05} = .48$$

The correct answer is **D**.

SOA Sample Question 533 Explanation

This is hypergeometric because accident probability of employees of each company is the same. By hypergeometric, if we have N items, of which a items are of type A, b items are of type B, then the probability of selecting n items, of which x items are of type A is:

$$f(x) = \frac{\binom{a}{x}\binom{b}{n-x}}{\binom{N}{n}}$$

Here, $N = 10,\ \ a = 6,\ \ b = 4,\ \ n = 3.$

$$P(at\ least\ 1\ of\ 3\ in\ B) = 1 - P(all\ 3\ from\ A) = 1 - f(3) = 1 - \frac{\binom{6}{3}\binom{4}{3-3}}{\binom{10}{3}} = .833$$

The correct answer is **E**.

SOA Sample Question 534 Explanation

Let X be the number of accidents in a year:

$$f(x) = \frac{.1^x e^{-.1}}{x!}$$

$$P(1st\ accident\ in\ 6th\ yr) = P(no\ accidents\ in\ 1st\ 5\ yrs\ and\ at\ least\ 1\ accident\ in\ 6th)$$

$$= [f(0)]^5[1 - f(0)] = (e^{-.1})^5(1 - e^{-.1}) = .05772$$

$$P(1st\ accident\ in\ 6th\ yr|none\ in\ 1st\ 2\ yrs) = \frac{P(1st\ in\ 6th\ yr\ and\ none\ in\ 1st\ 2)}{P(none\ in\ 1st\ 2)}$$

$$= \frac{P(1st\ accident\ in\ 6th\ yr)}{[f(0)]^2} = \frac{.05772}{(e^{-.1})^2} = .0705$$

The correct answer is **C**.

SOA Sample Question 535 Explanation

Let H be the losses under health, and D be the losses under dental insurance.

We are given that 20% of health, and 10% of dental losses are unreimbursed.

Then, the total unreimbursed loss is:

$$T = .2H + .1D$$

$$Var\ T = .2^2 Var\ H + .1^2 Var\ D = .04(40000) + .01(10000) = 1700$$

The correct answer is **A**.

SOA Sample Question 536 Explanation

Let X be the number rolled on the die.

$$P(A) = P(X < 5) = P(X = 1,2,3, or\ 4) = .3$$

$$P(B) = P(X < 4) = P(X = 1,2, or\ 3) = .1$$

$$P(C) = P(X = 6) = .7$$

Since $B \subseteq A$, so $A \cup B = A$. This gives: $P(A \cup B) = P(A) = .3$

Also note that $A \cap C = \phi,\ and\ B \cap C = \phi$. So:

$$P(A \cup C) = P(A) + P(C) - P(A \cap C) = .3 + .7 - 0 = 1$$

$$P(B \cup C) = P(B) + P(C) - P(B \cap C) = .1 + .7 - 0 = .8$$

$$P(A \cup B) + P(B \cup C) + P(A \cup C) = .3 + 1 + .8 = 2.1$$

The correct answer is **C**.

SOA Sample Question 537 Explanation

$$P(at\ least\ 1\ hurricane\ in\ a\ year) = 1 - P(no\ hurricane) = 1 - .75 = .25$$

$$P(evacuation\ in\ a\ year) = P(at\ least\ 1\ hurricane\ and\ evacuation) = .25(.35) = .0975$$

Let X be the number of times the actuary evacuates in the 3 years. Then X is binomial with:

$$n = 3, \quad p = .0875$$

$$f(x) = \binom{3}{x}.0875^x(1 - .0875)^{3-x}$$

$$P(X \geq 1) = 1 - f(0) = 1 - \binom{3}{0}.0875^0(1 - .0875)^{3-0} = .24$$

The correct answer is **C**.

SOA Sample Question 538 Explanation

This is a geometric distribution in which success probability of each trial is .0625.

If success probability of each trial in a geometric distribution is between 0 and 1, its mode is 1.

Since $0 < .0625 < 1$, so the mode is 1.

The correct answer is **A**.

SOA Sample Question 539 Explanation

$$\bar{X} = \frac{X_1 + X_2 + X_3}{3}$$

$$E[\bar{X}] = \frac{1}{3}(E[X_1] + E[X_2] + E[X_3]) = \frac{100 + 100 + 100}{3} = 100$$

$$Var[\bar{X}] = \frac{1}{9}(Var\ X_1 + Var\ X_2 + Var\ X_3) = \frac{\frac{27(1)}{2} + \frac{27(2)}{2} + \frac{27(3)}{2}}{9} = 9$$

$$\sigma_{\bar{X}} = \sqrt{9} = 3$$

We need $P(\bar{X} > 106)$. So, we need to change 106 into z-score.

$$z = \frac{106 - 100}{3} = 2$$

$$P(\bar{X} > 106) = P(z > 2)$$

$$= 1 - P(z \leq 2)$$

$$= 1 - \Phi(2)$$

The correct answer is **D**.

SOA Sample Question 540 Explanation

Since 60% are males, so 40% are females.

$$P(F|5\ year) = \frac{P(F\ and\ 5\ year)}{P(5\ year)} = \frac{P(F\ and\ 5\ year)}{P(F\ and\ 5\ year) + P(M\ and\ 5\ year)}$$

$$= \frac{.4(.2)}{.4(.2) + .6(.4)} = .25 = \frac{1}{4}$$

The correct answer is **B**.

SOA Sample Question 541 Explanation

Let X be the lifetime of the component.

$$F(x) = 1 - e^{-x/m}$$

Because of the memoryless property of exponential distribution, any conditional probability is just the same as the corresponding unconditional probability. Thus:

$$P(X \geq 15|X \geq 5) = P(X \geq 10)$$

$$.027 = 1 - P(X < 10) = 1 - F(10) = 1 - \left(1 - e^{-\frac{10}{m}}\right) = e^{-\frac{10}{m}}$$

$$\ln .027 = -\frac{10}{m}$$

$$m = 2.7686$$

$$P(X \geq 25|X \geq 5) = P(X \geq 20) = 1 - P(X < 20) = 1 - F(20)$$

$$= 1 - \left(1 - e^{-\frac{20}{2.7686}}\right) = .0007$$

The correct answer is **A**.

SOA Sample Question 542 Explanation

Let L be the number of low-risks. Then, number of high-risks is $76 - L$.

$$Var\ of\ 76\ empoloyees = Var\ of\ L\ low\ risks + Var\ of\ 76 - L\ high\ risks$$

$$43^2 = .5^2 + .5^2 + \cdots (L\ terms) + 5.5^2 + 5.5^2 + \cdots (76 - L\ terms)$$

$$= .25L + 30.25(76 - L)$$

$$1849 = .25L + 2299 - 30.25L$$

$$30L = 450$$

$$L = 15$$

The correct answer is **B**.

SOA Sample Question 543 Explanation

Let X be the reported loss and Y be the claim payment. Then:

$$Y = p(X - d) = pX - pd$$

We know that $Var\ (aX + c) = a^2 Var\ X$. So:

$$Var\ Y = p^2 Var\ X = p^2 v$$

The correct answer is **B**.

SOA Sample Question 544 Explanation

Let N be the number of claims and X be the total claim size. We need $P(X \geq 2000|N \geq 2)$.

$$P(X \geq 2000|N \geq 2) = \frac{P(N \geq 2\ and\ X \geq 2000)}{P(N \geq 2)}$$

$$= \frac{P(N = 2\ and\ X \geq 2000) + (N = 3\ and\ X \geq 2000)}{.2 + .1} \qquad (1)$$

If 2 claims occur, then the only way that $X \geq 2000$ is if both claims are 1000. So:

$$P(N = 2\ and\ X \geq 2000) = P(N = 2)\ P(both\ claims\ are\ 1000) = .2(.5)(.5) = .05 \qquad (2)$$

If 3 claims occur, then the total claim amount will be at least 2000 in the following cases:

<u>Case I</u>: Two of the 3 claims are 500 each, and the other claim is 1000. Since the claim of 1000 could be either the 1st, 2nd, or 3rd claim, the probability of this happening is:

$$3(.5)(.5)(.5) = .375$$

<u>Case II</u>: Two of the 3 claims are 1000 each, and the other claim is 500. Since the claim of 500 could be either the 1st, 2nd, or 3rd claim, the probability of this happening is:

$$3(.5)(.5)(.5) = .375$$

<u>Case III</u>: All the 3 claims are 1000 each. The probability of this happening is:

$$(.5)(.5)(.5) = .125$$

Summing up these 3 cases, we see that if 3 claims occur, then the probability of $X \geq 2000$ is:

$$P(N = 3\ and\ X \geq 2000) = P(N = 3)P(X \geq 2000|N = 3)$$

$$= .1(.375 + .375 + .125) = .0875 \qquad (3)$$

Substituting (2) and (3) in (1) we get:

$$P(X \geq 2000|N \geq 2) = \frac{.05 + .0875}{.3} = .46$$

The correct answer is **D**.

SOA Sample Question 545 Explanation

We are given an exponential distribution with mean 1000000. So:

$$F(x) = 1 - e^{-x/1000000}$$

15th percentile is the value x_{15} such that $F(x_{15}) = .15$

$$1 - e^{-\frac{x_{15}}{1000000}} = .15$$

$$e^{-\frac{x_{15}}{1000000}} = .85$$

$$x_{15} = 162519$$

95th percentile is the value x_{95} such that $F(x_{95}) = .95$

$$1 - e^{-\frac{x_{95}}{1000000}} = .95$$

$$e^{-\frac{x_{95}}{1000000}} = .05$$

$$x_{95} = 2995732$$

$$x_{95} - x_{15} = 2995732 - 162519$$

$$= 2833213$$

To the nearest 100000, this rounds to 2800000.

The correct answer is **D**.

SOA Sample Question 546 Explanation

Since 10% are defective, so 90% are fine.

For fine bolts, test is 40% accurate. So, it will show defective for 60% of fine bolts.

$$P(Def \mid Tests\ Def) = \frac{P(Def\ and\ Tests\ Def)}{P(Tests\ Def)}$$

$$= \frac{P(Def\ and\ Tests\ Def)}{P(Def\ and\ Tests\ Def) + P(Fine\ and\ Tests\ Def)}$$

$$= \frac{.1(.8)}{.1(.8) + .9(.6)}$$

$$= \frac{4}{31}$$

The correct answer is **D**.

SOA Sample Question 547 Explanation

Since 70% are 0, so 30% are 1.

Since 80% are correct, so 20% are incorrect.

$$P(0\ sent\ |1\ received) = \frac{P(0\ sent\ and\ 1\ received)}{P(1\ received)}$$

$$= \frac{P(0\ sent\ and\ 1\ received)}{P(0\ sent\ and\ 1\ received) + P(1\ sent\ and\ 1\ received)}$$

$$= \frac{.7(.2)}{.7(.2) + .3(.8)} = .37$$

The correct answer is **C**.

SOA Sample Question 548 Explanation

Transfer is hypergeometric with $N = 5 + 4 = 9, \quad n = 2$.

<u>**Case I**</u>: Both transferred chips are red. Probability of this happening is:

$$\frac{\binom{5}{2}\binom{4}{0}}{\binom{9}{2}} = \mathbf{\frac{10}{36}}$$

After this transfer, Urn B will have 6 red and 5 white chips. Probability of a white chip is **5/11**

<u>**Case II**</u>: Both transferred chips are white. Probability of this happening is:

$$\frac{\binom{5}{0}\binom{4}{2}}{\binom{9}{2}} = \mathbf{\frac{6}{36}}$$

After this transfer, Urn B will have 4 red and 7 white chips. Probability of a white chip is **7/11**

<u>**Case III**</u>: One is red and one is white. Probability of this happening is:

$$\frac{\binom{5}{1}\binom{4}{1}}{\binom{9}{2}} = \mathbf{\frac{20}{36}}$$

After this transfer, Urn B will have 5 red and 6 white chips. Probability of a white chip is **6/11**

Combining the 3 cases, the overall probability of a white chip from Urn B after transfer is:

$$P(W) = \frac{10}{36}\left(\frac{5}{11}\right) + \frac{6}{36}\left(\frac{7}{11}\right) + \frac{20}{36}\left(\frac{6}{11}\right) = .535$$

The correct answer is **B**.

SOA Sample Question 549 Explanation

Number of ways n people can be seated on a round table is $(n-1)!$

So, number of ways 6 people can be seated on a round table is $5! = 120$

Since the 2 left-handed people have to sit next to each other, we can consider them as 1 person, and so we effectively have 5 people for which there are $4! = 24$ possibilities on a round table. However, for each of these 24 possibilities, the positions of the 2 left-handers can be switched with each other, to give a total of $2(24) = 48$ possibilities of the left-handers sitting together.

$$P(the\ 2\ left\ handers\ sit\ together) = \frac{\#\ of\ ways\ they\ can\ sit\ together}{total\ ways\ on\ the\ round\ table} = \frac{48}{120} = \frac{2}{5}$$

The correct answer is **D**.

SOA Sample Question 550 Explanation

Since 5 out of 9 have high blood sugar, so 4 do not have it.

In the 5 chosen ones, if 2 have high blood sugar, then 3 do not have it.

Therefore, from 5 sugar ones, we choose 2, and from 4 non-sugar ones we choose 3.

$$\binom{5}{2}\binom{4}{3} = 40$$

The correct answer is **C**.

SOA Sample Question 551 Explanation

The number of accidents is binomial with $n = 4,\ \ p = .3$.

$$f(x) = \binom{4}{x}.3^x(1-.3)^{4-x}$$

2 are reimbursed. So, to have at least 1 unreimbursed, at least 3 accidents occur.

$$P(X \geq 3) = f(3) + f(4) = \binom{4}{3}.3^3(1-.3)^{4-3} + \binom{4}{4}.3^4(1-.3)^{4-4} = .08$$

The correct answer is **B**.

SOA Sample Question 552 Explanation

For uniform $[a, b]$, the 80th percentile is the number p such that:

$$\frac{p-a}{b-a} = .8$$

$$p - a = .8b - .8a$$

$$p = .2a + .8b$$

The correct answer is **B**.

SOA Sample Question 553 Explanation

Cdf of an exponential distribution with mean m is:

$$F(x) = 1 - e^{-x/m}$$

The 40th percentile of a random variable with cdf $F(x)$ is the number p such that:

$$F(p) = .4$$

$$1 - e^{-\frac{4\ln\frac{5}{3}}{m}} = .4$$

$$e^{\ln\left(\frac{5}{3}\right)^{-4/m}} = .6$$

$$\left(\frac{5}{3}\right)^{-\frac{4}{m}} = .6$$

$$-\frac{4}{m}\ln\frac{5}{3} = \ln.6$$

$$m = 4$$

The median k is the x value for which $F(x) = .5$

$$1 - e^{-\frac{k}{4}} = .5$$

$$e^{-\frac{k}{4}} = .5$$

$$-\frac{k}{4} = \ln.5$$

$$k = -4\ln.5$$

$$= 4\ln.5^{-1}$$

$$= 4\ln 2$$

The correct answer is **B**.

SOA Sample Question 554 Explanation

Let X be the base fare fee. Then X is uniform [100, 225]. Let T be the total charge.

$$T = 15 + 1.3X$$

$$Var\,T = 1.3^2\,Var\,X = 1.69\frac{(225 - 100)^2}{12} = 2200.5$$

$$SD(T) = \sqrt{2200.5} = 46.9$$

The correct answer is **D**.

Tools needed for problems 555-570

By Central Limit Theorem if a population is normal, or if sample size, $n > 30$, then the sampling distribution of means and sums is approximately normal with mean and standard deviation:

$$\mu_{\bar{X}} = \mu \qquad \sigma_{\bar{X}} = \frac{\sigma}{\sqrt{n}} \qquad \mu_{sum} = n\mu \qquad \sigma_{sum} = \sqrt{n}\,\sigma$$

$$z = \frac{X - mean}{SD}$$

Pdf and cdf of an exponential distribution with mean m are:

$$f(x) = \frac{1}{m}e^{-x/m}, \quad x > 0, \qquad F(x) = 1 - e^{-x/m}$$

Standard deviation of an exponential distribution equals its mean.

N has **negative binomial** distribution if the probability of needing n trials to get r successes is:

$$P(N = n) = \binom{n-1}{r-1} p^r (1-p)^{n-r}$$

where p is the probability of success in each trial.

The pdf of a uniform [a, b] distribution is:

$$f(x) = \frac{1}{b-a}, \qquad a < x < b$$

$$\int (x+k)e^{ax}dx = \frac{(x+k)e^{ax}}{a} - \frac{e^{ax}}{a^2}$$

$$\int e^{ax}dx = \frac{e^{ax}}{a}$$

$$e^{-\infty} = 0$$

$$P(A\ and\ B) = P(B)\,P(A|B)$$

$$SD(X) = \sqrt{E[X^2] - (E[X])^2}$$

For a continuous random variable:

$$E[X] = \int_{-\infty}^{\infty} x\,f(x)\,dx$$

The probability of getting x Poisson successes with mean k is

$$f(x) = \frac{k^x e^{-k}}{x!}, \quad x = 0,1,2,3,\ldots$$

Pmf, mean and variance of binomial are:

$$f(x) = \binom{n}{r} p^r (1-p)^{n-r}, \qquad E[X] = np, \quad Var\,X = np(1-p)$$

SOA Sample Question 555 Explanation

By Central Limit Theorem the sampling distribution of 24 bottles is approximately normal and:

$$\mu_{sum} = n\mu = 24(12) = 288$$

$$\sigma_{sum} = \sqrt{n}\,\sigma = \sqrt{24}\,\sigma$$

$$P(sum > 290) = .2$$

$$\Rightarrow P(sum \leq 290) = .8$$

From the bottom of the exam table, a cumulative probability of .8 corresponds to $z = .8416$. So:

$$.8416 = \frac{290 - 288}{\sqrt{24}\,\sigma}$$

$$\sigma = .49$$

The correct answer is **C**.

SOA Sample Question 556 Explanation

In the table .5987 corresponds to $z = .25$, and .6026 corresponds to $z = .26$. By interpolation:

$$\frac{.6 - .5987}{.6026 - .5987} = .33$$

Thus, by interpolation, $z = .2533$ corresponds to a cumulative probability of .6

$$.2533 = \frac{1000 - \mu}{\sigma}$$

$$\mu = 1000 - .2533\sigma \quad (1)$$

From the bottom of the exam table, a cumulative probability of .8 corresponds to $z = .8416$. So:

$$.8416 = \frac{2000 - \mu}{\sigma}$$

$$\mu = 2000 - .8416\sigma \quad (2)$$

From (1) and (2):

$$1000 - .2533\sigma = 2000 - .8416\sigma$$

$$\sigma = \mathbf{1700}$$

Substituting this in (1) we get:

$$\mu = 1000 - .2533(1700) = \mathbf{569.4}$$

From the bottom of exam table, a cumulative probability of .95 corresponds to $z = 1.6449$. So:

$$1.6449 = \frac{x_{95} - 569.4}{1700}$$

$$x_{95} = 3366$$

To the nearest 100, this rounds to choice **D**.

SOA Sample Question 557 Explanation

Let X be the lifetime of the fridge. Cdf of an exponential distribution with mean m is:

$$F(x) = 1 - e^{-x/m}$$

$$P(X \leq 5) = F(5)$$

$$.4 = 1 - e^{-5/m}$$

$$e^{-5/m} = .6$$

$$m = \mathbf{9.79}$$

Standard deviation of an exponential distribution equals its mean.

The correct answer is **D**.

SOA Sample Question 558 Explanation

N has negative binomial distribution if the probability of needing n trials to get r successes is:

$$P(N = n) = \binom{n-1}{r-1} p^r (1-p)^{n-r}$$

where p is the probability of success in each trial. Here, $n = 10, \quad r = 3, \quad p = .45$

$$P(N = 10) = \binom{10-1}{3-1} .45^3 (1 - .45)^{10-3}$$

$$= .0499$$

The correct answer is **B**.

SOA Sample Question 559 Explanation

If the mean for Brand B is m, then the mean for Brand A is $2m$.

Let X be life span of a Brand A unit, and Y be the lifespan of Brand B unit. Cdf's are:

$$F(x) = 1 - e^{-\frac{x}{2m}}, \qquad G(y) = 1 - e^{-\frac{y}{m}}$$

$$P(X \geq 15) = 1 - P(X < 15)$$

$$.046656 = 1 - F(15)$$

$$.046656 = e^{-\frac{15}{2m}}$$

$$-\frac{15}{2m} = \ln .046656$$

$$m = 2.447$$

$$P(Y \geq 5) = 1 - P(Y < 5) = 1 - G(5) = e^{-\frac{5}{2.447}} = .13$$

The correct answer is **D**.

SOA Sample Question 560 Explanation

Let the fire loss be X. Then:

$$F(x) = 1 - e^{-\frac{x}{6}}$$

A loss will be partially unreimbursed if it is greater than the maximum benefit allowed. So:

$$p_A = P(X > m) = 1 - P(X \leq m)$$

$$= 1 - F(m)$$

$$= e^{-\frac{m}{6}} \quad (1)$$

$$p_B = P(X > m + 2) = 1 - P(X \leq m + 2)$$

$$= 1 - F(m + 2)$$

$$= e^{-\frac{m+2}{6}}$$

$$= e^{-\frac{m}{6}} e^{-\frac{2}{6}} \quad (2)$$

Dividing (2) by (1) we get:

$$\frac{p_B}{p_A} = \frac{e^{-\frac{m}{6}} e^{-\frac{2}{6}}}{e^{-\frac{m}{6}}}$$

$$= e^{-\frac{1}{3}}$$

The correct answer is **B**.

SOA Sample Question 561 Explanation

In the total of 8 keys there are 2 fitting keys and 6 non-fitting keys.

In the 4 selected keys, the probability of exactly 3 non-fitting keys means the probability of exactly **1** fitting key. This is hypergeometric with $N = 8,\ n = 4,\ a = 2,\ b = 6$

By hypergeometric formula, if we have N items, of which a items are of type A, b items are of type B, then the probability of selecting n items, of which x items are of type A is:

$$f(x) = \frac{\binom{a}{x}\binom{b}{n-x}}{\binom{N}{n}}$$

$$f(1) = \frac{\binom{2}{1}\binom{6}{3}}{\binom{8}{4}}$$

$$= .57$$

The correct answer is **E**.

SOA Sample Question 562 Explanation

Let the damage be X. Then its pdf is:

$$f(x)=\frac{1}{b-a},\quad a<x<b,\quad 0<a<3$$

$$P(X>4|X>3)=\frac{P(X>4\ and\ X>3)}{P(X>3)}$$

$$.9=\frac{P(X>4)}{P(X>3)}$$

$$=\frac{\frac{b-4}{b-a}}{\frac{b-3}{b-a}}$$

$$=\frac{b-4}{b-3}$$

$$.9(b-3)=b-4$$

$$.9b-2.7=b-4$$

$$\boldsymbol{b=13}$$

$$P(X>4|X<11)=\frac{P(X>4\ and\ X<11)}{P(X<11)}$$

$$.7=\frac{P(4<X<11)}{P(X<11)}$$

$$=\frac{11-4}{11-a}$$

$$.7(11-a)=7$$

$$\boldsymbol{a=1}$$

$$P(X>4)=\frac{b-4}{b-a}$$

$$=\frac{13-4}{13-1}$$

$$=.75$$

The correct answer is **B**.

SOA Sample Question 563 Explanation

Let X be the loss, Y be the benefit. Mean of X is $400/\ln 2 = 577$. So, its pdf is:

$$f(x) = \frac{1}{577}e^{-\frac{x}{577}}, \quad x > 0$$

$$Y = \begin{cases} X, & X \leq 1000 \\ 1000, & X > 1000 \end{cases}$$

$$E[Y] = \int_{-\infty}^{\infty} y\, f(x)\, dx = \int_{-\infty}^{1000} x\, f(x)\, dx + \int_{1000}^{\infty} 1000\, f(x)\, dx$$

$$= \frac{1}{577}\int_{0}^{1000} x\, e^{-\frac{x}{577}}\, dx + \frac{1000}{577}\int_{1000}^{\infty} e^{-\frac{x}{577}}\, dx$$

For the first of these integrals, we will use our integration by parts shortcut with $a = -1/577$:

$$\int xe^{ax}dx = \frac{xe^{ax}}{a} - \frac{e^{ax}}{a^2}$$

$$E[Y] = \frac{1}{577}\left(\frac{xe^{-x/577}}{-1/577} - \frac{e^{-x/577}}{(-1/577)^2}\right)\Big|_0^{1000} + \frac{1000}{577}\left(\frac{e^{-x/577}}{-1/577}\right)\Big|_{1000}^{\infty}$$

$$= \frac{1}{577}\left(\frac{1000e^{-\frac{1000}{577}}}{-\frac{1}{577}} - \frac{e^{-\frac{1000}{577}}}{\left(-\frac{1}{577}\right)^2} + 0 + \frac{e^0}{\left(-\frac{1}{577}\right)^2}\right) - 1000\left(e^{-\infty} - e^{-\frac{1000}{577}}\right)$$

$$= 475$$

The correct answer is **D**.

SOA Sample Question 564 Explanation

Let X be the length of the call. Then:

$$F(x) = \begin{cases} 1 - e^{-\frac{x}{.75}}, & if\ domestic \\ 1 - e^{-\frac{x}{.5}}, & if\ international \end{cases}$$

$$P(1 < X < 3) = P(1 < X < 3, and\ domestic) + P(1 < X < 3\ and\ international)$$

$$= P(domestic)P(1 < X < 3|domestic) + P(Int)P(1 < X < 3|Int)$$

$$= .4[F(3) - F(1)|domestic] + 6[F(3) - F(1)|Int]$$

$$= .4\left(e^{-\frac{1}{.75}} - e^{-\frac{3}{.75}}\right) + .6\left(e^{-\frac{1}{.5}} - e^{-\frac{3}{.5}}\right)$$

$$= .178$$

The correct answer is **A**.

SOA Sample Question 565 Explanation

$$f(x) = 20(x^3 - x^4),\ \ 0 < x < 1$$

$$E[X] = \int_{-\infty}^{\infty} x\, f(x)\, dx = 20\int_0^1 x\,(x^3 - x^4)\, dx = 20\int_0^1 (x^4 - x^5)\, dx = 20\left(\frac{x^5}{5} - \frac{x^6}{6}\right)\Big|_0^1 = \frac{2}{3}$$

$$E[X^2] = 20\int_0^1 x^2\,(x^3 - x^4)\, dx = 20\int_0^1 (x^5 - x^6)\, dx = 20\left(\frac{x^6}{6} - \frac{x^7}{7}\right)\Big|_0^1 = \frac{10}{21}$$

$$SD = \sqrt{E[X^2] - (E[X])^2} = \sqrt{\frac{10}{21} - \left(\frac{2}{3}\right)^2} = .178$$

The correct answer is **B**.

SOA Sample Question 566 Explanation

Let X be annual number of claims. Then:

$$f(x) = \frac{1.2^x e^{-1.2}}{x!}$$

$$P(X \geq 3 | X \geq 1) = \frac{P(X \geq 3\ and\ X \geq 1)}{P(X \geq 1)} = \frac{P(X \geq 3)}{P(X \geq 1)} = \frac{1 - f(0) - f(1) - f(2)}{1 - f(0)}$$

$$= \frac{1 - e^{-1.2} - 1.2e^{-1.2} - .72e^{-1.2}}{1 - e^{-1.2}} = .17$$

The correct answer is **D**.

SOA Sample Question 567 Explanation

N be binomial with $n = 5$. So:

$$E[N] = 5p,\quad Var[N] = 5p(1-p)$$

$$Var[N] = E[N^2] - (E[N])^2$$

$$5p(1-p) = 1.8 - (5p)^2$$

$$5p - 5p^2 = 1.8 - 25p^2$$

$$20p^2 + 5p - 1.8 = 0$$

$$p = \frac{-5 \pm \sqrt{5^2 - 4(20)(-1.8)}}{2(20)} = .2$$

$$Var[N] = 5p(1-p) = 5(.2)(1-.2) = .8$$

The correct answer is **A**.

SOA Sample Question 568 Explanation

Probability of a claim is $1-.2=.8$. Let X be the claim size.

$$.1837 = P(there\ is\ a\ claim)\ P(X > 55000$$

$$.1837 = .8P\left(z > \frac{55000-50000}{c}\right)$$

$$P\left(z > \frac{5000}{c}\right) = .2296$$

$$P\left(z \leq \frac{5000}{c}\right) = 1-.2296 = .7704$$

In the table, a cumulative probability of .7704 corresponds to $z = .74$. So:

$$\frac{5000}{c} = .74$$

$$c = .6757$$

The correct answer is C. The slight difference is caused by using more decimal places for z.

SOA Sample Question 569 Explanation

Let H be the total number of hail claims and T be the total number of theft claims in 10 years.

Then H is binomial with $n = 10,\ p = .2$

T is binomial with $n = 10,\ p = .1$.

$$P(H = h) = \binom{10}{h}.2^h(.8)^{10-h}$$

$$P(T = t) = \binom{10}{t}.1^t(.9)^{10-t}$$

$$P(H+T<2) = P(H+T=0) + P(H+T=1)$$

$$= P(H = 0\ and\ T = 0) + P(H = 0\ and\ T = 1) + P(H = 1\ and\ T = 0)$$

$$= \binom{10}{0}.2^0(.8)^{10}\binom{10}{0}.1^0(.9)^{10} + \binom{10}{0}.2^0(.8)^{10}\binom{10}{1}.1(.9)^9 + \binom{10}{1}.2^1(.8)^9\binom{10}{0}.1^0(.9)^{10}$$

$$= .17$$

The correct answer is **A**.

SOA Sample Question 570 Explanation

Let X be the number of fully insured pieces.

Let Y be the number of partially insured pieces.

Let Z be the number of un-insured pieces.

Out of the 3 damaged pieces, the following triplets give at least one fully insured, and at least one partially insured piece:

$$(X, Y, Z) = (1,1,1), (1,2,0), (2,1,0)$$

This is a hypergeometric situation with $N = 10, \quad n = 3$.

Out of the 10 total pieces, 2 are fully insured, 3 are partially insured, and 5 are uninsured.

$$f(1,1,1) = \frac{\binom{2}{1}\binom{3}{1}\binom{5}{1}}{\binom{10}{3}} = \frac{30}{120}$$

$$f(1,2,0) = \frac{\binom{2}{1}\binom{3}{2}\binom{5}{0}}{\binom{10}{3}} = \frac{6}{120}$$

$$f(2,1,0) = \frac{\binom{2}{2}\binom{3}{1}\binom{5}{0}}{\binom{10}{3}} = \frac{3}{120}$$

$$P(at\ least\ 1\ fully, and\ at\ least\ 1\ partially\ insured0 = f(1,1,1) + f(1,2,0) + f(2,1,0)$$

$$= \frac{30}{120} + \frac{6}{120} + \frac{3}{120}$$

$$= .325$$

The correct answer is **C**.

Tools needed for problems 571-627

$$|x| = \begin{cases} x, & if\ x \geq 0 \\ -x, & if\ x < 0 \end{cases}$$

$$Var\,[X] = E[X^2] - (E[X])^2$$

For a normal distribution, mean, median, and mode are equal.

$$\boldsymbol{For\ a\ Continuous\ random\ variable}: \quad E[X] = \int_{-\infty}^{\infty} x\,f(x)\,dx$$

For Poisson, variance equals mean and if mean is k then the pmf is:

$$f(x) = \frac{k^x e^{-k}}{x!}, \quad x = 0,1,2,3,\ldots$$

Central Limit Theorem: If population is normal, or if sample size, $n > 30$, then the sampling distribution of means and sums is approximately normal with mean and standard deviation:

$$\mu_{\bar{X}} = \mu, \qquad \sigma_{\bar{X}} = \frac{\sigma}{\sqrt{n}}, \qquad \mu_{sum} = n\mu, \qquad \sigma_{sum} = \sqrt{n}\,\sigma$$

$$Coefficient\ of\ Variation = \frac{Standard\ Deviation}{Mean}$$

Variance of the sum of independent variables equals the sum of individual variances.

Sum of independent normal variables is normal.

The pdf, cdf, and median of an exponential random variable with mean m are:

$$f(x) = \frac{1}{m} e^{-\frac{x}{m}}, \quad x > 0, \qquad F(x) = 1 - e^{-\frac{x}{m}}, \qquad median = m \ln 2$$

Variance of an exponential distribution equals square of its mean.

$$\boldsymbol{Integration\ by\ parts\ shortcut}: \quad \int (x+k)e^{ax}dx = \frac{(x+k)e^{ax}}{a} - \frac{e^{ax}}{a^2}$$

$$\boldsymbol{Covariance}: \quad Cov\,(X,Y) = E[XY] - E[X]\,E[Y]$$

If $X, Y, \ldots$ are independent then $Var\,(aX + bY + \cdots) = a^2\,Var\,X + b^2\,Var\,Y + \cdots$

$$\boldsymbol{Binomial\ pmf}: \quad f(x) = \binom{n}{x} p^x (1-p)^{n-x}, \quad x = 0,1,2,\ldots$$

In binomial, mean is close to the mode.

Binomial probabilities originally increase with x, reach a single maximum, then decrease.

For standard normal variable, $P(Z < c) = P(Z > -c)$ for any real number c.

Pdf, expected value, median, and variance of uniform $[a, b]$ distribution are:

$$f(x) = \frac{1}{b-a}, \qquad a < x < b, \qquad E[X] = \frac{a+b}{2} = median, \qquad Var\,X = \frac{(b-a)^2}{12}$$

The pth percentile is the random variable value x_p such that $F(x_p) = p/100$

SOA Sample Question 571 Explanation

We know that:

$$|x| = \begin{cases} x, & if\ x \geq 0 \\ -x, & if\ x < 0 \end{cases}$$

$$E[X] = \int_{-\infty}^{\infty} x\, f(x)\, dx = \int_{-2}^{0} x \left(\frac{-x}{10}\right) dx + \int_{0}^{4} x \left(\frac{x}{10}\right) dx = \int_{-2}^{0} \left(\frac{-x^2}{10}\right) dx + \int_{0}^{4} \left(\frac{x^2}{10}\right) dx$$

$$= -\frac{x^3}{30}\Big|_{-2}^{0} + \frac{x^3}{30}\Big|_{0}^{4} = -\frac{8}{30} + \frac{64}{30} = 1.8667$$

$$E[X^2] = \int_{-\infty}^{\infty} x^2\, f(x)\, dx = \int_{-2}^{0} x^2 \left(\frac{-x}{10}\right) dx + \int_{0}^{4} x^2 \left(\frac{x}{10}\right) dx = \int_{-2}^{0} \left(\frac{-x^3}{10}\right) dx + \int_{0}^{4} \left(\frac{x^3}{10}\right) dx$$

$$= -\frac{x^4}{40}\Big|_{-2}^{0} + \frac{x^4}{40}\Big|_{0}^{4} = \frac{16}{40} + \frac{256}{40} = 6.8$$

$$Var\,[X] = E[X^2] - (E[X])^2 = 6.8 - 1.8667^2 = 3.32$$

The correct answer is **C**.

SOA Sample Question 572 Explanation

The probability of getting x Poisson successes with mean k is

$$f(x) = \frac{k^x e^{-k}}{x!}, \quad x = 0,1,2,3, \ldots$$

$$P(no\ accidents\ in\ a\ safe\ interaction) = \frac{.5^0 e^{-.5}}{0!} = e^{-.5}$$

$$P(no\ accidents\ in\ a\ dangerous\ interaction) = \frac{1^0 e^{-1}}{0!} = e^{-1}$$

$$P(0\ accident) = P(safe\ \&\ 0\ accident) + P(dangerous\ \&\ 0\ accident) = .4e^{-.5} + .6e^{-1}$$

$$P(Safe\ given\ no\ accidents) = \frac{P(Safe\ and\ no\ accidents)}{P(no\ accidents)} = \frac{.4e^{-.5}}{.4e^{-.5} + .6e^{-1}} = .52$$

The correct answer is **D**.

SOA Sample Question 573 Explanation

For Poisson, variance equals mean. By central limit theorem, mean and SD of 40000 drivers are:

$$\mu_{sum} = n\mu = 40000(.16) = 6400$$

$$\sigma_{sum} = \sqrt{n}\,\sigma = \sqrt{40000}\,\sqrt{.16} = 80$$

$$CV = \frac{\sigma_{sum}}{\mu_{sum}} = \frac{80}{6400} = .0125$$

The correct answer is **A**.

SOA Sample Question 574 Explanation

Marginal distribution of the strawberries is:

$$f(1) = .07 + .06 + .06 + .05 + .01 = .25$$

$$f(2) = .07 + .1 + .08 + .05 + .03 = .33$$

$$f(3) = .04 + .05 + .06 + .05 + .04 = .24$$

$$f(4) = 1 - f(1) - f(2) - f(3) = 1 - .25 - .33 - .24 = .18$$

$$E[S] = \sum s\, f(s) = 1(.25) + 2(.33) + 3(.24) + 4(.18) = 2.35$$

$$E[S^2] = \sum s^2\, f(s) = 1(.25) + 4(.33) + 9(.24) + 16(.18) = 6.61$$

$$Var\,[S] = E[S^2] - (E[S])^2 = 6.61 - 2.35^2 = 1.09$$

The correct answer is **D**.

SOA Sample Question 575 Explanation

By central limit theorem, mean and SD of the 4-quarter profit X are:

$$\mu_{sum} = n\mu = 4(8) = 32$$

$$\sigma_{sum} = \sqrt{n}\,\sigma = \sqrt{4}\,(24) = 48$$

We need to find $P(X > 0)$. So, we need to change 0 in z-score.

$$Z = \frac{0 - mean}{SD} = \frac{0 - 32}{48} = -.67$$

$$P(X > 0) = P(Z > -.67)$$

The correct answer is **C**.

SOA Sample Question 576 Explanation

Let X be the lifetime of the bulb. X is uniform [0, 40]. We are given that:

$$P(X \le 30 \mid X > a) = .6$$

$$\frac{P(X \le 30 \;\&\; X > a)}{P(X > a)} = .6$$

$$\frac{P(a < X \le 30\,)}{P(X > a)} = .6$$

$$\frac{30 - a}{40 - a} = .6$$

$$a = 15$$

The correct answer is **C**.

SOA Sample Question 577 Explanation

Let T be the theft loss, F be the fire loss, and X be the total loss.

Since theft and fire losses are independent, so variance of X is sum of the two loss variances

$$E[X] = E[T] + E[F] = 100 + 150 = 250$$

$$Var\ X = Var\ T + Var\ F = 40^2 + 30^2 = 2500$$

$$Coefficient\ of\ Variation = \frac{Standard\ Deviation}{Mean} = \frac{\sqrt{2500}}{250} = .2$$

The correct answer is **A**.

SOA Sample Question 578 Explanation

Let X be total profit. Then X is normal because it is the sum of independent normal variables.

$$E[X] = E[A] + E[H] = 200 + 400 = 600$$

$$Var\ X = Var\ A + Var\ H = 400^2 + 300^2 = 250000$$

We need to find $P(X > 0)$. So, we need to change 0 in z-score.

$$Z = \frac{0 - mean}{SD} = \frac{0 - 600}{\sqrt{250000}} = -1.2$$

$$P(X > 0) = P(Z > -1.2)$$

The correct answer is **B**.

SOA Sample Question 579 Explanation

Recall our shortcut for integration by parts:

$$\int xe^{ax}dx = \frac{xe^{ax}}{a} - \frac{e^{ax}}{a^2}$$

$$P(1 < T \leq 2) = \int_1^2 te^{-t}\ dt = \frac{te^{-t}}{-1} - \frac{e^{-t}}{(-1)^2}\Big|_1^2 = -2e^{-2} - e^{-2} + e^{-1} + e^{-1} = .32975$$

$$P(T > 1) = \int_1^\infty te^{-t}\ dt = \frac{te^{-t}}{-1} - \frac{e^{-t}}{(-1)^2}\Big|_1^\infty = 0 + 0 + e^{-1} + e^{-1} = .73576$$

$$P(T \leq 2\,|\,T > 1) = \frac{P(T \leq 2\ and\ T > 1)}{P(T > 1)} = \frac{P(1 < T \leq 2)}{P(T > 1)} = \frac{.32975}{.73576} = .448$$

The correct answer is **C**.

SOA Sample Question 580 Explanation

Because of independence we have no covariance terms in the formula:

$$Var\,(3X_1 - X_2 - X_3 - X_4) = 3^2\,Var\,X_1 + (-1)^2\,Var\,X_2 + (-1)^2\,Var\,X_2 + (-1)^2\,Var\,X_2$$

$$= 9(9) + 1(9) + 1(9) + 1(9)$$

$$= 108$$

The correct answer is **E**.

SOA Sample Question 581 Explanation

$$E[XY] = \sum_{x,y} xy\,f(x,y) = 0 + 1(1)\left(\frac{1}{3}\right) + 2(1)(0) = \frac{1}{3}$$

$$E[X] = \sum_{x,y} x\,f_X(x) = 0 + 1f_X(1) + 2f_X(2) = 1\left(0 + \frac{1}{3}\right) + 2\left(\frac{1}{2} + 0\right) = \frac{4}{3}$$

$$E[Y] = \sum_{x,y} y\,f_Y(y) = 0 + 1f_Y(1) = 1\left(0 + \frac{1}{3} + 0\right) = \frac{1}{3}$$

$$Cov\,(X,Y) = E[XY] - E[X]\,E[Y]$$

$$= \frac{1}{3} - \left(\frac{4}{3}\right)\left(\frac{1}{3}\right)$$

$$= -\frac{1}{9}$$

The correct answer is **A**.

SOA Sample Question 582 Explanation

By central limit Theorem, if σ is the weekly standard deviation, then annual standard deviation is

$$\sigma_{sum} = \sqrt{n}\,\sigma$$

$$3 = \sqrt{52}\,\sigma$$

$$\sigma = \frac{3}{\sqrt{52}}$$

The correct answer is **D**.

SOA Sample Question 583 Explanation

Let the claim payment X be uniformly distributed on $[a, b]$.

$$P(X < 12) = \frac{12 - a}{b - a}$$

$$.5 = \frac{12 - a}{b - a} \qquad (1)$$

$$P(X > 6) = .875$$

$$P(X \le 6) = 1 - P(X > 6) = 1 - .875 = .125$$

$$.125 = \frac{6 - a}{b - a} \qquad (2)$$

Dividing (1) by (2) we get:

$$4 = \frac{12 - a}{6 - a}$$

$$24 - 4a = 12 - a$$

$$a = 4$$

Substituting this in (1) we get:

$$.5 = \frac{12 - 4}{b - 4}$$

$$b = 20$$

Thus, X be uniformly distributed on $[4, 20]$.

$$P(X < 10 \mid X > 6) = \frac{P(X < 10 \,\&\, X > 6)}{P(X > 6)} = \frac{P(6 < X < 10)}{P(X > 6)} = \frac{10 - 6}{20 - 6} = \frac{2}{7}$$

The correct answer is **C**.

SOA Sample Question 584 Explanation

Let X be the number of thefts in the year. If the mean of X is k then:

$$f(x) = \frac{k^x e^{-k}}{x!}, \quad x = 0,1,2,3, \ldots$$

$$.1 = P(X \ge 1) = 1 - f(0) = 1 - \frac{k^0 e^{-k}}{0!} = 1 - e^{-k}$$

$$e^{-k} = 1 - .1 = .9$$

$$k = -\ln .9 = .10536$$

This is the yearly mean. Because of independence, thefts over 15 years will also be Poisson, and will thus have variance equal to mean. The mean over 15 years is $15(.10536) = 1.58$

The correct answer is **E**.

SOA Sample Question 585 Explanation

To be between 1 and 3, and also between 2 and 4, you have to be between 2 and 3. So:

$$P(1 < Y < 3 \,|\, 2 < Y < 4) = \frac{P(1 < Y < 3 \ \& \ 2 < Y < 4)}{P(2 < Y < 4)} = \frac{P(2 < Y < 3)}{P(2 < Y < 4)} \qquad (1)$$

$$P(2 < Y < 3) = \int_2^3 \frac{y}{6} - \frac{y^2}{36}\, dy = \frac{y^2}{12} - \frac{y^3}{108}\Big|_2^3 = \left(\frac{9}{12} - \frac{27}{108}\right) - \left(\frac{4}{12} - \frac{8}{108}\right) = \frac{13}{54}$$

$$P(2 < Y < 4) = \int_2^4 \frac{y}{6} - \frac{y^2}{36}\, dy = \frac{y^2}{12} - \frac{y^3}{108}\Big|_2^4 = \left(\frac{16}{12} - \frac{64}{108}\right) - \left(\frac{4}{12} - \frac{8}{108}\right) = \frac{13}{27}$$

So, (1) becomes:

$$P(1 < Y < 3 \,|\, 2 < Y < 4) = \frac{13/54}{13/27} = .5$$

The correct answer is **D**.

SOA Sample Question 586 Explanation

Let X be the loss and Y be the payout, both in thousands. Then cdf of the loss is:

$$F(x) = 1 - e^{-x/6}$$

$$Y = .8(X - .5), \quad if\ X > .5$$

$$P(Y > 5) = P(.8(X - .5) > 5) = P(X - .5 > 6.25) = P(X > 6.75)$$

$$= 1 - P(X \le 6.75) = 1 - F(6.75) = e^{-\frac{6.75}{6}}$$

$$= .325$$

The correct answer is **C**.

SOA Sample Question 587 Explanation

$$6 = E[A] = 0 + 5(2p + 2p + 0) + 10(3p + 0 + 0) = 50p$$

$$p = .12$$

$$E[A^2] = 0 + 5^2(2p + 2p + 0) + 10^2(3p + 0 + 0) = 400p = 400(.12) = 48$$

$$Var\,[A] = E[A^2] - (E[A])^2$$

$$= 48 - 6^2$$

$$= 12$$

The correct answer is **B**.

SOA Sample Question 588 Explanation

Variance of exponential equals square of its mean. So, variance of 1 life is $1000^2 = 1000000$

Sum of variance of 5 independent lives is $5(1000000) = 5000000$.

$$SD\ of\ 5\ lives = \sqrt{5000000} = 2236$$

The correct answer is **D**.

SOA Sample Question 589 Explanation

Let the payout for **each** loss be Y.

$$Y = X - 2, \quad X > 2$$

$$E[Y] = \int_{-\infty}^{\infty} y\,f(x) = \int_{2}^{8} (x-2)\left(\frac{8-x}{32}\right) dx = \frac{1}{32}\int_{2}^{8} -x^2 + 10x - 16\,dx$$

$$= \frac{1}{32}\left[-\frac{x^3}{3} + 5x^2 - 16x\right]_2^8 = \left(\frac{-512}{3} + 320 - 128\right) - \left(\frac{-8}{3} + 20 - 32\right) = 1.125$$

$$Expected\ pmt\ for\ 1\ yr = Expected\ losses\ in\ 1\ yr * Expected\ payout\ from\ each\ loss$$

$$= 12(1.125)$$

$$= 13.5$$

The correct answer is **B**.

SOA Sample Question 590 Explanation

$$P(Game\ continues\ after\ a\ round) = P(HHH) + P(TTT)$$

$$= .25^3 + .75^3$$

$$= .4375$$

$$P(Game\ stops\ after\ a\ round) = 1 - .4375$$

$$= .5625$$

$$P(continues\ after\ 4\ rounds\ and\ stops\ after\ 5th\ round) = .4375^4(.5625)$$

$$= .0206$$

The correct answer is **C**.

SOA Sample Question 591 Explanation

Let the profit be X, and the required mean-centered interval be $(20-c,\ 20+c)$.

$$P(20-c<X<20+c)=.25$$

$$z_{20-c}=\frac{20-c-mean}{SD}=\frac{20-c-20}{\sqrt{16}}=-\frac{c}{4}$$

$$z_{20+c}=\frac{20+c-mean}{SD}=\frac{20+c-20}{\sqrt{16}}=\frac{c}{4}$$

$$P\left(-\frac{c}{4}<Z<\frac{c}{4}\right)=.25$$

$$P\left(0<Z<\frac{c}{4}\right)=\frac{.25}{2}=.125$$

$$P\left(Z<\frac{c}{4}\right)=P(Z\leq 0)+P\left(0<Z<\frac{c}{4}\right)=.5+.125=.625$$

This cumulative probability is very close to .6255 which corresponds to $z=.32$.

$$\frac{c}{4}=.32$$

$$c=1.3$$

$$(20-c,20+c)=(20-1.3,20+1.3)=(18.7,21.3)$$

The correct answer is **E**.

SOA Sample Question 592 Explanation

The number of positive patients, X, is binomial with $n=18,\ p=.15$.

$$f(x)=\binom{18}{x}.15^x(.85)^{18-x}$$

Mode is the x value corresponding to maximum probability.

In binomial, mean is close to the mode. Here, mean $=\ np\ =\ 18(.15)=2.7$

Also, binomial probabilities originally increase with x, reach a single maximum, then decrease.

Using these 2 facts, we find probabilities corresponding to values close to x =2.7:

$$f(1)=\binom{18}{1}.15^1(.85)^{18-1}=.1704$$

$$f(2)=\binom{18}{2}.15^2(.85)^{18-2}=.2556$$

$$f(3)=\binom{18}{3}.15^3(.85)^{18-3}=.2406$$

Thus, the mode is 2.

The correct answer is **C**.

SOA Sample Question 593 Explanation

Let the annual profit be X. We are given that $P(X < 21) = .28$

The standard score for 21 is:

$$z = \frac{21 - mean}{SD} = \frac{21 - 39}{\sigma} = -\frac{18}{\sigma}$$

$$P\left(Z < -\frac{18}{\sigma}\right) = .28$$

$$P\left(Z > \frac{18}{\sigma}\right) = .28$$

$$P\left(Z \leq \frac{18}{\sigma}\right) = .72$$

In the table, a cumulative probability of .7190 corresponds to $z = .58$, while a cumulative probability of .7224 corresponds to $z = .59$. Interpolating we get:

$$\frac{.72 - .719}{.7224 - .719} = .3$$

Thus, for a cumulative probability of .72 interpolation gives $z = .583$

$$.583 = \frac{18}{\sigma}$$

$$\sigma = 30.87$$

We are to find $P(X < 3)$.

$$z_3 = \frac{3 - mean}{SD} = \frac{3 - 39}{30.87} = -1.17$$

$$P(X < 3) = P(Z < -1.17) = P(Z > 1.17) = 1 - P(Z \leq 1.17) = 1 - .879 = .121 = 12.1\%$$

The correct answer is **E**.

SOA Sample Question 594 Explanation

The deck has 4 kings, 4 aces, 4 jacks. So, $52 - 12 = 40$ are neither aces nor jacks nor kings.

Let X be the number of kings in the 5 chosen. We want no aces or jacks. By hypergeometric:

$$P(x\ Kings, 0\ neither\ aces\ nor\ jacks, 5 - x\ others) = f(x) = \frac{\binom{4}{x}\binom{40}{5-x}\binom{8}{0}}{\binom{52}{5}}$$

$$P(X \geq 2) = f(2) + f(3) + f(4) = \frac{\binom{4}{2}\binom{40}{3}\binom{8}{0}}{\binom{52}{5}} + \frac{\binom{4}{3}\binom{40}{2}\binom{8}{0}}{\binom{52}{5}} + \frac{\binom{4}{4}\binom{40}{1}\binom{8}{0}}{\binom{52}{5}} = .024$$

The correct answer is **C**.

SOA Sample Question 595 Explanation

The check-out times, X, is uniform [1.1, 8.6].

$$P(X > y) = \frac{8.6 - y}{8.6 - 1.1} = \frac{8.6 - y}{7.5}$$

We want the above probability to be no more than 5%. So, we need to solve:

$$\frac{8.6 - y}{7.5} \leq .05$$

$$8.6 - y \leq .375$$

$$y \geq 8.225$$

The correct answer is **D**.

SOA Sample Question 596 Explanation

Let X be the profit, with mean μ and standard deviation σ

$$P(X > 3.5) = .3264$$

$$P(X \leq 3.5) = .6736$$

A cumulative probability of .6736 corresponds to $z = .45$. So:

$$.45 = \frac{3.5 - \mu}{\sigma} \qquad (1)$$

$$P(X > 3.62) = .2743$$

$$P(X \leq 3.62) = .7257$$

A cumulative probability of .7257corresponds to $z = .6$. So:

$$.6 = \frac{3.62 - \mu}{\sigma} \qquad (2)$$

Dividing (1) by (2) we get:

$$\frac{.45}{.6} = \frac{3.5 - \mu}{3.62 - \mu}$$

$$1.629 - .45\mu = 2.1 - .6\mu$$

$$\mu = 3.14$$

Substituting this in (1) we get:

$$.45 = \frac{3.5 - 3.14}{\sigma}$$

$$\sigma = .8$$

$$Var = \sigma^2 = .8^2 = .64$$

The correct answer is **B**.

SOA Sample Question 597 Explanation

Let X be the loss which is uniform $[a, 19]$. So, the expected value of this loss is:

$$E[X] = \frac{a+19}{2}$$

With 0 deductible, payout equals loss. So, the expected payout of 10 under policy A equals $E[X]$

$$\frac{a+19}{2} = 10$$

$$a = 1$$

$$f(x) = \frac{1}{19-1} = \frac{1}{18}, \qquad 1 < x < 19$$

With deductible 4, let the payout be Y.

$$Y = X - 4, \qquad 4 < X < 19$$

$$E[Y] = \int_{-\infty}^{\infty} y\, f(x)\, dx = \int_{4}^{19} (x-4)\left(\frac{1}{18}\right) dx = \frac{1}{18}\frac{(x-4)^2}{2}\Big|_4^{19} = 6.25$$

The correct answer is **B**.

SOA Sample Question 598 Explanation

Let the mean be μ and standard deviation be σ. The z-score for 0 is:

$$z = \frac{0-\mu}{\sigma} = \frac{-\mu}{\sigma}$$

$$P\left(Z > \frac{-\mu}{\sigma}\right) = P\left(Z < \frac{\mu}{\sigma}\right) = .92$$

In the table, a cumulative probability of .9192 corresponds to $z = 1.40$, while a cumulative probability of .9207 corresponds to $z = 1.41$. Interpolating we get:

$$\frac{.92 - .9192}{.9207 - .9192} = .53$$

Thus, for a cumulative probability of .72 interpolation gives $z = 1.4053$

$$\frac{\mu}{\sigma} = 1.4053$$

$$\mu = 1.4053\sigma$$

$$Var\,[X] = E[X^2] - (E[X])^2$$

$$\sigma^2 = 74 - \mu^2 = 74 - (1.4053\sigma)^2 = 74 - 1.975\sigma^2$$

$$2.975\sigma^2 = 74$$

$$\sigma^2 = 24.87$$

The correct answer is **A**. (They use normal calculators instead of tables to get slightly different z)

SOA Sample Question 599 Explanation

Let the random variable be X.

$$F(x) = 1 - e^{-\frac{x}{\mu}}$$

The 75th percentile is the random variable value x_{75} such that:

$$F(x_{75}) = \frac{75}{100}$$

$$1 - e^{-\frac{x_{75}}{\mu}} = .75$$

$$e^{-\frac{x_{75}}{\mu}} = .25$$

$$x_{75} = -\mu \ln .25 \quad (1)$$

The 25th percentile is the random variable value x_{25} such that:

$$F(x_{25}) = \frac{25}{100}$$

$$1 - e^{-\frac{x_{25}}{\mu}} = .25$$

$$e^{-\frac{x_{25}}{\mu}} = .75$$

$$x_{25} = -\mu \ln .75 \quad (2)$$

Subtracting (2) from (1) we get:

$$x_{75} - x_{25} = -\mu \ln .25 + \mu \ln .75 = \mu(\ln .75 - \ln .25) = \mu \ln \frac{.75}{.25} = \mu \ln 3$$

The correct answer is **D**.

SOA Sample Question 600 Explanation

Full reimbursement happens if the loss is less than or equal to .8.

Let p be the probability that full reimbursement happens. Then:

$$p = P(X \leq .8) = F(.8) = \frac{.8 + 15(.8)^2}{16} = .65$$

1st partially unreimbursed hospitalization will happen at the 3rd hospitalization if the first two are fully reimbursed, and the 3rd is not. Probability of this is:

$$p(p)(1-p) = .65(.65)(1 - .65)$$

$$= .148$$

The correct answer is **D**.

SOA Sample Question 601 Explanation

Let the payout be Y. Then $Y = X - 1100,\ X > 1100$.

$$E[Y] = \int_{-\infty}^{\infty} y\,f(x)\,dx = \int_{1100}^{\infty} (x-1100)\left(\frac{3}{1000}\right)\left(\frac{1000}{x}\right)^4 dx = 3(1000)^3 \int_{1100}^{\infty} \left(\frac{x-1100}{x^4}\right) dx$$

$$= 3(1000)^3 \int_{1100}^{\infty} (x^{-3} - 1100x^{-4})dx$$

$$= 3(1000)^3 \left(\frac{x^{-2}}{-2} - \frac{1100x^{-3}}{-3}\right)\Big|_{1100}^{\infty}$$

$$= 3(1000)^3 \left(0 + \frac{1100^{-2}}{2} - \frac{1100(1100)^{-3}}{3}\right)$$

$$= 413$$

The correct answer is **C**.

SOA Sample Question 602 Explanation

Using the given conditions we have:

$$p(0) = 3p(1) \qquad (1)$$

$$p(1) = 4p(2) \qquad (2)$$

$$p(2) = 5p(3) \qquad (3)$$

$$p(0) + p(1) + p(2) + p(3) = .95 \qquad (4)$$

Next step will be to find the probabilities of 0 or 1 in terms of probability of 3. From (2) & (3):

$$p(1) = 4(5)p(3) = 20p(3) \qquad (5)$$

From (1) & (5):

$$p(0) = 3(20)p(3) = 60p(3) \qquad (6)$$

Substituting (6), (5), and (3) in (4) we get:

$$60p(3) + 20p(3) + 5p(3) + p(3) = .95$$

$$86p(3) = .95$$

$$p(3) = .95/86$$

Substituting this in (4) we get:

$$p(0) + p(1) + p(2) + .95/86 = .95$$

$$p(0) + p(1) + p(2) = .94$$

The correct answer is **D**.

SOA Sample Question 603 Explanation

Let X be the number of break-ins with security system, and m be the mean of X.

$$P(0\ breaks\ with\ security) = 3P(0\ breaks\ without\ security)$$

$$\frac{m^0 e^{-m}}{0!} = 3\frac{3^0 e^{-3}}{0!}$$

$$e^{-m} = 3e^{-3} = .14936$$

$$m = -\ln .14936 = 1.9$$

$$P(2\ breaks\ without\ security) = \frac{3^2 e^{-3}}{2!} = .224$$

$$P(2\ breaks\ with\ security) = \frac{1.9^2 e^{-1.9}}{2!} = .27$$

$$P(security\ |2\ breaks) = \frac{P(security\ \&\ 2\ breaks)}{P(2\ breaks)}$$

$$= \frac{P(security\ \&\ 2\ breaks)}{P(security\ \&\ 2\ breaks) + P(no\ security\ \&\ and\ 2\ breaks)}$$

$$= \frac{.4(.27)}{.4(.27) + .6(.224)}$$

$$= .45$$

The correct answer is **D**.

SOA Sample Question 604 Explanation

Let m be the 6-month mean.

$$P(no\ tornados\ in\ 6\ months) = \frac{m^0 e^{-m}}{0!} = .008$$

$$e^{-m} = .008$$

$$m = 4.8283$$

$$monthly\ mean = \frac{m}{6} = .8047$$

$$2 - month\ mean = 2(.8047) = 1.6094$$

$$P(the\ 2\ months\ of\ July\ and\ Aug\ have\ 0\ tornados) = \frac{1.6094^0 e^{-1.6094}}{0!} = .2$$

Since different months are independent, whatever happened in July and August does not depend on whether there was a tornado in June or not. Hence:

$$P(0\ in\ July\ and\ Aug|a\ tornado\ in\ June) = .2$$

The correct answer is **A**.

SOA Sample Question 605 Explanation

Let F be the cdf of failure time of A, and G be the cdf of failure time of B. Then:

$$F(t) = 1 - e^{-\frac{t}{2}}$$

$$G(t) = 1 - e^{-\frac{t}{4}}$$

$$P(A\ fails\ within\ first\ 3\ yrs) = F(3) = 1 - e^{-\frac{3}{2}} = .777$$

$$P(B\ fails\ within\ first\ 3\ yrs) = G(3) = 1 - e^{-\frac{3}{4}} = .528$$

Since 10% are A, so 90% are B.

$$P(A \mid fails\ within\ first\ 3\ yrs) = \frac{P(\ A\ and\ fails\ in\ first\ 3\ yrs)}{P(fails\ in\ first\ 3\ yrs)}$$

$$= \frac{P(\ A\ \&\ fails\ in\ first\ 3\ yrs)}{P(A\ \&\ fails\ in\ first\ 3\ yrs) + P(B\ \&\ fails\ in\ first\ 3\ yrs)} = \frac{.1(.777)}{.1(.777) + .9(.528)} = .14$$

The correct answer is **B**.

SOA Sample Question 606 Explanation

$$p(x, y) = \frac{(6 - x)(3 - y)}{58(1 + |x - y|)}, \quad x = 0,1,2, \quad y = 0,1,2$$

We need to find $Var(X|Y = 1)$. For this, we need to find $p(x|y = 1)$.

$$P(Y = 1) = p(0,1) + p(1,1) + p(2,1)$$

$$= \frac{(6-0)(3-1)}{58(1+|0-1|)} + \frac{(6-1)(3-1)}{58(1+|1-1|)} + \frac{(6-2)(3-1)}{58(1+|2-1|)} = \frac{10}{29}$$

$$p(x|y = 1) = \frac{p(x, 1)}{P(Y = 1)} = \frac{\frac{(6-x)(3-1)}{58(1+|x-1|)}}{10/29} = \frac{\frac{2(6-x)}{58(1+|x-1|)}}{10/29} = \frac{(6-x)}{10(1+|x-1|)}$$

x	$p(x\|y = 1) = \frac{(6-x)}{10(1+\|x-1\|)}$
0	.3
1	.5
2	.2

In Multiview calculator, we enter 0,1,2 in the 1st column, and .3,.5,.2 in the 2nd column to get:

$$\sigma_x = .7$$

$$Var = .7^2 = .49 = \frac{49}{100}$$

The correct answer is **B**.

SOA Sample Question 607 Explanation

Let X be the duration of a call.

$$P(2 \le X < 8) = P(2 \le X < 4) + P(4 \le X < 6) + P(6 \le X < 8)$$

$$= .2 + .42 + .28$$

$$= .9$$

$$P(3 \le X < 7) = P(3 \le X < 5) + P(5 \le X < 7)$$

$$= .34 + .38$$

$$= .72$$

$$P(2 \le X < 3 \; or \; 7 \le X < 8) \; = P(2 \le X < 8) - P(3 \le X < 7)$$

$$= .9 - .72$$

$$= .18$$

The correct answer is **B**.

SOA Sample Question 608 Explanation

Let Y be the number of patients having disease. Then Y is binomial with $n = 6$.

$$f(y) = \binom{6}{y} p^y (1-p)^{6-y}$$

By the first condition, $f(0) = 10\,f(1)$.

$$\binom{6}{0} p^0 (1-p)^{6-0} = 10 \binom{6}{1} p^1 (1-p)^{6-1}$$

$$(1-p)^6 = 60p(1-p)^5$$

$$1 - p = 60p$$

$$p = 1/61$$

By the second condition, $f(0) = x\,f(3)$

$$\binom{6}{0} p^0 (1-p)^{6-0} = x \binom{6}{3} p^3 (1-p)^{6-3}$$

$$\left(1 - \frac{1}{61}\right)^6 = 20x \left(\frac{1}{61}\right)^3 \left(1 - \frac{1}{61}\right)^3$$

$$x = 10800$$

The correct answer is **E**.

SOA Sample Question 609 Explanation

Once $x > 5$, no more probability is accumulated. Thus, losses do no exceed 5. Thus:

$$P(X \leq 5) = F(5) = 1$$

$$c(5^2 + 5) = 1$$

$$c = 1/30$$

$$P(insurer\ pays\ something\ on\ a\ loss) = P(loss\ exceeds\ deductible) = P(X > 3.2)$$

$$= 1 - P(X \leq 3.2)$$

$$= 1 - F(3.2)$$

$$= 1 - c(3.2^2 + 3.2)$$

$$= 1 - \frac{1}{30}(3.2^2 + 3.2)$$

$$= .552$$

The correct answer is **D**.

SOA Sample Question 610 Explanation

Let X be the loss and Y be the payout. The pdf of loss is:

$$f(x) = \frac{1}{2000}, \quad 0 < x < 2000$$

$$Y = \begin{cases} X, & X \leq m \\ m, & X > m \end{cases}$$

$$E[Y] = \int_{-\infty}^{\infty} y\, f(x)\, dx = \int_{0}^{m} x \frac{1}{2000}\, dx + \int_{m}^{2000} m \frac{1}{2000}\, dx$$

$$910 = \frac{x^2}{4000}\Big|_0^m + \frac{mx}{2000}\Big|_m^{2000} = \frac{m^2}{4000} + \frac{2000m}{2000} - \frac{m^2}{2000} = m - \frac{m^2}{4000}$$

$$\frac{m^2}{4000} - m + 910 = 0$$

$$m = \frac{1 \pm \sqrt{1^2 - 4\left(\frac{1}{4000}\right)(910)}}{2\left(\frac{1}{4000}\right)}$$

$$= 2600, 1400$$

Since the maximum loss is 2000, so maximum payout cannot be 2600. So, it is 1400.

The correct answer is **C**.

SOA Sample Question 611 Explanation

The 30th percentile is the random variable value p such that $F(p) = 30/100$

We first find the value of the constant by setting the integral of the pdf equal to 1.

$$\int_{-\infty}^{\infty} f(x)\,dx = 1$$

$$\int_{5}^{8} c(x-5)\,dx + \int_{8}^{11} c\,(11-x)\,dx = 1$$

$$c\frac{(x-5)^2}{2}\Big|_5^8 - c\frac{(11-x)^2}{2}\Big|_8^{11} = 1$$

$$4.5c + 4.5c = c$$

$$c = 1/9$$

1st non-zero piece of the pdf ends at 8. Let us find how much probability is accumulated up to that point to see whether that piece contains our required cumulated probability or not.

$$F(8) = \int_{-\infty}^{8} f(x)dx = \int_{5}^{8} c(x-5)dx = 4.5c = 4.5\left(\frac{1}{9}\right) = .5$$

Since we are only looking for a cumulative probability of .3, the first piece is enough.

$$F(p) = .3$$

$$\int_{5}^{p} \frac{1}{9}(x-5)dx = .3$$

$$\frac{(x-5)^2}{18}\Big|_5^p = .3$$

$$\frac{(p-5)^2}{18} = .3$$

$$(p-5)^2 = 5.4$$

$$p - 5 = \pm\sqrt{5.4}$$

$$p = 5 \pm \sqrt{5.4}$$

$$= 7.32 \; or \; 2.68$$

Since there is no cumulated probability up to 5, so 2.68 is not possible.

Thus, the required percentile is 7.32.

The correct answer is **E**.

SOA Sample Question 612 Explanation

A median is 10 means that cumulative probability up to 10 to .5.

This is an exponential distribution with mean $1/c$

We know that median of an exponential distribution with mean m is $m \ln 2$. So:

$$10 = \frac{1}{c}\ln 2$$

$$c = \frac{\ln 2}{10}$$

$$mean = \frac{10}{\ln 2} = 14.427$$

Thus, cdf of this exponential distribution is:

$$F(x) = 1 - e^{-x/14.427}$$

Let the warranty payment be Y. Then:

$$E[Y] = 35\,F(5) + 25[F(7.5) - F(5)]$$

$$= 35\left(1 - e^{-\frac{5}{14.427}}\right) + 25\left(e^{-\frac{5}{14.427}} - e^{-\frac{7.5}{14.427}}\right)$$

$$= 13.06$$

The correct answer is **A**.

SOA Sample Question 613 Explanation

For Poisson, mean equals variance. So, mean equals the square of standard deviation. Hence:

$$mean\ for\ 1st\ site = 1.5^2 = 2.25$$

Let the mean for 2nd site be m.

$$P(no\ accident\ at\ 2nd\ site) = 1.1\,P(no\ accident\ at\ 1st\ site)$$

$$\frac{m^0 e^{-m}}{0!} = 1.1\frac{2.25^0 e^{-2.25}}{0!}$$

$$e^{-m} = .11594$$

$$m = -\ln .11594$$

$$= 2.1547$$

$$SD\ of\ 2nd\ site = \sqrt{m}$$

$$= \sqrt{2.1547}$$

$$= 1.47$$

The correct answer is **D**.

SOA Sample Question 614 Explanation

Let the profit in 1st year be F, that in 2nd year be S, and total profit be X.

$$X = F + S$$

Since the sum of independent normal variables is normal, so X is normal.

$$\mu_X = 660 + \mu$$

$$Var\ X = Var\ F + Var\ S = 1100^2 + 2640^2$$

$$\sigma_X = \sqrt{1100^2 + 2640^2} = 2860$$

$$P(X > 0) = .8643$$

So, we need to change 0 into standard score:

$$z = \frac{0 - (660 + \mu)}{2860} = \frac{-(660 + \mu)}{2860}$$

$$P\left(Z > \frac{-(660 + \mu)}{2860}\right) = .8643$$

$$P\left(Z < \frac{(660 + \mu)}{2860}\right) = .8643$$

A cumulative probability of .8643 corresponds to $z = 1.1$. So,

$$\frac{660 + \mu}{2860} = 1.1$$

$$\mu = 2486$$

The correct answer is **C**.

SOA Sample Question 615 Explanation

There are 7 days in a week. So, if the weekly mean is 63, then the daily mean is:

$$\lambda = \frac{63}{7} = 9$$

Standard deviation of Poisson equals square root of the mean. So, daily SD is:

$$SD = \sqrt{\lambda} = \sqrt{9} = 3$$

Thus, 2 standard deviations below expected value is $9 - 2(3) = 3$

Let X be the number of daily accidents. Thus, we are to find $P(X \le 3)$

$$f(x) = \frac{9^x e^{-9}}{x!}$$

$$P(X \le 3) = f(0) + f(1) + f(2) + f(3) = e^{-9} + 9e^{-9} + 40.5e^{-9} + 121.5e^{-9} = .021$$

The correct answer is **B**.

SOA Sample Question 616 Explanation

$$Var\ C = \frac{(10-0)^2}{12} = 8.3333$$

$$SD(C) = \sqrt{8.3333}$$

$$= 2.887$$

For the discrete uniform, we have 11 numbers, 0,1, 2,...,10, each with probability 1/11. Entering the numbers in first column and probabilities in 2nd column of the Multiview calculator we get:

$$SD(D) = 3.162$$

$$SD(D) - SD(C) = 3.162 - 2.887$$

$$= .275$$

The correct answer is **C**.

SOA Sample Question 617 Explanation

To get $Var(T|F=1)$ we need to find the corresponding probability function.

$$P(F=1) = .14 + .08 + .03$$

$$= .24$$

$$P(T=0|F=1) = \frac{P(T=0, F=1)}{P(F=1)} = \frac{.14}{.24} = \frac{7}{12}$$

$$P(T=1|F=1) = \frac{P(T=0, F=1)}{P(F=1)} = \frac{.08}{.24} = \frac{1}{3}$$

$$P(T=2|F=1) = \frac{P(T=0, F=1)}{P(F=1)} = \frac{.03}{.24} = \frac{1}{8}$$

Enter 0,1,2 in the first column in Multiview calculator, and the 3 probabilities in 2nd column:

$$\sigma_X = .6974$$

$$Var(T|F=1) = .6974^2$$

$$= .49$$

The correct answer is **D**.

SOA Sample Question 618 Explanation

$$E[X] = \frac{a+b}{2} = 8.5$$

$$a + b = 17$$

$$b = 17 - a \ (1)$$

$$Var\ X = \frac{(b-a)^2}{12} = .75$$

$$(b-a)^2 = 9$$

$$b - a = 3 \quad (2)$$

Substituting (1) in (2) we get:

$$17 - a - a = 3$$

$$a = 7$$

$$b = 17 - 7 = 10$$

So, the uniform distribution is [7, 10].

Additional 1.5 days on top of 7.5 days means a total of $7.5 + 1.5 = 9$ days. So, we need:

$$P(X \geq 9 | X \geq 7.5) = \frac{P(X \geq 9 \ and\ X \geq 7.5)}{P(X \geq 7.5)} = \frac{P(X \geq 9)}{P(X \geq 7.5)} = \frac{10-9}{10-7.5} = .4$$

The correct answer is **B**.

SOA Sample Question 619 Explanation

Let the mean of any 1-minute period be k. It will be same for 1st and any other minute.

$$f(4) = 54f(0)$$

$$\frac{k^4e^{-k}}{4!} = 54\frac{k^0e^{-k}}{0!}$$

$$k^4 = 1296$$

$$k = 6$$

$$Expected\ hits\ in\ a\ 60 - minute\ period = 60k$$

$$= 60(6)$$

$$= 360$$

The correct answer is **E**.

SOA Sample Question 620 Explanation

Let A, D, H, L be the events of selling auto, home, health, life, respectively.

$$P(A) = .55 \qquad P(D) = .45 \qquad P(H) = .5 \qquad P(L) = .6$$

By independence probability of picking a group equals product of individual probabilities.

$$P(3) = P(ADHL^C) + P(ADLH^C) + P(AHLD^C) + P(DHLA^C)$$

$$= .55 * .45 * .5 * .4 + .55 * .45 * .6 * .5 + .55 * .5 * .6 * .55 + .45 * .5 * .6 * .45 = .27525$$

$$P(4) = P(ADHL) = .55 * .45 * .5 * .6 = .07425$$

$$P(more\ than\ 2) = P(3\ or\ 4) = P(3) + P(4) = .27525 + .07425 = .35$$

The correct answer is **B**.

SOA Sample Question 621 Explanation

Let X be the time between accidents. Then:

$$F(x) = 1 - e^{-\frac{x}{15}}$$

Since exponential distribution is memoryless, what occurred in previous 10 days is irrelevant. So:

$$P(5 < X < 25) = F(25) - F(5) = \left(1 - e^{-\frac{25}{15}}\right) - \left(1 - e^{-\frac{5}{15}}\right) = .53$$

The correct answer is **D**.

SOA Sample Question 622 Explanation

For uniform distribution, 50th percentile, or median is the midpoint of the 2 ends. So:

$$\frac{a+b}{2} = 16.36$$

$$b = 32.72 - a \quad (1)$$

$$Var\ X = \frac{(b-a)^2}{12} = 7.63^2 = 58.2169$$

$$b - a = 26.43 \quad (2)$$

Substituting (1) in (2) we get:

$$32.72 - 2a = 26.43$$

$$a = 3.14445$$

$$b = 32.72 - 3.14445 = 29.5755$$

$$\frac{b}{a} = \frac{29.5755}{3.14445} = 9.41$$

The correct answer is **E**.

SOA Sample Question 623 Explanation

Let the exam scores be X.Mode and mean of a normal distribution are equal. So, mean is 56.

40th percentile is the value corresponding to a cumulative probability of .4. So:

$$P(X \leq 52.2) = .4$$

The standard score for 52.2 is:

$$z = \frac{52.2 - 56}{\sigma} = \frac{-3.8}{\sigma}$$

$$.4 = P\left(z \leq \frac{-3.8}{\sigma}\right) = P\left(z \geq \frac{3.8}{\sigma}\right) = 1 - P\left(Z < \frac{3.8}{\sigma}\right)$$

$$P\left(z < \frac{3.8}{\sigma}\right) = 1 - .4 = .6$$

Cumulative probabilities of .5987 and .6026 correspond to $z = .25$ and .26 respectively.

$$\frac{.6 - .5987}{.6026 - .5987} = .33$$

$$z = .2533$$

$$\frac{3.8}{\sigma} = .2533$$

$$\sigma = 15$$

The percentile for a score of 65.5 is found by finding $P(X \leq 65.5)$. z-score is:

$$z = \frac{65.5 - 56}{15} = .63$$

$$P(X \leq 65.5) = P(Z \leq .63) = .7357 = 73.57\%$$

The correct answer is **B**.

SOA Sample Question 624 Explanation

Let A be the profit from auto, and H be the profit from home. Let X be total profit. Then X is normal because it is the sum of independent normal variables.

$$E[X] = E[A] + E[H] = 400 - 100 = 300$$

$$Var\ X = Var\ A + Var\ H = 200^2 + 500^2 = 290000$$

We need to find $P(X > 0)$. So, we need to change 0 in z-score.

$$Z = \frac{0 - mean}{SD} = \frac{0 - 300}{\sqrt{290000}} = -.56$$

$$P(X > 0) = P(Z > -.56) = P(Z < .56) = .7123$$

The correct answer is **E**.

SOA Sample Question 625 Explanation

If there were exactly 8 hurricanes in the first seven years of the decade, then we are effectively asked to find the probability of exactly 2 hurricanes in the last 3 years.

Let X be the number of hurricanes over a 3-year period. The mean of X is $1(3) = 3$.

$$f(x) = \frac{3^x e^{-3}}{x!}$$

$$f(2) = \frac{3^2 e^{-3}}{2!} = .224$$

The correct answer is **E**.

SOA Sample Question 626 Explanation

$$P(0\ claim\ for\ type\ 1) = \frac{1}{2} P(0\ claim\ for\ type\ 2)$$

$$\frac{\lambda_1{}^0 e^{-\lambda_1}}{0!} = \left(\frac{1}{2}\right)\frac{\lambda_2{}^0 e^{-\lambda_2}}{0!}$$

$$e^{\lambda_1 - \lambda_2} = 2$$

$$\lambda_1 - \lambda_2 = \ln 2 = .693$$

Since variance of Poisson equals its mean, we get:

$$V_1 - V_2 = .693$$

The correct answer is **A**.

SOA Sample Question 627 Explanation

$$P(X < 2) = P(X = 0) + P(X = 1) = (.06 + .1 + .12 + .2 + .08) + (.11 + .15 + .06) = .7$$

$$P(Y = 0|X < 2) = \frac{P(Y = 0, X < 2)}{P(X < 2)} = \frac{.06 + .08}{.7} = .2$$

$$P(Y = 1|X < 2) = \frac{P(Y = 1, X < 2)}{P(X < 2)} = \frac{.10 + .11}{.7} = .3$$

$$P(Y = 2|X < 2) = \frac{P(Y = 2, X < 2)}{P(X < 2)} = \frac{.12 + .15}{.7} = .3857$$

$$P(Y = 3|X < 2) = \frac{P(Y = 3, X < 2)}{P(X < 2)} = \frac{.02 + .06}{.7} = .1143$$

$$E(Y|X < 2) = \sum_y y\,P(Y = y|X < 2) = 0 + 1(.3) + 2(.3857) + 3(.1143) = 1.41$$

The correct answer is **C**.

Practice Exam 1 (Give yourself 3 hours to mimic actual P Exam)

1. Each of subjects A, B, C, D has 40% of a university's students enrolled in it. That is, 40% are enrolled in A, 40% in B, etc. Also, each pair of the subjects has 30% of the students. That is, 30% are enrolled in A and B, 30% in A and C, etc. Each triplet of subjects has 20% of students in it. 10% of the students are enrolled in all the 4. How many are enrolled in at least one?
   A) 45%
   B) 50%
   C) 55%
   D) 60%
   E) 70%

2. Dr. Megan's class has 30 students, 60% of whom are girls, while Dr. Laura's class has 39 girls. If one student is selected from each class, the probability of both being of same gender is .513. How many students are there in Dr. Laura's class?
   A) 65
   B) 66
   C) 67
   D) 68
   E) 69

3. The probability, $p(n), n \geq 0$, of there being n annual floods in a state follows the recurrence relation: $p(n+1) = .7p(n)$. An insurance company will pay only if there is more than one flood in the year. Find the probability that company will have to pay.
   A) .21
   B) .30
   C) .42
   D) .49
   E) .51

4. Two researchers use carbon dating to measure the age, x, of a document. The error made by one of them is normally distributed with mean $0.1x$ and standard deviation $0.1x$. The error made by the other is normally distributed with mean $0.05x$ and standard deviation $0.2x$. The errors of the two researchers are independent of each other. Find the probability that the average of the two ages is within $0.1x$ of the age of the document.
   A) .32
   B) .41
   C) .53
   D) .69
   E) .84

5. A certain brand of cars comes with a 1-year theft insurance that provides 700 in case the car gets stolen within a year of purchase if the purchase is made during the first week of a calendar year. This year, 65 cars were sold in the first week and each has 2% probability being stolen during the year, independent of any other car. Find the smallest amount of money that the selling company must have so that there is at least a 90% chance that it will cover the year's theft benefits.
   A) 1923
   B) 1953
   C) 1983
   D) 2013
   E) 2043

6. The time it will take from now to see the first snowstorm in a certain country is exponentially distributed. The probability of there being a snowstorm during the next 6 months is .2. Find the probability of there being no snowstorm during 3 months from now.
   A) .11
   B) .28
   C) .56
   D) .72
   E) .89

7. The participants in an aerobics class are classified by their ages as children, adults, and seniors. The number of adults and seniors in class is the same and there are twice as many adults as children. Find the probability that among 4 randomly selected members, there are exactly 3 children.
A) .0128
B) .0256
C) .0384
D) .0512
E) .0640

8. The depreciation of a car, X has the pdf:

$$f(x) = \begin{cases} c(5-x), & 0 < x < 5 \\ 0, & otherwise \end{cases}$$

Given that the depreciation exceeds 1, calculate the probability that it is less than 4.
A) .1375
B) .3375
C) .5375
D) .7375
E) .9375

9. A couple plans to have as many children as possible. Assume that probability of them having a boy is .45. Find the probability that they will have at least 4 girls before the 2nd boy.
A) .156
B) .256
C) .356
D) .456
E) .556

10. An insurance has a monthly deductible of 50. Monthly medical expenses follow an exponential distribution with mean 200. Find the interquartile range of monthly medical expenses that exceed the deductible.
A) 200
B) 220
C) 240
D) 260
E) 280

11. The number of volcanoes erupting each month in a certain country follows Poisson distribution. The mean of eruptions during each summer month (May through August) is 0.7. The mean of eruptions during each of April, September, and October is 0.5. The mean of eruptions during each of the remaining months is 0.4. Find the probability of exactly 3 volcanoes during the first half of the year.
A) .11
B) .22
C) .33
D) .44
E) .55

12. Let X be a continuous random variable with density function

$$f(x) = \frac{p-1}{x^p}, \qquad x > 1$$

Find p such that $E[X] = 1$

(A) 1

(B) 2.5

(C) 3.5

(D) All values of p work.

(E) There is no such p.

13. There is a 20% chance that a patient coming to a doctor's office on Jan 2 is a new patient. Six patients arrive on that date. Total annual visits that a new patient will make are Poisson with mean 3. Each new patient gets a discount on 25% of their visits during the year. Find the variance of the total number of undiscounted new patient visits among these 6 patients.
A) 6.3
B) 6.6
C) 6.9
D) 7.2
E) 7.5

14. Each person at a university belongs to one and only one of the following categories: undergraduate students, graduate students, faculty, and staff. There are twice as many undergraduate students as graduate students, faculty, and staff combined.
The number of graduate students is three times the number of faculty and staff combined. There are twice as many faculty as staff.
Find the probability that a random person at this college is faculty or staff.
A) .06
B) .08
C) .10
D) .12
E) .14

15. The joint probability function of X and Y is given by:

$$P[X = 0, Y = 0] = .800$$

$$P[X = 1, Y = 0] = .050$$

$$P[X = 0, Y = 1] = .025$$

$$P[X = 1, Y = 1] = .125$$

Calculate $Var[X|Y = 0]$

A) .055
B) .075
C) .095
D) .115
E) .135

16. You buy a used car and want to sell it next week. Bids for your car are uniformly distributed on $[x - 3, x + 2]$, where x is the price you paid for the car. Let L be the lowest, and H be the highest of 5 mutually independent bids. Assume that no bid equals the price you paid. Find $P[L < x < H]$.
A) .51
B) .61
C) .71
D) .81
E) .91

17. In a certain town,

(i) Every adult has had at least one vaccine.
(ii) 70% of adults have had more than one vaccine.
(iii) 60% of adults have had covid vaccine.
(iv) Of those adults who have had more than one vaccine, 75% have had covid vaccine.

Find the probability that a randomly selected town adult has had exactly one vaccine and that vaccine is not a covid vaccine.

A) 7.5%
B) 22.5%
C) 30%
D) 50%
E) 52.5%

18. An insurance with a deductible covers 120 faculty members and 2500 students at a university. During the flue season, there is a 15% chance that a faculty member will get sick, and 90% chance that the resulting medical expenses will exceed the deductible. Also, there is a 20% chance that a student will get sick and 60% chance that the resulting medical expenses will exceed the deductible. The medical expense of a sick insured is examined and found to exceed the deductible. Find the probability that the person was a student.
A) .91
B) .93
C) .95
D) .97
E) .99

19. By age of a man, we mean the age at which he dies. Adam's grandfather died in 1854 when the average age of men in country X was normally distributed with mean 60 years and standard deviation 10 years. His age was at the 70th percentile among men's ages in country X in 1854. Adam lived the same number of years as his grandfather and died in 1918 when the average age of men in country X was 65 years with standard deviation 8 years. Both Adam and his grandfather spent their entire lives in country X. Find Adam's percentile age among men's ages in country X in 1918. Assume that ages are reported in integers only.
A) 50
B) 52
C) 54
D) 56
E) 58

20. The lifetime of a species has pdf proportional to

$$(x - x^2), \qquad 0 \le x \le 1$$

Find the mode of this distribution.

A) 0
B) 1/4
C) 1/2
D) 3/4
E) 1

21. A company provides accident insurance to its 6 drivers. Each driver has 3% probability of having an accident during the year. In case of an accident, the number of hospital visits is modeled by a geometric distribution with a mean of 4. The numbers of hospital visits of different drivers are mutually independent. Each visit costs 20000. Calculate the probability that the Company's total costs in a year are less than 35000.

A) .13
B) .25
C) .5
D) .75
E) .87

22. Annual home repair costs are uniformly distributed with a minimum cost of 0, and a maximum cost of M. An insurance covers these costs subject to a deductible that equals 15% of M. Calculate the annual ratio of the variance of the insurance payout to the variance of the repair costs.

A) .87
B) .89
C) .91
D) .94
E) .96

23. An insurance will cover losses incurred from up to 2 floods during the year. Let X be the number of floods that result in at least 15000 in losses and let Y be the total number of floods during the year. The joint probability function for X and Y is

$$p(x,y) = c(3x + 2y), \qquad x = 0,1,2, \qquad y = 0,1,2,3, \qquad x \leq y$$

where c is a constant. Calculate the expected number of floods that result in fewer than 15000 in losses.

A) 1
B) 13/11
C) 15/11
D) 17/11
E) 19/11

24. The pdf of a random variable X is of the form:

$$f(x) = cx^5 e^{-0.2x}, \ x > 0$$

where c is a constant. Calculate $Var\ X - E[X]$.

A) 30
B) 120
C) 150
D) 870
E) 930

25. The time until the next baby is born is exponentially distributed with mean 0.5 month. Given that no baby is born until two months from now, find the probability that a baby will be born in the 3rd month from now.

A) .0158
B) .0169
C) .0183
D) .0201
E) .0207

26. A bunch of computers are checked, one at a time, for a defect until a defective computer is found. Each computer independently has the same probability of being defective. Probability that at least 20 computers are checked is k. Find the probability that at least 25 computers are tested given that at least 20 computers are checked.

A) $k^{5/19}$
B) $k^{24/19}$
C) $k^{19/25}$
D) $k^{19/24}$
E) $k^{4/19}$

27. Cost for visiting a doctor is uniformly distributed on [0, 800]. An insurance has a deductible of d per visit. The expected value of the uncovered portion of the cost is 100 per visit. Find d.

A) 101
B) 103
C) 105
D) 107
E) 109

28. Let X denote the percentage of men in city A that will be employed next year and Y the percentage of women in city A that will be employed next year. X and Y have a joint cumulative distribution:

$$F(x,y) = \frac{xy(x+y)}{2000000}, \qquad 0 \le x \le 100, \qquad 0 \le y \le 100$$

Find the probability that at least 40% men and at least 55% women in city A will be employed next year.

A) .40
B) .42
C) .44
D) .46
E) .48

29. The expected value of a random variable X is 10 and $E[(2X-1)^2] = 999$. Find the variance of X.

A) 150
B) 155
C) 160
D) 165
E) 170

30. Given that 2% of the population has green eyes, find the probability that out of 150 randomly chosen persons, more than 6 will have green eyes.

(A) .01

(B) .02

(C) .03

(D) .04

(E) .05

Practice Exam 2 (Give yourself 3 hours to mimic actual P Exam)

1. Of the 45,000 students at a university, 5500 are teenagers, 20000 are male, and 7000 are graduate students. There are 2200 teenage males, 3000 male graduate students, and 150 teenage graduate students. Also, there are 70 teenage male graduate students. Find the number of teenage female undergraduate students. Note that every student at the university is undergraduate or graduate, and male or female.
   A) 2280
   B) 2380
   C) 2920
   D) 3120
   E) 3220

2. A hospital deals with only hearing and vision problems. 40% of the patients have hearing problem, 70% of patients vision problem, and 35% of patients have both problems. Of those who have only hearing problem, 15% will have a surgery this month. Of those who have only vision problem, 10% will have a surgery this month. Of those who have both the problems, 17% will have a surgery for at least one of the problems this month. How many of the hospital patients will have at least one surgery this month?

   (A) 10%

   (B) 10.1%

   (C) 10.2%

   (D) 10.3%

   (E) 10.4%

3. In a city, 70% people live in apartments, 20% live in houses, and the rest live elsewhere. In the same city, 24% have a car and the rest do not. Three quarters of those with car live in apartments. A tenth of those who neither live in apartments nor in houses own a car. How many live in houses but do not have a car?
   A) 7%
   B) 9%
   C) 11%
   D) 13%
   E) 15%

4. Half of the population in a country does not have a car, 45% have one car, and the remaining have more than one car. Those with one car are twice as likely to be in an accident than those who have no car, and also twice as likely to be in an accident than those who have more than one car. If a randomly selected person was in an accident, what is the probability that they had more than one car?
   A) .0145
   B) .0245
   C) .0345
   D) .0445
   E) .0555

5. The number of children that a couple in a certain country has follows a Poisson distribution with mean 2. Find the probability that a couple there has 3 children given that they have at least one child.
   A) .21
   B) .26
   C) .31
   D) .34
   E) .39

6. The lifetime of a car costing 15000 is exponentially distributed with mean 13 years. An insurance pays 10,000 if the car fails during the first year following its purchase, 6000 if it fails during the second year, 2000 if it fails during the 3rd year and nothing otherwise. Find the expected total benefit.
   A) 1079
   B) 1179
   C) 1279
   D) 1379
   E) 1479

7. An insurance policy pays for a random loss X subject to a deductible. The loss amount is modeled as a continuous random variable with density:

$$f(x) = \begin{cases} 3x^2, & 0 < x < 1 \\ 0, & otherwise \end{cases}$$

Given a random loss X, the probability that the insurance payment greater than 0.2 is 0.7. Find the deductible.

A) .17
B) .23
C) .37
D) .47
E) .57

8. A car battery will be replaced when it stops working, but definitely after 3 years of purchase. The battery's age at failure, X, has density function:

$$f(x) = \begin{cases} \frac{1}{4}, & 1 < x < 5 \\ 0, & otherwise \end{cases}$$

Let Y be battery's age at the time of replacement. Calculate the variance of Y.

A) 0.42
B) 0.52
C) 3.24
D) 3.61
E) 4.0

9. Probability distribution of ages in a certain class are given below:

Age	Probability
16	.05
17	.15
18	.55
19	.2
20	.05

Find the percentage of ages within one standard deviation of the mean age.

(A) 45%

(B) 55%

C) 70%

(D) 90%

(E) 100%

10. Car damage in accidents is exponentially distributed. An insurance will cover damages exceeding a deductible of 1000. Probability that the reimbursement is less than 4000, given that the damage exceeds deductible is .6. Find probability that the reimbursement is greater than 2000 but less than 5000, given that loss exceeds the deductible.

A) .31
B) .33
C) .35
D) .37
E) .39

11. Annual repair costs (in thousands) of 4 insured homes are mutually independent random variables with common density function:

$$f(x) = \frac{4}{x^5}, \qquad x > 1$$

Find the expected value of the highest of the 4 costs.

A) 1173
B) 1373
C) 1573
D) 1773
E) 1973

12. A fund gets donations from 300 persons. Donations are mutually independent and identically distributed with mean 800 and variance 200. Calculate the approximate 95th percentile for the distribution of the total fund amount.

A) 200403
B) 210403
C) 220403
D) 230403
E) 240403

13. Home losses due to a fire follow exponential distribution. Insurance company A reimburses each loss completely, while company B reimburses each loss subject to a deductible which reduces the expected reimbursement by 25%. Find the percentage reduction in the variance.
   A) 5%
   B) 6%
   C) 8%
   D) 9%
   E) 10%

14. The average number of daily sleeping hours, X, for people who do not use any sleep aid is uniformly distributed on $[a, 9]$. Average number of daily sleeping hours, Y, for people who use a certain sleeping aid is uniformly distributed on $[.75a, 9]$. Given $E[X] = 6.5$, find the 30th percentile of Y.
   A) 4.5
   B) 4.8
   C) 5.1
   D) 5.4
   E) 5.7

15. Losses in a crash have probability density function

$$f(x) = c(30000 - x), \qquad 0 < x < 30000$$

where c is a constant. A car is insured with a deductible of 1000. This car was involved in a crash with resulting losses in excess of the deductible. Calculate the probability that the losses exceeded 6000.

   A) .655
   B) .665
   C) .675
   D) .685
   E) .695

16. You have three 4-sides prisms. The faces on two of the prisms are marked 1,2,3,4, while the faces on the 3rd prism as marked 2,2,4,4. If a prism is rolled, it is equally likely to land on any of the four faces. You randomly select one of the three prisms and roll it twice. Find the probability that it lands on the face 2 both times.
A) 1/8
B) 1/4
C) 3/8
D) 1/2
E) 3/4

17. A student takes an exam consisting of 35 multiple choice questions, each with 4 answer choices. The student knows the answer to N of the questions, which are answered correctly, and guesses the answers to the rest. The conditional probability that the student knows the answer to a question, given that the student answered it correctly, is 0.842. Find N.
A) 20
B) 21
C) 22
D) 23
E) 24

18. In a sample of 15 men, the probability that exactly 7 men like apples is 0.9 times the probability that exactly 8 men like apples. Find the probability that a randomly chosen man in this sample does not like apples.
A) .356
B) .474
C) .500
D) .526
E) .644

19. A policy covers auto repairs for a year subject to a deductible. During the year, only one of the following can happen:
   (i) Battery may need to be replaced at a cost of 200. The probability of this happening is 0.2
   (ii) Brakes may need to be changed at a cost of 600. The probability of this happening is 0.15
   (iii) AC may need to be repaired at a cost of 500. The probability of this happening is 0.1

   Find the deductible that would produce an expected claim payment of 82.5 for the year.
   A) 183
   B) 200
   C) 217
   D) 230
   E) 243

20. At a certain time, there are 9 people in a children's park, some of them are adults and the remaining are children. Three of the persons are on the slides, and the probability that all of these 3 are children is 5/21. Find the probability that at most one of these 3 is an adult.
   A) .24
   B) .54
   C) .77
   D) .85
   E) .91

21. Two phenomena of interest in a region are annual number of snowstorms (X), and annual number of hurricanes (Y). The pmf of X is:

$$f(x) = \frac{3^x e^{-3}}{x!}, \qquad x = 0,1,2,\dots$$

   Standard deviation of Y is 2. Correlation between X and Y is .5. Find the variance of the total annual number of the two phenomena.
   A) 5
   B) 7
   C) 8.7
   D) 10.5
   E) 12

22. A man buys a 4-year policy that will provide an annual benefit of 2000 for every year in which his home suffers a total fire loss in excess of 1000, up to a maximum of 2 annual payments over the 4-year period. The probability that he will have a fire loss in excess of 1000 in a given year is .15, independent of any other year. Find the man's expected benefit over the 4-year period.
A) 1075
B) 1175
C) 1275
D) 1375
E) 1475

23. Probability that an adult has hearing problems is .05. Probability that an adult has vision problems is .25. Find the probability that an adult has exactly one of two problems. Assume that the 2 problems are independent of each other.
A) .235
B) .255
C) .275
D) .295
E) .300

24. Five sparrows and three nightingales have their permanent home on the same tree. Three of these birds are currently eating, including at least one sparrow. Find the probability that the other two eating are nightingales.
A) .04
B) .14
C) .24
D) .34
E) .44

25. Heights of 20-year old girls in US are normally distributed. Probability that the height of a randomly chosen 20-year old girl in US is less than 63 inches is .5478, and the probability that the height of a randomly chosen 20-year old girl in US is less than 65 inches is .7704. Find the probability that the height of a random 20-year old girl in US is between 64 and 66 inches.
A) .1567
B) .1667
C) .1767
D) .1867
E) .1967

26. The number of deaths in a town each month follows a Poisson distribution with mean 1.5. The number of deaths in different months are mutually independent. Find the probability that more than two deaths will happen during a consecutive two-month period, given that at most one death happened in the first of the two months.
A) .16
B) .34
C) .5
D) .66
E) .84

27. After a flood, there is a 55% chance that the repair cost of a home follows a uniform distribution on $[0, 2b]$, and a 45% chance that it follows a uniform distribution on the interval $[2b, 3b]$. The median repair cost due to flood is 1200. Calculate the mean repair cost (to the nearest 100).
A) 1000
B) 1100
C) 1200
D) 1300
E) 1400

28. Roof repair costs are uniformly distributed on [0,6000]. A home-owner has a primary home-insurance which covers up to 2500 of the roof repair costs, and a secondary home-insurance which covers up to 2200 of any remaining roof repair costs in excess of 2500. Find the expected roof repair cost covered by the secondary insurance.
A) 800
B) 820
C) 840
D) 860
E) 880

29. In a certain country people work from ages 16 to 60 only. The age at which a working adult dies is uniformly distributed on [16, 60]. In case of death, the loss to the family is exponentially distributed with mean 10 times the age. Find the standard deviation of the loss from a death.
A) 400
B) 420
C) 440
D) 460
E) 480

30. The independent random variables X and Y have the same variance. The coefficients of variation of X and Y are 8 and 9 respectively. Calculate the coefficient of variation of $2X + 3Y$.
A) 2.14
B) 3.15
C) 4.16
D) 5.17
E) 6.18

Solutions to Practice Exam 1

1.

$$P = P(A) + P(B) + P(C) + P(D) - P(AB) - P(AC) - P(AD) - P(BC) - P(BD) - P(CD) + P(ABC) + P(ABD) + P(BCD) + P(ACD) - P(ABCD)$$

$$= 4(40\%) - 6(30\%) + 4(20\%) - 10\%$$

$$= 160\% - 180\% + 80\% - 10\%$$

$$= 50\%$$

The correct answer is **B**.

2.

$$60\%(30) = 18$$

So, Dr. Megan's class has 18 girls, and $30 - 18 = 12$ boys.

Let number of boys in Dr. Laura's class be x.

18 Girls	39 Girls
12 Boys	x Boys
Total = 30	Total = $x + 39$

$$P(BB) + P(GG) = .513$$

$$\frac{12}{30} \cdot \frac{x}{x+39} + \frac{18}{30} \cdot \frac{39}{x+39} = .513$$

$$702 + 12x = .513(30)(x + 39)$$

$$x = 30$$

Total students in Dr. Laura's class $= x + 39$

$$= 30 + 39$$

$$= 69$$

The correct answer is **E**.

3.

$$p(1) = .7p(0)$$

$$p(2) = .7p(1) = .7[.7p(0)] = .49p(0)$$

$$p(3) = .7p(2) = .7[.49p(0)] = .343p(0)$$

etc. The sum of all possible probabilities is 1. That is:

$$p(0) + p(1) + p(2) + p(3) + \cdots = 1$$

$$p(0) + .7p(0) + .49p(0) + .343p(0) + \cdots = 1$$

$$p(0)[1 + .7 + .49 + .343 + \cdots] = 1$$

Sum of a geometric series equals:

$$\frac{First\ Term}{1 - common\ ratio}$$

Thus, we have:

$$p(0)\left[\frac{1}{1 - .7}\right] = 1$$

$$p(0) = .3$$

$$p(1) = .7p(0) = .7(.3) = .21$$

The company will pay if there is one or more flood, that is, if $n > 1$. So,

$$p(n > 1) = 1 - p(0) - p(1) = 1 - .3 - .21 = .49$$

The correct answer is **D**.

4.

Let X_1, X_2 be the two errors. The average of these two is:

$$Y = \frac{X_1 + X_2}{2}$$

We are asked to calculate:

$$P(-.1x \leq Y \leq .1x)$$

The sum and constant multiple of two normal variables is normal with mean and variance:

$$\text{Mean of } Y = \mu = \tfrac{1}{2}(\mu_{X_1} + \mu_{X_2}) = \tfrac{1}{2}(.1x + .05x) = .075x$$

$$\text{Var}(Y) = \left(\tfrac{1}{2}\right)^2 (VarX_1 + VarX_2\,) = \tfrac{1}{4}((.1x)^2 + (.2x)^2 = .0125x^2$$

So, the standard deviation of $Y = \sigma = \sqrt{.0125x^2} = .1118x$

Since we need to use standard normal table to calculate the required probability, so we need to change the given extreme values of Y into standard normal values through the formula:

$$z = \frac{Y - \mu}{\sigma} = \frac{Y - .075x}{.1118x}$$

So, the two extreme values convert into:

$$z_1 = \frac{-.1x - .075x}{.1118x} = -1.57, \quad z_2 = \frac{.1x - .075x}{.1118x} = .22$$

Thus, we on the standard normal curve, we need:

$$P(-1.57 \leq z \leq .22)$$

However, table values that are provided to us on the exam give us the area to the left of the positive standard values and not the in between area.

From the figure, we see that:

$$P(-1.57 \leq z \leq .22) = P(z \leq .22) - P(z \leq -1.57)$$
$$= P(z \leq .22) - [1 - P(z \leq 1.57)]$$
$$= P(z \leq .22) + P(z \leq 1.57) - 1$$

Using the appropriate table value, we have:

$$P(-1.57 \leq z \leq .22) = .5871 + .9418 - 1$$
$$= .53$$

The correct answer is **C**.

5.

Let X be the number of thefts. It is binomial with $n = 65,\ p = .02$. So,

$$E[X] = np = 65(.02) = 1.3$$

$$Var\ X = np(1-p) = 1.3(1-.02) = 1.274$$

Let Y be the payout. Then $Y = 700X$.

$$E[Y] = 700E[X] = 700(1.3) = 910$$

$$Var\ Y = 700^2\ Var\ X = 700^2(1.274) = 624260$$

$$\sigma_Y = \sqrt{Var\ Y} = \sqrt{624260} = 790.1$$

Let s be the smallest amount of money needed in the fund. We want:

$$P(Y \le s) = .9 \quad (1)$$

From table and interpolation $z = 1.282$ corresponds to .9.

$$P(z \le 1.282) = .9 \quad (2)$$

From (1) and (2) we see that $z = 1.282$ corresponds to $Y = s$. Hence,

$$z = \frac{Y - \mu_Y}{\sigma_Y}$$

$$1.282 = \frac{s - 910}{790.1}$$

$$s = 1923$$

The correct answer is **A**.

6.

The cdf of an exponential distribution with mean k is given as:

$$F(x) = 1 - e^{-\frac{x}{k}}$$

Here, x is the time elapsed (in years) before the first snowstorm.

We are given that $F(.5) = .2$.

The probability of there being no snowstorm during the first quarter is the probability of the first snowstorm happening after the first quarter which is $P(X > .25) = 1 - F(.25)$. So, we get:

$$.2 = 1 - e^{-\frac{.5}{k}}$$

$$e^{-\frac{.5}{k}} = .8$$

$$-\frac{.5}{k} = \ln(.8)$$

$$k = -\frac{.5}{\ln(.8)} = 2.24$$

$$1 - F(.25) = 1 - (1 - e^{-\frac{.25}{2.24}})$$

$$= .89$$

The correct answer is **E**.

7.

This is a trinomial distribution which is a special case of the multinomial distribution. Let:

X_1 represent number of children in class,
X_2 represent the number adults in class,
X_3 represent the number of seniors in class

Here, $n = 4$ because we are selecting 4 members in our study. Also,

$$p_2 = p_3 = 2p_1$$

$$p_1 + p_2 + p_3 = 1$$

$$p_1 + 2p_1 + 2p_1 = 1$$

$$p_1 = \frac{1}{5}, \quad p_2 = \frac{2}{5}, \quad p_3 = \frac{2}{5}$$

$$f(x_1, x_2, x_3) = \frac{4!}{x_1!\,x_2!\,x_3!}\left(\frac{1}{5}\right)^{x_1}\left(\frac{2}{5}\right)^{x_2}\left(\frac{2}{5}\right)^{x_3}$$

We are to find $P(X_1 = 3)$ subject to the condition $X_1 + X_2 + X_3 = 4$

The two possible cases in which this happens are listed in the table below:

x_1	x_2	x_3	$f(x_1, x_2, x_3)$
3	0	1	.0128
3	1	0	.0128

Required probability equals:

$$.0128 + .0128$$

$$= .0256.$$

The correct answer is **B**.

8.

$$P(X < 4 \; given \; X > 1) = \frac{P(X < 4 \; and \; X > 1)}{P(X > 1)}$$

$$= \frac{P(1 < X < 4)}{P(X > 1)}$$

$$P(X > 1) = c\int_{1}^{5}(5 - x)\,dx = 8c$$

$$P(1 < X < 4) = c\int_{1}^{4}(5 - x)\,dx = 7.5c$$

$$P(X < 4 \; given \; X > 1) = \frac{7.5c}{8c} = .9375$$

The correct answer is **E**.

9.

This will happen if in the first 5 children, there are at least 4 girls, because if there are less than 4 girls in the first 5 children, then they have already had 2 boys without having at least 4 girls.

P (at least 4 girls in the first 5 kids)= $P(4) + P(5)$

Where $P(x) = \binom{5}{x}(.55)^x(.45)^{5-x}$, because this is a binomial distribution with $n = 5$, $p = 1 - .45 = .55$, $X = \#$ of girls. Thus:

$$P(X \geq 4) = \binom{5}{4}(.55)^4(.45)^{5-4} + \binom{5}{5}(.55)^5(.45)^{5-5}$$

$$= .256$$

The correct answer is **B**.

10.

Let *X* represent the monthly medical expense. Exponential cdf with mean 200 is:

$$F(x) = 1 - e^{-x/200}$$

Interquartile range is the difference between 75th and 25th percentiles

The pth percentile x_p of expenses exceeding deductible satisfies the equation:

$$P(X < x_p \text{ } given \text{ } X > 50) = p/100$$

$$\frac{P(X < x_p \text{ } and \text{ } X > 50)}{P(X > 50)} = \frac{p}{100}$$

$$\frac{P(50 < X < x_p)}{1 - P(X \le 50)} = \frac{p}{100}$$

$$\frac{F(x_p) - F(50)}{1 - F(50)} = \frac{p}{100}$$

$$\frac{1 - e^{-\frac{x_p}{200}} - \left(1 - e^{-\frac{50}{200}}\right)}{1 - \left(1 - e^{-\frac{50}{200}}\right)} = \frac{p}{100}$$

$$\frac{e^{-\frac{1}{4}} - e^{-\frac{x_p}{200}}}{e^{-\frac{1}{4}}} = \frac{p}{100}$$

$$e^{-\frac{1}{4}} - e^{-\frac{x_p}{200}} = \frac{p}{100} e^{-\frac{1}{4}}$$

$$.7788 - \frac{p}{100} e^{-\frac{1}{4}} = e^{-\frac{x_p}{200}}$$

$$\ln\left(.7788 - \frac{p}{100} e^{-\frac{1}{4}}\right) = -\frac{x_p}{200}$$

$$x_p = -200 \ln\left(.7788 - \frac{p}{100} e^{-\frac{1}{4}}\right)$$

$$x_{75} = -200 \ln\left(.7788 - \frac{75}{100} e^{-\frac{1}{4}}\right) = 327.26$$

$$x_{25} = -200 \ln\left(.7788 - \frac{25}{100} e^{-\frac{1}{4}}\right) = 107.54$$

Subtracting the two percentiles we get:

$$x_{75} - x_{25} = 220$$

The correct answer is **B**.

11.

The sum of N independent Poisson variables with means $k_1, k_2, \ldots, k_N$, is also Poisson with mean $k_1 + k_2 + \cdots + k_N$

The means of Jan to June are $.4, .4, .4, .5, .7, .7$ respectively.

So, the total mean in these months $= .4 + .4 + .4 + .5 + .7 + .7 = 3.1$

The probability of getting x Poisson successes with mean k is

$$f(x) = \frac{k^x e^{-k}}{x!}$$

Here, $x = 3, k = 3.1$. So,

$$f(3) = \frac{3.1^3 e^{-3.1}}{3!}$$

$$= .22$$

The correct answer is **B**.

12.

$$E[X] = \int_{-\infty}^{\infty} x f(x)\, dx$$

$$= \int_{1}^{\infty} x \frac{p-1}{x^p} dx$$

$$= (p-1) \int_{1}^{\infty} x^{1-p}\, dx$$

$$= (p-1) \frac{x^{2-p}}{2-p} \Big|_{x=1}^{x=\infty}$$

$$= \frac{p-1}{2-p} (\infty^{2-p} - 1^{2-p}) \quad (1)$$

We know that

$$\infty^k = \begin{cases} 0, & k < 0 \\ \infty, & k > 0 \end{cases}$$

Thus, for expected value to be finite, we must have:

$$2 - p < 0$$

$$p > 2$$

In this case, (1) becomes:

$$E[X] = \frac{p-1}{2-p}(0-1)$$

$$= \frac{1-p}{2-p}$$

Setting that equal to 1 we get:

$$\frac{1-p}{2-p}=1$$

$$1-p=2-p$$

$$1=2$$

This is a contradiction. So, there is no such p.

The correct answer is **E**.

13.

If X is the number of new patients, then X is binomial with $n=6,\ p=.2$

$$E[X]=np=6(.2)=1.2$$

$$Var[X]=np(1-p)=1.2(1-.2)=.96$$

Let V be number of annual visits for each new patient. V is Poisson with mean 3.

$$E[V]=Var[V]=3$$

If Y the number of undiscounted visits for each accident, then:

$$Y=.75V$$

$$E[Y]=.75E[V]=.75(3)=2.25$$

$$Var[Y]=.75^2Var[V]=.5625(3)=1.6875$$

Let T be the total undiscounted visits for X new patients. Then:

$$E[T|X]=XE[Y]=2.25X$$

$$Var[T|X]=XVar[Y]=1.6875X$$

$$Var(T)=E[Var(T|\mathrm{X})]+\mathrm{Var}[\mathrm{E}(\mathrm{T}|\mathrm{X})]$$

$$=E[1.6875X]+Var[2.25X]$$

$$=1.6875E[X]+2.25^2Var[X]$$

$$=1.6875(1.2)+2.25^2(.96)=6.9$$

The correct answer is **C**.

14.

Let U,G,S,F be the number undergraduates, graduates, staff, and faculty, respectively. So, total members $=U+G+S+F$. We need to find:

$$P(F\ or\ S)=\frac{F+S}{U+G+F+S}$$

We are given that:

$$U = 2(G + F + S) \quad (1)$$

$$G = 3(F + S) \quad (2)$$

$$F = 2S \quad (3)$$

Substituting (3) ind (2), and then the result is (1) we get

$$G = 3(2S + S) = 9S$$

$$U = 2(9S + 2S + S) = 24S$$

$$P(F \text{ } or \text{ } S) = \frac{F + S}{U + G + F + S}$$

$$= \frac{2S + S}{24S + 9S + 2S + S}$$

$$= \frac{3S}{36S}$$

$$= .08$$

The correct answer is **B**.

15.

$$P[X = 0|Y = 0] = \frac{P[Y = 0 \text{ } and \text{ } X = 0]}{P[Y = 0]}$$

$$= \frac{.8}{P[X = 0, Y = 0] + P[X = 1, Y = 0]}$$

$$= \frac{.8}{.8 + .05}$$

$$= .9412$$

$$P[X = 1|Y = 0] = 1 - P[X = 0|Y = 0]$$

$$= 1 - .9412$$

$$= .0588$$

$X\|Y = 0$	$P[Y\|X = 0]$
0	.9412
1	.0588

From calculator, SD = .2352.

So, $Var = .2352^2 = .055$

The correct answer is **A**.

16. Let N be the number of bids and let us call a bid being less than your price a success. Let Y be the bid amount which is uniformly distributed on $[x-3,\ x+2]$. Then N is binomially distributed with $n = 5$, and the probability of success:

$$p = P(Y < x)$$

$$= \frac{x-(x-3)}{(x+2)-(x-3)}$$

$$= \frac{3}{5}$$

$$= .6$$

We need $P(L < x < H)$ which is the probability that the lowest of the 5 bids is below your price and the highest bid is above the actual price. This will happen if exactly 1, 2, 3, or 4 bids are below your price, that is, the number of binomial successes is 1,2, 3, or 4. So, using the binomial pmf:

$$f(x) = \binom{5}{x}.6^x(.4^{5-x}),\quad x = 0,1,2,3,4,5$$

$$P(X = 1,2,3\ or\ 4) = f(1) + f(2) + f(3) + f(4)$$

$$= 1 - f(0) - f(5)$$

$$= 1 - \binom{5}{0}.6^0(.4^5) + \binom{5}{5}.6^5(.4^0)$$

$$= .91$$

The correct answer is **E**.

17.

	Exactly one Vaccine = 100% − 70% = 30%	More than one vaccine = 70%	Total
Covid vaccine	60% − 52.5% = 7.5%	.75(70%) = 52.5%	60%
No Covid Vaccine	30% − 7.5% = 22.5%		

From the above table we see that the required probability is **.225.**

The correct answer is **B**.

18.

Total Insured $= 120 + 2500 = 2620$

Probability of selecting a faculty member $= 120/2620$

Probability of selecting a student $= 2500/2620$

$$P(Faculty\ selected\ and\ Sick) = \frac{120}{2620}(.15) = .00687$$

$$P(Student\ selected\ and\ Sick) = \frac{2500}{2620}(.2) = .19084$$

$$\begin{aligned} P(Exceeds\ Deductible) \\ &= P(Student\ Sick\ and\ Exceeds\ Ded) \\ &+ P(Faculty\ Sick\ and\ Exceeds\ Ded) \end{aligned}$$

$$= .00687(.9) + .19084(.6)$$

$$P(Student\ Sick|Exceeds\ Ded) = \frac{P(Student\ Sick\ and\ Exceeds\ Ded)}{P(Exceeds\ Ded)}$$

$$= \frac{.19084(.6)}{.00687(.9) + .19084(.6)}$$

$$= .95$$

The correct answer is **C**.

19.

The z-score of grandfather is the value corresponding to a cumulative probability of .7. In table .6985 corresponds to $z = .52$, and .7019 corresponds to $z = .53$.

$$\frac{.7 - .6985}{.7019 - .6985} = .4$$

Thus, by interpolation, $z = .524$. Now we find grandfather's age.

$$z_{GF} = \frac{X_{GF} - mean}{SD}$$

$$.524 = \frac{X_{GF} - 60}{10}$$

$$X_{GF} = 65$$

to the nearest year. That is also Adam's age.

$$z_{ADAM} = \frac{65 - 65}{8} = 0$$

This corresponds to a cumulative probability of .50. Thus, Adam's percentile is 50.

The correct answer is **A**.

20.

$$f(x) = c(x - x^2), 0 \le x \le 1$$

where c is a constant.

Mode is the x value for which $f(x)$ is maximum.

Recall from calculus that the absolute maximum and minimum are found by evaluating the function value at the end points and critical points.

The endpoints here are 0 and 1.

Critical points are those where the derivative is 0 or undefined.

$$f'(x) = c(1 - 2x)$$

This is always defined. So, we only need to see where it is 0.

$$c(1 - 2x) = 0$$

$c \neq 0$ because pdf cannot be always 0. So

$$1 - 2x = 0$$

$$x = \frac{1}{2}$$

This is the only critical point. The candidate points for max are 0,1, and 1/2

$$f(0) = 0 \quad (1)$$

$$f(1) = 0 \quad (2)$$

$$f\left(\frac{1}{2}\right) = \frac{c}{4} \quad (3)$$

A pdf can never be negative. So, $c > 0$, and $f\left(\frac{1}{2}\right) > 0$.

So max is at $x = 1/2$.

The correct answer is **C**.

21.

Since 1 visit costs 20000, 2 visits will cost 40000 which exceeds 35000.

So, we are really being asked the probability of less than 2 total visits.

The number of employees in accidents, X, is binomial with $n = 6,\ p = .03$

$$f(x) = \binom{n}{x} p^x (1 - p)^{n-x} = \binom{6}{x} (.03)^x (.97)^{6-x} \quad (1)$$

Also, the number of hospital visits V for an employee having accident is geometric with mean 4.

For the geometric distribution:

$$g(v) = (1-P)^{v-1}P,$$

mean $= 1/P$. So,

$$P = \frac{1}{mean} = \frac{1}{4}$$

$$g(v) = \left(1 - \frac{1}{4}\right)^{v-1}\left(\frac{1}{4}\right)$$

$$= \left(\frac{3}{4}\right)^{v-1}\left(\frac{1}{4}\right)$$

$$\Rightarrow g(1) = \frac{1}{4}$$

Less than 2 hospital visits can happen in exactly the following scenarios:

Case 1: No one has a hospital visit.

This also implies no accident because we are told that in case of accident, the number of visits V is geometric, and the values that a geometric variable takes are 1,2, 3,.... Thus, an accident implies at least one hospital visit.

The probability of no visit is found by substituting $x = 0$ in (1)

$$f(0) = \binom{6}{0}(.03)^0(.97)^{6-0} = .83297$$

Case 2: One employee has an accident, and has 1 visit; others have none.

P (Only 1 employee has accident, and has only 1 visit) $= f(1)g(1)$

$$= \binom{6}{1}(.03)^1(.97)^{6-1}\left(\frac{1}{4}\right) = .03864$$

$$P(Less\ than\ 2\ visits) = .83297 + .03864 = .87$$

The correct answer is **E**.

22.

Let X be the damage and Y be the payout. Deductible is $.15M$

$$f(x) = \frac{1}{M}, \qquad 0 < x < M$$

$$Var\ X = \frac{(M-0)^2}{12}$$

$$Y = \begin{cases} 0\,, & X < 0.15M \\ X - 0.15M\,, & 0.15M < X < M \end{cases}$$

$$E(Y) = \int_{-\infty}^{\infty} y\, f(x)\, dx$$

$$= \int_{0.15M}^{M} (x - 0.15M)\left(\frac{1}{M}\right) dx$$

$$= \int_{0.1b}^{M} \frac{x}{M} - 0.15\, dx$$

$$= \left(\frac{x^2}{2M} - 0.15x\right)\Big|_{x\,=\,.15M}^{x\,=\,M}$$

$$= \left(\frac{M^2}{2M} - 0.15M\right) - \left(\frac{(.15M)^2}{2M} - 0.15(.15M)\right)$$

$$= \frac{M}{2} - .15M - \frac{.0225M}{2} + .0225M$$

$$= .36125M$$

$$E(Y^2) = \int_{-\infty}^{\infty} y^2 f(x)\, dx$$

$$= \int_{0.15M}^{M} (x - 0.15M)^2\left(\frac{1}{M}\right) dx$$

$$= \frac{1}{M}\left(\frac{(x - .15M)^3}{3}\right)\Big|_{x\,=\,.15M}^{x\,=\,M}$$

$$= \frac{1}{M}\left(\frac{(M - .15M)^3}{3}\right)$$

$$= \frac{(.85M)^3}{3}$$

$$= .2047M^2$$

$$Var\ Y = E(Y^2) - (E[Y])^2$$

$$= .2047M^2 - (.36125M)^2$$

$$= .0742M^2$$

$$\frac{Var\ Y}{Var\ X} = \frac{.0742M^2}{\left(\frac{M^2}{12}\right)}$$

$$= .89$$

The correct answer is **B**.

23.

$$E[Y-X]=\sum(y-x)p(x,y)$$

We first find c by summing the probability function to 1.

$$f(0,0)+f(0,1)+f(0,2)+f(0,3)+f(1,1)+f(1,2)+f(1,3)+f(2,2)+f(2,3)=1$$

$$c(0+2+4+6+5+7+9+10+12)=1$$

$$c=\frac{1}{55}$$

Number of floods that result in less than 15000 in losses = $Y-X$

(x,y)	(0,0)	(0,1)	(0,2)	(0,3)	(1,1)	(1,2)	(1,3)	(2,2)	(2,3)
$y-x$	0	1	2	3	0	1	2	0	1
$3x+2y$	0	2	4	6	5	7	9	10	12

$$E[Y-X]=\sum(y-x)\frac{1}{55}(3x+2y)=\frac{1}{55}(2+8+18+7+18+12)$$

$$=\frac{13}{11}$$

The correct answer is **B**.

24.

We recognize this as a gamma distribution with

$$\alpha=6,$$

$$\theta=\frac{1}{.2}=5$$

$$Var\,(X)=\alpha\theta^2$$

$$=6(5)^2$$

$$=150$$

$$E[X]=\alpha\theta$$

$$=6(5)$$

$$=30$$

$$Var\,X-E[X]=150-30$$

$$=120$$

The correct answer is **B**.

25.

Let X be the number of months until next birth.

$$F(x) = 1 - e^{-\frac{x}{.5}}$$

$$= 1 - e^{-2x}$$

No birth during next 2 months and a birth in 3rd month from now is equivalent to the statement:

The number of months it takes for the 1st birth to occur is between 2 and 3.

So, we are to find $P(2 < X < 3)$.

$$P(2 < X < 3) = F(3) - F(2)$$

$$= \left[1 - e^{-2(3)}\right] - \left[1 - e^{-2(2)}\right]$$

$$= .0158$$

The correct answer is **A**.

26.

Let q be the probability of a computer NOT being defective.

Let X be the number of computers tested until one with defect is found.

We are to find:

$$P(X \geq 25 | X \geq 20) = \frac{P(X \geq 25 \text{ } and \text{ } X \geq 20)}{P(X \geq 20)}$$

$$= \frac{P(X \geq 25)}{P(X \geq 20)}$$

$$= \frac{P(X \geq 25)}{k}$$

Now if at least 20 computers are tested, the first 19 do not have defect. Thus

$$k = P(X \geq 19) = q^{19}$$

$$\Rightarrow q = k^{1/19} \quad (2)$$

Similarly, if at least 25 computers are tested, the first 24 do not have defect.

$$P(X \geq 25) = q^{24} = k^{24/19}$$

by using (2). Thus, (1) becomes:

$$P(X \geq 25 | X \geq 20) = \frac{k^{\frac{24}{19}}}{k} = k^{5/19}$$

The correct answer is **A**.

27.

Let X be the cost and Y be the uncovered portion of cost.

When cost is less than the deductible, all the cost is uncovered.

When cost is greater than the deductible, then deductible is the unreimbursed portion of the cost.

$$f(x) = \frac{1}{800}, \qquad 0 < x < 800$$

$$Y = \begin{cases} X, & X \leq d \\ d, & X > d \end{cases}$$

$$E[Y] = 100$$

$$\int_{-\infty}^{\infty} y\, f(x)\, dx = 100$$

$$\int_{0}^{d} x\left(\frac{1}{800}\right) dx + \int_{d}^{800} d\left(\frac{1}{800}\right) dx = 100$$

$$\frac{1}{800}\left(\frac{x^2}{2}\right)\Big|_0^d + \frac{1}{800} d\, x\Big|_d^{800} = 100$$

$$\frac{d^2}{1600} + \frac{800d - d^2}{800} = 100$$

$$d^2 + 1600d - 2d^2 = 160000$$

$$d^2 - 1600d + 160000 = 0$$

$$d = \frac{1600 \pm \sqrt{1600^2 - 4(1)(160000)}}{2(1)}$$

$$= 1492, 107$$

A deductible of 1492 makes no sense because it is greater than max cost of 800.

Hence the correct deductible is 107

The correct answer is **D**.

28.

We are to find $P(X \geq 40 \; and \; Y \geq 55)$.

We will use the complement rule, addition rule, and the fact that if a probability evaluation of only one variable is done using a joint cdf, then that missing variable is set to its maximum possible value, which in this case is 100 for both the variables.

$$P(X \geq 40 \; and \; Y \geq 55) = 1 - P(X < 40 \; or \; Y < 55)$$

$$= 1 - [P(X < 40) + P(Y < 55) - P(X < 40 \; and \; Y < 55)]$$

$$= 1 - F(40, 100) - F(100, 55) + F(40, 55)$$

$$= 1 - \frac{40(100)(40 + 100)}{2000000} - \frac{100(55)(100 + 55)}{2000000} + \frac{40(55)(40 + 55)}{2000000}$$

$$= .40$$

The correct answer is **A**.

29.

$$999 = E[(2X - 1)^2]$$

$$999 = E[4X^2 - 4X + 1]$$

$$999 = 4E[X^2] - 4E[X] + E[1]$$

$$999 = 4E[X^2] - 4(10) + 1$$

We have used the fact that the expected value of a constant is that constant.

$$E[X^2] = 259.5$$

$$Var\ X = E[X^2] - (E[X])^2$$

$$= 259.5 - 100$$

$$= 159.5$$

The correct answer is **C**.

30.

This is a binomial experiment with $n = 150,\ p = .02$.

We are to find $P(X > 6)$. This has to be done through the complement.

Note that when $n > 20$, and either $np < 5$ or $n(1 - p) < 5$, then binomial distribution can be approximated by Poisson distribution and the resulting calculations are less tedious. So here, the mean m is given by:

$$m = np$$

$$= 150(.02)$$

$$= 3 < 5$$

So, using Poisson formula:

$$f(x) = \frac{m^x e^{-m}}{x!}$$

$$P(X \leq 6) = f(0) + f(1) + f(2) + f(3) + f(4) + f(5) + f(6)$$

$$= e^{-3}\left(\frac{3^0}{0!} + \frac{3^1}{1!} + \frac{3^2}{2!} + \frac{3^3}{3!} + \frac{3^4}{4!} + \frac{3^5}{5!} + \frac{3^6}{6!}\right)$$

$$= .97$$

You are welcome to verify that this will be the result even if you used binomial formula instead of Poisson approximation.

$$P(X > 6) = 1 - P(X \leq 6)$$

$$= 1 - .97$$

$$= .03$$

The correct answer is **C**.

Solutions to Practice Exam 2

1.

Teen Undergraduate Females = Teen Females – Teen Graduate Females

= (Teens – Teen Males) – (Teen Graduates – Teen Graduate Males)

= (5500 – 2200) – (150 – 70)

= 3220

The correct answer is **E**.

2.

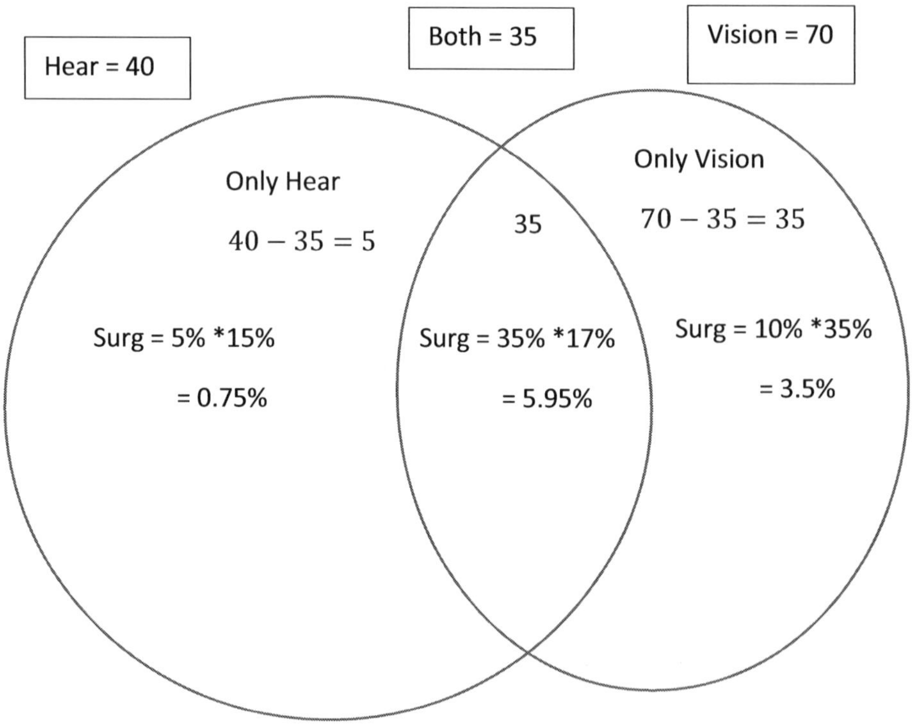

Total Having at least one Surgery is:

$$.75 + 5.95 + 3.5$$
$$= 10.2\%$$

The correct answer is **C**.

3.

With so many variables, a table is easier than a Venn Diagram.

	Apartment	House	Other	Total
No Car	*.52*	**.15**	*.09*	*.76*
Car	*.18* (3/4 of .24)	*.05*	*.01* (1/10 of .10)	.24
Total	.70	.20	*.10*	1

Normal font entries were directly given, the ones in italics and having normal entries in parentheses were calculated next, and the ones in italics were calculated next (by making sure that the correct row and column totals were achieved). Bold entry is what was asked.

The correct answer is **E**.

4.

50% have no car. So, 5% have more than one car.
Let x be the probability of being in an accident with no car.
Then $2x$ is the probability of being in an accident with one car.
And x is the probability of being in an accident with more than one car.

$$x + 2x + x = 1$$

$$x = .25\,, \qquad 2x = .5$$

$$P(more\ than\ 1\ car, given\ accident) = \frac{P(\ more\ than\ 1car\ and\ accident)}{P(accident)}$$

$$= \frac{.05(.25)}{.05(.25) + .5(.25) + .45(.5)}$$

$$= .0345$$

The correct answer is **C**.

5.

The pdf for a Poisson distribution with x successes and mean 2 is:

$$f(x) = \frac{2^x e^{-2}}{x!}$$

$$P(X = 3, given\ X \geq 1) = \frac{P(X = 3\ and\ X \geq 1)}{P(X \geq 1)}$$

$$= \frac{P(X = 3)}{P(X \geq 1)}$$

$$= \frac{f(3)}{1 - f(0)}$$

$$f(3) = \frac{2^3 e^{-2}}{3!} = .1804$$

$$f(0) = \frac{2^0 e^{-2}}{0!} = .1353$$

$$P(X = 3, given\ X \geq 1) = \frac{.1804}{1 - .1353}$$

$$= .21$$

The correct answer is **A**.

6.

Let T be the random variable representing the lifetime of the car. The cdf of an exponential distribution with mean 13 is:

$$F(t) = P(T \leq t) = 1 - e^{-\frac{t}{13}}$$

P(Failure during 1st year) = $P(T \leq 1) = F(1) = 1 - e^{-\frac{1}{13}} = .07404$

P(Failure during 2nd year) = $P(1 \leq T \leq 2) = F(2) - F(1) = .06856$

P(Failure during 3rd year) = $P(2 \leq T \leq 3) = F(3) - F(2) = .06348$

Expected Benefit= $10000(.07404) + 6000(.06856) + 2000(.06348) = 1279$

The correct answer is **C**.

7.

Let Y represent the insurance payment and let C be the deductible.

For a loss less than C, no payment is made.

For a loss bigger than C, the payment is $X - C$. So,

$$Y = \begin{cases} 0\ if\ \ X < C \\ X - C\ if\ \ X > C \end{cases}$$

We are given that:

$$P(Y > .2) = .7$$

$$P(X - C > .2) =..7$$

$$P(X > C + .2) = .7$$

$$\int_{C+.2}^{1} 3x^2 dx = .7$$

$$x^3 \Big|_{C+.2}^{1} = .7$$

$$1 - (C + .2)^3 = .7$$

$$(C + .2)^3 = .3$$

$$C + .2 = .67$$

$$C = .47$$

The correct answer is **D**.

8.

$$Y = \min\{X, 3\}$$

$$= \begin{cases} X, & X \le 3 \\ 3, & X > 3 \end{cases}$$

$$E[Y] = \int_{-\infty}^{\infty} y\, f(x)$$

$$= \int_{-\infty}^{3} x\, f(x)\, dx + \int_{3}^{\infty} 3\, f(x)\, dx$$

$$= \int_{1}^{3} x \left(\frac{1}{4}\right) dx + \int_{3}^{5} 3 \left(\frac{1}{4}\right) dx$$

$$= \frac{x^2}{8}\Big|_1^3 + \frac{3x}{4}\Big|_3^5$$

$$= 1 + 1.5$$

$$= 2.5$$

$$E[Y^2] = \int_{-\infty}^{\infty} y^2\, f(x)$$

$$\int_{-\infty}^{3} x^2 f(x)\, dx + \int_{3}^{\infty} 3^2\, f(x)\, dx$$

$$\int_{1}^{3} x^2 \left(\frac{1}{4}\right) dx + \int_{3}^{5} 9 \left(\frac{1}{4}\right) dx$$

$$= \frac{x^3}{12}\Big|_1^3 + \frac{9x}{4}\Big|_3^5$$

$$\frac{26}{12} + \frac{18}{4}$$

$$= 6.67$$

$$Var\, Y = E[Y^2] - (E[Y])^2$$

$$= 6.67 - (2.5)^2 = 0.42$$

The correct answer is **A**.

9.

The mean and standard deviation can be found on calculator. We get:

$$\mu = 18.05, \quad \sigma = .86$$

We are interested in the portion within 1 standard deviation of mean.

$$(\mu - \sigma, \mu + \sigma) = (18.05 - .86, 18.05 + .86) = (17.19, 18.91)$$

Only the age of 18 falls in this interval. The probability of that is .55

The correct answer is **B**.

10.

Let X be the loss.

Let Y be reimbursement given that the loss exceeds deductible.

By memoryless property of the exponential distribution, Y has the same distribution as X.

We are given that:

$$P(Y < 4000) = .6$$

We are to find $P(2000 < Y < 5000)$.

$$G(y) = 1 - e^{-ky}$$

$$G(4000) = 1 - e^{-4000k}$$

$$P(Y < 4000) = 1 - e^{-2000k}$$

$$.6 = 1 - e^{-4000k}$$

$$e^{-4000k} = .4$$

$$\sqrt{e^{-4000k}} = \sqrt{.4}$$

$$e^{-2000k} = .632$$

$$P(2000 < Y < 5000) = G(5000) - G(2000)$$

$$= (1 - e^{-5000k}) - (1 - e^{-2000k})$$

$$= e^{-2000k} - e^{-5000k}$$

$$= e^{-2000k} - (e^{-2000k})^{5/2}$$

$$= .632 - (.632)^{5/2}$$

$$= .31$$

The correct answer is **A**.

11.

Let the 4 costs be represented by X_1, X_2, X_3, X_4 .

Let $Y = \max\{X_1, X_2, X_3, X_4\}$.

We are to find the expected value of Y.

For this, we will need the pfd of Y. For this, we first find the cdf of Y.

$$G(y) = P(Y \le y)$$
$$= P(\max\{X_1, X_2, X_3, X_4\} \le y)$$
$$= P(X_1 \le y, and\ X_2 \le y, and\ X_3 \le y, and\ X_4 \le y)$$
$$= P(X_1 \le y) \bullet P(X_2 \le y) \bullet P(X_3 \le y) \bullet P(X_4 \le y)$$
$$= F(y) \bullet F(y) \bullet F(y) \bullet F(y) = [F(y)]^4$$

Note that we have used the same F for the cdf of the three variables because each of the 4 variables have the same density function $f(x)$.

The next step is to find $F(y)$.

$$F(y) = P(X \le y)$$
$$= \int_{-\infty}^{y} f(x)\, dx$$
$$= \int_{1}^{y} \frac{4}{x^5}\, dx$$
$$= 4\frac{x^{-4}}{-4}\Big|_1^y$$
$$= 1 - y^{-4}$$
$$G(y) = (1 - y^{-4})^4$$
$$g(y) = G'(y)$$
$$= 4(1 - y^{-4})^3(4y^{-5})$$
$$= 16y^{-5}(1 - 3y^{-4} + 3y^{-8} - y^{-12})$$
$$E[Y] = \int_{-\infty}^{\infty} y\, g(y)\, dy$$
$$= \int_{1}^{\infty} y\,(16y^{-5})(1 - 3y^{-4} + 3y^{-8} - y^{-12})dy$$
$$= \int_{1}^{\infty} 16y^{-4} - 48y^{-8} + 48y^{-12} - 16y^{-16}\, dy$$

$$= 16\frac{y^{-3}}{-3} - 48\frac{y^{-7}}{-7} + 48\frac{y^{-11}}{-11} - 16\frac{y^{-15}}{-15}\Big|_1^{\infty}$$

$$= \frac{16}{3} - \frac{48}{7} + \frac{48}{11} - \frac{16}{15}$$

$$= 1.773\ thousand$$

$$= 1773$$

So, the correct answer is **D**.

12.

Central Limit Theorem tells us that the distribution of the sum of more than 30 identically distributed variables (300 here) is approximately normal.

Also, if there are n such variables, then the mean and standard deviation of the sum are:

$$\mu = n(mean\ of\ each) = 300(800) = 240000$$

$$\sigma = \sqrt{n}\ (SD\ of\ each) = \sqrt{300}\ \sqrt{200} = 244.95$$

To find the 95th percentile, we first find the standard score z from the table that corresponds to a cumulative probability of .95.

We see that a probability of .9495 corresponds to $z = 1.64$, while a probability of .9505 corresponds to $z = 1.65$.

We use linear interpolation:

$$\frac{.95 - .9495}{.9505 - .9495} = .5$$

So, we go .5 of the way between 1.64 and 1.65. Thus, we have:

$$z = 1.645$$

$$z = \frac{x - \mu}{\sigma}$$

$$1.645 = \frac{x - 240000}{244.95}$$

$$x = 240403$$

The correct answer is **E**.

13.

The quickest way to do this problem is to remember that if a loss distribution is exponential, and the payout has a deductible so that the expected value of the payout is reduced by $a\%$ compared to the expected value of the loss, then the variance of the payout reduces by $(a\%)^2$ compared to the variance of the loss.

So here, the variance of the payout will reduce by:

$$(25\%)^2 = \left(\frac{25}{100}\right)^2 = .0625 = 6\%$$

The correct answer is **B**.

14.

The first target is to find a. For this, we will need to work with the distribution of X.

We know that for a uniform $[a, b]$ distribution,

$$E[X] = \frac{a+b}{2}$$

So, using the given distribution of X, we have

$$E[X] = \frac{a+9}{2}$$

$$6.5 = \frac{a+9}{2}$$

$$13 = a + 9$$

$$a = 4$$

The distribution of Y is therefore uniform on $[.75(4), 9] = [3,9]$.

Let the 30th percentile of this distribution be k. Then we have:

$$P(X < k) = .30$$

$$\frac{k-3}{9-3} = .3$$

$$k - 3 = 1.8$$

$$k = 4.8$$

The correct answer is **B**.

15.

$$P(X > 6000 \; given \; X > 1000) = \frac{P(X > 6000 \; and \; X > 1000)}{P(X > 1000)}$$

$$= \frac{P(X > 6000)}{P(X > 1000)} \qquad (1)$$

$$P(X > 6000) = \int_{6000}^{\infty} f(x)\,dx = \int_{6000}^{30000} c(30000 - x)\,dx$$

$$= -c\frac{(30000 - x)^2}{2}\Big|_{6000}^{30000} = -\frac{c}{2}[(30000 - 30000)^2 - (30000 - 6000)^2]$$

$$= 288000000c$$

$$P(X > 1000) = \int_{1000}^{\infty} f(x)\,dx = \int_{1000}^{30000} c(30000 - x)\,dx$$

$$= -c\frac{(30000 - x)^2}{2}\Big|_{1000}^{30000} = -\frac{c}{2}[(30000 - 30000)^2 - (30000 - 1000)^2]$$

$$= 420500000c$$

So, equation (1) becomes:

$$P(X > 6000\ given\ X > 1000) = \frac{288000000c}{420500000c} = .685$$

The correct answer is **D**.

16.

$$P(2\ from\ any\ of\ the\ 1st\ 2\ prisms) = \frac{1}{4}$$

$$P(2\ from\ 3rd\ prism\ prisms) = \frac{2}{4}$$

$$P(Two\ 2's\ from\ \ 1st\ prism) = \frac{1}{4}\left(\frac{1}{4}\right) = \frac{1}{16}$$

$$P(Two\ 2's\ from\ \ 2nd\ prism) = \frac{1}{4}\left(\frac{1}{4}\right) = \frac{1}{16}$$

$$P(Two\ 2's\ from\ \ 3rd\ prism) = \frac{2}{4}\left(\frac{2}{4}\right) = \frac{1}{4}$$

Each prism has probability $1/3$ of being picked. So, Probability of Two 2's

$$= P(1st\ prism\ and\ two\ 2's) + P(2nd\ prism\ and\ two\ 2's) + P(3rd\ prism\ and\ two\ 2's)$$

$$= \frac{1}{3}\left(\frac{1}{16}\right) + \frac{1}{3}\left(\frac{1}{16}\right) + \frac{1}{3}\left(\frac{1}{4}\right) = \frac{1}{8}$$

The correct answer is **A**.

17.

Question Type	Proportion	Probability correct
Knows	$\frac{N}{35}$	1
Guesses	$\frac{35-N}{35}$	$\frac{1}{4}$

$$P(knows|correct) = \frac{P(knows\ and\ correct)}{P(correct)}$$

$$.842 = \frac{\frac{N}{35}(1)}{\frac{N}{35}(1) + \left(\frac{35-N}{35}\right)\left(\frac{1}{4}\right)}$$

Multiply the numerator and denominator on right side by 140.

$$.842 = \frac{4N}{4N + 35 - N}$$

$$.842(3N + 35) = 4N$$

$$N = 20$$

The correct answer is **A**.

18.

Let p be the probability that a random man likes apples. This is binomial with $n = 15$.

Let X be the number of men who like apples. The binomial pmf is:

$$f(x) = \binom{15}{x} p^x (1-p)^{50-x}$$

We are given that:

$$f(7) = .9f(8)$$

$$\binom{15}{7} p^7 (1-p)^{15-7} = .9\binom{15}{8} p^8 (1-p)^{15-8}$$

$$6435p^7(1-p)^8 = (.9)6435p^8(1-p)^7$$

Dividing both sides by $6435p^7(1-p)^7$ we get:

$$1 - p = .9p$$

$$1.9p = 1$$

$$p = .526$$

Since p is the probability of liking apples, the probability of not liking apples will be:

$$1 - p = 1 - .526 = .474$$

The correct answer is **B**.

19.

Let d be the deductible.

If $d \le 200$, the expected claim payment will be:

$$.2(200 - d) + .15(600 - d) + .1(500 - d) = 82.5$$

$$40 - .2d + 90 - .15d + 50 - .1d = 82.5$$

$$97.5 = .45d$$

$$d = 217$$

This contradicts out supposition that $d \le 200$. So d must be greater than 200.

If $200 < d < 500$, the expected claim payment will be:

$$.15(600 - d) + .1(500 - d) = 82.5$$

$$90 - .15d + 50 - .1d = 82.5$$

$$57.5 = .25d$$

$$d = 230$$

This is consistent with our assumption that $200 < d < 500$.

The correct answer is **D**.

20.

Let there be a total of x children.

$$P(all\ 3\ on\ slides\ are\ children) = \frac{x}{9}\left(\frac{x-1}{8}\right)\left(\frac{x-2}{7}\right) = \frac{5}{21}$$

$$x(x-1)(x-2) = 120$$

Since x has to be integer between 0 and 9, we note that $x = 6$ is a solution of this equation.

So, out of the 9, there are 6 children and hence 3 adults.

$$P(at\ most\ 1\ of\ 3\ on\ slides\ is\ an\ adult) = P(0\ adult) + P(1\ adult) \qquad (1)$$

$$P(\ 0\ adult) = P(all\ 3\ children) = \frac{5}{21}$$

$$P(1\ adult) = P(1\ adult\ and\ 2\ children) = \frac{\binom{3}{1}\binom{6}{2}}{\binom{9}{3}} = .5357$$

So, equation (1) becomes:

$$P(at\ most\ 1\ of\ 3\ on\ slides\ is\ an\ adult) = \frac{5}{21} + .5357 = .77$$

The correct answer is **C**.

21.

The total annual number of the two phenomena is $X + Y$. So, we need $Var\ (X + Y)$.

$$Var\ (X + Y) = Var\ X + Var\ Y + 2\ COV(X, Y) \quad (1)$$

$$Var\ Y = 2^2 = 4$$

$Var\ X$ can be found by noting that X is Poisson with mean 3, and hence variance 3. So,

$$Var\ X = 3$$

We also know that the correlation coefficient r is given by:

$$r = \frac{COV(X, Y)}{\sqrt{(Var\ X)\ (Var\ Y)}}$$

$$.5 = \frac{COV(X, Y)}{\sqrt{4(3)}}$$

$$COV(X, Y) = 1.732$$

So, (1) becomes:

$$Var\ (X + Y) = 4 + 3 + 2(1.732)$$

$$= 10.5$$

The correct answer is **D**.

22.

The number of losses in excess of 1000, say, X, during 4 years is binomial with:

$$n = 4, \ \ p = .15$$

$$f(x) = \binom{n}{x} p^x (1 - p)^{n-x}$$

$$= \binom{4}{x} .15^x (.85)^{4-x}$$

The possible benefits amount and their probabilities are tabulated below:

Benefit	When X is	Probability
2000	1	$f(1) = \binom{4}{1} .15^1 (.85)^{4-1} = .3685$
4000	≥2	$1 - f(0) - f(1) = .1095$

So, the expected benefit is:

$$2000(.3685) + 4000(.1095) = 1175$$

The correct answer is **B**.

23.

Let H be the event that a person has hearing problems.

Let V be the event that a person has vision problems

$$P(H) = .05$$

$$P(V) = .25$$

$$P(exacly\ one) = P[(H, not\ V)\ OR\ (V, not\ H)]$$

$$= P(H, not\ V) + P(V, not\ H)$$

$$= .05(1 - .25) + .25(1 - .05) = .275$$

The correct answer is **C**.

24.

Since one sparrow has already been spotted among the eating birds, we can exclude that sparrow from the total.

Thus, we practically have 4 sparrows and 3 nightingales for the remaining 2 eating birds.

So, by hypergeometric, the required probability of the other 2 birds being nightingales is:

$$\frac{\binom{3}{2}\binom{4}{0}}{\binom{7}{2}} = .14$$

The correct answer is **B**.

25.

Let X be the height of a 20-year old US girl.

$$P(X < 63) = .5478$$

From tables, $z = .12$ corresponds to a cumulative probability of .5478. So, in

$$z = \frac{X - \mu}{\sigma}$$

we have $z = .12$ when $X = 63$.

$$.12 = \frac{63 - \mu}{\sigma}$$

$$\mu = 63 - .12\sigma \quad (1)$$

$$P(X < 65) = .7704$$

From tables, $z = .74$ corresponds to a cumulative probability of .7704.

So, we have $z = .74$ when $X = 65$.

$$.74 = \frac{65 - \mu}{\sigma}$$

$$\mu = 65 - .74\sigma \quad (2)$$

Comparing (1) and (2) we have:

$$63 - .12\sigma = 65 - .74\sigma$$

$$.62\sigma = 2$$

$$\sigma = 3.2258$$

Substituting in (1)

$$\mu = 63 - .12(3.2258) = 62.613$$

We are to find $P(64 < X < 66)$. We need to change 64 and 66 into z-scores.

$$z_1 = \frac{X - \mu}{\sigma} = \frac{64 - 62.613}{3.2258} = .43$$

$$z_2 = \frac{X - \mu}{\sigma} = \frac{66 - 62.613}{3.2258} = 1.05$$

$$P(64 < X < 66) = P(.43 < z < 1.05)$$

$$= P(z < 1.05) - P(z < .43)$$

$$= .8531 - .6664$$

$$= .1867$$

The correct answer is **D**.

26.

If N is the number of deaths in any month, then

$$P(N=n)=f(n)=\frac{1.5^n e^{-1.5}}{n!}, n=0,1,2,3,...$$

Let X be the number of deaths in the 1st of the 2 consecutive months.

Let Y be the number of deaths in the 2nd of the 2 consecutive months.

We are to find $P(X+Y>2|X\le 1)$.

We will find $P(X+Y\le 2|X\le 1)$ and then take the complement.

$$P(X+Y\le 2|X\le 1)=\frac{P(X+Y\le 2 \text{ and } X\le 1)}{P(X\le 1)} \quad (1)$$

$$P(X\le 1)=f(0)+f(1)$$
$$=e^{-1.5}+1.5e^{-1.5}$$
$$=.5578 \quad (2)$$

The variable values satisfying the required conditions are tabulated.

x	0	0	0	1	1
y	0	1	2	0	1
$f(x)=\frac{1.5^x e^{-1.5}}{x!}$	$e^{-1.5}$	$e^{-1.5}$	$e^{-1.5}$	.3347	.3347
$f(y)=\frac{1.5^y e^{-1.5}}{y!}$	$e^{-1.5}$	.3347	.251	$e^{-1.5}$	.3347
$f(x)f(y)$	.0498	.0747	.056	.0747	.112

Note that since the eruptions are independent over different months, so X *and* Y are independent and therefore the probability at each pair of points can be obtained by multiplying the corresponding probabilities for the original variables.

$$P(X+Y\le 2 \text{ and } X\le 1)=\sum_{x+y\le 2,\ x\le 1} f(x,y)=\sum_{x+y\le 2,\ x\le 1} f(x)f(y)$$

$$=.0498+.0747+.056+.0747+.112=.3672 \quad (3)$$

Substituting (2) and (3) in (1) we get:

$$P(X+Y\le 2|X\le 1)=\frac{.3672}{.5578}=.66$$

$$P(X+Y>2|X\le 1)=1-P(X+Y\le 2|X\le 1)$$

$$=1-.66$$

$$=.34$$

The correct answer is **B**.

27.

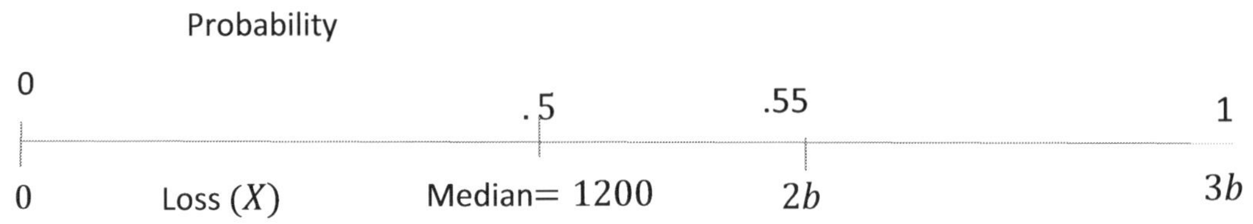

From the picture we see that the median, which corresponds to a cumulative probability of .5, lies in the $[0,2b]$ portion.

The median is 1200. So,

$$.5 = P(X \leq 1200)$$

$$.5 = P(X \text{ is in } [0,2b])\left(\frac{1200 - 0}{2b - 0}\right)$$

$$.5 = .55\left(\frac{1200}{2b}\right)$$

$$.5 = \frac{330}{b}$$

$$b = \frac{330}{.5} = 660$$

By law of total probability,

$$E[X] = P(X \text{ in } [0,2b])E[X|X \text{ in } [0,2b]] + P(X \text{ in } [2b,3b])E[X|X \text{ in } [2b,3b]]$$

$$= .55E([0,2b]) + .45E([2b,3b]) \quad (1)$$

The expected value of a uniform distribution lies at its midpoint. So, (1) becomes:

$$E[X] = .55\left(\frac{0 + 2b}{2}\right) + .45\left(\frac{2b + 3b}{2}\right)$$

$$= 1.675b$$

$$= 1.675(660)$$

$$= 1100$$

The correct answer is **B**.

28.

Let Y be the cost covered by the secondary insurance.

Let X be the annual repair cost. Then:

$$f(x) = \frac{1}{6000}, \qquad 0 \le X \le 6000$$

$$Y = \begin{cases} 0, & X \le 2500 \\ X - 2500, & 2500 < X < 4700 \\ 2200, & X \ge 4700 \end{cases}$$

$$E[Y] = \int_{-\infty}^{\infty} y\, f(x)\, dx$$

$$= \int_{2500}^{4700} (x - 2500)\left(\frac{1}{6000}\right) dx + \int_{4700}^{6000} 2200\left(\frac{1}{6000}\right) dx$$

$$= \frac{1}{6000} \frac{(x-2500)^2}{2} \Big|_{2500}^{4700} + \frac{22}{60} x \Big|_{4700}^{6000}$$

$$= \frac{1}{12000}(4700 - 2500)^2 + \frac{22}{60}(6000 - 4700)$$

$$= 880$$

The correct answer is **E**.

29.

Let S be the dying age and X the loss.

So X is exponential with mean $10S$ for a given S.

Variance of an exponential variable equals square of its mean, so:

$$E[X|S] = 10S$$

$$Var(X|S) = (10S)^2 = 100S^2$$

$$Var\ X = Var(E[X|S]) + E[Var(X|S)$$

$$= Var\ (10S) + E[100S^2]$$

$$= 10^2 Var\ (S) + 100E[S^2] \quad (1)$$

$$E[S] = \frac{a+b}{2} = \frac{16+60}{2} = 38$$

$$Var\ (S) = \frac{(b-a)^2}{12} = \frac{(60-16)^2}{12} = 161.33$$

$$Var\ S = E[S^2] - (E[S])^2$$

$$161.33 = E[S^2] - (38)^2$$

$$E[S^2] = 1605.33$$

Equation (1) becomes:

$$Var\ (X) = 10^2(161.33) + 100(1605.33) = 176666$$

$$SD(X) = \sqrt{Var\ X} = \sqrt{176666} = 420$$

This rounds to choice **B**.

30.

Coefficient of variation of a random variable is the ratio of its standard deviation to its mean. Since variances are same for both variables, so the standard deviations are also same, say, σ.

$$CV(X) = \frac{\sigma_X}{\mu_X}$$

$$8 = \frac{\sigma}{\mu_X}$$

$$\mu_X = \frac{\sigma}{8}$$

$$CV(Y) = \frac{\sigma_Y}{\mu_Y}$$

$$9 = \frac{\sigma}{\mu_Y}$$

$$\mu_Y = \frac{\sigma}{9}$$

Let $W = 2X + 3Y$. Then:

$$\mu_W = 2\mu_X + 3\mu_Y = 2\left(\frac{\sigma}{8}\right) + 3\left(\frac{\sigma}{9}\right) = \frac{7\sigma}{12}$$

$$Var\ W = 2^2\ Var\ X + 3^2\ Var\ Y + 2(2)(3)Cov\ (X, Y)$$

But X, Y are independent.

So, $Cov\ (X, Y) = 0$. Hence

$$Var\ W = 4(\sigma)^2 + 9(\sigma)^2 = 13\sigma^2$$

$$\sigma_W = \sqrt{Var\ W} = \sqrt{13\sigma^2} = \sqrt{13}\sigma$$

$$CV(W) = \frac{\sigma_W}{\mu_W} = \frac{\sqrt{13}\sigma}{\frac{7\sigma}{12}} = 6.18$$

The correct answer is **E**.

Loss means negative profit.

If a pair of $\boldsymbol{n}$ **−sided** dice is rolled, there are n^2 possible outcomes.

$$\infty^k = \begin{cases} 0, & k < 0 \\ \infty, & k > 0 \end{cases}$$

With a **deductible** d, if X is the payout, and $a > d$ it is simpler to calculate $P(X < a)$ by finding $P(X \geq a)$ and taking the complement.

An integral of the form:

$$\int_a^b \left[\frac{k - nx}{m - x}\right] dx$$

can be done by making the substitution $u = m - x$ and then splitting fraction.

Integration by parts shortcut:

$$\int (x + k)e^{ax} dx = \frac{(x + k)e^{ax}}{a} - \frac{e^{ax}}{a^2}$$

Addition Rule

For 2 events: $P(A \cup B) = P(A) + P(B) - P(AB)$.

For 3 events: $P(A \cup B \cup C) = P(A) + P(B) + P(C) - P(AB) - P(AC) - P(BC) + P(ABC)$

Note that we will regularly be using the shorthand $P(AB)$ for $P(A \cap B)$

Set addition rule

If the number of elements in 3 sets are X, Y, Z, then the number of elements in their union is:

$$X \text{ or } Y \text{ or } Z = X + Y + Z - X\&Y - X\&Z - Y\&Z + X\&Y\&Z$$

Complement Rule:

$$P(A') = 1 - P(A)$$

Partition Rule:

$$P(A) = P(AB) + P(AB')$$

Independence:

Two events A, B are independent, if and only if $P(AB) = P(A)P(B)$

A, B, C are mutually independent if an only if $P(ABC) = P(A)P(B)P(C)$

If $P(AB) = 0$, and X is any event, then $P(ABX) = 0$

Conditional Rule:

$$P(A\ given\ B) = \frac{P(AB)}{P(B)}$$

Sum of a geometric series *with 1st term a and common ration r is:*

$$S = \frac{a}{1-r}$$

The geometric sum of n terms equals:

$$\frac{a(1-r^n)}{1-r}$$

Note that geometric series implies infinite terms, and geometric sum implies finite terms.

Normal Distribution:

If X is normally distributed with mean μ and standard deviation σ, the standard score is:

$$z = \frac{x-\mu}{\sigma}$$

For a **standard normal** distribution:

$$P(z > k) = 1 - P(z \le k)$$
$$P(z > -k) = P(z < k)$$

The pth percentile of standard normal distribution (called the standard pth percentile) is the z corresponding to a cumulative probability p.

Absolute values of z-scores for cumulative probabilities p and $1-p$ are equal.

Linear interpolation should be used to find a z value corresponding to a cumulative probability that is not listed in the table.

Central Limit Theorem

If population is normal, or if sample size, $n > 30$, then the sampling distribution of means and sums is approximately normal with mean and standard deviation:

$$\mu_{\bar{X}} = \mu$$

$$\sigma_{\bar{X}} = \frac{\sigma}{\sqrt{n}}$$

$$\mu_{sum} = n\mu$$

$$\sigma_{sum} = \sqrt{n}\,\sigma$$

where μ and σ are mean and standard deviation of each of n identical variables.

If X, Y are independent normal variables, and $N = aX + bY$, then:

$$\mu_N = a\mu_X + b\mu_Y$$

$$\sigma_N = \sqrt{a^2{\sigma_X}^2 + b^2{\sigma_Y}^2}$$

Continuity Correction:

$$P(X > n) = P(X \geq n + .5)$$

$$P(X < n) = P(X \leq n - .5)$$

This correction is used when a discrete variable is approximated by a continuous variable.

Binomial Distribution:

The probability of x successes in n binomial trials is given as:

$$f(x) = \binom{n}{x} p^x (1-p)^{n-x}, \qquad x = 0,1,2,\ldots$$

where p is the probability of success in each trial.

The mean of a binomial distribution is np

Variance of binomial distribution is $np(1-p)$.

Geometric distribution gives the probability of the 1st success requiring k independent trials, each with success probability p. The pmf is:

$$f(k) = p(1-p)^{k-1}$$

The mean, or expected value of geometric distribution with this characterization is $1/p$

Geometric distribution is memoryless. This means that:

$$E[K|K > a] = a + E[K]$$

Geometric distribution with success probability p can also be characterized as the number of failures x before the first success. In this case the pmf is:

$$f(x) = p(1-p)^x, \qquad x = 0,1,2,3,\ldots$$

With this characterization, the mean isL

$$E[X] = \frac{1-p}{p}$$

Variance of geometric distribution with both the above characterizations is:

$$Var\ X = \frac{1-p}{p^2}$$

Hypergeometric Formula:

If we have N items, of which a items are of type A, b items are of type B, then the probability of selecting n items, of which x items are of type A is:

$$\frac{\binom{a}{x}\binom{b}{n-x}}{\binom{N}{n}}$$

N is **negative binomial** if the probability of needing n trials to get r successes is:

$$P(N = n) = \binom{n-1}{r-1} p^r (1-p)^{n-r}$$

where p is the probability of success in each trial.

Mode: The mode of a variable X is the value x for which $f(x)$ is maximum.

Median of a Discrete distribution: is the value m such that $P(X \leq m) \geq .5$ and $P(X \geq m) \geq .5$

Combinations and Permutations are related by the formula:

$$n\,C\,r = \frac{n\,P\,r}{r!}$$

$$\binom{n}{x} = \frac{n!}{x!\,(n-x)!}$$

$$n\,P\,r = \frac{n!}{(n-r)!}$$

Bayes Theorem says that if events $A_1, \ldots, A_n$ form a partition of the sample space S, and B is any event, then for $i = 1, \ldots, n$:

$$P(A_i\ given\ B) = \frac{P(A_i B)}{P(A_1 B) + \cdots P(A_n B)}$$

Multinomial:

The multinomial probability mass function is given as:

$$f(x_1, \ldots., x_k; n; p_1, \ldots.., p_k) = \frac{n!}{x_1! * \ldots * x_k!} {p_1}^{x_1} * \ldots. {p_k}^{x_k}$$

Where n = number of trials,
$x_1, \ldots, x_k$, are the number of instances of events $1, \ldots, k$ respectively,
$p_1, \ldots, p_k$, are the probabilities of events $1, \ldots, k$ respectively. Note that the binomial formula is a special case of this with only 2 events.

Density Functions:

Density function, or **probability density function (pdf)** of a continuous random variable X is denoted by a lowercase function, for example, $f(x)$. For a discrete variable, $f(x)$ is referred to as probability function.

The integral of a pdf over its entire range is 1

Absolute Value:

$$|x| = \begin{cases} -x, & x < 0 \\ x, & x \geq 0 \end{cases}$$

If $|x| < a$, then $-a < x < a$.

Cumulative Density function (cdf) of a continuous random variable X is denoted by the uppercase function corresponding to the lowercase pdf.

For example, $F(x)$ is the cdf corresponding to the pdf $f(x)$. Cdf is generally the integral of pdf:

$$F(x) = P(X \leq x) = \int_{-\infty}^{t} f(t)\,dt$$

Also, since the cdf is cumulative probability, so it always equals 0 at one end and 1 at the other end of the domain of the corresponding pdf.

For a discrete variable, $F(x)$ is referred to as cumulative probability function.

For both discrete and continuous variables:

$$F(a) = P(X \leq a)$$

$$F(b) - F(a) = P(a \leq X \leq b)$$

The range that usually interests us for the cdf is the one strictly between 0 and 1. That is why in a lot of problems we are asked to find $0 < F(x) < 1$ and this is the part that is found by the above mentioned integral.

In general, pdf is the derivative of cdf, that is,

$$f = F'$$

Strictly speaking, in intervals where the cdf is differentiable, pdf is the derivative of cdf, except at end points.

All measurements, for example, heights, weights, times, are continuous variables. For continuous variables it makes no difference whether the probability expressions have strict inequalities or non-strict inequalities. For example, $P(X \leq x) = P(X < x)$.

$$P(X > x) = \int_{x}^{\infty} f(t)\,dt$$

$$P(a < X < b) = \int_{a}^{b} f(t)\,dt$$

However, in practice, if some part of the pdf in (a, b) is 0, then the limits on the integral will be covering only that range where the pdf is not 0. For example, for a uniform (0,2) distribution, since the pdf is non-zero only from 0 to 2, we have:

$$P(-1 < X < 1) = \int_{0}^{1} \frac{1}{2}\,dx$$

Joint Probability Function

This is the probability function of two variables X, Y. It is usually denoted by $f(x, y)$.

$$f(x,y) = g(x)\,h(y \text{ given } x) = f_X(x) f_Y(y|x)$$

$$f(x,y) = h(y)\,g(x \text{ given } y) = f_Y(y) f_X(x|y)$$

For independent variables X, Y, and also for a rectangular domain, the joint pdf is:

$$f(x,y) = g(x)h(y)$$

where $g(x), h(y)$ are the pdf's of X and Y, respectively.

If the joint pdf of 2 variables is constant/uniform over a domain, then it equals the reciprocal of the area of the domain.

For discrete variables:

$$P(y = a|x = b) = \frac{P(x = a, y = b)}{P(x = b)}$$

If X and Y are independent, then:

$$(i)\ Var[X|Y < y] = Var[X|Y > y] = Var[X|Y = y] = Var\ X$$

$$(ii)\ f(x,y) = f_X(x)f_Y(y)$$

Percentiles:

The pth percentile of a random variable X is the value x_p such that:

$$F(x_p) = \frac{p}{100}$$

Median is the 50th percentile.

Interquartile range is the difference between 75th and 25th percentile.

Poisson Distribution:

$$f(x) = \frac{m^x e^{-m}}{x!}, \qquad x = 0,1,2,3, \dots$$

where m = mean.

The variance of a Poisson distribution equals its mean.

The sum of N independent Poisson variables with means $k_1, k_2, \dots, k_N,$ is also Poisson with mean $k_1 + k_2 + \cdots + k_N$

Expected Value

For a continuous random variable, with pdf $f(x)$, the **expected value** is:

$$E[X] = \int_{-\infty}^{\infty} x\, f(x)\, dx$$

For a discrete random variable, with pmf $f(x)$, the **expected value** is:

$$E[X] = \sum x\, f(x)$$

If a distribution is a mixture of continuous parts and **point masses** (discrete points having non-zero probabilities), then the expected value is calculated by calculating the expected values of each portion, multiplying by their respective probabilities, and adding up the products.

$$E[X+Y] = E[X] + E[Y]$$

$$E[aX] = aE[X]$$

$$E(c) = c$$

where c is a constant.

If

$$X = \begin{cases} A, & with\ probability\ a \\ B, & with\ probability\ b \\ & \vdots \end{cases}$$

Then

$$E[X] = aE[A] + bE[B] + \cdots, \qquad E[X^2] = aE[A^2] + bE[B^2] + \cdots$$

Variance and Standard Deviation:

$$Var\,[X] = E[X^2] - (E[X])^2$$

$$Var[Y|X = a] = E[Y^2|X = a] - (E[Y|X = a])^2$$

$$\text{Standard Deviation} = \sqrt{Variance}$$

$$\sigma_{aX+b} = |a|\,\sigma_X$$

For independent variables X, Y, Z, the variance of $aX + bY + cZ$ are:

$$Var = a^2 VarX + b^2 VarY + c^2 VarZ$$

The variance of a horizontally shifted pdf is same as that of the original.

Covariance:

Covariance of variables X, Y is defined as:

$$Cov[X, Y] = E[XY] - E[X]E[Y]$$

For independent variables $X, Y,\ Cov[X, Y] = 0$.

The converse of above equation is not true. That is, it is possible for two dependent variables to have a covariance of 0 as well.

If X, Y are random variables, and a, b, c, d are constants, then:

$$Cov(aX + bY, cX + dY) = acVarX + (ad + bc)Cov(X, Y) + bdVarY$$

$$Var[X + Y] = Var[X] + Var[Y] + 2Cov[X, Y]$$

$$Var\,(aW + bZ + c) = a^2\,Var\,W + b^2\,Var\,Z + 2ab\,Cov\,(W, Z)$$

Last equation also shows that variance of a constant is 0.

If T is the sum of N independent identical variables X, then:

$$E[T|N] = NE[X]$$

$$Var[T|N] = NVar[X]$$

Coefficient of variation (CV) of a random variable is the ratio of its standard deviation to its mean. That is:

$$CV = \frac{Standard\ Deviation}{Mean}$$

The ***correlation coefficient*** between two random variables is:

$$r = \frac{Cov(X, Y)}{\sqrt{(Var\,X)(Var\,Y)}}$$

$$-1 \le r \le 1$$

Law of Total Probability:

If $B_1, B_2, B_3, \ldots$ are disjoint events whose union is the whole sample space, and if A is any event in the sample space, then:

$$P(A) = \sum_i P(AB_i)$$

Where, by our usual convention the product AB_i means the intersection of A and B_i

Law of Total Expectation:

$$E[X] = P(A)E[X|A] + P(B)E[X|B] + \cdots \text{ (1-variable prob function)}$$

$$E(X|Y = a) = \textstyle\sum_x P(X = x|Y = a)E[X|X = x, Y = a] \text{ (2-variables prob function)}$$

Conditional Variance Formula, or Law of Total Variance:

$$Var(X) = E[Var(X|\lambda)] + \mathrm{Var}[\mathrm{E}(\mathrm{X}|\lambda)], \text{where } \lambda \text{ is a parameter of } X$$

Exponential Distribution

The pdf, and cdf, respectively, of an exponential distribution with mean k are:

$$f(x) = \frac{1}{k}e^{-\frac{x}{k}}, \qquad 0 < x < \infty$$

$$F(x) = 1 - e^{-x/k}$$

Standard deviation of an exponential distribution equals its mean.

Median of an exponential distribution with mean k is $k \ln 2$.

If a loss distribution is exponential, and the payout has a deductible so that the expected value of the payout is reduced by $a\%$ compared to the expected value of the loss, then the variance of the payout reduces by $(a\%)^2$ compared to the variance of the loss.

Because of the **memoryless property** of exponential distribution we have:

$$Var\ (X|X > a) = Var\ X$$

$$E[X|X > a] = a + E[X]$$

Uniform Distribution:

For a uniform $[a, b]$ or (a, b) distribution, the pdf expected value, and variance are:

$$f(x) = \frac{1}{b-a}, \qquad a \le x \le b,$$

$$E[X] = \frac{a+b}{2}$$

$$Var\ X = \frac{(b-a)^2}{12}$$

If U is uniform $[a, b]$, and $X = cU$, where c is constant, then X is uniform $[ac, bc]$

Moments:

If X is a discrete random variable, its nth moment is given as:

$$E[X^n] = \sum x^n f(x)$$

If X is a continuous random variable, its nth moment is given as:

$$E[X^n] = \int_{-\infty}^{\infty} x^n \, f(x)dx$$

Every odd moment of a variable with symmetric pdf is 0.

A random variable X is said to have gamma distribution with parameters α, θ if its pdf is:

$$f(x) = \frac{1}{\theta^\alpha \Gamma(\alpha)} x^{\alpha-1} e^{-\frac{x}{\theta}}, \;\; x > 0$$

$$\Gamma(n) = (n-1)! \;, \;\; n = 1,2,3,\ldots$$

$$\Gamma\left(\frac{1}{2}\right) = \sqrt{\pi}$$

The mean and variance of the above gamma distribution are:

$$E[X] = \alpha\theta$$

$$Var\,(X) = \alpha\theta^2$$

A random variable X is said to have beta distribution with parameters a, b if its pdf is:

$$f(x) = \frac{\Gamma(a+b)}{\Gamma(a)\Gamma(b)} x^{a-1}(1-x)^{b-1} \;, \;\; 0 < x < 1$$

A beta distribution with $a = 1, b = 1$ is actually the uniform (0,1) distribution.

Appendix 1: Introduction to Gamma Distribution

A random variable X is said to have gamma distribution with parameters α, θ if its pdf is:

$$f(x) = cx^{\alpha-1}e^{-\frac{x}{\theta}}, \; x > 0$$

Here, c is a constant which turns out to be:

$$c = \frac{1}{\theta^{\alpha}\Gamma(\alpha)}$$

where $\Gamma(\alpha)$ is the value of the gamma function at α. The values of the gamma function that you should know for Exam P are:

$$\Gamma(n) = (n-1)! \; , \; n = 1,2,3,\ldots$$

$$\Gamma\left(\frac{1}{2}\right) = \sqrt{\pi}$$

The mean and variance of the above gamma distribution are:

$$E[X] = \alpha\theta$$

$$Var\ (X) = \alpha\theta^2$$

Example: The pdf of a random variable X is of the form:

$$f(x) = kx^4e^{-2x}, \; x > 0$$

where k is a constant. Calculate the variance of X.

F) .5
G) 1.25
H) 2.5
I) 12.5
J) 15

Solution: We recognize this as a gamma distribution with

$$\alpha = 5, \qquad \theta = 1/2$$

$$Var\ (X) = \alpha\theta^2$$

$$= 5\left(\frac{1}{2}\right)^2$$

$$= 1.25$$

The correct answer is **B**.

Note: If $\alpha = 1$, then gamma distribution become exponential distribution with mean θ.

Made in the USA
Las Vegas, NV
07 April 2025

20630796R00400